NEW
AMERICAN HISTORY

BY

ALBERT BUSHNELL HART, LL.D.

PROFESSOR OF GOVERNMENT
HARVARD UNIVERSITY

AMERICAN BOOK COMPANY

NEW YORK CINCINNATI CHICAGO

THE AUTHOR TO THE TEACHER

This book is prepared with a view to a simple system of study and teaching which may be summarized as follows:

(1) The textbook will be carefully read and studied by the pupils: first, for the acquirement of a body of useful facts, and then for a sense of the movement and proportions of the history of the country. Essential names, events, and dates go directly into the text; the dates in parentheses are inserted merely to keep straight the progress of events.

(2) Class exercises will be based first of all upon the text, with such methods of recitation, question, and quiz as the teacher may prefer. Here is the opportunity to show how previous chapters bear on the day's subject, and to enlarge the subject, through the teacher's knowledge.

(3) Outside reading of additional books by the pupils will greatly aid in accomplishing the teacher's purpose. A textbook, in order to cover the ground, must briefly notice many facts and statements which can be enlarged to advantage out of other books. The lists of references which follow each of the chapters are guides to a variety of formal histories, biographies, and reference books. Special attention is called to the lists of sources, illustrative works, and pictures.

(4) Written work has long been recognized as one of the adjuncts of historical study in the secondary school: it may take many forms, such as essays, based on secondary authorities; reports, based in whole or in part on sources; brief "judgment questions" set and answered in class; or "written recitations." The chapter references will aid in such work. The first group of "Topics" can be prepared mostly by enlarging the brief statements of the textbook from general histories, biographies, ency-

iii

clopedias, and similar accessible books. The "Topics for Further Search" suggest the use of a larger range of secondary writers and of the available sources. Naturally the school pupil's use of sources is a very different thing from the historian's research. It is worth while to learn that "sources" are simply records made at or near the time of events by people in a position to know what was going on. Well-selected sources bring home to the mind the reality of history; they bring out the human element; they vitalize past times.

(5) Geography and map work, oral and written, are aided by the abundant maps in the text and those referred to in accessible volumes and atlases mentioned in the chapter references.

In using this book as a foundation for teaching it may be well to keep in mind the features of the work which the author believes to be most important for the pupil and most helpful to the teacher. They may be summed up as follows: (1) Political geography, as the background of national history, is emphasized throughout the book and made available by maps and geographical references. (2) The people of the United States form one of the main factors throughout, so that social conditions and events have been freely described; and that part of the work is backed up by many of the references, especially those under "Sources" and "Illustrative." (3) The economic features of American history are dwelt upon in many sections, and particularly in those chapters dealing with pursuits, industries, trade, and business. One of the main threads running through the book is the process by which the continent has been occupied and the gifts of nature have been made available. (4) All sections of the country have helped to make the Union; hence, all sections, North, East, South, West, and far West have been included in the plan of the volume. (5) Since what makes a nation is the greatness of its people, this book aims to bring out clearly the character and public services of great Americans. The details of the lives of some of these men appear in special sections of the text. (6) Foreign relations, diplomatic controversies, and their settlement receive due attention. (7) The accounts of military and naval events include little detail of battles and campaigns, in order to make room for discussions of the causes, aims, and conduct of our various wars and the state of public feeling behind them. (8) The government of the American people is another main subject throughout the book, though it is treated not technically, but so as to show the main principles, and the way they have worked out in the course of time. (9) The bibliographical apparatus has been brought down to narrow space limits by abbreviating the titles. The more important books are listed in Appendix B; and the place and date of publication of any book mentioned can always be found through a library. (10) The list of sources gives an opportunity to reach selected extracts or extended documents; a selected set of source publications can easily be made up from these indications. (11) Special efforts have been made to gather a convenient list of illustrative works, descriptive volumes, stories, novels, and other interesting matter. (12) The pictures, with the exception of a few reproductions of famous paintings, are all realities, intended to place before the pupil in visible form the faces of public men, the surroundings of famous events, and some of the national monuments and buildings. (13) In Appendix A will be found a select list of materials found serviceable to teachers.

Pains have been taken to make the book as free from errors in fact and statement as possible. The chapters have been verified by Mr. David M. Matteson. To combine into one volume the broad and manifold phases of a great nation's life is a difficult task. I have, at least, tried to write about the things that count; to describe events which have aided to make us Americans; to set before my young countrymen the ideal of true national greatness.

ALBERT BUSHNELL HART.

CONTENTS

vi

Contents   vii

TERRITORIAL
DEVELOPMENT
OF THE CONTINENTAL
UNITED STATES
1776-1866

NEW AMERICAN HISTORY

CHAPTER I

FOUNDATIONS OF AMERICAN HISTORY

1. DAWN OF AMERICAN HISTORY

WHERE does American history begin? The true fathers of America are the Europeans who, three or four centuries ago, had the courage to voyage across unknown seas, and the persistence to plant colonies beyond the ocean. The men of each colony brought with them the religion, language, laws, and methods of government to which they and their ancestors were accustomed; hence the early history of America is really a part of European history. The first American colonists were simply Spaniards, Portuguese, or Frenchmen in America; and the English settlers who removed overseas looked upon themselves as still a part of the English people. When that bond was broken by the Revolution of 1775, the United States became at once one of the family of civilized nations. Our history has always been closely connected with that of Europe by commerce, by immigration, by sharing the world's literatures, by interchange of inventions and principles of government.

Five hundred years ago, the only parts of the world that were known to Europeans were their own continent, the neighboring islands, and parts of Asia and Africa. The discovery of America was a result in great part of that new spirit of interest in the past

1

and curiosity about the world, which we call the Renaissance. When, about the year 1300, men of modern European nations began to appreciate the beauty and power of ancient writers and of ancient works of art, interest in nature sprang up again with passionate force, and with it the desire to know the shape and extent of the world. Hence, when a new commercial route from Europe to India was needed, men were willing to take great risks, to sail across the unknown western ocean, and to explore lands hitherto undreamed of.

2. INVENTIONS

The new spirit showed itself especially in two inventions (both previously known in China), which helped discovery and exploration: (1) Gunpowder, first used in war about 1350, enabled the invaders of America to beat the savages. (2) Printing with movable types, probably first practiced in Europe by Gutenberg in 1450, served to spread the fame of the New World.

Long voyages became possible because the art of navigation was steadily advancing. Seagoing ships were now fitted with keels and single rudders, with heavy spars and square sails; and for defense from the seas and from enemies, they were provided with high bulwarks, with "forecastles" and "aftercastles." There was little distinction between merchantmen and warships: in time of war the trader simply took on a few more guns and men and became a fighting cruiser.

Naval science was immensely aided by four inventions, which by 1450 were widely used: (1) The wondrous art of sailing on the wind gave confidence to men on long voyages, because they could get back against an adverse wind. (2) The magnetic compass was a guide far out of sight of land, and when the stars were not visible. (3) The astrolabe enabled the mariner roughly to estimate his distance from the equator. (4) The portolano, or sea chart, showed what was known about the seas and coasts.

3. EUROPE AND THE EAST

The approach to American history came through the attempt to establish new relations between Europe and Asia. In 1450 Europe had no direct intercourse by sea with India, China, and

EARLY ROUTES OF COMMERCE BETWEEN EUROPE AND ASIA. (Showing the Portuguese discoveries along the African coast.)

Japan. Eastern products found their way westward only by transfer overland at the head of the Red Sea, or by a slow and expensive caravan journey across Asia, over routes which were broken in two by the Turks when they took Constantinople in 1453. After that, how were Europeans to get such eastern products as carpets and silks, pearls and cotton goods, the sweet white powder called sugar, the gums, and the pepper that sometimes sold for its weight in gold?

One European, Marco Polo, had actually crossed Asia and returned from the Chinese coast in 1295, and thus reported: "And I tell you with regard to that Eastern Sea of Chin, according to what is said by the experienced pilots and mariners of those parts, there be 7459 Islands in the waters frequented by the said mariners. . . . And there is not one of those Islands but produces valuable and odorous woods . . . and they produce also a great variety of spices." In course of time the question began to be asked, Why might not the Spice Islands and Japan be reached by sea from western Europe? Hence attempts were made to find an eastward water passage around Europe by the Arctic Ocean, and around Africa by the Atlantic Ocean.

Moreover, the learned men of the Renaissance pointed out that the ancients believed the world to be round. A strange book of wonders, called the *Travels of Sir John Mandeville* (published about 1370), says, "For when the sun is east in those parts towards paradise terrestrial, it is then midnight in our parts of this half, for the roundness of the earth. For our Lord God made the earth all round in the midplace of the firmament." By 1470 the Florentine astronomer Toscanelli figured out the circumference of the earth at very nearly its true length. If the world was really round, why was it not possible to reach India by sailing westward instead of eastward?

4. THE EARLY COLONIZING NATIONS

Such a question could best be answered by the maritime nations of western Europe — by Italy, Spain, France, England, and Portugal. The Portuguese had already begun to make long voyages west and south. They discovered or rediscovered the four groups of the Canary, Madeira, Cape Verde, and Azores islands. Under the direction of Prince Henry the Navigator, their vessels pushed down the west coast of Africa; but at the time of his death they had reached no farther south than Sierra Leone.

The neighbor and great rival of Portugal was Spain. The marriage of Ferdinand of Aragon with Isabella of Castile brought under one sovereignty the Christian parts of that land. In 1492, by the conquest of the Moors of Granada (southern Spain), the way was cleared for one great Spanish kingdom. Twenty-seven

WESTERN EUROPE ABOUT 1500. (Showing the chief commercial centers and routes of trade.)

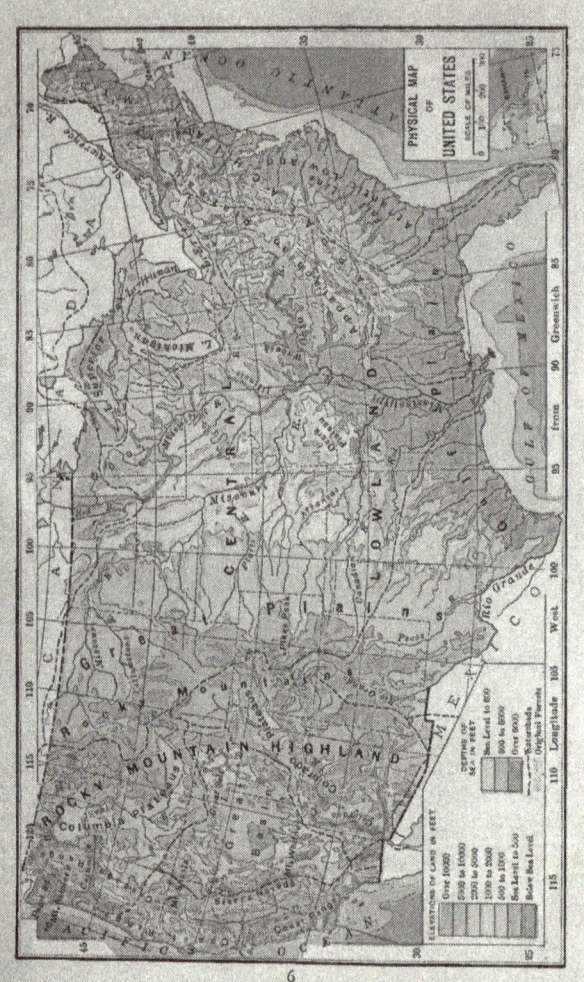

PHYSICAL MAP
OF
UNITED STATES

6

years later, Charles V, grandson of Ferdinand and Isabella, king of Spain and ruler of the Netherlands, became also German emperor, and thus brought Spain into the heart of European politics. Spain built a powerful navy, and organized an infantry that could defeat knights in armor and was almost invincible by other footmen; and for many years she was the strongest state in Europe.

Germany, England, and France in this period were wearing themselves out with civil wars and other wars, and had little energy left for voyages of discovery. Italy was broken up into several states, but furnished the best and boldest sailors of that period.

5. ATLANTIC COAST OF NORTH AMERICA

The Europeans of the fifteenth century thought of the world as consisting of only three parts: Europe, Asia, and Africa. After the discovery of America, as described in the next chapter, it required a generation of explorers to approach the truth that North America is not part of Asia, and more than a century passed before men generally began to think of the western hemisphere in its true relations to the rest of the world. The course of American discovery and colonization was much affected by the physical character of the land; therefore, the nature of the country is one of the essentials of American history.

The Atlantic coast of North America abounds in deep and sheltered harbors, which helped the early settlers in their seafaring. The coast is bold and rugged as far south as Massachusetts Bay, and the country inland is hilly and stony, and abounds in waterfalls. South of the Hudson, a low coast plain gradually widens till it reaches Georgia, and thence stretches westward along the Gulf of Mexico to Texas. Its sandy coast is fringed with shallow lagoons, separated from the open sea by long, narrow islands.

Up to the foothills of the Appalachians this southern country is flat and fertile and well adapted to agriculture. The sluggish rivers are generally navigable from the coast to the "Fall Line," where abundant water power has aided the growth of a series of towns and cities, such as Trenton, Richmond, Petersburg, Raleigh, Columbia, Augusta, and Macon. The flatness of the Atlantic coast gave rise to one disadvantage: innumerable swamps and fresh-water ponds bred mosquitoes. When our forefathers sickened with fevers, they little guessed that it was this insignificant enemy which brought disease, death, and often ruin to a colony.

On the west, the Atlantic lowland is shut in by the Appalachian Mountain system, which extends in a belt about a hundred miles wide from the Gulf of St. Lawrence 1600 miles southwestward to northern Alabama. On the western side of these mountains is an upland plateau which declines gradually to the west and is deeply trenched by the steep-sided valleys of the streams. Like the lower coast lands, this whole highland region was originally clothed with forests which concealed the lurking savage.

6. INTERIOR OF OUR COUNTRY

The west slope of the Appalachian plateau merges into a vast low plain, which is drained partly northeastward to Hudson Bay, partly eastward through the Great Lakes to the Gulf of St. Lawrence, but chiefly southward through the Mississippi River system. A northern belt, as far west as the upper Mississippi, and a southern belt, as far as the Ozark Plateau, were originally forest-covered; but the central part from Indiana westward was made up of broad grassy prairies, treeless except for narrow fringes of timber along the watercourses.

The St. Lawrence and Mississippi valleys make up the most extensive tract of highly fertile land in the world. Most of it has abundant rainfall. "When tickled with a hoe, it laughs with a harvest"; and it has almost every variety of soil and product. The numerous streams furnish alluvial "bottom land." North of the Missouri and Ohio rivers most of the country is covered with glacial deposits, making nature's wheat fields; and the vast prairies grow all kinds of crops, especially corn.

About 500 miles beyond the Mississippi River the land rises gradually into a treeless plateau, which is called the Great Plains and is so dry that not much farming is possible without irrigation. The "bunch grass" of these plains once supported countless herds of wild bison, and now is the pasturage for beef cattle.

Beyond the plains is the Rocky Mountain chain, with a general elevation of about 10,000 feet. These lofty and complicated ranges occupy a belt of country from 200 to 300 miles wide, made up of mountains extremely rough and steep. Their summits reach to nearly 15,000 feet, though the chain may be crossed at elevations not greater than from 6000 to 8000 feet. West of the mountains are broad, rugged plateaus. In these mountains and uplands the Indians found large game for food, and small fur-bearing animals. From the sheep that now range the region the white man still draws material for clothing; while in the upheaved and dislocated strata he finds our richest stores of gold, silver, copper, and lead.

7. PACIFIC COAST OF OUR COUNTRY

Farther west, rises the steep escarpment of the Sierra Nevada and Cascade chains. which sink away again in a long western slope, abundantly watered in winter by moist winds from the Pacific, that clothe it with thick forests of valuable trees. These chains are scarcely more than seventy-five miles wide, but they

BIG TREES IN CALIFORNIA.

rival the Rocky Mountains in height and ruggedness. West of the crest of the Sierra Nevada and Cascade systems, and beyond a series of long lowland valleys, stand the low Coast Ranges, which rise steeply from the Pacific Ocean. These ranges are broken down to the sea at three places only: the bay of San Francisco, the Columbia River, and the Strait of Juan de Fuca, which leads to Puget Sound. The climate is much the same all along the western coast — warm, dry summers and mild winters, which have made it a resort for travelers and health seekers.

8. Routes of Trade and Travel

Through the forests and across the mountains ran two systems of primeval routes of travel: footpaths and waterways. (1) Throughout the continent, buffalo paths and Indian trails, sometimes only six inches wide, led through prairie and forest; they often followed the divides between the valleys, because they were free from crossings of streams. (2) A network of water routes was made by rivers and lakes, on which plied the dugout and, in the north, the Indian birch-bark canoe, which was one of the best inventions of any savage race; it was easy to make, swift to paddle, and light to "tote" over a carry from one system of rivers to another.

For long journeys to the west the Atlantic streams could be followed up to the divides separating them from the tributaries of the Great Lakes or of the Ohio River. The routes across the Appalachian chain ran for the most part on the same lines as the present trunk-line railroads, especially through the gaps at the heads of the Mohawk, Susquehanna, Potomac, and James rivers. By carries or portages known to the Indians, one could also pass from the Great Lakes to Hudson Bay, or to the upper Mississippi, or to the Ohio. Examples of such transfer points are Ravenna, Ohio, between the Cuyahoga and Mahoning rivers; Fort Wayne, Indiana, between the Maumee and the Wabash; and Chicago, between Lake Michigan and

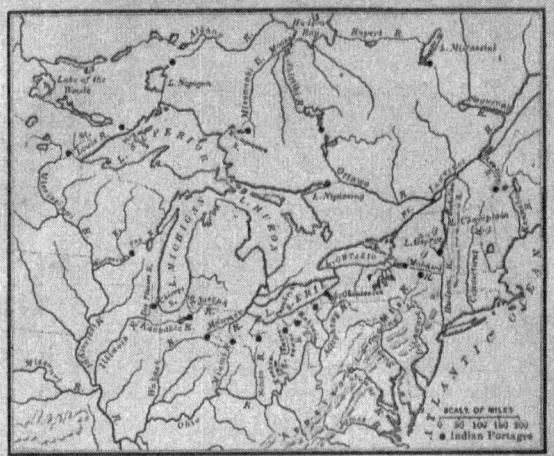

IMPORTANT INDIAN PORTAGES.

the Des Plaines branch of the Illinois. At such places white
men's towns eventually grew up. Indians rarely crossed from
the east to the Pacific drainage, though the passes were known
to the natives.

9. AMERICAN PRODUCTS

The whole land originally abounded in wild animals. The
deer and the bison, commonly called buffalo, furnished meat
for the hungry, clothing for the cold, and a roof for the family;
the game birds, of which the turkey and the pigeon were the most
plentiful, increased the food supply; and the coast waters and
streams abounded in fish and in fur-bearing animals. The
earth furnished the savage with berries and other fruits, corn,
beans, pumpkins, squashes, and maple sugar for his diet; tobacco
for his luxury; herbs and simples for diseases and wounds; wood
for his hut and his fire.

INTERIOR OF A ZUÑI PUEBLO. (About the same size as in 1492.)

The colonists found valuable resources in the timber and the iron ores; their descendants discovered coal and oil, and copper, lead, zinc, and the precious metals; but almost the only things the Indian had to sell that the white man coveted were deerskins and furs, especially that of the beaver. Still America yielded three products not then known to the Old World: (1) Corn was the plant most widely sown and harvested by the Indians; the colonists quickly found it to be "a grain of general use to man and beast." (2) The potato, native of South America, in the course of time became the chief food of millions of Europeans. (3) Tobacco, everywhere much prized by the Indians, grew wild or was rudely cultivated.

10. NATIVE CIVILIZATION IN AMERICA

The native inhabitants of America, called Indians by Columbus because he supposed he had reached the Indian coast of Asia, were almost all of one great race, though their origin is a puzzle for scientists. Throughout central North America exist a great number of mounds, some of which are graves, some village sites, some defenses, some the outlines of animals; but there is no reason to suppose that the "mound builders" were different from the ordinary Indians.

From Georgia to Arizona, most Indian tribes raised plenty of food and lived in fixed towns, some southwestern peoples in cliff dwellings. The descendants of some of these tribes, as for instance the Zuñis, still live in the same communal villages or pueblos, and carry on much the same life as their forefathers.

Farther south, in the communal city of Mexico, were the Aztecs, men of war who lived on tribute or plunder from neighboring tribes, and reveled in human sacrifice; they had the arts of making pottery, of working in soft metals, of weaving and feather work, and even of a kind of picture writing. In Mexico and Central America ruined stone cities mark a higher civilization, already decaying when the white man came. These abound in elaborately carved stone walls, stairways, and monuments, strangely like certain temples and idols in eastern Asia. In South America native civilization reached its highest point

in the empire of the Incas in Peru, who had an organization far above that of the ordinary Indians; for they built roads and stone towns, trained llamas for beasts of burden, and used a system of records made by knotted cords.

ANCIENT PERUVIAN JAR.
(Perhaps a portrait.)

The Indians who most disturbed the English colonists were three groups: (1) along the northern Atlantic coast, the Algonquin family; (2) inland, between the Hudson and Lake Erie, the "Five Nations" of Iroquois; (3) between the Mississippi and the southeast coast the powerful Cherokees, kin to the Iroquois, and the Muskogee family,

HART'S NEW AMER. HIST. — 2

including the intelligent, numerous, and warlike tribes of Choctaws, Creeks, and Chickasaws. All these Indians were vigorous and hardy people, well built, tall, and handsome. Their clothing was chiefly of deerskins, supplemented after the whites came by the "match-coat," or blanket. They gathered into villages, living for the most part in wigwams of bark or skins; though some tribes had "long houses" — rows of continuous wooden dwellings.

The main occupations of these Indians were fishing and hunting and fighting, but nearly all had cornfields, and some of them plots of tobacco and vegetables, all tilled by the women. The Indians were fond of gayety, lively conversation, dancing, and open-air games. They knew no real religion; early discoverers said that they worshiped stones and the devil. Their priests were medicine men who sang, shook their rattles, and circled about the fire ten or twelve hours together, "with most impetuous and interminate clamours and howling." In many ways the Indians showed remarkable inventive skill. They strung bows, fashioned stone arrowheads, clubs, and hatchets, contrived snowshoes, made rude pottery, tanned skins, executed beautiful designs in beads and porcupine quills, manufactured maple sugar, plaited nets, carved pipes, wove baskets, painted pictographs on skins and rocks, had a currency of wampum made from seashells, and invented the serviceable bark canoe.

11. INDIAN WARFARE AND GOVERNMENT

In war the Indians were among the fiercest fighting men of all history. Their weapons were the bow and arrow, club, tomahawk, and stone knife; and they quickly adopted the white man's muskets, axes, and knives. Swift and silent in movement, they chose to attack by surprise; if once beaten back, they were likely to give up and go home for the time, rather than lose more men. Their custom of killing or enslaving men, women, and children alike, was too often imitated by their white enemies, who also learned how to take the scalps of their savage adversaries. The narratives of white captives are filled with accounts of fearful tortures.

Fortunately for the whites, the Indians were broken up into small political fragments. The so-called "tribes," often including many villages, were united by the loosest of ties; they fought among themselves. The fundamental idea of the Indian was that every member of every other tribe, unless bound by

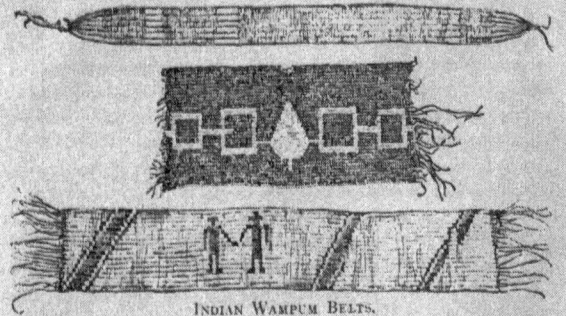

INDIAN WAMPUM BELTS.

friendly treaty, was his enemy; and he looked on all white men as members of one hostile tribe. Indeed, the whole Indian conception of government and society was different from that of the white man. The tribes were subdivided into clans or "totems," and families; and the tribal councils were mere "powwows," for the decision bound nobody; yet discussion and decision were backed up by a powerful public opinion. The tribal lands were usually only the territory over which the tribe habitually ranged; nobody "owned" land in the English sense of absolute property which could be transferred to another person.

The Indians were often friendly, gave food, furnished guides, and fought on the white men's side against other tribes; but their chiefs had no recognized power to compel obedience, and

hence treaties with the English were always hard to enforce.
Few Indians have come down in history as leaders of their
people. Wahunsonacock, commonly called Powhatan by the
Virginians, King Philip in New England, Pontiac and Corn
Planter in the West, George Guess who invented a Cherokee
alphabet, and later Tecumseh, Chief Joseph, and Geronimo
the Apache, are almost the only great names.

12. REVIEW

Early American history was simply a part of the history of
the nations of Europe that made discoveries and planted colonies
in the western hemisphere. They were aroused by that intellectual movement which we call the Renaissance, one phase of
which was greater interest in seafaring. The interruption of
trade with central Asia, caused by the invasion of the Turks,
was an additional reason for trying to reach India by a new sea
route.

Although the Europeans were not aware of it until some years
later, the Atlantic coast of our country abounds in broad rivers
and good harbors. From the water line the land rises to the
summit of the Appalachian Mountains and then descends to
the fertile St. Lawrence and Mississippi river basins. Westward the land again rises until it reaches the high Rockies, and
the great upland beyond; and beyond the Sierra Nevada it
slopes down to the Pacific coast. Easy divides and passes con-
nect the various parts of the country with one another.

A good share of this broad land abounded in animal life, furnishing food and clothing to the natives. The Indians also had
corn, potatoes, and tobacco, none of which were then known in
Europe. Most of the tribes were still in the savage stage of
civilization, though many of them lived in villages, and the
Mexicans and Peruvians built stone cities and temples. The
Indians provided themselves with tools and utensils. They
were excellent warriors, but never understood how to unite
in strong and numerous communities.

References Bearing on the Text and Topics

Geography and Maps. See maps, pp. 3, 5, 6, 11. — Avery, *U.S.*, I. — Bogart, *Econ. Hist.*, 4, 5, 10, 18, 78. — Coman, *Indust. Hist.*, front., 3. — *Epoch Maps*, no. 1. — Farrand, *Basis of Am. Hist.* — Shepherd, *Hist. Atlas*, 187, 188.

Secondary. Bassett, *U.S.*, ch. i. — Becker, *Beginnings*, 1–17. — Cheyney, *Europ. Background.* — Farrand, *Basis of Am. Hist.* — Fiske, *Discov. of Am.*, I. 1–147, 256–334; II. 294–364. — Hodge, *Handbook of Am. Indians.* — Morgan, *Am. Aborigines.* — Powell, *Physiographic Regions.* — Shaler, *Nature and Man in Am.*, 166–283. — Winsor, *America*, IV. i–xxx.

Sources. Hart, *Source Book*, § 9; *Source Readers*, I. §§ 8, 19–33, 37–44. III. §§ 57–69. — *Old South Leaflets*, nos. 30, 32. — See also New Engl. Hist. Teachers' Assoc., *Hist. Sources*, § 65; *Syllabus*, 167–168, 293.

Illustrative. Leland, *Algonquin Legends of New Engl.* — Longfellow, *Hiawatha.* — Lummis, *Strange Corners of Our Country.* — Whittier, *Bridal of Pennacook.*

Pictures. Avery, *U.S.*, I. — Catlin, *North Am. Indians.* — Mc-Kenney and Hall, *Hist. and Biography of the Indian Tribes.* — *Mentor*, serial nos. 7, 34, 60, 83, 92, 113, 116. — U. S. Bureau of Ethnology, *Reports.* — Winsor, *America*, I.

Topics Answerable from the References Above

(1) When and how was gunpowder first used in Europe? [§ 2] — (2) What were the first books printed in America? [§ 2] — (3) How did the mariner's compass come into use in Europe? [§ 2] — (4) What five harbors of North America were first located by Europeans? [§ 5] — (5) What are the best passes across the Rocky Mountains? [§ 6] — (6) What were the best waterways (with portages) from the Atlantic to the Mississippi? [§ 8] — (7) Indian mounds. [§ 10] — (8) The Indian totem system. [§ 11]

Topics for Further Search

(9) Adventures of Marco Polo. [§ 3] — (10) Was there ever a Sir John Mandeville? [§ 3] — (11) Prince Henry the Navigator. [§ 4] — (12) Introduction of corn, potatoes, and tobacco into Europe. [§ 9] — (13) Indian remains in your neighborhood. [§ 10] — (14) Ancient buildings and monuments in Mexico and Central America. [§ 10] — (15) Peruvian roads and buildings. [§ 10] — (16) Account of *one* of the Indians mentioned in § 11.

CHAPTER II

THE CENTURY OF DISCOVERY (1492-1604)

13. FORERUNNINGS OF DISCOVERY (1000-1492)

UNTIL about 1500, the existence of any western continent was undreamed of in Europe, although in far-off Iceland there

were records of a "saga," or memorized tradition, telling how Leif Ericson — "Leif the Lucky"—reached the mainland, far south of Greenland, in the year 1000. Another saga tells that in 1007 one Karlsefni landed there in a fine country, which has never been identified, abounding in flat stones and "wineberries" and fierce natives. No evidence has ever been found to show that Leif's discovery of North America was known to Italian or Spanish

LEIF ERICSON'S SHIP.

navigators. Their incentive to western voyages was the hope of finding a direct western route to India, especially after Bartholomew Diaz of Portugal reached the Cape of Good Hope (1487) and saw a broad sea beyond, on which ships could undoubtedly sail to Asia, though by a long and roundabout route.

To Christopher Columbus, born (about 1451) in the Italian city of Genoa, is due the credit of applying the science of his time to this problem of reaching India. Before he was thirty years old he formed a plan of sailing westward to Asia, which he calculated to be not far from 2500 miles distant from Europe. Directly, or through his brother Bartholomew, he appealed to the kings of Portugal, Spain, England, and France to fit him out; and all declined the splendid opportunity. Finally, he turned again to Spain and appealed to the zeal of Queen Isabella in behalf of the distant heathen, and aroused her counselors by depicting rich results of conquest and power. Isabella at last agreed to fit out an expedition in behalf of her kingdom of Castile.

14. COLUMBUS THE DISCOVERER (1492-1502)

Furnished with the queen's money, Columbus got together three little ships called caravels, the *Santa Maria*, *Niña*, and *Pinta*, carrying 90 men in all. He sailed from Palos early in August, 1492, and from the Canary Islands five weeks later; thenceforward his sole reliance was his own unconquerable will. When the crews threatened to mutiny unless he would turn back, he pleaded and threatened and even deceived them by underestimating the ship's daily run.

On Friday, October 12, 1492 (October 21 of our calendar), thirty-three days after losing sight of land, and then distant 3230 nautical miles from Palos, the caravels came upon an island, to which, says Columbus, "I gave the name of San Salvadore, in commemoration of his Divine Majesty who has wonderfully granted all this. The Indians call it Guanahani." This landfall was probably Watling Island of the Bahama group. A few days later Columbus reached the coast of Cuba, and then Hispaniola, now Haiti. He was deeply disappointed not to find towns and civilized communities, for to the day of

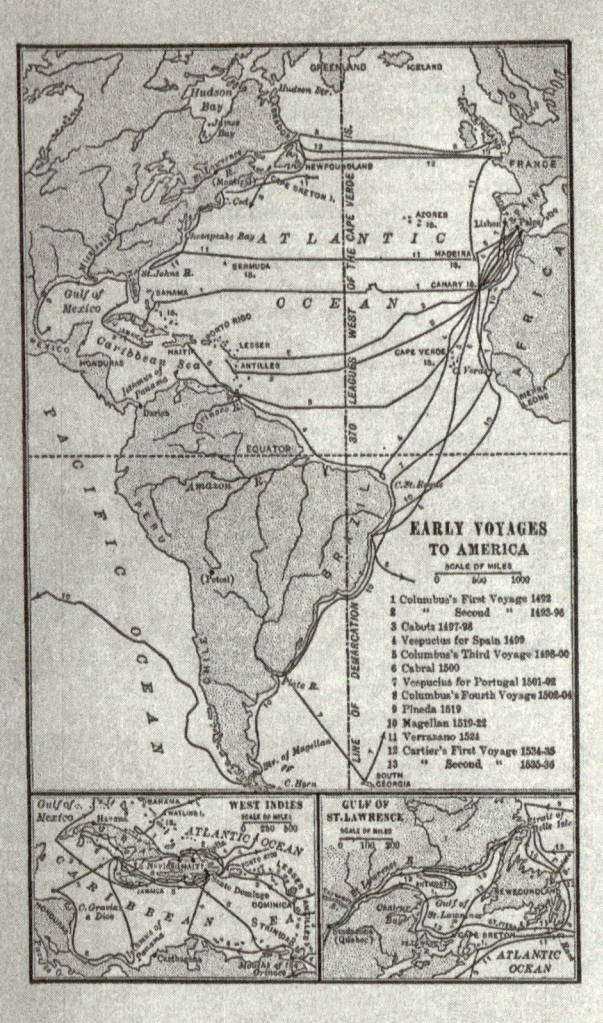

EARLY VOYAGES
TO AMERICA

SCALE OF MILES

0   500   1000

1 Columbus's First Voyage 1492
2   "   Second   "   1493-96
3 Cabots 1497-98
4 Vespucius for Spain 1499
5 Columbus's Third Voyage 1498-00
6 Cabral 1500
7 Vespucius for Portugal 1501-02
8 Columbus's Fourth Voyage 1502-04
9 Pineda 1519
10 Magellan 1519-22
11 Verrazano 1524
12 Cartier's First Voyage 1534-35
13   "   Second   "   1535-36

his death he supposed that he had hit on the coast of Asia. Thus was America discovered accidentally in the voyage of one of the most extraordinary men in history.

On a second and a third voyage (1493, 1498) Columbus discovered Porto Rico, Jamaica, some of the Lesser Antilles, and

DEPARTURE OF COLUMBUS. (From De Bry's *Voyages*, 1590.)

the mouth of the Orinoco. He founded a colony in Hispaniola, including the city of Santo Domingo, but was sent home in chains and for a time was in disgrace. He made, however, a fourth voyage (1502), in search of a water passage to India, which carried him to the coast of Honduras and to the Isthmus of Panama. Four years later he died in Spain.

15. ENGLISH AND PORTUGUESE DISCOVERIES (1493–1507)

The announcement that Columbus had reached Asia aroused new national rivalries, and it was followed by many western voyages. Henry VII, king of England, gave authority to the Venetian navigator John Cabot and his three sons "to sail to all parts, regions, and waters of the eastern, western, and southern seas, and to discover any heathen regions which up to this time have remained unknown to Christians." Though this voyage later became the basis of the English claims to North America, we know only that Cabot came back in 1497 and reported "that 700 leagues hence he discovered land, the territory of the grand Chan. He coasted for 300 leagues and landed and found two very large and fertile new islands." His landfall is supposed to have been the island of Cape Breton. The next year Cabot and his son Sebastian are supposed to have made a voyage farther south; but of their discoveries, if they made any, we have no contemporary accounts.

Meantime the Portuguese were trying to reach India by sailing eastward around Africa, and they claimed a monopoly of the discoveries that they might make. In May, 1493, the Pope issued a bull in which he undertook to divide the new non-Christian world between Portugal and Spain, by a north and south line through the Atlantic. A year later, in the treaty of Tordesillas, made directly between Spain and Portugal, it was agreed that the "line of demarcation" should run "from pole to pole, 370 leagues west from the Cape Verde Islands." The need of such a treaty was realized in 1497, when the Portuguese Vasco da Gama passed the Cape of Good Hope, and shortly reached India. Then Cabral, one of the Portuguese voyagers to India, hit on the coast of Brazil (1500), which he thought was an Asiatic island. Thus America would have been discovered without Columbus. Later it was found that the line of Tordesillas ran to the west of the Brazilian coast, which was therefore left to the Portuguese to settle.

The Italian Americus Vespucius, of Venice, coasted large parts of South America from 1499 to 1507 in behalf of Spain and then of Portugal. He published several letters describing his discoveries and, apparently without any such expectation, furnished a name which gradually supplanted the term "New World" used by Columbus and others. An Alsatian geographer, Hylacomylus, realizing that a new continent had been discovered, suggested in 1507 that the new fourth part of the world be called "Amerige; that is, the land of Americus, or America." This name, originally applied to the eastern part of South America, was gradually extended to all of South America, and then to the entire New World.

16. SPANISH DISCOVERIES AND CONQUESTS, TO 1532

By the year 1513 most of the islands of the Caribbean Sea, and the coast from Mexico to the Plata, had been visited; so that the Spaniards began to realize that wherever they sailed far enough west, they struck land, perhaps a continuous continent. In that year Balboa crossed the narrow isthmus of Darien or Panama, and looked upon the Pacific Ocean.

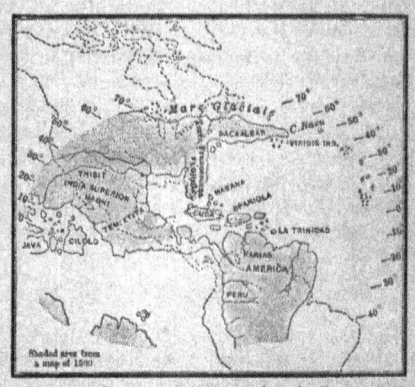

SUPPOSED LIMITS OF AMERICA (1530), COMPARED WITH THE ACTUAL OUTLINES.

Since the Spaniards could not penetrate directly westward, they sent Magellan in 1519 with a small fleet to coast along America southward. He discovered and passed through the strait to which he gave his name, entered the Pacific Ocean, then sailed up the west coast of South America, and thence westward until he reached the Ladrones and the Philippine Islands. Magellan was killed in a fight with the natives, but one of his vessels got home to Spain via the Cape of Good Hope — the first circumnavigation of the globe. At last the true Indies had been reached by sailing west, and the Philippines speedily became a Spanish colony, regularly communicating with the home country across Mexico.

Meanwhile the Spanish were pushing exploration and conquest within the continents, beginning with a fruitless expedition by Ponce de Leon in Florida (1513), and a voyage by Pineda, who was the first to skirt the north coast of the Gulf of Mexico (1519). The first permanent settlement on the mainland was the result of the romantic occupation of Mexico by Hernando Cortes in 1519. With 550 men and 16 horses he marched into the country and took the fortified city of Mexico, smashed the rude political organization of the Aztecs, and set up the Catholic religion; and in 1521 he founded the province of Mexico. In 1532 a Spanish force of 200 men and 60 horses, under Francisco Pizarro, penetrated and conquered Peru, and looted a large quantity of gold; here also the native government was overthrown and a permanent Spanish colonial government under a viceroy was set up.

17. Spanish Explorations of the Coast and Interior (1526-1592)

Except for these two conquests the interior of the two American continents had hardly been touched by Europeans. The Spaniards now began to send exploring expeditions to and into the southern part of what is now the United States: (1) De Ayllon attempted to found a colony on Chesapeake Bay (1526) and thus founded a claim to what later became Virginia. (2) Narvaez with a party explored the land north of the Gulf coast, and passed the mouth of the Mississippi, probably the first white man to see any part of that river (1528). (3) Hernando De

Soto, with a force of 620 men, marched inland from the coast of Florida; and in 1541 reached the Mississippi and explored part of the present state of Arkansas. (4) In 1540 Coronado, incited by tales of seven rich and wonderful "cities of Cibola," went northward from Mexico, but found the cities to be only Indian pueblos, of which some are still standing. He penetrated to the country of Quivira (Kansas), which abounded in "crook-backed cows" (buffaloes). (5) From 1533 to 1592 the Pacific coast was visited by Spaniards as far north as the Strait

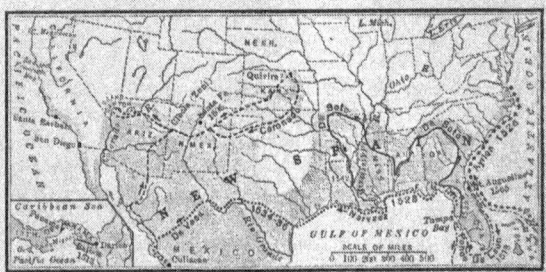

SPANISH EXPLORATIONS IN THE INTERIOR OF NORTH AMERICA.

of Juan de Fuca; the exploration gave them title to California and Lower California.

The West Indies, as the Spanish possessions in the islands and the continent of the New World were generally called, made the Spanish kingdom for a time the richest of all European countries, and enabled the Spaniards for a century to take the leading place in Europe. The accumulated gold of Mexico and Peru was quickly swept up; but in 1545 the rich silver mines of Potosi, in Peru, were opened, and later good silver mines were found in Mexico. By 1550 Spanish colonies were established in Mexico and Central America, on the west and north coasts of South America, and on the lower Plata.

18. FRENCH DISCOVERIES (1524-1565)

Meanwhile, about twenty years after Columbus's first voyage, a mighty change was begun in Europe through the Protestant Reformation. Up to this time, every nation in western Europe was Roman Catholic. A new faith appeared in Germany and spread to France, Italy, England, Scotland, Hungary, and the Scandinavian countries. In the end, the peoples of northwestern Europe became mostly Protestant, while those of the south remained Catholic.

France, though mainly Catholic, ignored the papal division of 1493 (§ 15). In 1524, King Francis I dispatched the Italian Verrazano, of Florence, with a fleet which crossed the Atlantic and explored an unknown coast including what is now New York Harbor, a bay, he said, in "a very pleasant situation among some steep hills, through which a very large river, deep at its mouth, forced its way to the sea." Much farther north the French captain Jacques Cartier explored the coast, found islands and a river (1534), and the next year "a goodly great gulf, full of islands, passages, and entrances," which he named St. Lawrence; thence he entered "the great river Hochelaga and ready way to China." His progress was stopped by the rapids later dubbed Lachine ("Chinese"), near a hill which he called Mount Royal, now Montreal.

A body of "Huguenots," or French Protestants, with the consent of the Catholic king, planted a colony under Jean Ribault at Port Royal, now in South Carolina (1562); but it failed. The French returned and built a second Port Royal on the "River May" (St. Johns) in Florida. This was a flat defiance of the Spaniards, who founded (1565) the frontier town of St. Augustine to confront the French; this town, still in existence, is the oldest within the mainland boundaries of the United States. Menendez, the Spanish governor, uprooted the French colony; and the French never regained the opportunity of settling the southern Atlantic coast.

19. ENGLISH TRADERS AND FREEBOOTERS (1566-1580)

Spain's monopoly of American trade and colonization aroused the spirit of the English, especially when, under Philip II (1556-1598), Spain became the leading Catholic power of

SULGRAVE MANOR, ENGLAND.
(Early home of the Washington family.)

Europe. Internal troubles arose out of the Reformation in England, but diminished in the reign of the Protestant Queen Elizabeth; and English merchants began to plan voyages and colonies both in the East and in the West. In despite of Spain a charter was granted in 1566 to Sir Humphrey Gilbert to open a northwest passage around America to India, and to discover new lands, which were to be an English colony. Several later explorers made voyages on the same quest, penetrating as far as Hudson Strait and Bay.

One of the boldest English adventurers and bravest fighters was Sir John Hawkins, who made several profitable voyages to the Spanish colonies with African slaves. When his five ships were caught in a Mexican port by thirteen Spanish ships, he fought them all and escaped with two vessels. One of Hawkins's captains was Francis Drake, who in 1572 sailed off again to prey on Spanish commerce. Pirate-like he harried the Spanish mainland, captured Spanish vessels and mule trains, and carried off gold, silver, and merchandise. Nevertheless, on his return to England Drake was kindly received by Queen Elizabeth, who even shared in the plunder.

The slow downfall of Spain may be said to have begun when the Spanish provinces of the Netherlands revolted and formed a union against Spain (1576). The English government sym-

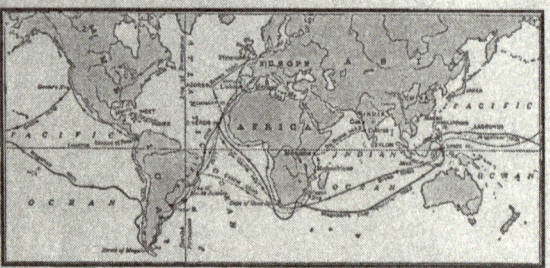

EARLY VOYAGES AROUND THE WORLD.

pathized with the rebels; then individual Englishmen took an active part in the pulling down of Spain. In 1577 Drake, with the queen's approval, though without a royal commission, set off with a little fleet; he rounded South America, passed through the Strait of Magellan with his one remaining ship, and was the first to see Cape Horn, and to find the open sea to the south of it. The story of Drake's next exploits sounds like the Arabian Nights, and is adorned with such phrases as "thirteene chests full of royals of plate, foure score pound weight of golde, and sixe and twentie tunne of siluer." He sailed up the unfortified west coast of South America, capturing Spanish coasting ships, terrifying towns, taking one prize worth a million dollars on its voyage from Peru, and throwing the Spaniards into a panic.

Running far to the north, in hope of finding a passage through or around America to England, he put into a bay just north of the harbor of San Francisco to repair his ships, and called the country New Albion. Thence he struck boldly westward across the Pacific, sailed through the Philippines and the Spice Islands, and then home again (1580) around the Cape of Good Hope, the first Englishman to circumnavigate the globe. Queen Elizabeth formally knighted him, and thus proclaimed him an English hero fighting for his sovereign.

20. FIRST ENGLISH COLONIES (1578-1587)

The next step towards colonization was a vain attempt at planting an English settlement in Newfoundland under a new charter granted to Sir Humphrey Gilbert (1578). His half-brother, Sir Walter Raleigh, then got from the queen a new "patent," or grant of lands (1584), authorizing him to colonize "remote heathen and barbarous lands . . . not actually possessed of any Christian Prince." Forthwith he sent out two vessels, under Amadas and Barlowe, to find a proper place for a colony, and they fixed on Roanoke Island. On their return and favorable report Queen Elizabeth named the new land for herself, "Virginia."

Three times Raleigh sent out actual colonists to Roanoke Island, which was not a very favorable place. The third colony, commanded by John White (1587), was made up of 150 people, including seventeen women. One of them gave birth to Virginia Dare, the first English child born on American soil. Part of the colonists returned to England. All who remained in America disappeared, and their fate to this day is uncertain.

21. WAR WITH SPAIN (1587-1604)

The harrying of the commerce of Spain inevitably led to war, and the crisis came in 1587, when Philip II resolved to in-

vade England and destroy the plague of English sea rovers at
its source. The proposed invasion took the form of a religious
crusade. The troops were to be carried to England by a
mighty Spanish fleet called the "Invincible Armada." The
Armada sailed from Corunna in 1588 — 137 vessels, carrying

27,000 men — and
made its way in half-
moon formation up
the English Channel.
It was beset by an
enemy as brave as the
Spaniards and much
more nimble; for the
English received their
guests with 197 ships
and 16,000 men,
mostly trained sea-
men. The Armada
stopped at the Nether-
lands, but the English

ENGLISH WARSHIP OF 1588. (From a tapestry
in the old House of Lords.)

finally sent fire ships among the Spaniards, and drove them out
into the North Sea, where many of the fleet were destroyed.
The rest attempted to escape around Scotland, but many were
lost in fearful storms. The commander in chief arrived in Spain
at last; and gradually 67 ships out of the fleet crept into port.

The war meanwhile had extended to the colonies, and it lasted
for seventeen years. Drake captured and plundered the city of
Santo Domingo, the richest in the New World, and other ports.
The new king of Spain, Philip III, and the new king of England,
James I, both desired peace; but the Spaniards long insisted
that England should agree to keep Englishmen from trading
in the Spanish colonies, or settling in territory claimed by Spain.
On both points the English stood firm, emboldened by their
victory over the Armada; and in 1604 a treaty of peace was
made without either of the desired pledges. Thus the way was

opened for the foundation of English colonies which grew into the later United States, in territory then claimed by Spain.

22. RIVAL CLAIMS TO AMERICA (1584–1605)

Gradually the coast of North America became better known, and the various European nations began to bring forward arguments for their claims to America. France talked about the effect of the voyages of Verrazano and Cartier. Spain urged the Pope's bull of 1493 and the early Spanish explorations, assuming that coasts once skirted by Spanish ships remained Spanish, and that the territories inland from such coasts were Spanish to eternity. Against these sweeping claims, the English geographer Hakluyt asserted that "one Cabot and the English did first discover the shores about the Chesapeake"; and a contemporary writer set forth the English title to Virginia as follows: (1) first discovery by the subjects of Henry VII (1497); (2) voyages under Elizabeth "to the mainland and infinite islands of the West Indies"; (3) the voyage of Amadas and Barlowe (1584); (4) the actual settlement by the White colony (1587); (5) a broad and quite unfounded claim that the coast and the ports of Virginia had been long discovered, peopled, and possessed by many English. The writer said of the Pope's bull, "if there be a law that the Pope may do what he list, let them that list obey him."

From 1602 to 1605 three attempts were made by individuals to plant colonies on what is now the coast of Maine, on the basis of these English claims. All these efforts failed; for the English had not learned to bear the cold winters, and as yet had too little experience in colonizing.

23. REVIEW

Notwithstanding voyages by the Northmen, who reached the northeast part of North America, the first European to discover and occupy western territory for a European power was Christopher Columbus, in 1492. He explored the West Indies and later coasted parts of the mainland of South America and the Isthmus of Panama.

The Portuguese were already on the eve of reaching southern Asia by the Cape of Good Hope sea route; and in 1494 Portugal and Spain agreed to a north and south "line of demarcation," to divide their claims. John Cabot in 1497 discovered land for the king of England. America received its name from an Italian explorer named Americus Vespucius.

In 1513 Balboa crossed the Isthmus of Panama and saw the open Pacific. Six years later Magellan sailed around the southern end of South America and through the Pacific westward; his expedition was the first to go around the world.

The Spaniards made settlements in South America and Mexico, and explored the southern part of what is now the United States. They claimed all the coasts that they skirted and all the country inland from those coasts; but their claim was ignored by France, whose vessels explored the coasts of present New York and the St. Lawrence River.

The English also disregarded the Spanish claim to sole possession, and their freebooters began to plunder Spanish ships and towns. They also tried to find a northwest passage to India around North America. In 1577, Drake, an English sea captain, sailed around South America into the Pacific, plundered the Spaniards there, and made his way back home westward. Sir Walter Raleigh and his friends tried to plant colonies in Newfoundland and on Roanoke Island, but failed.

Spain finally sent out the Armada of 1588 to crush England, but the great fleet was defeated; and after years of irregular warfare Spain and England finally made peace in 1604. By this time the English were firmly convinced that they had a better claim than any one else to part of North America.

References Bearing on the Text and Topics

Geography and Maps. See maps, pp. 20, 25, 28, 63. — Avery, *U.S.*, I. — Becker, *Beginnings*, 28. — Bourne, *Spain in Am.* — Coman, *Indust. Hist.*, 8. — *Epoch Maps*, no. 2. — Semple, *Geogr. Conditions*, 1–18. —

Shepherd, *Hist. Atlas*, 105–111, 191. — Winsor, *Columbus; Cartier to Frontenac*, 1–76. — See U. S. Supt. of Docs., *Geography and Exploration List*.
   Secondary. Bassett, *U.S.*, ch. ii. — Becker, *Beginnings*, 17–54. —
Bourne, *Spain in Am.*, chs. i–xii. — Channing, *U.S.*, I. chs. i–v. —
Cheyney, *Europ. Background*, ch. iv. — Fiske, *Discov. of Am.*, I. 147–
516, II. 1–293, 365–569; *Old Va.* I. 1–40. — Hovgaard, *Voyages of
the Norsemen.* — Lummis, *Span. Pioneers.* — Markham, *Christopher
Columbus.* — Parkman, *Pioneers of France*, 9–228. — Reeves, *Find-
ing of Wineland.* — Tyler, *England in Am.*, chs. i, ii.
   Sources. *Am. Hist. Leaflets*, nos. 1, 3, 9, 13. — Bourne, *Narratives
of De Soto.* — Hart, *Contemporaries*, I. §§ 16–36, 44–48; *Patriots and
Statesmen*, I. 31–59; *Source Book*, §§ 1–4, 7. — Higginson, *Am. Explorers*, 1–228. — James, *Readings*, §§ 1–7. — Jameson, *Original Narratives*
(Northmen, Spanish, English, and French). — *Old South Leaflets*, nos.
17, 20, 29, 31, 33–37, 39, 71, 90, 92, 102, 115–120, 122. — Payne,
Elizabethan Seamen. — Winship, *Journey of Coronado; Sailors' Nar-
ratives.* — See New Engl. Hist. Teachers' Assoc., *Hist. Sources*, §§ 66–68;
Syllabus, 293–296.
   Illustrative. Ballantyne, *Erling the Bold* (Iceland); *Norsemen in
the West.* — Barnes, *Drake and his Yeomen.* — Cooper, *Mercedes of
Castile.* — Johnston, *Sir Mortimer* (Sea dogs). — Kingsley, *Westward
Ho!* — Longfellow, *Skeleton in Armor; Sir Humphrey Gilbert.* — Lowell,
Columbus; Voyage to Vinland. — Munroe, *Flamingo Feather* (Hugue-
nots). — Simms, *Vasconselos* (De Soto). — Tennyson, *Columbus.* —
Wallace, *Fair God* (Mexico).
   Pictures. — Avery, *U.S.*, I. — *Mentor*, serial nos. 13, 22. — Wilson,
Am. People, I. — Winsor, *America*, II–IV.

Topics Answerable from the References Above

   (1) The English claims based on the Cabot voyages. [§ 15] —
(2) Balboa's expedition. [§ 16] — (3) Magellan's expedition. [§ 16] —
(4) Cortes in Mexico. [§ 16] — (5) Pizarro in Peru. [§ 16] — (6) De Soto's
expedition. [§ 17] — (7) Cartier's voyages. [§ 18] — (8) The French
settlements in Florida and South Carolina. [§ 18] — (9) Adventures of
Sir John Hawkins. [§ 19] — (10) Adventures of Sir Francis Drake. [§ 19]

Topics for Further Search

   (11) Life of Christopher Columbus before 1492. [§ 13] — (12) Ancient and medieval ideas that the world was round. [§ 13] — (13) Portuguese voyages to the coast of Africa. [§ 15] — (14) Earliest accounts
of South America. [§ 15] — (15) Spanish silver mines in the New
World. [§ 17] — (16) Who first discovered Chesapeake Bay? [§ 22]

CHAPTER III

EUROPEAN COLONIZATION (1604–1660)

24. European Colonizing Conditions

The year 1604 is a turning point in the history of the world because it marks not only the end of Spanish supremacy but also the beginning of a long rivalry among six European powers for a lodging in America. All of them expected to realize a profit from American trade; all of them hoped that their colonies would aid them to hold their own in the whirlpool of European policy; all of them clung to their naval power; and each looked upon the colonial trade of the others as fair game for capture whenever a war broke out.

(1) Spain grew steadily weaker throughout the whole period from 1604 to 1660, but still kept most of her colonies in America. (2) England established her merchants in southern Asia and in North America. (3) France was in rivalry with England all over the globe. (4) Holland, though not recognized by Spain as an independent nation until 1648, was actually a great sea power with a strong navy which several times defeated the English navy. (5) Sweden had considerable territory on the south side of the Baltic Sea, and under the great king Gustavus Adolphus became one of the strong naval and military powers of Europe. (6) Portugal was for half a century annexed to Spain and afterwards remained content with the immense area of what is now Brazil, and took no part in the struggles of the other five powers for American territory and power.

Although Spain and France were Catholic countries, and England, Holland, and Sweden were Protestant, no alliances were formed on a religious basis. The French defied the Spaniards, and the English fought the Dutch, without recognizing any ties of religion. Even so natural a combination as that between England and the neighboring United Netherlands, commonly called Holland, was never brought to pass. Each power struggled for itself alone, and the two weaker ones, Sweden and Holland, found no defenders when stronger neighbors seized their territory.

The settlement and the political division of America were very little affected by the nations of eastern Europe, where, beyond the then powerful kingdom of Poland, a new and crude empire of Russia was growing up. To the south of Poland, the Turks had pushed their way up into the heart of Europe, and Austria, Hungary, and Germany were from time to time fighting for their national existence. They had no energy to spare for sending colonists westward, and the Germans thus missed the opportunity of planting colonies in the attractive New World. Then Protestant north Germany and Catholic south Germany joined in the terrible grapple of the Thirty Years' War (1618–1648), which ruined and demoralized both sections. This left as the main contestants for the two Americas, the three western powers, Spain, France, and England.

25. SPANISH SETTLEMENTS (1492–1689)

The Spaniards had the great advantages of being first on the ground, of profiting by a century's experience in colonization, and of having fixed their settlements in rich and productive regions. They occupied the four large islands of the West Indies — Cuba, Hispaniola, Jamaica, and Porto Rico — and such of the smaller islands as they desired. The first supply of native island laborers had long ago been killed out, but there was a lively importation of Africans to take their place, and with the aid of this slave labor the islands were prosperous.

Mexico was found to contain a very rich tropical belt and large amounts of arable land on the high plateau, and also valuable silver mines. A few settlements were made on the west side of Central America. Peru had silver mines, which, with those of Mexico, poured forth to Spain a steady stream of "plate"; that is, of silver bullion.

Spain had a flourishing colony on the north coast of South America, in which Carthagena, Caracas, and Bogota were the principal cities. She had also prosperous colonies on the Plata, outside the main area of Spanish colonization.

In all these colonies could be found walled cities, stately cathedrals, strong fortifications, improved harbors and warehouses, and spacious mansions. The population of Spanish birth was as well off and quite as enlightened as the inhabitants of Spain. The Spanish Americans had noble parks, bridges, and plazas, botanic gardens, printing presses, and universities.

The serious weakness in the Spanish colonies on the mainland was the presence and the influence of the natives. Every part of America occupied by the Spaniards was conquered from a considerable native population, which when overwhelmed by the ships and horses and armor and firearms of the white men, was obliged perforce to accept the new rulers. Great numbers of the Indians were converted and partly civilized, though numerous natives farther inland remained independent and often very hostile to the white men. Spaniards and Indians united in a mixed race which had the Spanish language and traditions, and yet was cut off from the social and other advantages of the born Spaniard and his descendants of the pure Spanish blood. Hence it was always easy for the Spaniards to raise armies, which could include the half-breeds and Indians, but they were never willing to build up colonies in which all the people shared in the public life of the community.

During the seventeenth century the Spanish colonies were gaining in population and strength; but the Spaniards showed

a remarkable lack of interest in the northern part of their
dominion, now occupied by the southwestern and Pacific states
of the Union. Settlers pushed up the Rio Grande, and after
several towns had been uprooted by the Indians, succeeded in
1605 in planting Santa Fe. Nearly the whole of Texas was
left to the fierce and warlike Indian tribes that the Spaniards
found there; and until 1769, not a single settlement was made
on the Pacific coast north of the present Mexican territory.
Excepting the feeble little town of St. Augustine, there were
no Spanish settlements in Florida or on the north coast of
the Gulf of Mexico.

26. THE FRENCH IN AMERICA (1603-1632)

The boldest and most successful American explorers during
this second century of colonization in America were the French.
They did not set out to fill the country with settlements or to
build up rich cities. Their main purpose was to make a profit
out of the one product of northern North America which was
then highly prized in Europe, namely, the furs. Therefore
they ignored the claim which they might have made on the
basis of Verazzano's voyage of 1524, but followed out the later
discoveries of Cartier on the St. Lawrence. The heavily forested country which stretched indefinitely westward from the
St. Lawrence abounded in fur-bearing animals, particularly
the beaver, the fur of which was largely used for the making
of hats. The French controlled the island of Newfoundland because it was a convenient basis of operations in their fisheries.
They looked upon Nova Scotia with favor, partly because
of the rich inshore fisheries. The brilliant French king Henry
IV revived some of the ancient claims, and in 1603 began
a systematic colonization which lasted till the defeat of the
French by the English in 1763.

As in the earlier French attempts (§ 18), the leading spirit
was a Huguenot. The Sieur de Monts received a royal patent
for the land between the fortieth and forty-sixth parallels

(that is, from the latitude of Philadelphia almost to that of Quebec), which was named Acadie (map, page 40). Under this patent, which gave him the sole right to trade in Acadie, De Monts made a temporary settlement on Passamaquoddy Bay (1604) and others of his party settled Port Royal, later called Annapolis by the English. Then his agent, Samuel de Champlain, founded Quebec (1608), which is the first French settlement in North America that has had a continuous existence.

In 1606 the king of England, flatly disregarding the French claims, granted to some of his subjects the right to make settlements as far north as the forty-fifth parallel (the latitude of

CHAMPLAIN DEFEATING THE IROQUOIS, 1609. (From Champlain's *Voyages*, 1613.)

Halifax). Efforts were also made to plant colonies on the Maine coast not far from the earliest French settlement. The French paid no attention to the English claims, and Champlain, who was the most brilliant and most successful of French explorers and colonists, boldly pushed into the interior. Soon after settling at Quebec he joined a war party of Algonquin Indians in an excursion up the water now called Lake Champlain, where they fell in with a band of fierce and hostile Iroquois. Champlain's firearms quickly dispersed the strangers in a panic, and he thus laid the foundations of hatred and dreadful warfare between the French and the Five Nations. In 1611 he founded Montreal, and a few years later was the first European to reach the shores of Lake Huron and of Lake Ontario.

A settlement made by French Jesuits on the island of Mount Desert in 1613 was forthwith the scene of the first armed conflict between the French and the English on American soil. Captain Argall from the English colony of Virginia, which had been founded a few years before, descended upon Mount Desert and carried away the French settlers. A few years later England went so far, during a war between England and France, as to capture Port Royal and Quebec. Nevertheless, by the treaty of St. Germain (1632), which was the first European agreement as to American boundaries, the English formally acknowledged the rightful title of France to "New France, Acadia (Acadie), and Canada"; that is, to the present Nova Scotia and the lower St. Lawrence valley, with the country between. In return, the English were to be undisturbed in their new colonies of Plymouth and Massachusetts.

OLD DUTCH HOUSE, ALBANY.

27. THE DUTCH AND THE SWEDES (1609–1655)

The year 1609, when Champlain fought the Iroquois on the shores of the lake (§26), was marked also by another important event in American history.

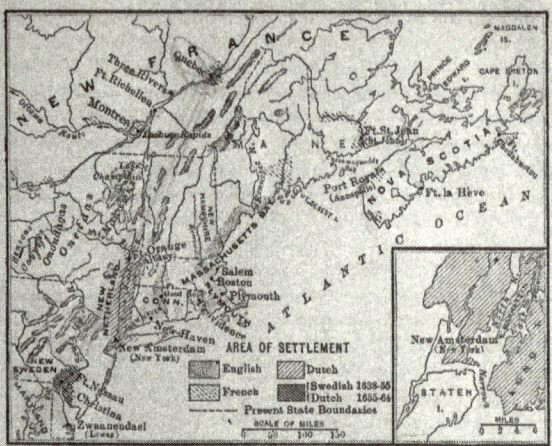

NEW NETHERLAND AND NEIGHBORING SETTLEMENTS.

In that year Henry Hudson, sailing under the flag of Holland, discovered and explored the magnificent river which now bears his name. In 1614, a Dutch company built the trading post of New Amsterdam, on the site of the present city of New York; but the first permanent town there was built twelve years later.

A new and enterprising Dutch West India Company, which received a monopoly of the Dutch trade in America in 1621, laid a broad foundation for a colony which was called New Netherland. Agents of that company planted little trading posts on the Connecticut River (Fort Good Hope), on Long Island, on the upper Hudson River or "North River" (Fort Orange, now Albany), and on the "South River," as they called the Delaware. Great land grants were assigned to Dutch "patroons," gentlemen who were to bring out their own settlers and to establish a sort of feudal system.

Sweden contested the Dutch claims by sending a colony of Swedes and Finns who settled on the lower Delaware at Fort Christina (now Wilmington). The colony was not well supported by the home company, and in 1655 it was seized by the Dutch of New Amsterdam. The conditions seemed favorable for a permanent Dutch colony, occupying the best part of the North Atlantic seacoast.

28. THE FIVE NATIONS

French and Dutch alike speedily learned that the way from the coast to the interior with its valuable furs was held by the powerful confederacy of the Five Nations of Iroquois — the Mohawks, Oneidas, Onondagas, Cayugas, and Senecas. Their territory stretched

IROQUOIS LONG HOUSE.

along central New York, where they lived in villages made up of log cabins called "long houses." Though they never numbered more than ten thousand people, of whom two thousand or three thousand were warriors, their war parties were a terror as far east as Boston, as far south as Virginia, and as far west as Illinois.

Though constantly reduced by desperate fighting and disease, they kept up their numbers by adopting prisoners. Their internal organization was weak, for there was only a loose confederation among the tribes; and if the young men wanted to go to war, they made up a party, including members of one or more tribes, or of all the tribes, and went their way, without orders or discipline.

The worst enemies of the Iroquois were their own fierceness, disease, and the white man's rum. Like other Indians, they suffered fearfully from smallpox, which ran its course till often whole villages were depopulated. As to the effects of liquor, an eyewitness says: "They were all lustily drunk, raving, striking, shouting, jumping, fighting each other, and foaming at the mouth like raging wild beasts. And this was caused by Christians!"

29. THE FRENCH IN THE INTERIOR (1634–1660)

As the Iroquois were hostile to the French (§ 26), they were disposed to be friendly to the Dutch; and the Dutch made the most of their opportunity for trade with that powerful body of Indians. The natural route of the French traders up the St. Lawrence, through Lake Ontario and Lake Erie to the west, was easily blocked by the Iroquois. Hence the French used the Ottawa route from the St. Lawrence to Lake Huron (map, page 11). Many Hurons and other Indians were converted by the tireless Catholic missionaries. In 1634 the trader Jean Nicolet reached Lake Michigan; a missionary, Father Allouez, discovered Lake Superior in 1665. Before long, French traders opened up an overland route from Lake Superior to Hudson Bay and brought down rich supplies of furs.

Meanwhile the French missionaries were making heroic, though on the whole unavailing, efforts to Christianize the Iroquois. Father Isaac Jogues's account of his experience as a prisoner gives a frightful picture of his captors, who seemed to him like demons; they leaped upon him like wild beasts, tore out his nails, and crunched his fingers with their teeth; his attendant Hurons were tortured on a scaffold in the midst of the Iroquois village; yet the heroic priest "began to instruct them separately on the articles of the faith, then on the very stage itself baptized two with raindrops gathered from the leaves of a stalk of Indian corn." Rescued by the Dutch, this brave and self-sacrificing man returned and plunged a second time into that misery, and died a martyr's death. The Iroquois long remained a barrier to western exploration.

30. FIRST PERMANENT ENGLISH COLONY (1607–1612)

While the French and the Dutch were founding their North American colonies, the English were at the same time planting settlements in Virginia and New England. The early English

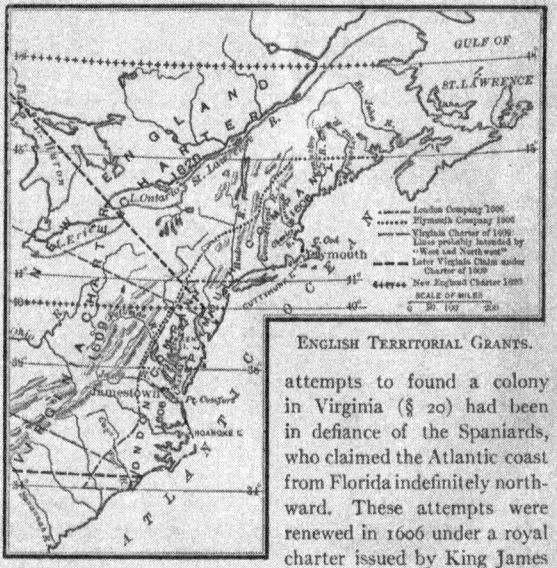

ENGLISH TERRITORIAL GRANTS.

attempts to found a colony in Virginia (§ 20) had been in defiance of the Spaniards, who claimed the Atlantic coast from Florida indefinitely northward. These attempts were renewed in 1606 under a royal charter issued by King James I, which created two corporations: (1) The so-called Plymouth Company was to make a settlement somewhere between the thirty-eighth and forty-fifth parallels. (2) The London Company was to colonize somewhere between the thirty-fourth and forty-first parallels. The Spanish government looked upon the scheme as an attempt to plant a naval station for the vexation of Spanish commerce. The Spanish ambassador at London suggested to his master, "It will be serving God and Your Majesty to drive these villains out from there and hang them"; but sloth, poverty, and hesitation to renew the war held back the Spaniards from anything stronger than protest.

The Plymouth Company never made a permanent settlement; but on May 13, 1607, a party of one hundred and four emigrants, sent by the London Company, selected a peninsula on the James River for a settlement which they called Jamestown. The spot was one of the least favorable in that fine country; it was low, marshy, mosquito-cursed, unhealthful, and hard to defend from the Indians, who attacked it within two weeks.

The little colony was badly managed from the first. In the course of two and a half years, 630 immigrants came out, of whom 570 died forthwith; yet the founders of Virginia did not lose courage. The company reorganized in 1609, under a second charter granting a specified tract, extending two hundred miles each way along the coast from Old Point Comfort, together with "all that Space and Circuit of Land, lying from the Sea Coast of the Precinct aforesaid, up into the Land throughout from Sea to Sea, West and Northwest." In 1612, by a third and last charter, the company was reorganized and received larger powers of control of its own affairs.

In the midst of distress and death in the early days of Vir-

CAPTAIN JOHN SMITH IN 1624. (From the title-page of his *Generall Historie*.)

ginia, one spirit shone brightly. It was Captain John Smith, who alternately pacified and fought the Indians; who found supplies, explored the country, and was the principal man in the little government. Later in life Smith told a believing world that he was once taken prisoner by the Indians, who were about to beat out his brains; whereupon Pocahontas (then a child of ten or twelve years), daughter of the great chief Powhatan, sprang between him and the club and saved his life. Whether this story be true or imagined, the courage and ability of Smith are undeniable.

31. DEVELOPMENT OF VIRGINIA (1613–1650)

The London Company spent on Virginia the immense sum of £100,000 in twelve years, and at the end of that period the colonists numbered only 400. The company became entangled in English politics, and passed into the control of opponents of royal power. In 1619 it authorized the meeting of a popular assembly in Virginia — the first free representative government in America. Accordingly twenty-two "burgesses," elected from the various settlements of Virginia, met in the church at Jamestown, and drew up numerous laws for the colony. The year 1619 also marks the beginning of the African slave trade in the English colonies. A Dutch man-of-war in Virginia exchanged twenty negro slaves for provisions; and thus began a new source of labor for the cultivation of tobacco, which quickly became the main industry of Virginia.

In 1623 the Indians arose and killed nearly 350 settlers; and the tragedy gave point to enemies of the colony in England, who assailed it as a swampy, pestilential, ill-housed, and dreary place, where "tobacco only was the business." In 1624, by the judgment of the Court of King's Bench, the Virginia charters were held null and void. Thereafter Virginia had only such a government as the king chose to set up; but the governors whom he appointed were instructed to call elected assemblies, and Virginia never lost this privilege of partial self-government. The colonists learned how to live in a new country, and by 1650 they numbered about 15,000.

32. PURITANS AND PILGRIMS (1604–1660)

Early Virginia was simply a commercial speculation, pushed by the wealthy stockholders of a powerful company. The next English colony in America was founded by poor people who were looked upon with suspicion by their own government. During the reign of Elizabeth there grew up within the established Church of England a body of so-called Puritans, who felt that the Reformation had not gone far enough; and out of the Puritans arose a body of "Separatists" (later called Independents), who would not remain in that church. Under James I, many Puritan ministers were deprived of their right to hold services; the Separatist congregations were broken up; and about three hundred of the Separatists took refuge in Holland.

A God-fearing and industrious folk, the exiles found themselves strangers in Holland, and feared that their children would not hold to their faith. Under the advice of their pastor, Rev. John Robinson, about two hundred who were later called "Pilgrims" made up their minds to seek a place of settlement in America. Their friends in England lent them about £5000, and they obtained from the London Company a patent for lands to be located somewhere within the general bounds of the second charter of that company. After many difficulties, about a hundred of the Pilgrims left the harbor of Plymouth, England, on the ship *Mayflower*, bound for the Hudson River country. After three months of stormy voyage they found themselves just off Cape Cod, which was part of the territory of the old Plymouth Company, and in a region already named New England. Since they had no patent for lands in that region, those on board the *Mayflower* drew up a brief "compact" (November 11, 1620), by which they agreed to organize as a "civil body politic" for their government after they should land; and they chose John Carver to be governor.

After exploring the coast
the Pilgrims decided to
settle on the bay already
called Plymouth Harbor,
and landed December 11,
1620 (December 21, new
style), near a great bowl-
der now called Plymouth
Rock. The season was
cruelly hard, and during
the first winter half the
colonists died from cold,
poor food, and other hardships. The next season

THE *MAYFLOWER*. (From a model in the National Museum, Washington.)

others came out, and thenceforward the little colony pros-
pered. The people paid their debt due in England out of their
fishery and Indian trading business. They set up the first
town meetings in America, and later organized a representative assembly (1639). In the seventy-one years of
its existence as a separate colony, Plymouth never had a
charter or a royal governor. Yet it hardly knew internal
strife; it was at peace with its neighbors; it showed that
Englishmen could prosper in the cold climate of the northeastern coast; it established in the New World the great
principle of a church free from governmental interference, and
founded on the will of the members. Above all, the Pilgrim
Fathers handed down to later generations priceless traditions
of strength, manliness, patience, uprightness, and confidence in
God.

33. MASSACHUSETTS (1629-1634)

In 1629, some merchants and country gentlemen, most of
them Puritans who still adhered to the Church of England,
secured from King Charles I a charter issued to the "Governor
and Company of the Massachusetts Bay in New England "

Their territory was to extend from a line three miles north of the Merrimack River to a line three miles south of the Charles River, and was to reach westward to the South Sea (Pacific Ocean).

The company had behind it abundant means and energy, and fifteen of the stockholders agreed to go out to Massachusetts. They took their charter with them, as their authority for holding a "general court," or stockholders' meeting, in order to carry on their affairs thousands of miles away from the inquisitive English government. In 1630 a thousand people landed on the shores of Massachusetts Bay, and the work of the government of the company was started under the governorship of John Winthrop. They found in existence several little towns, which were soon brought under the authority of the company.

Although King Charles was furious at the unexpected transfer of the charter from England to Massachusetts, the colony grew rapidly, and in ten years increased to nearly 3000 people. Within a few months the colony became self-sustaining, raising its own food, and shortly it had a surplus of fish and timber and furs to send to England. It was also able to build up a system of government which made it almost an independent republic.

(1) The written charter was speedily found to be a kind of constitution which was well suited to the needs of the people; and to it was added a little code of laws called the "Body of Liberties."

(2) The government was genuinely popular, for the governor and "assistants" formed a kind of council elected every year by the "freemen," that is, the members of the company; and the principal inhabitants were made members. In 1634 the people demanded and received an elective general court, and the assistants became an upper house.

(3) The settlements were made in villages, each governed in local affairs by its own town meeting.

34. MARYLAND (1632–1650)

Hardly had Massachusetts been settled, when a southern colony was chartered under Catholic influence. In 1632 King Charles granted to Lord ,Baltimore, head of the Calvert family, a charter for a colony called Maryland after Queen Henrietta Maria. It was bounded on the north by the "fortieth degree of latitude," on the east by Delaware Bay and the ocean, on the south by the Potomac, and on the west by a north and south line drawn through the source of the Potomac.

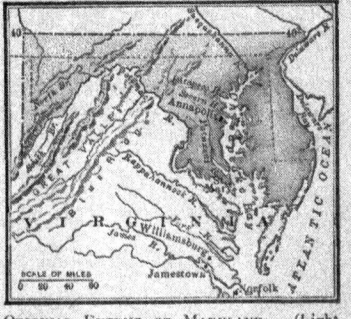

ORIGINAL EXTENT OF MARYLAND. (Light dashes indicate present state boundaries.)

This charter was of a new type, for both the land and the powers of government were transferred to Calvert as a "proprietary"; and he had authority to make laws for the colony, provided the freemen of the colony assented. Although not distinctly so stated in the charter, it was understood that Catholics would be allowed in the province; and in 1634 a body of colonists, both Catholic and Protestant, settled first at St. Marys and then elsewhere. The Calvert family was rich and powerful, and sent out many emigrants; the soil was fertile, tobacco growing soon became the main industry, and slaves were introduced.

In an early contest with the proprietor the assembly successfully asserted its right to initiate — that is, to propose — laws. The most significant statute was the Toleration Act of 1649, which distinctly declared that "no person . . . professing to believe in Jesus Christ, shall from henceforth be anywaies molested, or discountenanced . . . for his religion nor in the free exercise thereof." Under this act, neither Catholics nor Protestants could be persecuted for their faith. Protestant settlers were already outnumbering the Catholics, and with the arrival of new settlers the colony speedily became distinctly Protestant in feeling.

35. CONNECTICUT AND NEW HAVEN (1635–1660)

South of Massachusetts was a belt of country which attracted the Dutch and the Plymouth people, both of whom built forts on the Connecticut River. In 1635 a little settlement was made at Saybrook, at the mouth of the river. The next year came a body of settlers from Massachusetts, headed by Rev. Thomas Hooker, who founded the towns of Hartford, Windsor, and Wethersfield on the Connecticut River (map, page 52). In 1639, representatives of these three little towns, feeling the need of a common government, met at Hartford and drew up the "Fundamental Orders of Connecticut," the first detailed constitution made by a self-governing American community for itself.

Meantime, the colony of New Haven was forming in like manner out of separate communities. The town of New Haven was founded in 1638 by Theophilus Eaton and Rev. John Davenport. In 1643 it united with several other little towns in a common colonial assembly.

Both colonies were founded among warlike Indians. The Pequot tribe grew threatening, as they saw their hunting grounds invaded by the English. Captain John Mason, of Connecticut, with 90 armed white men and 400 Narragansetts, attacked the Pequots not far from the present Stonington, Connecticut, and stormed their fort (1637). As the chronicler puts it, "Downe fell men, women, and children, those that scaped us, fell into the hands of the Indians, that were in the reere of us . . . not above five of them escaped out

of our hands." This cruel and merciless massacre terrified
the remnants of the tribe and gave peace for nearly forty
years.

36. RHODE ISLAND, MAINE, AND NEW HAMPSHIRE
(1623–1652)

(1) Neither Connecticut nor New Haven had any authority
from the Crown to carry on a colony; and another settlement was made on the same terms, or rather, lack of terms, in
Rhode Island. This colony was founded by Roger Williams, a
Massachusetts minister who took it upon himself to deny the
right of any government to prescribe religious belief for its citizens. He was therefore banished from Massachusetts (1636),
and betook himself to the wilderness of Narragansett Bay, where
he secured land from the Indians and founded the town of
Providence. Soon after, he still further antagonized Massachusetts by joining the Baptist Church, which was then bitterly
persecuted both in England and in the colonies. Other little
towns were founded at Portsmouth and Newport, and with
Providence they secured an English patent (1644) under which
they governed themselves and elected a common assembly and
governor. Emigrants gathered and the little community called
Rhode Island became prosperous, although heartily disliked by
its neighbors.

(2) North of Massachusetts, one Ferdinando Gorges tried to
build up a colony in what is now Maine, but this territory was
annexed by Massachusetts in 1652.

(3) Farther south in the region north of the Merrimack,
several little towns were founded at Dover, Exeter, and elsewhere, from 1623 to 1638. For a time they had a government in common, something like that of Rhode Island; then
the people became a part of Massachusetts; and finally they
received a government of their own under the name of New
Hampshire.

37. EFFECT OF THE CIVIL WAR IN ENGLAND (1642–1655)

The stream of immigrants into New England was suddenly checked in 1642 by the breaking out of war between King Charles I and the Puritans who had control of Parliament. In 1649, the Parliamentary army under Oliver Cromwell became the virtual government of England, and Charles I was executed by the Puritans. The Independents, who had about the same religious belief as the New England Congregationalists, came into control and supported Cromwell till his death in 1658.

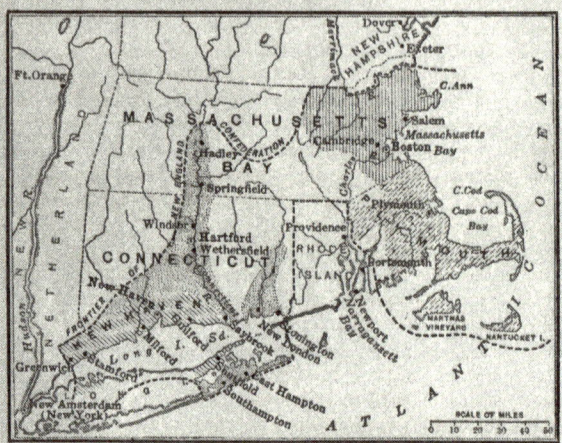

THE NEW ENGLAND CONFEDERATION.

The colonists were left mostly to themselves during the civil war, and in 1643 the four colonies of New Haven, Massachusetts, Connecticut, and Plymouth formed a federal union under written "Articles of Confederation." The visible government was made up of two commissioners from each colony, meeting from time to time. This New England Confederation existed

for more than forty years and was very helpful to New England.
It kept the Dutch in check, fought the Indians, and was interested in the general improvement of the colonies. Its constitution was so good that traces of it can be found in the Constitution of the United States.

Cromwell did not interfere with the New England colonies,
but he sent a fleet (1652) which compelled Maryland and Virginia to accept the authority of the Puritan Parliament. He was
the first ruler of England to lay down a commercial policy for
the protection of trade with the English colonies; in 1651 he
secured the first "Navigation Act," which was intended to cut
down Dutch trade.

Cromwell also saw the importance of reducing the colonial
power of Holland and of Spain. He compelled the Dutch to
withdraw from the Connecticut valley, and in 1655 his fleet
captured the island of Jamaica from the Spaniards, and it has
ever since remained English. This was the beginning of the
break-up of the Spanish American empire.

38. RELIGION IN NEW ENGLAND (1620–1660)

Considering that so many of the New England colonists
came over in order to have the privilege of worshiping God
according to their own consciences, it is remarkable how unwilling they were that other people should worship God according to their consciences. Massachusetts made it a point to
repress those who differed from the established Congregational
Church or criticized the clergy. In 1636 Mrs. Anne Hutchinson of Boston and others — the so-called "Antinomians" —
held women's meetings to discuss and to dissect the latest sermons. She was put on trial, not for establishing the first
Woman's Club in the country, but for heresy. Notwithstanding a valiant defense in which she had the better of her judges,
she was dismissed from the church and sent into exile.

The same illiberal spirit was shown toward the English sect
called Quakers, founded (1648) by George Fox as a protest

against religious ceremonies and control. The Quakers, or Friends, used plain speech, were rigid in their customs, had no regular ministers, and would not take oaths or use force, even in defense of their country. Though a folk of singularly blameless lives, they were harassed in England. When two Godfearing Quaker women reached Boston, their doctrines were officially declared to be "heretical, blasphemous, and devilish."

Massachusetts, Connecticut, and Plymouth, as well as Maryland and Virginia, hastened to pass laws for the severe punishment of Quakers and "ranters." From 1659 to 1661 four of them were executed in Boston. The Quaker episode is a proof that the good and pure principles of the Puritans did not keep the community from tyranny and stupid cruelty. The Quakers neither harmed nor seriously threatened the good order of the colonists; they were persecuted because they ventured to differ from the usual religious and political practices.

39. REVIEW

Six European powers gained a footing in America: Spain, Portugal, France, Holland, Sweden, and England. Germany was too exhausted by religious wars to take part in the contest for the New World.

The Spaniards held most of the islands of the West Indies and the coasts of North and South America, and easily overcame the opposing Indians. The Portuguese were satisfied to hold Brazil.

The French, against English protests, sought the St. Lawrence region because of the valuable fur trade. Their first great explorer, Champlain, fought against the Iroquois.

The Dutch made settlements on the Connecticut, Hudson, and Delaware rivers. The Swedes settled on the lower Delaware, but their little colony was soon annexed by the Dutch. Between the French and the Dutch lay the warlike Five Nations, to avoid whom the French used the Ottawa River route to Lake Huron; and so discovered Lakes Michigan and Superior.

An English colony was founded by the London Company at

Jamestown, Virginia, in 1607. One man, Captain John Smith, showed himself a natural leader. In 1619 the first popular Assembly met; but in 1624 the Virginia charter was taken away.

The first settlement in the region called New England was that of the Pilgrims, who came to Plymouth in 1620 and set up a little colony. Massachusetts, planted in 1630, quickly developed a popular government. Maryland was settled by Lord Baltimore, a Catholic nobleman, but numerous Protestants also came in. Connecticut, New Haven, Rhode Island, and New Hampshire were four little Puritan colonies built up without any charter. Settlements in Maine did not prosper.

During the civil war in England, four of the colonies formed a New England Confederation (1643). Cromwell captured the island of Jamaica (1655), and this was the first inroad on the Spanish empire. The Puritans soon found themselves troubled by those who disagreed with the majority on religious matters, and severely treated the Antinomians and Quakers.

References Bearing on the Text and Topics

Geography and Maps. See maps, pp. 11, 20, 40, 43, 49, 52. — Avery, *U.S.*, II. - *Epoch Maps*, no. 3. — Coman, *Indust. Hist.*, 28, 34. — Semple, *Geogr. Conditions*, 19–35. — Shepherd, *Hist. Atlas*, 185, 189–193. — Tyler, *England in Am.*

Secondary. Bassett, *U. S.*, chs. iii, iv. — Becker, *Beginnings*, 54–70, 80–119. — Bourne, *Spain in Am.*, chs. xiii–xx. — Channing, *U. S.*, I. chs. vi–xix. — Fiske, *Old Va.*, I. 41–318; *Beginnings of New Engl.*, 50–198; *Dutch and Quaker Cols.*, I. 80–242. — Innes, *New Amsterdam.* — Parkman, *Pioneers*, pt. iii; *Jesuits in Am.; Old Regime; Pontiac*, I. 7–28, 46–68. — Thwaites, *Colonies*, §§ 13, 18–22, 28–34, 48–68, 83, 84, 108–110; *France in Am.*, chs. i–iii. — Tyler, *England in Am.* — Weeden, *New Engl.*, I. 23–46; *Early R. I.*, chs. i–iii. — Wilson, *Am. People*, I. 34–68, 74–218.

Sources. *Am. Hist. Leaflets*, nos. 7, 16, 25, 27, 29, 31, 36. — Bogart and Thompson, *Readings*, 1–11. — Caldwell, *Survey*, 13, 29–32. — Colden, *Five Indian Nations.* — Hart, *Contemporaries*, I. §§ 37–41, 49–142 passim, 150–154, 158, 169–171; *Patriots and Statesmen*, I. 61–116; *Source Book*, §§ 5, 6, 8, 10, 13. — Higginson, *Am. Explorers*, 231–316. — James, *Readings*, §§ 8–14, 20. — Jameson, *Original Narratives.*

— MacDonald, *Select Charters*, nos. 1–21. — *Old South Leaflets*, nos. 7, 8, 48–51, 53–55, 66, 69, 77, 87, 91, 93, 94, 96, 121, 142, 143, 153, 154, 164, 167–170, 176, 178, 207. — See New Engl. Hist. Teachers' Assoc., *Hist. Sources*, §§ 69–71; *Syllabus*, 297–305, 309, 310.

Illustrative. Austin, *Standish of Standish; Betty Alden* (Plymouth). — Child, *Hobomok* (Plymouth). — Cooke, *My Lady Pokahontas; Stories of the Old Dominion*, 1–64. — Curtis, *Indian Days of Long Ago.* — Dix, *Christopher Ferringham* (Quaker). — Doyle, *Refugees* (Canada). — Eastman, *Indian Boyhood.* — Hawthorne, *Maypole of Merry Mount; Endicott and the Red Cross; The Gentle Boy* (Quakers); *Grandfather's Chair*, pt. i, chs. i–vii. — Holland, *Bay Path* (Connecticut). — Johnston, *To Have and to Hold* (Va.). — Longfellow, *Courtship of Miles Standish; John Endicott.* — Motley, *Merry Mount.* — Paulding, *Konigsmarke* (Swedes). — Stedman, *Peter Stuyvesant's New Year's Call.* — Stimson, *King Noanett* (Mass. and Va.). — Tenney, *Constance of Acadia.* — Thruston, *Mistress Brent* (Md.). — Whittier, *John Underhill; The Exiles; Banished from Massachusetts; King's Missive.*

Pictures. Avery, *U.S.*, II. — Wilson, *Am. People*, I. — Winsor, *America*, III, IV.

Topics Answerable from the References Above

(1) Why did Spain grow weaker after 1604? [§ 24] — (2) Adventures of Champlain. [§ 26] — (3) Early accounts of New Amsterdam. [§ 27] — (4) Early explorations of *one* of the following lakes: Huron; Michigan; Superior. [§ 29] — (5) Why was there such loss of life in the early English colonies? [§ 30] — (6) Adventures of Captain John Smith. [§ 30] — (7) Tobacco planting in Virginia. [§ 31] — (8) Early accounts of *one* of these colonies: Virginia [§ 30]; Plymouth [§ 32]; Massachusetts Bay [§ 33]; Connecticut. [§ 35] — (9) Was there real religious toleration in Maryland? [§ 34]

Topics for Further Search

(10) The Pueblo Indians as the Spaniards found them. [§ 25] — (11) The Pueblo Indians to-day. [§ 25] — (12) Why were the Five Nations so important? [§ 28] — (13) Catholic missions in the Great Lakes region. [§ 29] — (14) What was meant by " up into the Land throughout from Sea to Sea, West and Northwest" ? [§ 30] — (15) Was the Pequot War justified? [§ 35] — (16) What did the New England Confederation accomplish? [§ 37] — (17) Was Mrs. Anne Hutchinson justly condemned? [§ 38] — (18) Why were the Quakers so unpopular? [§ 38]

CHAPTER IV

ENGLISH COLONIZATION AFTER 1660

40. The Taking of New Netherland

In 1660 peace and union came back to England under the "Restoration" of Charles II as king, and the nation entered on a new career of conquest and colonization, both in the

Water Front of New York in 1673. (Drawing by Hugo Allard.)

eastern and in the western hemisphere. By creating the East India Company (1660), the English laid the foundation of an empire in India and Ceylon in opposition to the Portuguese, Dutch, and French. In the west, their colonies were already far stronger than the Dutch possessions.

New Netherland was a feeble and ill-managed commercial community, numbering less than 10,000 Europeans. The Dutch West India Company, which controlled the colony, was chiefly interested in the Indian fur trade. Contentions arose between the company and the settlers; and the last of the Dutch governors, Peter Stuyvesant, found that he had little means of defense for the colony and no intelligent support.

On the basis of vague claims upon the whole Atlantic coast, King Charles II granted the region occupied by the Dutch to his brother James, Duke of York. A fleet was sent out to which the little town of New Amsterdam surrendered (Aug. 29, 1664). The rest of the colony fell without a blow; and the name New York was applied to the former New Netherland. During a later war with England, a Dutch fleet occupied the place for a few months in 1673; but from that time on, the Dutch never held any territory in America, except a little settlement on the north coast of South America and some small islands in the West Indies.

41. Charters and Colonies in the North (1662–1665)

The taking of New York was part of a systematic policy for the colonization of the whole coast from Maine southward. In fact, the greater part of Maine was included in the grant to the Duke of York, but it was eventually bought for a second time by Massachusetts (§ 36).

The king smiled upon Connecticut (§ 35), and in 1662 granted to it a favorable charter — the first and last charter that the colony ever had — with bounds extending to the South Sea. New Haven was incorporated into Connecticut, as punishment for harboring two of the "regicides" who had condemned Charles I to death (§ 37). Rhode Island (§ 36) also received a charter in 1663, giving it about its present boundaries and a liberal government with an elective governor. Plymouth received no charter, but was allowed to remain separate nearly thirty years longer.

Even before the Duke of York got possession of his magnificent proprietary domain, he began to cut it up into smaller provinces. In 1664 he granted to Berkeley and Carteret the tract between the Hudson River and the Delaware, and they called it Nova Caesarea — which is, in English, plain New Jersey. Ten years later the new province was divided into East New Jersey and West New Jersey. The rich soil and the ease of access speedily attracted population; a contemporary said, "'Tis far cheaper living there for Eatables than here in England; and either men or Women who have a Trade, or are laborers, can, if industrious, get near three times the Wages they commonly earn in England." The Quakers fixed their attention on the Jerseys. Two of them, Fenwick and Byllynge, gained control of West Jersey, and many Quakers settled there. Then a body of proprietors, including William Penn, secured both the Jerseys.

Through these various changes, by 1665 the English government had recognized in the coast region east of the Delaware River (1) the three charter colonies of Massachusetts, Connecticut, and Rhode Island; (2) the proprietary colonies of New York and New Jersey; (3) the unchartered or irregular settlements of New Hampshire, Plymouth,

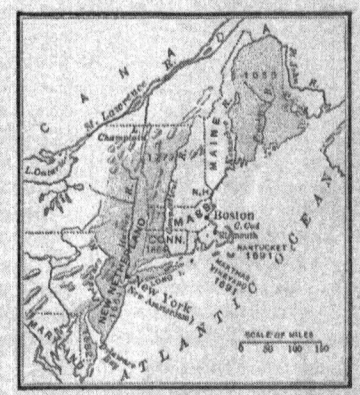

LANDS OF THE DUKE OF YORK. (With dates of cession of outlying portions.)

and Maine, the last two of which eventually were absorbed by neighbors.

42. ORGANIZATION OF NEW YORK COLONY (1664–1686)

It was no easy matter to fit the new territory and colony of New York into the general English system. In the first place,

ENGLISH OFFICER IN UNIFORM, 1664.

the territorial grant was clumsy and conflicted with previous charters. The Duke of York's grant extended to the Connecticut River, though both the Massachusetts charter of 1629 and the recent Connecticut charter of 1662 granted to those colonies strips of territory as far west as the Pacific; that is, directly across New York. The boundary between New York and Connecticut was soon agreed on, but that between New York and Massachusetts remained unsettled for more than a hundred years.

To govern the colony of New York, the Duke sent out Governor Nicolls. He found many Dutch in the Hudson valley, a few Swedes west of the Delaware, and some New Englanders in Long Island. As the Duke did not desire anything like popular government, Nicolls drew up a code called "The Duke's Laws." Some of the towns vainly tried to join Connecticut. Nicolls gave a charter to the city of New York in 1665, the officials of which, however, were to be appointed. A later governor, Dongan, in 1686 was authorized to call an elective assembly. Dongan also granted to New York and

to Albany city charters with elective aldermen. These were
the first popular city governments to be created in the New
World.

43. Scheme for a New England Colony (1685–1689)

Massachusetts was looked upon as an insubordinate colony
which must be disciplined. During the civil wars in England,
the colonial government had acted like an independent republic,
even venturing to coin silver "pine-tree shillings" — a great
presumption for a colony. Under strong pressure from England, the colony grudgingly repealed its harsh and brutal laws
against the Quakers, allowed services of the Church of England,
and admitted others than Congregationalists to the suffrage.

New troubles arose because immediately after the Restoration
the English government put into operation a system of "Acts
of Trade," or Navigation Acts, already begun under Cromwell
(§ 37). Their prime purpose was to prevent the Dutch from
carrying on a profitable trade with English colonies in the West
Indies and the mainland. They provided that most of the trade
of the colonies should be with England, and that colonial trade
with England should be transported only in English or
colonial vessels. To carry out these laws (1660, 1663, 1673)
customhouses were set up in the colonies, and very low duties
were laid on imported goods; the customhouse formality
made it possible for the British government to keep track of the
vessels arriving and departing.

The Acts of Trade, often called the "Colonial System,"
gave many advantages to colonial shipbuilders, but were
usually disregarded by all the colonies, and particularly by
Massachusetts. For this and other offenses the English
government made up its mind to punish that colony by taking
away the charter. Much the same method was followed as in
the case of Virginia in 1624 (§ 31). An English court held that
the Massachusetts people had violated their charter and that,
therefore, it was no longer binding on the Crown (1684).

HART'S NEW AMER. HIST. — 5

The colony had recently suffered from the devastation of an Indian outbreak, commonly called King Philip's War (1675), in which most of the frontier towns were destroyed. When in 1685 the Duke of York became King James II, he set out to consolidate all the New England colonies into one group. Sir Edmund Andros was appointed to carry out this plan under a commission as governor-general of the Dominion of New England. The weak colonies of Plymouth and Rhode Island yielded. Connecticut refused to give up its charter and, according to tradition, the document was hidden in a hollow oak tree in Hartford. Nevertheless, the scheme would have succeeded but for the breakdown of King James in England, which will be discussed further on.

44. The Southern Colonies (1663–1729)

South of the James River several small settlements were made on Albemarle Sound and the Chowan River by wanderers from Virginia, from New England, and from the West Indies. In 1663 England incorporated this region with her dominions in North America, by granting to a body of eight noble proprietors, land for a new colony of Carolina (named for Charles II). The first Carolina patent extended from the 31st to the 36th degree of north latitude, and west to the South Sea. In 1665, a second patent added strips of territory southward to the 29th degree, and northward to 36° 30'.

The English philosopher John Locke was requested by the proprietors to draw up a "Fundamental Constitution" often called "The Grand Model," which was to establish a kind of feudal system in Carolina. This constitution never went into effect; instead, a popular assembly was organized (1669) and governors were sent out by the proprietors.

A settlement was made on the Ashley River (1670), which developed into the town of Charleston. Around it the colony of South Carolina grew up, separated by many miles of wilderness from the settlements in North Carolina. Scotch, Quakers,

and Huguenots came in. In the course of thirty years twenty
thousand people gathered in the two Carolinas, including large

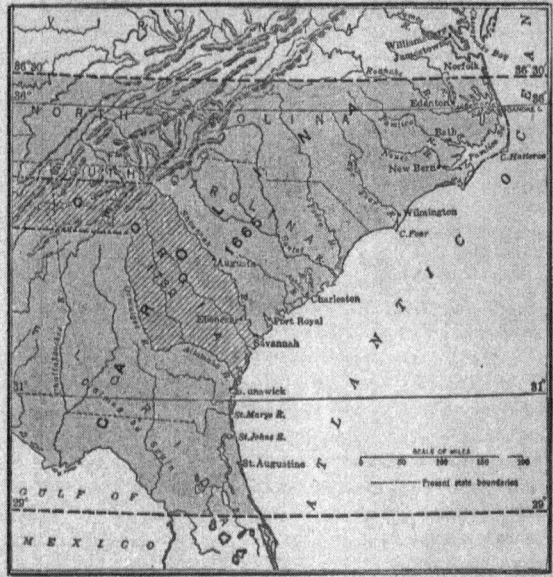

CAROLINA AND GEORGIA GRANTS.

numbers of negroes; for the rice plantations of South Carolina
gave opportunity for profitable slave labor.

Virginia made no resistance to the creation of Carolina,
though it included some of the territory which had been assigned
to the old colony in the charter of 1609 (§ 30). During this
period Virginia was steadily gaining in population, and the
chief industry was still tobacco raising. The worst Indian war

for half a century caused the massacre of 300 settlers. A planter, Nathaniel Bacon, took the lead in fighting the Indians, and then headed an insurrection against the harsh and wasteful government of the royal governor, Sir William Berkeley. He burned Jamestown, set up a government of his own (1676),

and might have altered the history of the colony but for his sudden death and the consequent melting away of his party. To one of the rebels Berkeley remarked, "Mr. Drummond! you are very welcome. I am more glad to see you than any man in Virginia; you shall be hanged in half an hour." Drummond and thirty-five others were executed.

BULL-PRINGLE HOUSE, CHARLESTON.
(Built about 1760.)

No wonder King Charles recalled Berkeley in disgrace, exclaiming, "That old fool has hanged more men in that naked country than I have done for the murder of my father."

Maryland (§ 34) shared in the tobacco planting, and under the easy government of the proprietary family, passed successfully through several little insurrections which long plagued the colony.

45. PENNSYLVANIA AND DELAWARE (1681–1701)

Notwithstanding all the charters and grants of the period from 1660 to 1680, one of the fairest portions of the New World was still left unoccupied. This was the broad and diversified country west of the Delaware River, in which the only evidence of civilization was a few Swedish and Dutch settlements along the river. To fill up this gap, and thus to complete the belt of coast colonies, a royal patent was issued in

1681 to William Penn, a leading Quaker, for a colony which
was named by the king in compliment to Penn's father
"Pennsylvania." The province was to extend five degrees of
longitude westward from the Delaware. The northern part of

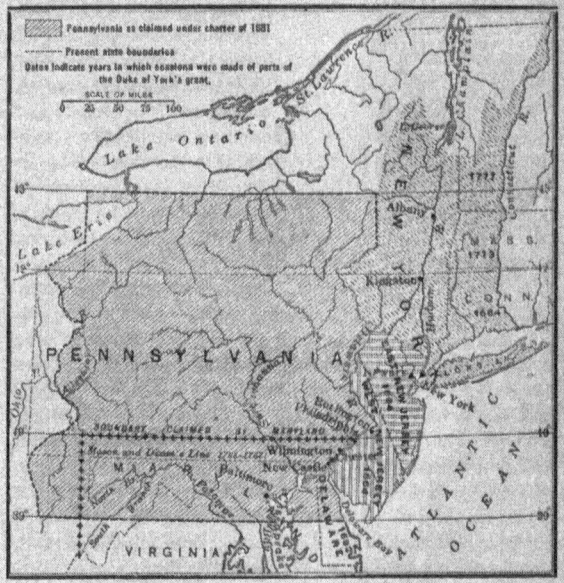

PENNSYLVANIA BOUNDARY CONTROVERSY.

the grant covered territory included in the Connecticut charter,
which was nineteen years older; and on the south it cut into
the territory of Maryland, which was forty-nine years older:
so that Pennsylvania came into existence in the midst of several
spirited boundary controversies, which were not settled for

many years. In addition, the territory now in the state of
Delaware was bought by Penn from the Duke of York.

As in Maryland and New York, the ownership of the land
in the new colony, and also the right to provide a govern-

ment, were put in the hands
of a proprietor. Penn sent
over many colonists, and for
a time made his own home
in Pennsylvania. He saw the
desirability of a popular government and therefore (1682)
granted what he called the
"Frame of Government,"
which was practically a liberal
constitution. His two principles were "First, to terrify
evildoers: secondly, to cherish
those that do well; . . . I know some say, let us have good
laws, and no matter for the men that execute them: but
let them consider that though good laws do well, good men
do better." A city government was set up for Philadelphia,
which in 1691 received a charter with mayor and aldermen.

WILLIAM PENN. (From an ivory
by Bevan.)

Yet even in this elysium the settlers were discontented; they
felt that the proprietor kept too much for himself, and they began
to quarrel with the governors. In 1701 Penn granted a new plan
of government called the "Charter of Privileges," in which the
legislature received greater powers. At Penn's death (1718), he
left the rights and dignity of his proprietorship to his children;
and they remained in the hands of the family down to the
Revolution.

46. COLONIAL REORGANIZATION (1689–1752)

James II of England followed the example of his father,
Charles I, in provoking a conflict with Parliament. He was a
Catholic, and many of his subjects invited his nephew, the

Protestant William III of Orange, the head of the Dutch nation, to take his place. James fled the kingdom; and in February, 1689, the two houses of Parliament declared that he had abdicated and that William III of Orange and his wife Mary, James's daughter, were lawful king and queen of England. Under them and their successors occurred several changes in the make-up of the English colonies.

In New England, Governor Andros (§ 43) was deposed, and the three main colonies were formally restored to the old system of self-governing charters. Under the new charter given to Massachusetts (1691), Maine and Plymouth were both included without objection on their part. Connecticut and Rhode Island continued under their former liberal charters, and were the only communities in any part of America which were allowed to elect their own governors (§ 41). New Hampshire was restored as a separate royal "province" — that is, a colony like Virginia without any charter; but it was allowed a considerable degree of self-government through a legislature (§ 31). Thus the number of New England colonies was fixed at four.

The home government had a strong prejudice against the proprietorships of the middle colonies. New York was turned into a royal province when the Duke of York became King James II in 1685. For a short time under William III, both Pennsylvania and Maryland were deprived of their charters, but eventually they were given back to the Penn and Calvert families. Delaware became a separate proprietary colony, no longer a part of Pennsylvania. The proprietors of the Jerseys (§ 41) gave up their rights in 1702, and those two colonies were then united in the single royal province of New Jersey. In 1729, likewise, the Carolina proprietors (§ 44) surrendered their claims, and thus North Carolina and South Carolina became royal provinces.

Stricter navigation acts were passed (§ 43) and a board, called the Board of Trade, was created in England to act as a colonial office and keep in touch with what was going on.

More than one hundred years after the founding of Virginia and Massachusetts, the colony of Georgia was set up (1732) under James Edward Oglethorpe, a man of philanthropic spirit, whose purpose was to build up a Christian commonwealth in the New World. The territory granted to the trustees for Georgia was bounded on the north by the Savannah River, and on the south by the Altamaha, and nominally it extended westward across the continent to the South Sea, in defiance of French and Spanish claims. The first settlement was made at Savannah in 1733. Besides colonists from England, Protestant exiles came from the principality of Salzburg in the Austrian Alps; and German Moravians, Protestant Scotch Highlanders, and Jews soon moved in.

The three fundamental principles of the new colony were that slavery should not be permitted, that rum should be excluded, and that there should be complete religious toleration. Still the colony was not prosperous; the colonists insisted on the removal of restrictions concerning slavery and rum; and the trustees, disappointed in both the moral and the pecuniary returns for their investment, surrendered their proprietorship to the home government (1752).

47. INTERNATIONAL RIVALRIES

The progress of the English colonies was not accepted by either France or Spain as a permanent thing. The Spaniards in 1670 made a treaty which acknowledged the existence of the English colonies; but they began to attack the Carolinas almost as soon as the little settlements were planted. By setting up the Hudson's Bay Company (1670), England came into a new rivalry with the French for the highly valuable fur trade of the country tributary to Hudson Bay (§ 29). New York was hemmed in by the Iroquois; but the territory of Pennsylvania, Virginia, and the Carolinas extended beyond the Appalachian Mountains to the unknown waters of the interior, which the French were the first to explore. Sooner or later there was bound to be a clash over the possession of the splendid country west of the mountains.

By the year 1689, the decided contrasts in the governments and the Indian policies of the three powers were clearly shown. The large and populous Spanish colonies were ruled strictly by governors who took their orders from Spain. The Indians under Spanish rule were little better than slaves. The trade of the Spanish colonies, including that from the Philippine Islands, was a monopoly of the merchants of the single port of Seville; and their commerce was regulated by a royal council called the *Casa de Contractacion*, or "House of Trade." Most of the export and import business was concentrated on the Isthmus of Panama, whence year after year for more than two centuries sailed the "plate fleet" which carried to Spain gold and silver, Asiatic products, and colonial exports. In comparison with this system of restriction, the English navigation acts (§ 43) were mildness itself.

The French got on with the natives better than any other colonizing people, because they were willing to meet them half-way. They lived on terms of peace and almost of intimacy with their Indian subjects, and many French frontiersmen took squaw wives. Soon arose a distinct class of "coureurs de bois" — white men and half-breeds who had adopted the Indian dress and manner of life. Canada, like the Spanish colonies, was governed from overseas. It was substantially a big military camp, made up of weak little settlements, which existed mainly for the fur trade; even the French permanent colonists were chiefly peasants, who had no ambition for self-government.

The English despised the Indians, and sooner or later killed off the tribes or drove them westward. The individual colonists had large opportunities for making a living, were of an intelligent class, and had partial self-government, which during such times as the English civil war amounted almost to independence.

48. REVIEW

After the civil war in England, the monarchy was restored under Charles II, and his government decided to seize the Dutch colony of New Netherland. The king granted to his brother, the Duke of York, the country between the Connecticut and Delaware rivers, and also Maine. The Dutch colony was easily taken by the English, and renamed New York. The new colony was governed by a code called "The Duke's Laws."

The next step was to make a plan for a New England colony, by forcing Massachusetts, Connecticut, and Rhode Island to give up their charters and come under one government. Massachusetts was weakened by King Philip's War, lost its charter in 1684, and was for a time governed by Sir Edmund Andros.

A new colony was chartered south of Virginia in 1663, and was later subdivided into North Carolina and South Carolina. Virginia was harassed by Indian wars which led to the short-lived Bacon Rebellion in 1676. Another new colony was Pennsylvania, chartered in 1681, with William Penn, a Quaker, as proprietor. Delaware was added to it, and later separated. Penn drew up a kind of constitution called the "Frame of Government," and gave a charter to Philadelphia.

The downfall of James II in 1689 was followed by various changes in the colonies, so that they finally numbered twelve. A thirteenth colony, Georgia, was founded in 1732.

Of the three great colonial groups that were planted in America, the Spanish colonies were governed by orders from Spain, and their trade was much restricted. The French had little local government, but got on well with the Indians. The English allowed the colonists many privileges of self-government, but never fraternized with the Indians.

References Bearing on the Text and Topics

Geography and Maps. See maps, pp. 59, 63, 65. — Andrews, *Col. Self-Govt.* — Avery, *U.S.*, III. — Becker, *Beginnings*, 134. — Greene, *Provincial Am.*, 6, 252. — Shepherd, *Hist. Atlas*, 190–193.

Secondary. Ashe, *No. Carolina*, I. chs. v–xvii. — Bassett, *U. S.*, ch. v. — Bruce, *Oglethorpe.* — Channing, *U. S.*, II. chs. i–vii, xii. — Fiske, *Beginnings of New Engl.*, 199–278; *Dutch and Quaker Cols.*, I. 243–294, II. 1–61, 99–208; *Old Va.*, II. 45–116, 131–162, 270–308, 333–336. — Mathews, *Expansion of New Engl.*, ch. iii. — McCrady, *So. Carolina*, I, II. chs. i–v. — Sharpless, *Quaker Experiment.* — Wendell, *Cotton Mather*, 21–87. — Wertenbaker, *Va. under the Stuarts*, chs. v–viii.

Sources. *Am. History Leaflets*, no. 16. — Bogart and Thompson, *Readings*, 11–20. — Hart, *Contemporaries*, I. §§ 42, 43, 54, 70, 71, 76–81, 104, 116, 121–126, 132–136, 155–157, 160–167, 172, II. §§ 39–44; *Patriots and Statesmen*, I. 116–126, 134–147, 183–186; *Source Book*, §§ 22–27.—Jameson, *Original Narratives.* — MacDonald, *Select Charters*, nos. 24–49, passim. — *Old South Leaflets*, nos. 21, 22, 88, 95, 155, 171, 172. — See New Engl. Hist. Teachers' Assoc., *Hist. Sources*, §§ 70–72; *Syllabus*, 301, 310, 313.

Illustrative. Butterworth, *Wampum Belt* (Penn.). — Bynner, *Begum's Daughter* (Leisler). — Catherwood, *Story of Tonty.* — Cooper, *Wept of Wish-Ton-Wish* (Philip); *Water Witch* (N.Y.). — Goodwin, *White Aprons* (Bacon). — Green, *Young Pioneers* (La Salle). — Hawthorne, *Gray Champion* (Andros); *Grandfather's Chair*, pt. i, chs. viii, ix. — Johnston, *Prisoners of Hope* (Bacon). — Kennedy, *Rob of the Bowl* (Md.). — Seton, *Charter Oak.* — Simms, *Cassique of Kiawah* (S.C.). — Whittier, *Pa. Pilgrim.* — Wilkins, *Heart's Highway* (Va.).

Pictures. Avery, *U.S.*, II, III. — Wilson, *Am. People*, I. — Winsor, *America*, III, IV.

Topics Answerable from the References Above

(1) Life in New Amsterdam about 1660. [§ 40] — (2) Early life in New Jersey. [§ 41] — (3) History of "The Duke's Laws." [§ 42] — (4) Why did Locke's "Fundamental Constitution" fail? [§ 44] — (5) Early slavery in South Carolina. [§ 44] — (6) Life of William Penn, down to 1681. [§ 45] — (7) Plans of James Oglethorpe. [§ 46] — (8) Hudson's Bay Company to 1750. [§ 47] — (9) The Spanish "plate fleet." [§ 47]

Topics for Further Search

(10) Story of the early British East India Company. [§ 40] — (11) How were the charters obtained for Connecticut and Rhode Island? [§ 41] — (12) Were the Acts of Trade a good thing for the colonies? [§ 43] — (13) Was Sir Edmund Andros a tyrant? [§ 43] — (14) Was Nathaniel Bacon a patriot? [§ 44] — (15) Boundary between Pennsylvania and Maryland. [§ 45] — (16) Board of Trade. [§ 46] — (17) German and Moravian colonists in Georgia. [§ 46]

CHAPTER V

SOCIAL AND POLITICAL LIFE (1689-1763)

49. COLONIAL POPULATION

WE are interested nowadays in the development of the English colonies, because we know that they finally came together in the federal Union under which we live. The colonists themselves were not much interested in their own history. They lived like their descendants, from one day to another:

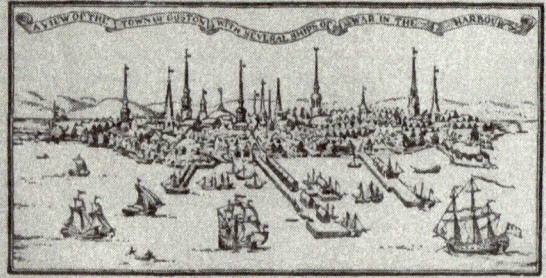

BOSTON IN 1722.

going to church — some of them going to prison, — building, working, traveling, fighting, marrying, and dying.

Everywhere the population grew rapidly. Though New England received hardly any direct immigration after the beginning of the English civil war (§ 37), by 1700 it had about 105,000 inhabitants. The southern colonies (Maryland, Virginia, and the Carolinas) together had about 110,000; the middle col-

onies (New York, New Jersey, Pennsylvania, and Delaware),
55,000; making a total of about 270,000 people. The largest
towns were Boston, with about 7000 people, and Philadelphia,
with 4000. By 1763, the population had grown to about
1,770,000, of which the New England group contained about
510,000, the middle group 460,000, and the southern group
(including Georgia in addition to the earlier southern colonies)
about 800,000. Philadelphia, New York, and Boston, the
only large towns down to 1763, varied from 15,000 to 20,000
people each.

Many races combined to make up this population, but it is
now impossible to know how many there were of each, except
in the case of the negroes. In every colony the largest element
was of English descent. There may have been 25,000 descendants of Dutchmen in New York and on the Delaware in 1700.
A few Swedes and Finns (§ 27) still remained on that river,
and a small Swedish immigration continued there. A few
Huguenots could be found in almost all the colonies, and they
were numerous in South Carolina. The negroes in 1700 were
about 46,000, and in 1763 had increased to perhaps 300,000.
The Indians had nowhere fused with the white population, and
were not considered members of the community.

The two most important non-English races were the Germans and the Protestant Scotch-Irish, to whom may be added
some Catholic Irish and some Scotch Highlanders. The Germans — nearly all of them Protestants — came mostly from
the Rhine region, with a few from Austria; most of them lived
in Pennsylvania, a few in Maryland, Georgia, and central
New York. They are supposed to have been about 100,000
in number in 1763. The Scotch-Irish were about 125,000, and
most of them lived in Pennsylvania, the Carolinas, and Georgia.

50. COLONIAL HOME LIFE

The greater part of the colonists lived in easily constructed
log houses. In New England there were many frame buildings,

clapboarded or shingled. In the towns and in the Dutch and German villages, there were more substantial houses of brick.

Among the poor families, the rude furniture was hardly more than floor, seats, and tables, all made of "puncheons," — that is, of split halves of small tree trunks, — with a few pewter dishes, a fireplace, and its utensils. The better houses had substantial oaken chests, chairs, and tables, and handsome clocks.

In dress our well-to-do forefathers followed as closely as they could the English fashions of elaborate suits of cloth or velvet or silk, and full-bottomed wigs. The most common materials were homespun linen and woolen, though on the frontier deer-skin was used.

GERMAN (MORAVIAN)
EARTHENWARE STOVE.

Food abounded: game wandered in and out of all the

A HAND LOOM.

settlements, shellfish were abundant, and the New England coast fisheries provided a regular supply of salt fish; Indian corn was grown everywhere, and there was plenty of wheat flour.

The colonies were swept by diseases, chiefly due to ignorance and uncleanliness, such as "ship-fever," "small pocks," "yellow fever," "break-bone fever," "fever and ague," and other varieties of malaria; and medical practice was lamentably unskillful.

51. COLONIAL EDUCATION

Though England was a land with numerous town schools and several world-famous universities, some of the colonies in America, broken up into separate and widely distributed plantations, could not maintain many schools. Governor Berkeley reported (1671) for Virginia: "I thank God there are no free schools nor printing, and I hope we shall not have these hundred years; for learning has brought disobedience, and heresy, and sects in the world, and printing has divulged them, and libels against the best government. God keep us from both." The New England towns established the first schools in northeastern America, though closely followed by the Collegiate School of the Dutch Reformed Church in New Amsterdam (1633). The colony of Massachusetts Bay showed its interest in education by requiring that every town of fifty families should maintain a school, and every town of a hundred families, a grammar school (that is, a Latin school); but the towns too frequently avoided the responsibility if they could, and no public education was provided for the girls. In 1689 the Penn Charter School was founded in Philadelphia.

Three small colleges provided higher education for the colonies. Harvard College, named from the Rev. John Harvard, its earliest private benefactor, was founded (1636) "to advance learning and perpetuate it to posterity." From the beginning it trained the ministers, and also had as students future men of affairs and statesmen. William and Mary College was established in Virginia (1693); King William III, the colony, and private subscribers united to give the college a home in Williamsburg. Yale College was "first concerted by the ministers" (1701), and its earliest property was forty volumes given by the founders for a library. The college was soon removed from Saybrook to New Haven, and (1718) received its name from Elihu Yale, a public-spirited Englishman who interested himself in the new institution.

52. COLONIAL LITERATURE

Among all the colonizing races could be found men of learning: Puritan divines, like Increase Mather and Jonathan Edwards; Dutch schoolmasters, such as Dominie Bogardus; German ministers and literary men, such as Pastorius and Christopher Sower. One of the earliest historical writings was Beverly's *History of Virginia* (1705). In addition, the English books of the time were read and admired in the colonies.

The most notable colonial writers of the seventeenth century were the discoverers, explorers, and colonists who wrote en-

PART OF A PAGE OF THE FIRST AMERICAN NEWSPAPER, 1704.

tertaining accounts of their experiences. Thus John Smith and William Strachey wrote about Virginia; and William Bradford and John Winthrop each left an admirable historical account of the colony in which he was governor and leader. In the South, the writer of greatest literary merit was Colonel William Byrd, who left in manuscript a charming book of travel called *History of the Dividing Line.* In the middle colonies, till Benjamin Franklin came, the only man who can be called a literary light is William Penn; but the Moravians were great printers, and issued the first complete Bible, except Eliot's Indian Bible, published within the colonies. The first newspaper in the colonies, the *Boston News Letter*, appeared in 1704; and the trial of John Peter Zenger in New York (1735) established the important principle that a journalist cannot be convicted of libel for publishing the truth.

Works of fiction were unknown, except as serious writers set down neighborhood gossip; but there were several writers of poor verse. The *Bay Psalm Book*, the first book printed in the English colonies (1640), was made by a syndicate of ministers, whose poetic gifts may be shown by the facsimile on this page.

A PAGE FROM THE *BAY PSALM BOOK*.

The favorite literature for educated men was theological and controversial. The most famous writer of this kind was Cotton Mather, a Boston minister, long the leading man of New England, who wrote an enormous and confused folio which he called *Magnalia Christi Americana.* The two most popular

books in the colonies were the *New England Primer*, with its
pious doggerel and rude woodcuts, which went through many
editions and was often given as a school prize; and Wiggles-
worth's *Day of Doom*, which was learned by heart by hundreds
of persons. It is a fearful description of that gruesome place,

> "Where God's fierce ire kindleth the fire,
>   and vengeance feeds the flame,
> With piles of wood and brimstone flood,
>   that none can quench the same."

53. BENJAMIN FRANKLIN

BENJAMIN FRANKLIN IN 1766. (After a painting
by Martin.)

The most dis-
tinctly intellec-
tual man of this
period, and also
the greatest polit-
ical leader, was
Benjamin Frank-
lin, who was born
in Boston in 1706,
and settled in
Philadelphia in
1723. Franklin
was a good print-
er, and the first
American jour-
nalist widely read
in the colonies.
Throughout his
life he was in-
terested in educa-
tion, and he ren-
dered great service
to science by
discovering that
lightning is the

same thing as the discharge of electricity produced by friction. He was also the inventor of the useful Franklin stove, a kind of little movable fireplace.

Franklin was appointed deputy postmaster-general for the colonies in 1753 and greatly improved the service. In 1757 he was sent to England as agent of the colony of Pennsylvania, and remained there five years. Gradually other colonies noticed his influence with British statesmen and gave him a similar commission. He was a keen and caustic writer, and his satires on social and political matters, such as his *Rules for Reducing a Great Empire to a Small One*, had powerful effect. His *Poor Richard's Almanac* was an annual, abounding in shrewd, common-sense observations; it was widely read throughout the colonies.

THE FRANKLIN STOVE. (Invented in 1744. Called by its inventor the "Pennsylvania Fireplace.")

The chief merit of Franklin was that his great mind saw how much the colonies could do if they would only act together. He showed a willingness, very uncommon in the colonies, to sink local differences and interests for the common good; and in England he impressed the leading men with respect for himself and for the colonies which he represented. Franklin personified the colonist of the second half of the eighteenth century who looked upon himself as no longer an Englishman living overseas, but as an American, with no purpose or desire but to remain a colonist.

54. COLONIAL RELIGIOUS LIFE

Franklin, though born in New England, never concerned himself with the creed of the New England Puritans, whose theology was built on the writings of the great Genevese, John Calvin (died 1564). This great divine's favorite doctrine was "predestination"; that is, he thought that the whole human race was doomed to perdition, except as God might "elect" a few persons to be saved. Hence good deeds, contemptuously called "filthy rags of works," could not in themselves save anybody. Even such heads of the church as Cotton Mather were tormented by the fear that after all they might not be "elect." On the other hand, Calvin set forth the great doctrine of "free will" — of choice between good and evil, with its emphasis on personal duty and responsibility.

The Church of England, or Episcopal Church, which held milder doctrines of salvation, was now gaining ground. It was made the official church, supported by public taxation, in Virginia, Maryland, the Carolinas, and parts of New York, though aided also by voluntary contributions. In 1689 the first "King's Chapel" was built in Boston as a place of Episcopal service. The Congregational Church supported by public taxation in New Hampshire, Massachusetts (including Maine and Plymouth), and Connecticut. In the other five colonies there was no state church.

Side by side with the established churches lived many other religious sects. The Baptists were settled chiefly in Rhode Island; the Presbyterians, some English and some Scotch, in the middle and southern colonies; the Dutch Reformed Church in New York; Lutherans, Moravians, Mennonites, and other German sects in Pennsylvania; English Catholics in Maryland; Quakers and a few Jews in most of the colonies. In Rhode Island and Pennsylvania there was practically toleration for every form of Christian belief; and after 1689 there was no religious persecution anywhere in the colonies.

OLD SWEDES' CHURCH, PHILADELPHIA, BUILT IN 1700.

Both in the North and in the South, many of the church buildings were handsome and commodious. In New England the able-bodied population was required to go to service, where pews were carefully assigned according to the social position of the attendants. In the sermons — two on Sunday and a third, the "Thursday lecture," during the week — our forefathers received a good mouthful of doctrine, though two hours and a half was thought too long for a sermon. No hymns were allowed, only the Psalms lined out by the minister. Sunday, commonly called Sabbath, lasted from sundown on Saturday to sundown on Sunday, and in strictness was as near a Jewish Sabbath as the conditions permitted.

55. WITCHCRAFT EPISODE (1692)

All the colonies shared in the fearful belief, then current throughout the world, that human beings could become

"witches," and could make a personal compact with the devil
which would enable them to change their shape, to travel on the
wings of the wind, and especially to bring bodily harm to
their enemies. But nowhere else in the civilized world did
this awful delusion play so little part as in the American colonies, though there were a few cases of the execution of witches.
In Europe thousands of innocent persons suffered torture and
death — often by fire — for crimes of "witchcraft" which no
one could commit.

In 1692 several girls, including the daughter of a minister
near Salem, Massachusetts, accused an Indian slave woman,
Tituba, of bewitching them. In a few weeks scores of the
"afflicted" were accusing their neighbors of the foulest crimes
and most improbable orgies. A special court was set up for
the trial of the accused. The principal testimony was the
"spectral evidence " — that is, the assertion of the "afflicted"
that they had consorted with witches and had seen things
invisible to others. Nineteen alleged witches were hanged,
and one was pressed to death by heavy weights for refusing
to plead guilty or not guilty.

To save themselves, the so-called witches accused other
people, and so the number rolled up till more than fifty people
were so crazed that they confessed to being witches, and told
preposterous stories of flying through the air on broomsticks,
of taking part in "devil's sabbaths," and of tormenting their
neighbors. When Lady Phips, wife of the governor, was
accused, the prosecutions broke down, and there were no
more executions in New England, though they continued half
a century longer in Europe.

56. RELIGIOUS AWAKENING (1736–1771)

The Puritan "theocracy " — that is, the ruling influence of
the ministers who felt that they spoke for the Almighty as
interpreted by John Calvin (§ 54) — steadily lost ground during the eighteenth century, although a new leader of thought

in New England, Rev. Jonathan Edwards, worked out an elaborate system of theology based on the "total depravity" of human nature.

Against this harsh theology and appeal to the fears of mankind came a movement of protest, which began in the attempt of John and Charles Wesley, devoted clergymen of the Church of England, to restore vital religion to that church. In their sermons, doctrinal books, and hymns, they dwelt on the love of the Savior, and the great desire of God that His children should be reconciled to Him. In 1736 both brothers, followed by Rev. George Whitefield, came out for a time to Georgia, and attempted to convert the natives and to rouse the colonists. The Wesley movement ended in the founding of the Wesleyan or Methodist Church in England. In 1740 Whitefield came to New England, and by his powerful preaching brought about "The Great Awakening," the first general revival of religion in America.

The New England Congregationalists under this pressure divided into "Old Lights" and "New Lights," the latter feeling that genuine conversion must show itself by tears, groans, and convulsions, such as half a century later were popularly called "the jerks." The outcome of the movement was the establishment of the Methodist Church in America and a great strengthening of the Baptists, while the Congregational, Presbyterian, and Episcopal churches throughout the colonies were directly or indirectly influenced to make religion less a matter of observance and dogma and more a matter of personal service.

A new intellectual interest was shown by the publication of several excellent local histories, and by the foundation, between 1746 and 1769, of six new colleges: New Jersey, shortly moved to Princeton; Kings, now Columbia; Queens, now Rutgers; Philadelphia, founded by Franklin (later reorganized as the University of Pennsylvania); Rhode Island, now Brown; and Dartmouth.

57. ENGLAND'S CONTROL OF THE COLONIES

In politics as in religion, the colonies felt a serious responsibility for their own future. During the seventeenth and eighteenth centuries, most European countries were falling more and more under a one-man government. In England alone did the people succeed in building up a system in which an elected parliament was superior to the hereditary king. That idea of popular government was still further expanded in the English colonies.

Nominally, the colonial governments from 1689 to 1763 were subject to the control of the king; but practically they were controlled only to some extent by the king's ministers, who made the decisions and required the king to accept them. The principal ways in which the colonial governments were subject to England were the following:

(1) The colonists acknowledged the king to be their sovereign and felt a personal loyalty to him, which was doubtless the stronger because they were too far away to see him. They also admitted the right of Parliament to legislate for them in matters of trade.

(2) Every colony was originally founded on a royal grant or charter, given direct or through proprietors, though most of these charters were later surrendered.

(3) The home government sent out instructions to the governors, who were appointed by the Crown.

(4) Every colony had a legislature authorized by its charter or by instructions from England; but the acts of that body, except in Rhode Island and Connecticut, could be set aside by the governor's veto; and if he signed a bill it could still be set aside by the Privy Council on the advice of the Board of Trade in England.

(5) The laws were not to be contrary to the laws of England; and in some cases appeals could be taken from the colonial courts to the Privy Council in England.

58. COLONIAL POPULAR GOVERNMENTS

These limitations did not prevent the American colonies from enjoying the freest and most popular government then existing in the world. Nowhere else was there so much discussion of public questions by the people at large; nowhere else was there so much of what Edmund Burke, the great English statesman, called the "fierce spirit of liberty."

Then and since, the colonies have often been classified into three official forms: (1) three charter colonies — Massachusetts, Rhode Island, and Connecticut; (2) three proprietary colonies — Pennsylvania, Delaware, and Maryland; (3) seven royal or provincial colonies — New Hampshire, New York, New Jersey, Virginia, North Carolina, South Carolina, and Georgia.

In all the colonies, whatever their origin or form, there was a colonial democracy built on the conviction that Americans were entitled to inborn rights, which could not be taken away by either British or colonial governments. Among them were: (1) the personal rights of Englishmen set forth in the old common law, such as speedy and open trial by jury, and freedom from arbitrary arrest; (2) rights asserted for the English by such statutes as the Petition of Right (1628), the Habeas Corpus Act (1679), and the Bill of Rights (1689); (3) the right to make decisions in local matters through town meetings and other local assemblies.

Voting was in every colony restricted to owners of real estate, as in England, or to payers of considerable personal taxes; but the land qualification was easy to get, and therefore about one half or one third of the adult free men were voters. There were no political parties in the modern sense: the usual division was between the friends of the governor and the opposition. In all the colonies local dignitaries controlled their neighbors' votes; and the public honors fell to a small number of families of social distinction.

Though officially quite a distance from one another, and connected only by common adherence to the British government, the colonies had many relations with one another. It was easy for an Englishman or a foreigner to become a citizen of a colony, or to move from one to another, for every colony was Protestant, every colony had about the same system of laws, in every colony English was the only official language.

The most significant thing about the colonial governments is that they were very like the present state governments, particularly in their subdivision into three "departments":

(1) The Executive. In each colony the governor was the principal figure. Whether elected by the people as in Rhode Island and Connecticut, or appointed by the proprietors, or appointed by the Crown, the governors carried on the government in understanding with the people as represented by their assembly. In most colonies there was also a small council appointed by the Crown or the proprietor, which acted as the upper house of the legislature.

(2) The Legislative. The lower house of the legislature, usually called the assembly, was elected by the people. It shared in making the laws and its consent was necessary for taxes.

(3) The Judiciary. The judges were appointed by the governor or by the Crown (except in Rhode Island and Connecticut, where they were elected by the legislature). In the royal colonies the governor and council were the highest court. This was the weakest department, for the judges were often not skilled in the law; but justice was speedy and inexpensive, and the individual was protected by juries in all criminal and most civil cases.

59. Local Governments

One of the glories of colonial democracy was the local governments, in which the will of the people was least restrained. They were all founded upon the English system of shires or counties, parishes, and boroughs or cities; but the colonies made many changes and improvements.

(1) All the colonies were divided into counties, governed by what we should call commissioners, appointed by the governors and called Courts of Quarter Sessions, or County Courts. In the southern colonies, the county courts did most of the local governing.

(2) Beginning with New York in 1665, "borough" or "city" governments were set up in a few places in Pennsylvania, New York, and New Jersey.

(3) The smallest unit of local government was the parish or town. The parish in the South was gov-

HAND FIRE ENGINE. (Used in Germantown, about 1765.)

erned by what was called a "select vestry" which filled its own vacancies. In the North the unit was the "town," in which there was a taxpayers' meeting founded on a similar meeting in some of the English parishes; the county was there of little significance. In Pennsylvania and New York there were active town governments and also county organizations.

Amidst all these different forms, the most interesting is the New England town meeting, which was a general assembly of all those who were qualified to vote, with other people present as lookers-on. These lively little meetings chose the town officers, especially the "townsmen," or "selectmen," who made up an executive board which sat whenever necessary.

The main business of the town meeting, however, was to
legislate for the town, and it was a place for vigorous discussion, and for the development of parliamentary law and political patience. In troubled times it was the center of
protest, as when the Cambridge town meeting in the Stamp
Act days instructed its representatives that "they use their
utmost endeavours, that the same may be repealed; that this
vote may be recorded in the Town Book, that the children yet
unborn may see the desires that their ancestors had for their
freedom and happiness."

60. REVIEW

The thing most important to remember about the early
English colonies is that for a long time they looked upon themselves as simply a body of English people living across the sea.
Nevertheless the conditions of frontier life and Indian warfare
made their life very different. They increased rapidly in population, doubling about every twenty-five years. Most of them
lived simply, though a few had handsome houses and surroundings.

The New Englanders and Dutch early started schools, and
three little colleges were founded before 1702. In Pennsylvania
and New England there were several well-known writers, especially the Dutch and Puritan clergymen. Benjamin Franklin is the most striking figure of the period, as journalist,
inventor, statesman, and writer.

The most important religious denominations were the Congregationalists in New England and several other colonies, and the
Episcopalians in the southern colonies and New York. There
were several other denominations, English, Dutch, German, and
Jewish. In 1692 many people of New England went almost
insane over witchcraft, and nineteen supposed witches were
hanged. A new religious movement was started by the Wesley
brothers and Whitefield, which resulted in the foundation of the
Methodist Church in America and the stirring up of the other

churches. Six new colleges were founded between 1746 and 1769.

The colonists had a very free government with their own legislatures, but were partly under the control of governors appointed by the king. They enjoyed liberal personal rights and popular suffrage on rather easy conditions. They also developed their own local government in the three forms of towns, counties, and cities.

References Bearing on the Text and Topics

Geography and Maps. Avery, *U.S.*, III. 206. — Greene, *Provincial Am.*, 66.

Secondary. Bassett, *U.S.*, 134-137, 145-158. — Becker, *Beginnings*, ch. v. — Bruce, *Social Life of Va.* — Channing, *U.S.*, II. chs. viii, xiv-xvi. — Dickerson, *Am. Col. Govt.* — Doyle, *English in Am.*, I. 268-274, 326, II. 1-10, III. 1-97, 298-310, 377-395, V. chs. iv, v, vii. — Fiske, *Dutch and Quaker Cols.*, II. 258-285, 317-356; *New France and New Engl.*, chs. v, vi; *Old Va.*, II. 1-44, 116-130, 204-269, 308-325. — Ford, *Many-sided Franklin*. — Greene, *Provincial Am.*, chs. i-vi, xi-xiv, xviii; *Provincial Governor*. — Jenks, *When Am. won Liberty*, chs. v-vii. — McCrady, *So. Carolina*, II. 399-540. — Thwaites, *Cols.*, §§ 23-26, 40-46 passim, 75-81 passim, 91-97 passim, 119, 129. — Tyler, *Am. Literature* (colonial). — Weeden, *New Engl.*, I. 47-87, 213-231, 269-303, 410-429, II. 512-551, 692-713. — Wendell, *Cotton Mather*, 88-307.

Sources. Caldwell, *Survey*, 13-22, 126-132. — Franklin, *Autobiography*. — Hart, *Contemporaries*, I. §§ 85-89, 137-149, 168, 172, II. §§ 16-18, 25-47 passim, 87, 90-108; *Patriots and Statesmen*, I. 149-153, 157-162, 170-180, 187, 194-243 passim; *Source Book*, §§ 11, 12, 28-35, 41-52. — Hill, *Liberty Docs.*, ch. xi. — Jameson, *Original Narratives* (witchcraft cases). — *Old South Leaflets*, nos. 51, 159-161, 177, 184, 185. — Sewall, *Diary*. — Woolman, *Journal*. — See New Engl. Hist. Teachers' Assoc., *Hist. Sources*, §§ 73, 74; *Syllabus*, 306-308, 313-315, 318-321.

Illustrative. Cooke, *Youth of Jefferson* (college life). — Cooper, *Satanstoe* (N.Y.). — DuBois, *Martha Corey* (witchcraft). — Earle, *Home Life in Colonial Days; Child Life in Colonial Days; Colonial Dames; Sabbath in Puritan New England; Two Centuries of Costume; Curious Punishments*. — Harland, *His Great Self* (Col. Byrd). — Longfellow, *Giles Corey*. — Meyers, *Young Patroon* (N.Y.). — Paulding, *Dutchman's Fireside*. — Whittier, *Mabel Martin; Prophecy of Samuel Sewall; Witch of Wenham*.

Pictures. Avery, *U.S.*, III, V, ch. i. — Earle's books (cited in the preceding paragraph). — Eggleston, in *The Century*, 1884, 1885. — *Mentor*, serial nos. 62, 77, 86, 99. — Sparks, *Expansion*. — Wilson, *Am. People*, I, II.

Topics Answerable from the References Above

(1) Life in Philadelphia, *or* New York, *or* Boston, about 1750. [§ 49] — (2) Account of the Collegiate School in New Amsterdam. [§ 51] — (3) Early life in Harvard, *or* William and Mary, *or* Yale. [§ 51] — (4) Benjamin Franklin, as a boy and young man. [§ 53] — (5) Incidents of church services in the colonies. [§ 54] — (6) Witch prosecutions in other colonies besides Massachusetts. [§ 55] — (7) Contemporary accounts of Salem witchcraft. [§ 55] — (8) Account of a meeting of a colonial legislature. [§ 58] — (9) Colonial town meetings. [§ 59] — (10) Colonial county courts. [§ 59]

Topics for Further Search

(11) Huguenots in the English colonies. [§ 49] — (12) *One* of these groups of immigrants in Pennsylvania before 1763: Germans; Scotch-Irish; Moravians. [§§ 49, 54] — (13) Description and criticism of Mather's *Magnalia*, *or* of the *New England Primer*. [§ 52] — (14) Famous early church buildings. [§ 54] — (15) *One* of the following clergymen in America: Increase Mather; Edwards; Whitefield; John Wesley; Byles. [§ 56] — (16) Life in *one* of the following colleges before the Revolution: New Jersey; Kings; Philadelphia; Rhode Island; Dartmouth. [§ 56] — (17) Why was government so democratic in the colonies? [§ 58] — (18) Experiences of some particular colonial governor. [§ 58]

CHAPTER VI

FRANCE AND THE WEST (1670–1763)

61. FRENCH IN THE INTERIOR (1670–1680)

GOVERNOR SPOTSWOOD'S EXPE-
DITION TO THE BLUE RIDGE.

WITH all their dash and
enterprise on the seacoast,
the English showed little curiosity about the country behind
the Appalachian Mountains. Two or
three unofficial travelers, particularly
Batts, an Englishman, and Lederer, a
German Swiss, crossed the divide before
1689 and reached waters flowing mys-
teriously westward; and a few traders
penetrated into the Cherokee Indian country in the southwest. Not till 1716 did
Governor Spotswood of Virginia cross the
Blue Ridge.

The French, however, had a natural genius for exploration, and never ceased to enlarge their knowledge about the great interior (§ 29). From the Indians on the upper lakes, they learned vaguely about a great south-flowing river which, they guessed, must empty into the Gulf of California. Meanwhile another Frenchman was making plans for reaching that stream. This was Robert Cavelier, commonly called La Salle, a nobleman who in 1670 ventured on Lake Erie and thence southwestward to a large river which was perhaps the Ohio.

The first Frenchman to reach the great south-flowing river was the missionary Father Marquette, accompanied by the trader Joliet. They ascended the Fox River and went down the Wisconsin till (June 17, 1673) they entered the mighty Mississippi (map, page 94). League after league they floated down the river, hoping to reach the sea. They passed the mouth of the Missouri, so muddy that they would not drink it. By the time they reached the mouth of the Arkansas they felt sure that they were near Spanish and hostile territory; they therefore turned back, and paddled up the Illinois River, which they called the Divine, and crossed over the site now occupied by Chicago to Lake Michigan.

La Salle obtained the favor of the French monarch Louis XIV, who authorized him to make discoveries in the far West. In 1679 La Salle built the ship *Griffon* on Lake Erie and navigated her to Lake Michigan. Crossing the portage from the St. Joseph River to the Kankakee River, he went downstream, and began to build another ship on the Illinois River at a place which he named Fort Crèvecœur (Heartbreak). A missionary friar, Father Hennepin, came out with La Salle and was sent by him down the Illinois and thence up the Mississippi; he was taken prisoner by the Sioux Indians, and carried to the falls, which Hennepin named St. Anthony, on the site of the present Minneapolis (1680).

62. EXPLORATION OF THE LOWER MISSISSIPPI (1682-1687)

Fate seemed against La Salle. The *Griffon* was lost. The shipbuilders on the Illinois deserted. But La Salle never gave up. He traveled thousands of miles till he collected the necessary men and supplies. Early in 1682 he reached the mouth of the Illinois with a party in canoes, and thence floated down the same stretch that Marquette had traversed. Soon after passing the mouth of the Ohio he took possession of the country with great ceremony, and set up the king's arms. A few days later, at the Chickasaw Bluffs, he founded Fort Prudhomme.

After a few weeks he passed Marquette's farthest point and (April 6, 1682) arrived at a place where the river divided into three channels. As one of the party wrote: "The water is brackish; after advancing two leagues it became perfectly salt, and advancing on, we discovered the open sea, so that . . . the sieur de la Salle, in the name of his majesty, took possession of that river, of all rivers that enter it, and of all the country watered by them." Thus was asserted the French title to the magnificent valley which La Salle named Louisiana, in honor of Louis XIV.

La Salle's discovery made such an impression that the king sent him back, by sea, to plant a colony near the mouth of the Mississippi. By ill fortune he missed the river, and built Fort St. Louis (1685) on Matagorda Bay, Texas. He could not find his river; and after setting out for Canada to get help he was murdered by some of his own followers in 1687. The fort in Texas was destroyed by Indians, while the Spaniards from Mexico were trying to reach it in order to prevent a possible French settlement.

63. LOUISIANA (1687-1735)

After La Salle had explored the Mississippi, the French made several permanent settlements in what came to be called the

Illinois country, among them Detroit (1701), and Vincennes on
the Wabash (1735).

The Spaniards were anxious to make good their neglected
claims to the lower Mississippi country, and settled Pensacola
(1696) as a basis for colonies to be planted farther west. The
French interrupted this plan by sending out 130 colonists under

FRENCH LOUISIANA.

Iberville in 1699 to take possession of the coast of Louisiana.
After stopping at Dauphin Island and at Biloxi on the mainland,
they founded Mobile (1702). The main purpose of this colony
was to secure control of the valuable fur trade with the Indians
of the interior, but it grew very slowly.

In 1712 a rich banker, Antoine Crozat, got from the king of
France a grant giving him a monopoly of trade in "all the

countries, territories, lakes within land, and the rivers which fall directly or indirectly into the river St. Louis, heretofore called the Mississippi." This is the first distinct claim since La Salle's voyage (§ 62) to the whole region drained by the tributaries of the Mississippi, as belonging to France. Crozat made little use of his privileges, but in 1717 the Illinois country was annexed to Louisiana. During the next year a new political and commercial center for the colony was created in the town of New Orleans, on a site chosen because the water front was elevated a few feet above the river. Some German emigrants came in as well as French, and in the course of a few years 7000 Europeans gathered in Louisiana.

64. RIVALRIES IN EUROPE (1689–1763)

The year 1689 is a significant date in the history of the United States: for it marks the beginning of a period of European wars which extended to the colonies and which, after nearly seventy-five years of strife, pushed France out of the North American continent and thus made an independent American nation possible. The first step in this process was the overthrow of James II of England (§ 46). He fled to France, where Louis XIV harbored him; and that at once brought on war between England and France. The resulting struggle in the New World was the first of four intercolonial wars, which were not ended till 1763. In 1701 Spain came into the wars as a kind of satellite of France, for the Spanish accepted as their king a younger grandson of Louis XIV. Another significant change was the union of England and Scotland into the kingdom of Great Britain in 1707. Up to this time the two countries had been distinct, although both had the same sovereign after the accession of James I (1603). After 1707 they were one land, with one parliament and one flag — the British.

The most notable thing in the intercolonial wars is the rise of the British sea power, through the "wooden walls of England." To protect her own colonies, scattered all over the globe, and to attack the colonies of France and Spain, England developed the best navy of the time. The great "ships of the line," for naval battles, were of 1000 to 2000 tons' burden, and carried in one or two tiers as many as seventy-four guns. In each of the four intercolonial wars there was fighting on the wilderness frontiers between the French colonies and the English colonies of New England and New York; in the later wars the English colonists in the South also found themselves pitted against the Spaniards of Florida; while the West Indies became a zone of naval warfare in which European fleets contended and the small islands changed hands.

65. INDIAN WARFARE

All the English colonists except the Pennsylvanians were used to wars with their own immediate Indian neighbors. The Indians were now drawn into these international troubles as the allies of one side or the other. The first experience of invasion was an expedition of French and Indians which in 1690 made a night attack on the town of Schenectady, near Albany, sacked and burned the little place, killed sixty people, and took thirty prisoners. A similar incident was the raiding of the Connecticut River town of Deerfield in 1704, when more than half of the inhabitants were killed or swept away. First and last ten places in Maine, New Hampshire, Massachusetts, and New York were raided in this fashion. The English used the same tactics, engaged Indian allies when they could, and did not disdain to offer a reward for scalps.

Fearful was the hasty march northward after a French raid; little children were brained against the trees, because too troublesome to carry; the women who fainted with fatigue were tomahawked and scalped to save the trouble of carrying them along. In one such foray (1691) Hannah Dustin of Haverhill, Massachusetts, was made prisoner. She had the courage, with a nurse and a white boy, to surprise her captors,

and to kill not only two Indian men but three women and
five children; by this means she escaped and reached home
to tell the tale.

The English saved themselves from the worst danger from
Indians by making friends with the ferocious Iroquois, who were
enlarged into "Six Nations" instead of five by taking in the
Tuscaroras in 1715. The home government later appointed Sir
William Johnson its agent to the Six Nations. He lived among
them in a great place called Johnson Hall, where he kept open
house for their benefit. He was an adept at those long-drawn
councils which the Indians so much loved; he knew how to
give belts of wampum, how metaphorically "to dry up their
tears," "to clear the road grown up with weeds," and to set up
"the fine shady trees almost blown down by the northerly
winds." This palaver, accompanied with plenty of food and
rum, was very effective in preventing the French north wind
from blowing down the English influence among the Iroquois.

66. FIRST THREE INTERCOLONIAL WARS (1689–1748)

It is not necessary here to follow the confused and indecisive
conflicts between the British on the one side and the French
and the Spanish on the other. The only notable successes of
the English colonists in the first three wars were the capture of
the little town of Port Royal in Acadia in 1690, and again in
1710, and the taking of the great naval station of Louisburg on
the island of Cape Breton in 1745.

The results of the first three wars were recorded in three
notable treaties: (1) The Peace of Ryswick in 1697 gave back
to each side the possessions that it had at the beginning of the
war. (2) The Peace of Utrecht in 1713 yielded French Acadia
— the present Nova Scotia — to Great Britain; and the French
also gave up the Hudson Bay country and Newfoundland.
This was the beginning of the downfall of the French colonial
empire. (3) The Peace of Aix-la-Chapelle in 1748, after a
war in which the colonists aided the British to attack the

Spanish colonies in South America, restored things as they had been after the treaty of Utrecht. Nevertheless Great Britain was gaining power throughout the world, especially on the sea, while Spain was slowly going downhill, and France was barely able to hold her own.

67. FRENCH AND ENGLISH RIVALRY ON THE OHIO (1749–1754)

Everybody understood that the peace of 1748 was only a respite in the struggle for the possession of the Mississippi valley. The French already had a chain of posts and settle-

THE BATTLE AT FORT NECESSITY.

ments from Lake Michigan through Illinois down to the Mississippi River. They now proceeded to strengthen this defense by building another chain from Lake Ontario to the Ohio River. Among the new forts were Presque Isle (Erie), and Le Bœuf on a tributary of the Allegheny River. The French had the advantages of first discovery, first settlement, and the friendship of the Indians. Nevertheless, the British government made a grant to the so-called Ohio Company (1749), formed by Virginians, for lands on the upper Ohio River.

Under instructions from England, Governor Dinwiddie of Virginia in 1753 sent out a colonial officer, George Washington (then 21 years old), to warn the French to depart. He delivered his message at Fort Le Bœuf and returned to report that the French would not yield. Instead, the French seized the strategic point of the Forks of the Ohio (now Pittsburgh) and built Fort Duquesne on the coveted spot. Washington, in command of a little force of Virginians, attacked a smaller body of Frenchmen near Great Meadows (May, 1754); and under his orders the first shot was fired in the fourth intercolonial war, which developed into a great international contest. A few weeks later Washington was obliged to surrender Fort Necessity — a little stronghold that he had built.

68. FRENCH AND INDIAN WAR (1754–1763)

The colonists were neither armed nor prepared for such a struggle, and an attempt was made by the Board of Trade to bring them to act together through a Congress which assembled at Albany in 1754. Representatives appeared from seven colonies and made arrangements to keep the favor of the Iroquois. Benjamin Franklin also presented a plan for colonial union which is a foreshadowing of our present Constitution. A grand council, representing the colonies roughly in proportion to their population, was to be the active body. This plan was approved by the Albany Congress, and was sent out to the colonies for consideration, but as Franklin said, "Its fate was singular; the assemblies did not adopt it, as they all thought there was too much prerogative in it, and in England it was judged to have too much of the democratic."

Another notable incident of the war was the forcible removal

of the seven thousand French settlers who were living in
Nova Scotia, notwithstanding its cession to Great Britain in
1713. To prevent the danger of their rising, an officer was
sent (1755), with orders to remove them. He says that the
men first to embark "went off Praying, Singing & Crying being
Met by the women & Children all the way (which is 1½ mile)
with great Lamentations upon their Knees, praying &c." The

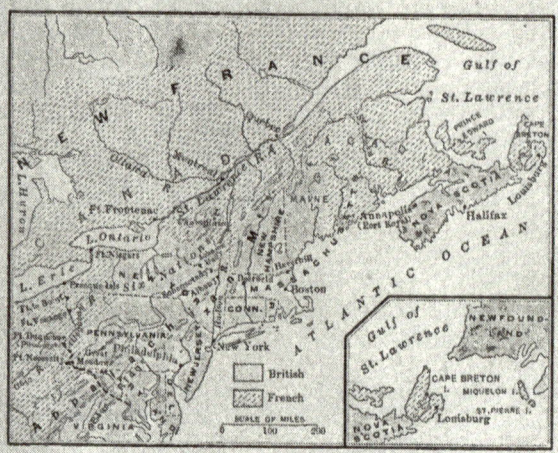

SCENE OF THE FRENCH AND INDIAN WAR.

Acadian families were torn from their homes, loaded on vessels,
and distributed in the colonies, where many of them suffered
severely before they could find a livelihood, and some families
were forever separated.

At the beginning of the war, the British colonists numbered
about 1,300,000; and the French Canadians only about 80,000,
besides some savage allies. The fighting raged all along the
frontiers from Maine through Lake Champlain and the southern

shore of Lake Ontario to the headwaters of the Ohio. The colonists raised considerable numbers of troops and were backed by small armies of British regulars.

In the summer of 1755 an expedition of fifteen hundred men, under the British general Braddock, was sent against Fort Duquesne and met a dramatic fate. Braddock was within seven miles of his destination, when a force of French and Indians, about one half of his strength, sallied out and totally defeated him. His regulars were brave but did not understand Indian fighting, and Braddock would not allow even the militia to fight from behind trees; hence a third of his officers and men were killed, and the remainder, regulars and provincials alike, Washington says, "ran as sheep pursued by dogs."

In the first three years of the war, the French had the best of it almost everywhere in America; it was hard to get the English colonies to act together. As had been expected, the war extended to Europe, where it lasted from 1756 to 1763 and is therefore called the Seven Years' War. It extended even to India, where in the famous battle of Plassey (1757), British supremacy was secured over the French and the natives. Elsewhere Great Britain suffered humiliating defeats. Then the English people insisted that William Pitt, an ardent and impulsive man, a powerful speaker, and a great administrator, be put at the head of affairs; and things began to mend. In America Fort Duquesne was taken in 1758; and the French could not prevent the second capture of Louisburg.

To invade Canada, Pitt now selected General James Wolfe, a model commander, endowed with the English bulldog tenacity, and at the same time with soldierly skill and daring. With 9000 men and a fleet, Wolfe besieged the strong fortress of Quebec, defended by 14,000 men ably commanded by the Marquis de Montcalm. Wolfe forced and won a battle on the Plains of Abraham, above the town (September 13, 1759), but was himself mortally wounded. The result was disputed at the time. "'They run, see how they run,' cried a bystander. 'Who runs?' demanded our hero, with great earnestness. . . . The officer answered, 'The enemy, Sir; Egad, they give way everywhere.' The dying general issued his orders quickly; then turning on his side, he said, 'Now,

THE DEATH OF GENERAL WOLFE AT QUEBEC.

God be praised, I will die in peace.'" In a few days Quebec surrendered, and the next year Montreal fell. In 1762 Manila and Havana were captured from Spain by British fleets.

69. RESULTS OF THE WAR (1763)

The war was ended in all parts of the world by the Peace of Paris (1763). Besides momentous changes in the maps of Europe and India, the treaty registered the most significant alterations in the internal boundaries of North America that had ever been brought about:

(1) The French lost every part of their American empire except the two little islands of St. Pierre and Miquelon off Newfoundland, and a few of the West Indies.

(2) By a secret treaty France ceded to Spain the whole of the western half of Louisiana beyond the Mississippi River, together with the "Island of Orleans" (New Orleans and vicinity), which commanded the mouth of that river. Since Spain claimed the Pacific coast, she was thus put into possession of nearly half the continent of North America.

(3) By the Peace of Paris the British gained much: (*a*) Cape
Breton and Prince Edward Island; (*b*) Canada, or the whole
valley of the St. Lawrence, including the Great Lakes; (*c*) the
Ohio valley, Illinois country, and all other parts of Louisiana
east of the Mississippi, excepting the Island of Orleans;
(*d*) East and West Florida, which were given by Spain in exchange for the return of Cuba. Thus the British became
masters of the whole eastern half of the continent.

Except for extending Georgia southward to the St. Marys
River, none of this new territory was added to the coast colonies. In fact, by the "Proclamation of 1763" the governors
were forbidden to "grant warrants of survey or pass patents for
any lands beyond the heads or sources of any of the rivers
which fall into the Atlantic Ocean from the west or northwest."
That country was to be reserved for the Indians (map,
page 104).

The vast interior had very few white inhabitants. There
were perhaps 6000 French east of the Mississippi in the northwest country. South of the Ohio there were only a few Indian
traders and half-breeds. It soon became clear, however, that
the eastern settlers would push into the new country, proclamation or no proclamation. Pennsylvania was the only colony
that still possessed a charter under which it held a continuous strip beyond the Alleghenies, and before the war was over
hardy Scotch-Irishmen and Germans were pushing their way
down the western slopes toward the Ohio.

70. REVIEW

After 1670, the French steadily pushed west and southwest.
The missionary, Father Marquette, was the first to reach the
Mississippi River (1673). The greatest explorer was La Salle,
the first Frenchman to navigate Lake Erie. One of his companions, Father Hennepin, went up the Mississippi River to the
falls of St. Anthony. La Salle in 1682 went down the river till he
reached the sea; and he claimed the whole region as a French

possession, under the name of Louisiana. The French colony
of Louisiana, founded in 1699, developed very slowly and included little settlements in the Illinois country.

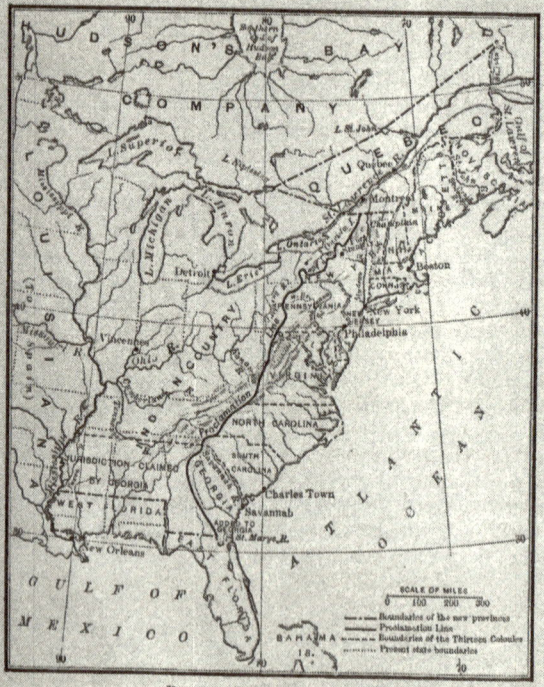

BRITISH COLONIES IN 1765.

From 1689 to 1763, the history of international relations in
America is chiefly the story of the downfall of the French colonial power. In these wars the Indians took part. The French

used them for raiding the frontiers, but the English had the aid of the Iroquois.

In three wars between 1689 and 1748 the French lost Nova Scotia and their claims to the Hudson Bay country and Newfoundland. They then attempted to strengthen their possessions and claims west of the Alleghenies. Virginia, acting for the British government, protested; and her agent, George Washington, attacked the French in 1754.

This was the beginning of the French and Indian War, in which the French held their own in the Ohio valley for three years and defeated the little army of General Braddock near the forks of the Ohio (1755). In 1757 came a change. The French were compelled to give way in various parts of the world, and by the capture of Quebec, in 1759 lost their hold in Canada. By the Peace of Paris (1763) they were obliged to give up all their splendid possessions on the mainland of North America. The country west of the mountains was left for the British to settle; but for some years they held off from founding new colonies there.

References Bearing on the Text and Topics

Geography and Maps. See maps, pp. 94, 100, 104. — Avery, *U.S.*, III, IV. — Bogart, *Econ. Hist.*, 23, 27. — Coman, *Indust. Hist.*, 11, 17. — *Epoch Maps*, nos. iv, v. — Semple, *Geogr. Conditions*, 36–46. — Thwaites, *Colonies; France in Am.* — See Supt. of Docs., *Geography and Exploration List.*

Secondary. Andrews, *Col. Period*, ch. ix. — Channing, *U.S.*, II. chs. xviii, xix. — Douglas, *New Engl. and New France.* — Fiske, *New France and New Engl.*, chs. iv, vii–x. — Greene, *Provincial Am.*, chs. vii–x. — Griffis, *Sir William Johnson.* — Johnson, *General Washington*, 1–66. — King, *Sieur de Bienville.* — Lodge, *Washington*, I. 1–14, 54–118. — Parkman, *Frontenac; Half Century of Conflict; La Salle; Montcalm and Wolfe; Pontiac.* — Sloane, *French War and Rev.*, 22–115. — Thwaites, *France in Am.; Marquette.* — Winsor, *Cartier to Frontenac*, chs. x–xvi; *Mississippi Basin.* — Wood, *Fight for Canada.*

Sources. *Am. Hist. Leaflets*, no. 14. — Caldwell, *Survey*, 39–43; *Terr. Development*, 12–23. — Cox, *Journeys of La Salle.* — Hart, *Contemporaries*, I. §§ 42, 43, II. §§ 109–129; *Patriots and Statesmen*, I. 126–134, 162, 170, 188–190, 201–205, 210–213, 220–235, 243–247; *Source Book,*

§§ 36–40. — MacDonald, *Select Charters*, nos. 51, 52, 54. — *Old South Leaflets*, nos. 9, 46, 73, 187. — See New Engl. Hist. Teachers' Assoc., *Hist. Sources*, § 75; *Syllabus*, 216, 301, 315–318.

Illustrative. Catherwood, *Story of Tonty.* — Cooke, *Stories of the Old Dominion*, 110–139. — Cooper, *Last of the Mohicans; Deerslayer.* — Craddock, *Old Fort Loudon.* — Crowley, *Daughter of New France.* — Eggleston, *Am. War Ballads*, I. 14–20. — Gordon, *Englishman's Haven* (Louisburg). — Hawthorne, *Grandfather's Chair*, pt. ii., chs. vii–x; *Old News*, pt. ii. — Kirby, *Golden Dog* (Canada). — Laut, *Heralds of Empire.* — Longfellow, *Evangeline.* — McHenry, *The Wilderness* (Ohio country). — Munroe, *At War with Pontiac.* — Parker, *Trail of the Sword* (Canada); *Seats of the Mighty* (French and Indian War). — Stevenson, *Soldier of Virginia* (Braddock and Washington). — Whittier, *Pentucket.*

Pictures. Avery, *U.S.*, III, IV. — *Mentor*, Serial no. 35. — Wilson, *Am. People*, II. — Winsor, *America*, V.

Topics Answerable from the References Above

(1) Why was La Salle so much interested in western travel? [§ 61] — (2) Father Marquette as a missionary. [§ 61] — (3) Incidents of La Salle's voyage on the Mississippi. [§ 62] — (4) First French colony in Louisiana. [§ 63] — (5) Life in early New Orleans. [§ 63] — (6) Life at Johnson Hall. [§ 65] — (7) Account of the French chain of western posts. [§ 67] — (8) George Washington in the West. [§ 67] — (9) English capture of Quebec. [§ 68]

Topics for Further Search

(10) Life in early Detroit, or Pittsburgh. [§§ 63, 67] — (11) Life on an English ship of war. [§ 64] — (12) Account of an Indian raid on the English frontier. [§ 65] — (13) Franklin's plan of colonial union. [§ 68] — (14) Story of the removal of the Acadians. [§ 68] — (15) The English in India. [§ 68] — (16) Why did France give up Louisiana in 1763? [§ 69] — (17) The Proclamation Line of 1763. [§ 69]

CHAPTER VII

COLONIAL BUSINESS (1750–1775)

71. THE BUSINESS SIDE OF LIFE

HOWEVER interested the colonists were in wars and treaties, in elections and governments, in schools and churches, the thing that was most in their minds and about which they probably talked most was — how to make a living. Even the Pilgrims (§ 32) had to face that question because they were heavily burdened with debt when they arrived, and they were glad to pay it off out of the profits of their fur trade and their fishing. Some writers on American history believe that the hard, practical, and material side of colonial life was the most important; and they think they can discover the real motives and influences of the times in wheat and corn, furs, timber, and other products of the land. Without for a moment accepting the doctrine that bread and butter seemed more important to the colonists than political liberty or eternal salvation, we must admit that business interests and business motives were stronger influences than even the people themselves realized.

The movements of population were much affected by the distribution of natural resources. The French were drawn to the St. Lawrence and the Dutch to the Hudson by the need of reaching the furs. The first prosperity of New England was due chiefly to the rich fisheries of that coast. Virginia and Maryland grew up mainly on tobacco planting. The most populous towns, such as Boston, New Haven, New York,

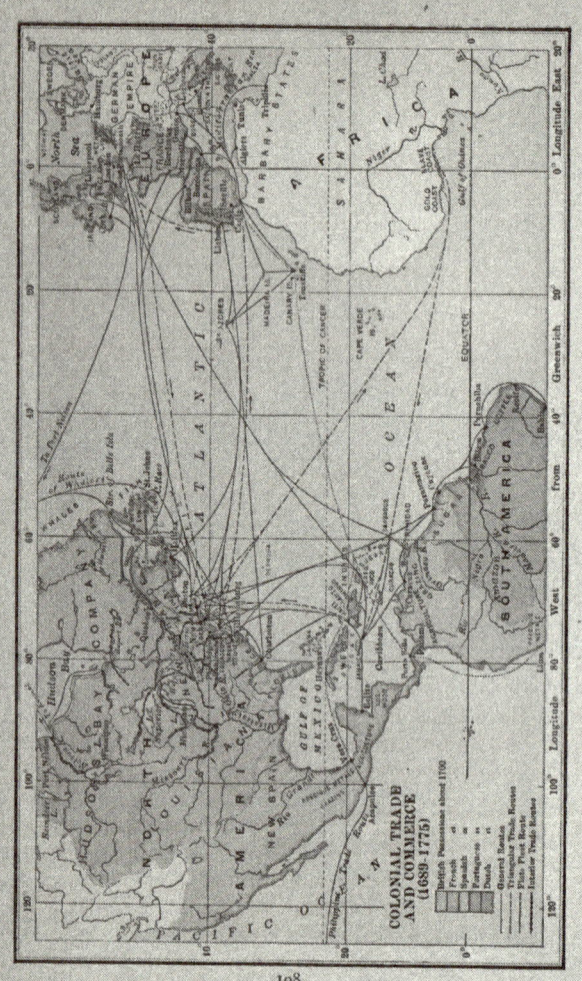

COLONIAL TRADE
AND COMMERCE
(1689-1775)

108

Philadelphia, Baltimore, and Charleston were placed on the best harbors. It was perfectly natural that newcomers should seek the best land, the best ports, and the places best situated for trade.

The business of the colonies early divided itself into a variety of callings. Probably nine tenths of all the people down to the period of the Revolution lived on farms and either worked on the land or were busy in occupations directly connected with the land, such as carding and spinning wool, making tools, and putting up farm buildings. The greater part of the other tenth were seafarers, including fishermen and the officers and crews of coasting craft and of vessels engaged in foreign trade. Another class was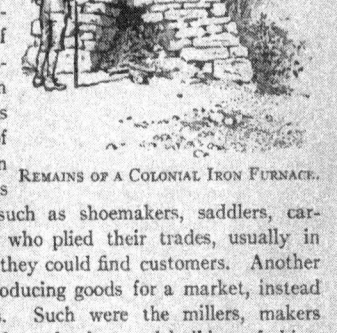

REMAINS OF A COLONIAL IRON FURNACE.

that of handicraftsmen, such as shoemakers, saddlers, carpenters, blacksmiths, etc., who plied their trades, usually in villages or hamlets, where they could find customers. Another group was employed in producing goods for a market, instead of for particular persons. Such were the millers, makers of pig iron and of pot and pearl ashes, and builders of ships. Then there was a small class of wealthy men, most of them merchants and shipowners, with a few large landowners, who carried on business on a large scale, with each other and with foreign merchants. Many of the colonists could turn their hands to various occupations. Farmers built ships in winter and their sons sailed them. Carpenters could still go out lumbering. There was no large class of wage-earning workmen.

72. THE FARMER

The basis and support of every colony was the tillage of the soil; and the most numerous class of the population was that of free farming families, living on farms that would supply their owners with almost every need. The forest trees furnished building material, fuel, and timber for ships. The farmers raised most of their own food, for corn and other grains, pork, mutton, and beef were common farm products.

The heaviest labor throughout the colonies was clearing new land. The usual method was to girdle the trees, and then to plant a first crop among the dead timber; later, to cut the trees down, roll the logs together into piles, and burn them. This work was too heavy for a man to do alone, so neighbors used to join together and roll the logs, first for one and then for another. Thence is derived the modern term of "logrolling," which is applied to members of a legislature who combine to support each other's measures. The stumps often remained an impediment for many years. In New England, also, the bowlders were an obstacle to farming and were rolled away or holes were dug to receive them. It was this hard labor that made land valuable; uncleared land could be had almost for the asking.

The principal crop was Indian corn, which was a staple article of food from Maine to Georgia, eaten in the various forms of mush or "hasty pudding," succotash, roasting ears, Indian pudding, corn cake, and hoecake. Wheat and other grains were grown from New England to Virginia, for wheat bread was widely preferred to corn. A little before the Revolution there sprang up a brisk export of wheat to other parts of the world. Vegetables were grown by farmers for their own use, and most townspeople cultivated vegetable gardens.

The colonists did not put up ice and had no knowledge of the method of canning food, so that they were dependent to a large degree on salt fish, salt pork, and salt beef for their animal food.

Clams and oysters, however, were abundant and made up almost
the entire food of some poor families. Game was still abundant
in or near most communities, and venison, wild turkey, and
bear meat were welcome additions to the table. Most farmers
had orchards. Much fruit was put in store for the winter, and
part of it was converted into preserves, peach butter, and
apple butter. Molasses was imported from the West Indies;
and in the northern states, large quantities of sugar were made
Indian fashion from maple sap. Coffee and chocolate were not
much used, but tea was a highly prized and widely distributed
luxury.

Part of the apples went to the cider mill to be turned into
cider, which was a drink widely used. Still stronger beverages,
distilled from cider and peach juice, were "applejack" and
peach brandy. Imported gin and West India or New England
rum were common; and those who could afford it drank
wine, especially Madeira imported from the Madeira Islands.
Alcoholic liquors were used without stint and caused a vast
amount of drunkenness.

Besides the food crops, the farmers of the northern and
middle colonies raised cattle for sale and large numbers of
sheep, from the wool of which most of the people were clothed.
Few farmers had a surplus that could be turned into cash,
but they could trade their crops and butter, cheese, honey, and
other products to the storekeeper for necessary supplies.

73. THE PLANTER

South of Pennsylvania, agriculture was in general of a different type. The staple crop was tobacco, which exhausted
the land so that there was a constant process of clearing new
soil and letting the old fields go out of cultivation. Grain and
cattle were raised in Maryland and Virginia, but south of
Virginia it was difficult to raise cattle on account of the ticks and
other pests in the woods. Farther south the soil was not suitable
for grain, except that rice was raised in the coast swamps of

South Carolina and Georgia. In Maryland and Virginia there was a class of farmers working their own land, just as in the states farther north; but in the Carolinas and Georgia, these independent farmers degenerated into a shiftless folk who came eventually to be known as "poor whites," "sand hillers," and "red necks."

HEADDRESS OF A COLONIAL LADY. (The wife of Benjamin Rush, one of the signers of the Declaration of Independence.)

The typical southern land-owner and raiser of crops was the slave-owning planter. A few such planters could be found in Rhode Island and New York; more in Pennsylvania and Maryland; but from Virginia southward they were the dominant class in the community. They raised corn for the food of the slaves, and half-wild hogs, often called "razorbacks," ran through the woods. The expression "hog and hominy" came to be jocularly applied to the diet of most of the people. Yams and other vegetables could be easily grown, but few plantations had vegetable gardens.

In the quarter century before the Revolution, the southern planters were not fortunate. Tobacco was very low-priced. Indigo could be grown only in South Carolina and rice in South Carolina and Georgia. One of the few exports was "naval stores," — that is, pitch, tar, and turpentine, products of the abundant pine forests, — but this was not a planter's crop. Cotton was not yet recognized as a paying crop.

The richest of the southern planters were men of high breeding and gallant spirit. Take for example Colonel William Fitz-hugh, a lawyer, a keen planter and slave-buyer, and a capable business man, owner of fifty-four thousand acres of land. He grew flax and hemp, hay and tobacco, and put his large profits into more land and slaves. He had a home plantation of a thousand acres, including a "very good dwelling house with many rooms in it, four of the best of them hung & nine of them plentifully furnished with all things necessary & convenient, & all houses for use furnished with brick chimneys, four good Cellars, a Dairy, Dovecot, Stable, Barn, Henhouse, Kitchen & all other conveniencys," together with an orchard, garden, water gristmill for wheat and corn, a stock of tobacco and good debts. His yearly income was estimated at sixty thousand pounds of tobacco (about $15,000 in money), besides the

BYRD MANSION, WESTMORELAND, VIRGINIA.

increase of the negroes. His tobacco he shipped direct to England from the private wharf of his own plantation, and he was accustomed to order fine clothing, silverware, books, and other English goods.

74. WHITE LABORERS

In all the colonies there was a class of white men working for wages for landowners and other employers. Some of the first colonists of New England brought with them such hired servants. It was difficult to hold them, for the more industrious among them saved their wages, bought land, and set up for themselves. Hence a system of forced white labor began immediately. Convicts, criminals, prisoners in the civil wars, and children, were sent over as bond servants. Other thousands of respectable men and families came over as "redemptioners," under agreement with the shipmaster that he might sell their services for a term of years to somebody in America for money to pay their passage. Both bond servants and redemptioners were subject to the arbitrary will of their masters and were often cruelly treated. Nevertheless, many of them worked out their terms of service, became prosperous members of the community, and founded families.

The respectable colonists strongly protested against sending over men and women of known bad character. The demand for labor was met partly by the large families of the time. Many farmers had eight, ten, or twelve children, who helped on the farm and in the abundant housework, and saved the expense of hired laborers.

In the trades, skilled laborers might earn as much as two shillings a day (having about the purchasing power of $1.00 nowadays) and their board. In the trades such as harness making and blacksmithing and the manufacture of wooden bowls, and also in the shops or small stores, it was the custom to employ apprentices who were commonly bound to serve for seven years, and who lived with the master's family but were often very harshly treated. The average daily wage for unskilled laborers would not buy so much as 50 or 60 cents in our times. While most provisions were cheap, imported articles were always expensive, and the wage earner could not afford to purchase them.

75. THE SLAVE

Perhaps a third of all the hard labor in the colonies after 1750 was performed by negro slaves. The first colonists began to

enslave the Indians, but the red men were sullen and revengeful
and rapidly died off in confinement. The first importations
of slaves were made from the West Indies, then direct from
Africa to the American mainland. Theirs was a terrible fate.
Captured by fellow-Africans in raids which caused the destruction of nine tenths of their friends and kindred, they were
brought down to the West African coast, and there sold for
rum and iron and trinkets to white men who brought them

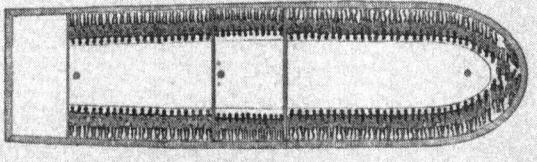

DECK PLANS OF A SLAVER. (Showing stowage of nearly 500 persons
in a 300-ton ship.)

over to an unknown country and distributed them through the
colonies. The negroes spent their lives in bondage, transmitted
the obligations of a slave to their children, and were shut out
from the social and political life of the country in which they
lived.

In most of the northern colonies, the slaves were few in
number, for it was not profitable to use them in gangs in the
fields, and they were held chiefly to mark the wealth and position of their owners. Thus it is recorded that Madam Wads-
worth, wife of the president of Harvard College, owned a slave
woman named Venus. There was a small negro population in

all the northern seaports, because most of the slave ships were run by New Englanders. In the South, the negroes were a small proportion till after 1700; but by the time of the Revolution they were a third of the southern population, and in South Carolina counted more than half.

Slaves were cheap and their labor was often very profitable; but they could be held only in defiance of the great English principle that all men are free. For a long time masters would not allow their slaves to be baptized, because they had scruples against holding Christians in bondage. Some people held that slavery was both unchristian and stupid. Colonel Byrd, a slave owner, wrote of slaves, "They blow up the pride and ruin the Industry of our White People." A favorite devotional book, *Baxter's Christian Directory*, warned masters that "to go as Pirates and catch up poor Negroes or people of another land, and to make them slaves, and sell them, is one of the worst kinds of Thievery in the World." That slavery was dangerous was shown by severe laws against slave offenses, and by slave insurrections in Virginia and in South Carolina, and a supposed slave plot in New York in 1741.

76. The Trader and the Merchant

The business of exchanging products and bringing manufactures within reach of the people was carried on by a class of small peddlers and storekeepers. The man with a pack on his back was welcome in the farmer's kitchen, where he tempted the girls with ribbons, the boys with knives, and the housewife with tinware. In all the villages and in many places in the open country, little shops were set up which corresponded to the modern country "general stores." Mrs. Knight, a lively New England traveler, in 1704 wrote about the local business men of New Haven: "They give the title of merchant to every trader; who Rate their Goods according to the time and spetia they pay in: viz. Pay, mony, Pay as mony, and trusting. *Pay* is Grain, Pork, Beef, &c. at the prices sett by the General Court that Year; *mony* is pieces of Eight, Ryalls, or Boston or Bay shillings (as they call them), or Good hard money, as sometimes silver coin is termed by them; also Wampom, viz. Indian beads which serves for change. *Pay as mony* is provisions, as aforesaid,

CHEW HOUSE, GERMANTOWN. (Injured by cannon balls in a battle fought at this place in 1777; still standing.)

one Third cheaper then as the Assembly or Gene Court setts it; and *Trust* as they and the merchant agree for time."

The traders were usually obliged to take their pay in "produce," which they in turn sent to the larger places in payment for their goods. Those on the frontier also bought the Indian wares, a little corn, maple sugar, and bead work, but especially furs, which were a staple commodity. Another class of traders circulated through the frontiers both north and south with their pack horses loaded with blankets, powder and ball, guns, red cloth, hatchets, knives, scissors, kettles, paints, looking-glasses, tobacco, beads, and "brandy, which the Indians value above all other goods that can be brought them." One of the traders, James Adair, wrote an account of his experiences, and complained bitterly that disorderly traders "decoy the intoxicated savages to defraud the old fair dealer every winter, of many thousand pounds of dressed deer-skin, by the enchanting force of liquors." Adair was a "squaw man," who was proud of his wife, whom he called a "Chickasaw princess."

CHILDREN'S COSTUME OF ABOUT 1776.
(Worn by the author's children.)

Very different from these hand-to-mouth traders were the well-to-do merchants of the large towns. At that time there were no business companies chartered by the colonies except for marine insurance, and no private or public banks. The rich merchants were the only large manufacturers and forwarders, and they also acted as bankers, for they would receive money from their neighbors, pay it over sea, and collect accounts at either end of the line. Their principal business was to buy the products of the country and exchange them for foreign imports; to that end they often took ships in payment for goods or built ships and freighted their own craft to distant ports. One of the most famous of these merchants was William Phips, who began life as a poor boy, with one ambition — to be "owner of a Fair Brick-House in the Green-Lane of North Boston." He traded, gathered property, organized an expedition to raise the treasure of a sunken Spanish vessel, got about £300,000 in gold and silver, was knighted, became governor of Massachusetts, and owned his "fair brick-house."

Among the most famous merchant houses about the time of the Revolution were the Morrises of Philadelphia and the Hancocks of Boston. John Hancock lived in a stately house fronting on Boston Common, with a ballroom 60 feet long, and furniture, wall paper, and hangings imported from England. He had beautiful mahogany furniture, elegant table silver, and, like other rich men of his time, dressed in magnificent silk and velvet suits. He had his picture painted by a good artist, and felt himself to be one of the principal men of his time.

77. SHIPPING AND SAILORS

In New England and the middle colonies, one of the principal pursuits for men of all classes was following the sea, and they drew large wealth from the briny deep in several different ways:

(1) The fisheries were a steady source of employment and profit. The New Englanders had access to the banks fisheries south of Newfoundland, to the offshore fisheries, especially in the neighborhood of Cape Cod, and to very valuable inshore fisheries. Their principal catch was cod and mackerel, which provided part of the daily food of a large part of the population and furnished a valuable export. The fisheries were nurseries for merchant seamen and helped to man the ships of war in the naval wars.

(2) Shipbuilding was a flourishing industry all along the coast from Maryland north, especially where, as in Maine, splendid forests of tall timber grew alongside of deep salt water. Shipbuilding was a boon to New England, for it gave winter employment to the farmers; and when the ship was built it was manned by farmers' sons, and commanded by a farmer's son. American ships brought good prices in foreign markets and were an important export.

(3) The business of sailing ships, on coasting voyages and on voyages to the West Indies and to European ports, was large and gave employment to thousands of men. Yankee ships found their way to the Mediterranean and to Africa. These long voyages, far out of reach of mails, made it necessary to place a large responsibility on the sea captain, who often showed amazing pluck, skill, and endurance.

78. COMMERCE

A lively and profitable commerce went on all the time from colony to colony, from the continent to the West Indies, and from all the colonies to England and other European countries. The principal exports were: to the West Indies, clapboards, hoops, shingles, hay and cattle, flour and provisions, especially dried fish, and (later) rum; to England, tobacco, masts, wood ashes, furs, and (later) pig iron, rice, and indigo; to other European countries, dried fish and naval stores — pitch, tar, and turpentine.

To the PUBLIC.

THE FLYING MACHINE, kept by John Mercereau, at the New Blazing-Star Ferry, near New-York, sets off from Powles Hook every Monday, Wednesday, and Friday Mornings, for Philadelphia, and performs the journey in a Day and a Half, for the Summer Season, till the 1st of November; from that Time to go twice a Week till the first of May, when they again perform it three Times a Week. When the Stages go only twice a Week, they set off Mondays and Thursdays. The Waggons in Philadelphia set out from the Sign of the George, in Second-street, the same Morning. The Passengers are desired to cross the Ferry the Evening before, as the Stages must set off early the next Morning. The Price for each Passenger is Twenty Shillings, Proc. and Goods as usual. Passengers going Part of the Way to pay in Proportion.

As the Proprietor has made such Improvements upon the Machines, one of which is in Imitation of a Coach, he hopes to merit the Favour of the Publick.

JOHN MERCEREAU.

ADVERTISEMENT OF THE "FLYING MACHINE." (A Post wagon of 1771.)

The imports from England were manufactures of all kinds — guns and ammunition, hardware, cutlery, clothing, furniture, glass, china, silverware, and tools. Tea, coffee, and chocolate were regular imports, often from Holland. The ladies would have their "calamancoes," or glossy woolens, their "paduasoys," or silks, their "oznabrigs," or German linen, and the much-prized pins. For children, merchants imported "poppets," or dolls, and other toys; for the gentlemen, silks and velvets, gold lace for their best suits, and "pipes" of wine.

A COLONIAL FAMILY—THE GRIMES CHILDREN. (From the picture in the Virginia Historical Society.)

Several new branches of trade developed after 1700, especially the African slave trade. Under the treaty of Utrecht (1713) an English company, in which Queen Anne was one of the partners, got the *Asiento*, or privilege of carrying slaves from Africa to the Spanish West Indies. The New Englanders were quick to work up a profitable slave trade for themselves. Very few people protested against the trade or its shocking cruelties; and whenever the legislatures of the colonies tried to tax it for revenue, or for any other reason, the bills were vetoed in England because the trade was so profitable to the English merchant.

Eventually so many slaves were brought that the people began to be frightened, and South Carolina several times tried to lay duties on their importation. The slave traffic was connected with the manufacture of rum, which was carried to Africa to be exchanged for slaves; part of the slaves were carried to the West Indies and exchanged for molasses; and the molasses and the profits were brought home to New England to furnish raw material for more rum. The colonists liked to buy from the French and Spanish West Indies, but in the year 1733 the British government passed the so-called "Molasses Act," which was intended to compel them to get their molasses only from the British West India colonies.

79. CURRENCY AND PAPER MONEY

The standing difficulty in all kinds of business was the lack of a uniform and unvarying currency. The standard money basis of business and accounts was the English pound. Among the coins were gold guineas (21 shillings), and silver pieces from five shillings down. The conditions of trade with the West Indies brought in a varied mass of coins of all nations, especially the Mexican dollar. The name is derived from the "joachimsthaler," a silver piece coined in Austria, which became a standard in America. This mixed silver and gold currency was further confused by the issuance of paper money by the colonists, beginning with £40,000 printed by Massachusetts in 1690. Later, Massachusetts and other colonies issued paper money and lent it to farmers on real estate security. This brought about a depreciation and loss throughout the colonies, so that the British government (1761–1763) prohibited the issue of paper money. A dollar was worth about four shillings in silver, but six Massachusetts paper shillings went for a dollar; eight New York paper shillings were required for the same value; and there was a time when a Rhode Island note for ten pounds would not buy the value of ten shillings in specie.

80. NAVIGATION ACTS

For many years the colonists freely sent and received cargoes in trade with foreign countries; but the policy of the early Navigation Acts was expanded by an act of Parliament (1672) laying small customs duties on the trade from one colony to another, or to other countries than England. This was the first act of Parliament for taxing the colonies. In 1696 a more thoroughgoing navigation act was passed by Parliament. Under these and other later "Acts of Trade," the commerce of the colonies was restricted as follows:

(1) Trade to and from England had to be carried on in ships built and owned in England or in the colonies. (2) Importations had to come through English ports; that is, through the hands of English firms. (3) Exports of "enumerated goods" had to be sent only to English ports, even if intended ultimately for some other country; most of the colonial products were enumerated, such as tobacco, sugar, molasses, and furs, but not fish or provisions, timber, and the standard "naval stores." (4) For the protection of English manufactures, colonists were virtually forbidden to make rolled iron, or to ship certain goods from one colony to another — for instance, hats which might compete with English hats. Though all these restrictions seem harsh they indirectly gave a distinct advantage to colonial shipping.

Spain, France, and Holland had even stricter colonial systems than the English; but the English colonists, sometimes by stealth, often with the connivance of local officials, managed to carry on a very profitable trade with the Spanish, French, and Dutch West Indies, especially in dried fish and lumber; and they brought back molasses, tropical products, and a good surplus of hard dollars, commonly called "pieces of eight." In the same way foreign vessels often brought European cargoes into North America, in defiance of the Navigation Acts.

81. REVIEW

By far the larger part of the English colonists were farmers, whose first task was to clear the soil, so that they might grow crops. In most places food, both vegetable and animal, was abundant. Besides the small farmers of the South, a class of slave-owning planters raised corn, tobacco, rice, and indigo. Cotton was not then a paying crop. Rich planters such as Colonel Fitzhugh lived handsomely.

Part of the hard labor was done by white wage-servants, or white indentured servants. There was a small class of skilled workmen in trades and some free negroes. In both North and South negro slaves existed, many of them brought direct from Africa. An antislavery movement began very early.

Peddlers and country storekeepers bought small stocks of imported goods and sold them for farm products, furs, or money. Traders penetrated beyond the frontier and bought skins and furs from the Indians. In the large seaports a small number of wealthy merchants built fine houses, and lived splendidly.

The principal calling besides farming was that of seafaring, including fisheries, shipbuilding, and sailing the ships. A good trade was carried on to the West Indies, another to England, and a smaller limited trade to other European countries. The slave trade was also profitable and was linked up with the trade in molasses from the West Indies.

The colonies lacked a good currency, for their gold and silver coins were much mixed. Some of them issued paper money, but it was hurtful to business and was finally prohibited. After 1660 Parliament passed "Acts of Trade" which were intended to throw colonial commerce as far as possible toward English ports and through English firms, and to prevent the importation of goods from other countries. Many colonists evaded these laws by active smuggling.

References Bearing on the Text and Topics

Geography and Maps. See map, p. 108. Coman, *Indust. Hist.*, 52, 64, 75, 80. — Semple, *Geogr. Conditions*, ch. vii.

Secondary. Bogart, *Econ. Hist.*, chs. iii–vi. — Channing, *U.S.*, II. chs. xiii, xvii. — Coman, *Indust. Hist.*, ch. iii. — Dewey, *Finan. Hist.*, ch. i. — Fiske, *Dutch and Quaker Cols.*, II. 222–235, 285–293; *Old Va.*, II. 174–203, 325–331, 338–369. — Greene, *Provincial Am.*, chs. xvi, xvii. — Jacobstein, *Tobacco Industry*, ch. i. — Locke, *Anti-Slavery in Am.*, 9–45. — Morriss, *Col. Trade of Md.* — Peabody, *Merchant Venturers of Salem.* — Stockton, *Buccaneers and Pirates.*

Sources. *Am. Hist. Leaflets*, no. 19. — Bogart and Thompson, *Readings*, 20–142. — Callender, *Econ. Hist.*, chs. ii, iii. — Hart, *Contemporaries*, II. §§ 45, 46, 88, 89; *Patriots and Statesmen*, I. 153–156, 180–183, 191–194, 236. — James, *Readings*, §§ 25–27. — MacDonald, *Select Charters*, nos. 22, 23, 25, 28, 34, 43, 50.

Illustrative. Carruthers, *Knights of the Horseshoe* (Va.). — Earle, *Stage-Coach and Tavern Days.* — Ingraham, *Captain Kyd.* — Johnston, *Audrey* (Va.). — Stockton, *Kate Bonnet* (pirates).

Pictures. Avery, *U.S.*, III. — Dunbar, *Hist. of Travel in Am.*

Topics Answerable from the References Above

(1) The fur trade of the French on the St. Lawrence, *or* of the Dutch on the Hudson. [§ 71] — (2) Life on a Virginia plantation. [§ 73] — (3) Indentured white servants. [§ 74] — (4) Slave trade in Africa, *or* across the Atlantic. [§ 75] — (5) Slaves in the northern colonies, *or* in Virginia, *or* in South Carolina. [§ 75] — (6) Antislavery writers before 1720. [§ 75] — (7) Colonial shipbuilding. [§ 77] — (8) Trade in *one* of the following products: ashes; naval stores; fish; iron; furs. [§ 78] — (9) Coin in the colonies. [§ 79] — (10) Incidents of the paper money craze. [§ 79]

Topics for Further Search

(11) Iron furnaces before 1775. [§ 71] — (12) Regulation of liquor selling before 1775. [§ 72] — (13) Account of *one* of the following classes from 1750 to 1775: poor white farmers; apprentices; Indian traders; merchant princes. [§§ 73, 76] — (14) The banks fisheries in colonial times. [§ 77] — (15) The Molasses Act. [§ 78] — (16) What were "enumerated goods"? [§ 80] — (17) Colonial smuggling. [§ 80]

CHAPTER VIII

CAUSES AND COURSE OF THE REVOLUTION (1763–1781)

82. SPIRIT OF UNREST

CONSIDERING the prosperity of the English colonies and the freedom of their government, we often wonder that as soon as the French and Indian War was over, they began to get into trouble with the home government; and that after about ten years of friction and strife, they revolted and set up a government for themselves. To this day, it is not easy to see just why the colonists felt so dissatisfied. They professed and doubtless felt the warmest attachment to the king, whom God

and Parliament had provided for them. They read English books, wore English clothes, and felt high respect for English visitors. After the crisis, John Adams said that nobody in the colonies had desired or planned independence before the Revolution.

The great reason for the division of the British Empire into two parts seems to be that the colonists were so free and did so many things for themselves that they could not see

GEORGE III, ABOUT 1765. (From a painting by Sir William Beechy.)

why they should not be relieved from almost all restraints. One reason for a change of feeling was the coming to the throne of young King George III (1760). His predecessors, George I and George II, were Germans who had little interest in their English kingdom. George III said, "Born and bred in this country, I glory in the name of Briton." His mother used to say to him, "George, be a king"; and he soon began systematically to get away from the control by Parliament and to build up a personal government.

Opposed to the king's policy was a group of brilliant statesmen, of whom the most famous were William Pitt (later Earl of Chatham), Charles James Fox, and Edmund Burke; they counseled wise and moderate dealing with the colonies.

A new spirit began to stir among the colonists when the danger of invasion by French neighbors ceased forever in 1763. As the French statesman Turgot had said, "Colonies are like fruits: they stick to the tree only while they are green; as

STAMPS USED TO TAX THE COLONIES.

soon as they can take care of themselves they do what Carthage did and what America will do."

On the other side of the ocean the home government also showed a new spirit by attempts to stiffen the Navigation Acts and to stop the evasions (§ 80). In 1764 a new "Sugar Act" was passed (§ 78) which laid a tax on sugar and coffee and other tropical products imported from any but the British West India colonies; the molasses duty was much reduced. Then followed in 1765 the first general tax ever laid by Parliament upon the English colonies. The "Stamp Act" provided for "certain stamp duties, and other duties, in the British colonies and plantations in America, toward further defraying the expenses of defending, protecting, and securing the same." The duties were to be imposed on all sorts of legal documents, law proceedings, wills, licenses and commissions, land patents, bills of sale; and also on playing cards, newspapers, pamphlets, advertisements, almanacs, and the like. The proceeds of the tax (estimated at £100,000 a year) were to go toward the expense of troops which were to be sent to America for the defense of the colonies.

83. Colonial Ideas of the British Constitution

Somehow the colonies would never accept the British assurance that these taxes would not be used to help support the British government. For some years the colonists had been trying to think out a theory of their relations to the British Empire which would make such action by Parliament unlawful.

A brilliant and able young Massachusetts lawyer named James Otis argued against "writs of assistance" (1761), which authorized British customs officers to search any private house for smuggled goods. He raised the point that such a writ was contrary to the unwritten law of American liberty. "Reason and the constitution are both against this writ. . . . All precedents are under the control of the principles of law. . . . No acts of Parliament can establish such a writ. . . . An act against the constitution is void." John Adams said of him, "Otis was Isaiah and Ezekiel united — Otis was a flame of fire — Otis's oration against writs of assistance breathed into this nation the breath of life."

Notwithstanding Otis's argument, the writs of assistance were again issued in Massachusetts; but his speech and his later pamphlets stated three principles of great weight in the approaching Revolution: (1) that the colonists possessed certain inalienable personal rights; (2) that there was a traditional system of colonial government, which could not be

altered by Great Britain without the consent of the colonies;
(3) that under that system the colonies were united to Great
Britain through the same sovereign, but were not a dependent
part of Great Britain, nor subject to Parliament.

In accordance with the practice of a century and a half
(§ 57), the British government about this time vetoed a statute of
Virginia which reduced the stipends of the established clergy.
A test case was made (1763), commonly called "the Parson's
Cause," in which Patrick Henry gained his first reputation and
also won the jury by an argument that there was a limit to the
legal control of the mother country over colonial legislation.
In a bold and significant phrase he declared that "a King, by
. . . disallowing acts of so salutary a nature, from being the
Father of his people degenerates into a Tyrant, and forfeits
all rights to his subjects' obedience."

84. STAMP ACT CONTROVERSY (1765)

Against the Stamp Act (§ 82), the best writers in America
poured forth a flood of argument and protest; and they
fashioned phrases which were the watchwords of the Revolution.

(1) Taxation. They flatly denied the right of any one to
lay taxes within the colonies, except the colonial governments.
As one writer rhetorically put it, "If they have a right to im-
pose a stamp tax, they have a right to lay on us a poll tax,
a land tax, a window tax; and why not tax us for the light of
the sun, the air we breathe, and the ground we are buried in?"

(2) Representation. To cover this point they laid down the
maxim of "No taxation without representation"; and, they
argued, how could they be represented in a Parliament thousands of miles away?

(3) Nature of colonial government. They insisted that the
colonists had an inherited right not to be ruled in such matters
by Parliament. As the Boston merchant, John Hancock,
said, "I will never carry on Business under such great disad-

vantages and Burthen. I will not be a slave; I have a right to the libertys & Privileges of the English Constitution, and I as an Englishman will enjoy them."

The movement passed very quickly from talk to outright opposition, which took the following serious forms:

(1) Some of the colonial assemblies passed strong resolutions, such as Patrick Henry's Virginia Resolutions, which declared "That every attempt to vest such power in any other person or persons whatever than the General Assembly aforesaid, is illegal, unconstitutional, and unjust, and has a manifest tendency to destroy British as well as American liberty."

(2) Two more quiet but effective means were the organization of "Sons of Liberty," a kind of patriotic society; and an attempt to boycott British goods.

(3) In many places mobs made discussion impossible: the stamps were seized, stamp distributors were threatened and compelled to resign, or were burned in effigy before their own doors, and their property destroyed. In thus forsaking an orderly government, and resorting to violence, the people who engaged in these outbreaks damaged their own cause.

(4) The most effective method was the holding of a Stamp Act Congress of delegates from nine colonies, in New York, October 7, 1765. They petitioned the British government to withdraw the act, and drew up a formal statement of "The most essential rights and liberties of the colonists, and of the grievances under which they labor."

When November 1 came, the date for putting the Stamp Act in force, it was entirely ignored, and documents were simply left without stamps. Parliament finally decided to repeal the act; but it claimed the right to pass acts binding upon the colonies.

85. REVOLUTION APPROACHING (1767–1773)

The way was thus kept open for a renewal of the struggle. By the Townshend Act in 1767, Parliament laid new duties on paper, painter's colors, glass, and tea imported into the colonies, the proceeds to be used for the salaries of the colonial governors and judges. The result was a warm protest. John Dickinson of Pennsylvania, in his *Letters from a Farmer*, called upon his countrymen by practical and law-abiding methods to "take care of our rights, and we therein take care of our prosperity . . . slavery is ever preceded by sleep." Nonimportation agreements were made in many parts of the colonies and signed by men like George Washington. Soon after (1768), two regiments of redcoats were ordered to Boston "to strengthen the hands of the government in the Province of Massachusetts Bay." As a witty Boston clergyman said, "Our grievances are now all red-dressed."

The coming of troops, intended to overawe and not to defend, incensed all the colonies. In March, 1770, there was a fight between the troops and the populace in Boston in which five persons were killed. The unsuitable name of "Boston Massacre" was applied to the unfortunate affair. The offensive Townshend duties were withdrawn in 1770 after producing £16,000 at a cost of about £200,000; but the British government stupidly insisted on the principle of taxation, by leaving in force the former tea duty of threepence a pound.

Feeling ran especially high in Massachusetts, where the struggle became almost a personal contest between Thomas Hutchinson, the governor, and Samuel Adams, leader of the popular party. Hutchinson's letters to friends in England, urging that "there must be an abridgement of what are called English liberties," gave great offense to the colonists.

Things grew so squally that in 1772 Samuel Adams obtained from the Boston town meeting the appointment of a Committee of Correspondence "to state the Rights of the colonists and of this Province in particular . . . to communicate and publish the same to the several Towns in this Province and to the World." A "continental committee" was subsequently started by Virginia, and eleven other colonies appointed similar committees, which corresponded with each other and prepared for later joint action.

The climax was reached by the effort of the British East India Company to send shipments of tea to the principal colonial ports. The tea duty was not much felt, because the colonists usually drank smuggled tea; but to help the British East India Company out of financial difficulties, the home government gave it such privileges that it was able to undersell the smugglers, and in August, 1773, tea ships were dispatched to the principal colonial ports. If the tea were landed and the duty paid, the right of taxation was admitted. Hence, upon the arrival of the tea ships in Philadelphia, New York, and some other places, they were sent back without unloading. Efforts to this end in Boston were foiled; but a meeting of five or six thousand people was held in and around the Old South Church in Boston (December 16, 1773) to make a final protest against the landing of the tea. Suddenly a war whoop was heard outside, and two hundred men boarded the ships and flung into the sea tea worth £18,000 (about $90,000). An eyewitness says: "They say the actors were Indians from Narragansett. Whether they were or not, to a transient observer they appear'd as such, being cloath'd in Blankets with the heads muffled, and copper-color'd countenances." Children who next morning found their fathers' shoes full of tea kept their own counsel.

86. First Continental Congress (1774)

To the royal government in England, the Boston Tea Party appeared to be an act of outrageous violence, for which Boston and Massachusetts deserved such a punishment as would give warning to the other colonies. Hence a set of statutes sometimes called "The Intolerable Acts" was hastily passed by Parliament (1774): the port of Boston was thereby closed; the charter of Massachusetts was set aside; and town meetings were forbidden. To put these measures into force, General

Thomas Gage was sent over to be governor of Massachusetts. The Salem merchants offered their wharves to their Boston brethren, and from south to north came expressions of sympathy with Massachusetts. By this time resistance to taxes laid by Parliament had carried the country to the verge of revolution.

The colonies immediately accepted a proposition of Virginia, formally stated by the Massachusetts House of Representatives, for a colonial congress; and on September 5, 1774, at Philadelphia, delegates came together from twelve colonies, Georgia alone not being represented. Among the distinguished members of this body were John Adams and Samuel Adams of Massachusetts, John Jay of New York, John Dickinson of Pennsylvania, Peyton Randolph, Patrick Henry, Richard Henry Lee, and George Washington of Virginia, and John Rutledge of South Carolina. This so-called "First Continental Congress" took important action in three directions:

(1) It drew up dignified and loyal protests against the treatment of Massachusetts and of the colonies in general, it respectfully petitioned the king to remove their grievances, and it sent out a series of addresses explaining the situation.

(2) Congress drew up a Declaration of Rights, which laid claim to the liberties and immunities of Englishmen, including a "Right of Representation . . . in all Cases of Taxation and internal Polity, subject only to the Negative of their Sovereign." Various acts of Parliament were enumerated which were declared to be "infringements and violations of the rights of the colonists."

(3) Congress voted the "Association" (October 20, 1774), which was an agreement for a boycott on an immense scale: no British goods (including slaves) were to be imported or sold. From north to south there was an era of terrorism; mob methods were called in; and the ship captain who arrived in port with a shipload of British merchandise was a fortunate man if allowed even to sail away again with his goods on board.

Before adjourning, the Congress took measures to call another Congress to meet in May, 1775, if meanwhile the grievances had not been redressed.

87. OUTBREAK OF THE REVOLUTIONARY WAR (1775)

Many of the men who took part in the movement so far, including some members of the Congress, believed that this dignified remonstrance would bring the home government to terms. They did not realize the stubbornness of the king or the unwillingness of the English nation to accept the idea of

BATTLE OF LEXINGTON, APRIL 19, 1775. (From Earl's drawing, made a few days later.)

colonies that must not be governed by Parliament. During the winter, while the colonists were waiting to hear the decision, a political storm was coming on in Massachusetts. The patriot leaders organized what they called a "Provincial Congress" in which the central authority was a "Committee of Safety" which began to collect military stores and to organize

"Minutemen" — militiamen who should be ready to march at a minute's notice.

The British garrison in Boston, numbering now about 5000 men, chafed under this preparation of a hostile force and put the matter to a test by sending out a column of 800 men to seize the stores at Concord. Warning of their coming was given during the night by Paul Revere of Boston and other swift riders, who galloped through the countryside arousing the people. When the British van appeared early in the morning (April 19, 1775), on the green at Lexington, they found a line of provincial militia drawn up. It is uncertain just how the fight began; an English officer who was present at the battle says, "On our approach they dispersed and soon after,

VICINITY OF BOSTON.

firing began; but which party fired first I cannot exactly say, as our troops rushed on shouting and huzzaing previous to the firing." When the smoke cleared away, seven patriots were found killed and nine wounded. The responsibility for this outbreak of open war goes back to the king of Great Britain, who had forced matters to this issue; and it is shared by men like Samuel Adams and Washington who were ready to resist the authority of the mother country rather than yield what they felt to be their rights.

From Lexington the British marched seven miles to Concord, where a body of militia boldly marched down to oppose them, and beat them back at a little bridge where now stands the statue of the Minuteman.

"Here once the embattled farmers stood
And fired the shot heard round the world."

After destroying some of the patriots' stores, the weary British troops returned to Boston, harassed by the militia, with a total loss of 273 British to 93 Americans. The beaten force at last reached the shelter of the guns on the British ships.

On the news of the battle of Lexington, virtual war began throughout most of the thirteen colonies; for the people of the middle and southern colonies showed their sympathy with Massachusetts by driving out their governors and setting up provincial congresses and conventions which assumed the government.

88. THE NATION IN ARMS (1775–1776)

In the midst of this excitement, the so-called Second Continental Congress met in Philadelphia (1775) and sat in the building now called Independence Hall. Every one of the thirteen colonies was soon represented (May 15), and Congress at once became the center of organization for the war. Without any formal authority from the colonial governments, but supported by their good will and assent, Congress made itself a national government. For example, from May to July, 1775, it forbade certain exportations, ordered a state of defense, organized a post office, voted an American continental army, appointed George Washington commander in chief, authorized bills of credit, sent a last petition to the king, and considered Franklin's scheme for a federal constitution.

Without waiting for any action by Congress, the Massachusetts men besieged Boston. They were reënforced by militia from the neighboring New England colonies, and (June 17, 1775) an attempt was made to plant a battery on Bunker Hill, in order to command the city. The patriots were finally driven out of their intrenchments by three desperate assaults of the British, who lost over one thousand men out of three thousand engaged. The American defeat was really a victory, for the Minutemen proved their bravery against regulars, and the British did not again attempt to sally out of Boston.

Shortly after the battle General Washington, the new commander in chief, arrived to take charge of the siege of Boston. He drew up the troops on Cambridge Common, under or near an elm tree which is still standing, and assumed formal command.

While the siege was progressing, two little armies, under Montgomery and Benedict Arnold, made their way into Canada, which they all but conquered. The Canadians held off, for they did not understand this kind of friendship and had no mind to exchange British rulers for near-by American masters. At the end of the winter (March, 1776), Washington succeeded in fortifying Dorchester Heights and thus forcing the British army, still numbering 10,000

THE CRAIGIE HOUSE, CAMBRIDGE. (Used as headquarters by General Washington in 1775–1776.)

soldiers and sailors, to leave Boston. They went on board the British fleet and sailed for Halifax.

By this time, it became clear that though there was a strong minority in England who were opposed to this war between brethren, the king had a firm hold upon Parliament; and the only safety for the colonists was to fight it out. Hence during 1776, on the advice of Congress, several colonies drew up written constitutions of their own, suitable for permanent governments. The next step was the world-famous vote of Congress, of the Declaration of Independence, dated July 4, 1776, declaring that "these United Colonies are, and of Right ought to be, Free and Independent States."

89. THE RIVAL FORCES

Thus to throw down the gage to Great Britain was a bold step, for the two parties were very unequal. Great Britain was a rich country for the times, fruitful and productive. It was the most important manufacturing nation in the world, and was just on the point of adapting steam power to machinery;

ENGLISH LIGHT DRAGOON, ABOUT 1778.
(Type of the British cavalryman.)

it had an immense commercial marine, and possessed the largest and most powerful navy in the world.

Against the might of Great Britain was opposed a poor country, with no large manufactures of iron or cloth, hardly able to cast a cannon. Yet America was a land of comfort and prosperity. Lafayette wrote of it, "Simplicity of manners, kindness, love of country and of liberty, and a delightful equality everywhere prevails. . . . All the citizens are brethren. In America there are no poor, or even what we call peasantry." Even during the war the colonists made money from privateering and from West India and European trade, and bought the necessary materials of war with their exports.

The British were overwhelmingly superior in the size of their military and naval forces, although much hampered by the necessity of transporting men and materials across a stormy sea. In 1776 they had 270 ships of war, and for men they drew on 11,000,000 people in Great Britain and Ireland, besides the

loyalists in the American colonies. Yet the British government committed the stupid blunder of hiring 30,000 Hessians
from Germany, who had no personal interest in the struggle, and
were leased by their princes like so many cattle. "Were I an
American," said Chatham, "as I am an Englishman, while a
foreign troop was landed in my country, I never would lay
down my arms — never — never — never"; and Franklin
wrote grimly, "The
German auxiliaries are
certainly coming; it is
our business to prevent
their returning."

Out of the 3,000,000
people in the colonies,
the loyalists and ne-
groes numbered at least
1,200,000. There were
from 300,000 to 400,000
able-bodied patriots, of
whom perhaps 250,000
served in the army at
one time or another;
but they never num-
bered more than 40,000
men under arms at one

A Tough Old Patriot. (Monument in
Arlington, then Menotomy, near Boston.)

time, and sometimes the total force available for striking a blow
was not above 5000. On the patriot side besides soldiers of
English descent, there were many Germans, Irish, and Scotch,
some Dutch, Jews, French, and Welsh, and several thousand
negroes, especially from Rhode Island. Both sides made the
moral and military mistake of enlisting Indian allies. The
Americans were first to seek this dubious aid; the British
used it most effectively.

The main difficulty with the army was that the states insisted on furnishing militia on short terms of service, instead

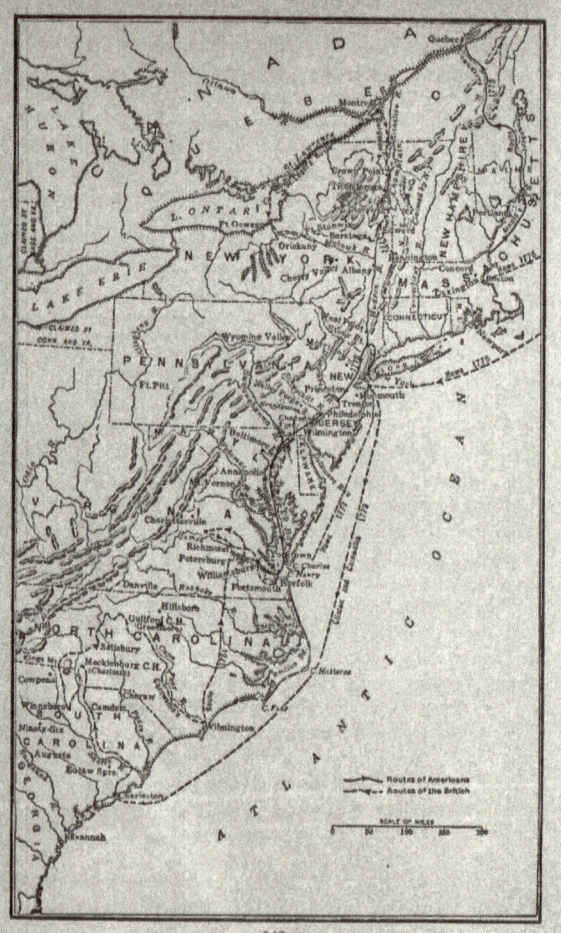

of allowing Congress to form a sufficient regular force with national officers, enlisted for the war. Washington said of the militia, "The system appears to have been pernicious beyond description. . . . It may be easily shown, that all the misfortunes we have met with in the military line are to be attributed to this cause."

Many soldiers of fortune drifted over from Europe to seek employment, besides Lafayette, a French nobleman, who brought his own enthusiasm and the silent support of the French government. The German Baron von Steuben, an excellent soldier, skillfully drilled the troops and introduced improved tactics. The Poles Kosciusko and Pulaski and the French general De Kalb were gallant soldiers.

90. CAMPAIGNS OF 1776-1777

The Revolution was a long and hard-fought war, with many incidents, skirmishes, and sea fights; but the pitched battles were few and the details of the engagements and sieges are not essential. We are interested chiefly in the critical struggles and the final military results.

The first success of the American patriots at Boston was followed by a brilliant victory near Charleston. A British attack on that city was beaten off by skillful fighting, in which Sergeant Jasper distinguished himself for bravery.

Then in August, 1776, came a severe defeat. Sir William Howe landed with a British army of 20,000 men on Long Island. Washington had never before commanded an army

JASPER MONUMENT,
CHARLESTON, S. C.

in the field or defended a country, and his force of 18,000
men was badly defeated. The British maneuvered him out
of the city of New York, followed him northward and then
southwestward across New Jersey till he crossed the Delaware
River, his army sometimes falling below 3000 men. Almost
in despair Washington wrote, "If every
nerve is not strained to recruit the new
army with all possible expedition, I
think the game is pretty nearly up."
But for the heroic efforts of Robert
Morris, a wealthy merchant of Philadelphia, who raised money on his
personal credit to keep the army
together, the Revolution might have
failed then and there. To prevent
the British following him to Philadelphia, Washington boldly took the
offensive, crossed the Delaware, and
successfully attacked the British at
Trenton and Princeton.

In the spring of 1777, the British
entered on a well-planned scheme to
cut the new United States in two,
by pushing one army up the Hudson
and sending another southward from
Canada to meet it. General Howe,

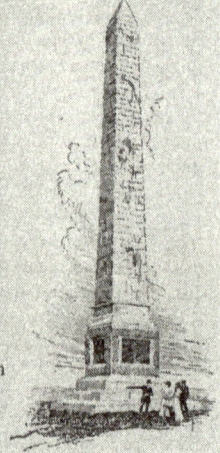

BATTLE MONUMENT AT
ORISKANY.

who lay in New York, had the bad judgment to take away
his part of the forces for a separate attack on Philadelphia.
He carried his troops around by sea to the head of Chesapeake Bay and defeated Washington in a pitched battle
at the river Brandywine (September, 1777). Two weeks
later Howe entered Philadelphia and remained there until
the following summer.

Meanwhile General Burgoyne started southward from Montreal with an army of about 8000 men, including Hessians.

He put forth a bombastic proclamation in which he said, "I
have but to give stretch to the Indian forces under my direction . . . and the messengers of justice and wrath await them
in the field; and devastation, famine, and every concomitant
horror." Instead he found a hornets' nest. American patriots
poured in from near-by New England until Burgoyne was far out-
numbered; other patriots checked a British expedition into
the Mohawk valley at the battle of Oriskany, where the patriot
General Herkimer did good service; most of Burgoyne's Indians
deserted him; and the expected British aid up the Hudson failed
to materialize. Burgoyne was at last confronted by Arnold
and others, active subordinates of the apathetic Gates, who

SCHUYLER MANSION, ALBANY. (Where General Burgoyne was
entertained after his surrender at Saratoga.)

was put in command against Washington's desire. After two
hard fights Burgoyne was obliged to surrender his whole remaining army at Saratoga, October 17, 1777. The prisoners
were 3500 British and Hessian troops, with 2300 volunteers
and camp followers. The defeat was the turning point of the

war, for the overthrow of the boastful proclamation-maker
gave the patriot cause new life. In the words of a popular
squib,

> "Burgoyne, alas ! unknowing future fates,
>   Could force his way through woods, but not through Gates."

91. DARK TIME OF THE REVOLUTION (1777-1778)

Notwithstanding this brilliant victory, the Revolution
almost collapsed during the winter of 1777-1778. Newport,
New York, and Philadelphia were all held by the British, and
reënforcements and supplies came to them steadily from over
the sea, while Washington's army at Valley Forge was living
miserably in a camp village of log huts. Fuel was plentiful,
but food and clothing were scanty, not because there was any
scarcity in the country, but because so many of the neighboring
people were disaffected, and the roads were so bad that it was
almost impossible to bring supplies which were stored only a
few miles away. At one time, out of a force of at most 11,000
men, 2898 were reported unable to go on duty for want of
clothing. Yet the spirit of the troops was excellent; one of
the officers wrote: "See the poor Soldier . . . if barefoot he
labours thro' the Mud & Cold with a Song in his Mouth ex-
tolling War & Washington — if his food be bad — he eats
it notwithstanding with seeming content."

One cause of the suffering of the soldiers was the bad management of the commissary officers; back of that was the weakness of Congress, of which Alexander Hamilton said, "Their
conduct, with respect to the army especially, is feeble, indecisive, and improvident." It was a time of great losses; nine
hundred American merchant vessels had already been taken;
thousands of men had lost their lives or were prisoners in barbarous prison ships, or had returned home wounded or diseased.
The states hung back, each hoping that other states would
furnish the necessary men, and therefore Congress lost spirit
and influence.

92. GEORGE WASHINGTON, THE INDISPENSABLE

The one beacon light which shone steadily was General George Washington. Every other Revolutionary hero and patriot could have been replaced; Washington alone was the indispensable man. He was a Virginian, and his appointment gave confidence to the southern states; he was a soldier who outranked in service and experience nearly all the other officers in the army; he was careful of his men; he was a man of extraordinary industry and mastery of details, keeping up correspondence all over the country. As a general Washington showed a splendid pertinacity: he learned by his own defeats; if beaten in one place, he would reappear in another. He was extraordinarily long-suffering and patient, and he had a magnificent temper; that is, though naturally hot and impetuous, he kept himself under rigid control, except when a crisis came, and on such occasions, as a contemporary records, "Washington swore like an angel from heaven."

Washington bore personal slights with wonderful dignity. He wrote to Congress of "the wounds which my feelings as an officer have constantly received from a thousand things that have happened contrary to my expectation and wishes." Especially did he shine out in the so-called Conway Cabal of 1778, the purpose of which was to put Gates, "the hero of Saratoga," over his head. The cabal fell to pieces when a letter from Conway was made public, in which he said, "Heaven has been determined to save your country, or a weak General and bad counselors would have ruined it." Gates shortly after withdrew from command in the field.

After all, the greatest of Washington's qualities was a rugged manliness which gave him the respect and confidence even of his enemies. Though he was at the head of a military force, nobody ever for a moment believed that he would use it to secure power for himself. Wisdom, patience, and personal influence over men were wonderfully united in Washington —

the greatest man in the Revolution, and, with the exception of Lincoln, the greatest of all Americans.

93. ALLIANCE WITH FRANCE (1778-1780)

The capture of Burgoyne saved the American Republic, because it made a profound impression upon the government of France, which for three years had remained neutral in the struggle, although doing much harm to its enemy Great Britain by secret aid in arms and money to the revolted colonies. Benjamin Franklin, as United States minister to France, was able to secure two treaties (February 6, 1778) by which the French recognized the independence of the United States, and promised to make common cause in the war until Great Britain should yield.

England vainly tried to head off this alliance and sent commissioners who offered to give up the disputed taxation if the colonies would return to their allegiance. The French had a good fleet and sent over troops and ships which obliged the British to withdraw from Philadelphia and concentrate in New York (June, 1778). From that time, there was no more heavy fighting in the north.

France also gave aid and comfort to the American navy. First the states and then the federal government organized naval forces, with one of which the island of New Providence in the West Indies was raided. In 1777 John Paul Jones, a former British merchant captain, was appointed captain of the ship *Ranger* and with it landed at two places on the British coast and captured the British ship-of-war *Drake*. Then with the *Bon Homme Richard*, transformed from a French merchant ship, Jones attacked and captured the *Serapis*, a forty-four-gun British ship. When the British captain called across demanding a surrender, Jones answered, " I have not yet begun to fight." This daring officer never had another chance in a good ship, and at the end of the war hardly an armed ship was afloat that carried the stars and stripes.

94. AMERICAN VICTORY (1780–1781)

Failing to break the center, the British transferred their active hostilities to the south, took Savannah (1778) and then Charleston (1780). Then the British under Lord Cornwallis in 1780 pushed into the interior of the Carolinas. Cornwallis tried to establish a Royalist government, and the country was ravaged by irregular "partisan" troops, who were guilty of excesses on both sides. The patriots Marion and Sumter with militia and guerrillas somehow kept the field. General Gates was badly defeated by the British at Camden (August, 1780). A few weeks later a force of 1200 Royalist troops was attacked by the militia and destroyed or taken at Kings Mountain (October). This important battle was won by western settlers under John Sevier from across the mountains.

In 1780 the patriot cause almost perished through the treason of Benedict Arnold, a brave veteran of many battles who was deep in debt and was willing to sell the important post of West Point for $30,000 and a major general's commission. Fortunately the British agent, Major John André, was taken at the critical moment (September 23, 1780); West Point was saved, and with it the line of communication with New England. Since André was traveling through the American lines in disguise, he was a spy, and was justly executed as a spy, though his captors bore tribute to his brave and manly character. Arnold received the promised reward from the British, and lived a miserable life, the betrayer of his own country.

During 1781 General Nathanael Greene was in command of the American forces in the South. The British were defeated at Cowpens and suffered great losses at Guilford. Cornwallis then withdrew, and invaded Virginia with the aid of Benedict Arnold. Washington aided the patriots in the South by holding the British forces in New York. He sent Lafayette to defend Virginia, and the British were soon cooped up in Yorktown awaiting reënforcement. At this critical juncture, a French

fleet under De Grasse blockaded the Chesapeake and repulsed a
British fleet bearing troops, while Washington at the right
moment made a brilliant dash southward from the Hudson,

together with a
French force under
Rochambeau, and
closed the net on
the land side.
After a spirited
siege at Yorktown,
Cornwallis surren-
dered his whole
army of 7000 men
(October 19, 1781).
Thus after seven
annual campaigns
the British held

BIRTHPLACE OF LAFAYETTE. (Purchased by
Americans for a Memorial Museum.)

only the cities of New York, Charleston, and Savannah.
The war was practically over.

95. REVIEW

During the twelve years from 1763 to 1775, the colonies ceased
to be contented with their relation to Great Britain, and rose
to the point of revolt.   The main causes of this change of feeling
were: (1) the attempt to enforce the Navigation Acts, including the use of writs of assistance; (2) taxation for revenue
by Parliament, including the Stamp Act of 1765, the Townshend
duties of 1767, and the tea duties in 1773; (3) the belief that
the colonists had certain rights under what they called "The
Constitution," noted arguments for which were framed by James
Otis and Patrick Henry; (4) the consciousness of common interest and ability to take care of themselves, shown in the Stamp
Act Congress of 1765; (5) irritation over the presence of troops
in Boston, shown by the so-called Boston Massacre of 1770, and
the Boston Tea Party of 1773, and by resistance in April, 1775.

A few Americans, especially Samuel Adams, expected trouble and began to organize through Committees of Correspondence. In 1774, the First Continental Congress was called, which represented twelve colonies in drawing up petitions, issuing a Declaration of Rights, and voting the Association, which was a boycott on British goods.

The fight at Lexington and Concord, April 19, 1775, was the beginning of a civil war. After the battle of Bunker Hill (June), the British were shut up in Boston, and in 1776 were obliged to evacuate the place. They then made preparations to subdue the colonists, and enlisted mercenary Hessians. The patriots were aided by their superior numbers, and by French, German, and Polish soldiers who came over to fight with and for them. Washington was all but driven from the field in 1776, but rallied; and Burgoyne's British army was captured at Saratoga in 1777. Washington was the soul of the Revolution. The French in 1778 made a treaty of alliance and sent over ships and soldiers which aided the Americans to capture the second British army at Yorktown (1781). That practically ended the war.

References Bearing on the Text and Topics

Geography and Maps. See maps, pp. 135, 140. — Avery, *U.S.*, V, VI. — Becker, *Beginnings*, 180, 272. — Howard, *Preliminaries of the Rev.* — Semple, *Geogr. Conditions*, 46–74. — Shepherd, *Hist. Atlas*, 194, 195. — Van Tyne, *Am. Rev.* — Winsor, *America*, VI.

Secondary. *Cambridge Mod. Hist.*, VII. chs. v–vii. — Channing, *U.S.*, III. chs. i–vi, viii–xi. — Fish, *Am. Dipl.*, chs. iii, iv. — Fiske, *Am. Rev.* — Greene, *Rev. War.* — Hapgood, *Paul Jones.* — Hosmer, *Samuel Adams*, chs. ii–xix. — Howard, *Preliminaries of the Rev.* — Lodge, *Washington*, I. chs. v–x; *Story of the Rev.* — Maclay, *U.S. Navy*, I. 34–151. — McCrady, *So. Carolina*, II. chs. xxvii–xli, III, IV. — Morse, *Benjamin Franklin*, chs. vi, vii, ix–xi. — Paullin, *Navy of the Am. Rev.* — Sloane, *French War and Rev.*, chs. x–xvi, xx–xxviii. — Smith, *Wars between Engl. and Am.*, chs. i–v. — Van Tyne, *Am. Rev.*, chs. ii, iii, vii–xvii passim. — Wilson, *Am. People*, II. chs. iii, iv.

Sources. Bogart and Thompson, *Readings*, 143–175. — Harding, *Select Orations*, nos. 1–4. — Hart, *Contemporaries*, II. §§ 130–133, 138–158, 170–183, 191–204, 211–214; *Patriots and Statesmen*, I. 247–380, II.

52–185 passim. — Hill, *Liberty Docs.*, ch. xii. — Johnston, *Am. Orations*, I. 11–23. — MacDonald, *Select Charters*, nos. 55–80. — *Old South Leaflets*, nos. 47, 68, 86, 156, 173, 179, 199, 200, 202.

Illustrative. Barr, *Bow of Orange Ribbon* (N.Y.). — Brady, *Blue Ocean's Daughter* (privateers). — Churchill, *Richard Carvel* (Paul Jones). — Cooke, *Fairfax; Henry St. John; Stories of the Old Dominion*, 140–218; *Virginia Comedians.* — Cooper, *Lionel Lincoln* (Boston); *The Pilot; The Spy.* — Frederic, *In the Valley* (Mohawk). — Hawthorne, *Edward Randolph's Portrait; Grandfather's Chair*, pt. iii; *Howe's Masquerade; Major Molineux* (mob); *Septimius Felton* (Concord). — Holmes, *Grandmother's Story of Bunker Hill.* — Longfellow, *Paul Revere's Ride.* — Lowell, *Concord Ode; Ode for the Fourth of July, 1876.* — Simms, *Eutaw; Forayers; Katherine Walton; Mellichampe; Partisan* (all on So. Carolina). — Thompson, *Green Mountain Boys.*

Pictures. Avery, *U.S.*, V, VI. — Chase, *Beginnings of the Am. Rev.* — Fiske, *Am. Rev.* (illus. ed.). — Hammond, *Quaint and Historic Forts.* — Lossing, *Field Book of the Revolution.* — *Mentor*, serial no. 53. — Wilson, *Am. People*, II. — Winsor, *America*, VI; *Boston*, III.

Topics Answerable from the References Above

(1) Objections to the Stamp Act. [§ 82] — (2) Patrick Henry as a young lawyer. [§ 83] — (3) The Sons of Liberty. [§ 84] — (4) Anti-Stamp Act mobs. [§ 84] — (5) Incidents of Stamp Act Congress. [§ 84] — (6) Contemporary accounts of the Boston Tea Party. [§ 85] — (7) Incidents in the First Continental Congress. [§ 86] — (8) Account of the Minutemen. [§ 87] — (9) Contemporary accounts of the battle of Lexington and Concord. [§ 87] — (10) Incidents in the Second Continental Congress. [§ 88] — (11) General Washington's siege of Boston. [§ 88] — (12) Colonial soldiers previous to the Revolution. [§ 89] — (13) Use of Hessians, *or* of Indians, *or* of loyalists, in the Revolution. [§ 89] — (14) The American soldier at Valley Forge. [§ 91] — (15) Washington's camp life. [§ 92]

Topics for Further Search

(16) Interest in America of *one* of the following English statesmen: Pitt; Fox; Burke. [§ 82] — (17) Was "No taxation without representation" a right of the colonists? [§ 84] — (18) Objections to sending British troops to Boston [§ 85], *or* to the "Intolerable Acts." [§ 86] — (19) Results of the Committees of Correspondence [§ 85], *or* of the Association of 1774. [§ 86] — (20) Troubles with the militia. [§ 89] — (21) Services to the Revolution of Lafayette, *or* Von Steuben, *or* De Kalb. [§ 89] — (22) How did Arnold's treason fail? [§ 94]

CHAPTER IX

BUILDING OF A NEW NATION (1775-1781)

96. PATRIOTS AND LOYALISTS

THE rapid survey of the military events of the Revolution, as given in the last chapter, might be much enlarged with sketches of the military leaders and incidents of heroic courage. But it is more important for us to know, instead, some details of the interior civil life of the country, and of the manner in which a national government was built up.

At the beginning of the struggle, the colonists were living mostly in a narrow belt of territory, stretching along the tidewater front. There were some interior settlements in southern New Hampshire and Vermont, the lower Connecticut valley, the valley of the Mohawk, western Pennsylvania, and the valleys of the Kentucky and Tennessee rivers. At the beginning of the war, some far western settlers were afraid because of Indian hostilities, and came back across the mountains; but they soon returned and built up the settlements in what are now central Kentucky and east Tennessee.

The American cause in all quarters of the country was seriously weakened because the colonists were themselves divided. John Adams later estimated that fully a third of the people were opposed to the war at the beginning and were still more strongly against independence. Hence the years of the war were full of commotion, tumult, and violence against the loyalists. Those Americans who ventured to maintain that the British government was not tyrannical, were intimidated,

151

arrested, imprisoned, tarred and feathered, and in some cases executed. As the struggle grew fiercer, the colonists passed laws banishing the loyalists or confiscating their property. In many districts the struggle was a civil war in which hundreds of the Tories, as the loyalists were called, were kept down by force. The Tories in the New England and middle commonwealths included most of the well-to-do classes, the former colonial officials and their friends, old officers of the British army, many of the clergy and of the graduates of colleges. In some states nearly half the people were loyalists. Thousands of them entered the British army and fought against their brethren; and thousands of families removed to Nova Scotia, Quebec, and other British colonies.

97. Patriot Leaders

It was an immense aid to the patriots that most of the men who were leaders in the colonies adhered to the Revolution. Able loyalists like Joseph Galloway of Pennsylvania were silenced or exiled, and stanch patriots like Benjamin Franklin, John Adams, George Clinton, Thomas Jefferson, and George Washington came to the front. At first these men hoped and worked for a settlement with the home country, which would have left the colonies about the same kind of government that is now enjoyed by Canada and Australia. Such concessions could not be secured in the face of the obstinacy of King George III and the lack of insight of the British nation. In vain did great Englishmen such as Lord Chatham (William Pitt) and Edmund Burke protest against this war between brethren. When fighting had fairly begun and the patriots won their first great triumph in the capture of Boston, the demand for independence grew rapidly.

One of the great champions of independence was Patrick Henry of Virginia, a passionate, impulsive, fiery man, with a reputation for surpassing oratory. It is a well-founded tradition that in the Virginia Assembly in 1765 he exclaimed,

"Cæsar had his Brutus; Charles I his Cromwell; and George III—" "Treason," shouted the Speaker. "Treason, treason," rose from all sides of the room, — "and George III may profit by their example. If this be treason, make the most of it." As a member of the First Continental Congress, Patrick Henry foresaw independence. "Government is dissolved," said he. "Fleets and armies and the present state of things show that government is dissolved. . . . I am not a Virginian, but an American"; and in the Virginia convention of 1775 he made a magnificent speech ending with the oft-quoted passage, "I know not what course others may take; but as for me, give me liberty or give me death."

In the North the greatest exponent of independence was the astute political leader Samuel Adams of Massachusetts, the first man to discover how much may be done in a democracy by organizing the voters and by preparing work for town meetings and assemblies through caucuses and private meetings. He induced Boston to take strong ground in the quarrel with England. He invented the Committee of Correspondence in 1772 (§ 85), and was himself the most active member. He pulled the wires which led to the Boston Tea Party; and in Congress he labored unceasingly for independence. Though he could destroy, he did not know how to build up a state, and after 1776 he lived for the most part in private, except for a brief period as governor of Massachusetts.

98. DECLARATION OF INDEPENDENCE (1775-1776)

The belief that the British North American colonies would sometime form a separate nation can be traced back to travelers and observers during the ten years previous to the Revolution. During 1775 several local conventions suggested that the British rule was at an end. The most famous among them is that of Mecklenburg County, North Carolina (May, 1775). Congress still hoped for a settlement till news came (November, 1775) that the king would not even receive their petition.

In January, 1776, appeared the first widely read and effective argument for independence — Thomas Paine's ringing pamphlet, *Common Sense*, an arsenal of arguments against England and against reconciliation. "The birthday of a new world is at hand," exclaimed Paine; "and a race of men . . . are to receive their portion of freedom."

The conviction that the time was approaching for a formal declaration of independence took root in Congress. May 15, on motion of John Adams, Congress voted that all British authority in the colonies ought to be legally suppressed. June 7, Richard Henry Lee, under instructions from his colony of Virginia, introduced a resolution for independence, looking to a formal union; and two committees were appointed (June 10-12), one to draft a declaration of independence, the other to prepare articles for a union. The question of independence was postponed, to enable delegates to receive instructions from home, for, as Franklin dryly remarked, "We must all hang together or we shall all hang separately."

INDEPENDENCE HALL, PHILADELPHIA. (Where the Second Continental Congress met.)

The Committee on Independence intrusted to Thomas Jefferson, a young delegate from Virginia, the delicate task of drawing up a public statement of the reasons for war and separation. Fortunately he had a ready pen, and his mind was

full of principles of free government, which were not peculiar
to the colonies, but were the common property of the English
race, and had been partly put in form by the English phi-
losophers Locke and Hobbes.

The declaration he prepared was reported on June 28, and
was for some days debated and then slightly amended. Meanwhile Lee's postponed resolution of independence was formally
adopted, July 2. John Adams has left us his impressions of
this momentous act. "The second day of July, 1776, will be
the most memorable epocha in the history of America. . . .
It ought to be commemorated, as a day of deliverance, by
solemn acts of devotion to God Almighty. It ought to be
solemnized with pomp and parade, with shows, games, sports,
guns, bells, bonfires, and illuminations, from one end of this
continent to the other, from this time forward forever more."
On July 4, 1776, Jefferson's Declaration of Independence was
adopted as amended. On August 2, an engrossed copy (still
preserved in Washington) was laid before Congress; and the
members then in Congress affixed their names to this document, although in the eye of English law every signer was
a traitor and subject to a traitor's doom.

99. MEANING OF INDEPENDENCE (1776)

The document thus formally adopted by Congress in behalf
of the communities which from that time on were called "states,"
is a cornerstone of American liberty and American government, yet it is simple in its language and its principles. The
Declaration of Independence (see Appendix D) is made up of
three significant parts:

(1) An announcement of certain political rights, by nature
applying to the colonists and rightfully applying to all mankind. These rights, which had been stated in much greater detail earlier by the First Continental Congress and by the states,
are here repeated in the form of certain "self-evident truths,"
such as "that all men are created equal; that they are endowed

by their Creator with certain unalienable rights; that among these are Life, Liberty, and the pursuit of Happiness. That to secure these rights, Governments are instituted among Men, deriving their just powers from the consent of the governed."

(2) A list of twenty-seven grievances which justify the Revolution; most of the acts thus complained of had for many years been accepted and practiced as legal by the British government.

(3) The ringing, positive, and fearless statement that "These United Colonies are, and of Right ought to be, Free and Independent States."

The fortunes of war during the next few years were to decide whether this last statement was true. Meanwhile the American people had to settle the further question whether the individual colonies were "Free and Independent States"; or whether it was the Union of thirteen states taken together that was "Free and Independent." "The Union is older than any of the States," said Abraham Lincoln in 1861, "and in fact it created them as States." He meant to bring out the fact that there was a national government in action before any state governments came into being.

100. New States (1775-1780)

The process of change from colonies into states was difficult and irregular. As the Revolution spread from Massachusetts to other colonies, the royal and proprietary governors were forced to flee. The patriots formed revolutionary assemblies, called "Congresses" or "Conventions," which for the time being carried on the government of the colonies, shutting out the Tories from any part in their control. People felt that these were only temporary governments, and asked Congress for advice. Acting under such advice, New Hampshire in 1776 adopted a document which was practically a little state constitution. Massachusetts, Rhode Island, and Connecticut made slight changes in their colonial charters and treated them as

constitutions. The other nine colonies (and also Vermont)
all adopted written constitutions during 1776 and 1777; and
Massachusetts at last (1780) gave up the old charter form and
provided herself with a document which was the first state
constitution ever adopted by popular vote.

These constitutions are the foundation of our present system
of state constitutions; and, with many variations in detail,
they are surprisingly alike in their general form and spirit.

FIRST CAPITOL OF NEW YORK STATE, AT KINGSTON.

(1) Each contained a bill of rights; that is, a statement
of the liberties of the individual. (2) Each provided for a representative republican government including three departments — legislative, executive, and judicial. In all the states
except two the legislature was made up of two houses; in all,
the legislature was the most powerful part of the system; each
of the states except Pennsylvania had a single governor, chosen
by popular vote or by the legislature. (3) None of the constitutions were strongly democratic according to our ideas, for
the suffrage was limited to property owners or taxpayers; and
most of the states had also religious and property qualifications

for office holders. (4) In the fear of military and centralized
government, all the constitutions fixed short terms for all elective officers. (5) Several of them provided a method of easy
amendment, and within ten years some of the first constitutions
were entirely recast. (6) All of these constitutions were made
by communities who were also taking part in the general government through Congress; and they expected to remain indefinitely in an organized federal union.

101. Articles of Confederation (1775-1781)

The reasons for union were many, the two strongest being
that the colonies were already in a union as parts of the British
Empire when the Revolution began, and that unless they made
their union closer they could never secure their independence.
As early as 1775, Benjamin Franklin proposed to Congress a
plan somewhat resembling his old suggestion to the Albany Congress of 1754 (§ 68). There is evidence to show that he had before him the Articles of the New England Confederation of
1643 (§ 37). He wanted a strong government in which the
states should be represented in proportion to their population;
and he wanted Congress to have control of boundary disputes and future colonies. The committee on a union (§ 98)
reported (July 12, 1776) a draft for a Confederation, drawn
up by John Dickinson, a Pennsylvanian. So many disagree-
ments arose in the debate that it was not till November 15,
1777, that Congress completed its revision of the Articles of Confederation and sent out the result to the states for ratification.

The state delegations disagreed on many points, but especially on the following: Was the Union to be strong or weak?
Should slave property be taxed? Should Congress regulate
foreign commerce? Should Congress control the western country? On these and other points the Articles as finally submitted were much weaker than Franklin's original proposition:
(1) Congress was not authorized to tax slaves or to regulate
foreign commerce; nor was it given any direct authority to

settle boundary disputes or to plant new colonies. (2) Each
state in the Confederation, however small, was to have an
equal vote in Congress. (3) Revenues for the support of the government were to be supplied by the states according to the value
of their lands — a method which proved to be impracticable.

Even for this weakened plan of Union, ratifications came in
slowly. During the first year only ten of the thirteen state
legislatures ratified; New Jersey, Delaware, and Maryland
stood out because they thought there ought to be some provision to prevent Virginia from securing the northwestern lands.
Not till March 1, 1781, did Maryland, the last state, ratify and
thus complete the adoption of the Articles of Confederation.

102. THE WESTERN COUNTRY (1763-1776)

Let us turn to the West, which was hereafter to play an im-
portant part in the history and government of the United
States. Though by the Peace of Paris in 1763 (§ 69) the
British came into control of the region between the Ohio River,
the Great Lakes, and the Mississippi, they had to fight an
Indian war for its possession, against the famous chief Pontiac
(1763-1764). The few little towns there, such as Detroit,
Green Bay, St. Joseph near the head of Lake Michigan,
Vincennes on the Wabash, and Kaskaskia and Cahokia on
the east side of the Mississippi, near the mouth of the Illinois,
were inhabited by Frenchmen and French half-breeds. A
little British government for the region was set up at Detroit,
with some slight authority in Vincennes and Kaskaskia.

Both Pennsylvania and Virginia claimed the forks of the
Ohio, where in 1765 the town of Pittsburgh was founded.
People poured across the mountains, and part of them drifted
southwest into the mountain regions of Virginia and North
Carolina. Then frontiersmen, chiefly Scotch-Irish and German, with a few Huguenots, ignored the Proclamation of 1763
(§ 69), defied their own colonial governments, braved the Indians, and plunged into the western wilderness.

The pioneer in this movement was Daniel Boone of the Yadkin district in North Carolina, who in 1769, with five companions, started out "in quest of the country of Kentucke." For years he was the leading spirit in a scattered community of men who were frontiersmen, farmers, trappers, and Indian fighters all at the same time — the first settlers in Kentucky. A second and more continuous settlement was begun in 1769

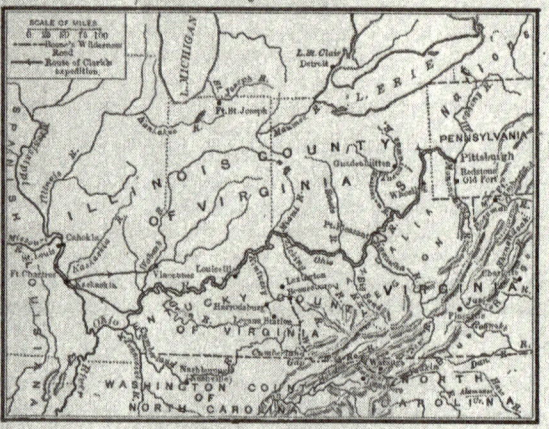

EARLY SETTLEMENTS IN THE WEST, AND CLARK'S EXPEDITION.

by William Beane, on the Watauga River, a head stream of the Tennessee, a region which he and his neighbors supposed to be a part of Virginia, though it proved to be within the North Carolina claims. Under the leadership of John Sevier and James Robertson, they formed a little representative constitution under the name of "Articles of the Watauga Association."

By this time the value of the West was apparent to some capitalists, who formed the Vandalia Company, a kind of successor to the old Ohio Company (§ 67), and asked for a royal charter for a colony south of the Ohio. In 1774, however, Parliament showed the purpose of the British government to prevent the growth of any new western commonwealth, by the Quebec Act, which added the region between the Ohio and the Great Lakes to the province of Quebec.

Just at the time the Revolution broke out, Richard Henderson of Virginia, with Daniel Boone as his right-hand man, set up what they called the Transylvania Company, in the region between the Cumberland and Kentucky rivers. Boone was sent ahead and blazed out a pack trail known as the Wilderness Road, from the Holston River (upper Tennessee) through Cumberland Gap to Kentucky. The new settlers founded Boonesboro and other settlements, and actually set up a government by a delegate convention. Later they applied to Congress to admit them as a state. The people of the Vandalia region in 1776 also petitioned Congress to make them "a sister colony and fourteenth province of the American confederacy." Both applications were distasteful to Virginia, which in 1776 organized Kentucky County, with a county seat at Harrodsburg, and put an end to the Transylvania government.

All these settlements were south of the Ohio River; all of them were in territory claimed by either Virginia or North Carolina; all of them showed a disposition to set up for themselves; all of them raised the question of the future control and government of the West.

103. INDIAN TROUBLES (1776-1779)

Although the new western settlers made some effort to purchase the Indian rights to the lands which they occupied, the tribes were quick to see that they and the "long-knives" could not live at peace. By this time, white traders and explorers were coming into close contact with the Cherokees, who occupied what is now western Tennessee and northern Georgia, and Alabama. They were the Iroquois of the South, the boldest, best-organized, and most intelligent Indians of their region.

Along the whole frontier from south to north, the Indians were greatly disturbed by the Revolutionary War. Both sides tried to win them as allies. Congress made every effort to placate them by the same kind of fatherly control as the British government had previously used. Congress received delegations of Indians in its sessions and harangued them, appropriated money to buy presents for them, appointed superintendents of Indian affairs, negotiated treaties with several tribes, and made some feeble attempts to civilize them.

Nothing could prevent war. The southwestern Indians attacked the neighboring settlements in 1776 and harried the frontier till the South Carolina legislature offered 75 pounds for every Indian scalp. The middle frontier, especially of Virginia, was harassed by a mixed force of British, Indians, and renegade whites directed by the British governor of the Northwest Country. The worst horrors of Indian warfare were felt in the backwoods of Pennsylvania and New York; for though the Iroquois Six Nations were divided, a large part of them took the British side. Joint forces of Tories and Indians in 1778 ravaged the Wyoming Valley, Pennsylvania, and Cherry Valley, New York. The next year Congress as a punishment dispatched an expedition under General Sullivan, who marched up into the territory of the Six Nations, defeated the Indians and their white allies, and laid waste their villages. The Iroquois were so reduced in numbers and prestige by this defeat that they never again became a force in American affairs.

104. CONQUEST OF THE NORTHWEST (1778–1779)

The defeat of the Iroquois Indians opened the way for an invasion of the region north of the Ohio River, in which there were few British and only about 6000 French and French half-breeds. Among the settlers in Kentucky associated with Boone was George Rogers Clark, an excellent backwoodsman and experienced Indian fighter. He was but twenty-five years old, and had neither money nor men; and no story of the

Arabian Nights is more romantic or improbable than his conception of such an invasion and his success in carrying it
out. Governor Patrick Henry of Virginia authorized him to
attack the British post at Kaskaskia, not far from St. Louis.
With about 100 men, Clark floated down the Ohio River,
marched across the country, and surprised and took Kaskaskia
and Cahokia (July, 1778). The British commander of the
Northwest Country, Hamilton, began to raise a force at Vincennes on the Wabash; but Clark enlisted the French residents,
whom he won over by giving them religious and civil liberty.
These forces he led in an incredible march over flooded country,
and Vincennes surrendered without a fight, in February, 1779.

The Americans remained to the end of the war in possession
of the southern half of the region north of the Ohio River, which
had been added to the province of Quebec in 1774 (§ 102).
Clark was anxious to capture Detroit, but never could muster
a sufficient force. Inasmuch as he was commissioned by Virginia, the government of that state erected the whole immense
region between the Ohio, the Mississippi, and the Great Lakes
into the "County of Illinois" (1778). This claim led Maryland to oppose the Articles of Confederation (§ 101).

105. RIVAL CLAIMS TO THE WEST (1778-1781)

By this time it was clear that the various claims to the title
of the West were in confusion, and that the thirteen states were
at loggerheads with one another, in curiously involved groups:

(1) Six of the thirteen states were so definitely bounded that
they could not, by any construction of their charters, claim any
part of the West; these were New Hampshire, Rhode Island,
New Jersey, Pennsylvania, Delaware, Maryland.

(2) Four states claimed the Southwest, in four parallel bands
extending as far as the Pacific Ocean; or rather, since the British recognized the Spanish possession of the far West, as far as
the Mississippi. These were Virginia, by the extinct charter
of 1609 (§ 30); the two Carolinas, on extinct grants of

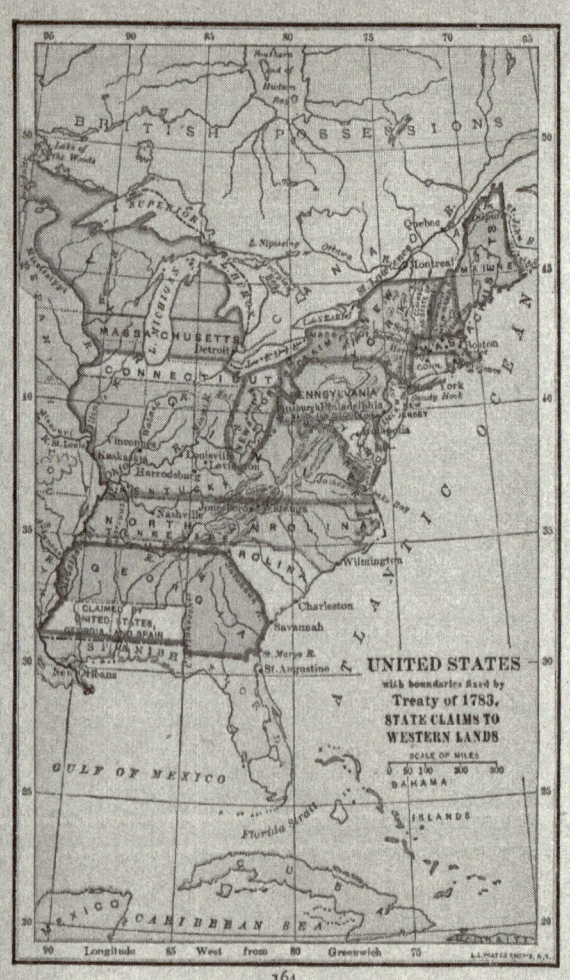

UNITED STATES
with boundaries fixed by
Treaty of 1783,
STATE CLAIMS TO
WESTERN LANDS

1663 and 1665 (§ 44); and Georgia by the extinct charter of 1732 (§ 46).

(3) Virginia also claimed practically the whole of the Northwest, under the uncertain terms of the charter of 1609, "Up into the land throughout from sea to sea, west and northwest."

(4) Three other states also claimed parts of the Northwest. (a) Massachusetts went back to the canceled charter of 1629 (§ 33), which was partly revived by the charter of 1691 (§ 46); and (b) Connecticut referred to the charter of 1662 (§ 41), which was in force down to the Revolution. They claimed parallel strips of territory as far as the Mississippi, covering part of the territory in the Virginia claim. (c) New York had no charter, and no settlements west of the Mohawk valley, but set up an indefinite claim to the upper Ohio country on the ground that it belonged to Indians who were subject to the Six Nations, who had ceded it to New York. Her claim conflicted with those of Massachusetts, Connecticut, and Virginia.

Manifestly these claims could not all be made good; and clearly it was contrary to the interests of all the other states of the Union that Virginia should be allowed to extend from tide water to Lake Superior and to possess a third of the territory of the Union. The only way out was to recognize the common-sense principle that the whole nation had rights in the western lands. The West was conquered and held only because the British were kept busy on the coast by the continental army. Hence Maryland stood out for holding the western lands.

As a pledge that the lands should be used for all the states, Congress passed a momentous vote (October 10, 1780) that "The unappropriated lands which may be ceded to . . . the United States shall be disposed of for the common benefit of the United States, and be settled and formed into distinct republican states, which shall become members of the federal union." New York and Virginia promised to cede at least a part of their claims, and without waiting for the details to be settled, Maryland ratified the Articles of Confederation.

106. REVIEW

More important than the military events of the Revolution is the building up of the new nation, in which the western settlements took a part. The organized patriots were led by such men as Patrick Henry and Samuel Adams.

Early in the war independence was urged by such writers as Thomas Paine, and such statesmen as Richard Henry Lee of Virginia. In June, 1776, a Declaration of Independence was drawn by Thomas Jefferson of Virginia; and it was adopted by Congress, July 4, 1776. This Declaration set forth the fundamental rights of man, and the recent violations of those rights.

To carry out this Declaration, new state and national governments were needed. All the thirteen states, and also Vermont, adopted constitutions. Congress also drew up Articles of Confederation, as a federal constitution for the Union (November, 1777); they were not adopted by all the states till 1781.

A new element in American history was the West, where in the Illinois country and in Kentucky and Tennessee flourishing little settlements were made by Daniel Boone and other noted pioneers. A large part of the Six Nations took the British side in the Revolution, and were therefore invaded and almost annihilated.

Virginia entered into the conquest of the West by sending out George Rogers Clark in 1778, who captured several British posts in what is now southern Illinois and Indiana. This revived the confused claims to the western country, parts of which were claimed by Massachusetts, Connecticut, New York, Virginia, North Carolina, South Carolina, and Georgia. Congress urged the states to surrender their claims, and the process was begun by cessions from New York and Virginia in 1781.

References Bearing on the Text and Topics

Geography and Maps. See references in ch. viii.

Secondary. Becker, *Beginnings*, 247–254, 262–267, 270–274. — Channing, *U.S.*, III. chs. vii, xiv. — Hart, *Formation of the Union*, §§ 36–39, 43–45. — Hazelton, *Declaration of Independence*. — Morse,

Benjamin Franklin, chs. viii, xii; *John Adams,* chs. iv-vi; *Thomas Jefferson,* chs. iii-vi. — Roosevelt, *Winning of the West,* I, II. — Schouler, *Americans of 1776.* — Thwaites, *Daniel Boone.* — Tyler, *Am. Revolution* (literary), I. chs. xix-xxiii, II; *Patrick Henry,* chs. xii-xv. — Van Tyne, *Am. Rev.,* chs. iv-vi, ix-xi, xiv, xv; *Loyalists.*

Sources. *Am. Hist. Leaflets,* nos. 11, 20. — Beard, *Readings,* §§ 10-13. — Caldwell, *Terr. Development,* 26-48. — Hart, *Contemporaries,* II. §§ 134-137, 159-169, 184-190, 205-210; *Patriots and Statesmen,* II. 15-50, 59-61, 68-74, 78-96, 123-139, 142-149, 153-166, 193-197, 216-223. — Hill, *Liberty Docs.,* chs. xiii-xv. — James, *Readings,* §§ 32-35. — Johnson, *Readings,* §§ 13-17, 22-25. — MacDonald, *Select Docs.,* nos. 1, 2. — *Old South Leaflets,* 2, 3, 43, 97, 152.

Illustrative. Campbell, *Gertrude of Wyoming.* — Eggleston, *Am. War Ballads,* I. 23-101. — Ford, *Janice Meredith.* — Freneau, *Poems.* — Kennedy, *Horseshoe Robinson* (loyalists). — Matthews, *Poems of Am. Patriotism,* 8-82. — Mitchell, *Hugh Wynne.* — Thompson, *Alice of Old Vincennes.* — Trumbull, *M'Fingal.* — See also refs. to ch. viii.

Pictures. Avery, *U.S.,* VI. — *Mentor,* serial no. 32. — Wilson, *Am. People,* II. — Winsor, *America,* VI.

Topics Answerable from the References Above

(1) Early settlers in Kentucky, *or* in Tennessee. [§ 96] — (2) Treatment of the loyalists. [§ 96] — (3) Contemporary accounts of the Declaration of Independence. [§ 98] — (4) Franklin's plan of a federal constitution. [§ 101] — (5) Pontiac's war with the English. [§ 102] — (6) French colonial towns in the West. [§ 102] — (7) Adventures of Daniel Boone, *or* of John Sevier. [§ 102] — (8) Life of the early western settlers. [§ 103] — (9) Indian and British frontier raids. [§ 103] — (10) Sullivan's raid. [§ 103] — (11) George Rogers Clark's campaign. [§ 104]

Topics for Further Search

(12) Influence on the Revolution of *one* of the following men : Patrick Henry; Thomas Paine; John Dickinson; John Adams; Samuel Adams; Robert Morris; Richard Henry Lee; Franklin; Jefferson. [§§ 97, 98] — (13) Influence of the Declaration of Independence on the world. [§ 99] — (14) Account of the Revolutionary Congress or Convention in *one* of the thirteen original states. [§ 100] — (15) Maryland's objections to the Articles of Confederation. [§ 101] — (16) Account of the Cherokee Indians. [§ 103] — (17) Did the eastern states have good claims to western territory? [§ 105]

CHAPTER X

CONFEDERATION AND FEDERAL CONSTITUTION
(1781-1788)

107. CONGRESS AND THE CONFEDERATION

FOR many months before the Articles of Confederation were finally adopted, Congress had been acting on the supposition that they would be ratified, and people hardly realized that this constitution went into effect on March 1, 1781. The government thus established suffered from so many troubles that it has been looked upon as a failure. In fact it was the best organized and most thoroughgoing confederation that the world had ever seen, though far inferior in efficiency to its successor. Although Congress was the only recognized federal authority under the Articles, it chose to act through three departments as follows:

(1) Congress itself was made up of delegates appointed by the state legislatures, each state delegation casting one vote. On several vital questions, no motion could be carried except by the affirmative vote of nine states.

(2) Congress created executive offices and commissioned officials, particularly the Secretary at War, the Superintendent of Finance, the Secretary for Foreign Affairs, and the Postmaster-General.

(3) Congress set up a Court of Appeals in Prize Cases, to which cases concerning captured vessels could be carried from the state courts.

Congress had no fixed place of meeting, but held sessions at

Philadelphia, Trenton, Annapolis, and other places. From 1785 it sat at New York. Membership was not much prized, and it was hard to get first-class men to enter Congress; but Thomas Jefferson, James Madison, and James Monroe, later Presidents of the United States, all showed their great abilities as members of Congress.

108. TREATY OF PEACE (1782–1783)

One of the most important duties of Congress was to secure a peace with Great Britain. When Lord North, the Prime Minister, heard of the Yorktown surrender (§ 94) he cried out, "O God, it is all over!" The merchants in England had suffered enormous losses by captures of their shipping, and therefore strongly urged a peace; and King George III was obliged to accept an opposition ministry, which was determined to end the war.

A strong commission — Franklin, John Adams, John Jay, and Henry Laurens — was selected to represent this country in peace negotiations at Paris in 1782. Though their instructions provided that these envoys should take no steps without the approval of the French government, they became satisfied that the French did not desire to give a good boundary west of the

1777.

1795–1818.

1877.

1918.

GROWTH OF THE FLAG.

Appalachians. In consultation in their rooms one day, Franklin said to Jay, "Would you break your instructions?" "Yes, as I break this pipe." The pipe went into the fire, and the instructions were ignored; an unexpectedly favorable treaty with Great Britain was secured without the aid of France, under date of November 30, 1782.

The main features of this treaty were as follows:

(1) Great Britain recognized the independence of the United States.

(2) The boundary was to run from the river St. Croix northward to the watershed of the St. Lawrence; thence along that ridge and on the 45th parallel to the St. Lawrence River; thence up that river and the Great Lakes to the Lake of the Woods; thence down the Mississippi to the 31st parallel; thence eastward to the head of St. Marys River, and by that river to the Atlantic Ocean.

(3) "The right to take fish of every kind" from the grand banks of Newfoundland was acknowledged, together with the "liberty" to dry and cure fish on the neighboring unsettled bays and creeks of Canada.

(4) British merchants were to have the right to collect debts due when the Revolution broke out, and on the other hand the British agreed to withdraw their armies from the United States without taking away "negroes or other property of the Americans."

(5) Congress was to recommend the states to receive and treat well the loyalists who had not taken arms in the British service.

This so-called Preliminary Treaty of 1782 practically ended the Revolutionary War. A year later a "Definitive Treaty" to the same effect was signed and in due time was ratified by Congress. New York was evacuated by the British in 1783. The United States of America had at last fully proved that the Declaration of Independence was real.

109. NATIONAL FINANCES (1776-1788)

Upon Congress fell the serious responsibility of providing for the finances of the Revolutionary War and for the debt left at the end of the war. During the Revolution every device was used to raise money. The states laid taxes which were collected with difficulty; they issued $210,000,000 of paper money, most of which was never redeemed; they fixed prices in paper money and punished those who refused to receive it; they confiscated the estates of the loyalists; they borrowed money, and could not pay the interest. National finances were not much better, as was shown by the accumulation of several kinds of debt: (1) domestic, including bonds and certificates to creditors, amounting to about $11,000,000; (2) foreign, due to France and French officers, amounting to about $6,000,000; (3) unsettled and unfunded debts — perhaps $16,000,000; (4) paper money: from 1775 to 1781, Congress

CONTINENTAL PAPER MONEY.

issued $242,000,000 in paper money, which rapidly declined in purchasing power. Toward the end of the war a specie dollar would buy a thousand dollars in continental currency, and

"Paper money became so cheap,
  Folks wouldn't count it, but said 'a heap.'"

The paper money, both state and national, was really a kind of taxation. Congress got about forty million dollars' worth of supplies and of soldiers' services for the paper notes which were never redeemed; and therefore the system caused that amount of loss to the people through whose hands the notes passed, or in whose possession they were finally left. The Confederation did not attempt to float paper money, but about half the states put out new issues after the war was over.

In the seven years from 1781 to 1788 the states turned in

about $500,000 a year in specie to the national government, which was the only cash income of the United States except some money lent by France and by Dutch bankers. Robert Morris of Philadelphia, who was then considered the richest man in America, was put in charge of the finances, but resigned in 1784. At that time the outstanding federal debt was about $40,000,000, and the interest upon it was rolling up from year to year.

110. National Commerce (1781–1788)

After the Revolution, European countries were anxious to make treaties with the United States, so as to get a part of our trade; and several such commercial treaties were negotiated. Spain stood off because the United States asked for the right to navigate the Mississippi River to its mouth, without paying duties to the Spanish colony of Louisiana, through which the river flowed for the last hundred miles of its course. This concession Spain absolutely refused, and Congress was inclined to accept the Spanish terms; but some of the southwestern people roundly threatened to leave the Union if cut off from the sea. Washington wrote: "The western states (I speak now from my own observation) stand as it were upon a pivot. The touch of a feather would turn them any way." The whole matter was postponed for the time.

Now that the United States was completely separated from Great Britain and no longer subject to the Navigation Acts, our government was unexpectedly made to understand that it had lost the special privileges of trade with the British colonies. The navigation system (§ 80) was applied against the United States when (July, 1783) the British government closed the West India trade to all vessels except those built and owned by British subjects. Still, direct trade between Great Britain and the United States went on freely in the vessels of both nations; and the British merchants got most of the American orders for foreign goods; hence Great Britain saw no reason for making a commercial treaty.

In other respects the treaty of 1782–1783 did not end the controversies between the two countries. The British merchants complained that the state governments prevented them from collecting the old debts; and the British government was incensed because the loyalists were not allowed to return and resume their place in the states. On the other side, the Americans complained that the retiring British troops carried off negro slaves, and the British kept possession of about twelve little posts inside the northern American boundary.

Our trade and foreign relations were in an unsatisfactory state during the whole life of the Confederation.

III. STATES AND THE UNION (1781–1788)

Within the Union also there were serious quarrels: first of all, about the western lands, and then about commerce. One reason why Great Britain refused to make a commercial treaty was that certain states undertook to regulate commerce without any treaty. Some laid discriminating duties on British ships; others took off discriminations, so as to induce British ships to come to their ports. Three states — Massachusetts, New York, and Pennsylvania — adopted protective tariff duties which were applied against their neighbors; and New Jersey retaliated with an act taxing the New York lighthouse on Sandy Hook. Among the state acts that most affected neighboring states were the "Stay and Tender" laws, suspending all suits for debt for six months or a year, or permitting the debtor to offer goods, cattle, or even land in payment of his debts.

So far as we can now judge, the country was prosperous during this period, though the governments were in financial trouble. Population was increasing, towns were growing, houses and ships were being built, and quantities of goods were imported. The main trouble was the difficulty of paying for these goods; for the exports were less than before the Revolution, and there was very little hard money — gold and silver — in the country. Everybody found it difficult to pay debts and taxes; and under

the laws of the time a man might be kept indefinitely in jail
for no other cause than inability to pay his debts. From one
end of the country to the other, there was a chorus of complaint
— much of it justified — that court fees and lawsuits and imprisonment for debt were intolerable hardships.

In several states riots broke out and rose almost to revolutions. The climax was reached in the Shays Rebellion in Massachusetts, which made a great impression on the country.
Early in 1787 Captain Daniel Shays got together about 1800
men, and even attacked the United States arsenal at Springfield.
State militia was sent to break up the insurrection; when the
two forces actually met each other at Petersham, the rebels
gave way in confusion, and order was shortly restored. This
rebellion was important as showing the weakness of the federal
government, which had no power to maintain order.

112. Division on the Slavery Question

Down to the Revolution, when slavery and the slave trade
were legal in every colony, there was not much chance for
differences between the sections on that question. The few
antislavery advocates, such as John Woolman, a Quaker lay
preacher, worked in both northern and southern colonies. There
was no antislavery society until 1775, when one was formed in
Philadelphia. Up to this time the main argument against
slavery had been that slavery was unchristian. Now came the
doctrines of the Declaration of Independence and the Bills of
Rights, in favor of the equality of all men. Then followed the
first legal step against slavery, which was the prohibition of the
slave trade by votes of the Continental Congress and by statutes
of most of the individual states.

In the debates on the Articles of Confederation, however,
northern members began to criticize the South for slavery; and
between 1777 and 1784, five states and one semi-independent
community laid the ban of law on slavery. (1) Vermont in
its constitution of 1777 prohibited the slavery of grown men and

women. (2) Pennsylvania in 1780 passed an act providing that all persons born within the commonwealth after the date of the act should be born free. (3) The Massachusetts constitution of 1780 declared that "All men are born free and equal," which the courts afterward held to be a prohibition of slavery. (4) A similar clause in the revised constitution of New Hampshire in 1783 had the same effect in that state. (5) In Connecticut and (6) Rhode Island, emancipation acts, similar to that of Pennsylvania, were passed in 1784. The gap between New England and Pennsylvania was closed by emancipation acts of New York (1799) and New Jersey (1804). Thus was created a solid block of territory, stretching from the Atlantic Ocean to Lake Erie, north of Mason and Dixon's Line (the southern boundary of Pennsylvania), in which slavery was dead or dying (map, page 179). The result was that the Union was divided into two sections, with hostile labor systems. Such men as Washington and Jefferson, however, believed that slavery would soon disappear in the South as well as in the North.

113. WESTERN LAND QUESTION SETTLED (1781–1790)

If Congress showed little capacity to deal with the pressing financial and commercial questions, it nevertheless settled another issue, upon which it had no authority under the Articles. This was the western land controversy, involving the three questions of state claims, administration of the public lands, and organization of new western communities. This adjustment is shown in many parts of the present map of the West and in the public land system, and should therefore be carefully stated.

The four states claiming the lands north of the Ohio River (§ 105) all gracefully yielded: (1) New York ceded all claims west of the present western boundary of that state (1781). (2) Virginia gave up all claims to territory north of the Ohio River, except ownership of the Virginia Reserve Military Bounty Lands (1784). (3) Massachusetts yielded all claims west of New York (1785), and gave up to that state her claim to govern western New York, retaining ownership in the lands. (4) Connecticut yielded her claims (1786), with the exception of the "Western Reserve"—a strip along Lake Erie west of Pennsylvania.

The claims south of the Ohio River (§ 105) were harder to adjust. (1) To Virginia, by an agreement of 1784, was left

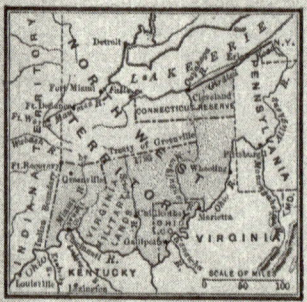

THE NORTHWEST IN 1800.

the District of Kentucky, which remained a part of Virginia until later admitted as a state. (2) South Carolina gave up her claim to a narrow strip lying between western North Carolina and Georgia (1787). (3) North Carolina claimed Tennessee, including the Watauga and other settlements, and issued land grants covering most of the tract, but eventually ceded to Congress the right to govern the region (1790). (4) Georgia claimed everything between the present state and the Mississippi River, and did not consent to accept her present state boundaries till 1802.

114. PUBLIC LANDS AND WESTERN SETTLEMENTS (1780-1785)

Before any part of the disputed lands came under the exclusive control of Congress, that body made preparations to sell them and to apply the proceeds to paying off the national debt. The first Public Land Act in our national history was the Grayson Ordinance (1785). In this act is included the system of surveying the land into square blocks, a plan based on a suggestion from Thomas Jefferson. Provision was made for dividing the western country into townships six miles square by lines running east and west, crossed at regular intervals by lines running north and south. Each township was to be subdivided by lines a mile apart into thirty-six sections, one of which was reserved for schools. The standard government price was to be $1 an acre.

It was one thing to offer the land and another to dispose of it. Some tracts were held by squatters who had to be driven off by troops. The states and the private holders of warrants for bounty lands hadgreatquantities to sell below the government price. Hence several shrewd men hit on the idea of buying land, not with cash, but with certificates of the national debt

METHOD OF PUBLIC LAND SURVEY.

which were then at a distressing discount. To float these schemes, three companies were formed: (1) The Ohio Company contracted to buy about 1,500,000 acres and took about 900,000. (2) The Symmes Company wanted 1,000,000 acres, and finally got 250,000, including the site of Cincinnati. (3) The Scioto Company, managed by speculators, undertook to buy 3,500,000 acres but never took any. In the year 1788 the state of Pennsylvania bought the triangle of land west of the New York line, — 200,000 acres, — which gave to the state a lake front, including the site of the city of Erie.

All these sales were in the Northwest. In Kentucky and Tennessee, the frontier was settled by hardy people called "backwoodsmen." They were of Scotch-Irish, German, and English descent, but when thrown together they speedily became one people. They took up farms by land patents, or by "tomahawk right"; that is, by blazing trees where they meant to settle. In a few days of hard labor they could build a log house; in a few days more, a fort. Their large families of children grew up and settled more land about them, or plunged into the far backwoods. Their ordinary dress was the fringed

A FRONTIER POST, 1787. (Fort Steuben, Ohio. From a recent restoration.)

hunting shirt and leggings, and their flintlock rifles brought down game or Indians, according as they shot.

The Kentuckians in 1784 took steps toward the immediate establishment of a state government, but desisted when Virginia intimated that she would soon give her consent to the separation. In Tennessee a convention formally voted to establish a state of Franklin (1784), elected John Sevier governor, chose a legislature, made laws, and defied the jurisdiction of North Carolina. Again a policy of conciliation was followed; and the people returned to their allegiance under the promise that North Carolina would transfer the territory to the United States.

115. THE NORTHWEST ORDINANCE (1784-1788)

Although Congress had no authority under the Articles of Confederation to create territories, nevertheless it did so in order to provide a proper government for the western settlers. Jefferson drafted a general ordinance for temporary territorial governments; this was adopted by Congress but was never put into force. Several Revolutionary officers from Massachusetts, headed by Rufus Putnam, organized a land company called the Ohio Company of Associates. In 1787 Manasseh Cutler, the agent of the company, applied to Congress, which was then sitting in New York, to sell them a tract of land, and also to provide a form of government especially for their settlement. This

SLAVE AND FREE SECTIONS, 1804.

was granted in the famous Northwest Ordinance dated July 31, 1787, of which the principal points are the following:

(1) It specifically applied to the Northwest Territory, lying between the Ohio, the Mississippi, and the Great Lakes.

(2) A governor and three judges, appointed by Congress, were to act as a board to select laws for the territory.

(3) Provision was made for a later representative assembly, with power to elect a non-voting delegate to Congress, and to make laws subject to the governor's veto.

(4) Six "Articles of Compact" provided for personal liberty, for religious freedom, for "schools and the means of education," and added the momentous provision: "There shall be neither Slavery nor involuntary Servitude in the said Territory, other-

wise than in the punishment of Crimes, whereof the Party shall have been duly Convicted." This extended the belt of free territory from Pennsylvania to the Mississippi.

Colonists sent by the Ohio Company traveled from Massachusetts, west to Pittsburgh; and on April 7, 1788, founded the town of Marietta, at the junction of the Muskingum and Ohio rivers. The first territorial government was established under the governorship of General St. Clair. The Ordinance of 1787 was thus put into force, and was the basis of free government in a region out of which five new states have since been formed.

116. WEAKNESS OF THE CONFEDERATION (1781-1788)

Notwithstanding the good things in the Confederation and its success in dealing with the difficult problems of the western lands and territory, it showed many lines of weakness, of which the following were the most important:

(1) The organization of Congress was poor. No action could be taken unless at least two members were present from each of seven states; no important action was possible without the vote of nine states; and sometimes for weeks together there was no quorum.

(2) The powers of the Confederation were not sufficient. It had no control over commerce between the states and therefore could not prevent them from passing acts intended to hurt one another (§ 111). It could not control commerce with foreign countries. Above all it could not lay any duties or direct taxes on individuals, and the requisitions on the states barely produced enough to pay necessary salaries.

(3) No means were provided for carrying out the powers granted by the Confederation. Congress could not compel individuals to obey, and could not keep the states up to their duties.

These difficulties were clear to the thinking men in the country; and Congress tried three times to induce the states to accept

constitutional amendments which would at least have tided
over the trouble: (1) By the "Five Per Cent Scheme" (1781)
Congress would have had the power to lay a very small duty
upon imports, the proceeds to go toward paying the principal
and interest of the public debt. (2) By the "Revenue Plan"
(1783) Congress would have had the right to lay specific duties
on a very low scale. (3) The "Commerce Amendment" (1784)
would have made it possible to pass laws discriminating against
the commerce of countries which refused to make commercial
treaties. Each of the first two of these amendments received
twelve ratifications out of the necessary thirteen. The third
was ratified by only seven states.

No man in this difficult time was more persistent in urging a
strong government than George Washington, then living in re-

MOUNT VERNON, ABOUT 1830. (From an engraving by Stuart.)

tirement at Mount Vernon. In 1786 he wrote a famous letter
urging a stronger union. He complained that "Thirteen sovereignties pulling against each other, and all tugging at the
federal head, will soon bring ruin on the whole." When asked

to use his influence for reform, he replied: "Influence is no government. Let us have one by which our lives, liberties, and properties will be secured, or let us know the worst at once."

117. THE CONSTITUTIONAL CONVENTION CALLED (1786–1787)

Since Congress could not rouse the states into action, several public men suggested a special constitutional convention. A meeting of delegates from five states at Annapolis (September, 1786) proposed that a general convention meet in Philadelphia to prepare amendments to the Articles of Confederation. Under this unofficial call some of the states began to elect delegates, and Congress then reluctantly issued a formal call for a convention "for the sole and express purpose of revising the Articles of Confederation, and reporting to Congress and the several legislatures, such alterations and provisions therein, as shall, when agreed to in Congress and confirmed by the states, render the federal constitution adequate to the exigencies of government, and the preservation of the union."

Eleven of the states responded promptly by choosing delegates. New Hampshire came in late and Rhode Island paid no attention to the Convention. Among the fifty-five members of the Convention were some of the greatest Americans, including eight signers of the Declaration of Independence. The heavy work fell on a few leaders. Benjamin Franklin was old, but as shrewd as ever. Alexander Hamilton, one of the most impetuous members of the Convention, took too extreme ground and lost influence. William Paterson of New Jersey spoke for the small states. James Wilson of Pennsylvania, later a justice of the federal Supreme Court, was the keenest constitutional lawyer. The strongest group of the Convention was the Virginia delegation, including George Washington, who gave it prestige throughout the country.

The man who did most to harmonize the sharp differences in the Convention was James Madison of Virginia. In 1787

Madison was only thirty-six years old.   A graduate of Princeton
College, he had seen service in the Virginia legislature and

GEORGE WASHINGTON IN 1784.   (From Wright's portrait.)

in Congress, where he learned to know the difficulties of the
Confederation.   He was a studious man, and before the Convention began sent for all the books that he could find on the

history of earlier confederations, and prepared a sort of summary of those books, which he sent to Washington. He also consulted with his friends in Virginia and elsewhere, and drew up the strongly federal "Virginia Plan" or "Randolph Plan" as a basis of argument.

At the beginning of the Convention it occurred to Madison that posterity would be interested in the debates; and as there were no reporters, he took down in shorthand an abbreviated or concentrated statement of the debates, which he wrote out in the evenings and submitted to the speakers. In these discussions Madison himself took part more than fifty times, and throughout he advocated a national government, well knit, strong, and empowered to carry out its own just authority. As a representative of the largest and most populous state in the Union, the members from the small states sometimes thought him unfair; but in a quiet and sagacious way he often suggested a middle course, and few things against which he argued were adopted.

118. BLOCKING OUT THE CONSTITUTION (1787)

The Convention met in Philadelphia in May, 1787, and chose Washington to be its president. It then settled to work under the "Virginia Plan." May 30, the Convention agreed, as its first formal resolution: "That a national government ought to be established, consisting of a supreme legislative, executive, and judiciary." This meant that the Convention did not consider itself bound by its original call simply to modify the Articles of Confederation.

Four other plans were suggested in the course of the Convention, but none of them were adopted: (1) the Connecticut Plan, which would have given more powers to Congress, without otherwise improving the Articles of Confederation; (2) the New Jersey Plan, which stood for the views of the small states and would have kept equal representation for the states in Congress; (3) Hamilton's Plan, a highly centralized scheme with a President and a Senate chosen for life, and the states shorn of much of their power; (4) Pinckney's Plan, the details of which are not completely known.

In coming to a conclusion, the Convention sensibly made use of the previous experience of the English government, the colonies, the states, and the Confederation. For instance, they gave the President a limited veto power because that system had worked well in Massachusetts. At the same time they discarded provisions that had worked ill, such as the nine-states rule, and substituted methods which they had seen working well elsewhere.

119. COMPROMISES OF THE CONSTITUTION (1787)

Notwithstanding the good will and the skill of the members · of the Convention, they came near breaking up on several questions which involved the rivalry of the geographical sections and of the farming, business, and planting interests. These difficulties were finally settled by three great compromises:

(1) The "Connecticut Compromise" adjusted the question of representation in Congress between the small states that wanted one house with an equal vote, as in the old Congress, and the large states that stood out for two houses with representation in both proportional to population. So obstinate and bitter were both sides that Franklin feared lest "our projects will be confounded, and we ourselves shall become a reproach and bye word down to future ages." He therefore moved that the Convention be opened every day with prayer. A Connecticut member threw out the suggestion that the people ought to be represented in one branch, and the states in the other; and this idea was carried out (July 16) by an agreement that there should be an equal vote of states in the Senate and a proportional representation in the House.

(2) The second serious question involved slavery. Northern members proposed that direct taxes should be apportioned to the states in proportion to the total population, both free and slave. Southern members insisted that slaves ought not to be counted

on the same basis as freemen. The result was a compromise by a vote (July 12) that, both in distributing representatives to the House and in laying direct taxes, slaves should be taken into account at three fifths of their total number.

(3) On two questions of commerce there-were further differences between North and South. Northern members wanted power to lay navigation acts that would give special assistance to American shipping, though they would probably raise the freights on southern exports. But some members from the far South were strongly opposed to the regulation of the slave trade by Congress. A compromise was arranged (August 25) which left Congress free to pass acts in aid of American shipping, but withheld for twenty years the power to prohibit the slave trade.

Between May 17, when the Convention met, and September 17, when the final form was presented for signature by the members, the Convention debated the whole groundwork of the document three different times, and gradually the details were worked in. At the end, several delegates had gone home in disgust; and three members who were present refused to sign the completed work. Thirty-nine of the original fifty-five members, however, representing twelve states, affixed their signatures to the Constitution. Madison records that, at this solemn moment, Franklin called the attention of the members to the sun painted behind the president's chair. "I have," said he, "often and often, in the course of the session, and the vicissitudes of my hopes and fears as to its issue, looked at that behind the president, without being able to tell whether it was rising or setting; but now, at length, I have the happiness to know that it is a rising, and not a setting sun."

120. SUBSTANCE OF THE CONSTITUTION (1787)

The document sent out to the states for ratification was not a revision of the Articles of Confederation, but a complete new Constitution which has proved available for the nation ever since. (See Appendix E.)

(1) In its form, it was a great improvement because it replaced the clumsy Congress with a government of three distinct departments of government, the Legislative, the Executive, and the Judicial, on the model of the state governments.

(2) The powers of the federal government were much enlarged, and included authority to raise money by its own taxation of individuals, power to control the territory belonging to the United States, power to admit new states into the Union, and large powers over foreign and interstate commerce.

(3) Sufficient means of enforcing its powers were at last bestowed on the federal government: through the federal courts, it could punish those who disobeyed the national laws, and the states could be kept in their orbits by decisions of the United States Supreme Court.

(4) The division of powers between the states and the Union was made definite, and the states once for all gave up their former control over foreign commerce, paper money, and many other subjects. By the clause authorizing the United States to control "commerce between the states," power was given which a century later resulted in control of railroads and interstate corporations by the federal government.

121. STRUGGLE OVER RATIFICATION (1787–1788)

The Convention wisely provided that the Constitution was to go into effect as soon as nine state conventions should have ratified it, thus avoiding the fatal requirement of unanimous consent which had prevented the amendment of the Articles of Confederation. The friends of the new Constitution gave themselves the name of "Federalists," to indicate that the system which they favored was not centralized but federal, and preserved the proper rights of the states. Their opponents could think of no better title than "Anti-Federalists."

Both sides issued pamphlets and published elaborate letters in the newspapers. The most famous of these arguments was a series of essays skillfully defending the Constitution, written by Alexander Hamilton, James Madison, and John Jay, which appeared for many weeks in succession in New York newspapers over the name *Federalist*. To this day the *Federalist* remains one of the wisest and best discussions of the Constitution.

All the states except Rhode Island called the necessary state conventions, and the fight over the Constitution raged from end to end of the land. The Anti-Federalists predicted that Congress would overawe the states, that the President would prove a despot, and that the courts would destroy liberty, while the Senate would be a stronghold of aristocracy. In one state convention a member objected that "if there be no religious test required, pagans, deists, and Mohametans might obtain offices among us, and that the senators and representatives might be pagans." The point most criticized was the lack of a bill of rights, such as was found in all the state constitutions.

In five states, however, the Federalists had an easy task: Delaware was first to ratify (December 7, 1787), and that by a unanimous vote; the great influence of Pennsylvania was thrown into the same scale (December 12) by a vote of 46 to 23; next came unanimous ratification by New Jersey (December 18), and by Georgia (January 2, 1788); Connecticut followed, after a hot discussion, by a vote of 128 to 40 (January 9).

The first dangerous contest was in Massachusetts, where the majority of the delegates elected were against the Constitution, for reasons well stated by a country member: "These lawyers, and men of learning and moneyed men that talk so finely, and gloss over matters so smoothly, and make us poor illiterate people swallow down the pill, expect to get into Congress themselves; they expect to be the managers of this Constitution, and get all the power and all the money into their own hands, and then they will swallow up all us little folks, like the great Leviathan, Mr. President — yes, just as the whale swallowed up Jonah. That is what I am afraid of." The balance of power in the convention was held by its president, John Hancock, who was kept away at first by a convenient attack of the celebrated "Hancock gout." He had to be secured by promising him the governorship and hinting at the presidency of the United States. As a last resort, the friends of the Constitution agreed that certain amendments be added, not as a condition of ratification, but as a strong suggestion. With all these influences, on the test vote (February 6, 1788), Massachusetts ratified by only 187 votes to 168.

The contest in Massachusetts was the crisis of the Constitution, for the result greatly influenced other states. Maryland ratified by a vote of 63 to 11 (April 28); South Carolina ratified

The Ninth PILLAR erected !

"The Ratification of the Conventions of nine States, shall be sufficient for the establishment of this Constitution, between the States so ratifying the same." *Art.* vii.

INCIPIENT MAGNI PROCEDERE MENSES.

ADOPTION OF THE CONSTITUTION, 1788. (From the *Independent Chronicle.*)

by a vote of 149 to 73 (May 23); and New Hampshire, by a vote of 57 to 46, made herself the ninth state and completed "the federal arch" (June 21).

The Virginia convention supposed that their state would be necessary to make nine. Madison was strongly for the Constitution, and Washington threw all his mighty influence in its favor. The strongest opponent was Patrick Henry, who did not shine as a logician. When taxes came to be discussed, he exclaimed: "I never will give up that darling word 'requisition': my country may give it up; a majority may wrest it from me, but I will never give it up till my grave." After the greatest exertions, Madison succeeded in having the long list of proposed amendments made a "recommendation" and not a con-

dition of ratification; and the Constitution was ratified by the
narrow vote of 89 to 79 (June 25, 1788).

The New York convention was at first hostile to the Constitution, and Governor George Clinton, the political chief of the
state, appeared in the convention to oppose it. Its successful
champion was Alexander Hamilton. Again the plan of a con-
ditional ratification was proposed, but finally by the close vote
of 30 to 27 New York ratified (July 26, 1788), "in full confidence" that certain changes would be made after the new government should be organized.

For some time two states still held off. The North Carolina convention adjourned without taking a vote, but a second
convention was called which duly ratified the Constitution
(November 21, 1789). Rhode Island at this time called no convention, but was brought to terms later, when Congress proposed to treat it as a foreign nation; and she completed the
roll of thirteen ratifying states (May 29, 1790).

122. REVIEW

From 1781 to 1788 the affairs of the Union were carried on
by the Congress of the Confederation, acting under the Articles
of Confederation. This government obtained a favorable treaty
of peace from Great Britain, which acknowledged the independence of the United States, and accepted as boundaries the Mississippi on the west, the Great Lakes on the north, and the parallel
of 31° on the south.

Congress was distressed over national finances, unable to pay
off any part of the national debt or to keep up the interest. It
could not obtain the much desired treaties of commerce with
Spain and Great Britain, because the states would not agree
to national control of foreign commerce. Though the country
was growing in population and wealth it felt poor, and some of
the states passed trick laws for the relief of debtors. Several
revolutionary movements alarmed the country, especially the
Shays Rebellion of Massachusetts. The beginning of a future

division was seen when the northern states began to emancipate the slaves, thus creating two groups of states in the Union.

During this period, most of the states which claimed western lands ceded to the federal government all or a great part of their claims. Congress provided for surveying the West into mile-square blocks, and began to sell land to companies. The people of Tennessee and Kentucky set up short-lived governments of their own. Congress created the first territorial government, by the Northwest Ordinance of 1787.

Congress was a badly organized, weak body, and could not secure amendments from the states to enlarge its powers, because the unanimous vote of all thirteen was necessary. Hence a Constitutional Convention was called by Congress (1786).

In that Convention, which sat in 1787, a new document was drawn up, which sought by judicious compromises to secure the support of most of the country. With great difficulty it was ratified by nine states, which were enough to put it in motion. The other four states soon ratified the Constitution and thus completed the "more perfect Union."

References Bearing on the Text and Topics

Geography and Maps. See maps, pp. 164, 176, 179. — Avery, U.S., VI. — Becker, Beginnings, 272. — Bogart, Econ. Hist., 32, 145. — Coman, Indust. Hist., 129, 159, 161, 163. — Epoch Maps, no. vi. — Fish, Am. Dipl., 47, 70; Am. Nationality, 23, 486. — Johnson, Union and Democracy, 1, 9, 37, 39, 42. — McLaughlin, Confederation and Constitution. — Shepherd, Hist. Atlas, 196.

Secondary. Bassett, U.S., 214–216, 222–254. — Channing, U.S., III. chs. xii, xv–xvii. — Coman, Indust. Hist. (rev. ed.), 106–131. — Farrand, Framing of the Constitution. — Fish, Am. Dipl., chs. v–vii. — Fiske, Critical Period. — Foster, Century of Dipl., ch. ii. — Hunt, James Madison, chs. vi–xvi. — Johnson, Union and Democracy, chs. i, ii. — Lodge, George Washington, I. ch. xi, II. ch. i; Alexander Hamilton, ch. iv. — McLaughlin, Confederation and Constitution. — McMaster, U.S., I. 103–423, 436–524; III. 89–116. — Morse, John Adams, ch. ix; Benjamin Franklin, chs. xiv, xv; Thomas Jefferson, chs. vi, viii. — Phillips, West in Dipl. of the Rev. — Roosevelt, Winning of the West, III. — Sparks, Expansion, chs. vii–xi. — Treat, Land Sys-

tem, chs. i, ii. — Tyler, *Patrick Henry*, chs. xvii–xix. — Walker, *Making of the Nation*, 1–62. — Winsor, *Westward Movement*, 225–374.

Sources. *Am. Hist. Leaflets*, nos. 8, 22, 28, 32. — Beard, *Readings*, §§ 14–21. — Bogart and Thompson, *Readings*, 179, 185–200. — Callender, *Econ. Hist.*, 183–235. — Farrand, *Records of the Federal Convention.* — Harding, *Select Orations*, nos. 6–9. — Hart, *Contemporaries*, II. §§ 215–220, III. 37–75 ; *Patriots and Statesmen*, II. 172–176, 191–361 passim. — Hill, *Liberty Docs.*, chs. xvi, xvii. — Johnson, *Readings*, §§ 18–21, 26–39. — Munro, *Selections from the Federalist.* — *Old South Leaflets*, nos. 1, 12, 13, 15, 16, 40, 70, 99, 127, 186, 197.

Illustrative. Atherton, *The Conqueror* (Hamilton). — Bellamy, *Duke of Stockbridge* (Shays's Rebellion). — Bird, *Nick of the Woods* (Ky.). — Gray, *Kentucky Chronicle.* — Hopkinson, *Essays.*

Pictures. Avery, *U.S.*, VI. — *Mentor*, serial no. 75. — Sparks, *Expansion.* — Wilson, *Am. People*, III.

Topics Answerable from the References Above

(1) Service under the Confederation of : Robert R. Livingston ; *or* Robert Morris ; *or* Henry Knox. [§ 107] — (2) Service in foreign countries of : John Adams ; *or* John Jay ; *or* Henry Laurens. [§ 108] — (3) Depreciation of Revolutionary paper money. [§ 109] — (4) The Shays Rebellion. [§ 111] — (5) The state of Franklin. [§ 114] — (6) First western settlement by the Ohio Company. [§ 115] — (7) How was the Northwest Ordinance secured? [§ 115] — (8) Washington's opinions of the Confederation. [§ 116] — (9) Services in the Federal Convention of *one* of the following statesmen : Hamilton ; Paterson ; Wilson ; Randolph ; Madison ; Johnson ; Sherman. [§ 117] — (10) Members of the Convention who did not sign the Constitution. [§ 119] — (11) Ratification of the Constitution in *one* of the thirteen original states. [§ 121]

Topics for Further Search

(12) Were the envoys justified in breaking their instructions in 1782 ? [§ 108] — (13) Facts about the British carrying off negro slaves. [§ 110] (14) Effect of the " Stay and Tender " laws. [§ 111] — (15) Why did the northern states prohibit slavery? [§ 112] — (16) Why did the seven states give up their western claims? [§ 113] — (17) Reason for the failure of *one* of the following Constitutional Amendments : Five Per Cent ; Revenue ; Commerce. [§ 116] — (18) Defenders of small states, *or* of slavery, *or* of the slave trade, in the Convention. [§ 119]

CHAPTER XI

THE ORIGINAL PEOPLE OF THE FEDERAL UNION (1780-1800)

123. THE POPULATION

WHAT were the numbers, characteristics, and capacities of the people who made and adopted the federal Constitution? The census of 1790 showed a total population of 3,930,000, not including about 80,000 Indians. Of these, 60,000 were free negroes and 700,000 more were slaves. In the remaining 3,170,000 persons the English race was predominant in all of the states. There were perhaps 300,000 Scotch-Irish, chiefly along the frontier; a small but persistent Dutch element in New York; over 175,000 Germans, mostly in Pennsylvania and the West; and a small Huguenot element in South Carolina. Over nine tenths of the people lived

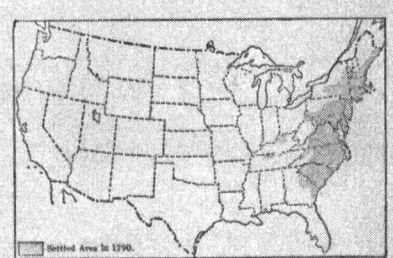

SETTLED AREA IN 1790.

in the country. In 1790 the only places having a population greater than 8000 were Philadelphia, with about 42,000 people (including suburbs); the city of New York, with 33,000; Boston, with 18,000; Charleston, with 16,000; and Baltimore, with 14,000. Only about one twentieth of the whole population lived west of the crest of the Appalachians; and Louisville was the farthest town on the Ohio River.

124. FARMING

Nearly all the white men in America worked on farms at least part of the year, and most of them on their own farms, and their life was much like that of the colonists (§ 72). Northern farmers raised vegetables for their own use, hay for their stock, corn and other grain, in some places hemp and flax, and salted down pork and beef. The most valuable crop was wheat, cultivated from New England to Virginia, and forming the basis of a large export of grain and flour. In Maryland and Virginia tobacco was still abundant, while South Carolina raised rice and still a little indigo.

WALL PAPER USED IN THE PERRY HOUSE, KEENE, N. H.

For an example of prosperity, take a French traveler's account of a Quaker family living near Philadelphia. The three daughters, beautiful, easy in their manners, and modest in their deportment, helped the mother in the household. The father was constantly in the fields, where he grew wheat and other crops. He had an excellent garden and orchard, ten horses, a big corn house, a barn full of wheat, oats, and other grain, a dairy, in which the family made excellent cheese. "Their sheep give them wool of which the cloth is made that covers the father and the children. This cloth is spun in the house, wove and fulled in the neighborhood. All the linen is made in the house."

125. Free Labor and Slavery

The farmers for the most part had large families and hence did not need to hire much labor. There was a good demand for handicraftsmen, such as shoemakers, harness makers, and tailors. Their wages were in purchasing value only about half what wages are to-day, but every wage earner who had the ambition and enterprise and industry could strike out for himself, by taking up land and starting a farm.

Much of the hard labor was done by slaves (§ 75). They were commonly treated with kindness, but there were instances everywhere of cruel treatment. In Georgia and South Carolina, — where in 1790, out of 330,000 people, 136,000 were negro slaves, — much of the labor was exceptionally hard. In all the South the cotton crop was small and of little value, because it took so much labor to clear the seed out of the fiber. In 1794 Eli Whitney, a Yankee schoolmaster living in Georgia, invented the cotton gin, a simple machine which could do the work of scores of men. This made cotton cultivation very profitable and the production of cotton rose from a few hundred bales in 1790 to 600,000 bales in 1820; and the growing of this crop led to an increased demand for slave labor.

Manufactures, except shipbuilding, were not much developed in America in 1800. A little iron and some steel were made, all of it with charcoal. Carpet weaving and broom making had sprung up, and Philadelphia exported from 200,000 to 350,000 barrels of flour every year; this industry was aided by Oliver Evans's invention of the endless band elevator, to carry grain and flour from floor to floor. In such manufactures nearly all the workmen were free laborers.

126. Trade and Business

The shipping trade again became prosperous after the war, and new avenues of commerce were opened. In 1784 the ship *Empress of China* made the first voyage from the

United States to China, and brought home as part of her freight 300,000 silver dollars. A profitable trade ensued with China, India, and the east coast of Africa. About 7000 men were engaged in the cod fishery, and several thousand in the whale fishery. The near-by fur trade fell off as settlers pushed westward, but John Jacob Astor, a New York merchant, made what was then considered the enormous fortune of over a million dollars, by developing the business in the far Northwest.

As an example of the rich and influential class of American merchants, let us take John Hancock of Boston (§§ 76, 121). He bought ships, sold ships, and chartered ships to carry his cargoes. He bought and sold country produce, and exported fish, whale oil and whalebone, pot and pearl ashes, naval stores (pitch, tar, and turpentine), lumber, masts, and ship timber. He imported dress goods for men and women, manufactures of all kinds, and coal. The Hancock firm also did a banking business, lent money, held mortgages and placed them for friends, and issued drafts upon their London correspondents.

In contrast with the great merchant was the country storekeeper, with his shelves of hardware, cotton goods, and a few groceries, with plenty of hard liquors.

127. Roads and Waterways

Interior commerce was hampered by a lack of roads and waterways; but there was a lively coasting trade along the Atlantic.

Tolerable wagon roads were built about 1790 from Philadelphia, through Bedford in southern Pennsylvania, to Pittsburgh; and later from Cumberland on the upper Potomac to the Monongahela River. The so-called Wilderness Road, marked out by Daniel Boone, the only direct overland route into Kentucky, was widened into a wagon track (1795) and served as the principal highway into the Southwest (map, page 268).

About this time, a new method of road making was introduced from England: a layer of large stones, a foot or more in depth, was first put down, and on it was laid a crowning of small, angular stones. Under travel these consolidated, making a smooth, hard surface. Many such roads, called "turnpikes" or "stone pikes," were built in America by individuals or corporations, beginning with a stretch from Philadelphia to Lancaster (1792); and large streams were bridged. On such roads and bridges the owners charged toll.

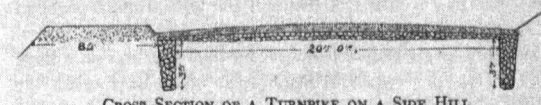

CROSS SECTION OF A TURNPIKE ON A SIDE HILL.

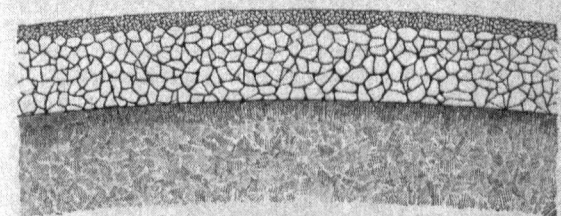

CROSS SECTION OF A TURNPIKE. (Showing arrangement of layers of stone.)

The second half of the eighteenth century was a period of canal building in England, and the system spread to America. After the Revolution Washington visited the upper Potomac and Mohawk valleys, and suggested building canals to the West by both routes. The governments of Maryland and Virginia thereupon united in a plan for improving the navigation of the Potomac. A little later a traveler named Elkanah Watson formed "the sublime plan of opening an uninterrupted water communication from the Hudson to Lake Ontario." A few canals were actually built, or begun, in the decade from 1793 to 1803, notably the Santee in South Carolina, the Dismal Swamp in Virginia and North Carolina, and the Middlesex from Boston to Lowell.

128. INVENTIONS AND MACHINERY

To carry on the new enterprises, there was a rapid development of joint stock companies after 1790. Insurance, bridge, and turnpike companies, manufacturing concerns, and especially banks were chartered by the state legislatures. All of these companies had special charters and the legislatures were beset by demands to grant privileges to new corporations.

We are now accustomed to rely, for manufactures on a large scale, on steam power and machinery, which have taken the

MACHINERY IN SAMUEL SLATER'S MILL.

place of the old hand labor. It is hard to realize now that, at the beginning of the nineteenth century, the only motive force for erecting buildings, for making iron or cloth, for all the farm work and transportation, was the muscles of men and animals, except wind, water power, or the tide, by which a few mills were run. In 1800 there was hardly a steam engine in America, and not a power loom.

The making of woolen and cotton cloth was aided about the time of the Revolution by four English inventions: Hargreaves's "spinning jenny" (1767); Arkwright's spinning frame (1769); Crompton's mule spinner (1779); and Cartwright's power loom (1785). The first spinning machinery in the United States was made by Samuel Slater of Pawtucket, Rhode Island, in 1790, and that started the woolen, cotton, and hemp mills of the United States. The first power loom here was set up by F. C. Lowell at Waltham, Massachusetts, in 1813.

Several other important inventions can be traced back to this period, such as Oliver Evans's power dredge, and Jacob Perkins's nail-making machine. The renowned Yankee industry of clock making on a large scale was also begun by Eli Terry at Plymouth, Connecticut. The use of steam for propelling ships was suggested by two American inventors. John Fitch put a boat on the Delaware propelled by a steam engine at a speed of seven miles an hour (1786), and James Rumsey ran a steam craft of another type on the Potomac River (1787). Washington predicted that Rumsey's invention would solve the problem of water transportation.

129. SPIRIT OF HUMANITY

Another proof that America was changing was a new spirit of humanity and sympathy. Throughout the world during the eighteenth century, the family, the school, the shop, and especially the jail, abounded in cruelty. The constable beat the vagrant, the master workman beat the apprentice, the farmer beat the indentured servant or maid, the planter beat the slave. The insane man or woman was treated literally as a beast — chained, starved, and flogged. The criminal or the man charged with crime was brutalized in a poisonous and stifling jail, a school of criminals. Americans who won the battles of the Revolution, and the sailors in John Paul Jones's ships, were often half starved and were beaten by their own officers. Debtors might in any state in the

Union be lodged in jail and kept there the best of their lives for a petty debt.

Such oppression and disregard of one's neighbor were not only contrary to Christianity, but were also opposed to the great Revolutionary doctrine of the equality of man, set forth in the bills of rights of every state constitution. Equality was so well carried out that foreign travelers were amazed to see innkeepers sit down with their guests, and to hear that military officers were chosen by their men. Gradually benevolent societies began to spring up in aid of the weak and helpless, and a new sense arose of the duty of the community to all its people. Moreover, this feeling of sympathy and responsibility began to extend to the slaves. Hence Thomas Jefferson, born and bred a slaveholder, wrote in 1781: "Can the liberties of a nation be thought secure when we have removed their only firm basis, a conviction in the minds of the people that these liberties are of the gift of God? That they are not to be violated but with his wrath? Indeed I tremble for my country when I reflect that God is just; that his justice cannot sleep forever."

130. DEMOCRATIC SPIRIT

Notwithstanding the bold assertion that the people had the "right to govern themselves," the United States from 1780 to 1800 was far from being a thoroughgoing democracy. In the New England states, the ministers and the merchants were still practically an aristocracy, holding, as John Adams put it, that "the rich and the well-born and the able must be separated from the mass and placed by themselves." Even the little New England town meetings were not free from the mastery of the local squire. A satirist poked fun at them as follows:

> "Yet at town meetings ev'ry chief
> Pinn'd faith on great M'Fingal's sleeve,
> And as he motion'd, all by rote
> Rais'd sympathetic hands to vote."

Pennsylvania, New Jersey, and Virginia farmers were not

influenced so much by great family names as by political organizations. The first state nominating convention was held in Pennsylvania in 1788. Two years later Senator Maclay observed that in New York, "The Sons of St. Tammany had a grand parade through the town in Indian dresses. . . . There seems to be some kind of scheme laid of erecting some kind of order or society under this denomination." Within ten years, the Tammany Society did develop into a political force. However, the organization of the New York voters remained in the hands of two rival clans, the friends of the Livingstons and the friends of the Clintons, who early developed the practice, whenever they got into power, of turning their political opponents out of office.

131. SCHOOL LIFE AND COLLEGES

After the Revolution the opportunities for education rapidly increased in the United States (§ 51). New England kept up rural schools in hundreds of "district schoolhouses," which received both boys and girls as young as two years old. The teachers were slenderly paid, and were "boarded round" from family to family in the district. Similar public common schools were organized in the Northwest. Neither the middle states nor the South set up common schools till much later. Most of the towns in the Union had schools, usually supported by fees. In attending such a school in Philadelphia, Alexander Graydon read Latin fables, learned Roman history, fought the other boys, was flogged by his teacher, and when fourteen years old had read Ovid, Vergil, Cæsar, and Sallust, and was reading Horace and Cicero.

For secondary education New England developed a system of endowed academies which spread into the middle states and West. Among them were the two Phillips Academies of Andover and Exeter, and the Lexington (Kentucky) Grammar School. Such a thing as a public high school existed only in a few favored New England towns; but wealthy families

SAMPLER EMBROIDERED BY A LITTLE GIRL.

throughout the Union often had private tutors for their children. Several new colleges also were founded: the University of Pennsylvania was reorganized and put on a collegiate basis (1799); and in 1795 was established the germ of the University of North Carolina, the first state institution of the kind. The first professional schools in the United States were two medical schools founded in Philadelphia and Boston.

The formal education of girls stopped in what we should call the grammar grade; but the daughters of well-to-do families embroidered, tapped the harpsichord, and read good books; and there were some girls' boarding schools.

132. LITERATURE AND ART

The United States still had no genuinely national literature, for most of the authors followed English models and were very dull. The most admired American poets were Philip Freneau, who wrote stirring patriotic songs during the Revolution, and Joel Barlow, whose epic, *The Vision of Columbus*, is a weak imitation of Pope's *Homer's Iliad*. The only satirist and essayist of the time who is now much read was Benjamin Franklin, decidedly the most distinguished American author of the eighteenth century.

The one field of literature in which Americans excelled

was in the writings of public men, who furnished a new stock of political ideas to the world. Some of these books are descriptive, like Jefferson's famous *Notes on Virginia;* others are discussions of public questions, like the *Federalist,* and Alexander Hamilton's financial reports. George Washington wrote admirable letters on public questions.

The fondness of Americans for newspapers and periodicals showed itself in the first daily newspaper, the *Pennsylvania Packet,* founded in 1784. The newspapers were dull; they had no editorials, few advertisements, and filled many columns with reprints from foreign newspapers, and with long-winded essays on politics.

St. Michael's Church, Charleston, Built in 1761. (Type of massive stone church.)

Two literary magazines were founded about this time: the *Universal Asylum and Columbian Magazine,* of Philadelphia, and the *Boston Magazine.*

Some notable artists appeared in this period — especially Benjamin West, who went to England and was very successful there; and the portrait artists Copley, Gilbert Stuart, and Trumbull, to whom we owe our knowledge of the appearance of many of the great men of the time.

The most notable American art was the architecture of the best houses and public buildings. Such residences as the Chew House in Germantown (p. 117) and the Harrison house in Virginia, are among the best examples of American architecture. All over the eastern states are still to be seen good courthouses and other public buildings and a few good church buildings of the time: for example, the Old South Church in Boston, Trinity Church and St. Paul's in New York, and St. Michael's in Charleston (p. 203).

133. Religion and the Churches

The churches and other religious bodies were still, as in colonial times (§ 54), the greatest moral and intellectual interest

Square-pewed Church, Salisbury, Mass., Built in 1791. (Type of eighteenth-century meetinghouse.)

of the times. After the Revolution, most of the great churches in America sought to organize in a national way so as to fit in with the national life.

(1) As a logical result of their theories of republican government, the southern states withdrew their public support of the Episcopal Church (§ 54). In 1784 Samuel Seabury was consecrated as Bishop of Connecticut at Aberdeen, Scotland; he came over, and in 1785 was held the first general convention of the Protestant Episcopal Church in the United States.

(2) The Methodist Church, founded by Wesley and Whitefield (§ 56), began its American organization in 1784, when the Methodists summoned a national conference, which adopted the title of Methodist Episcopal and gave to Francis Asbury and Thomas Coke the title of Superintendent, later Bishop.

(3) The long prejudice against the Catholics softened, and several states put them on an equal footing with the Protestants. In 1789 one of the Maryland Carrolls was made Catholic bishop of Baltimore and thus that church was formally organized in the United States.

(4) Another type of church government was established when in 1789 the Presbyterian local synods united in "the General

QUAKER MEETING, 1809. (From Kendall's *Travels.*)

Assembly of the Presbyterian Church in the United States of America," which has ever since been the supreme governing body of that church. The Dutch Reformed Church of New York and New Jersey, though closely akin to the Presbyterian in doctrine, kept its separate synod.

(5) The thousand Congregational churches in New England were nearly all supported by taxation, and each was its own highest tribunal; for there was no general convention.

(6) The Quakers also practiced local self-government; and

both Quakers and Methodists freely admitted women to take part in their service.

Among the many other Protestant denominations were the German Lutherans, the Moravians or United Brethren, and Dunkards; and the Mennonites, none of whom would take an oath, or fight, or accept office, or go to law. The Universalists had a few congregations. The curious communities known as the Shakers were founded during the Revolution by Anna Lee, whom her followers called the Elect Lady, or Mother Ann.

SHAKER DANCE, ABOUT 1830.   (From a contemporary print.)

The Jews had synagogues in some large places, but no central organization. On the frontier, religion was emotional. There was a great revival of religion in 1800, and the "camp meeting" was invented in Kentucky.

All the churches enjoyed the greatest religious freedom that had ever been known in the history of mankind. Each denomination selected its ministers, laid down its doctrine, and disciplined its members in its own way. For the individual there was equal freedom. The federal Constitution of 1787 prohibited any religious test for federal office; and the states in course of time removed most of the religious qualifications both for voters and for public officers.

134. REVIEW

To describe the American people just after the Revolution is a hard task, because there was no single kind of American people. Nearly a fifth of the whole population was negro. About a fifth of the white people were Scotch-Irish, German, or Dutch. The cities were few and small.

After 1794 the cotton gin made cotton a profitable crop.

Manufactures for general markets began to appear, manned by free workmen. A new shipping trade sprang up with the Orient, and large business houses and local merchants increased. Wagon roads were extended into the far West, and in the older parts of the country stone roads or turnpikes were built, and a few canals were opened. Numerous corporations were formed for banks, insurance companies, road companies, and manufacturing companies; textile machinery was introduced; and efforts were made to invent practical steamboats.

After a long period of disregard for the rights of the poor and weak, the humanitarian spirit of the Revolution was applied to better the conditions of the unfortunate, the poor, and the slave. Steps were taken toward a more democratic type of government; for the Americans still felt a deference toward what John Adams called "the rich, the well-born, and the able."

The schools of some states shared in this democratic spirit, for common schools were established for both boys and girls. Academies began to increase and a few colleges were founded. This period witnessed the growth of genuine American literature and architecture. Many religious denominations in the country provided themselves with national organizations. The people began to feel that they belonged to one nation.

References Bearing on the Text and Topics

Geography and Maps. See map, p. 268. Johnson, *Union and Democracy*, 49, 125. — See U. S. Supt. of Docs., *Geog. and Explor. List*.

Secondary. Adams, *U.S.*, I. 1–184. — Bassett, *Federalist System*, chs. x–xiii. — Bogart, *Econ. Hist.*, chs. x, xi. — Fish, *Am. Nationality*, ch. i. — Fiske, *Critical Period*, 50–89. — Hunt, *James Madison*, 67–86. — Locke, *Antislavery*, 88–111, 166–197. — McMaster, *U.S.*, I. 1–102, 423–436, II. 1–24, 57–66, 158–165, 538–582, III. 514–516, V. 268–284. — Merwin, *Thomas Jefferson*, 45–58. — Rhodes, *U.S.*, I. 3–27. — Schouler, *U.S.*, I. 1–12, 221–241. — Sparks, *Expansion*, 135–187. — Weeden, *New Engl.* II. 816–875. — See also references to chapter vi.

Sources. Bogart and Thompson, *Readings*, 181–184, 200–208, 219–234, 240, 252–275. — Bowne, *Girl's Life Eighty Years Ago.* — Caldwell and Persinger, *Source History*, 246–264. — Grant, *Memoirs of an Am. Lady.* — Graydon, *Memoirs.* — Hart, *Contemporaries*, III. §§ 10–36; *Patriots and Statesmen*, II. 168–172, 185–190, 241–250, 291–293, 368, 378–381, III. 32–34, 67–71, 103–107, 213–215, 247. — James, *Readings*, §§ 39–44. — Scudder, *Men and Manners in America.*

Illustrative. Barr, *Maid of Maiden Lane; Trinity Bells* (N.Y.). — Brown, *Arthur Mervyn* (Philadelphia). — Cleghorn, *Turnpike Lady.* — Earle, *Two Centuries of Costume.* — Kennedy, *Swallow Barn* (Va.). — May, *In Old Quinnebasset* (N.E.). — Shelton, *Salt-Box House*, 168–237. — Stowe, *Minister's Wooing; Oldtown Folks* (N.E.).

Pictures. Avery, *U.S.*, V–VII. — Earle's books, cited above and in refs. to ch. v. — *Mentor*, serial nos., 77, 106, 109. — Sparks, *Expansion.* — Wilson, *Am. People*, III.

Topics Answerable from the References Above

(1) Slaves on plantations in 1790. [§ 125] — (2) First American voyage to China. [§ 126] — (3) Early American turnpike roads. [§ 127] — (4) Introduction of spinning machinery by Slater. [§ 128] — (5) Steamboats of Fitch and Rumsey. [§ 128] — (6) Jefferson's opinions on slavery. [§ 129] — (7) New England district schools about 1800. [§ 131] — (8) Girls' schools about 1800. [§ 131] — (9) Characteristic letters of George Washington. [§ 132] — (10) The Shakers. [§ 133]

Topics for Further Search

(11) *One* of the following races in the United States in 1790: Scotch-Irish; Germans; English. [§ 123] — (12) Conditions in some *one* of the cities in 1790. [§ 123] — (13) Account of Whitney's cotton gin. [§ 125] — (14) Whale fishery about 1790. [§ 126] — (15) East India trade about 1800. [§ 126] — (16) The Wilderness Road. [§ 127] — (17) Early plans for an Erie Canal. [§ 127] — (18) Treatment of American sailors on their own ships. [§ 129] — (19) Origin of the Tammany Society. [§ 130] — (20) Details of the organization of some *one* of the national churches about 1800. [§ 133]

CHAPTER XII

APPLYING THE CONSTITUTION (1789-1793)

135. STARTING THE GOVERNMENT (1789-1793)

THE federal Constitution laid down the general principles of the government; but many details had to be settled by Congress, whose work in the early years was hardly less important than that of the Philadelphia Convention. The first presidential election came in 1788. There was no contest for the presidency, as everybody expected George Washington to have the first vote of every elector. John Adams was elected Vice President.

The members of Congress drifted into New York slowly, so that both houses were not organized till April 6, 1789. Frederick Muhlenberg of Pennsylvania was elected Speaker of the House of Representatives, and Vice President John Adams took his seat as presiding officer of the Senate. Then the two houses laid down rules for their procedure, and thus made precedents which now have almost the weight of law. The House from the beginning, and the Senate from 1793, have almost always sat in open session. Congress voted its members a salary of $6 (later $8) a day while in session. Committees at first were chosen by ballot in both houses, but after 1790 the House authorized the Speaker to appoint all its committees, a great power which he enjoyed until 1911. Within a few years there began to grow up a system of standing committees appointed at the beginning of each session. At last the people of the United States had a government that could govern. Ever since 1775 they had been moving toward this "more perfect union," which could pass laws binding on every person in the land.

136. THE PRESIDENT AND THE DEPARTMENTS (1789–1793)

Meanwhile, Washington arrived in New York and was received by thousands of enthusiastic people. On April 30, 1789, he was solemnly inaugurated at Federal Hall on Wall Street, where he took the oath of office, and made a simple and earnest speech. Congress voted the President $25,000 a year, the largest salary then received by any man in the United States. Washington liked ceremony, and it was un-

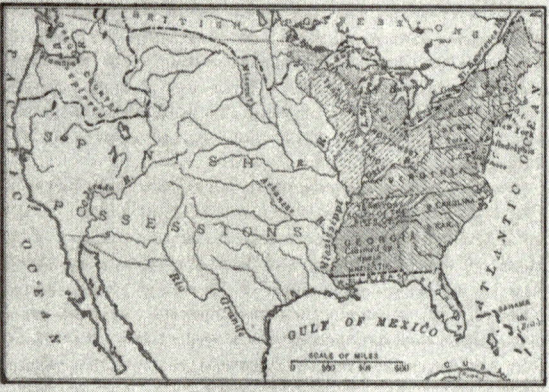

UNITED STATES IN 1790.

derstood that he approved the proposed title of "His Highness, the President of the United States of America and Protector of their Liberties," though Patrick Henry said of the title that "it squinted toward monarchy." Eventually no title was given by law; so that the official form of address to the President is simply, "Mr. President."

One of the earliest tasks of Congress was to organize the executive departments, and in its first session it created three: (1) The Department of Foreign Affairs (a name soon changed to Department of State); it was under Thomas Jefferson as Secretary of State. (2) The War Department; Henry Knox was reappointed Secretary of War. (3) The Treasury; the first Secretary of the Treasury was Alexander Hamilton. In addition, Congress created the office of Attorney-General, who later became the head of a department, but for many years had only clerks under him. The former Post Office was continued, and Samuel Osgood was appointed Postmaster-General.

All these officers were appointed by the President subject to the confirmation of the Senate. By the casting vote of John Adams in the Senate, Congress established the wholesome principle that the President should have the power of removing heads of departments and other officers without the consent of the Senate. He is thus enabled to carry on his constitutional duty "to see that the laws are faithfully executed."

The President at once began to use his constitutional right to call on the heads of departments for written opinions; and he went further by asking the three Secretaries and the Attorney-General to meet him from time to time and discuss public business. This is the beginning of the unofficial "Cabinet," to which the Secretary of the Navy, Postmaster-General, Secretary of the Interior, Secretary of Agriculture, Secretary of Commerce, and Secretary of Labor have since been added.

137. AMENDMENTS AND COURTS (1789–1793)

Another early task of Congress was the consideration of the constitutional amendments that had been recommended by state conventions. Ten amendments passed by the requisite two-thirds vote in both houses, were duly ratified by three fourths of the states, and thus became part of the Constitution (1791). These amendments formed a little bill of rights, assuring jury trial, freedom of speech and of the press, etc., against any action by the federal government, and included as the Tenth Article the important provision that "The powers not delegated to the United States by the Constitution, nor prohibited by it to the States, are reserved to the States respectively, or to the people." (See Appendix E.)

The Constitution provides that there shall be a Supreme Court and inferior courts, leaving it to Congress to settle the details. By a "Judiciary Act" (September 24, 1789) most of which is still in force, Congress created two kinds of inferior courts from which appeals could be taken to the Supreme Court. Appeals could also be taken from the highest state courts to the federal Supreme Court, in cases involving the federal law. Thus all suits turning on federal law might finally be brought before the Supreme Court of the United States, so that there should be one highest authority on federal law throughout the country.

The President at once appointed John Jay of New York to be Chief Justice. The first Supreme Court case which attracted much notice was Chisholm *vs.* Georgia in 1793, in which the court gave a decision against the state. To prevent such suits against a state by citizens of another state or of a foreign country, the Eleventh Amendment was at once proposed, and speedily added to the Constitution.

138. NATIONAL CAPITAL (1789-1790)

The location of a permanent seat of government came up in 1789 and raised a hot discussion between the northern and southern sections, both of which wanted the capital. The center of American social and political life was Philadelphia, seat of Congress during most of the Revolution. While the British were in Philadelphia, Congress sat in York, Lancaster, and Baltimore; and after Congress was insulted in its own hall by mutinous soldiers in 1783, it sat in Princeton, Trenton, Annapolis, and New York, but did not select any of them as the permanent seat of government. In a debate on the subject, a Pennsylvania member spoke for Wright's Ferry (Columbia, Pa.), and praised the fish of the Susquehanna; but a Georgian member, who did not like to travel so far, retorted, "This . . .

will blow the coals of sedition and endanger the Union. . . .
This looks like aristocracy." And a New England member
said "he did not dare to go to the Potomac. He feared that
the whole of New England would consider the Union as destroyed."

When the matter came up again in 1790, it was tangled with
a proposal that the federal government assume the outstanding state debts, which the southern members opposed and
the New England members favored. Hamilton, as a northern
man, appealed to Jefferson, over whose dining table an agreement was reached that the Virginia members would vote for
assumption, if Hamilton would find the votes necessary to fix
the capital on the Potomac; and by this compromise (it would
be called a "deal" nowadays) both measures were passed.
Eighteen million dollars was distributed among the states,
to close up their debts; and the capital was fixed for ten
years at Philadelphia, and then in a district ten miles square
to be selected by the President on the Potomac River. This
was the origin of the District of Columbia.

139. ALEXANDER HAMILTON (1789–1793)

To Alexander Hamilton the present government of the
United States owes almost as much as to Madison or to Washington; for he had the genius to think out methods of organizing the new national government. Hamilton was born in the
island of Nevis in the West Indies (1757), and was educated at
King's College, now Columbia University. When the Revolution broke out, he began to write patriotic pamphlets, then
joined the army, and attracted the notice of Washington, who
never ceased to love and admire him. He sat in the Congress
of the Confederation for a time (1782–1783), but a friend said
of him that he was not "adapted to a council composed of discordant materials, or to a people which have thirteen heads."
He was a famous lawyer, but his genius was especially fitted to
finance, and it was a national blessing when, in September,

1789, at thirty-two years of age, he was appointed Secretary of the Treasury.

It was a discouraging post. Hamilton found a debt of about $50,000,000 and no money in the treasury; the accounts were in confusion; the old paper-money notes were repudiated (§ 109), and few seemed to expect that the federal government would ever pay its bonded debt. Hamilton prepared a series of financial reports to Congress in which he laid down a system of national finance, which he pushed with such force and statesmanship that he induced Congress to accept every one of the following plans:

ALEXANDER HAMILTON. (From the portrait by Weimar.)

(1) Import duties were to provide for the interest on the public debt. (2) An excise on the manufacture of whisky would raise additional money and would make the western people understand that they had a government. (3) The debt of the United States was to be fully acknowledged, and the government was to assume the state debts, so as to interest the lenders in the success of the government. (4) A national bank was to perform the government business and furnish a safe currency.

140. PUBLIC AID TO BUSINESS (1789-1793)

What was the main reason for framing and adopting the Constitution? Was it, as some people argue nowadays, to protect the property of those who framed it and of their friends? It is true that in the old Continental Congress, in the Federal Convention, in the state legislatures, and in later congresses, there were well-to-do members who owned government securities which were increased in value by the success of the new Constitution. It was the habit of the time to choose such men to public office. There was, however, no moneyed class as we now understand it. In 1789 there were very few banks in the whole country and hardly any corporations except insurance companies. The only large business men were great merchants, who were also ship-owners. Very few men had money at interest, and those did not look upon themselves as separated from or opposed to the landowning farmers and the planters of the South.

There was a general feeling throughout the country that a new Constitution was needed in order to give business an opportunity to develop. This sentiment was shown in the settlement of the national debt, a difficult task, because many owners of certificates of that debt had bought them at a depreciation. Some members of Congress wanted to pay them at less than their face value. Hamilton insisted, and Congress agreed, that the actual legal holders of certificates ought to be paid in full, because it was to the interest of the government to borrow money in such a way that its bonds or certificates would easily pass from hand to hand without anybody's trying to figure out whether only a portion of them would be paid. In a few months, the surprised holders of government bonds began for the first time to receive regular interest on their holdings; and the result was that the certificates of the national debt quickly rose to par.

Several manufacturers sent in petitions asking Congress to pass a protective tariff; Pennsylvanians were anxious to protect "our infant manufactures." On the other hand, South Carolinians thought that protection was "big with oppression." "Middle-of-the-road men" like Madison of Virginia were opposed to protection as a system, but were willing to lay duties

in order to encourage young industries and build up the manufacture of military material. The outcome of these discussions
was the passage of the first tariff act (July 4, 1789), which was
before Hamilton came into office. It was intended to give a
little protection, though the average rate of duty was only about
8½ per cent — the lowest in our federal history. Later, at
Hamilton's suggestion, the import duties were raised a little,
and an " excise " — that is, a special tax on making liquor —
was laid on whisky (March 3, 1791), amounting to 7 or 8 cents
a gallon.

The country greatly needed a permanent specie currency;
therefore, Congress passed an act (April 2, 1792) establishing
a United States mint, to which any possessor of gold or
silver could bring gold or silver bullion and have it coined into
gold or silver pieces without charge except for the stamping.
The act also established the ratio of fifteen to one between gold
and silver; that is, $15 in gold coin was to weigh exactly as
much as $1 in silver.

Vessel owners also asked for protection through a tonnage tax which should be higher on foreign than on American
shipping. Hence Congress used the commercial power which
it received under the third compromise of the Constitution
(§ 119) by passing such a discriminating act. Some years
later, all foreign vessels were excluded from the coasting trade
between American ports.

As a result of these acts and of the prospect that the Union
would continue, exports and imports at once began to increase,
but for some years the growth was very irregular.

141. THE NATIONAL BANK (1791)

The greatest boon for business men, perhaps, was the Bank
of the United States, which was chartered by Congress (February 25, 1791) and which Hamilton looked upon as the crown
of his whole system. At this time there were only three state
banks, and the purpose of the act was to bring the banking

business chiefly under the control of the United States government, which took one fifth of the stock. The capital of
$10,000,000 was quickly subscribed and was as important in
the conditions of that time as a bank would be to-day with a
capital of $1,000,000,000.

The services which the bank was expected to perform for
business men were as follows: (1) to receive and hold deposits
of individuals; (2) to have the custody of most of the government balances; (3) to make loans to business men out of its
capital and deposits; (4) to make exchanges for individuals
and the government by receiving money at one place and paying it out at another; (5) to issue paper notes, holding a reserve of gold and silver so as to redeem on demand any that
might be presented. The chief object of the bank was even
deeper than these great services. Hamilton wanted the business
men of the country to feel that their welfare and prosperity
would be aided by a great banking corporation chartered by
the federal government.

Upon this question rose the first of many debates on the
powers of Congress under the Constitution. There was no
direct statement in that document on banks or corporations,
but Hamilton argued that the framers of the Constitution, by
giving Congress power to pass acts that are "necessary and
proper for carrying into execution the . . . powers vested by
this Constitution in the government of the United States," expected that such acts as that for the bank would be passed.
Jefferson took the line of argument to which the term "strict
construction" is often applied; viz., that the bank could not be
constitutional, because the Constitution gave no express power to
charter a corporation, and that a bank was not "necessary and
proper," since all the services which it might perform for the
government could be secured in some other way. Hamilton,
arguing from "loose construction," insisted that Congress had
the "implied power" to carry out any of its expressed powers
through a corporation, if that would do the work better; and

that "necessary and proper" did not mean "indispensable,"
but "suitable."

All the northern votes in Congress, except one, were in favor
of the act. Washington signed it, and twenty-eight years later
the Supreme Court adopted Hamilton's doctrine of implied
powers, and it is now constantly used in the legislation of Congress. The bank was at once organized, with a head office in
Philadelphia and eight branches in other cities, and proved a
safe and prosperous concern. Yet the debates brought out
the division of the people of the United States into two ways
of thought — for and against a vigorous active national government. The first appearance of national parties can be
traced back to this discussion.

142. Growth of the West (1789–1801)

The first enlargement of the Union was by the admission of
Vermont, a New England frontier community, as the 14th
state in 1791. In the following year the western territory of
Virginia, with her consent, was admitted as the state of Kentucky (15th state).

All the old questions about the right of Congress to establish
territories in the West and to regulate the settlers and the Indians were now at an end, for Congress quickly began to use its
new powers over territories and over Indian trade and tribes.
The settlers were warned not to go into the regions occupied by
the Indians; on the other hand, the Indians were induced to
cede certain lands to accommodate white settlers. Nevertheless, an Indian war burst out in the Northwest Territory and
two small armies under General Harmar and General St. Clair
were defeated by the Indians.

Washington's private secretary has recorded the President's
emotion at the news of St. Clair's defeat (1791). "And yet,
to suffer that army to be cut to pieces, hacked, butchered,
tomahawked by a surprise — the very thing I guarded him
against! O God, O God, he is worse than a murderer!" "But,"

he added, recovering himself, "General St. Clair shall have justice!" Anthony Wayne, who was now put in command, built frontier posts, thoroughly thrashed the Indians, and made possible the treaty of Greenville (1795), by which the Indians gave up the territory now composing southern and eastern Ohio.

The Southwest grew rapidly. South of Kentucky, Congress set up the "Territory South of the Ohio River" in 1790; and six years later that region came into the Union under the name of Tennessee (16th state). Still farther south the controversy over the western claims of Georgia continued; but Congress created the Mississippi Territory out of a part of the disputed land (1798), and four years later Georgia ceded everything west of her present boundary, and the long controversy as to western lands was ended (§ 105).

Meanwhile settlers were pouring into the Northwest Territory. Virginia opened up her reserve of Military Bounty Lands north of the Ohio. Then followed new communities near Chillicothe on the Scioto, and at Losantiville, now called Cincinnati. Along Lake Erie settlement began about 1795, when Connecticut sold the greater part of the Western Reserve to the Connecticut Land Company. General Moses Cleaveland, agent of the company, in 1796 founded at the mouth of the Cuyahoga, on Lake Erie, the city now called Cleveland, for the founder. Next year the "Girdled Road" was made from the Pennsylvania line along the lake to Cleveland. In 1800 the state of Connecticut ceded to the United States all jurisdiction over the Reserve, so that the lake and river settlements might be united into a new state. Indiana Territory was immediately set off, and in 1802 the people of Ohio were authorized to form a state government, and were duly admitted to the Union the next year (17th state).

143. BEGINNING OF POLITICAL PARTIES (1792)

Till about 1793 there were no national political parties, for the Anti-Federalists disappeared soon after the Constitution was adopted, and hardly a man in the country any longer criticized the Constitution. The first division on living issues came about in meetings of the Cabinet, where Jefferson says that he and Hamilton from day to day attacked each other "like cocks in a pit." The two men and their followers absolutely disagreed on the cardinal questions of the nature of government. Hamilton and his friends believed that the opinion of the educated and property-holding classes must always be the best for the ignorant and the poor. He is said to have remarked once at a dinner: "Your people, your people, sir, is a great beast." The other side was represented by Jefferson, who counted himself among "those who identify themselves with the people, have confidence in them, cherish and consider them as the most honest and safe, although not the most wise depository of the public interest."

Hamilton and his friends believed further that it was the duty of government to encourage private enterprise, and to that end laid down their principle of "loose construction" (§ 141). Jefferson's theory of "strict construction" of the Constitution was that government ought to do as little as possible, that it ought to lay taxes only for absolutely necessary expenses, and that the development of the country ought to be left to individuals.

On almost the same day (in May, 1792) Hamilton wrote that Madison and Jefferson were at the head of a "faction decidedly hostile to me, . . . and dangerous to the Union, peace and prosperity of the country"; and Jefferson described Hamilton and his friends as "monarchical federalists." In the election of 1792, though there was not a vote against Washington, there was a strong and almost successful attempt to displace Adams as Vice President; and thenceforth one body of men throughout the country took on the party name of Federalists, and the Jeffersonians called themselves Republicans.[1]

[1] This first Republican or Democratic-Republican party is not to be confused with the new party of the same name organized in 1854.

144. REVIEW

The new government was organized in 1789 and George Washington was the first President. Under the Constitution he appointed heads to the new executive departments which were created by Congress, and also the judges of the new federal courts. He invited the heads of the four principal departments to consult with him, and that is the foundation of the so-called Cabinet. Congress also organized the courts, and submitted to the state legislatures eleven constitutional amendments which were adopted. The first ten made a kind of bill of rights.

The first sharp division of opinion in Congress was over the national capital, which was finally placed on the Potomac River. To secure this result certain members of Congress agreed to vote for the assumption of the outstanding state public debts. In this transaction and in other great statutes for setting the government in motion, the leader was Alexander Hamilton, the Secretary of the Treasury. He induced Congress to fund the national debt in full; he urged a protective tariff which was passed; and he secured an excise on liquors. Hamilton's greatest triumph was the charter of a national bank (1791) in which the United States government was a stockholder. That raised the question of whether Congress had "implied powers" bearing upon matters not expressly mentioned in the Constitution.

Vermont, Kentucky, and Tennessee were admitted into the Union. The western claims of North Carolina and Georgia were ceded; Connecticut also ceded control over the so-called Western Reserve, and then Ohio was admitted (1803).

After 1793, two political parties appeared, the Federalist and the Republican, headed by Alexander Hamilton and Thomas Jefferson, and this division spread throughout the Union.

References Bearing on the Text and Topics

Geography and Maps. See maps, pp. 176, 242. Johnson, *Union and Democracy*, 59. — Semple, *Geogr. Conditions*, 75–92.

Secondary. Bassett, *Federalist System*, chs. i, iii. — Dewey, *Financial Hist.*, §§ 34–52. — Ford, *True George Washington.* — Foster, *Century of Diplomacy*, 103–135. — Gordy, *Polit. Parties*, I. 103–158. — Hinsdale, *Old Northwest*, 296–313, 368–388. — Hunt, *James Madison*, 167–212. — Johnson, *Union and Democracy*, ch. iii. — Lodge, *George Washington*, II. chs. ii, iii, vii; *Alexander Hamilton*, chs. v, vi. — McDougall, *Fugitive Slaves*, §§ 16–19. — McMaster, *U.S.*, I. 525–604, II. 24–57, 67–89, 144–154, III. 116–123. — Morse, *Thomas Jefferson*, chs. viii, ix. — Roosevelt, *Winning of the West*, IV. 1–100. — Schouler, *U.S.*, I. 70–220. — Stanwood, *Presidency*, I. chs. ii, iii. — Treat, *Land System*, ch. iv. — Walker, *Making of the Nation*, 73–114. — Winsor, *Westward Movement*, 375–574.

Sources. Ames, *State Docs. on Fed. Rels.* 1–15. — Bogart and Thompson, *Readings*, 485–490. — Hart, *Contemporaries*, III. §§ 76–89; *Patriots and Statesmen*, II. 363–367, 372–378, 381–383. — Johnson, *Readings*, §§ 46–67. — MacDonald, *Select Docs.*, nos. 6–12. — Maclay, *Journal.* — *Old South Leaflets*, nos. 10, 74. — See New Engl. Hist. Teachers' Assoc., *Hist. Sources*, § 80; *Syllabus*, 334–336.

Illustrative. Allen, *Choir Invisible* (Ky.). — Cooper, *Pioneers.* — Hale, *East and West* (N. W. Terr.). — Paulding, *Westward Ho!* (Ky.).

Pictures. Avery, *U.S.*, VII. — Wilson, *Am. People*, III.

Topics Answerable from the References Above

(1) Washington's journey from Virginia to New York. [§ 136] — (2) John Jay as Chief Justice. [§ 137] — (3) The first ten constitutional amendments. [§ 137] — (4) The Eleventh Amendment. [§ 137] — (5) Laying out of the city of Washington. [§ 138] — (6) Alexander Hamilton as a young man. [§ 139] — (7) Admission of *one* of the following states: Vermont; Kentucky; Tennessee; Ohio. [§ 142] — (8) Account of Indiana Territory. [§ 142]

Topics for Further Search

(9) Early cabinet meetings. [§ 136] — (10) Was the Constitution made by capitalists? [§ 140] — (11) Early arguments for, *or* against, a protective tariff. [§ 140] — (12) Early arguments for, *or* against, a national bank. [§ 141] — (13) Account of the Indian wars on the northwest frontier. [§ 142] — (14) Early settlements on the south shore of Lake Erie. [§ 142] — (15) What Jefferson and Hamilton thought about each other. [§ 143]

CHAPTER XIII

BEGINNING OF PARTY POLITICS (1793-1801)

145. RELATIONS WITH FRANCE (1789-1793)

THE Federalist leaders had to deal not only with the great problem of organizing a system of government and business that would serve the needs of the nation, but also with difficult and dangerous relations toward foreign nations. Before the new system was fairly in operation, the great French Revolution of 1789 broke out. In 1792 France was declared a republic; soon after, King Louis XVI was executed by his people and the French republic declared war against Great Britain and Spain. The national sympathy of America went out to France as a friend, ally, and sister republic, apparently struggling against tyranny. Furthermore, by the treaty of 1778 the United States was bound to defend the French West Indies in case of "defensive war." Since the British had recently been enemies, and were still on bad terms with the United States, the French government expected that the United States would directly, or by secret aid, join in the war against Great Britain and Spain; and they sent over a new ambassador, Edmond Genêt, to bring about that result.

When the news of the outbreak of war was received in America, Congress was not in session, and President Washington decided quickly that the country was in no condition for war. Even Jefferson, whom Hamilton accused of "a womanish attachment for France and a womanish resentment against England," reluctantly admitted that the treaty of 1778 could not be justly applied to the changed conditions of the time.

The President accordingly (April 22, 1793) issued what is usually called the "Proclamation of Neutrality," a declaration that the United States would "pursue a conduct friendly and impartial towards the belligerent powers." This was clear evidence that the United States would not take sides in the war. Genêt had already landed in Charleston (April 8, 1793), and began to issue privateering commissions to Americans and to enlist them for the French service. He was received in Philadelphia with enthusiasm, and the friends of France — chiefly Republicans — formed "Democratic clubs" on the model of the French revolutionary clubs. Genêt at first accepted the Proclamation of Neutrality, but he did not scruple to enlist men in the West for an expedition to capture New Orleans from the Spanish, a plan which pleased the Kentuckians. Then he lost his judgment, and in his violence and fury overreached himself: he fitted out a cruiser, the *Petit Democrat*, in Philadelphia, and, in defiance of Jefferson's protest, sent her to sea. He lost standing further by trying to force Washington to call an extra session of Congress. In December, 1793, his own government was weary of him, and sent a recall.

146. NEUTRAL TRADE AND IMPRESSMENTS (1793-1794)

The naval war involved all the principal European maritime nations: Dutch, Spanish, French, and British merchantmen were chased on every sea. The United States unexpectedly became the principal neutral, but Great Britain quickly showed unwelcome views as to the rights of neutrals; and since there was no commercial treaty between the two countries, they fell back on uncertain and disputed principles of international law:

(1) The United States admitted that neutral ships could be captured anywhere on the sea if bound to a port actually blockaded by men of war; but the British claimed the same right of capture on a "paper blockade"; that is, a mere notice, not backed up by a blockading fleet.

(2) The United States admitted the right to capture ships having on board "contraband," meaning military stores destined for an enemy; but the British claimed that provisions were also contraband, and therefore seized American food ships bound to French ports.

(3) The United States insisted that "free ships make free goods"; that is, that an American ship was not subject to capture simply because it had the property of French subjects on board. The British took such ships wherever they could find them.

(4) Great Britain, under what was called the "Rule of 1756," proceeded to capture American vessels carrying cargoes from French colonies to American ports, because such trade had not been allowed by France in time of peace.

Forthwith scores of American ships were taken as prizes by British cruisers and privateers. So far as they had opportunity, the French were as violent as the English; they seized provision ships and British goods in American ships.

The trouble was aggravated by the method of recruiting for British ships of war by "impressing" (seizing) sailors on shore, or from British merchant ships. Under the theory that a man born in England remained an Englishman as long as he lived, the British freely extended their impressment to persons under the protection of the United States: (1) to English sailors employed in American ships; (2) to Englishmen born, who were naturalized in the United States; (3) sometimes to Englishmen born who were American citizens before the treaty of peace; (4) frequently to American sailors born in America, and no more subject to Great Britain than to China.

For this and other outrages, Congress in April, 1794, was on the point of declaring war against Great Britain, but once more Washington's calm good sense saved the country from a great danger. He nominated John Jay, then Chief Justice of the United States, as special envoy to make a last remonstrance to Great Britain.

147. PEACE WITH GREAT BRITAIN AND SPAIN (1794-1795)

After nearly four months' negotiation, Jay signed a treaty in London (November 19, 1794) which was intended to settle all but one of the four controversies then outstanding:

(1) The British agreed to carry out the treaty of 1783, by evacuating the undisputed American territory (§ 110); but then and thereafter they would make no compensation for slaves carried away in 1783. On the other hand, the United States undertook to make compensation to British merchants who had not been able to collect debts due in 1775; later a lump sum of about $3,000,000 was paid by the United States on that score. The loyalist question was dropped, and never revived.

(2) For the capture of American vessels, the British government agreed to make a compensation, if a commission of arbitration so decided; and eventually paid about $1,000,000. Jay gave up the principle that "free ships make free goods" (§ 146), and agreed that provisions under some circumstances might be held contraband.

(3) A commercial treaty to last a term of years was negotiated; but the British, who in 1783 had limited the trade between the United States and the West Indies to British ships (§ 110), refused to open it to American ships.

(4) On impressment, Jay could get no agreement.

In general, the Jay treaty did not satisfy the shipowners and commercial people, and all the weight of Washington's influence was necessary to induce the Senate to ratify it by the bare two-thirds majority of 20 to 10. The House at first showed a strong inclination to refuse the appropriation necessary to carry out the treaty, but voted the money at last; and war with Great Britain was thus averted.

Meanwhile a very favorable settlement was made with Spain by a treaty of 1795, which gave us: (1) some desired commercial arrangements; (2) the still more desired navigation of the Mississippi; (3) an acknowledgment of the southern boundary as laid down by the British treaty of 1783.

148. WHISKY INSURRECTION (1794)

While Jay was negotiating his treaty, trouble broke out in western Pennsylvania, where the national "excise" duties on the manufacture of liquors, though low, were felt by the many small distillers. Discontent arose till several hundred armed men attacked the house of Inspector General Neville, and it was plundered and burned (1794). The mail from Pittsburgh eastward was robbed, and about seven thousand men assembled at Braddock's Field and marched to Pittsburgh to intimidate the town.

Since Governor Mifflin of Pennsylvania would not act, Washington disregarded him and called out thirteen thousand militia from New Jersey, Pennsylvania, Maryland, and Virginia. In October the little army crossed the mountains and came down into the western counties, but found not an insurrectionist in arms, for most of the people who were wanted had decamped. Two men were later found guilty of treason by the courts for their share in the rising and were sentenced to death, but were pardoned by the President. In his messages to Congress, Washington stated that the rebellion was due to "certain combinations of men," or, as the Senate put it, to "self-created societies"; that is, to the Democratic clubs founded in 1793. The criticism went home; and Jefferson and his friends — though they had no part in instigating the rebellion — soon thought it desirable to employ a party name which had not such associations with France, and began again to call themselves Republicans.

149. RETIREMENT OF WASHINGTON (1796–1797)

Throughout this difficult period, George Washington was the most clear-headed and unyielding friend of good national government. As President he showed a remarkable power to judge and select men. It was a great trial to Washington that after 1792 the newspapers began to abuse him, and even his friend Jefferson wrote a letter criticizing him, to a foreign correspondent named Mazzei, which found its way into print. Jefferson tells us that one day at a cabinet meeting the President vehemently declared "that he had never repented but once the having slipped the moment of resigning his office, and that was every moment since, that . . . he had rather be on his farm than to be made emperor of the world, and yet that they were charging him with wanting to be a king!"

In his celebrated farewell address of September 17, 1796 (composed in part by Hamilton, but full of Washington's principles), Washington rose to the highest patriotism and statesmanship. He urged union of the North and South, union of the East and West, a union which would be in danger if the United States took sides with either party in the European wars. Hence he advised his countrymen to keep out of "permanent alliances with any portion of the foreign world."

As Washington expected to retire to private life, the two political parties each tried to elect his successor in the presidential election of 1796; and by the close electoral vote of 71 to 68, Vice President Adams was elected President. The Federalists did not unite on any one candidate for Vice President; and the rival candidate for President, Thomas Jefferson, was elected to the lower office.

150. PRESIDENT JOHN ADAMS (1797-1801)

John Adams of Massachusetts was one of the two or three men most responsible for the Revolution. He served in the two Continental Congresses, then was minister to France and to Holland, and was one of the commissioners of the Treaty of Paris (1782). In 1785 he was sent as the first American minister to Great Britain, and when the king laughingly hinted that Adams was no friend to France, he replied aptly, "That opinion, sir, is not mistaken; I must avow to your Majesty, I have no attachment but to my own country."

After eight years' service as Vice President, Adams became President in 1797; and he made the mistake of adopting his predecessor's Cabinet, which felt itself superior to its chief and which took counsel with his personal enemy Hamilton. Adams finally dismissed Timothy Pickering, Secretary of State; after that he had some peace and comfort in Cabinet meetings. During his term the government moved to the new capital at Washington, and Adams was the first President to occupy the White House.

In getting out of trouble with Great Britain, the United States was plunged a second time into difficulty with the French, who felt the bitterest resentment over the Jay treaty, because it gave to Great Britain privileges which were denied to France. In retaliation, the French in 1796 again began to seize American vessels; and when Charles C. Pinckney arrived in Paris with a commission as minister, he was warned to leave France. In a message on this insult (May 16, 1797) Adams said, "Such attempts ought to be repelled with a decision which shall convince France and the world that we are not a degraded people, humiliated under a colonial spirit of fear and sense of inferiority."

JOHN ADAMS, 1783. (In court dress; from the portrait by Copley.)

151. THE X. Y. Z. CONTROVERSY (1797-1798)

Still Adams could not bear to see his country drawn into war if he could help it, and he therefore commissioned Pinckney,

John Marshall of Virginia (two Federalists), and Elbridge Gerry of Massachusetts (a Republican) to make a last effort to come to an understanding with France. After some months, dispatches arrived, stating that the French government, incensed at Adams's message, refused officially to receive the commissioners; and that three men, called in the dispatches "X., Y., and Z.," came unofficially to inform them that if they wanted a treaty, they must furnish a quarter of a million dollars "for the pocket of the Directory and ministers." When Mr. X. said plainly to the envoys, "Gentlemen, you do not speak to the point; it is money: it is expected that you will offer money," they responded firmly, "No, no, no; not a sixpence." And the President thereon notified Congress (June 27, 1798), "I will never send another minister to France without assurances that he will be received, respected, and honored as becomes the representative of a great, free, powerful, and independent nation."

152. Alien and Sedition Acts, and State Sovereignty (1798–1800)

Adams's protest at the shameful attempt to exact bribes from American ministers raised him to the highest popularity of his whole life. Songs were written in his honor, among them Hopkinson's *Hail Columbia*. The Republicans were so stunned by the behavior of France that they could not stop four sweeping pieces of anti-French legislation by Congress in 1798, commonly called the "Alien and Sedition Acts": (1) a Naturalization Act raising the required term of residence to fourteen years; (2) the Alien Friends Act, authorizing the President to expel aliens in time of peace; (3) the Alien Enemies Act, for the expulsion of aliens (by which was meant Frenchmen) in time of war; (4) the Sedition Act, making it a crime to publish libels against the government, or Congress, or the President. The Sedition Act was passed because the Republican pro-French newspaper press was violent and abusive; as an example the

Federalists quoted from the *Aurora*, which they thought to be an organ of Jefferson, an article that called Adams "a person without patriotism, without philosophy, without a taste for the fine arts — a mock monarch."

The problem of the Republicans was how they could get rid of these offensive and partisan statutes; and their solution was to accuse the Federalist Congress of exercising powers which really belonged to the states. This led to the first public arguments that the states were not necessarily bound by acts of Congress. Late in 1798 the "Virginia and Kentucky Resolutions" were passed by the legislatures of those states. They attacked the Alien and Sedition Acts as being contrary to the superior force of the Constitution and held that they were "not law but utterly void and of no force."

The Virginia Resolution was drawn up by Madison; and, though it was not known till afterwards, Jefferson framed the Kentucky Resolution and also a second and stronger Kentucky Resolution a year later. This second resolution contained the dangerous declaration that "nullification by those sovereignties [the states] of all unauthorized acts done under that instrument [the federal Constitution] is the rightful remedy." These resolutions, which were really a kind of political platform, attracted great attention throughout the country; and the consequent popular criticism of the Alien and Sedition Acts in the end caused the defeat of the Federalist party.

This contest brought out clearly for the first time the States Rights theory of the government which appeared again in later times. According to this doctrine the states were sovereign from the beginning of the Revolution and remained sovereign after the Constitution went into force.

153. FRENCH NAVAL WAR (1798–1800)

After the X. Y. Z. affair, there seemed nothing for it but war with France. In 1798 Congress declared the treaties of 1778 at an end, and began to add to the little fleet; and the

Navy Department was organized, with a Secretary. Congress could not quite bring itself to declare war; but it did authorize the capture of French cruisers and, under some circumstances,

NAPOLEON BONAPARTE. (From the painting by Delaroche.)

of merchantmen, by warships and by American privateers, of which 365 were commissioned in a single year. The American frigate *Constellation* captured the French frigate *Insurgente*, and the *Boston* took the French corvette *Berceau.*

Just at this time, Napoleon Bonaparte rose to supreme power in France; and he saw no object in fighting America. Indirectly he sent word that he was willing to make peace, and Adams, against the advice of his party friends and his Cabinet, in 1799 directed negotiations resulting in a treaty of peace (September 30, 1800), which for a time safeguarded American neutral trade.

154. ELECTION OF JEFFERSON (1800–1801)

The death of Washington, in 1799, took away the balance wheel of American politics, for Adams offended his party associates and never had any hold on the Republicans. Several prosecutions of Republican journalists under the Sedition Act were unfairly pressed; and such a protest was made that the

Federalists were startled at their own work. Meanwhile the Federalist journals were allowed to indulge in publications which were at least as scurrilous as those of their opponents.

As the time drew on for the presidential election of 1800, a long-standing feud between Hamilton and Adams came to the surface, but Hamilton could not prevent his rival from again receiving the Federalist nomination. Jefferson, the candidate of the Republicans, was supported by Aaron Burr, of New York, who was nominated for Vice President; and that state changed over from the Federalist column. The result was that the Republican candidates got 73 electoral votes and Adams got only 65. John Adams and his party were defeated.

Every Republican elector voted both for Jefferson and for Burr, so that there was a technical tie. As the Constitution then stood, the House had the power to select between these two men, each state delegation casting one vote. The Federalists had the majority by states, and, in the face of the intention of the Republican voters to make Jefferson President, many of the Federalists voted for Burr, and came near electing him. Jefferson and his friends were furious, and even Hamilton advised his friends to vote for Jefferson, who in the end was chosen (February 17, 1801) by 10 states to 4. The Federalists looked on the success of Jefferson as the undoing of all their efforts to establish a firm government; and their conduct left in Jefferson's mind a strong feeling of injury. This dangerous crisis, in which the will of the people was almost set aside through an imperfection in the Constitution, led to the proposal of the Twelfth Amendment (ratified September, 1804) under which the President and Vice President are voted for separately.

155. REVIEW

Party divisions in the United States were much affected by the outbreak of war in Europe, in which France and Great Britain were the leading powers (1793). In the course of the French Revolution of 1789 France became a republic. The

President issued a proclamation of neutrality, which was a decision that the United States would not take part in the war with either side; and the French minister, Genêt, did his best to destroy that policy.

Great Britain on its side began to seize American neutral merchant ships on various pretexts which were denied by the United States, and came near bringing on war, but peace was kept by the Jay treaty (1794), which included a commercial agreement with Great Britain. The Spanish government also made a treaty giving us the use of the lower Mississippi (1795).

Meantime the people of western Pennsylvania were incensed by the collection of the excise on the manufacture of liquor, and in the bloodless Whisky Insurrection (1794) tested the power of the government to defend itself.

President Washington retired in 1797 after publishing a patriotic farewell address. John Adams, who succeeded as President, was not a tactful or discreet man; but he stood for the rights of his country when assailed by France in the X. Y. Z. controversy (1797). The Federalist Congress, however, passed the Alien and Sedition Acts of 1798. The legislatures of Virginia

WHITE HOUSE, WASHINGTON   (Begun, 1792; occupied by Adams, 1800; burned, 1814; rebuilt, 1818; restored, 1903.)

and Kentucky retorted with resolutions which called the attention of the country to the principle of state sovereignty. The United States drifted into a brief and eventless naval war with France; but Napoleon Bonaparte, as head of the French nation, made peace in 1800. Shortly after, Thomas Jefferson was elected President against Adams; and after a struggle to overcome the technicalities of the method of choosing the President, he duly took office and the Republicans thus came to power for the first time.

References Bearing on the Text and Topics

Geography and Maps. Avery, *U.S.*, VII. — Bassett, *Federalist System*, 58, 70, 168, 176, 290. — Shepherd, *Hist. Atlas*, 196.

Secondary. Allen, *Naval War with France*. — Bassett, *Federalist System*, chs. iv–ix, xiv–xix. — Conant, *Alex. Hamilton*, 100–135. — Fish, *Am. Diplomacy*, chs. viii–xi; *Am. Nationality*, 56–85. — Gordy, *Polit. Parties*, I. 159–382. — Hart, *Formation of the Union*, §§ 83–92. — Hunt, *James Madison*, 213–270. — Johnson, *Union and Democracy*, chs. iv–vi. — Lodge, *Alex. Hamilton*, chs. vii–ix; *George Washington*, II. chs. iv–vi. — McMaster, *U.S.*, II. 89–144, 165–537. — Maclay, *U.S. Navy*, I. 155–213. — Mahan, *Sea Power in Rel. to War of 1812*, I. 68–99. — Morse, *Thos. Jefferson*, chs. x–xii; *John Adams*, 251–318. — Roosevelt, *Winning of the West*, IV. 101–257; *Gouverneur Morris*, ch. x. — Schouler, *U.S.*, I. 238–314. — Stanwood, *Presidency*, I. chs. iv, v. — Stevens, *Albert Gallatin*, chs. iv, v. — Wilson, *Am. People*, III. 128–163. — Woodburn, *Polit. Parties*, ch. ii.

Sources. *Am. Hist. Leaflets*, no. 15. — Ames, *State Docs. on Fed. Relations*, 15–26. — Harding, *Select Orations*, nos. 10, 11. — Hart, *Contemporaries*, III. §§ 90–105; *Patriots and Statesmen*, III. 15–51, 34–67, 72–85; *Source Book*, §§ 74–77. — Hill, *Liberty Docs.*, ch. xviii. — James, *Readings*, §§ 47–51. — Johnson, *Readings*, §§ 68–70. — Johnston, *Am. Orations*, I. 84–143. — MacDonald, *Select Docs.*, nos. 13–23. — *Old South Leaflets*, nos. 4, 38, 103. — Univ. of Pa., *Translations and Reprints*, VI. no. 2. — See New Engl. Hist. Teachers' Assoc., *Hist. Sources*, § 80; *Syllabus*, 336, 337.

Illustrative. Brackenridge, *Modern Chivalry* (Whisky Rebellion). — Cooper, *Miles Wallingford*. — Eggleston, *Am. War Ballads*, I. 102–112. — Goodloe, *Calvert of Strathore* (France). — Mitchell, *Red City*. — Seawell, *Little Jarvis* (French War).

Pictures. Avery, *U.S.*, VII. — Wilson, *Am. People*, III.

Topics Answerable from References Above

(1) The Proclamation of Neutrality. [§ 145] — (2) Incidents of Genêt's mission. [§ 145] — (3) Incidents of the capture of American ships by the British, *or* by the French. [§ 146] — (4) Incidents of impressment of American seamen. [§ 146] — (5) Jay's experiences in London. [§ 147] — (6) Incidents of the Whisky Insurrection. [§ 148] — (7) Abuse of President Washington by the press. [§ 149] — (8) John Adams as Vice President. [§ 150] — (9) Why did John Adams quarrel with his Cabinet? [§ 150] — (10) Incidents of the naval war with France. [§ 153]

Topics for Further Search

(11) Why was there a French Revolution? [§ 145] — (12) Why did Washington retire from the presidency? [§ 149] — (13) Who were X., Y., and Z.? [§ 151] — (14) Objections to the Alien Friends Act, *or* to the Sedition Act. [§ 152] — (15) Interest of Napoleon Bonaparte in the United States. [§ 153] — (16) Aaron Burr as a politician. [§ 154] — (17) Account of the Twelfth Amendment. [§ 154]

CHAPTER XIV

EXPANSION OF THE REPUBLIC (1801-1809)

156. THOMAS JEFFERSON AND HIS DEMOCRACY

THE history of the United States from 1801 to 1809 might be grouped about the life of the President, Thomas Jefferson; the people liked him and Congress followed him. Born in 1743, the son of a Virginia planter, a graduate of William and Mary College, owner of land and slaves, Jefferson nevertheless had a Yankee love of novelty, an interest in all sorts of farm machinery, sciences, and discoveries. A visitor said of him that he was "at once a musician, skilled in drawing, a geometrician, an astronomer, a natural philosopher, and statesman." In

THOMAS JEFFERSON, ABOUT 1800. (From the portrait by Stuart.)

public service he had a wonderful career. He was a member of the Virginia Assembly at twenty-six years of age, then of the Continental Congress, then governor of Virginia (1779-1781), then two years a member of the Congress of the Confederation, then ambassador to France for five years, then Secretary of State (1790–1793), then Vice President (1797–1801).

This highly aristocratic and intellectual gentleman preached extreme doctrines of political equality and popular government. As President he insisted on what he called "republican simplicity" in the White House and in public intercourse. Hence he began the practice of making all presidential communications to Congress in written messages, instead of formal addresses to Congress in person. He was a strong advocate of local government on the New England town-meeting plan, and of public education. All his theories of government were founded on confidence in the average man; he opposed the use of force even to keep public order. Jefferson was never a good speaker and disliked appearing in public; yet no man of his time had such influence over the people. He found his principle of political equality in the minds of his countrymen; he stated it and made it familiar. In the end it led to the granting of manhood suffrage regardless of ownership of property, payment of taxes, or religious belief.

One of Jefferson's favorite beliefs was that governments ought to do as little as possible. Hence, as soon as he became President, he began to cut down the small army and navy, and to reduce the national debt. In this policy he had the aid of his Secretary of the Treasury, Albert Gallatin of Pennsylvania, a Genevan by birth, a member of Congress from 1795 to 1801, where he was a powerful critic of Hamilton's finance, and an able and honest statesman. Gallatin at once set to work to extinguish the national debt, a task which Jefferson said was "vital to the destinies of our government." In 1801 it stood at $83,000,000, but it was brought down in 1812 to $45,000,000.

Jefferson's love of peace was sorely tried by the pirates of Morocco, Algiers, Tripoli, and Tunis, who captured vessels and enslaved the crews. Like most nations, the United States paid

an annual tribute to these ruffians; but the more the pirates
got, the more dissatisfied they were. The pasha of Tripoli said,
"We are all hungry and if we are not provided for, we soon get
sick and peevish." Jefferson had to use the navy when Tripoli
declared war on the United States. From 1801 to 1805 American squadrons fought the Tripolitan pirates till the pasha
gave in. Decatur, Bainbridge, and other naval commanders
rendered good service. Tunis, Algiers, and Morocco yielded
without serious fighting. A little tribute was paid by the United
States to these piratical states till 1815.

157. THE OFFICEHOLDERS (1801–1805)

Jefferson's party friends put great pressure on him to follow
the practice usual in the politics of New York, Pennsylvania,
and other states, by turning out the federal officeholders,
nearly all of whom were Federalists. In his inaugural address,
March 4, 1801, Jefferson tried to soothe his political opponents.
"We have called by different names brethren of the same
principle," said he; "we are all Republicans, we are all Federalists." Later he announced that he would appoint none but
Republicans, until the Republicans and Federalists in office
were about equal; "after which," said he, "I . . . shall return
with joy to that state of things when the only questions concerning a candidate shall be, Is he honest? Is he capable?
Is he faithful to the Constitution?" Before he could reach
that point, he removed or replaced 109 civil officials, or about
one third of all the officeholders filling important posts.

In the last days of Adams's term twenty-four new judicial
officers were created — often called "midnight judges." Jefferson was furious at what he called Adams's indecent conduct
"in crowding of appointments . . . after he knew he was making them . . . not for himself, even to nine o'clock of the night
at twelve o'clock of which he was to go out of office." Therefore, in the first session of the Republican Congress, the new
judgeships were abolished (1802), and Adams's appointees lost

their places. When the Supreme Court, in the case of Marbury *vs.* Madison (1803), tried to protect some minor officers, whom Jefferson had refused to recognize, Jefferson's friends retorted by an unsuccessful attempt to impeach and remove Samuel Chase, one of the Supreme Court justices.

158. THE LOUISIANA QUESTION (1763-1803)

Jefferson was a man who felt strongly the duty of looking out for the nation's interest; and he was greatly aroused by a change in the ownership of Louisiana. Napoleon Bonaparte (§ 153) was just then at peace with Great Britain, and formed a scheme of colonial empire, for which he wanted Louisiana.

What was Louisiana? To answer this question we must keep in mind that the regions east and west of the Mississippi River had not the same territorial history. Both sides were claimed by France under La Salle's discoveries and the first colony of 1699 (§§ 62, 63). In 1763 the whole eastern half, except the Island of Orleans (the triangle between the Mississippi, the Bayou Manchac, and the Gulf, including New Orleans), was ceded to Great Britain and ceased to be reckoned as part of Louisiana. The cession included the strip along the Gulf coast from the Island of Orleans to the river Perdido, to which the British gave the name of West Florida. The remainder of Louisiana, including the whole western half, together with the Island of Orleans, went to Spain (§ 69). During the Revolution, Spain conquered from Great Britain part of West Florida. In 1800, by the treaty of San Ildefonso, Napoleon received back "the colony or province of Louisiana, with the same extent that it now has in the hands of Spain, and that it had when France possessed it." The greatest military power in the world thus again became the possessor of both banks of the lower Mississippi and a near neighbor to the United States.

The natural uneasiness of the Americans, when in 1802 they heard of this change, was heightened when the Spanish governor withdrew the privilege of sending goods through New

Orleans free of duty, which had been secured by the treaty of
1795 (§ 147). Plainly, he meant to turn over the province to
France with the river blocked to American trade. Hence it
was that Jefferson wrote to Robert R. Livingston, our minister
in France: "There is on the globe one single spot, the possessor
of which is our natural and habitual enemy. It is New Orleans.
The day that France takes possession of New Orleans . . .
from that moment, we must marry ourselves to the British
fleet and nation."

A party in Congress wanted to take New Orleans by military force; and an act was passed authorizing 80,000 volunteers. Jefferson was cooler. He instructed Livingston to
attempt the purchase of the Island of Orleans and the strip to
the eastward, between the southern boundary of the United
States and the Gulf. In January, 1803, he designated his
friend James Monroe as a special envoy to France to aid Livingston. Fortunately for America, Napoleon was already
tired of his own plan, for war with Great Britain was about to
break out again, and it would be impossible for him to protect
the sea route to Louisiana. Meanwhile he failed to reconquer
the necessary halfway station of Haiti, where Toussaint L'Ou-
verture, a negro general, aided by fever, had the impertinence
to destroy 10,000 of his best troops.

159. PURCHASE OF LOUISIANA (1803)

Therefore, while Livingston was trying to buy West Florida
and New Orleans, suddenly the French foreign office asked him
what he would give for the whole of Louisiana. One day later
Monroe arrived, and the two ministers did not hesitate to go
beyond their instructions by accepting the offer, but for some
weeks haggled over the price. The treaty was completed April
30, 1803; the United States was to pay $11,250,000 in cash and
$3,750,000 to American claimants against the French govern-
ment, a total of $15,000,000; in return Napoleon ceded all
Louisiana, including the Island of Orleans and the whole

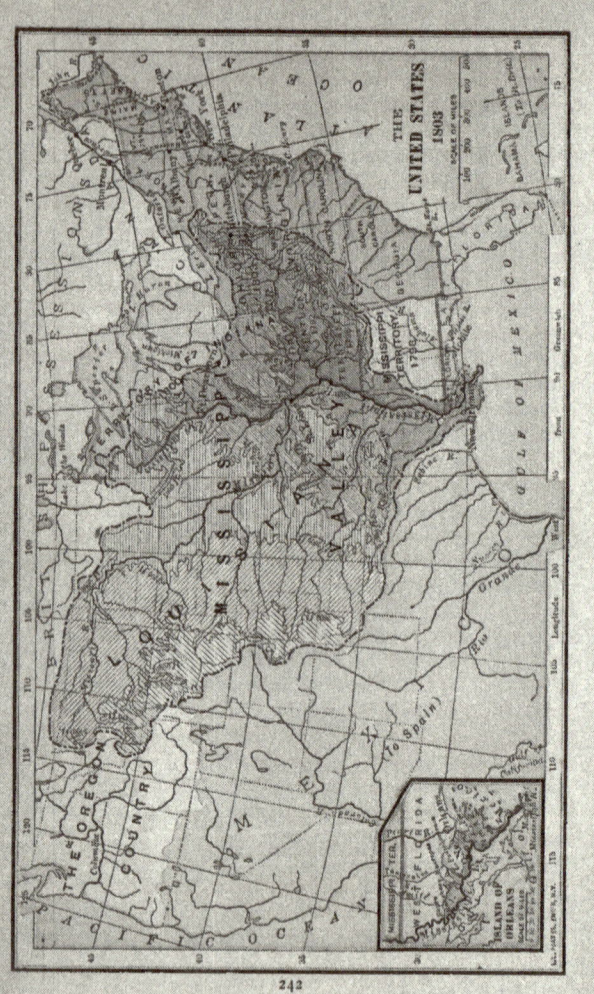

THE
UNITED STATES
1803

western part of the valley of the Mississippi, with an area of
885,000 square miles. Livingston, Monroe, and Jefferson
each thought that he was responsible for this splendid addition to the territory of the United States. In reality, Louisiana
came like a plum dropping from the tree; but Jefferson is
fairly entitled to the credit of seeing more clearly than any other
man of his time the danger of France becoming a neighbor, and
the possibilities of the West.

Since there was nothing in the Constitution on the question
of annexing territory, Jefferson asked for a constitutional
amendment; but his friends found authority in the old Federalist doctrine of implied powers, and the treaty was promptly
ratified. Notwithstanding protests by some of the New England Federalists, the next step was to take possession of the
new country; New Orleans was turned over by the Spanish
commander to a French officer (November 30, 1803), and
twenty days thereafter was formally ceded by the Frenchman
to the United States; though the distant Spanish post of
St. Louis was not transferred till March, 1804.

The population of the new acquisition was about 40,000,
almost entirely settled along the water fronts of the Mississippi
and Red rivers. Congress speedily passed an act organizing
the lower part of Louisiana as the Territory of Orleans, with
an appointed legislature. The people of New Orleans were in
an uproar. They did not like the new laws, the new language,
or the new governor, and Congress good-naturedly gave them
a territorial government with an elective legislature (March,
1805). Seven years later an act was passed for the admission
of this small part of the old province of Louisiana as "Louisiana," an equal state in the Union (18th).

The annexation of Louisiana soon led to serious boundary
controversies with Spain. The treaty of 1803 contained no
description of Louisiana except the phrase of the treaty of
San Ildefonso: "with the same extent that it now has in the
hands of Spain, and that it had when France possessed it";

but "in the hands of Spain" Louisiana did not include West
Florida; while "as France possessed it" Louisiana extended
to the Perdido. The Spanish government insisted that their
cession of Louisiana in 1800 was not intended to include West
Florida, and the French supported that contention. Yet
Livingston, who had started out to purchase West Florida,
could not give up the idea that he had secured it as part of
Louisiana, and Jefferson soon took up that belief, which was
held for many years.

Spain was in possession of the disputed strip, and refused to
give it up. In 1810 the United States annexed part of the
region, and in 1811 Congress passed a secret act authorizing
the President to take East Florida also; but it was not till 1813
that the whole even of the West Florida claim was occupied.

160. Reaching out for Oregon (1792–1811)

Jefferson was the first man to see the possibilities on the
northwestern Pacific coast, where in 1792 Captain Gray, in
the ship *Columbia* of Boston, had found the mouth of a great
river, and named it for his ship. As soon as Jefferson became
President, he induced Congress to provide for an overland
expedition to this Oregon country, under the command of
William Clark and Meriwether Lewis, Jefferson's private secretary. By the time this expedition left St. Louis (May 14,
1804), the whole Missouri valley had become part of the United
States, by the annexation of Louisiana. In the course of six
months, the party of 45 men ascended the Missouri 1600 miles.
They camped all winter, and in the spring of 1805, 31 of them
started northwest, under the guidance of the Indian "Bird
Woman," who carried her child on her back. In August, 1805,
they reached a point on the Missouri River where a man could
bestride it; and then they struck across the mountains on horse-
back and found a westward-flowing river; following down, they
reached the mouth of the Columbia River (November 15, 1805),
4000 miles from St. Louis.

This expedition through a country absolutely unknown to
white men, opened up half a continent; and it was the second
link (following Gray's discovery) in the chain that bound
Oregon to the United States. Eventually it gave the United
States a Pacific sea front, and opened a broad window toward
the Pacific islands and Asia. In 1811 John Jacob Astor forged

EXPLORATIONS OF LEWIS AND CLARK, AND PIKE.

the third link of our possession by establishing a fur-trading
post at Astoria, on the south side of the Columbia.

Meanwhile, in 1806, Lieutenant Zebulon Pike, with a command of United States troops, approached the northern boundary of Louisiana in an exploration up the Mississippi River to
find its source. On another expedition he made his way westward overland, discovered Pikes Peak, and came out beyond
our boundaries in New Mexico.

161. BURR INSURRECTION (1806)

Another difficulty arose in Louisiana in 1806 through the
ambition of Aaron Burr. His willingness to accept the presidency in 1801 (§ 154) was never forgiven by Jefferson; and in
the presidential election of 1804 George Clinton of New York
was put in his place for Vice President. Jefferson and Clinton
swept the country; the Federalist candidates got only 14

electoral votes. Meanwhile Burr was defeated as independent candidate for governor of New York, and laid this defeat to Alexander Hamilton. Burr, therefore, forced a duel on Hamilton and killed him.

When his term as Vice President expired in 1805, Burr was a desperate man. Being indicted for the murder of Hamilton, he thought it prudent to go west for a time, and returned with vague schemes for settling or conquering a region in the Southwest on, or more probably beyond, the Spanish boundary. He raised a few score men, and floated down the Ohio River (December, 1806) into the Mississippi. His friend, and, as he hoped, his partner, James Wilkinson, general of the United States army, played him false. Hastily making an agreement that the Sabine River should be the temporary boundary of Louisiana, Wilkinson hurried to New Orleans, arrested some of Burr's followers, and forwarded to Jefferson a letter from Burr which proposed to seize New Orleans, where "there would be some confiscation." Jefferson had been waiting to see how far Burr would go; he now issued a proclamation against him, and had him arrested and sent east to stand trial for treason. Chief Justice Marshall ruled that there was no evidence of treason, and, to the wrath of the President, Burr went free; but he never could enter public life again.

162. Impressments and Captures (1803-1805)

After a renewal of the European war in 1803, interference with American neutral trade began again. The British justified their harsh measures on the ground that the Americans indulged in three forms of sharp practice: (1) Deserters from British ships of war were welcomed to employment on Yankee merchantmen. (2) American ships frequently carried two or three different sets of ship's papers, to make themselves out something different from what they were, so as to avoid capture. (3) The Americans, through their ports, carried on trade from French colonial ports to France.

To meet these real or fancied difficulties, the British began to capture or search American vessels, often for reasons not urged earlier: (1) By the new doctrine of "continuous voyages," their courts held that the profitable trade in West India sugar brought to the United States, unloaded, and then reshipped to Spain or France, was subject to capture. (2) Vessels which had carried a doubtful cargo going out, were captured on their way home with innocent cargoes. In order to enforce these new principles, British men-of-war cruised up and down the American coast, and captured American vessels outside the ports to which they belonged. (3) Impressments began again on a large scale, for the hard, underpaid, and often cruel naval service of Great Britain caused hundreds of sailors to desert.

163. CRISIS OF NEUTRAL TRADE (1806–1807)

Against all these outrages the United States government remonstrated; but Jefferson wanted to keep the peace, and instead of building warships he induced Congress to spend $1,600,000 in building and maintaining a flotilla of small gunboats for coast defense. In 1804 the commercial clauses of the Jay treaty of 1794 by agreement were allowed to expire, and Great Britain would not grant as good terms again; therefore we had no commercial treaty at all. To compel Great Britain to come to terms, Congress enacted a "Nonimportation Act," — practically the old Association of 1774 over again (§ 86), — which never took effect.

Napoleon still hoped by combining the fleets of France and Spain to check the British sea power; but in 1805 the splendid genius of Admiral Nelson at the battle of Trafalgar destroyed the allied fleet, and left Great Britain supreme at sea. The resourceful emperor of the French then set up what was called the "Continental System," by which all the numerous allies of France agreed not to purchase any British goods.

Great Britain retaliated in 1806 and 1807 with Orders in Council, setting up "paper blockades" on the French coast.

Napoleon replied by the Berlin and Milan Decrees (November, 1806, December, 1807), forbidding all trade to the British islands or in British goods. The worst sufferers from this furious war of documents were the American shipowners, yet they were the people who least wanted war. Although, between 1803 and 1811, the British took 917 American vessels, and the French took 558, the profits of the neutral trade were so great that the American tonnage engaged in foreign trade almost doubled.

The difficulty reached its crisis in June, 1807, when the United States ship *Chesapeake* was stopped on the high seas off Cape Henry by the British frigate *Leopard*, so that some deserters from the British navy who had enlisted on board the American ship might be taken off. The *Chesapeake*, though in international usage a part of the territory of the United States, was fired upon and disabled, and three American-born sailors were then seized, besides one English deserter.

164. The Embargo (1807-1809)

The accumulation of injuries called for action of some kind. Negotiation had failed; Great Britain would neither make a treaty nor give any satisfaction for the *Leopard* outrage. The United States might fight, but war would cut off American trade almost altogether. To yield and say nothing meant to give up abjectly the rights of an independent nation. Jefferson's ingenious mind found a way out of this apparently impassable bog by the Embargo Act (December 22, 1807), prohibiting the sailing of any ship carrying a cargo from the United States to foreign ports. Jefferson was sure that both France and Great Britain would come to terms if the American food products and other exports were cut off. On the contrary, Napoleon simply confiscated American vessels in French ports, because, he argued, they must have violated the American embargo; and the British, though they felt the loss of American exports, held out stubbornly.

The people who suffered most and who made the most ado

were the Americans. The New England, middle, and southern states were all heavy exporters, and as the year 1808 wore on, thousands of people found their livelihood taken away. Ships moldered at the wharves, wheat rotted in the warehouses; the peace-loving Jefferson found his temper rising, as the people, especially the New Englanders, slipped out of port or defiantly carried their goods over the Canadian boundary. At the end of fourteen months, the country, especially New England, would bear no more; and against Jefferson's private remonstrance, Congress repealed the Embargo Act (March 1, 1809).

165. REVIEW

Jefferson was a modern man, interested in literature, science, and agriculture, as well as in public affairs. He came into office in 1801, determined to pay off the public debt and to diminish party spirit. In spite of the economy of Gallatin, Secretary of the Treasury, he was obliged to spend money on war with piratical Tripoli. He tried to equalize parties by removing some Federalist officeholders, and his friends attempted in vain to curb the Supreme Court which assailed his policies.

Jefferson's greatest service to his country was the annexation of Louisiana, which unexpectedly came as the result of an effort to secure the mouth of the Mississippi. This annexation strengthened the South, began a policy of enlarging the Union, and at once led to boundary disputes with Spain. Before Louisiana was annexed, Jefferson had started a government expedition to Oregon, which in 1805 terminated its overland journey at the mouth of the Columbia, and thereby laid the foundation for a territorial holding on the Pacific coast. Jefferson skillfully crushed his enemy Aaron Burr, who engaged in a vague scheme of invading the western country.

Jefferson's second administration (1805–1809) was full of new issues and of disappointments, which were chiefly due to the fierceness of the war between France and Great Britain. Both powers looked on American neutral trade as simply something that helped the other side. Both captured American merchant vessels and cargoes, and in addition Great Britain impressed American sailors.

The crisis came when, by the British Orders in Council and the French decrees (1806–1807), additional unjust captures of American vessels were made, and when sailors were taken from the deck of the United States ship of war, *Chesapeake*. Jefferson's remedy was an Embargo (1807) intended to prevent American products from reaching the two contending powers; but the producers and merchants of the United States would not stand the pressure, and the Embargo was repealed shortly before the retirement of Jefferson (1809).

References Bearing on the Text and Topics

Geography and Maps. See maps, pp. 242, 245. — Avery, *U.S.*, VII. — Bogart, *Econ. Hist.*, 287. — Channing, *Jeffersonian System*. — Coman, *Indust. Hist.*, 173. — Fish, *Am. Diplomacy*, 218; *Am. Nationality*, 486. — Johnson, *Union and Democracy*, 134, 185, 190. — Semple, *Geogr. Conditions*, 93–113. — Shepherd, *Hist. Atlas*, 198.

Secondary. Adams, *U.S.*, I. 185–446, II–IV; *John Randolph*, 1–233. — Allen, *Navy and Barbary Corsairs*. — Brady, *Stephen Decatur*, 1–61. — Cable, *Creoles of La.*, 1–160. — Chadwick, *U.S. and Spain*, I. chs. iii–vii. — Channing, *Jeffersonian System*, chs. i–xvii. — Fish, *Am. Diplomacy*, chs. xii, xiii; *Am. Nationality*, ch. vii. — Foster, *Century of Diplomacy*, 185–232. — Hosmer, *Louisiana Purchase*, 21–178. — Hunt, *James Madison*, chs. xxviii, xxix. — Lighton, *Lewis and Clark*. — McCaleb, *Aaron Burr Conspiracy*. — McMaster, *U.S.*, II. 583–635, III. 1–88, 142–338, 496–514, V. 373–380, 418–432. — Mahan, *Sea Power in Rel. to War of 1812*, I. 99–214. — Merwin, *Thomas Jefferson*, 119–164; *Aaron Burr*, 57–147. — Roosevelt, *Winning of the West*, IV. 258–343. — Schouler, *U.S.*, II. 1–229.

Sources. Ames, *State Docs. on Fed. Relations*, 26–44. — Caldwell, *Terr. Development*, 77–108. — Harding, *Select Orations*, no. 12. — Hart, *Contemporaries*, III. §§ 106–122; *Patriots and Statesmen*, III. 87–103, 108–213. — James, *Readings*, §§ 52–56. — Johnson, *Readings*, §§ 71–76. — *Old South Leaflets*, nos. 43, 104, 105, 128, 131, 134, 174. — See New Engl. Hist. Teachers' Assoc., *Hist. Sources*, § 81; *Syllabus*, 338–340.

Illustrative. Bennet, *Volunteer with Pike*. — Bynner, *Zachary Phips* (Burr). — Cable, *Grandissimes; Strange True Stories of La.* —

Carpenter, *Code of Victor Jallot.* — Hale, *Man Without a Country; Philip Nolan's Friends.* — Hough, *Magnificent Adventure.* — Johnston, *Lewis Rand.* — *Scenes at Washington.* — Seawell, *Decatur and Somers.*
Pictures. Avery, *U.S.*, VII. — Sparks, *Expansion.* — Wilson, *Am. People,* III.

Topics Answerable from the References Above

(1) Thomas Jefferson as a young man, *or* at college, *or* as a planter. [§ 156] — (2) Jefferson's "republican simplicity." [§ 156] — (3) Incidents of the Barbary wars. [§ 156] — (4) Negotiations for Louisiana in Paris. [§ 159] — (5) Adventures of Lewis and Clark in 1804, *or* in 1805. [§ 160] — (6) Settlement at Astoria. [§ 160] — (7) First American exploration of the Pikes Peak region. [§ 160] — (8) Burr's visits to the West. [§ 161] — (9) Attack on the frigate *Chesapeake.* [§ 163] — (10) Objections to the Embargo. [§ 164]

Topics for Further Search

(11) Officeholders turned out by Jefferson. [§ 157] — (12) Why did Napoleon want Louisiana? [§ 158] — (13) Why did Napoleon give up Louisiana? [§ 158] — (14) Why did the people of Louisiana object to the new government? [§ 159] — (15) Was West Florida part of Louisiana? [§ 159] — (16) Was Burr a traitor? [§ 161] — (17) Jefferson's gunboat system. [§ 163] — (18) What was Napoleon's Continental System? [§ 163]

CHAPTER XV

166. MADISON'S DIPLOMACY (1809-1811)

JEFFERSON was glad to follow Washington's example in retiring from the presidency at the end of his second term. He

secured the office for his
Secretary of State, James
Madison, who was elected
President in 1808 over
the Federalist C. C.
Pinckney, by 122 electoral
votes to 47. Madison no
longer showed his earlier
spirit (§§ 117, 152), was
not a good party leader,
and his Cabinet, with
the exception of Gallatin,
was weak. All the efforts
of President Madison to
adjust the troubles with
Great Britain failed; a
fair treaty was signed
by the British minister,
Erskine, in 1809, but
Great Britain refused to

DOLLY MADISON, ABOUT 1810. (Mrs.
James Madison, a famous social leader.
From the portrait by Stuart.)

ratify his work. The next minister, James Jackson, accused
the President and Secretary of State of lying, and noted in his
private correspondence that "a more despicable set I never

252

met with before," which was his way of complaining because the United States government absolutely refused to have any more dealings with him; but he was received and welcomed by New England Federalists.

Congress had no better success. It passed a "Non-Intercourse Act" (March 1, 1809), prohibiting commerce with France and Great Britain, but the commerce went on indirectly. In 1810, by the "Macon Bill No. 2," Congress feebly attempted to play off one enemy against another. Napoleon in August, 1810, publicly announced, "His Majesty loves the Americans; their prosperity and their commerce are within the scope of his policy"; on the same day he showed his affection by a secret decree ordering the confiscation of all American ships in his ports.

167. Coming on of War (1811–1812)

Upon the western frontier, two Indian leaders had arisen — the brothers Tecumseh and the Prophet. Tecumseh was perhaps the greatest Indian in American history, because he was the only one to grasp the idea of throwing the whites back by forming a confederation of all the frontier tribes from north to south. He succeeded in controlling 5000 warriors, a force which, if it would only act together, could defeat any army that the United States was able on short notice to bring into the field.

In 1811, while Tecumseh was absent, William Henry Harrison, governor of Indiana Territory, forced the fight by marching with 1000 men against the Indian town of Tippecanoe, on the Wabash River. Harrison took it and burned it. A few months later war broke out on the southern frontier, where Fort Mimms, near the Alabama River, was captured by the Creeks and about 500 people were killed. General Andrew Jackson was put in command of the southwestern troops, and in several campaigns during 1813 and 1814 nearly crushed out the opposing Indians.

Meanwhile the public feeling of wrath and indignation
steadily rose against France, and still more against England.
In the new Congress, which met in December, 1811, Henry
Clay of Kentucky was chosen Speaker of the House; he
organized it with a view to war, and made young John. C.

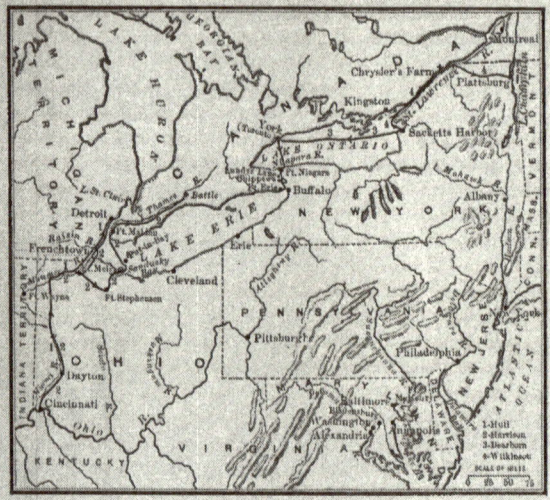

THE WAR OF 1812.

Calhoun, of South Carolina, chairman of the Committee on
Military Affairs.

War had at last become popular in the majority of the Republican party which controlled both houses. The West had no
patience with the timidity of the shipowners, for to the frontiersmen nothing seemed easier than to conquer Canada, and, as
Clay said, to "negotiate the terms of a peace at Quebec or
Halifax." The country was then prosperous; manufactures
were springing up, and nearly $200,000,000 worth of goods

were made in the country in a single year. But the "War Hawks" in Congress did not consider that the national revenues were falling off, that the army numbered only 7000 men, and that there were no good roads to the Canadian frontier.

President Madison could not stand the pressure, and war was formally declared against Great Britain, June 18, 1812. The official reasons for the war were as follows: (1) the insolence of the British cruisers on the coast; (2) the capture of over 900 American vessels since 1803; (3) blockades and other unrighteous practices under the British Orders in Council; (4) the stirring up of Indian hostilities; (5) impressment. An apology had been made for the *Chesapeake* affair; at the last moment the British partly withdrew the offensive orders; and we now know that it was an error to suppose that the British government instigated the Indian wars. Nevertheless, two substantial grievances remained — the capture of our merchantmen and the impressment of about 4000 seamen, of whom many were still prisoners on British cruisers.

The real reason for the war was a sense of indignation at the overbearing conduct of Great Britain, shown not only in the search and capture of vessels but in the refusal to withdraw the Orders in Council and in the contemptuous tone of such diplomats as Jackson. The British felt that they were fighting for the freedom of mankind against a despot, and that the American claims to neutral trade and seamen's rights were simply methods of preventing the British from destroying Napoleon's power. They looked on the American claim of the right to change allegiance, which was part of the contest with regard to impressments, as a new and dangerous idea.

168. LAND AND SEA CAMPAIGNS OF 1812

The Americans set out to decide the war by a single land campaign, and their campaign began in an effort of General Hull to seize the part of Canada north of Lake Erie. The tables were unexpectedly turned when the British captured Detroit

(August, 1812) after an ignoble defense by Hull. The Americans then made two attempts to penetrate Canada across the Niagara River; both were utter failures because the American troops had no discipline and no confidence in their officers.

THE FRIGATE *CONSTITUTION*.

The country discovered all at once that it had made no proper preparation for a land war.

Hence there was great joy when news of naval victories began to pour in. At the outbreak of the war the United States navy consisted of sixteen vessels, of which the largest was a handy 44-gun frigate. President Madison expected that the little fleet would surely be captured; nevertheless, when our frigate

Constitution fell in with the *Guerrière*, a ship of about her tonnage, in thirty minutes the *Guerrière* lay a helpless wreck (August, 1812). Two months later, the *Wasp* took the British brig *Frolic;* and the frigate *United States* captured, and subsequently brought into port, the British frigate *Macedonian.* Then the *Constitution* made another splendid capture, the frigate *Java.* During the year the only loss of the Americans was the *Wasp,* taken by a British three-decker battleship. In all, sixteen British ships of war were captured, besides those on the Lakes. In vain did the British attempt to show that the American ships in every case had more tonnage, or more men, or more weight of broadside. The British navy had not been accustomed to calculate odds so closely; in fact nearly every capture was due to the superior guns and marksmanship of the Americans.

169. THE INDECISIVE YEAR (1813)

The tide of naval victory changed in 1813, notwithstanding several other gallant captures of British cruisers. The American frigate *Chesapeake* was taken by the *Shannon* (May 30); and by the end of 1813 most of the American cruisers were driven into port and there blockaded. Then the *President* was captured; but the frigate *Essex*, Captain Porter, found its way into the Pacific and made havoc of the British whalers, till captured in Chilean waters in 1814. The land war was renewed on the Canadian frontier, but here the principal gains were on the boundary lakes. Lieutenant Oliver H. Perry was sent to Lake Erie to prepare the way for a recapture of Detroit. With wonderful energy he constructed a fleet of five vessels, trained his crews, and on September 10, 1813, met the attack of the enemy at the battle of Lake Erie, off Put-in-Bay. He reported his victory in the laconic letter, "We have met the enemy and they are ours: two ships, two brigs, one schooner, and one sloop."

Perry's victory cleared the way for a successful campaign

in western Canada. General William H. Harrison defeated the
Canadians and their Indian allies at the battle of the Thames
in Canadian territory (October 5, 1813), where Tecumseh was
killed. Renewed attempts to invade eastern Canada, under
General Wilkinson, were again a failure; and at the end of the
year 1813 the war was a sort of drawn game — each side
occupying substantially the territory which it held at the
beginning.

170. ON THE DEFENSIVE (1814)

So far the British had sent few troops to aid Canada. Their
energy was devoted chiefly to the war against Napoleon, who
made his disastrous retreat from Russia in 1812. In 1814,
however, Napoleon was overwhelmed and compelled to abdi-
cate. Large British forces by land and sea were thus set free
and began to make a series of invasions of the United States:
(1) The British occupied the coast of Maine as far as the Ken-
nebec River, and blockaded most of the American coast.
(2) A small British force was sent to seize Astoria, Oregon.
(3) In August, a British force of only 5000 troops landed about
fifty miles from Washington on Chesapeake Bay, marched up
into a country inhabited by at least 50,000 able-bodied men,
beat off an ill-commanded force hastily summoned to repel
them, and took and burned the capital of the United States —
as an alleged retaliation for destruction in York (now Toronto)
by American forces. (4) A similar attack on Baltimore in
September, which suggested Key's patriotic poem, *The Star-
Spangled Banner*, was beaten off by the American militia.
(5) A British force attempting to advance southward up Lake
Champlain was stopped (September, 1814), partly by a fleet
under Commander MacDonough, partly by the presence of
militia intrenched at Plattsburg, under Macomb.

In a last attempt to invade Canada, the Americans crossed
the Niagara River and fought two battles, at Chippewa and
at Lundys Lane (July 15, 1814); but they again retreated to

their own territory. The closing incident of the war was an
attack on the Gulf coast by General Pakenham. General
Andrew Jackson fortified himself at Chalmette, just below New
Orleans, and there (January 8, 1815), the British column of
5300 troops assaulted his works, defended by about 4000 troops,
of whom only a third were actually engaged. The American
militia, however, were well commanded and intrenched, and
they beat off the British army, inflicting a loss of 2000.

171. HUMILIATION OF THE WAR

The victory of Jackson left in the minds of Americans the
notion that they had repeated the experience of the Revolution
by defeating the veteran troops of Great Britain; and that
they could always depend upon militia to spring to the defense
of their country when needed. So far as the sea fights were
concerned, the early war was a brilliant victory for the Americans; but as the months went on, every American cruiser
was either captured, sunk, or helplessly blockaded in a home
port. For a time, there was not an American commissioned ship
of war on the ocean. Nevertheless the naval war was continued with brilliancy and success by a swarm of American
privateers. American shipowners, whose vessels could no
longer with safety carry a cargo, turned them into private
fighting ships, which often richly paid for themselves out
of their prizes. In three years about 1700 American merchant ships were taken by the British; on the other hand,
2300 British merchantmen were taken by privateers, besides
200 by cruisers, though 750 were retaken by the British; and
the insurance on a voyage from England to Ireland rose to
14 per cent. Dismay spread through the maritime interest of
England. As the London *Times* said of the American ships,
"If they fight, they are sure to conquer; if they fly, they
are sure to escape."

In the land war, the three clear American victories were
the battle of the Thames, though Harrison could not hold the

territory thus gained; Macomb's repulse of the British at Lake Champlain, from which the United States gained no territory; and the victory of Jackson, although it did not drive the British off the coast. The United States could hardly be called victorious when the British captured part of Maine, took our only holding in Oregon, and destroyed the capital city, almost without opposition.

Throughout, there was no lack of men for the American service. During the course of the war 529,000 individuals joined the American forces, but most of them were raw militia, without trained officers and without any experience in actual war against trained troops, and only 130,000 served as much as six months. Congress was never willing to authorize a proper federal army, and at one time volunteering fell off till plans were made for conscripting men by a draft. As in the Revolution (§ 89) a national army of 20,000 or 25,000 men, armed, equipped, officered, and disciplined under the authority of the United States alone, might have done what hundreds of thousands of militia could not do. On the other hand, the War Department was in a scandalously inefficient condition. Some of the commanders like Hull were old Revolutionary soldiers who had forgotten how to fight. The only land officers that came out of the war with national reputation were Harrison, Jackson, Jacob Brown, and young Winfield Scott, who had shown decided pluck at the battle of Lundys Lane. Secretary Armstrong, himself a Revolutionary veteran, was compelled to resign when the capture of Washington proved his incapacity. He was succeeded by James Monroe, who was one of the few administrators to show courage and ability. The United States paid a terrible penalty for going into a war without making preparations beforehand.

172. INTERNAL OPPOSITION TO THE WAR (1812–1814)

One reason for the mortifications of the land campaigns was the political opposition at home. In 1811 a New England

member of Congress, Josiah Quincy, roundly threatened that
New England would secede if Louisiana were made a state,
thus increasing the power of the South. As a protest against
the war, part of the Republicans under De Witt Clinton made
common cause with the Federalist opposition in the election of
1812, and the coalition got 89 electoral votes to 128 for Madison.
This personal and party opposition was carried into official form.
When the President of the United States called upon all the states
for a certain number of militia, New Hampshire, Massachusetts,
Rhode Island, Connecticut, and Vermont refused to send them.

There was some reason for protest and indignation. Congress neglected to provide either men or money enough to keep
the war going. No proper tax laws were passed till 1813,
when the hated Federalist excise and direct taxes were revived. The government borrowed $98,000,000 during the war,
but the bonds had to be sold at a depreciation of from 5 per
cent to 30 per cent; large amounts of "treasury notes" —
promises to pay in the future — had to be issued for supplies; and legal tender paper money was openly suggested.

The critical time came when New England began to feel
the blockade and the war taxes. In December, 1814, a convention of official delegates from several New England states
met at Hartford. We know little of the secret debates of the
convention, but its official report proposed that Congress should
give up its power to prohibit foreign commerce, and should
leave the proceeds of federal taxes to the states in which they
were paid. Such demands could not be granted without giving up the federal Constitution; and they amounted to saying
that unless the war were speedily stopped, the New England
states would withdraw from the Union.

173. FAVORABLE PEACE (1814)

One reason for the delusion that the War of 1812 was highly
successful, was the favorable peace which was made at Ghent
(December 24, 1814), before the report of the Hartford Conven-

tion, and before the battle of New Orleans. Negotiations began within a few months after the war broke out, and the commissioners sent to Ghent by the British government were unexpectedly willing to stop the war. The European struggle now seemed to be over, and when the great Duke of Wellington was consulted about the American war, he expressed the opinion that it would take a large force to drive the American militia out of their trenches. At sea, the devastations of the American privateers caused the British shipmasters to clamor for relief. Hence, the British commissioners at last gave way on one point after another:

(1) They agreed to give up all their territorial conquests, and to go back to the boundaries of 1812.

(2) They again promised not to take away slaves or other private property (§ 108) when they evacuated those territories.

(3) Since the war had put an end to all outstanding treaties, for a time the fisheries and conditions of commerce were left at loose ends, but after a few months they were both settled by separate treaties favorable to the United States.

The only subject on which satisfaction could not be had was impressments — the main cause of the war; but as soon as the European war was over, impressments ceased of themselves and, as a matter of fact, never began again.

174. Review

From 1809 on, Congress tried various remedies short of war, but could not bring Great Britain or France to terms, by any form of restriction of commerce. An attack in the frontier country of Indiana by the Indians, erroneously supposed to be urged on by the British, aroused public sentiment. In 1812 war was declared by the United States against Great Britain. At the last moment the British withdrew a part of the offensive Orders in Council; but nothing could be done to stop impressments, which was the chief remaining grievance when war broke out.

From one point of view the war was a great humiliation to the United States. All the efforts to invade Canada from Detroit, Niagara, and the St. Lawrence River were distressing failures, notwithstanding the great superiority of numbers of the United States troops. The only creditable operations on the northern frontier were the battles of Lake Erie, the Thames, Lundys Lane, and Plattsburg; and the British finally succeeded in occupying a great part of Maine, and Astoria on the Pacific, and captured and burned Washington.

On the other side, the little navy of the United States won a great success by beating the English in repeated duels and by capturing hundreds of British merchantmen. The Americans won victories on Lake Erie and Lake Champlain. After peace was made came the battle of New Orleans, which was a notable victory for the Americans.

The war was very unpopular in the middle states and especially in New England. Several states refused to allow their militia to take part. In 1814, at the Hartford Convention, suggestions were made that New England ought to secede. The favorable Peace of Ghent (1814) not only put an end to the war, but silenced the sectional jealousies; and the war left a feeling of national pride.

References Bearing on the Text and Topics

Geography and Maps. See maps, pp. 242, 254. — Babcock, *Rise of Am. Nationality*, 6, 88, 136, 276. — Fish, *Am. Nationality*, 114. — Johnson, *Union and Democracy*, 208. — Lucas, *Canadian War.* — Shepherd, *Hist. Atlas*, 200.

Secondary. Adams, *U.S.*, V–VIII, IX. 1–103. — Babcock, *Rise of Am. Nationality*, chs. i–x. — Bassett, *Andrew Jackson*, I. chs. vi–xiii. — Brady, *Stephen Decatur*, 62–137. — Brown, *Andrew Jackson*, 25–248. — Clark, *U. S. Navy*, chs. vi–xii. — Eggleston and Seeley, *Tecumseh and the Shawnee Prophet.* — Fish, *Am. Diplomacy*, chs. xiv, xv; *Am. Nationality*, ch. viii. — Hollis, *Frigate Constitution.* — Hunt, *James Madison*, chs. xxx–xxxiv. — Johnson, *Union and Democracy*, chs. xi, xii. — Lucas, *Canadian War of 1812.* — McMaster, *U.S.*, III. 339–458, 528–560, IV. 1–279. — Maclay, *U.S. Navy*, I. 305–658,

II. 3–22. — Mahan, *Sea Power in Rel. to War of 1812*, I. 215–423, II. — Morison, *H. G. Otis*, II. chs. xix–xxviii. — Roosevelt, *Naval War of 1812.* — Schouler, *U.S.*, II. 279–447. — Smith, *Wars*, 203–250. — Updyke, *Dipl. of the War of 1812.*

Sources. Ames, *State Docs. on Fed. Rels.*, 45–88. — Bogart and Thompson, *Readings*, 217, 490. — Caldwell and Persinger, *Source Hist.*, 323–334. — Harding, *Select Orations*, no. 13. — Hart, *Contemporaries*, III. §§ 123–129; *Patriots and Statesmen*, III. 215–317; *Source Book*, §§ 82–87. — Johnson, *Readings*, §§ 81–86. — Johnston, *Am. Orations*, I. 164–215. — MacDonald, *Select Docs.*, nos. 28–32. — See New Engl. Hist. Teachers' Assoc., *Hist. Sources*, § 82; *Syllabus*, 340.

Illustrative. Altsheler, *Herald of the West* (Washington and New Orleans). — Crowley, *Love thrives in War.* — E. Eggleston, *Roxy* (Tippecanoe). — G. C. Eggleston, *Am. War Ballads*, I. 113–145. — Matthews, *Poems of Am. Patriotism*, 83–107. — Munroe, *Midshipman Stuart.* — Post, *Smith Brunt.* — Pyle, *Within the Capes.* — Read, *By the Eternal* (New Orleans). — Seawell, *Midshipman Paulding.*

Pictures. Lossing, *Field Book of the War of 1812.* — *Mentor*, serial no. 103. — Wilson, *Am. People*, III.

Topics Answerable from the References Above

(1) Influence of Tecumseh. [§ 167] — (2) Battle at Tippecanoe. [§ 167] — (3) Henry Clay, *or* John C. Calhoun, as a boy and young man. [§ 167] — (4) The capture of *one* of the following ships: *Guerrière; Frolic; Macedonian; Java.* [§ 168] — (5) The capture of *one* of the following American ships: *Wasp; Chesapeake; Essex; President.* [§ 169] — (6) Contemporary accounts of the battle of Put-in-Bay. [§ 169] — (7) British occupation of the coast of Maine. [§ 170] — (8) Jackson's New Orleans campaign. [§ 170] — (9) Adventures of Winfield Scott in the War of 1812. [§171] — (10) Public services of De Witt Clinton. [§ 172]

Topics for Further Search

(11) James Madison in Congress; *or* as Secretary of State; *or* as President. [§ 166] — (12) What was the "Macon Bill No. 2"? [§ 166] — (13) Was there sufficient reason for the War of 1812? [§ 167] — (14) Why did the campaigns fail on the Niagara frontier? [§ 168] — (15) Why were the Americans so successful at sea? [§ 168] — (16) Why was Washington captured by the British? [§ 170]. — (17) Account of the Hartford Convention. [§ 172] — (18) Why was the peace of Ghent so favorable? [§ 173]

CHAPTER XVI

SETTLING THE WEST (1800-1820)

175. THE WEST AS A FACTOR IN THE NATION

EVER since the early years of the Revolution, the West had been active in national affairs: first, by the part played by the westerners in the war (§§ 94, 104); then by the demand that the national Congress should provide for new western states (§ 102); and then by the admission of the three western states Kentucky, Tennessee, and Ohio (§ 142), and the part played by their senators and representatives and by their state legislatures in national affairs.

In 1800 about 1,250,000 out of 7,000,000 people in the United States were living west of the summits of the Appalachians. Pioneer conditions could still be found in the northern woods of New England and New York, and in considerable parts of Pennsylvania and the southern states; but the people of those regions joined in the political life of the seacoast. The West was different; it was a region in which practically everybody was a pioneer. The western people had a sense of belonging to a section of their own, and of looking upon national questions from their own standpoint.

In 1802 Jefferson predicted that the Mississippi valley "will ere long yield more than half of our whole produce and contain more than half of our inhabitants." Two decades later the West contained one fourth of the inhabitants of the Union, and had revealed many elements of its own natural wealth, among them the following: (1) The soil was deep and fertile; the bottom lands of Kentucky and Tennessee, the wooded areas of Ohio, and the prairies farther west all bore surprising crops. (2) Most of the settled area abounded in superb timber, furnishing abundant building material. A few of the best trees ran to 150 or even 200 feet in height and 30 to 40 feet in girth. (3) The country was well watered and fitted for grazing, so that the westerners easily raised cattle and about 1820 began to drive herds over the mountains to market. (4) The abundant waterways and the ease of making roads quickly opened the country to settlement. (5) Regular coal mining began in Pittsburgh in 1784, and the black diamonds were found also in many other places. (6) Iron ore was abundant, and charcoal iron furnaces were started, while lead was discovered in Illinois and Wisconsin.

176. THE WESTWARD MOVEMENT

A stream of immigrants sought this promised land, with an effect seen in the census returns of some of the states: Tennessee had 36,000 people in 1790 and 262,000 in 1810; Ohio

DETROIT IN 1815.

rose from 45,000 in 1800 to 581,000 in 1820. New settlements sprang up. Fort Dearborn, on the Chicago River, first built in 1803 and destroyed by Indians in 1812, was rebuilt in 1816, and became the nucleus of Chicago. Terre Haute, Fort Wayne, and South Bend were settled about 1817. St. Louis had been founded by the French in 1764. Although the eastern states were all growing rapidly, they were able to send off swarms of emigrants, because large families were common throughout the country. Every stalwart son could make a livelihood, and almost every daughter was wanted as a farmer's wife.

To accommodate this stream of land-hungry people, the United States in 1800 adopted a new public land system : land was divided into small parcels and sold at land offices on the frontier at a minimum price of $2 an acre, one fourth of the purchase money down and four years' time for the balance. Many followed the principle of the old woman in Eggleston's novel, *The Hoosier Schoolmaster*, who, when her husband was buying, said, "Git a plenty while you're a gittin' . . . Congress land."

177. ROADS AND WATERWAYS TO THE WEST

To reach the western lands several main highways from east to west were marked out by nature: (1) A route led from Albany through the valley of the Mohawk, and thence via Geneva to Buffalo. (2) In 1812 Rochester was founded, the plain to the west of it was quickly occupied, and a new main road was laid out directly west to Lake Erie. (3) From Philadelphia a good road ran through Bedford in southern Pennsylvania to Pittsburgh, 350 miles. (4) From Alexandria (opposite Washington) a road led about 300 miles to Pittsburgh, by Braddock's old route up the Potomac to Cumberland, and across the Laurel Mountains to the Monongahela River. (5) From Alexandria or Richmond people followed the long-traveled easy pass from the upper Roanoke southwest to the Holston River, and thence down the Tennessee, or northwest-

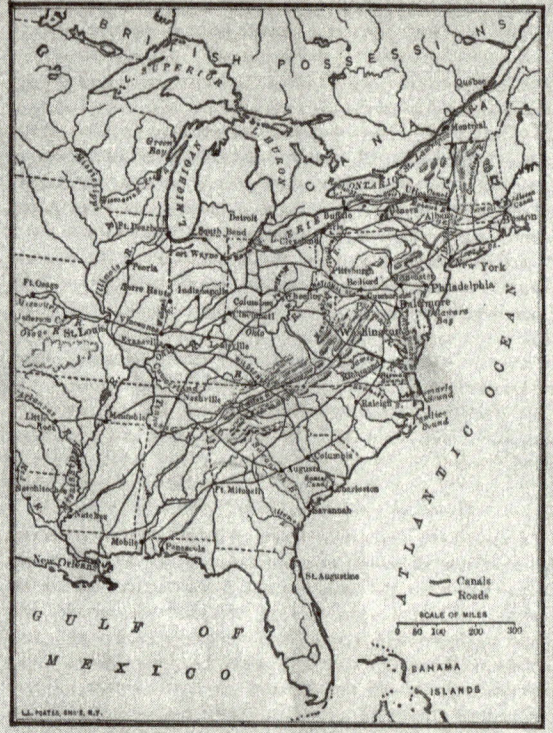

ROADS AND WATERWAYS TO THE WEST IN 1825.

ward through the Cumberland Gap to Kentucky. (6) From Georgia westward there was easy travel to Mississippi Territory and New Orleans.

Most of the wheel roads crossed many swamps and unbridged

streams, and were without good inns. In regions where there
was very little stone, pikes were out of the question. As a
substitute, companies built "plank roads" of thick boards laid
side by side, and charged toll. The greater part of the highways west of the mountains were simple rough tracks, winding
in and out among stumps and trees, pleasant in dry weather,
and a slough when it rained. Hence the journey from the
eastern states to the West was a serious undertaking. The ordinary vehicle was the Conestoga wagon of wood, with an arched
canvas top. The emigrants sold most of their furniture and
other heavy movables, took food with them, and cooked as
they went along. Breakdowns were frequent in the terrible
roads, and an average of twenty miles a day was quick
travel.

When once the tributaries of the Mississippi were reached,
movement became easier; even on small rivers like the upper
Wabash and the Muskingum, flatboats were used. The
simplest craft in the lively river traffic was the birch-bark canoe,
which would hold one or two persons, or the dugout, often
larger. More elaborate was the raft, sometimes as much as
a hundred feet long, floating all day on the current and tied up
at night; some of the rafts carried houses, open fires, and cattle.
The flat-bottomed ark was sometimes as much as sixty feet
long. The flatboat was more common, with its crew of un-
kempt and brawny polemen, the terror of the frontier. A step
higher was the keel boat, a more carefully built and ambitious
structure, housed over with a deck, and provided with two
"broadhorns," or steering oars.

On some such craft the settler floated lazily down the rivers
and met the dangers of the voyage — the river pirates, who
often attacked even armed boats, and Indians, who poured in
a volley from the shore. Many of the immigrants to central
Ohio, Kentucky, and Tennessee took advantage of the water
highways by following down the Ohio and then poling up a
tributary to the place of destination.

178. Steamboats (1807–1820)

In later times many settlers traveled in steamboats. Robert Fulton in New York set himself to the problem of building a successful steamboat (§ 128), raised with difficulty the few thousand dollars necessary for a trial, and ordered an engine from England. In August, 1807, he set in motion, on the

The CLERMONT.

Hudson River, the clumsy-looking *Clermont*, which could steam against wind and tide, and on her trial trip reached Albany in less than a day and a half. The use of steamers spread rapidly. A regular line to Albany was established in 1808; within five years a line was running on the Delaware, a steamboat was built at Pittsburgh, and steam ferryboats were introduced in New York and Philadelphia; and in 1816 steamers were introduced on Long Island Sound.

After 1812 steamers multiplied on the western rivers. The hulls could be built anywhere out of timber on the spot; the fuel was wood from the river banks; engines and boilers at first had to be brought over the mountains. The river life is best described in the boyhood recollections which Mark Twain has preserved for us in his books on the West. In 1820 it took thirty-five days to go up from New Orleans to Pittsburgh by steam, and about ten days to go down. The Great Lakes were not safe or convenient for small sailing craft or for rowboats, and were not much used as a highway for immigration till steamers

were introduced. The first Lake Erie steamer was the *Walk-in-the-Water*, built in 1818; in 1832 a steamer reached Chicago from the East; and after that time hundreds of thousands of immigrants passed through the Lakes.

THE *WALK-IN-THE-WATER*, ABOUT 1820.

179. LOCAL AND NATIONAL HIGHWAYS

The trouble with most of the roads was that they were made by the local governments, which spent as little as possible. The stretches of privately owned "pike" and plank road (§ 177) in the West did not reach across the mountains. Some states, such as Pennsylvania, disliked to spend money on roads intended to carry people through them into other states. Hence it was suggested that the federal government should build national highways. The first act of Congress on the subject (1802) was that for the admission of Ohio, which provided that five per cent of the proceeds of the public lands sold in that state should be applied to roads to reach those lands. This idea took definite form in an act of 1806 for the survey of a road from Cumberland, Maryland, to the Ohio River.

Construction of this so-called Cumberland Road began speedily; in 1820 it was opened to Wheeling. It was later continued westward to Columbus, thence much of the way to Indianapolis, and southwestward toward St. Louis. As soon as it was opened it became the great artery of western travel, for it was direct, had easy grades, and was macadamized. Congress in the course of thirty years spent upon it $6,800,000;

but it was at last superseded by railroads, and at various times after 1834 Congress transferred the roadbed to the ownership of states in which it lies.

180. ERIE CANAL (1817-1830)

The most obvious line of western transit by water was from the Hudson up the Mohawk and across to Lake Ontario. The first statesman to take up the building of a canal on this route was De Witt Clinton of New York, who saw the many advantages to the state and city of New York from a waterway which would make New York Harbor the commercial mouth of the Great Lakes, thus diverting traffic from New Orleans. The War of 1812 gave impetus to this idea, because it showed how hard it was to transport men and supplies from the coast and the interior to the Lakes.

In 1817, under the energetic leadership of John C. Calhoun, who said that "he was no advocate for refined arguments on the Constitution," Congress passed the so-called Bonus Bill, appropriating about $1,500,000 to be distributed among the states for internal improvements. It was expected that New York would have a big slice to spend on the proposed Erie Canal, but President Madison stepped in, and on the last day of his term vetoed the bill, for the "strict construction" reason that he could find no clause of the Constitution which distinctly authorized such expenditure.

The state of New York at once set to work to build its own canal, and in 1823 the Erie Canal was finished from the Hudson near Albany to the Genesee River; in 1825 the direct line was completed to Black Rock, near Buffalo, 363 miles from Albany. The original canal cost $7,000,000, and the whole expenditure was more than repaid by tolls; but down to 1916, $200,000,000 more had been spent on extensions and repairs.

The effects of the Erie Canal were marvelous. Lands all along the line at once trebled in value, and the freight rate from tidewater to Lake Erie dropped from $120 a ton to $19.

The city of New York increased from 124,000 people in 1820
to 203,000 in 1830, and has ever since remained the most populous city in the Union.   After 1825 a large part of the overland immigration passed through the Erie Canal.   The passage
from Schenectady to Utica (about two hours by rail nowadays)
was twenty-two hours by canal boat; the passengers were
crowded, and half stifled at night, and the frequent cry of "low
bridge" disturbed the journey by day.

181. WESTERN FRONTIER LIFE

When the settler reached the golden West, he found substantially the old colonial life over again — land to clear, log
houses to build, towns to found, schools to start.   An observer
said of the westerners, "They are in a low state of civilization,
about half Indian in their modes of life."   Abraham Lincoln,
born in Kentucky in 1809, lived as a boy one winter in Indiana, in a hovel called a "half-faced camp."   Better abodes were
built of logs, with log chimneys and puncheon (split log) floors,
and might cost twenty or twenty-five days' labor.

Yet in the midst of much that was rough, trained men like
Philander Chase, Episcopal Bishop of Ohio, struggled on, founding schools, building new churches, educating the ministers, and
elevating the community.   The Methodist or Baptist frontier
minister had perhaps half a dozen little churches on his hands,
and "rode circuit" from hamlet to hamlet, preaching, baptiz-
ing, burying the dead, organizing churches, and, if necessary,
threatening rowdies who undertook to disturb the meeting.
One of the favorite diversions of the time was to attend camp
meeting, which was a combination of picnic, summer resort,
and religious exercise, where people took household furniture,
children, dogs, and psalm books.   If the ministers roared and
the converts shrieked, foamed at the mouth, and fell in convulsions, we must remember that such exaggerated experiences
often aroused and turned to better ways rough but powerful
natures that could not be reached by milder means.

For education in the Northwest early provision was made. Each settlement soon had its common school. Out of land reserved by the Northwest Ordinance, and private contributions, half a dozen little colleges arose in a few years. In 1830 two western magazines were started: Hall's *Illinois Magazine* and Flint's *Western Monthly Review*.

182. WESTERN TERRITORIES AND STATES (1798-1819)

Until many years later, the regions north and south of the Ohio River were both considered parts of the West. In many respects the pioneer life was about the same in Indiana, Tennessee, and Louisiana. All the settlers had the same problem of conquering the forest, of living through dearth and the diseases from which the new settlements suffered, of laying the foundation for improved farms and towns and cities. Nor did Congress prefer one group over another. Great territories were created in both regions, and as they grew in population they were subdivided and portions were admitted as states. Hence most of the territorial governments lasted but a few years, and the number of states steadily grew.

Out of the Northwest Territory of 1787 (§ 115) were set off the territories of Indiana (1800), Michigan (1805), and Illinois (1809). The Territory South of the Ohio River (1790) was incorporated in the state of Tennessee. Farther south was the Territory of Mississippi (1798 and 1804), from which was set off Alabama Territory (1817). The greater part of the Louisiana purchase was organized as the Territory of Louisiana (1805), later renamed the Territory of Missouri (1812). Each of these territories had sooner or later a representative government with a one-house legislature, a delegate in Congress who had a seat but no vote, and a governor and other territorial officials appointed by the President. Each of them understood that it was simply a halfway stage to a state government.

The one striking difference between the northern and the southern territories was with regard to slavery. The North-

west Ordinance, including the antislavery clause, was confirmed
by act of Congress in 1789; but when the Territory South of
the Ohio and the Mississippi Territory were organized in 1790
and 1798, that clause was omitted, and the slavery then existing was allowed to continue in those regions, as also in Kentucky. Shortly after Ohio was admitted into the Union (1803)
as a free state, New Jersey added its gradual emancipation act
to those of the neighboring states (§ 112). Thus was completed a compact block of nine free states flanked by eight
slaveholding states. When Louisiana was admitted to the
Union (1812) as the 18th state, the number stood nine to nine.

As early as 1793, Congress passed a Fugitive Slave Act
by which it took the responsibility for the recovery of fugitives
who might find their way into free states.

183. THE ANTISLAVERY MOVEMENT (1807–1820)

In 1807 the question of slavery came up clearly before Congress because of the controversy over a bill to prohibit the slave
trade, as soon as the prohibition in the Constitution (§ 119)
should expire. On this question, the South was divided:
Maryland and Virginia had surplus slaves to sell to their southern neighbors and joined with the northern states in voting to
prohibit the foreign slave trade absolutely. On the question
of domestic slavery, however, those states stood with their
southern neighbors.

Still slavery at that time seemed hardly to be a sectional
question. Antislavery societies were formed all along the
border, both north and south of the Mason and Dixon Line
and of the Ohio River. A sort of national antislavery society
was formed in the shape of "The American Convention for
Promoting the Abolition of Slavery and Improving the Condition of the African Race," which met about once every two
years. This convention and local societies discussed political
questions affecting slavery, petitioned the state legislatures and
Congress, and tried to stir people up to form abolition socie-

ties. One western man, Benjamin Lundy of Kentucky, was a kind of antislavery apostle, and in 1821 established an abolition paper, the *Genius of Universal Emancipation.*

These efforts were rather checked than aided by the National Colonization Society (founded in 1816), which aimed (1) to encourage emancipation by carrying the free negroes to Africa and (2) to relieve slaveholders by taking away the free negroes who made their slave brethren discontented. In 1819 Congress appropriated $100,000 to carry back slaves that might be captured on the high seas; a negro colony was founded in Liberia, on the west coast of Africa (1821), and first and last several thousand negroes were sent there.

Gradually the West came into the slavery discussion, at first because used as a kind of balance between North and South. From the admission of Louisiana (1812) the number of slave states was kept equal to that of free states, so that neither section might have a majority in the Senate; Indiana in 1816 (19th state) was balanced by Mississippi in 1817 (20th state); Illinois in 1818 (21st state) was followed by Alabama in 1819 (22d state). The North, including the Northwest, grew so much faster than the South, that in 1820, under the application of the three-fifths rule, there were 105 free-state members in the House to 81 slave-state members.

184. POLITICAL LIFE, AND HENRY CLAY

Politics was perhaps the most interesting topic in the West. Local parties very quickly were merged in the general national parties; elections were lively, and about 1800 the practice of "stump speaking" was introduced; that is, of open-air addresses to a series of popular meetings. The western states led in a movement for the suffrage of all adult white men and for elective judges. In politics and in social life the most influential man in a village was the storekeeper, who was often also distiller, country banker, real estate dealer, and justice of the peace, and hence called "Squire."

Local government in the West was imported from eastern communities. The northwestern states set up a system of school districts on the New England model. In Ohio, where the New England element was strongest, the people adopted a kind of modified town meeting. In Indiana and Illinois, where there were many southern people, and also in the southwestern states, the county of the southern type became more important.

No man more distinctly represents the West than Henry Clay. Born a poor boy in Virginia, he emigrated to Kentucky, and at twenty-nine sat as senator from Kentucky in Washington (1806). From that time to his death in 1852 Clay was most of the time in the service of the federal government as senator, representative, or Secretary of State. In six terms he showed himself the greatest Speaker in the history of Congress, managing the House of Representatives as a skillful coachman handles a four-horse team.

What made Clay so distinctively a western man was his political optimism. He believed in all good things, in the future of his country, the growth of the West, the good judgment of the average voter. He was the inventor and the strongest advocate of what he called the "American System," by which he meant the commercial development of the country by protective tariffs and other public aids. Above all, throughout his life he worked steadily and wisely for the establishment of better means of transit. His personal qualities gave strength to his political views; he was courteous and quick, had a natural power of attracting friends to him, and was ingenious in devising compromises when party spirit ran high.

185. MISSOURI COMPROMISE (1819–1821)

The influence of Henry Clay was strongly felt in one phase of the first great political controversies over the western question. The issue was the admission of Missouri, which chanced to be the battle ground for the struggle between slavery and antislavery. In its institutions, the character of the popula-

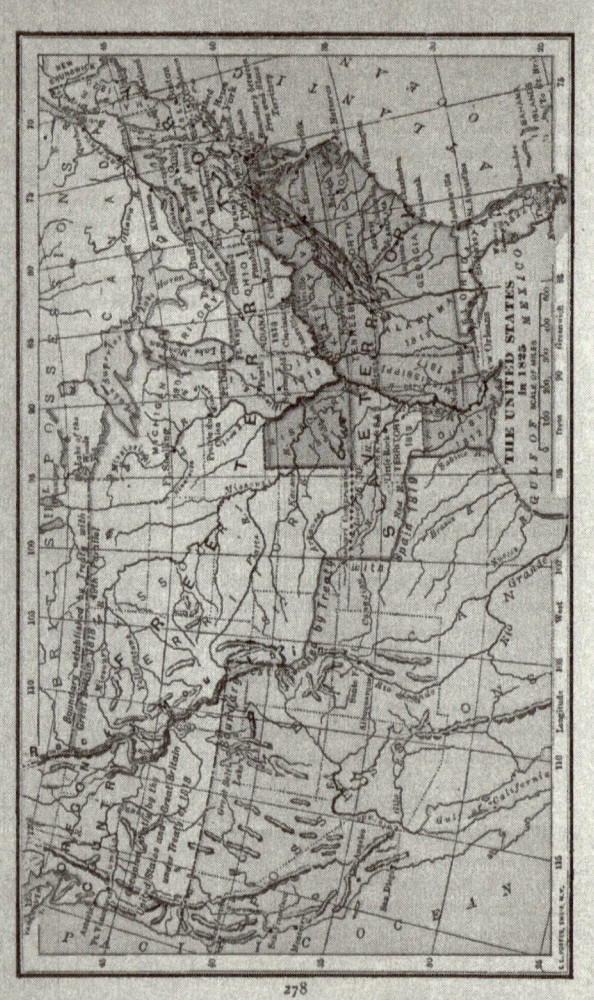

tion and its produce, the community grouped about the lower
Missouri River country and the section of the Mississippi below
St. Louis, was western. The Missouri people had about the
same make-up and interests as the neighboring state of Illinois,
but a large part of the population came from southern slaveholding states, and some of them had brought their slaves with
them and intended to keep them. When in February, 1819, a
bill for the admission of Missouri came up in Congress, an
antislavery amendment, introduced by James Tallmadge of
New York, passed the House by the close vote of 87 to 86;
but the Senate refused to accept it, and the bill failed.

During 1819 many northern legislatures and public meetings
declared that Missouri must never be a slave state. When a
new Congress assembled in December, 1819, a bill passed the
House to admit Maine (at that time a part of Massachusetts)
as a new state; and another bill for the admission of Missouri.
To the latter the House, by a test vote of 94 to 86, added an
amendment prohibiting slavery in Missouri. The Senate
united the two measures into one bill, but instead of the House
prohibition accepted the amendment of Senator Thomas of
Illinois, forever prohibiting slavery in the Louisiana Purchase
north of 36° 30' north latitude, except in Missouri. After a
few days of great excitement, the House accepted the Thomas
amendment as a compromise; Maine was admitted at once
(23d state), and the people of Missouri were allowed to form
a slaveholding constitution.

The new Missouri constitution made it the duty of the legislature to prevent the coming in of free negroes. This provision produced a second uproar in Congress and led to a second
compromise, engineered by Henry Clay in 1821, by which the
legislature of Missouri agreed to make no law infringing on the
rights of citizens of other states; and Missouri was at last
admitted to the Union (24th state).

The essence of the Missouri Compromise was the drawing of
a geographical line across the Louisiana Purchase, north of

which there were to be no slaveholding territories, and no slaveholding states except Missouri. That is, the act continued the
old geographical separation of slaveholding and free territory
along Mason and Dixon's Line and the line of the Ohio River,
by extending the boundary around Missouri and then along
the line of 36° 30' to the western limits of the United States.
The compromise thus excluded slavery from the larger part of
the Louisiana Purchase, and also recognized the right of Congress to deal with slavery in the territories.

The compromise had plenty of enemies on both sides. John
Randolph of Virginia politely called it "a dirty bargain."
John Quincy Adams, when his friend Calhoun threatened secession, made perhaps the first prophecy of a civil war when he
asked whether in such a case "the population of the North
. . . would fall back upon its rocks bound hand and foot to
starve, or whether it would not retain its powers of locomotion
to move southward by land."

186. REVIEW

The West began to be a vital part of the nation soon after
1800. It was rich in land and resources, and attracted hundreds
of thousands of immigrants. They came from the East in three
main streams of settlement: (a) through central New York
and along Lake Erie; (b) through Pennsylvania and Maryland,
overland to the headwaters of the Ohio River; (c) through or
around the southern mountains.

The settlement of the West was greatly aided by the use
of steamboats on the rivers and lakes; and by the Cumberland Road, constructed by Congress to the Ohio River. The
Erie Canal (finished in 1825) made a direct connection with
the Great Lakes, and was for years the most important highway
to the West; and it built up the city of New York.

At first the West was all frontier and suffered from the
disadvantages of frontier life, such as poverty, ignorance, and
religious excitement. As settlement advanced, new territories

were created in the region north of the Ohio River under the
Northwest Ordinance. The states of Ohio and Louisiana were
admitted to the Union (1803, 1812). The slavery question came
up in the territories north of the Ohio River and in older states,
where abolition societies and agitators were at work. After
1812, the states were regularly admitted in pairs, one free and one
slave. After a violent controversy, in Congress and throughout
the country, an east and west line was drawn by the Missouri
Compromise of 1820 across the Louisiana Purchase. North of
it slavery was forever prohibited. The West was much interested in politics and public discussion, and was well represented
in Congress by statesmen of whom Henry Clay was the most
distinguished.

References Bearing on the Text and Topics

Geography and Maps. See maps, pp. 268, 278. — Bogart, *Econ.
Hist.*, 209. — Brigham, *Geogr. Influences*, chs. iv, v.— Fish, *Am. Nationality*, 137. — Johnson, *Union and Democracy*, 248, 253, 270, 278,
306, 341, 344. — Semple, *Geogr. Conditions*, 150–168, 246–277. — Shepherd, *Hist. Atlas*, 202, 203, 206. — Turner, *New West*, 70, 226, 310. —
See Supt. of Docs., *Geography and Exploration Lists.*

Secondary. Adams, *U.S.*, IX. 148–174. — Babcock, *Rise of Am.
Nationality*, ch. xv. — Bogart, *Econ. Hist.*, 128–130, 189–212 (§§ 116,
166–185). — Coman, *Indust. Hist.*, 156–174, 203–206. — Dodd, *Expansion and Conflict*, ch. ii. — Hinsdale, *Old Northwest*, 313–328,
351–367, 380–392. — Johnson, *Union and Democracy*, 245–259, 269–
279, 298–304. — McLaughlin, *Lewis Cass*, 1–33, 95–132. — McMaster,
U.S., III. 123–142, 459–495, 516–528, IV. 381–429, 570–601, V. 13–18,
130–137, 147–168. — Mathews, *Expansion of New Engl.*, 178–224. —
Roosevelt, *T. H. Benton*, 1–20, 32–40. — Schouler, *U.S.*, II. 125–131,
205–278, III. 96–103, 134–137, 178–188, 346–352. — Schurz, *Henry
Clay*, I. 1–47, 137–146, 172–202. — Sparks, *Expansion*, 220–274. —
Treat, *Land System.* — Turner, *New West*, chs. v–vii.

Sources. Bogart and Thompson, *Readings*, 234–251, 338–369. —
Caldwell, *Survey*, 142–144, 233–245. — Callender, *Econ. Hist.*, ch. xii. —
Hart, *Contemporaries*, III. §§ 135–141; *Patriots and Statesmen*, III.
319–326, 335–337, 345–363, IV. 83–90, 145–148; *Source Book*, §§ 90–
93. — James, *Readings*, §§ 57, 64–66. — Johnson, *Readings*, §§ 91–93.
— Johnston, *Am. Orations*, II. 33–101. — MacDonald, *Select Docs.*,

nos. 35–42. — See New Engl. Hist. Teachers' Assoc., *Hist. Sources*, § 83; *Syllabus*, 342–344.

Illustrative. Banks, *Round Anvil Rock.* — Bryant, *Hunter of the Prairies.* — Churchill, *The Crossing.* — Clemens (Mark Twain), *Life on the Mississippi.* — Cooke, *Leather Stocking and Silk.* — Cooper, *The Prairie.* — Eggleston, *Circuit Rider.* — Parrish, *When Wilderness was King.* — Riddle, *Ansel's Cave.*

Pictures. Sparks, *Expansion.* — Wilson, *Am. People*, III.

Topics Answerable from the References Above

(1) Life in some *one* western town previous to 1830. [§ 176] — (2) Account of a journey over *one* of the roads mentioned in § 177. — (3) Fulton's invention of the steamboat. [§ 178] — (4) Construction of the Cumberland Road, *or* of the Erie Canal. [§§ 179, 180] — (5) Travel on the Erie Canal. [§ 180] — (6) Frontier life about 1810. [§ 181] — (7) Abraham Lincoln as a boy. [§ 181] — (8) Wandering life of Benjamin Lundy. [§ 183] — (9) Henry Clay as Speaker of the House. [§ 184] — (10) The settlement of the Missouri country down to 1819. [§ 185] — (11) Why was Maine made a separate state? [§ 185]

Topics for Further Search

(12) Early western cattle business. [§ 175] — (13) Methods of buying and settling public land down to 1860. [§ 176] — (14) Why did Madison veto the Bonus Bill? [§ 180] — (15) *One* of the early colleges in the West. [§ 181] — (16) Brief history of *one* of the following territories: Indiana; Michigan; Illinois; Mississippi; Alabama; Louisiana. [§ 182] — (17) Emancipation acts in New Jersey, *or* in New York. [§ 182] — (18) External slave trade after 1789. [§ 183] — (19) Why did colonization of the negroes fail? [§ 183] — (20) Clay's " American System." [§ 184] — (21) Incidents in the debate on the Missouri Compromise. [§ 185]

CHAPTER XVII

THE NEW AMERICAS AND THE MONROE DOCTRINE
(1806-1823)

187. THE UNITED STATES AS A NOVELTY IN THE WORLD

WE have grown so accustomed to thinking of the United States as one of the pillars of the world that we fail to realize how startling was the appearance of a new member among the family of nations through the success of the Revolution. In 1775 the principal powers of Europe — Spain, France, England, Austria, Prussia, and Russia — hardly recognized that there were any nations in the world outside of themselves that were entitled to equal rights. The small states of Europe, such as Holland and Portugal, existed by their consent. Turkey, which then held Greece and all the Balkans, was looked upon as an inferior pagan state. Not a single country in Africa or Asia was considered to be entitled to independence if any European power had the strength to conquer it.

The two Americas were subdivided among the colonizing powers. Great Britain, Spain, and Portugal had nearly all the land, but some islands in the West Indies belonged to the French and to the Dutch; and Russia was just beginning to lay claims in the far Northwest.

The appearance of the United States was, therefore, a new thing in the world's history; it was the first country, founded by Europeans, which set up for itself. By so doing it put into circulation the great idea that any European colonies might easily grow to the point where they would have a right to de-

283

mand a government of their own. American independence was
also a notice served on the world that a nation was appearing
in a new quarter of the globe, where there never had been independent states before.

In addition, the new United States was the most democratic country on earth and at once set out to teach the rest
of the world the value of self-government. We have already
seen how the appearance of the United States among the nations
interfered with Napoleon's plans of conquest (§ 159). The War
of 1812 was the proof that this new kind of nation might be
very disagreeable at sea. Old-fashioned Europe was disturbed
by this upstart nation of the western hemisphere.

188. EFFECT ON LATIN AMERICA (1806–1822)

The example of the United States was not only disturbing,
— it was dangerous; for Canada, Brazil, and the Spanish colonial
empire contained several million people who were quick to learn
the lesson that colonies could get new privileges by threatening
to revolt. The Spanish government especially was very un-
easy under the prospect of colonial self-government, and therefore lightened the shackles of trade for the colonies.

Nevertheless, movements began in America which looked
toward freedom for these colonies. A Latin American named
Miranda landed in Venezuela in 1806 with several hundred
men raised in the United States, and tried to revolutionize it.
This was the first of what came to be called "filibustering"
expeditions in aid of Latin Americans. A vain attempt was
also made by the British to annex the colony of La Plata
(Buenos Aires, or Argentina). These blind movements were
much aided by the exploits of Napoleon in Europe. He descended upon Portugal in 1807, and thus caused the Portuguese
royal family to take refuge in Brazil. The next year Napoleon
did all that was in his power to annex Spain, intending by this
means to bring all the Spanish colonies into the French empire.
The Spaniards and the Spanish Americans detested the French;

and since for seven years the invaders remained in control of a
great part of Spain, the colonists were left much to themselves
and set up local governments which opened their trade to Great
Britain and also to the United States.

In 1814 Napoleon was compelled to evacuate Spain, and the
old royal house was restored.   For a time the colonies accepted
this "legitimate
government," ex-
cept La Plata,
which, in 1816,
formally declared
itself independent
and never again
came under the
Spanish authority.
From the Plata
the banner of in-
dependence was
carried by General
San Martin to
Chile and then to
Peru.

In the mean-
time General
Simon Bolivar
had been success-
ful in Colombia,
which is now sub-
divided into Ven-
ezuela, Colombia,

LATIN AMERICA (1815-1830).

and Ecuador. The only continental possessions left to Spain
were Mexico and Central America, which declared themselves
independent in 1821.   Brazil cut loose from Portugal and
declared itself an independent empire in 1822.   The island
of Haiti had made itself independent during the French

Revolution. There was therefore nothing left of the Portuguese, French, and Spanish colonial empires except the Spanish islands of Cuba and Porto Rico, some small French islands in the Caribbean Sea, and French Guiana.

This recital of the bare facts leaves out of account the romantic side of the whole episode. This period of Latin American history is full of thrilling adventures, of marvelous crossings over high mountains, of battles on land and sea, of gallant aid rendered to the revolutionists by Englishmen and Americans who crossed the sea to fight in their cause. To the people of the United States the Latin Americans seemed to be a band of patriots who were following the glorious example of the American Revolution. As a matter of fact Mexico and Brazil were both organized as monarchies, and in several other countries the head of the state was nothing but a military dictator backed up by an army of cutthroats. The revolutions led to fearful civil wars and there were some frightful struggles between neighboring peoples who were just emerging from what they claimed to be the tyranny of Spain.

189. INTEREST IN LATIN AMERICA (1806–1821)

What was the proper action for the government of the United States in this unexpected change of American conditions? Every American President from Washington to Monroe had a strong sense that it was highly undesirable for the United States to take part in European relations or political combinations, except in necessary defense of its own neutral rights. This "Doctrine of Isolation" was repeatedly stated by Washington and was part of the policy of Jefferson and Madison. The United States had a very small army and navy, and notwithstanding the brief French war of 1799, the war with Tripoli, and the War of 1812, the feeling of the whole country was that the United States was not in shape to take part in the combinations of European powers and policies.

Under this spirit of noninterference with Europe, it was a

short step to the corresponding doctrine that European powers ought not to interfere in America. This idea was at the bottom of the annexation of Louisiana, which was the only way of preventing the French from getting a new foothold in our neighborhood. The United States did not deny the right of a European nation to control the colonies which it already had in America, but greatly objected to any serious changes in its holdings.

For many reasons the Latin Americans welcomed American trade. Spain had always been very arbitrary about the trade with her colonies, but during the revolution in the colonies Cuban trade was for the first time opened wide. The new Latin American states all received American vessels and merchants in their ports. The new states seemed to be reaping the experience of the American Revolution, and several of them paid the United States the compliment of imitating its republican and its federal government.

The natural impulse was to recognize the declarations of independence put forth by these new governments at their face value. Still the United States had great ambitions in America and had no desire to offend Spain by recognizing states that might again be subdued by Spain. Hence for several years President Madison and President Monroe contented themselves with aiding to build up business in the various countries.

190. AMBITIONS OF THE UNITED STATES (1803–1821)

Whatever their feeling about other nations annexing American territory, the people of the United States had no scruples about certain Spanish territory which they much desired. From 1803 to 1819 steps were taken to complete the control of the Atlantic and Gulf coasts by the annexation of three successive areas: (1) The coast of Louisiana, stretching indefinitely from the Island of Orleans westward, came in as part of the Louisiana cession. (2) Part of West Florida, extending from Louisiana to the Perdido River, was annexed by force of arms from 1810 to 1813. (3) For East Florida, a treaty with Spain was necessary. In addition, the United States for a long time felt it had a good claim to Texas, and it coveted Cuba and the Spanish claims in Oregon, whatever they might be worth.

Cuba remained a fixed part of the Spanish empire, although in 1822 an agent of some of the Cubans arrived in Washington and suggested that the time had come for Cuba to be independent. John Quincy Adams believed that the annexation of Cuba was certain to come, but for the time being all the American statesmen were willing that Cuba should remain Spanish, if they could be sure that it would not be transferred to England or to France.

Good fortune attended the effort to secure a treaty with Spain, notwithstanding a bad blunder by General Andrew Jackson, who in 1818 pursued hostile Indians into East Florida and then proceeded to capture the Spanish posts of St. Marks and Pensacola. The treaty, negotiated in 1819, put an end to the controversies about Texas, West Florida, and East Florida. Under it: (1) Spain for an allowance of $5,000,000 ceded both East Florida and all claims on West Florida. (2) The United States ceased to urge claims to Texas, and accepted on the south and west an irregular line from the mouth of the Sabine River to the source of the Arkansas and thence due north to latitude 42°. (3) The Spaniards surrendered all claims on the Pacific coast north of the 42d parallel.

191. NORTHERN BOUNDARY AND THE FISHERIES

The ambitions of the United States began to extend also to the Pacific, where in 1818 the little post of Astoria was given back by the British to representatives of the United States. In the same year Great Britain and the United States agreed that the 49th parallel should be the boundary between Canada and the United States from the Lake of the Woods as far west as the Rocky Mountains. Beyond those mountains, any region along the northwest coast, claimed by either party, should be "free and open" to the subjects of both powers. This meant joint occupation of the Oregon country, or the whole disputed region between California and Russian Alaska.

Another serious territorial question which was settled by the same treaty was that of the northeastern fisheries. The agreement made some changes in the privileges set forth in the treaty of 1783 (§ 108). It gave Americans the right to take fish inshore — that is, within a line drawn three miles from the low-water mark parallel with the coast — on parts of the coast of Newfoundland and Labrador; also the right to dry and cure fish on the unsettled parts of those coasts. On the other hand, the United States renounced such rights on all other British coasts, except that American fishermen might enter harbors of said coasts for shelter, wood, and water, and "for no other purpose." This treaty is still in force.

192. EUROPEAN POLITICAL SYSTEM (1815-1822)

The disturbances in Latin America greatly interested Europe. When Napoleon was finally defeated (1815) and was sent to spend the rest of his life as a prisoner on the island of St. Helena, the rulers of France, Austria, Prussia, and Russia, fearing that the spirit of revolution would break forth again in Europe, formed what was called "The Holy Alliance." They agreed that they would "on all occasions and in all places lend each other aid and assistance." Really their plan was for a kind of mutual insurance against revolutions.

The benevolence of the Holy Alliance was tested in 1823, when the European powers by force put an end to a revolution in Spain against the arbitrary Bourbon king; and it was suggested that they might also end the revolutions in Spanish America. At about the same time (1821) the Russian government laid claim to the exclusive trade and occupation of the northwest coast, including part of Oregon; and both these suggestions of interference in America aroused the United States.

For several years Henry Clay, then Speaker of the House,

had been leading a movement for the recognition of the new South American states, whether or not they were really independent. This policy seemed to have a precedent in the generous conduct of France toward the American Revolution (§ 93). President Monroe — who was elected in 1816 — held back from recognition but sent special agents to South America to report on the conditions there.

Soon after the treaty of 1819 (§ 190) was ratified by Spain (1821), the President proposed, and Congress agreed, to recognize the principal Latin American countries (1822); and in the course of a few months ministers were exchanged between the United States and Colombia, Chile, La Plata, Brazil, Guatemala, and Mexico. Within a short time the government began to make commercial treaties with these powers. By this action the United States put itself on record as believing that the Latin American states had forever separated themselves from their parent countries.

After the Holy Alliance restored the tyrannical royal government in Spain, a proposition was made to send out an expedition — presumably French — to bring back the Spanish colonies to their former allegiance. Great Britain, which had no desire to see those colonies and their trade go back to Spain, held off and warned the United States. At this opportune moment George Canning, British foreign minister, made a friendly suggestion (1823) to Richard Rush, our minister in England, to join with him in a declaration against the transfer of any Spanish or Portuguese state to another European power.

193. THE MONROE DOCTRINE (1823)

Rush's account of the British proposition greatly stirred President Monroe and his Cabinet. They had to decide whether they would go hand in hand with Great Britain; or whether, as Secretary John Quincy Adams insisted, they should make an independent stand. For weeks the Cabinet wrestled with these problems, but in the end Monroe yielded to the stronger mind of his secretary, and allowed him to draft that part of the message of December 2, 1823, which has been commonly called the "Monroe Doctrine." It contains three main statements on the American question:

(1) On colonization: while speaking of the northwest coast, Monroe said that "the American continents, by the free and independent condition which they have assumed and maintain, are henceforth not to be considered as subjects for future colonization by any European powers."

(2) On interposition: in discussing the proposed intervention by European powers against the Latin American states, the message says that "interposition for the purpose of oppressing them, or controlling in any other manner their destiny, by any European power" would be considered unfriendly to the United States.

(3) On the European political system: the doctrine runs, "We should consider any attempt on their part to extend their system to any portion of this hemisphere as dangerous to our peace and safety."

Monroe meant his doctrine to be peaceful and harmonizing. His argument was, in substance: (1) Since the United States does not interfere in European controversies, we should not permit third parties to interfere in the New World in quarrels not their own. (2) We are not hostile to existing colonies of European powers, but it is contrary to our interest that Latin American territory be conquered and occupied by foreign powers.

The Monroe Doctrine accomplished its purpose: all schemes of European intervention were given up; and Russia forthwith made treaties with the United States and Great Britain, accepting as the southern boundary of Russian America the parallel of 54° 40' north latitude.

194. IMMEDIATE RESULTS OF THE DOCTRINE (1823–1826)

John Quincy Adams was much more disposed than Monroe to push the doctrine to the point of making the United States

the leader among the American states. When he became
President in 1825, he had the opportunity of pushing that
policy, and he hastily accepted an invitation from some of the
Latin American states to meet in a congress at Panama. One
of the purposes was to be the contriving of means for setting
Cuba free; and another was to come to a decision as to how
the American republics were to protect themselves against
danger from the Holy Alliance.

The Latin American states, however, showed themselves
unfriendly to slavery. For these and other reasons the Senate
held up Adams's nomination of commissioners to attend the
congress for nearly a year, and then Adams was obliged to
give them such instructions as to make it impossible for them
to take the lead. This was before the days of the telegraph,
and news traveled slowly. When the commissioners arrived at
Panama, they found that the congress had met, with only a
part of the Latin American states represented, and had adjourned. The Latin Americans showed themselves incapable
of forming a union of Latin states, and had the question of
accepting the supremacy of the United States been fairly presented to them, they would undoubtedly have declined it.

This first opportunity of actually making the Monroe Doctrine mean something definite went by, and it was more than
twenty years before any President or Secretary of State tried
seriously to change conditions in Latin America. Later the
doctrine became a fixed policy of the United States.

195. REVIEW

When the United States became a nation, Europe was
shocked, for there had never before been independent civilized
countries in North or South America. The success of the
Revolution made the Latin American colonists discontented;
and from time to time in 1806 to 1822, they worked and fought
to be free from the Spanish and Portuguese home governments.
La Plata was the first colony to secure its liberty; but be-

tween 1814 and 1822 all but Cuba and Porto Rico became independent.   ·

The "Doctrine of Isolation," first distinctly laid down by Washington, kept the United States out of European wars, but the Americans naturally preferred republican governments among their neighbors, and hence favored the Spanish American revolutionists. After the annexation of Louisiana, West Florida (1813), and East Florida (1819), the Spanish government in those parts of the world was extinguished, and there was some hope of annexing Cuba. Meanwhile the United States was trying to establish a title to Oregon and to secure fishing privileges on the northeast coast.

The "Holy Alliance," a combination of powers in Europe, interfered to put down a revolution in Spain (1823), and listened to a proposal to invade the Spanish American colonies; while Russia claimed the northwest coast of North America (1821-1824). The United States began to recognize the Latin American powers in 1822.

In 1823, Great Britain proposed a joint declaration against any interference in America; instead of this President Monroe issued a declaration called the "Monroe Doctrine." He protested (1) against any new European colonization in America; (2) against any interposition in the Latin American states; (3) against any attempt to extend the European "political system" to America. The doctrine was aimed simply to keep peace in the Americas; but the Latin American powers tried to induce the United States to take more positive ground in the Panama Congress of 1826. The Senate was opposed, and the United States was unable to take the lead among the new countries.

References Bearing on the Text and Topics

Geography and Maps. — See maps, pp. 278, 285. — Babcock, *Rise of Am. Nationality*, 272, 276, 286. — Bogart, *Econ. Hist.*, 287. — Fish, *Am. Dipl.*, 218; *Am. Nationality*, 486. — Johnson, *Union and Democracy*, 263, 293. — Turner, *New West*, 208.

Secondary. Babcock, *Rise of Am. Nationality*, ch. xvii. — Bassett, *U.S.*, 347, 348, 368-371, 375-377, 383, 384; *Andrew Jackson*, I. chs. xiv-xviii, II. ch. xix. — Chadwick, *U.S. and Spain*, I. chs. vii-xi. — Fish, *Am. Dipl.*, chs. xvi, xvii; *Am. Nationality*, 168-172, 179. — Fuller, *Purchase of Fla.*, chs. vii-xi. — Hart, *Monroe Doctrine*, chs. i-vi. — Johnson, *Union and Democracy*, 259-265, 289-297, 320-323. — McMaster, *U.S.*, IV. 372-376, 430-483, V. 1-54, 433-463, 483-487. — Morse, *J. Q. Adams*, 98-148. — Schouler, *U.S.*, III. 23-26, 57-97, 128-133, 175-178, 189, 255, 274-293, 358-366, 389-395. — Schurz, *Henry Clay*, 146-171, 267-275, 293-300. — Turner, *New West*, ch. xii.

Sources. Caldwell, *Terr. Development*, 105-126. — Hart, *Contemporaries*, III. §§ 142-150; *Patriots and Statesmen*, III. 327-332, 337-345, IV. 25-49, 98-114. — Hill, *Liberty Docs.*, ch. xx. — MacDonald, *Select Docs.*, nos. 34, 43. — *Old South Leaflets*, nos. 56, 129. — See New Engl. Hist. Teachers' Assoc., *Hist. Sources*, § 83; *Syllabus*, 344.

Illustrative. Aimard, *Queen of the Savannah* (Span. Am. independence). — Atherton, *Rezánov* (Russia in Cal.). — White, *El Supremo* (Paraguay).

Pictures. Wilson, *Am. People*, III.

Topics Answerable from the References Above

(1) What claims had Russia to the northwest coast in 1821? [§ 187] — (2) Why did the Spanish American colonies revolt? [§ 188] — (3) Washington's " Doctrine of Isolation." [§ 189] — (4) What was the interest of the United States in Cuba? [§ 190] — (5) Why was Astoria restored to the United States? [§ 191] — (6) What was "The Holy Alliance"? [§ 192] — (7) Why did Monroe hesitate to recognize the Latin American states? [§ 192] — (8) Why did not the United States accept Canning's offer? [§ 193]

Topics for Further Search

(9) How did the French get their islands in the West Indies? [§ 187] — (10) How did the Dutch get their holdings in the West Indies and South America? [§ 187] — (11) How did Haiti become independent? [§ 188] — (12) Miranda's expeditions of 1806. [§ 188] — (13) Account of General Simon Bolivar. [§ 188] — (14) Ought the United States to have joined in the Panama Congress? [§ 194]

CHAPTER XVIII

GROWTH OF NATIONAL SPIRIT (1815-1830)

196. Effect of the War of 1812 on the Nation

Notwithstanding the defeats and the humiliations of the War of 1812, the United States came out of it with a new idea of what it might do as a nation, both within its own boundaries and as one of the countries of the world. The war and the long difficulties before it had made people realize the need of national finances, and of national relations with business. ·

The currency was in bad condition because the Bank of the United States (§ 141) had been allowed to expire in 1811, and the business of banking and of issuing paper money was left to banks chartered by the states. Many of them were frauds, many others were badly managed, and the country was full of paper notes which could not be redeemed in specie.

The course of business had been altered by the interruption of commerce. Some of the accumulation of profits, both from shipping and from other sources, went into cotton, woolen, and iron mills, especially in New England and the middle states. The manufactures of the United States came nearer supplying the market than at any previous time in the history of the country. Naturally, the manufacturers were anxious to keep these advantages. The difficulty of getting troops and supplies to the frontier aroused the country to the need of new lines of transportation with improved highways and waterways. Among the wealthy business men of this period the best known was Stephen Girard of Philadelphia, merchant ship-

STEPHEN GIRARD.

owner and founder of Girard College.

Above all, there was a feeling that the United States was worth while. Whatever the defects of the army in the recent war, the navy belonged to no section but was a national service, and the whole country could rejoice in its success. Even "strict constructionists" — statesmen like Jefferson and Madison, who had written the Virginia and Kentucky Resolutions (§ 152) — now felt that the nation was more important than the states, and supported a liberal use of national powers.

197. The Tariff and the Second Bank (1816)

One of the first national questions to come up was that of the relation of the federal government to American manufacturers. As soon as the war was over, there came a rush of importations which greatly interfered with the little American mills that had been recently constructed for weaving coarse cottons and woolens. The import duties had been doubled when the war broke out, and for a time the home manufactures had had almost a monopoly of the market. If now the import duties were allowed to go back to the old scale, it seemed more than the home manufacturers could stand.

The result was the tariff of April 27, 1816, passed by test votes of 25 to 7 in the Senate, and 88 to 54 in the House — a

tariff which now seems very low, but at the time was thought
highly protective. The average rate of duties on dutiable goods
in 1811 was about 15 per cent; by the tariff of 1816 it was
made 20 per cent. The new tariff was supported by a combination of three interests: (1) New England and middle
states manufacturers; (2) western farmers under the leadership of Henry Clay; (3) South Carolina planters under John
C. Calhoun, who interested
his constituents in the hope
of building up cotton manufactures in South Carolina.
The strongest opponent was
· John Randolph of Virginia,
who said the only question
was, "Whether you, as a
planter, will consent to be
taxed, in order to hire another man . . . to set up a
spinning jenny."

Another evidence of na-
tional feeling was the charter
of the second United States
Bank. Till 1811 the notes
of the United States Bank
and the banks chartered by the states circulated alongside
gold and silver coin, in which the good banks redeemed
their notes whenever presented. After the capture of Washington (§ 170) all the state banks, except those of New England, "suspended specie payments of their notes," so that state
bank notes became the only currency. By an act of April 10,
1816, a second United States Bank was chartered by Congress,
with what was then thought the enormous capital of $35,000,000,
of which the United States was to own one fifth. The main
public services expected of the bank were: (1) to furnish a
sound paper currency, and to induce the state banks to pay

STATE VOTE ON THE TARIFF OF 1816.

their notes in specie; (2) to act as financial agent of the government in receiving and paying money; (3) to hold on deposit the government balance, which ranged from $3,000,000 to $10,000,000. After one false start, the bank established branches far and wide, and did a large and profitable business.

198. John Marshall and the Supreme Court (1801–1819)

This vigorous use of the powers of Congress was warmly supported by the third department of the federal government, the courts, under the guidance of Chief Justice John Marshall. Marshall was born in 1755, served as a captain in the Revolutionary War, studied law, and sat in the state legislature and in the Virginia ratifying convention of 1788. In 1797 he became a Federalist member of the House, then Secretary of State, and near the end of John Adams's term was appointed Chief Justice, and held that high office until his death in 1835.

Marshall is one of the most interesting of Americans. He was a simple householder who often carried home his own turkey from market, a renowned expert in the game of quoits, an upright Christian gentleman. His colleague, Story, said of him: "I love his laugh, . . . it is too hearty for an intriguer, and his good temper and unwearied patience are equally agreeable on the bench and in the study." Yet he was the greatest of American jurists, and his main service was to take advantage of cases which happened to come before the Supreme Court to set forth clearly, logically, and irresistibly the true principles of the federal Constitution; and he so influenced five judges appointed by Jefferson and Madison that they agreed with him.

Many of the cases decided by Marshall are landmarks in the history of the United States, because they clearly state the loose-construction theory of the federal government, to which Congress, the President, and the Supreme Court all gave their sanction.

(1) The Supreme Court undertook to keep the states from encroaching on what the court believed to be the rightful

powers of Congress. To this end, it declared that certain state statutes were void and not binding, because they were contrary to the federal Constitution (especially Fletcher *vs.* Peck, 1810). In another famous case (Dartmouth College case, 1819) the court insisted that a charter granted to a private corporation was a "contract" which the states were forbidden by the federal Constitution to repeal or alter. When the state courts tried to prevent these decisions by refusing to allow cases to be carried upon appeal, the federal Supreme Court took jurisdiction even in cases where states were parties (case of Cohens *vs.* Virginia, 1821).

(2) On the other hand, the court strongly sustained the implied powers of Congress by giving effect to the bank and other acts that were questioned by the states (especially McCulloch *vs.* Maryland, 1819).

"Let the end be legitimate," said Marshall, "let it be within the scope of the Constitution, and all means which are appropriate, which are plainly adapted to that end, which are not prohibited but consist with the letter and spirit of the Constitution, are constitutional."

199. PARTIES AND ELECTIONS (1816–1824)

Most of the great decisions came during the administration of Madison's successor, James Monroe, who was chosen President in 1816 over the Federalist Rufus King, by 183 electoral votes to 34. Monroe, notwithstanding long experience as diplomat and Cabinet officer, was overshadowed by four young Republican statesmen, each of whom had a just ambition to be President. They were: Henry Clay, Speaker of the House and always a critic of the President's policy; John Quincy Adams, Secretary of State, the strongest spirit in the administration; John C. Calhoun, Secretary of War, then an ardent nationalist or supporter of strong federal government; and William H. Crawford of Georgia, Secretary of the Treasury, a keen politician.

The Republican party by this time accepted most of the old Federalist doctrines, such as implied powers, and the old party spirit ceased. The great questions before the people came in such issues as the Missouri Compromise (§ 185) and internal improvements. Monroe was reëlected without opposition in 1820, and by 1822 the Federalist party had died out. Hence the period got the name of the "Era of Good Feeling," though in reality it was full of jealousy, intrigue, and disagreement.

As the presidential election of 1824 approached, the alleged "Era of Good Feeling" disappeared. Crawford got the coveted nomination by a caucus of Republican members of Congress; but that way of making nominations had grown unpopular. Other candidates were put forward by a new method of nomination by state legislatures — John Quincy Adams in New England, Henry Clay in Kentucky and several other western states, and Andrew Jackson in Tennessee. Calhoun accepted the almost unopposed nomination for Vice President.

Of all these nominations the most unexpected was that of Andrew Jackson. He was of Scotch-Irish descent, born in 1767 among the poor whites of the Carolinas. He studied law and went out to Tennessee in 1788, and was successively public prosecutor, member of Congress (1796), and federal senator (1797), then judge of the supreme court of Tennessee. Always a testy man, he lived in a part of the country where private warfare was thought a fine thing; he fought several duels and killed one man. He commanded at New Orleans in 1815, and in Indian campaigns from 1817 to 1819.

200. PRESIDENT JOHN QUINCY ADAMS (1825–1829)

The campaign of 1824 was hot and bitter and full of personalities. The electoral votes turned out to be 99 for Jackson, 84 for Adams, 41 for Crawford, and 37 for Henry Clay. Since no one had a majority of electoral votes, the choice went to the House of Representatives, where Adams was elected by the vote of 13 states to 7 for Jackson and 4 for Crawford (February 9,

1825). The Jackson men insisted that inasmuch as their candidate had more electoral votes than Adams, the "will of the people" was defeated; and a friend of Jackson also brought forward the unfounded charge that Adams had bought his election by promising to make Clay Secretary of State. Jackson seems never to have doubted the truth of this slander.

No man of his time was better qualified than John Quincy Adams, by character and training, for his great office. As Federalist senator from Massachusetts in 1807, he voted for Jefferson's embargo, and was thereupon dropped by his own party. He became a Republican, minister to Russia, one of the peace commissioners at Ghent, minister to England, and from 1817 to 1825 was Secretary of State. Adams was by nature an expansionist. He would have liked to annex Canada; he was especially interested in Cuba; he wanted to buy Texas; he got rid of both the Spanish and the Russian claims to the Oregon region; and he went farther than Monroe in his interest in our Spanish American neighbors.

A methodical, able, and hard-working President, just and honorable in all his public and private relations, Adams was cold in manner, and had few close and warm friends. After he retired from the presidency, he was elected to the House (1830) and spent seventeen years there, in which he revealed magnificent power as a debater and became the champion of the North.

201. CONTROVERSY OVER THE TARIFF (1824–1828)

The tariff of 1816 did not bring prosperity to the country; for the duties were not high enough to shut out foreign goods, and hence did not wholly suit the manufacturers. In 1824 a tariff was passed by narrow majorities in both houses (May 22), which raised duties somewhat, and for the first time taxed certain raw materials of New England manufactures. The strongest northern opponent of this tariff was Daniel Webster, member from a shipowning district, who declared that "the general sense of this age sets, with a strong current, in favor of freedom of commercial intercourse, and unrestrained individual action." The great champion of the tariff was Henry Clay, who argued for what he called the "American System."

A strong and persistent objection to protective tariffs, whether high or low, made itself felt in the South, where the hopes

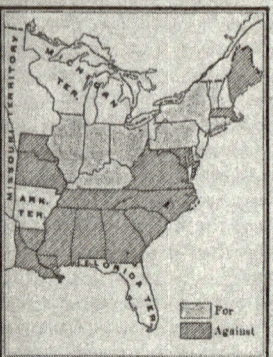

of establishing manufactures with slave labor had come to nothing. In 1828 a new tariff bill was introduced into Congress, and was now supported by Webster on the ground that his constituents had in good faith changed their investments over to manufactures. The opponents of the bill helped to amend it by raising the duties on raw materials, in the expectation that many friends of the bill would vote against it in its amended form. It therefore became known as the "Tariff of Abominations." Nevertheless, it became a law (May 19, 1828), and the average rate of duty paid on dutiable goods rose from 36 per cent in 1826 to 49 per cent in 1830 — the highest tariff in the United States even to the period of the Civil War.

STATE VOTE ON THE TARIFF OF 1828.

Protests rained upon Congress. The Boston moneyed men protested; southern legislatures protested; most important of all, South Carolina and John C. Calhoun protested. Calhoun was at first a strong advocate of a national bank, a tariff, and internal improvements, in the confidence that the federal government would help develop his own state of South Carolina. Gradually he came to see that Congress could do little for a state like his, which had no manufactures and which depended on slave labor.

In 1828 Calhoun wrote a long paper called *The Exposition*, in which he argued that any protective tariff was unconstitutional, and that any state had a right to "nullify" a federal law which it thought unconstitutional.

202. ELECTION OF ANDREW JACKSON (1828)

In spite of the vigor and ability of John Quincy Adams, his administration was almost a failure because the Jackson men did everything they could to prevent his plans from going through. They delayed the nomination of commissioners for the Panama Congress (§ 194); they blocked Adams's excellent plans for internal improvements that would help the nation; they attacked his personal character. The truth is that there was a lack of questions which really divided the nation. In 1827 an Antimasonic party was founded, but it never became very large; opposition to freemasonry was not an issue upon which the nation could be divided. Even the tariff of 1828, though it brought out rivalry between North and South, did not lead to the foundation of new political parties.

In the election of 1828 the only candidates for the presidency were Adams and Jackson; and the only vital issue was the personal one, whether Adams was a good man who deserved reëlection, or Jackson was a representative of the people who ought to supplant him. Adams was the subject of scurrilous campaign literature; it was charged "that he was rich; that he was in debt; that he had long enjoyed public office." On the other side an Adams man printed a "coffin handbill," charging Jackson with the illegal execution of six men thirteen years before on a technical charge of desertion.

Jackson's election was almost assured in advance by a combination of the West and South with Pennsylvania and New York. A majority of the electoral votes in New York was

turned over to Jackson by Martin Van Buren, a wily statesman who was head of the "Albany Regency," the first well
organized political "machine." Jackson was elected by 178
electoral votes to 83; and his popular vote was about 650,000
to 500,000 for Adams. As an enthusiastic friend and admirer
of Jackson says, "General Jackson was therefore triumphantly
elected President of the United States in the name of reform and
as the standard bearer of the people."

203. REVIEW

During the fifteen years after the close of the War of 1812,
all sections of the Union called upon Congress to create a new
financial and economic system; for business and public finance
were in bad condition. The principal results of this pressure
were:

(1) The tariff of 1816.

(2) The second United States Bank of 1816.

(3) A series of decisions by the Supreme Court which were
intended to curb the states, sustain the doctrine of implied
powers, and give general effect to the national feeling.

Monroe, elected President in 1816, surrounded himself with a
very strong Cabinet, including John Quincy Adams, Calhoun,
and Crawford. There was no opposition to his reëlection in
1820, and the Federalist party shortly died out. In 1824 there
were four candidates, Clay, Crawford, Jackson, and Adams;
there being no majority of electors, the choice went to the House
of Representatives, where Adams was chosen.

The protective tariff of 1816 satisfied nobody, and every
four years thereafter new tariffs were introduced, of which
two, those of 1824 and 1828, were passed. Great opposition
arose in the South, particularly in South Carolina, against the
"Tariff of Abominations" of 1828. Nevertheless the tariff
was not an element in the election of 1828, which was a
personal contest between Jackson and Adams. Jackson was
elected.

References Bearing on the Text and Topics

Geography and Maps. Dodd, *Expansion and Conflict*, 18. — Johnson, *Union and Democracy*, 314, 328. — Turner, *New West*, 6, 232, 242, 260.

Secondary. Adams, *U.S.*, IX. 105–148, 188–197. — Babcock, *Rise of Am. Nationality*, chs. xi–xiv. — Bassett, *U.S.*, 345–349, 357–368, 377–390. — Coman, *Indust. Hist.*, 184–203. — Dewey, *Financial Hist.*, §§ 66–80. — Dodd, *Expansion and Conflict*, ch. i. — Johnson, *Union and Democracy*, 231–244, 266–269, 307–320, 324–345. — Lodge, *Daniel Webster*, 60–166. — McMaster, *U.S.*, IV. 280–372, 376–380, 484–521, V. 55–81, 109–120, 488–519. — Morse, *J. Q. Adams*, 148–224. — Schouler, *U.S.*, II. 447–463, III. 1–450 passim. — Schurz, *Henry Clay*, I. 126–321 passim. — Shepard, *Martin Van Buren*, chs. iv, v. — Stanwood, *Am. Tariff Controversies*, I. 111–348; *Presidency*, I. chs. ix–xii. — Thayer, *John Marshall*. — Turner, *New West*, chs. i, ix, xi, xiv–xvi, xviii, xix. — Wilson, *Division and Reunion*, §§ 8–10, 25–27.

Sources. Ames, *State Docs. on Fed. Relations*, 89–113, 133–157. — Beard, *Readings*, §§ 46–48. — Bogart and Thompson, *Readings*, 309–321, 493. — Callender, *Econ. Hist.*, ch. x. — Hart, *Contemporaries*, III. §§ 130, 132–134; *Patriots and Statesmen*, III. 365–383, IV. 13–133 passim. — Hill, *Liberty Docs.*, ch. xix. — Johnson, *Readings*, §§ 77, 78, 87–90. — MacDonald, *Select Docs.*, nos. 33, 44, 45. — See New Engl. Hist. Teachers' Assoc., *Hist. Sources*, § 83; *Syllabus*, 341.

Pictures. Wilson, *Am. People*, III.

Topics Answerable from the References Above

(1) Early cotton, *or* woolen, *or* iron mills. [§ 196] — (2) John Marshall as a boy and young man. [§ 198] — (3) Justices of the Supreme Court from 1789 to 1830. [§ 198] — (4) Public services of James Monroe previous to 1817. [§ 199] — (5) John Quincy Adams, *or* Andrew Jackson, *or* Martin Van Buren, as a boy and young man. [§ 199] — (6) Antimasonic party. [§ 202]

Topics for Further Search

(7) Wildcat banks before 1830. [§ 196] — (8) Debate on the tariff of 1816, *or* on the second United States Bank, *or* on the tariff of 1824, *or* on the "Tariff of Abominations." [§§ 197, 201] — (9) Was the first, *or* the second, United States Bank a good thing? [§ 197] — (10) Daniel Webster's part in the Dartmouth College case. [§ 198] — (11) Daniel Webster's speeches in Congress. [§ 201]

CHAPTER XIX

SOCIAL AND SECTIONAL CONDITIONS (1829-1841)

204. HUMANE SENTIMENT

THE first half of the nineteenth century, from 1800 to 1850, both in Europe and in the United States, was full of a splendid spirit of moral reform. One of the results of the American and French revolutions was to sweep away the old belief that things must be right because they existed. The influence of the principle of equality was to upset social arrangements that thrust part of the people down under the feet of another part. The serfs in Germany were emancipated. The antislavery forces in Great Britain compelled Parliament to pass a gradual emancipation act for her colonies in America, and this led to complete emancipation in 1837. In 1832 a British "Reform Act" was passed which destroyed many abuses and extended the suffrage in Great Britain to the middle class. In spite of the Holy Alliance, the little states of Germany and Italy began to demand that they should be allowed to govern themselves. Greece revolted from Turkey, and by the aid of Great Britain, France, and Russia, became an independent kingdom (1827). In 1830 there was a second French revolution, which succeeded in driving out the Bourbon king and enthroning a king of the Orleans family, who ruled under a liberal constitution.

The same spirit was at work in the United States, beginning with the movement against slavery and the slave trade as far back as 1777 (§ 112). Public attention was also called to terrible abuses in the treatment of other poor, weak, and friendless classes. In the twenties and thirties, for example, societies were formed against imprisonment for debt; and their cause was much strengthened by such incidents as that of an old Revolutionary soldier who had been in jail for seven years because he was unable to pay a debt of less than five dollars. The conditions of the children in the cities were found to be bad, especially the large numbers who were working in factories, and who sometimes spent twelve hours out of the twenty-four within the walls of their place of labor. How did the American people deal with these and similar difficulties?

205. RELIGIOUS REFORM

In the United States at least three influences — religious, political, and social — were at work side by side to lead men to a more kindly and humane spirit toward their fellows. The influence of religion and of the organized churches was far-reaching. The Christian and Jewish churches agreed in holding that all human beings were born with the same dignity, the same rights in the eyes of God, and the same share in salvation. Therefore the Indians and the negroes and the poor and ignorant white people were all entitled to the privilege of hearing the gospel preached. There was an active missionary spirit for the benefit of the Indians, among whom there had been missions ever since the founding of the colonies. Another similar movement was that for home missions on the frontier, among those settlers who would otherwise grow up without churches and religious teaching. The Sunday School movement, which was first organized by Robert Raikes in England, spread to this country and became an essential part of the church organization of nearly all Protestant bodies.

A large part of the Christian church held the doctrine that the heathen whom the message of salvation never reached were doomed to everlasting punishment, and that made it a solemn duty to spread the tidings as far as possible. For this purpose arose a great movement for foreign missions. The

Catholic Church had always had a missionary organization, and the system was now taken up by the Protestant denominations. In 1806, a few students of Williams College, taking shelter under

HAYSTACK MONUMENT, WILLIAMSTOWN, MASSACHUSETTS.

a haystack, agreed to enter on missions among the heathen in foreign lands. The idea spread rapidly, and in the course of a few years most of the national churches had regular boards which were in charge of active missions in the Hawaiian Islands, in Africa, and, as soon as China and Japan were opened up, in those countries.

Within the churches new duties were assumed, new societies were founded, and several denominations were divided. The Unitarian movement in New England broke up the Congregational Church into two parts commonly called Unitarian and Trinitarian, or Orthodox. The Presbyterian Church, in 1837, split on doctrinal questions into "New School" and "Old School." The Methodist Church, in 1844, divided into a northern and a southern church, and the Baptist Church also showed a disposition to divide. The Catholic Church was much increased by steady immigration, especially from Ireland and Germany.

A remarkable new organization, commonly called the Mormon Church, was founded by Joseph Smith of Palmyra, New York, in 1829. In 1830 he published what he called the *Book of Mormon*, which he alleged to be a miraculously preserved account of the settlement of America by the lost tribes of Israel. He and his followers built a temple at Kirtland, Ohio; in 1837 moved to Missouri; and soon after to Nauvoo, Illinois, where they built up a city of ten thousand adherents. The neighborhood disliked the Mormons, and Smith was killed by a mob in 1844. Three years later most of the Mormons moved to Utah, then an unoccupied part of Mexico.

206. POLITICAL AND HUMANE REFORM

Another influence was that of the doctrine of the rights of man as set forth in declarations, laws, and constitutions of the Revolution and later times. Thinking men began to realize that workmen were not really free, because the courts would punish them if they made a combination to raise wages. The conditions of working people in mines and factories were often very bad, and the employment of children in factory labor had begun. These difficulties could be most conveniently reached by state laws.

Perhaps a stronger influence was that of the many societies based on the new spirit of humanity, which was shocked by the cruelty of labor systems all over the world, and by the harsh treatment of prisoners for debt and those confined as criminals. To better the condition of these and other sufferers, societies were formed: some of them local, some of them national, some of them with a sort of federal organization of local societies which sent delegates to an annual national meeting. These organizations were very effective in creating public sentiment by holding meetings, publishing papers, printing tracts and books, and petitioning the legislatures.

A class of professional reformers arose, men and women who spent their lives in urging reforms, and who traveled about the country making converts to their causes. Some had paid employment as secretaries and managers of societies. Some freely gave both their time and their means. They did their best,

without much effect, to induce the churches to take strong
ground in favor of such causes as temperance and antislavery.
They invited foreign agitators to come over; they engaged
reformed criminals to warn their countrymen against crime;
they organized and agitated and created public opinion to their
hearts' content.

207. REFORMS ACCOMPLISHED

The basis of these movements was a new conception of the
responsibility of the state and local governments for the welfare
of the people.   Concern was felt even for the condition of slaves
and of convicts, who had previously been looked upon as almost outside of the pale of humanity.   People began to see that
brutality to prisoners leads to brutality to free men, and that

DOROTHEA DIX IN 1850. (From an
engraving.)

punishment is useless un-
less it leads to reform.
The first modern prison in
America was the Eastern
Penitentiary at Philadel-
phia (finished just before
1830), where, in order to
prevent one criminal from
contaminating another, the
prisoners were shut up in
separate cells.   In the
course of the twenties and
thirties all the states and
the federal government
passed laws releasing
debtors who had nothing
with which to pay.

Hospitals, clean and well-kept poorhouses, orphan asylums,
and institutions for the deaf, dumb, and blind, also began to
appear; and in 1841 came forward a great woman, Dorothea
Dix, who made it the object of her life to persuade people that

it was the duty of the state governments to provide public asylums for the care of the insane.

Up to about 1840 spirituous liquor was used freely by all classes: harvest hands received it; it was a part of the regular ration at sea; and it was often served even at funerals. The Washingtonian societies, founded in 1840, agreed to use liquor only in moderation, and from that it was a short step to total abstinence, and in 1851 to the "Maine Law," the first of the state prohibition laws.

A strong movement began about 1830 for "Woman's Rights," in which Frances Wright, and later Lucy Stone, Susan B. Anthony, and others were leaders. Their demand for good schools for girls was heard; girls were admitted to the public schools, then into high

LADY IN BLOOMER COSTUME.

schools; academies were founded for them; and in 1833 Oberlin College was opened to women. The movement soon spread to a demand for woman suffrage, which, however, was nowhere granted till more than a generation later. Mrs. Bloomer tried in vain to introduce a new ladies' costume.

208. EDUCATIONAL REFORM

The idea underlying all these reform movements and methods was that the world was steadily improving and that by a vigorous effort of the men and women of good will, it could be rapidly brought to perfection. All the heathen were to be converted; all the forces for evil in our own country were to be destroyed; free government, free conscience, and free discussion were to make the United States the best and happiest land that the world had ever seen. Virtue, however, needed to be backed by intelligence, and hence the reform movement early applied itself to the schools of the country.

The states of New York and Pennsylvania now adopted the system of general public schools supported by taxation. The old theory was that schooling was like the use of roads and bridges — the people who want them ought to pay for them. That idea was supplanted by the great conception that the state ought to provide for the education of all the children because a state made up of educated people is stronger and more efficient. Hence childless people and corporations were required to pay school taxes exactly like the heads of large families.

This movement did not much affect the southern states, where the boys of well-to-do families were educated in private schools, and till years later there was no adequate system outside of town and city public schools. Even in the states that had longest enjoyed the public school system, the schools were doing poor work.

Massachusetts, under the guidance of Horace Mann, woke up in 1837 to the fact that she had wretched schoolhouses, dull textbooks, untrained teachers, and ill-disciplined pupils. Public sentiment was aroused in the state, the school system was improved, the people began to tax themselves more freely, and a state Board of Education was formed. The first normal school for the training of teachers was established in 1839. These ideas spread from state to state.

The system of state universities was developed in 1825 by the founding of the University of Virginia (in which Jefferson was specially interested), the first American institution on the

German model, offering a variety of elective studies. In the thirties Michigan established the so-called "Epistemiad," which developed into a state university. In 1837 there were over seventy-five endowed colleges in the country, besides twelve state universities and various kinds of special and technical schools. West Point Military Academy was founded in 1802, the Naval Academy in 1846, and law and medical schools by 1840 were numerous.

This was also a period of the foundation or enlargement of libraries — the Astor in New York, the Mercantile in Philadelphia, the Athenæum in Boston, and many others. Museums of art and science were opened in many cities, and the lyceum system of public lectures brought into towns and villages the most eminent men of the time.

209. GROWTH OF AMERICAN LITERATURE

Until about 1830 most of the American essays, poems, novels, and criticisms were simply imitations of English writers. Even Washington Irving was, intellectually, an Englishman of the school of Addison and Goldsmith, but he sought American subjects, and his *Knickerbocker's History of New York* (published 1809) is one of the most delightful of American satires. Of novelists the only widely known American at that time was James Fenimore Cooper, who began in 1821 to publish his entrancing

SUNNYSIDE, WASHINGTON IRVING'S HOME AT TARRY-TOWN, NEW YORK.

novels of Indian life and character. In 1833 Edgar Allan Poe
began his wonderful tales. William Cullen Bryant in 1811,
when seventeen years old, touched the height of his genius
in his poem of *Thanatopsis*. Other great writers, such as
Hawthorne and Lowell, though they began to publish at this
time, reached their zenith later. A school of American historians arose with the bold undertaking of George Bancroft
to write the history of America from the beginnings, of which
the first volumes came out in 1834; and a little later (1837)
appeared William H. Prescott's *Ferdinand and Isabella*. Another important book was the first edition of Noah Webster's
American Dictionary of the English Language, published in
1828.

Educated Americans were great readers of the English quar-
terly reviews; and in 1815 was established the *North American
Review*, for many years an intellectual force. Newspapers began
to improve, and between 1833 and 1841 were founded the *New
York Daily Sun*, the first one-cent newspaper; the *New York
Herald*, which set a standard in the search for news; and
Horace Greeley's *New York Tribune*, an example of breezy personal journalism. They were reënforced in 1849 by the Associated Press, which furnished information to a great number of
papers.

210. SLAVE LIFE

The spirit of social reform extended very slowly to the South,
which was not kindly disposed to new ideas that might upset
its rigid class system. The 3,700,000 whites of the South in
1830 were divided into three social strata: (1) At the summit
stood from 25,000 to 30,000 members of the families of large
slaveholders; in a few cases one master owned as many as a
thousand slaves. These people were the social and political
aristocracy; they furnished the governors, the judges, the
representatives in Congress, and the senators. (2) About
630,000 people belonged to families each holding from one to
four slaves; together with perhaps 500,000 prosperous nonslave-

holding white farmers, they made up the active working community. (3) The poor whites, numbering about 2,500,000, had neither slaves nor property, except rough land and miserable buildings. Outside of some mountain communities they never dreamed of using their votes against the slaveholding aristocracy.

Below all the whites were 180,000 free negroes, a despised and unhappy class, without political rights, held responsible for most of the petty crimes, and not allowed to move about freely. At the bottom of society were 2,000,000 African slaves, the people from whose physical toil came most of the wealth and consequence of their masters.

FANNY KEMBLE, ABOUT 1830.

On the conditions of slave life there is an immense mass of conflicting testimony. Fanny Kemble, English wife of a Georgia planter, complained of sick slave women "prostrate on the earth, without bedstead, bed mattress, or pillow." She saw her husband's slaves, including sick women, going to the field in gangs, each with a slave driver armed with a whip. She saw a perfectly faithful slave given over to a new master who, in a few hours, was to carry him away forever from his father, mother, and wife.

At the other extreme is the picture of slavery in Virginia drawn by such writers as Pollard in his *Black Diamonds* — the white and the black boys growing up together, friends and playmates; the master listening to the complaints of his slaves;

and the white mistress, sweet and stately, counseling the young and protecting the aged. "I love the simple and unadulterated slave, with his geniality, his mirth, his swagger, and his nonsense; I love to look upon his countenance, shining with content and grease; I love to study his affectionate heart."

These views conflict, but are not contradictory, for there were many kinds of slavery. On some plantations the slaves were felt to be members of the family; on other plantations the life of the slaves was a round of dull misery, lighted up by a few jollifications. The house slaves were well fed, had light tasks, and were often petted by their masters; the field slaves were often overworked and abused. The right to own a slave included the right to sell him, and there was no legal obligation to sell families together. Heartbreaking scenes came at the auction block; yet the next day the slave, torn from his family, might be cheerfully fiddling on his way to the dreaded far South.

211. SLAVERY CONTROVERSY (1831–1850)

Slavery had been under discussion in both North and South for fifty years; but for various reasons it came sharply to the front after 1830:

(1) The slaves were not contented, as was shown by three risings: the Gabriel insurrection in Virginia in 1800; a plan to destroy Charleston, formed in 1820 by Denmark Vesey, a free negro; and a bloody insurrection in Southampton, Virginia (1831), under Nat Turner, a slave.

(2) The South was bent on expanding the boundaries and the influence of slavery, and enlarging the profits of slave labor; the result was the appearance of northern men, like John Quincy Adams, who protested against the extension of slavery.

(3) The free states grew in population so that after 1833 they had 141 representatives in Congress, as against 99 from the slave states (§ 183).

(4) The method of reform through societies extended to the slavery question. Though the southern abolition movement

(§ 183) suddenly collapsed about the year 1830, within ten years one thousand northern abolition societies were formed with about 40,000 members; and they demanded the immediate and absolute emancipation of all the slaves.

Two kinds of people, often not clearly separate, took ground against slavery: the antislavery men, who would have been

AT WORK IN A COTTON FIELD.

satisfied to prevent its extension; and the abolitionists, who wanted to destroy it where it already existed. Among the abolitionists there were three groups: western, middle states, and New England. (1) The western abolition societies were started chiefly by former slaveholders, who crossed the Ohio River to get away from the system. Such were Rev. John Rankin and James G. Birney. (2) The middle states abolitionists were strong in Philadelphia, the city of New York, and central New York state, and included men like Arthur and Louis Tappan and Gerrit Smith, who had money and freely gave it for the cause. (3) The New England group included the most brilliant opponents of slavery, such as Wendell Phillips, the abolition orator; John Greenleaf Whittier, the abolition poet; Theodore Parker, the abolition parson; and later James Russell Lowell, the abolition satirist.

Among the hundreds of northern agitators, William Lloyd Garrison, by his intense devotion to the cause, has somehow come to be accepted as the typical abolitionist, although he differed with everybody else, and always represented the extremest principles. Garrison was born at Newburyport, Massachusetts (1805), became a printer, and wandered about the country. In 1830 he went to jail in Baltimore for too freely criticizing a slave trader. In January, 1831, Garrison founded in Boston a little paper which he called the *Liberator*, and which speedily became one of the best-known and worst-hated papers in the country. From the platform of principles which he published in the first number, he never swerved throughout his life. He "determined, at every hazard, to lift up the standard of emancipation in the eyes of the nation."

Garrison was a one-sided and prejudiced man, who never could see that the slaveholder was anything but a robber and murderer; but he compelled people to listen to him, even when he refused to have anything to do with the federal government, because it protected slavery; and he publicly burned the Constitution of the United States, calling it — in scriptural language — "a covenant with death and an agreement with hell."

212. ABOLITION SOCIETIES (1830–1840)

The abolitionists had a very effective method of agitation. Local societies were federated in a state society, which held an annual meeting; and into an annual national convention. Meetings and local conventions were held from time to time to arouse public sentiment, and women and negroes sat on the stage and took part in the exercises. The societies prepared petitions to the state legislatures and to Congress, and did everything they could to interest people and to make them abolitionists. Newspapers were founded, tracts, books, and almanacs were prepared, and freely illustrated with pictures of the horrors of slavery; and one college, Oberlin, admitted negro students and became the western center of the abolition sentiment.

The abolitionist meetings, societies, and publications caused an astonishing uproar. In the South, practically nobody was allowed to advocate abolition; in the North the sensitive city population showed its horror of the agitation by trying to mob the abolitionists. In 1835 an antislavery meeting in Boston was broken up by a mob, which laid hold of Garrison, tied a rope about his body, and dragged him through the streets. In 1837 another abolition agitator and editor, Elijah Lovejoy, was murdered by a mob in Alton, Illinois, because he persisted in publishing an antislavery paper even in a free state. Colored schools were broken up, and in New York and Philadelphia colored settlements were attacked. Nobody was more hated and despised than the abolitionist.

The abolition societies adopted the practice of sending petitions asking Congress to prohibit slavery in the District of Columbia, and in 1835 William Slade of Vermont made the first abolition speech in Congress. This led to a series of so-called Gag Resolutions (1836–1844), by which the House forbade any debate on antislavery petitions; and in the Senate, Calhoun introduced resolutions fiercely condemning the abolitionists. This attempt to stop discussion aroused John Quincy Adams, who insisted on the right to argue in the halls of Congress on any subject. In 1837 and again in 1842, attempts were made to pass a vote of censure on him in the House; but Adams warned Congress that if they attempted to stop petitions by censuring the member who presented them, "they would have the people coming besieging, not beseeching." The first

western abolitionist member of Congress, Joshua R. Giddings
of Ohio, appeared in 1838, and he made it the main purpose
of his life to bring about slavery debates on all sorts of side
questions, in spite of an attempt (1842) to close his lips by a
vote of censure.

213. REVIEW

The period from 1830 was one of social and moral reform.
Despotism was losing ground in Europe, and people in the
United States were growing sympathetic with the poor and the
ignorant, the debtor and the criminal. In the churches there
was a strong missionary spirit, which led to a system of missions in foreign countries. Sunday Schools were founded, and
new national churches were created, including the Mormon
sect, which later found a home in the West. Reform was much
aided by humanitarian societies, local and national, and by a
class of men and women who gave their whole energy to urging
reforms. Hence humane prisons were erected, imprisonment
for debt was prohibited, and new movements were put forth in
the cause of temperance reform and for the rights of women.

Public schools were established in the northern states that
lacked them, and were improved in others. The first important
state universities were founded, and also professional schools.
This was the Golden Age in American literature, in which
the leaders were Irving, Cooper, Hawthorne, Bryant, Lowell,
Bancroft, and Prescott. Great newspapers were founded and
improved.

The old abolitionist movement had died out but was renewed
under the new impetus; and visitors and observers began to
publish accounts of the conditions of slavery. No public criticism of slavery was allowed in the South, but active societies
were founded in all parts of the North; William Lloyd Garrison
was the best-known leader. These societies began to petition
Congress; and there was no stopping them, short of giving up
the right of free discussion in the national legislature.

References Bearing on the Text and Topics

Geography and Maps. Coman, *Indust. Hist.*, 204. — Dodd, *Expansion and Conflict*, 169. — Hart, *Slavery and Abolition*, 126, 230. — Johnson, *Union and Democracy*, 299.

Secondary. Adams, *U.S.*, IX. 175–187, 198–242. — Bogart, *Econ. Hist.*, ch. xxi. — E. E. Brown, *Middle Schools*, chs. xi–xv; *Origin of State Universities.* — W. G. Brown, *Lower South*, 16–49. — Collins, *Domestic Slave Trade.* — Fish, *Am. Nationality*, 149–154, 281–299. — Hart, *Slavery and Abolition; S. P. Chase*, 18–91. — Linn, *Mormons*, bks. i–iv. — McMaster, *U.S.*, IV. 522–569, V. 82–108, 184–226, 284–432, VI. 69–79, 94–113, 177–182, 270–298, 454–493, VII. 74–99, 134–270. — MacDonald, *From Jefferson to Lincoln*, ch. iv; *Jacksonian Democracy*, chs. i, xiv, xv. — Page, *Old South*, 57–92, 143–185. — Rhodes, *U.S.*, I. 40–75, 303–383. — Schouler, *U.S.*, III. 208–234, 507–531, IV. 1–31, 176–180, 199–229, 296–303, 310–316, 422–429, 480. — Sheldon, *Student Life*, ch. iv. — Sparks, *Expansion*, 290–296, 376–418. — Turner, *New West*, chs. ii–iv, x. — Wendell, *Literary Hist.*, 157–435. — See also refs. to ch. xi.

Sources. *Am. Hist. Leaflets*, no. 10. — Ames, *State Docs. on Fed. Rels.*, 193–223, 232–240. — Beard, *Readings*, §§ 32–35. — Bogart and Thompson, *Readings*, ch. xvii. — Caldwell, *Survey*, 148–156. — Caldwell and Persinger, *Source Hist.*, 387–395. — Callender, *Econ Hist.*, ch. xv. — Douglass, *Life and Times.* — Harding, *Select Orations*, nos. 16, 17. — Hart, *Contemporaries*, III. §§ 151–157, 169–184; *Patriots and Statesmen*, III. 333–335, 357–359, IV. 64–382 passim, V. 62–70, 75–78, 153–155, 159–171, 252–257; *Source Book*, II. §§ 94–101. — James, *Readings*, §§ 62, 63, 76, 81. — Johnson, *Readings*, §§ 108–115. — *Old South Leaflets*, nos. 78, 79, 81, 102, 135, 137–141, 144, 145, 148, 157, 175, 180. — Olmsted, *Seaboard Slave States.* — Smedes, *Southern Planter*, 17–189. — See New Engl. Hist. Teachers' Assoc., *Hist. Sources*, § 85; *Syllabus*, 348.

Illustrative. Aldrich, *Story of a Bad Boy* (N.E.). — Belt, *Mirage of Promise* (abolition). — Chesnutt, *Conjure Woman* (slave life). — Dougall, *Mormon Prophet.* — Eggleston, *Graysons; Hoosier Schoolmaster* (West). — Hale, *New Engl. Boyhood.* — Harris, *Uncle Remus.* — Hawthorne, *Blithedale Romance.* — Johnston, *Old Times in Middle Georgia.* — Kester, *Prodigal Judge* (S.W.). — Kirkland, *McVeys; Zury* (West). — Larcom, *New England Girlhood.* — Longstreet, *Georgia Scenes.* — Lowell, *On the Capture of Fugitive Slaves; Wendell Phillips; W. L. Garrison.* — Mitchell, *Doctor Johns* (Conn.). — Stowe, *Uncle Tom's Cabin.* — Tiernan, *Suzette* (Va.). — Tourgée, *Button's Inn* (Mormons). — Whittier, *Antislavery Poems*, 9–94.

Pictures. *Mentor*, serial nos. 77, 100, 109. — Sparks, *Expansion*. — Wilson, *Am. People*, IV.

Topics Answerable from the References Above

(1) Incidents of imprisonment for debt. [§ 204] — (2) Influence of Dorothea Dix. [§ 207] — (3) Early temperance societies. [§ 207] — (4) Career of *one* of the following: Frances Wright; Lucy Stone; Susan B. Anthony. [§ 207] — (5) Founding of *one* of the following colleges: Wesleyan; Oberlin; Union; North Carolina; Michigan; Iowa. [§ 208] — (6) Literary career of *one* of the following: Irving; Poe; Cooper; Bryant; Hawthorne; Lowell; Bancroft; Prescott; Noah Webster; Greeley. [§ 209] — (7) Account of *one* of the following slave insurrections: Gabriel; Denmark Vesey; Nat Turner. [§ 211] — (8) Contemporary account of an abolition meeting. [§ 212] — (9) The Garrison, *or* Lovejoy, mob. [§ 212]

Topics for Further Search

(10) Catholic *or* Protestant missions to the Indians. [§ 205] — (11) Beginning of the Sunday School movement. [§ 205] — (12) Mormon Church to 1844. [§ 205] — (13) New England, *or* western, public schools previous to 1830. [§ 208] — (14) Early days at *one* of the following: University of Virginia; West Point; Naval Academy. [§ 208] — (15) Conditions of *one* of the following groups: rich slaveholding families; small slaveholding families; poor whites; free negroes in the North; free negroes in the South; slaves in the border states; slaves in the lower South. [§ 210] — (16) Antislavery activity of *one* of the following: John Rankin; James G. Birney; Arthur Tappan; Louis Tappan; Gerrit Smith; Wendell Phillips; John Greenleaf Whittier; Theodore Parker; James Russell Lowell. [§ 211]

CHAPTER XX

NEW POLITICAL ISSUES (1829-1841)

214. American Democracy and Jackson

WHEN Jackson became President in 1829 (§ 202), the principles of American democratic government had in many ways advanced much further than in 1789: (1) Many of the states had rid themselves of the old property and tax qualifications for officers and for voters. (2) Nearly all the important state officers, including judges, were elected by popular vote instead of being chosen by the legislature or governor, as formerly. (3) By the system of "rotation in office" state and local elective officers were chosen for short terms, and rarely reëlected more than once or twice. (4) The idea of rotation in office was extending to clerks and other minor officers in most states and municipalities. (5) The cities were growing rapidly and demanded new forms of government.

Politics, too, had lost its old simplicity. There were some leaders of the type now called party bosses; and whatever party might be in power in a state tried to keep in power by distributing offices as rewards to its followers. Parties often tried to perpetuate their power by the "gerrymander"; that is, by so arranging the boundaries of electoral districts that their friends should carry some districts by small majorities and their opponents should carry fewer districts by large majorities, so that the minority might rule. Violence at the polls was frequent, and fraud was not unknown. The party newspapers were still unscrupulous and abusive.

215. ANDREW JACKSON

The most noted representative of the new democratic principles was President Andrew Jackson; and, except Clay, no man in all the West was so widely known, so experienced in public affairs, and so capable of making quick decisions.

In personal appearance Jackson was tall and spare, with a high forehead and a great mane of hair, which silvered while he was President. A lion to his enemies, Jackson was the soul of courtesy, and to ladies almost a Don Quixote. All his life long he was accustomed to lead in the community and in the army; hence he was over-quick to make up his mind, and when he had once come to a conclusion, could not be moved from it.

ANDREW JACKSON.   (From a daguerreotype.)

"Jack Downing," a political humorist of the time, makes him say, "It has always bin my way, when I git a notion, to stick to it till it dies a natural death; and the more folks talk agin my notions, the more I stick to 'em."

On the whole Jackson's instincts were right; he hated monopoly and corporate greed and private advantage from public office. He saw much better than most men of his time the dangers likely to result from the effort of the national government to help the states and the business men. His fault was that he looked upon the government as a kind of military organization in which it was treason to the country to interfere with the orders of the commanding general. If he had a prejudice against a man, he thought that man his enemy; if he was Jackson's enemy, of course he must also be an enemy to his country. Yet it is true that Jackson was a living representative of the opinions of a majority of the voters in the United States, and represented them more directly than did the members of Congress.

216. JACKSON'S ADMINISTRATION (1829–1837)

Jackson's military principles were carried into his appointments. His Cabinet had no eminent member except Martin Van Buren of New York, the Secretary of State, often called "the Little Magician," for his urbanity and political shrewdness. Alongside his official Cabinet was a group of personal friends satirically called the "Kitchen Cabinet," which contained the real advisers of the President: it included Van Buren; Major Eaton, Secretary of War; Amos Kendall, later brought into the post office department to dismiss the local postmasters; and

THOMAS H. BENTON.

Duff Green, editor of the *Telegraph*, the Jackson newspaper organ. It was a mistake to appoint other men to the Cabinet if the President did not care to consult them. Thomas H. Benton, senator from Missouri, was one of the strongest Jackson men.

Never before that time had a President been so beset with office seekers; and the principal way in which vacancies could be found was by turning out those who already held office. To the day of his death Jackson declared that no man was removed in his administration without a reason; but he was easily persuaded that hundreds of officers were lazy, or corrupt, or politically partisan. Hence in his eight years he removed 252 of the 610 officers appointed by the President; and nobody knows how many clerks and subordinates went with their chiefs. The vacancies thus made were filled without much discrimination, and the Senate threw out many of his nominations. Yet it is an injustice to Jackson to hold him responsible for bringing the system of partisan politics to Washington. He really meant to carry out what he called "the task of reform," but he demoralized the public service, because he took the advice of people intent chiefly on their own political fortunes. This so-called "Spoils System" was much aided by the growth of party spirit and party organization; when a party captured the presidency, many of the friends of the other party were removed.

217. THE BANK AND THE TARIFF (1829–1832)

Jackson's love of a fight and his hold on the people were brought out by his long contest with the United States Bank. That bank had several sets of enemies, among them the western state banks, of which there were about three hundred. Another group was created when Biddle, president of the bank, refused to remove some branch-bank officers and to substitute Jackson men (1829). Its most dangerous foe was Jackson, because he represented an enormous constituency of farmers and small traders who were convinced that the eastern capitalists were getting more than their share of the annual products of the country. Jackson believed also, and with reason, that the bank sooner or later would become a political force.

Accordingly, in his annual messages year after year Jackson

repeated a warning that the bank was dangerous, unsound, and unconstitutional. In 1832, as the presidential election was approaching, the friends of the bank, under Clay's leadership, made up their minds to force the issue into the campaign. They therefore passed a recharter bill in both houses, four years before the charter of 1816 was to expire; and Jackson, as was expected, vetoed it (July 10, 1832).

The bank question was for a time pushed aside by the threats of South Carolina to nullify the offensive tariff acts. The temper of the states was shown in a debate in the Senate in 1830, in which Senator Hayne insisted on the right of a state to declare a federal statute void (§ 152). Webster of Massachusetts seized the opportunity in his "Second Reply to Hayne," to protest, with all his matchless eloquence and national spirit, not so much against Hayne as against the doctrines of the South Carolina *Exposition* of 1828, written by Vice President Calhoun (§ 201).

Jackson's position on nullification was not clearly made known till April, 1830, when, at a dinner on Jefferson's birthday, he was called on for a toast and gave "Our Federal Union: it must be preserved." A few weeks later Jackson quarreled with Calhoun for personal reasons, and broke off relations with the Vice President. A last effort was made to get Congress to reduce the offensive tariff, and a new tariff was passed (July 14, 1832); but Clay saw to it that the protective duties of 1824 were left in, and some of them raised; though the average rate of duty was reduced to about 34 per cent.

218. NULLIFICATION AND THE TARIFF (1832–1833)

In the presidential campaign of 1832, the direct issue was the bank. For the first time delegates were gathered in general party nominating conventions. The anti-Jackson men met in a "National Republican Convention," made the first rational party platform, and nominated Henry Clay. Jackson had already been nominated by members of several state legislatures, and his nomination was confirmed by a "Democratic National Convention," which also proposed Van Buren for Vice President. In the election, part of New England, with Maryland, Delaware, and Kentucky, went for Clay; and the rest of the South (except South Carolina) and the West, with Pennsylvania and New York, voted for Jackson, who had 219 electoral votes to 49 for Clay, and 690,000 popular votes to 530,000.

Jackson accepted the election of 1832 as an approval of his past course, and also of all the things that he meant to do in the future; and something had to be done very soon in South Carolina. A convention of the state, elected for that sole purpose, passed a Nullification Ordinance (November 24, 1832) declaring the tariff acts of 1828 and 1832 to be "null, void, and no law, nor binding upon this State, its officers or citizens." This action, which was a revival of the doctrine of the Virginia and Kentucky Resolutions (§ 152), was taken by Jackson as a personal affront. He issued a proclamation (December 11), warning the people of South Carolina against "the illegal and disorganizing action of the convention." At Jackson's request, an act, popularly called the "Force Bill" or "Bloody Bill," was passed by Congress (March 2, 1833), giving the President more power to raise forces to meet such a crisis.

South Carolina began to raise troops, and the country was full of excitement. Calhoun resigned the vice presidency and came back to the Senate in 1833, in order to defend his doctrines in debates with Webster. In the end South Carolina really carried her point, for the majority of Congress believed that the South was wronged by the tariff. Under Clay's leadership, by the Compromise tariff of 1833 (March 2) Congress provided that the rates should be reduced at intervals till 1842, when they were all to come down to 20 per cent. Since the purpose of nullification was thus reached without actually applying it, all plans of resistance were dropped by South Carolina.

219. STATE RIGHTS THEORIES OF CALHOUN

For the ideas and arguments behind the nullification movement, we must look to the addresses and speeches of John C. Calhoun. Calhoun came of the vigorous Scotch-Irish race; he was born in 1782 in South Carolina and entered Congress in 1811. As Monroe's Secretary of War (1817–1825) he was very efficient, and as Vice President (1825–1832) he was long looked upon as the probable successor to Jackson. In 1828 he made a square turn against the use of national authority through implied powers (§ 141) and worked out his doctrine of nullification — a doctrine which was a magazine of argument for the secessionists at the time of the Civil War. It may be divided into three parts — the grievance, the nature of the federal government, and the remedy:

JOHN C. CALHOUN, ABOUT 1850. (From a daguerreotype.)

(1) Calhoun's grievance was that without any constitutional warrant, by the "tyranny of the majority," the tariff took a tax out of the pocket of the planters, and brought them no advantage.

(2) His theory of the government was that "the Union is a union of states and not of individuals"; that the Constitution is a "compact" made by the states; and, as in any other contract, if the states on one side failed to observe the limitations of the Constitution, the other states were freed from their obliga-

tion. He insisted that the federal system had no independent existence and was not a real government, but only an "agency."

(3) Calhoun shrank from the logical policy of secession; he proposed, instead, the remedy of nullification, by which the people of South Carolina were simply to refuse to obey the tariff acts, on the ground that they were unconstitutional. For the federal government to bring suits to enforce the acts, or to use force, seemed to Calhoun's mind an act of war, which would dissolve the Union; and he had no doubt that other states would come to the rescue.

220. NATIONAL THEORIES OF WEBSTER

The spokesman of the national theory of government was Daniel Webster, born in 1782 in New Hampshire. He graduated

DANIEL WEBSTER.

from Dartmouth College. In 1813 he was sent to Congress from New Hampshire; then in 1823 from Massachusetts, and in 1828 to a senator's seat from Massachusetts, which he occupied most of his life thenceforth, with two intervals of service as Secretary of State. Webster's theory of the government was substantially as follows:

(1) He scouted the idea that the Constitution is a compact, and called it an "instrument of government" for a nation. "It is, Sir, the people's Constitution, . . . made by the people, and answerable to the people. . . . We are all agents of the same supreme power, the people."

(2) In language which rang throughout the Union, he denied the right of nullification and declared the great principle that the states could no more destroy the Union than the Union could destroy the states; for both were founded on the consent of the American people, taken as a whole.

(3) On the question who should decide in disputes as to federal powers, he held that the Constitution provided a mode "for bringing all questions of constitutional power to the final decision of the Supreme Court."

Webster's speeches were widely read and became the familiar doctrine in the North, especially in the crisis of the Civil War. One of the phrases just quoted appears in a little different form in Lincoln's Gettysburg Address of 1863.

221. PUBLIC DEPOSITS AND SPECULATION (1833–1837)

When the nullification trouble was out of the way, Jackson returned with energy to the United States Bank, which he attacked with all his might because he was under the mistaken belief that it was secretly bankrupt. He therefore ordered the Secretary of the Treasury, Duane, to stop depositing government funds in the bank (September, 1833). When Duane refused, Jackson removed him and appointed in his place Roger B. Taney, who gave the necessary orders. This was a terrible blow to the prestige of the bank. Jackson held with justice that it was the right of the President to perform what he believed to be his constitutional duty, subject to impeachment or to public opinion. The approval of the country was shown in 1834, when majorities of Jackson men were elected to both the House and the Senate. The deposits were never restored, and when the national charter expired in 1836, the bank was obliged to accept a Pennsylvania state charter in order to continue business.

By this time it was a tradition that no President should serve more than two terms, and Jackson secured the nomination of Van Buren by the Democratic convention of 1836. The oppo-

sition, now called "Whigs," were too discouraged to make a
party nomination, and Jackson's popularity pulled the Democratic candidate through by 170 electoral votes to 124 scattered
among four Whig candidates.

Before Van Buren took office in 1837, the country was approaching the worst financial panic that it has ever known.
The main reasons for this calamity were the bad conditions of
currency, banking, and speculative business.

(1) When the notes of the United States Bank were retired,
the only currency was depreciated state bank notes, for specie
was almost out of circulation.

(2) The banking business was in poor shape. Western and
southwestern banks received large government deposits and
lent the funds to buyers of public lands.

(3) Prices of cotton and other products rose so fast that
everybody seemed to be getting rich. The states found that
they had credit abroad and ran up public debts amounting to
$170,000,000.

222. PANIC OF 1837 AND ITS CONSEQUENCES (1835-1840)

Speculation was especially lively in the western lands. To
check it, Jackson issued a Specie Circular (1836) directing that
nothing but gold and silver should thenceforth be received for
the public lands. In 1835 the national debt was extinguished
and a surplus began to run up. People supposed that there
would be a surplus every year indefinitely, and Congress passed
the Deposit Act (June, 1836) for transferring to the states
about $36,000,000. The money had to come out of the banks
holding government deposits, and that brought on the crash.
In May, 1837, all the banks in the country suspended specie
payment of their notes. Nine tenths of the business men in
the country went bankrupt. Many of the states ceased paying interest on their state debts, and three of them repudiated
their outstanding public debts to the amount of about
$20,000,000. The building of railroads and canals received a

shock, and it was five or six years before commercial prosperity returned.

The "pet banks" eventually turned over to the government $28,000,000 of public funds under the Deposit Act, and it was duly transferred to the states. Some of the states spent the money on canals, some in payment of old debts, some for education, and a few states simply divided it among the voters. Slowly the country struggled up again; though in a second and lighter crash (1839), the old United States Bank went completely to ruin. Some of the states, especially New York, had provided, against such a calamity, a system of banking laws, under which the state banks were required to keep on hand specie to redeem any notes that might be presented.

A notable act of Congress during Van Buren's administration was a statute of 1840 for an independent treasury, or sub-treasury, as it was often called, requiring the Treasury Department to keep its balances in its own vaults.

223. FOREIGN POLICY AND TEXAS (1829–1841)

Jackson was not exactly what is called a diplomatic man, but in his relations with foreign countries he was on the whole successful. From Great Britain he secured the long-desired privilege of carrying on West India trade in American ships (§ 110); and he refused to carry out an arbitration for the settlement of the Maine boundaries. By rather undignified threats, he compelled France to make a settlement (1836) of the "French Spoliation Claims," for captures of American merchantmen, claims which had been running ever since 1803.

The most serious foreign question of the time was the attitude of the United States toward "Texas," as the Mexicans named the region southwest of Louisiana. Americans had long looked with desire upon this broad, rich land, and in 1819 Moses Austin and his son Stephen F. Austin, originally Connecticut men, secured large land grants from Spain. When Mexico became independent (1821) the new government confirmed the grants, and thousands of settlers poured in, many of them from the southern states and many with their slaves. Both John Quincy Adams and Andrew Jackson, in the hope of bringing the wandering children back under the home roof, made several vain attempts to buy Texas.

By 1836 the Americans in Texas felt so strongly that they were a separate people, that they openly declared their independence, and drew up a constitution under which slavery was made legal. A few days later, the fortified church of the Alamo in San Antonio was taken by a Mexican force after a brave defense, and every American defender was killed. This massacre sowed undying hatred. The Texans could not be conquered by Mexico, and asked to be made a state of the Union, claiming a boundary to the mouth of the Rio Grande, "then up the principal stream of the said river to its source." Jackson would have been glad to meet this demand, but there was such a strong feeling in the North against bringing in more slaveholding territory that he contented himself by securing the recognition of Texan independence. For eight years, therefore, the United States regularly exchanged dispatches and messages with Texas. Van Buren, as a northern man, felt no interest in annexation, and he did his best to come to an understanding with Mexico by a settlement of claims for losses and injuries suffered in that country by American citizens.

224. Review

The twelve years of Jackson's influence, which included Van Buren's administration (1837–1841), were marked by great activity in public life. Suffrage and officeholding were made easier. At the same time party organization became stiffer, and tended to submit to personal control. Andrew Jackson represented these new tendencies toward a broader democracy, though he had the fault of looking on all public questions as more or less personal. He made the mistake of appointing a Cabinet which he did not fully trust, and of removing a large number of public officials because he was led to believe that they were corrupt or inefficient.

Jackson attacked the United States Bank and after several years of controversy succeeded in preventing its recharter. The protest of South Carolina against the tariff brought on the famous Webster-Hayne debate of 1830, shortly after which Jackson openly took the side of the Union.

Jackson was reëlected in 1832, mainly on the bank issue, and at once moved against the theory of the government put forth by Calhoun under the name of "nullification" (1828). The state of South Carolina in 1832 adopted an ordinance intended to nullify the tariff laws. Jackson opposed, and would have used force against the nullifiers. Nevertheless by the compromise of 1833, Congress gave way on the tariff issue, and nullification was not put to the test. On the other hand Daniel Webster stated the national theory of government in a way that was never forgotten.

Jackson ordered the removal of the government deposits in the United States Bank in 1833. Bad banking led to speculation in the public lands, and was not stopped by Jackson's Specie Circular of 1836, nor by the Deposit Act of the same year for turning over the cash surplus of the government to the states. A commercial panic in 1837 was the worst the country has ever seen. During this period Jackson was settling the French Spoliation Claims, and tried unsuccessfully to bring the country to the point of annexing the new republic of Texas.

References Bearing on the Text and Topics

Geography and Maps. See map, p. 346. — Dodd, *Expansion and Conflict*, 49, 66, 92. — Hart, *Slavery and Abolition*, 8, 52, 300. — Mac-Donald, *Jacksonian Democracy*, 4, 130, 214, 258.

Secondary. Bassett, *Andrew Jackson*, II. chs. xx–xxxii; *U.S.*, 392–426, 432–435. — Brown, *Andrew Jackson*, 118–156. — Coman, *Econ. Beginnings of the Far West*, II. 94–109. — Dewey, *Financial Hist.*, §§ 81–101. — Dodd, *Expansion and Conflict*, chs. iv–vi. — Fish, *Am. Nationality*, 184–248. — Garrison, *Texas*, chs. xi–xx; *Westward Exten-*

sion, ch. vi. — Hart, *Slavery and Abolition*, ch. xx. — Hunt, *J. C. Calhoun*, chs. ix-xv. — Lodge, *Daniel Webster*, 166-234. — McMaster, *U. S.*, V. 2-13, 519-556, VI. 1-68, 114-270, 299-420, 458-463, 494-513, 523-549. — MacDonald, *From Jefferson to Lincoln*, ch. iii; *Jacksonian Democracy*, chs. ii, iv-vii, ix, xi-xiii, xvii, xviii. — Peck, *Jacksonian Epoch*, 123-472. — Roosevelt, *T. H. Benton*, 63-139, 151-209. — Schouler, *U. S.*, III. 451-506, IV. 31-121, 132-199, 229-296, 316-352. — Schurz, *Henry Clay*, I. 322-384, II. chs. xiv-xvi, xviii-xx. — Shepard, *Van Buren*, chs. vi-x, xii. — Stanwood, *Presidency*, I. chs. xiii-xvi.

Sources. *Am. Hist. Leaflets*, nos. 24, 30. — Ames, *State Docs. on Fed. Rels.*, 158-189, 225-228. — Beard, *Readings*, §§ 39, 49-51. — Bogart and Thompson, *Readings*, 321-327, 496-503. — Caldwell and Persinger, *Source Hist.*, 354-378. — Hart, *Contemporaries*, III. §§ 158-164, 185, 186; *Patriots and Statesmen*, IV. 135-140, 154-329 passim. — Johnston, *Am. Orations*, I. 233-334, IV. 202-237. — See New Engl. Hist. Teachers' Assoc., *Hist. Sources*, § 84; *Syllabus*, 345-348.

Illustrative. Barr, *Remember the Alamo.* — Davis, *Letters of J. Downing, Major.* — Dillon, *Patience of John Morland.* — Munroe, *With Crockett and Bowie.* — Simms, *Border Beagles; Richard Hurdis.*
Pictures. Sparks, *Expansion.* — Wilson, *Am. People*, IV.

Topics Answerable from the References Above

(1) Objections to the "Kitchen Cabinet." [§ 216] — (2) Instances of removals of officials by Jackson. [§ 216] — (3) Career of Nicholas Biddle. [§ 217] — (4) Contemporary accounts of the Webster-Hayne debate. [§ 217] — (5) Why did Jackson quarrel with Calhoun? [§ 217] — (6) Incidents of the election of 1832. [§ 218] — (7) Incidents of the South Carolina Nullification Convention. [§ 218] — (8) Public career of Roger B. Taney. [§ 221] — (9) Wildcat state banks from 1830 to 1840. [§ 221] — (10) Incidents of the panic of 1837. [§ 222] — (11) Career of Moses Austin, *or* of Stephen F. Austin. [§ 223] — (12) Life in Texas before 1835. [§ 223] — (13) Siege and capture of the Alamo. [§ 223]

Topics for Further Search

(14) Why were the qualifications for voters made easier? [§ 214] — (15) Why were judges elected instead of appointed? [§ 214] — (16) Debates on the tariff of 1833. [§ 218] — (17) What did Calhoun mean by "compact"? [§ 219] — (18) Contemporary accounts of Webster's ideas on the Constitution. [§ 220] — (19) Was the second United States Bank dangerous? [§ 221] — (20) What were the "French Spoliation Claims"? [§ 223]

CHAPTER XXI

ADVANCE TO THE PACIFIC (1841–1850)

225. Whig Politics (1840–1842) and Local Disorders (1837–1842)

By the election of 1840, there was a change in party control for the first time since the new tariff system. The anti-Jackson men, or Whigs, succeeded in electing William Henry Harrison of Ohio over Van Buren, whom the Democrats nominated for a second term. It was a boisterous campaign, full of great mass meetings. Somebody said that Harrison was fit only to sit in his log cabin and drink hard cider; the Whigs took up the slur; and log cabins on wheels, amply provided with barrels of hard cider, were used as a popular argument to voters. The Democrats were beaten by the hard times, securing only 60 electoral votes against 234. Harrison had a popular majority of about 140,000. The Whigs, who were in control of both houses of the next Congress, set out to recharter a national

HARRISON CAMPAIGN SYMBOL OF 1840, AS DISPLAYED ON A HANDKERCHIEF.

337

bank, to spend money freely for internal improvements, and to revive a protective tariff.

Harrison died a month after his inauguration and was succeeded by the Vice President, John Tyler of Virginia, who was really not a Whig at all. He therefore vetoed two bank bills and two tariff bills, whereupon all the Whig Cabinet, except Webster, resigned. Tyler finally accepted the tariff of 1842, which ignored the compromise agreement of 1833 (§ 218) and raised the average duties from about 24 per cent to about 35 per cent. Throughout the rest of his administration, Tyler could find neither Whig nor Democratic support, and quarreled with Congress.

The late thirties and early forties were a time of disorder and disturbance. Besides the antislavery riots (§ 212), there were violent riots against foreigners; and in 1837 a Catholic convent near Boston was burned to the ground by an anti-Catholic mob. In two of the states there were serious outbreaks:

(1) In 1839, certain landholders in central New York held "Antirent" meetings to protest against the payment of a permanent annual ground rent, or "quitrent," amounting to from $7 to $18 a year per hundred acres. After several years of violence, the landlords accepted lump money payments for their claims.

(2) Rhode Island was the scene of the movement commonly called the "Dorr Rebellion" (1842). The so-called rebels were trying to secure, by irregular methods, a more liberal state constitution with manhood suffrage. Dorr, the most prominent man in the agitation, was arrested and convicted of treason. Practically he accomplished his work, for the government proceeded to make a new constitution and to enlarge the suffrage.

226. THE MAINE BOUNDARY (1821–1842)

Alongside the political questions of the day came several matters of foreign policy. Between 1842 and 1846 the boundaries of the United States were settled for Maine, Oregon, and Texas.

The controversy over the boundary between Maine and New Brunswick began with the Treaty of 1783, under which the line was to run "from the northwest angle of Nova Scotia, viz. that angle which is formed by a line drawn due north from the source of Saint Croix River to the Highlands; along the said Highlands which divide those rivers that empty themselves into the river St. Lawrence, from those which fall into the Atlantic Ocean, to the northwest-ernmost head of Con-necticut River." It was soon found that the two governments did not agree as to what stream was the St. Croix, nor where to locate the northwest angle, nor where the Highlands were, nor even what was meant by "Atlantic Ocean."

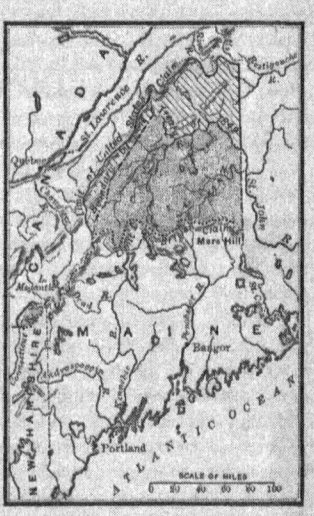

NORTHEAST BOUNDARY.

When an attempt was made to run the line (1821) the British insisted that the "Highlands" was a divide south of the St. John River. The Americans with far better reason found the "Highlands" 125 miles farther north, on the divide just south of the St. Lawrence. The local authorities almost came to blows in the "Aroostook War" (1838). Webster remained in Tyler's Cabinet long enough to settle this question: in 1842 he negotiated the Webster-Ashburton treaty, by which the dis-

puted territory was divided, and each party got about half.
The settlement was creditable and satisfactory to both sides,
and ended a controversy that threatened to bring on war.

227. Exploration of the Interior (1820-1845)

After the Lewis and Clark expedition to Oregon, and Pike's
explorations (§ 160), little was done by the government to
explore the interior; but the fur traders followed every important stream and opened up many routes across the Rockies.
After 1820 trade was developed with New Mexico over the
"Santa Fe trail," a road leading southwestward from Independence on the Missouri River to the Rio Grande (map, page
372). In 1832, a party under Bonneville crossed the Rockies
with a wagon by the Platte route and went as far west as Great
Salt Lake; some of his men even went on to the Pacific.

The Oregon fur trade was an object of great desire and before
1830 the traders discovered a route from the neighborhood of
Great Salt Lake across country to the Columbia. In 1834,
Nathaniel J. Wyeth of Massachusetts guided a party of traders
and settlers to Fort Hall, north of Great Salt Lake, and thence
to Oregon. By this time several mission societies, Protestant
and Catholic, were sending out missionaries to the Oregon
Indians along this route. In the winter of 1842-1843 Dr.
Whitman came east from Oregon by a dangerous, roundabout
route, partly on business of his mission, partly because he supposed that Webster was willing to give up all claims to Oregon.
There was no such danger; the country was awake to the importance of a Pacific outlet; and there is no contemporary
evidence to show that Whitman influenced either Secretary
Webster or the President. In 1843 he joined an expedition
formed by other people and with it returned to Oregon.

About the same time, a young army officer, named John C.
Frémont, made three long explorations westward (1842-1845).
He twice crossed the Sierra Nevada to California. He was a
poor explorer, and made no proper surveys; but he was a son-

in-law of Senator Benton of Missouri, young, dashing, and good-looking, and got the name of "Pathfinder" for his exploits.

228. ANNEXATION OF TEXAS (1844-1845)

The interior and Oregon were valuable for the future, but Texas was an immediate, pressing question which came to an issue in 1844. President Tyler appointed John C. Calhoun Secretary of State so that he might negotiate a treaty of annexation (April, 1844), and this brought the whole issue squarely before the country. The main arguments in favor of annexation were: (1) that it was a natural expansion which would simply bring back Americans to their own country; (2) that it was a "reannexation" of territory which was really a part of the Louisiana Purchase (§ 190); (3) that it would be an advantage to the slaveholders by giving them greater strength in the Union. On the other side the antislavery forces of the North violently opposed annexation because: (1) it would strengthen the slaveholding power in the Union; (2) it would probably bring on war with Mexico.

The treaty failed of ratification; and the question became an issue in the election of 1844. Clay, who was known to be opposed to annexation, was nominated by the Whigs. Van Buren was dropped by the Democratic convention and James K. Polk of Tennessee was nominated because he was known to favor annexation. The Democratic platform declared for "the reoccupation of Oregon and the reannexation of Texas at the earliest practicable period." Clay then felt compelled to change his ground by saying that he would be glad to see Texas annexed, "without dishonor, without war, with the common consent of the Union, and upon just and fair terms."

The abolitionists, under the name of the Liberty party, nominated James G. Birney, and it proved that they had the balance of power. With only 62,000 popular votes out of 2,700,000, they were able to draw so many votes away from

Clay in New York as to throw that close state to Polk, who was consequently elected.

Congress and President Tyler did not wait for the new administration: since annexation seemed to have the approval of the majority of the people, a joint resolution passed the House by a vote of 120 to 98, and the Senate by 27 to 25 (March 1, 1845), permitting the admission of Texas as a state on very favorable terms. The joint resolution provided also that Texas might later, with her own consent, be subdivided into five states, all presumably slave states; except that slavery was to be prohibited in any new state or states north of the line of $36°$ $30'$.

229. PRESIDENT POLK'S POLICY

Few Presidents have been so successful in carrying out what they undertook as James K. Polk, Tyler's successor. He was born in 1795, was a graduate of the University of North Carolina, was fourteen years a member of the House of Representatives (four years Speaker), and then for one term governor of Tennessee. He had large public experience, and an imperious and far-reaching mind. The defect of Polk's character was his lack of moral principle as to the property of our neighbor, Mexico. His diary shows clearly that his real intentions and purposes were very different from those which he put forward in public. From the first he meant not only to annex Texas, but to add to the Union the enormous belt of territory stretching from the Gulf to the Pacific, to gain the port of San Francisco for Pacific trade, and to turn over the greater part of the new territories to slavery.

Therefore, when Polk came into office, he put no obstacle in the way of the annexation policy which Tyler had carried through; and he seemed from the first to have adopted the extravagant Texan claim to all the territory north and east of the Rio Grande.

As for Oregon, Polk turned his back on the right to "all Oregon" and "Fifty-Four Forty or Fight" which had been part of his stock in trade in the election of 1844, and he soon showed a willingness to divide the country with Great Britain. The American government had a series of strong claims based on the discovery by Gray, in 1792 (§ 160), the first exploration of Lewis and Clark in 1805, the first settlement by Astor in 1811, and the first settlement in the Willamette valley in 1832.

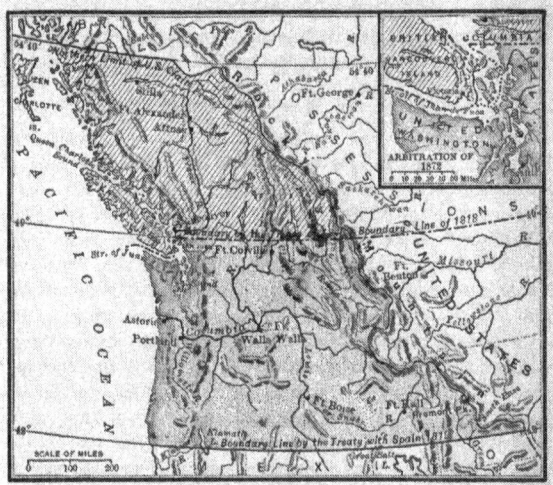

OREGON BOUNDARY CONTROVERSY.

The British came in second on all these counts; but their agent, the Hudson's Bay Company, was actually holding a considerable number of posts both north and south of the Columbia River. Years before this time the United States had offered to accept the 49th parallel, extended westward from the Rocky Mountains, as the boundary, and on that basis Polk made a treaty (June, 1846). The northwestern boundary territorial controversy was thus settled after fifty-four years of dispute.

A strong Democratic majority appeared in both houses of Congress in 1845-1846. Robert J. Walker, Secretary of the Treasury, drafted and presented to Congress a measure which became law as the tariff of 1846. The duties on luxuries were very high, reaching 100 per cent on brandy and spirits; on ordinary manufactures they were only about 30 per cent; the average on dutiable goods was about 25 per cent; and, by the increase of imports, the annual proceeds in a few years were twice as great as those under the tariff of 1842.

230. Causes of the War with Mexico (1845-1846)

California, with "the fine Bay of San Francisco," was much on Polk's mind, and he hoped that the native Californians would revolt just as the Texans had done and then annex themselves to the United States. He instructed our consul at Monterey to work in that direction, and he also sent John Slidell to Mexico to buy California if possible. The Mexicans would not consider any such proposition, and it became clear that the only way to annex California was to fight for it.

Several other reasons for war could be more openly stated than that relating to California: (1) Claims for outrages against the persons and property of Americans in Mexico had been pending for twenty years and those claims were now pushed hard by Polk. (2) Mexico was threatening war on the ground that the United States in annexing Texas had robbed Mexico of a province. (3) The Mexicans entirely rejected the Rio Grande boundary. In fact the Texan claim included part of the ancient province of New Mexico, which was no more Texan than St. Louis (map, page 346).

Without waiting even to hear from Slidell, Polk ordered General Zachary Taylor to advance with his troops into the disputed belt between the Nueces River and the Rio Grande. This brought about a collision (April 24, 1846). The Mexicans attacked the Americans on the northern side of the Rio Grande.

Polk was already trying to bring Congress to declare war, and the news of the Mexican attack was followed by a special message of May 11, 1846, in which Polk boldly declared that "war exists and notwithstanding all our efforts to avoid it, exists by the act of Mexico herself." On that basis Congress was swept into a declaration of war.

The wrath of the antislavery men over the purpose of enlarging the slave power was expressed by James Russell Lowell in the fiercest satire of his *Biglow Papers:*

> " They may talk o' Freedom's airy
> Till they're pupple in the face,
> It's a grand gret cemetary
> Fer the barthrights of our race,
> They jest want this Californy
> So's to lug new slave states in
> To abuse ye, an' to scorn ye,
> An' to plunder ye like sin."

The war had hardly begun before President Polk asked Congress for $2,000,000 to be used for "negotiations" (August 4, 1846); the real purpose seems to have been to buy General Santa Anna, former dictator of the Mexican Republic, then in exile. The northern antislavery men seized the opportunity to make clear their determination not to annex any more slave territory. David Wilmot of Pennsylvania introduced an amendment to the proposed appropriation, which has always been called the "Wilmot Proviso"; it was prepared by a group of northwestern Democrats. It declared that, "As an express and fundamental condition to the acquisition of any territory . . . neither slavery nor involuntary servitude shall ever exist in any part of the said territory." The whole proposition failed through a technicality; but the South was aroused. Abraham Lincoln, in 1847-1849, voted in Congress forty-two times for the principle of the Wilmot Proviso; but he voted in vain, for the Senate always showed an adverse majority.

231. MEXICAN WAR (1846-1848)

However unrighteous the causes of the Mexican War, it was carried on successfully by land and sea. General Taylor beat the Mexicans in the battles of Palo Alto and Resaca de la

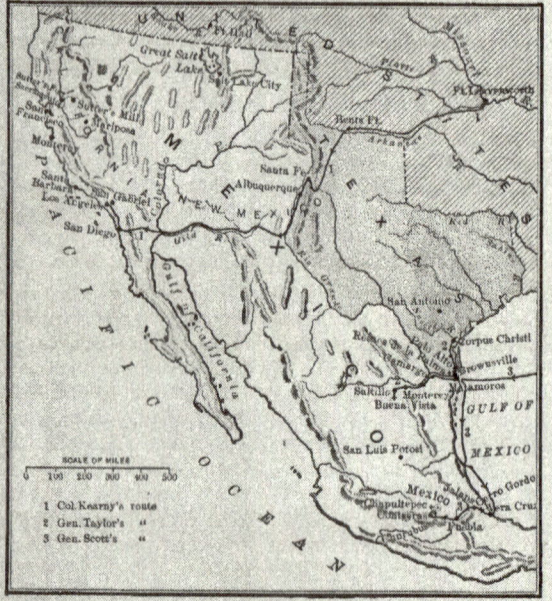

FIELD OF THE MEXICAN WAR. (The territory in dispute between Texas and Mexico is shown by the lighter shading.)

Palma (May). Then he crossed the river and again defeated the Mexicans at Monterey (September). Santa Anna was passed through the lines into Mexico, under Polk's order, but took the patriot side and organized a new army, with which he vainly attacked Taylor at Buena Vista (February, 1847).

General Winfield Scott, in chief command, landed with a new army at Vera Cruz (March, 1847), and fought his way steadily across the mountains and down into the valley of Mexico. He attacked the city of Mexico with about 6000 available troops and finally captured it (September). The Mexican government was thus broken up and could put no more armies into the field.

Three areas of territory were added to the United States as a result of the war. The first was the belt between the Nueces and the Rio Grande, out of which the Mexicans had been driven by Taylor's army. The second was New Mexico, which extended across the upper Rio Grande. The capital, Santa Fe, was taken by General Kearny without firing a shot (August, 1846). He set up a civil government and, with part of his command, marched on to California. This third area he found already conquered. In June, 1846, without knowing of the outbreak of war, the American settlers in California, numbering only 300, founded what they called the Bear Flag Republic, which was aided by Frémont with a little force of government troops, and then by a naval force under Commodore Sloat.

It was one thing to occupy these regions and quite another to find any responsible men in Mexico who would make a treaty ceding the conquered country. Polk sent out N. P. Trist, a quarrelsome and insubordinate man, to make a peace with Mexico. When he could not succeed, great pressure was put upon the President to annex the whole of Mexico. Polk's diary says on this point, "I replied that I was not prepared to go to that extent . . . that I had in my last message declared that I did not contemplate the conquest of Mexico." The Mexicans were startled and finally made a treaty with Trist under which $15,000,000 in cash was to be paid by the United States to Mexico; that is, practically, to the leaders who would sign the treaty. Mexico gave up all claim to Texas as far as the Rio Grande, and ceded the whole of New Mexico and

California. This treaty was accepted by Polk and approved
by the Senate. Thus the Mexican War resulted in a great increase of territory. The war cost about $100,000,000 and the
lives of 13,000 of the 100,000 soldiers engaged. In 1853 by the
Gadsden purchase (map, page viii) the United States bought
what is now southern Arizona from Mexico, paying $10,000,000.

232. COMMERCIAL EFFECT OF THE PACIFIC ANNEXATIONS

After the formal adjustment of the Oregon boundary in 1846
(§ 229), settlers made their way to Oregon both by land and

SANTA BARBARA MISSION, CALIFORNIA, FOUNDED IN 1786.

by the sea route around Cape Horn, but at that time the settled
part of Oregon was almost entirely in the Willamette valley.
Very little use was made of the magnificent timber which extended down to tidewater, until California began to use it.

Probably California would have developed as slowly as
Oregon but for the influence of the discovery of a few grains of
yellow metal. On January 24, 1848, just before the treaty of
peace with Mexico was signed, James W. Marshall, an immigrant

from New Jersey, picked up some flakes of gold in the race of a
new sawmill about sixty miles from Sutter's Fort, now called
Sacramento. The news spread like the cry of fire; within six
months the coast settlements of California were almost deserted;
the inhabitants hurried to the gold diggings, which were
"placers" (gravel reaches or terraces) yielding gold in dust,
coarser particles, and nuggets. Soon all sorts of merchandise
rose in price three times over; and some miners by their own
labor were taking from $3000 to $5000 a month at the diggings.

The next year thousands of "Forty-niners" made their way
to California, some around Cape Horn, some across the Isthmus
of Panama or Nicaragua, some in wagon trains straight west
across the plains. Between fifty thousand and one hundred
thousand people poured into California, and in two seasons
more than $30,000,000 of gold was taken out. If somebody
"struck it rich," "in half an hour a motley multitude, covered
with crowbars, pickaxes, spades, rifles, and wash bowls, went
streaming over the hills in the direction of the new deposits."
The old Spanish mining laws were inadequate, and the criminal
laws did not apply to the circumstances; and there was no
government to pass new statutes. The miners therefore organized, made their own mining rules, and set up so-called
"vigilance committees" for offhand punishment of crimes.

233. ISTHMIAN CANAL QUESTIONS (1846-1850)

The annexation of California at once brought up the question of the control of the Isthmus of Panama. During and after
the war, travelers and officers used the short cut across the
narrow lands of Central America (map, page 533); and the idea
of an isthmian canal was revived. The Isthmus of Panama
was part of the territory of the republic of New Granada (now
the United States of Colombia), which proposed (1846) that the
United States guarantee that isthmus against seizure or interference, while New Granada would grant to citizens of the
United States the use of any canal or roadway that might be

constructed across the isthmus, on the same terms as those applying to citizens of New Granada. A treaty to that effect was duly drawn in 1846 and ratified in 1848.

Another practicable canal route crossed Central America through the Lake of Nicaragua; to control that line, Great Britain claimed a protectorate over the Mosquito Indians, who were settled near the eastern end of the route. The United States roundly protested, but came to an understanding with Great Britain in 1850 by the so-called Clayton-Bulwer treaty. By this agreement Great Britain and the United States were to take joint control of any isthmian canal that might be constructed on the Nicaragua route, or any other, and the British agreed not to make any settlements in Central America. This was a fair compromise under the conditions of the time, and favorable to both parties.

234. TERRITORIAL SLAVERY (1848–1850)

When the war with Mexico was over and the desired territory was transferred to the United States, the country found itself in the midst of the most furious controversy about slavery that had ever arisen. The question was whether slavery should or should not enter into New Mexico and California. The extreme antislavery men supported the principle of the Wilmot Proviso, which meant that slavery in those territories should be prohibited by an act of Congress. The extreme proslavery men demanded that the 36° 30′ compromise line, which was to be extended across Texas (§ 228), should be continued to the Pacific, thus dividing California. A third proposition was that Congress should avoid settling the question. This was a suggestion by Senator Lewis Cass of Michigan that the question of slavery be left to the people of the territory, under what came to be called "popular sovereignty."

The contest was carried into the presidential election of 1848, but the issue was not clear-cut. The Whigs nominated General Zachary Taylor, who had never been in politics. The Democrats nominated Cass, who was a "dough face," or northern proslavery man. Van Buren, who still remembered how he was set aside in 1844, led his friends to join the Free-soil party, which included the former Liberty party (§ 228); the joint convention nominated Van Buren on the platform of "Free Soil, Free Speech, Free Labor, and Free Men." This combination polled nearly 300,000 votes and threw New York from the Democratic to the Whig side as it had been thrown to the Democrats in 1844, thus allowing Zachary Taylor, a slaveholder, to be elected by 163 electoral votes to 127 for Cass.

When Taylor became President, March 4, 1849, he decided to settle the question of California by bringing in that new community as a state. Accordingly a California convention was held. It drew up a constitution (September, 1849) which would put a stop to slavery in the future state, and also would prevent the extension of the compromise line, by declaring that California included the whole belt of coast from Mexico to Oregon. The ruling influence was that of free miners working with their own hands, who did not mean to work in competition with the labor of slaves owned by other people.

235. OTHER SLAVERY QUESTIONS

Other questions were arising in Congress which clamored for settlement alongside the territorial issues. Northern men strongly objected to the slave trade in the city of Washington, and Abraham Lincoln introduced a bill (January, 1849) for the gradual emancipation of all the slaves in the District of Columbia. Another question was that of fugitive slaves. The abolitionists had a regular system for aiding fugitives to escape, popularly known as the "Underground Railroad," in which more than 3000 people are known to have taken part; and through which, from 1830 to 1860, upward of 60,000 slaves escaped. Fugitives were kept in the houses of abolitionists, forwarded from place to place at night, or hidden in out-of-the-way places; and if the pursuers came, were finally shipped across the Lakes to Canada, which was free soil. The old Fugitive Slave Act of 1793 (§ 182) did not work well, and the South demanded an act from Congress more favorable to them.

The proposition to admit California as a free state raised the old question of keeping up an equal balance in the Senate. Up to this time the principle of balancing states (§ 183) was maintained. Arkansas (slave) — the 25th state — was admitted in 1836 and Michigan (free) in 1837, Florida and Texas (slave) in 1845 and Iowa and Wisconsin (free) in 1846 and 1848. Of the thirty states in 1849, fifteen were slave and fifteen free. To admit California as a free state meant a permanent superiority of the North in the Senate, for there was nowhere a southern territory ready to enter the Union.

236. COMPROMISE OF 1850

When Congress met again, in December, 1849, it looked as if the Union might break up over these complicated questions. Accordingly the aged Henry Clay, "the great pacificator," proposed, and with all his energies urged a compromise measure, by which California should be free while slavery was not to be forbidden in New Mexico. His point of view was that New Mexico and California came into the Union free by Mexican law and would remain free if Congress took no positive action. He declared, "No earthly power could induce me to vote for a specific measure for the introduction of slavery where it had not before existed."

Another line of argument was set forth by Daniel Webster, whose support of the compromise as leader of the "cotton Whigs" — that is, the commercial men of the North — made it possible to pass the compromise. In his famous "Seventh of March Speech," he accused the North of not doing its duty by the South. He was willing to say nothing about slavery in New Mexico because he was sure that it could never flourish there. As he put it, "I would not take pains to reaffirm an ordinance of nature nor to reënact the will of God."

Northern senators like Salmon P. Chase of Ohio scouted the idea that the Union was in danger, and denounced any compromise. They looked on Webster as a man who had always opposed slavery but was now betraying his own section, in hope of getting southern support for the presidency.

There was real danger to the Union. Robert Toombs of Georgia declared in open Congress, "I do not hesitate to avow . . . in the presence of the living God, that if . . . you seek to drive us from . . . California . . . I am for disunion." In milder terms John C. Calhoun, in the last speech of his life, argued against a compromise, because the only thing that could pacify the South was for

HENRY CLAY, ABOUT 1848. (From a daguerreotype.)

the North to stop the agitation of the slavery question. He said, "If you, who represent the stronger portion, cannot agree to settle . . . on the broad principle of justice and duty, say so; and let the states we both represent agree to separate."

In the midst of these discordant arguments, President Taylor's views were especially important because of his veto power. He was opposed to the compromise, but he died suddenly (July, 1850). Vice President Fillmore of New York then became President and signed the five bills into which Clay's compromise had been divided:

(1) New Mexico was organized as a territory, including land claimed by Texas east of the upper Rio Grande; $10,000,000 was given to Texas for accepting those boundaries. The real

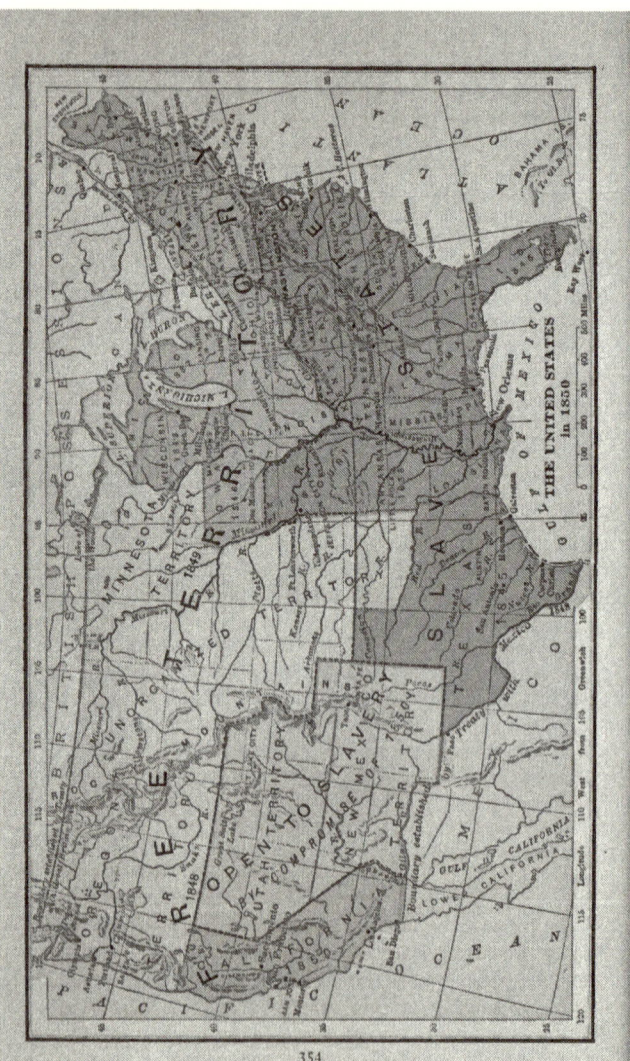

THE UNITED STATES
in 1850

issue of territorial slavery was, so far as possible, avoided by stating: (a) that "the Constitution and all laws which are not locally inapplicable" should apply to New Mexico; (b) that no citizen of the United States should be deprived of his "life, liberty, or property except by the judgment of his peers and the law of the land"; (c) that "when admitted as a State, the said Territory, or any portion of the same, shall be received into the Union, with or without slavery, as their constitution may prescribe at the time of their admission." This was a tacit permission to hold slaves while it remained a territory.

(2) The next bill admitted California as a free state.

(3) The Utah Bill, with provisions like those of the New Mexico Bill, organized a territory north of New Mexico, apparently intended to be free.

(4) A new fugitive slave act provided for a system of United States commissioners to try cases in a "summary manner."

(5) Another act prohibited the slave trade (but not slavery) in the District of Columbia.

237. REVIEW

Every election from 1840 to 1852 brought a change of parties in the national government. Harrison became President in 1841 and was at once succeeded by Tyler, the Vice President, who quarreled with the Whigs on the bank and the tariff. This was also a period of local disorders, including the Antirent riots and the Dorr Rebellion. Webster settled the long pending dispute with Great Britain over the Maine boundary (1842). The fur traders and others opened up the far West and marked out routes to Santa Fe, to Oregon, and to California.

The Democratic party returned to power in the election of 1844, when Polk beat Henry Clay. After long opposition by the antislavery people, Texas was annexed to the United States in 1845. Polk then set out to perfect the title to Oregon and accepted the 49th parallel as a compromise boundary. A low tariff was passed in 1846.

The next step was to acquire California. When Mexico declined to consider selling it, Polk occupied the disputed region on the Rio Grande. The resulting Mexican War lasted to 1848, when Mexico was obliged to yield the disputed territory northeast of the Rio Grande, and also New Mexico and California. The antislavery people in vain tried to secure the Wilmot Proviso, which sought to prevent slavery in the new annexations.

The discovery of gold in California brought a rush of "Fortyniners" to California. The United States guaranteed to New Granada possession of the Panama Isthmus route (1848). By the Clayton-Bulwer treaty of 1850, Great Britain and the United States took joint responsibility for any future isthmian canal.

The new annexations caused a controversy in Congress. An attempt to extend the 36° 30′ line to the Pacific failed, and in the election of 1848 Zachary Taylor was chosen President by the Whigs. Meanwhile the slave trade in the District of Columbia and the recovery of fugitive slaves came up. All these questions were settled by the Compromise of 1850: (1) The boundaries claimed by Texas were cut down. (2) California was admitted as a free state. (3) New Mexico and Utah were organized as territories, with the privilege of becoming slave states if they so desired. (4) The slave trade was prohibited in the District of Columbia. (5) A new fugitive slave act was passed. This settlement was called "a finality."

References Bearing on the Text and Topics

Geography and Maps. See maps, pp. viii, 339, 343, 346, 354, 372. — Bogart, *Econ. Hist.*, 287. — Dodd, *Expansion and Conflict*, 148, 159. — Fish, *Am. Diplomacy*, 229, 231, 232, 268, 272, 294; *Am. Nationality*, 486. — Shepherd, *Hist. Atlas*, 198, 201, 206, 210.

Secondary. Coman, *Econ. Beginnings of the Far West*, II. 75–93, 113–284. — Dodd, *Expansion and Conflict*, chs. vii–ix; *Jefferson Davis*, chs. iv–vii. — Fish, *Am. Diplomacy*, 228–279, 290–296; *Am. Nationality*, 249–262, 276–280, 302–325, 333. — Garrison, *Texas*, ch. xxi; *Westward Extension*. — Hapgood, *Daniel Webster*, 96–111. — Hart, *S. P. Chase*, 54–130. — Johnson, *S. A. Douglas*, chs. v–ix. — McMaster, *U.S.*, V. 463–483, VI. 429–454, 513–518, 550–637, VII. 1–73, 271–614, VIII. 1–45.

— Paxson, *Last Am. Frontier*, chs. i–vii. — Rhodes, *U.S.*, I. 75–202.
— Roosevelt, *T. H. Benton*, 210–301. — Schafer, *Pacific Northwest*, chs.
viii–xv. — Schurz, *Henry Clay*, II. chs. xxiii–xxvi. — Turner, *New West*,
ch. viii. — Wilson, *Am. People*, IV. 88–128.

Sources. Ames, *State Docs. on Fed. Relations*, 190–192, 229–232,
241–272. — Bogart and Thompson, *Readings*, 327–337, 503. — Caldwell,
Terr. Development, 131–199. — Dana, *Two Years before the Mast.* —
Grant, *Personal Memoirs*, I. 61–174. — Hart, *Contemporaries*, III.
§§ 187–189, IV. §§ 7–22; *Patriots and Statesmen*, IV. 22–25, 79–81, 270–
285, 334–382 passim, V. 13–61, 70–130. — James, *Readings*, §§ 67, 78–80.

Illustrative. Atherton, *Splendid Idle Forties* (Cal.). — Canfield, *Diary
of a Forty-niner.* — Hall, *Downrenter's Son* (antirent). — Harte, *Luck of
Roaring Camp; Tales of the Argonauts.* — Lowell, *Biglow Papers* (1st.
ser.); *Present Crisis.* — Matthews, *Poems of Am. Patriotism*, 108–115.
— Munroe, *Golden Days of '49.* — Potter, *Eleventh Hour.* — Watts,
Nathan Burke (Mex. War). — White, *Gold.* — Whittier, *Antislavery
Poems*, 94–155. — Wilson, *Lions of the Lord* (Mormons).

Pictures. Sparks, *Expansion.* — Wilson, *Am. People*, IV.

Topics Answerable from the References Above

(1) Incidents of the campaign of 1840. [§ 225] — (2) Experiences in
the West of *one:* Captain Bonneville; N. J. Wyeth; Dr. Whitman;
John C. Frémont. [§ 227] — (3) T. H. Benton, *or* James K. Polk as a
boy and young man. [§§ 227, 228] — (4) Spanish missions in California.
[§ 230] — (5) Abraham Lincoln's career in Congress. [§ 230] — (6) Account of *one:* big timber; Bear Flag Republic; placer gold diggings;
Forty-niners; vigilance committees. [§ 232] — (7) Account of the Wilmot
Proviso. [§ 234] — (8) Public career of Lewis Cass, *or* James K. Polk,
or James Buchanan. [§§ 229, 234] — (9) Incidents of the "Underground
Railroad"; *or* slave trade in the District of Columbia. [§ 235] — (10) Admission of *one* of the following states: Arkansas; Michigan; Florida;
Texas; Iowa; Wisconsin; California. [§ 235] — (11) Public career of
one of the following: Clay; Webster; Chase; Toombs; Fillmore. [§ 236]

Topics for Further Search

(12) Account of the "Aroostook War." [§ 226] — (13) Early days
on the Sante Fe trail. [§ 227] — (14) Was the annexation of Texas
desirable? [§ 228] — (15) The Hudson's Bay Company on the Pacific
coast. [§ 229] — (16) Did the Mexican War begin "by the act of
Mexico"? [§ 230] — (17) Career of Santa Anna. [§ 231] — (18) Was
the treaty of peace with Mexico just? [§ 231] — (19) Webster's "Seventh
of March" speech. [§ 236]

CHAPTER XXII

ECONOMIC PROGRESS (1830-1860)

238. RESOURCES OF THE COUNTRY

In the three decades from 1830 to 1860 the growth of population, the accumulation of property, and the development of resources were as great as during the previous two centuries of settlement in North America. The same spirit of intense life

McCORMICK'S FIRST REAPER, 1834.

and activity was shown in business affairs, as in the moral and intellectual growth described in an earlier chapter (§§ 204-209). The American mind naturally turned to new ideas of business organization and of mechanical inventions. Free land and good employment drew millions of people from the Old World and stimulated the use of labor-saving machinery. The desire for land and for opportunities to make money was a strong, if not the strongest, element in the annexations of territory that were noted in the preceding chapter.

The thing that did most for the growth of the country was the immense extent of the resources of nature; that is, the land

and its capacity to bear crops, the mineral wealth that lay beneath it, the timber that grew upon it, the wild animals that lived upon it, the motive power furnished by waterfalls and by wood and coal as fuel, and the waterways of lakes, rivers, and ocean, which made it easy to exchange these products. The people of the United States were in the position of an heir who comes into a great fortune which he suddenly finds himself called upon to manage and make productive. He is amazed at the wealth and the opportunities which are thus put at his disposal.

239. The Land Question

The first and most pressing question was that of land. The people of the United States were still in the situation of the colonists. In both the older and the newer states and territories there was an abundance of land which had never been tilled; and in the older sections large areas were worn out and had gone back into brush or forest. The great problem was how to make this immense quantity of land available for the farmers.

The point of view inherited from colonial times was that land was valuable only for farms, and that it ought to be given or sold in moderate tracts to those who could till it. Not a single one of the states made any attempt to keep even a part of the lands that it possessed. Great areas that fell to Massachusetts, New York, Connecticut in the Western Reserve, and Virginia all slipped away and left very little money to the state governments. The bounty lands granted by Congress to the soldiers of the Revolutionary War and the War of 1812 were in many cases sold for a song to speculators. The lands granted by the federal government to the new states for education, first a thirty-sixth and then an eighteenth of the whole area of the new states, were sold out with very little advantage to the states or the school children. The enormous area of lands owned by the federal government in the Northwest, in

Mississippi and Alabama, and in the new Southwest, was turned over as rapidly as possible to settlers and speculators.

The method of sale from 1800 to 1820 was clumsy. Settlers were allowed to buy land on installments at $2 an acre (§ 176); but many of them failed to make the payments, and in the end asked to have a portion of the land transferred to them fully paid. For twenty years after 1820 Congress sold land only for cash at a standard price of $1.25 an acre. Buyers who had the money could take anywhere from forty up to thousands of acres at a time.

The result was wild speculation in public lands; in the two years 1835 and 1836 the United States received $40,000,000 from this source alone. To prevent the accumulation in the treasury of a surplus from the lands, various plans were suggested: (1) to give the lands to the states; (2) to reserve the lands in small tracts for actual settlers; (3) to distribute among the states the surplus from the sales of land. Clay favored the third plan, but Jackson in 1833 prevented it by the veto of a distribution bill. The most serious cause of the panic of 1837 was speculation in public lands (§ 222); heavy buyers tried to "corner" the lands and to sell them at a great advance to settlers.

To meet this difficulty, in 1841 the "Preëmption Act" was passed, and from that time for about twenty years it provided a regular method of getting public land. Any person who was the head of a family might buy a tract not exceeding 160 acres. He had to live on it for a time, and then he could pay $1.25 an acre and it became his property, with the right to sell. Under the law, this privilege could be exercised only once in a lifetime; but there were people who preëmpted twenty different tracts in different land offices, and it was hard to detect the fraud. So much state and national land was dumped on the market that many of the heavy speculators lost money on their ventures. Land was not a very good investment and there were hardly any examples of men buying large tracts and di-

viding them into tenant farms, though that was the ordinary
system in many parts of Europe.

240. INDIANS AND INDIAN LANDS

A standing difficulty in settling the lands was the presence
of Indian tribes who occupied some of the richest sections. In
the Northwest after the War of 1812, the Indians were no longer
able to make headway against the whites. The so-called Black
Hawk War (1832), in which Abraham Lincoln was a militia
captain, was only a flurry. When the Indians were pushed back
into reservations which were set apart for their sole use, it was
possible to open their former lands to settlers.

In the South the problem was different. Within the boundaries of Georgia alone as late as 1824 there were about 50,000
Creeks, Cherokees, and Indians of other tribes who occupied
reservations of eleven million acres. These areas and their
Indian inhabitants were solely under the control of the federal
government and not subject to the law of Georgia. When a
few Creek chiefs undertook to make a treaty ceding tribal
lands, their fellow Indians did their best to nullify it by killing
those who signed it. The Cherokees were a well-to-do people
owning farms and slaves, and they tried to set up a permanent
government inside the boundaries of Georgia. This led to a
controversy between that state and the federal government;
for Georgia, ignoring the rights both of the Indians and of the
United States, simply annexed the Cherokee territory and declared the Indians to be under the state laws.

President Adams vainly tried to defend the Indians. Jackson, when he became President, ruled that Georgia was in the
right. When the Supreme Court decided a test case in favor of
the Indians, Jackson said, "John Marshall has made his decision; now let him enforce it." The Cherokees yielded to
their fate, and with the Creeks, Choctaws, Chickasaws, and
Seminoles, were moved west of the Mississippi into what for
three quarters of a century was called the Indian Territory,

where they were known as "the Five Civilized Tribes." Some
of the Seminoles ran away and came back to their old home in
Florida; there for a period of ten years they made good their
armed resistance against the federal government. Nevertheless, the question was settled that no Indian tribes would be
allowed, either north or south, to remain in permanent possession of large tracts of valuable lands desired by settlers.
A thousand whites could be prosperous where fifty Indians
could hardly find a living; and the tribes faded away or were
removed.

241. IMMIGRATION IN 1830–1860

One reason for the pressure on the public lands was the
coming in of great numbers of European immigrants. In fact,

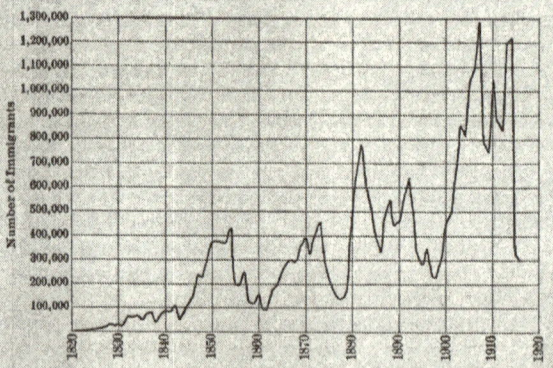

IMMIGRANTS ARRIVING IN THE UNITED STATES EACH YEAR.

one of the main reasons why the western states wished to have
easy land laws was to draw settlers, both from abroad and
from the eastern states. There was also a steady demand for
laborers to build roads and canals and to work in shops and

factories. Life was hard for the workers in all European countries; but any able-bodied man or woman who could reach the United States might expect to find employment; or if he had a little money, he could buy land and become a farmer.

The result was a steady stream of immigrants, who came in the sailing vessels of the time. Between 1820 and 1829 about 110,000 arrived; in the next decade, over 500,000 people, many of whom went straight out to make homes on the frontier. From 1820 to 1840 the population of the West increased from 2,600,000 to 7,000,000. Chicago in 1833 had 150 wooden houses, and a visitor said of it, "Almost every person I met regarded Chicago as the germ of an immense city."

From 1820 to 1840 most of the immigrants were English, Scotch, and Irish, all using the English language. They furnished much of the unskilled labor in the North, but many of them had good trades, and others found ready employment in the new textile mills and iron works. We have little information about the numbers coming from the various countries. There are records of a small immigration from the three Scandinavian

CARL SCHURZ.

countries — Sweden, Norway, and Denmark. A considerable German immigration set in, which grew rapidly when civil wars broke out in Germany (1848). The Germans included many highly educated men who could not endure the political conditions at home. Some of them, like Carl Schurz, were refugees who preferred exile to prison or even death.

The largest foreign element in this period was the Irish. Conditions in Ireland were bad; in 1846 a famine swept away hundreds of thousands. From 1845 to 1855 more than a million came over to this country. The passages of some were paid by local governments and societies at home; others paid

for themselves. Great numbers were brought over at the
expense of their friends and relatives who had already arrived
in the United States.

242. EFFECTS OF IMMIGRATION

A considerable part of the Irish immigrants and some of the
Germans settled down in the seaports and other towns of the
eastern states, but immigration sifted to all parts of the country. The rising cities of the interior, such as Buffalo, Cleveland, Cincinnati, Chicago, and St. Paul, attracted some Irish
and a large number of Germans. Great numbers of both races
took up farms, especially in the West.

Wherever they went, the immigrants helped to increase the
wealth of the country. In return for their money wages, they
gave their labor; the buildings, ships, roads, and machinery
which they made were a vast contribution to the national
wealth. Part of them took over the hard jobs of unskilled labor,
and thereby the better educated and better trained men already
in the country were set free to direct and build up enterprises.

The immigrants brought with them many of their own customs. The Scandinavians were Protestants. Most of the
Irish and some of the Germans were Catholics, who at once
took their place within the national Catholic Church and
helped to build it up. The Germans brought into the country
the Christmas tree, a greater love of music, the manufacture
of German beer and wine, and a greater interest in education
and literature. The Irish brought their fondness for street
processions and pageants, and very soon showed a skill in
making political combinations and building up parties, which
quickly brought them into the center of political life. Some of
the German immigrants formed communities, such as those of
the Amana Society in central Iowa. A few of the German
Swiss and Scandinavians formed settlements of their own,
in which they kept their language, schools, and customs. The
Germans and Irish generally expected to spend their lives and

bring up their children in America, and hastened to be naturalized and to become full-fledged citizens. Most of the German children quickly learned the English language. Hardly any immigrants returned to their native land.

243. TIMBER AND MINERAL WEALTH

One of the most widespread sources of wealth was the timber, which even in colonial times had furnished masts, ships, and sawed timber and boards for export (§ 77). By 1830 most of the northern coast states had been cleared of the valuable trees, but there still remained splendid pine forests in northern Maine, New Hampshire, and New York. Considerable parts of the southern states still stood in timber, which was used principally for the production of tar and turpentine. The Allegheny Plateau became a great center for the lumber industry between 1830 and 1860. From western New York and Pennsylvania and eastern and southern Ohio the trees could be rafted down the Ohio and Mississippi rivers; and for fifty years this was a steady and profitable business. Local sawmills cut timber for farm and city buildings and for bridges. Most of the farm fences of that period were made of split rails, and when Abraham Lincoln moved into Illinois, he built up a reputation for his ability as a rail splitter. Sawmills could be run by water power or by cheap engines and boilers in which the refuse of the mill could be used for fuel.

The wealth beneath the soil was many times more valuable than that growing above it. Coal had been known from early colonial times, and after 1815 began to come into many new uses. Benjamin Franklin invented a handy open stove in which wood could be used to heat rooms; and the soft or bituminous coal had long been used in Pittsburgh and elsewhere for house purposes. Now came the use of coal for all kinds of factories and other business. The cost of pig iron was reduced by the discovery that anthracite could be used instead of the old-fashioned charcoal to smelt iron (1838).

Hence a great iron industry was built up in the Pennsylvania mountains near Philadelphia and New York. Eight years later the clay furnace in western Pennsylvania made it possible to use soft coal for the same purpose, and that led to building many iron furnaces near the coal of western Pennsylvania and eastern Ohio. Illuminating gas, first manufactured in America in 1816, was a new comfort for the cities and enlarged the use of coal, which shortly became also the usual fuel for making steam, first in factories and then in locomotives and seagoing steamers.

From very early times it was known that there was a rich deposit of lead along the upper Mississippi, especially near Galena, Illinois, and a steady and prosperous mining industry grew up there. Besides the California mines (§ 232), some gold was found in Georgia, and for a long time a little branch mint was maintained at Dahlonega in the mountains. Iron ore was abundant both east and west of the Appalachian Mountains, and there was abundance of the limestone that was necessary to use as a "flux" in the furnaces, along with the fuel and the iron ore, in order to produce pig iron.

The inhabitants of northwestern Pennsylvania failed to realize that underneath their feet lay one of the greatest sources of wealth in the whole country. On Oil Creek, a tributary of the Allegheny River, oil had been found in colonial times and was collected by spreading out blankets. It was supposed to be a remedy for rheumatism. Until 1859 no one thought of drilling wells. The common illuminating oil in the eastern states was whale oil. In the West some very dangerous oils were distilled from coal, but ordinary families depended upon candles for their household light.

244. INDUSTRIAL INVENTIONS

From 1825 to 1860 the country was producing a series of amazing labor-saving inventions, and that made it possible to develop cheap raw materials and thus to reduce the cost of manufactured products of every kind. The first necessity was the improvement of tools and machinery. In this period comes the beginning of the American manufacture of edged tools of every kind. Wood-working was cheapened beyond any conception by the invention of planing machines, one of which would do the work of twenty men. The introduction of platform scales was a great convenience to factories and farmers.

The factory system, begun before the War of 1812, was now adapted to many new industries. Improved looms were introduced in the textile mills, and by 1860 there were about two thousand mills that used them.

To furnish power for cotton mills, woolen mills, paper mills, and other industries, dams were built on the falls of rivers in the eastern and southern states, and that caused the appearance of such manufacturing towns as Manchester, Nashua, Lowell, Holyoke, Cohoes, Trenton, and Richmond. The invention of the turbine water-wheel (1834) made it possible to use waterfalls of only a few feet.

CYRUS H. McCORMICK, ABOUT 1875. (From a photograph lent by the family.)

The spirit of invention spread to the household. Friction matches, invented in England in 1827, gradually took the place of the old flint and steel. The first iron cook stove was put on the market about 1840 and proved a great relief to the labors of the housewife. Churns run by dog power were introduced. Fanning mills were used for winnowing grain. The methods of farming were changed in many parts of the country by the introduction of farm machinery. The first horse reaper was invented by a Virginian, McCormick, in 1834, and was the basis of the present elaborate mowers and reapers. Improved horse rakes, drills, and seeders began to be used. About 1840 improved portable threshing machines came into use — the early ones run by horse power.

The inventions extended also to death-dealing contrivances. The people had long been used to what had first been called "screw guns"; that is, rifles. These weapons were much improved, and about 1835 the first Colt's revolver was introduced. Some attempts were made to invent a breech-loading service gun, but the ordinary weapon of soldiers was still the old-fashioned muzzle-loading, smooth-bore musket.

245. TRANSPORTATION BY SEA

One of the greatest changes of the period was the improvement of transportation both by sea and by land. As has already been noted, steamboats spread rapidly through the eastern coast waters and the western lakes and rivers (§ 178). The next step was to install steam machinery on seagoing vessels. The ordinary marine engine of the time had a heavy walking beam which seesawed up and down to carry power from the steam cylinders to the paddle wheels. It was difficult to use this machinery in heavy seas, but it was adapted for coasters.

In 1819 the ship *Savannah*, fitted with auxiliary steam power — that is, with engines for use during only part of the voyage, when there was too little wind to fill the sails — voyaged from New York to Savannah and thence to Liverpool. Certain doubters worked out a scientific proof that no steamer could carry enough fuel to cross the ocean solely by steam power; but in 1838 the steamers *Sirius* and *Great Western* arrived from England practically under steam alone. Two years later the Cunard Company established a regular steamship line from Boston to Liverpool. All these early steamers had masts and used sail power whenever they could, to help them on, or to steady the ship. The bulk of the sea freight was still carried in wooden sailing ships.

The growth in the average size of seagoing vessels called attention to the need of deepening and otherwise improving the harbors. In 1824 Congress began to make small appropriations for such purposes — an expenditure that has since grown to many millions a year. Among the early projects thus undertaken was the Delaware breakwater (begun in 1829).

To carry the growing trade of the United States and that of other countries, American shipping engaged in foreign trade reached the highest point in our history — 2,500,000 tons — in 1861. These were the days of the magnificent clipper ships, wooden sailing craft of unexcelled speed and handiness, making their swiftest voyages from England to New York sometimes in less than fourteen days, and from China to New York in about eighty days.

Screw steamers as yet were mostly ships of war, but the ocean paddle steamers grew in size and speed till they could cross the ocean in twelve days. In 1847 Congress granted a subsidy — an annual money gift — to two lines of steamers: $850,000 a year to the Collins American line, New York to Liverpool; and $200,000 a year to a line from New York to Bremen. The Collins line was extravagantly managed, lost several ships, and broke down in 1858.

246. INTERNAL TRANSPORTATION BY WATER

The movement of coal, iron ore, and other minerals and the carrying of manufactured products brought about a demand for improvements in the internal system of transportation. Even such highways as the Cumberland Road (§ 179) could not carry much heavy freight, and the favorite system of the time was the canal. The success of the Erie Canal (§ 180) led other states to attempt the same thing across a rougher country. Pennsylvania began a canal system across the Alleghenies in 1826, and six years later had a railroad from Philadelphia to Columbia, a canal thence to the base of the mountains, an inclined road for hauling the boats in sections over the mountains, and a canal from the other side to Pittsburgh.

MISSISSIPPI RIVER STEAMERS.

Several side canals were also constructed by Pennsylvania, including one from the Ohio River below Pittsburgh to Lake Erie (finished 1844). Ohio in 1825 entered upon the construction of canals from several places on the Ohio River to Lake Erie. Indiana spent $8,000,000, and the 476,000 people of Illinois ran into debt $14,000,000, or $30 a head. A few important canals were built by private corporations, especially the Delaware and Hudson (1820), and the Schuylkill Navigation (1818-1825) for carrying coal. Eventually about six thousand miles of canals were constructed in the United States, of which less than one thousand miles are now in use.

The old objection to the building of internal improvements by the federal government still continued (§ 180). Jackson (1830) vetoed a bill for the Maysville Road from the Ohio River across Kentucky, on the ground that it was local improvement. He felt sure that the public money would be spent for enterprises that did the general public little good. On the same grounds he vetoed several harbor bills. Nevertheless, Congress yielded on this point so far as to grant immense tracts of public lands (beginning in 1837) to the states to be used by them for the construction of canals and other similar works. The result was not very happy. States like Ohio, Indiana, and Illinois planned systems of canals so great that the proceeds of the land grants were not enough to pay for making them, and many of them were left incomplete and have never been revived.

247. RAILROADS

All other forms of internal improvement were soon cast into the shade by railroads, which suddenly cheapened transportation, stimulated travel, and built up new states and cities. The first railroads in America were a short temporary tramway for carrying heavy loads, built in 1807 in Boston, and a permanent one constructed in 1810 near Philadelphia. Railroads were soon begun westward from Albany, Philadelphia, Baltimore, and Charleston; but in 1830 only 23 miles had been built and were in operation by the various companies, all for cars to be drawn by horses.

A RAILROAD TRAIN OF 1831. (From a photograph of the original train, lent by the New York Central R. R.)

Soon after 1830 several great changes came about in railroads. An imported steam locomotive was introduced in

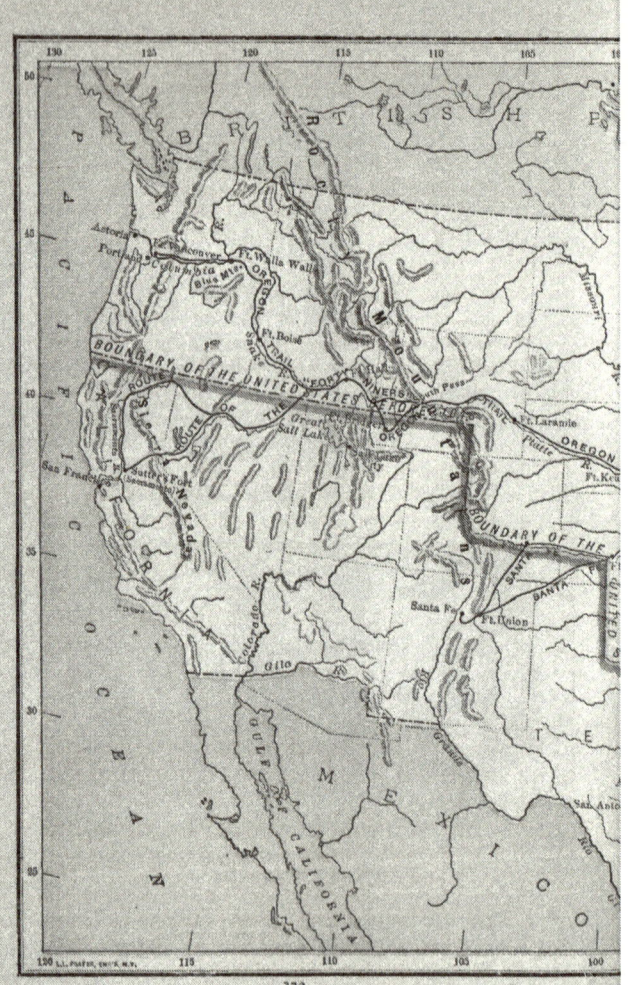

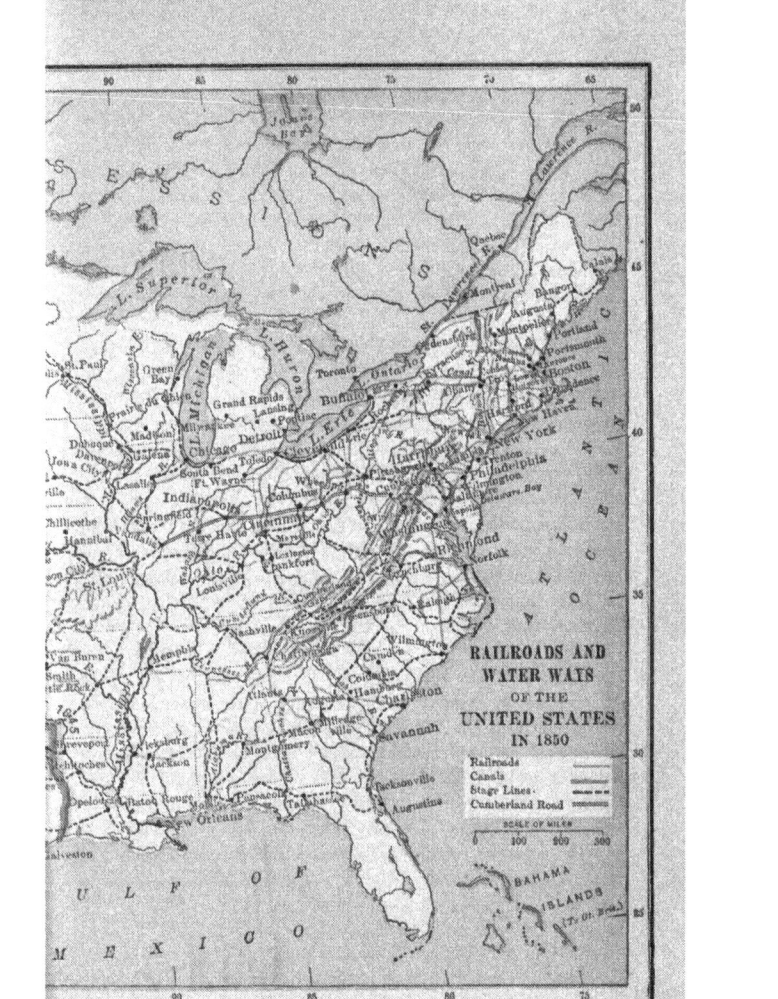

RAILROADS AND
WATER WAYS
OF THE
UNITED STATES
IN 1850

Railroads
Canals
Stage Lines
Cumberland Road

SCALE OF MILES
100   200   500

1829 for the Delaware and Hudson Canal Company; in 1830 Peter Cooper built an American locomotive for the Baltimore and Ohio, whereby horses were displaced. The inclined planes with stationary engines, which were introduced on many railroads, were replaced by continuous tracks; and on some roads coal was used as a fuel instead of wood. In 1834 the first long railroad in the world was completed — 136 miles from Charleston, South Carolina, to Hamburg, opposite Augusta.

The first railroads had stone sleepers, or were built on piles driven along the line of the road. At right angles to the sleepers were laid the rails, wooden stringers about six inches square; to these were spiked short lengths of wrought iron strips perhaps half an inch thick, and the curling up of the loosely attached irons was a common source of accident. The gauges varied from 4 feet 8 inches to 6 feet. The cars were at first modeled on the old stagecoaches, but the roads soon began to build the long car with a platform at each end and an aisle through the middle. Trains ran about fifteen miles an hour, and the early fares were three or four cents a mile. As there was no system of train dispatching, accidents were frequent.

At first anybody who could pay the tolls was allowed to run his cars on the tracks; but after locomotives came in, it was seen that both the roadbed and the motive power must be managed together. Several states looked on railroads as only a new type of public highway; and Massachusetts, Pennsylvania, Georgia, North Carolina, Michigan, and other states built lines of state railroad; others aided new roads with grants of money. Since many roads ran from one state into another, state ownership was difficult; and state management was expensive and clumsy; hence, eventually most of the states sold or leased their lines to private companies.

The railroad mileage in 1840 was under 3000; in 1850, 9000; in 1860, 30,000. Till 1850 there was hardly such a thing as a

through railroad line, but in 1851 the New York and Erie
Railroad was finished from New York to Lake Erie, and in
1853 a continuous chain of separate lines of railroad reached
Chicago from the east. In 1859 railroads from the north and
east reached New Orleans. The railroads now began to be consolidated into systems by uniting them end to end; for example, the five short connecting lines from Albany to Buffalo,
and five other lateral strips, in 1853 were united under the
New York Central.

Beginning with a grant to the Illinois Central in 1850, the
United States aided western railroads by immense grants of
public lands. It was a natural suggestion that a road might
be built to the Pacific in the same way, and Congress went
so far as to send out several exploring expeditions, especially
one in 1853, which surveyed various practicable routes. Though
a railroad was built by American capital across the Panama
Isthmus and opened for business in 1855, the plans for an isthmian canal still came to nothing.

248. BUSINESS ORGANIZATION

Such great enterprises as new water-power works, canals,
and railroads could not have been carried out, except by a much
improved system for doing business, especially after the panic
of 1837 had shaken out a great number of weak concerns.
This was the system of incorporated companies, like banking
corporations, with limited liability and salaried managers. Not
only canals and railroads, but also turnpikes and bridges, textile mills, and other enterprises were carried on by such corporations. There was lively competition between concerns in
the same line of business; but after 1850 some of the companies,
especially in the telegraph and railroad business, began to combine into larger corporations.

One of the results of the enlarged business and profits was the
growth of a class of wealthy men. John Jacob Astor made large
investments in New York real estate, and left a great fortune to

his family, which they have kept through four generations. Others made large fortunes out of railroad building or iron manufacture or out of wholesale business, such as dry goods or groceries. Most of them were self-made men who had begun as wage earners. They had money to put into new buildings, piers and ships, and railroads. They owned bank stock and helped to carry on the banking business. Retail lines of business were almost all carried on by small firms. It was the habit of the country storekeeper to make a trip once or twice a year to the most convenient wholesale point, New Orleans, Baltimore, or New York, and buy goods for the next season. At that time no firms sent out traveling salesmen.

The banking business during Jackson's administration was much confused and there were many heavy losses. After the panic of 1837 several of the states, especially Massachusetts, Pennsylvania, and Louisiana, adopted laws similar to the New York safety fund system (§ 222). In some states all the banks contributed to a fund for redeeming the notes of failed banks. In other states they were obliged to keep a specie reserve in order to protect the note-holders. In several states, especially Kentucky, Indiana, and Alabama, the states themselves went into the banking business, in some instances prohibiting any other banks. Throughout the country, however, the doubtful and bad banknotes were a great obstacle to business. In 1860 it was estimated that there were five thousand different issues of worthless or doubtful or counterfeited banknotes in circulation. Every time a merchant received money, he had to consider whether the bills were perfectly good, ought to be taken at a discount, or should be refused.

249. The Fur Trade

In the far West there was only one line of profitable trade and that was the fur industry, which held over from the colonial period, and which was one of the main things that led to the annexation of Oregon and California. The center of that trade was always St. Louis, because it was at the mouth of the Missouri River, the basin of which embraced a large part of the fur country east of the Rockies. There were two or three very important firms, of which the Sublettes were the most noted. They fitted out parties of factors and trappers who made their way up the river to such points as Fort Benton, where they had permanent posts. Some of them employed trappers of their own on annual salaries, others depended chiefly on Indians to bring in the pelts. The traders, in caravans, frequently took goods into the heart of the Indian country, and dealt with the wild men there. For many years there was a running fight between the traders and certain tribes of Indians. The Blackfeet were notorious for their habit of robbing and murdering whites.

The most valuable fur then, as in colonial times, was the beaver, which was supplied in large quantities and always brought a good price; although there were some rare pelts such as the otter which commanded higher prices. Besides the animals that were trapped, the buffaloes furnished a large trade in their long-haired pelts; the warm buffalo robes were used like blankets all over the northern part of the country. Though the buffaloes ranged far north in the Rockies, their great habitat was the plains from the Missouri River west to what is now Colorado. There they roamed in uncounted millions, furnishing food and tent materials for the neighboring Indians, and the hides were brought east by thousands.

The fur traders were the first to discover the great through routes across the continent. They early followed up the Platte River and discovered an easy divide north of Great Salt Lake to the upper waters of the Lewis or Snake River, which was a branch of the Columbia; though it lay so deep in a canyon that the usual route crossed over the Blue Mountains direct to the Columbia River. Neither Astor nor other fur traders from the United States were successful in the fur trade on and around the Columbia, chiefly because of the strong competition of the

Hudson's Bay Company. Some of the traders, however, were the first to discover a practicable route across the Sierra Nevada to California, and they also developed the route up the Sacramento River and thence across mountains into Oregon.

250. EXPANSION OF COMMERCE (1840–1860)

One object of the annexation of Oregon and California was to secure ports for direct trade with the Pacific islands, China, and Japan. The halfway station of the Sandwich or Hawaiian Islands had for twenty years been under the influence of American missionaries, and the native dynasty recognized that the interests of the United States were greater than those of any other power. Chinese trade, however, was much hampered by restrictions in Chinese ports. In 1844 Caleb Cushing, sent out by the United States, was able to secure a very desirable commercial treaty by which five Chinese "treaty ports" were designated for American trade; American consuls were allowed to hold court for cases involving their countrymen; and American merchants and other people got the right to buy pieces of ground for their own occupancy, "and also for hospitals, churches, and cemeteries."

Japan refused to admit any traders or foreign merchantmen on any terms, till the United States sent Commodore Matthew C. Perry to open up relations. He entered ports where no European vessel had ever been seen; he succeeded in breaking in the shell of the old empire; and he secured a favorable commercial treaty in 1854.

The annexation of California affected the country in still another way. The gold from that state furnished coins which freely circulated; and gold at once became a new export, having very large value in small bulk. After 1848 also, there was a great foreign demand for American breadstuffs. Exports in 1856 were nearly three times as great as in 1846.

The revenues of the government from duties on imports rose so fast that a new tariff was passed by a nonpartisan vote

(March 3, 1857). Every member from Massachusetts and every member from South Carolina voted for the bill, which decreased the existing low duties of 1846 (§ 229) by about a fifth; and the average rate of duties was brought down to about 20 per cent. Before the new tariff could have any effect, a commercial panic came upon the country, caused principally by the expenditure of about $70,000,000 on railroads in ten years. The panic began in August, 1857, and in October all the banks in the country suspended specie payment; many railroads failed; and first and last more than five thousand business houses broke, with losses of more than $150,000,000. The federal government saw its annual revenue reduced from $76,000,000 to $46,000,000; and it was obliged to issue treasury notes for its expenses. Still there was no such widespread suffering and no such check to business as after the panic of 1837, and by 1860 business was again normal.

251. REVIEW

The three decades after 1830 were a period of great expansion, not only in population but in business, politics, and intellectual life. Large quantities of the western lands passed out of the hands of the government at a low price, or were made absolute gifts to old soldiers or to states. In 1841 a Preemption Act was passed, intended to restrict sales to actual occupiers. Many of the Indian tribes occupied reservations; and in the South the Creeks and Cherokees made preparations to remain against the wishes of Georgia. The Indians were obliged to move west of the Mississippi.

Great numbers of people moved from the East to the West, and hundreds of thousands of immigrants arrived from foreign countries. At first most of them came from English-speaking countries. Then came Germans, Scandinavians, and others. Large numbers of Irish came after 1845.

In various parts of the country there was a great lumber trade, and hard coal and soft coal were developed as fuel for houses, for making steam, for gas, and for making iron. Oil wells were discovered in western Pennsylvania. New inventions and processes increased the output of manufactures of all kinds, and inventive genius was applied to household and farm implements.

Steam was applied to seagoing steamers, and after 1838 to trans-Atlantic steamers, but the American shipping was mostly of wood, including the splendid clipper ships. Congress appropriated some money for subsidies to steamer lines to Europe. On land, long stretches of canals were built, but Congress refused to spend money for such objects. Railroads for general transportation came in just before 1830, and several of the states built public lines. The federal government aided with immense land grants (after 1850), but most of the roads were owned by private companies. Commerce was expanded by trade with the Orient, and Japan was opened to trade in 1854. A lower tariff was passed in 1857.

References Bearing on the Text and Topics

Geography and Maps. See maps, pp. 372-373. — Bogart, *Econ. Hist.*, 232, 241, 490. — Coman, *Indust. Hist.*, 224, 250. — Dodd, *Expansion and Conflict*, 133, 134, 139. — MacDonald, *Jacksonian Democracy*, 178, 182. — Shepherd, *Hist. Atlas*, 202.

Secondary. Bassett, *U.S.*, 461-468. — Bogart, *Econ. Hist.*, 160-187 (§§ 141-165), 212-288 (§§ 186-242). — Carlton, *Organized Labor*, ch. iii. — Chittenden, *Am. Fur Trade.* — Coman, *Econ. Beginnings of the Far West*, I. 300-375; *Indust. Hist.*, ch. vii. — Day, *Commerce*, ch. xlviii. — Dodd, *Expansion and Conflict*, ch. iii. — Fish, *Am. Nationality*, 173-192 passim, 242, 264-276, 333-335. — Hart, *Formation of the Union*, §§ 136, 137. — MacDonald, *Jacksonian Democracy*, chs. viii, x, xvi. — McMaster, *U.S.*, V. 121-183 passim, 537-540, VI. 79-94, 220-232, 327-335, 421-429, 464-466, 518-523, VII. 221-227. — Raymond, *Peter Cooper*, 1-51. — Schouler, *U.S.*, III. 370-380, 477-480, IV. 122-131, 233-235. — Turner, *New West*, chs. xiii, xvii. — Wilson, *Division and Reunion*, §§ 20, 21, 23, 24, 52, 81, 82.

Sources. Ames, *State Docs. on Fed. Rels.*, 113-132. — Bogart and Thompson, *Readings*, 276-282, 285-295, 376-484, 507-542. — Caldwell and Persinger, *Source Hist.*, 380-387. — Callender, *Econ. Hist.*, chs.

vii–ix, xiii, xiv. — Hart, *Contemporaries*, III. §§ 165–167; *Patriots and Statesmen*, III. 304–309, IV. 148–152, 186–189, 272–277, 320–379 passim, V. 186–189, 246–259. — James, *Readings*, §§ 73, 75, 82. — Johnson, *Readings*, §§ 94–97. — *Old South Leaflets*, nos. 147, 151.

Pictures. Bogart, *Econ. Hist.* — Coman, *Indust. Hist.* — Dunbar, *Hist. of Travel in Am.* — *Mentor*, serial no. 87. — Sparks, *Expansion*.

Topics Answerable from the References Above

(1) Abraham Lincoln as a frontiersman, *or* in the Black Hawk War. [§ 240] — (2) Moving the Indians west. [§ 240] — (3) Immigration in sailing vessels. [§ 241] — (4) Early life in some western city. [§ 242] — (5) Early use of anthracite as fuel, *or* of coal to smelt iron, *or* of illuminating gas. [§ 243] — (6) Early lead mining in Illinois, *or* gold mining in the South. [§ 243] — (7) Invention of the reaper. [§ 244] — (8) Early journeys by steamers on the Atlantic Ocean, *or* on eastern coast waters, *or* on the Great Lakes, *or* on the Mississippi, *or* on small rivers. [§§ 245, 246] — (9) First steam locomotives. [§ 247] — (10) Early travel by rail. [§ 247] — (11) Fur trade on the upper Missouri River. [§ 249] — (12) Fur traders and Indians. [§ 249] — (13) Perry's expedition to Japan. [§ 250]

Topics for Further Search

(14) Frontier life on government land after 1830. [§ 239] — (15) Early immigration from Scandinavia, *or* from Germany, *or* from Ireland. [§ 241] — (16) Influence of *one* of the following races on the United States: Scandinavians; Germans; Irish; English; Scotch-Irish; Scotch; Welsh. [§ 242] — (17) Life in *one* of the following factory towns: Lowell; Lawrence; Nashua; Holyoke; Cohoes; Trenton. [§ 244] — (18) Account of the clipper ship trade. [§ 245] — (19) Account of *one* of the following canals: Pennsylvania east and west line; Pittsburgh and Erie; Ohio Canal; Sandusky to Cincinnati; Fort Wayne. [§ 246] — (20) First surveys for a Pacific railroad. [§ 247] — (21) Early trade relations with China, *or* with Japan. [§ 250]

CHAPTER XXIII

SECTIONAL CONTROVERSY (1850–1859)

252. WHY SLAVERY DIVIDED THE COUNTRY

IN spite of the Compromise of 1850, which both parties pronounced a "finality," the slavery question continued to be the most serious and hotly contested issue in the minds of the American people. The abolitionists never ceased to hold meetings and publish papers and write pamphlets against slavery. They looked on the Compromise of 1850 as simply a means of giving a free hand to the slaveholders. Though the abolitionist societies were fewer and smaller than a few years earlier, the number of antislavery men and women was much greater in the North, because the long debates over the annexation of Texas, New Mexico, and California had aroused public feeling.

The movement against slavery was greatly aided by a book called *Uncle Tom's Cabin*, written by a New England woman, Harriet Beecher Stowe. It first appeared as a serial in 1851, and afterward in many editions in book form. The book was not written with the expectation of affecting politics; but it expressed a bitter feeling of injustice, that any man should be allowed to own another man. It made the whole world see the human side of negro character, the kinship of men of every race. It was the only antislavery book that was widely read and discussed in the South.

How far *Uncle Tom's Cabin* is a truthful picture of slavery has been much disputed. Mrs. Stowe had seen something of slave life in Kentucky; and some of the incidents, such as Eliza's escape on the ice, were actual events. The purpose of the book was to call attention to the inevitable cruelty of human bondage and its degrading effect on the master, and to that end the author made use of harrowing scenes, all of which were possible under slavery, and many of which were like incidents set forth in the southern newspapers of the time.

253. THE STATES IN THE SLAVERY CONTEST

The abolitionists always built upon the fact that slavery, wherever it existed, was founded on laws made by the state and not by the nation. If half the states in the Union could prohibit slavery, the other half might do the same, if they could be persuaded or terrified into doing so. But not a single slaveholding state would budge; not a single law was passed to prevent such abuses as the breaking up of negro families by sale, or the sale of little children away from their mothers.

On the other hand, the free states were induced to pass laws unfavorable to slavery, which usually were called "Personal Liberty Bills." Under the Fugitive Slave Law of 1793 a free negro who was suspected of being a fugitive might be arrested without any real examination of the facts; and in many instances free men were thus kidnaped and sent into slavery. To meet this danger, the northern states began about 1840 to pass acts forbidding the state officials to take any part in proceedings against such persons. So far the states were acting within their rights; but either before or after the Fugitive Slave Act of 1850, statutes were passed in all the northern states except two, interfering in various ways with the operation of the national fugitive slave statute. All these acts showed that the free states, Constitution or no Constitution, would not recognize any responsibility for slavery.

254. NATIONAL QUESTIONS OF SLAVERY

Though slavery was made by state action and could be unmade or weakened by the same power, it could not be kept free of some control by the federal government. That was the main reason why the Compromise of 1850 was a failure: it could not stop the discussion with regard to slavery; and notwithstanding its so-called "finality," discussion in Congress continued under four different clauses of the Constitution:

(1) The Constitution gave Congress power to legislate for the District of Columbia "in all cases whatsoever." For thirty years abolitionists urged and petitioned Congress to prohibit slavery in the District, and they were not in the least pleased with the limited act of 1850 on this subject (§ 236).

(2) Congress had complete power over both the foreign and the interstate slave trade; the foreign slave trade was prohibited by the act of 1807 (§ 183), but as late as 1859 some southern writers demanded that the African slave trade be reopened. The domestic trade was never restricted except in the District of Columbia after 1850.

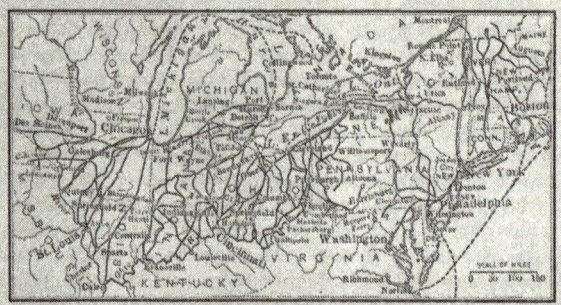

ROUTES OF THE "UNDERGROUND RAILROAD" FOR FUGITIVE SLAVES.

(3) Congress had power over the recovery of fugitive slaves and exercised it in the two acts of 1793 and 1850, the latter of which was especially hated by the antislavery element. Southerners complained of the increasing use of the "Underground Railroad" (§ 235).

(4) Under its general power to regulate the territories, Congress

prohibited slavery by four statutes applying to four definite areas : (a) the Ordinance of 1787, for the Northwest Territory, reaffirmed by an act of Congress of 1789 (§ 115); (b) the Missouri Compromise of 1820, covering all the Louisiana cession north of 36° 30′ except the state of Missouri (§ 185); (c) the Texas resolution of 1845, prohibiting slavery in states that might be formed in Texas territory north of 36° 30′ (§ 228); (d) the Oregon Act of 1848, prohibiting slavery in that territory (§ 234). It was clear that any future annexation of territory would lead to a fierce contest to decide which section should control the new region.

The conflict in Congress was intensified by the appearance of several ardent antislavery men in both houses. The first such senator was John P. Hale of New Hampshire (1847). Then in 1849 came Chase of Ohio, William H. Seward of New York, and in 1857 Sumner of Massachusetts. Seward, born in 1801, went to Union College and was for a short time tutor in a slaveholding family in the South. He entered politics in New York state and was twice Whig governor of New York (1839–1843). His intimate friend and political manager was Thurlow Weed, one of the most adroit, long-headed, and unscrupulous politicians in the history of the country.

In the debate of 1850 Seward was the leader of the antislavery forces against the compromise. His argument was that compromises settled nothing, and that it was useless to try to provide for such questions before they came up. In his speech Seward let fall a phrase which seemed monstrous to the South : "The Constitution devotes the domain to union, to justice, to defense, to welfare, and to liberty. But there is a higher law than the Constitution, which regulates our authority over the domain, and devotes it to the same noble purpose." What he meant to say was that the law of God agreed with the Constitution; what he was understood to say was that the higher law nullified the Constitution, which recognized slavery as existing in some states and territories.

255. FUGITIVE SLAVE CASES (1851–1858)

The slaves themselves helped to keep their cause before the public mind because every year a few of them ran away into free states. The radical antislavery people ignored and scouted the Fugitive Slave Act, and in many instances resisted it. Among such affairs the most startling cases were those of Shadrach, Gorsuch, and Burns.

Early in 1851, an undoubted fugitive named Shadrach was arrested in Boston and brought before the United States commissioner. Before the proceedings ended, an eyewitness said, "We heard a shout from the courthouse continued into a yell of triumph, and in an instant after down the steps came two huge negroes bearing the prisoner between them with his clothes half torn off, . . . and they went off toward Cambridge, like a black squall, the crowd driving along with them, and cheering as they went."

RUNAWAY SLAVE. (Cut used in newspaper advertisements.)

In September, 1851, a Maryland man named Gorsuch, who had pursued runaways to Christiana, Pennsylvania, was killed by a band of negroes, probably including his own slaves. A Quaker named Castner Hanway was present and refused to aid Gorsuch. An attempt was made to frighten the abolitionists by trying Hanway for treason for this refusal to take part in capturing a fugitive. The prosecution, however, broke down, and the slayers of Gorsuch were not found.

In 1854, while a fugitive named Burns was confined in the United States courthouse in Boston, a mob of abolitionists, in an attempt to rescue him, broke in the door and killed one of the deputy marshals.

Attempts were made to prosecute the rescuers of Shadrach and other fugitives; but juries would not convict. The truth was that northern public sentiment was so strong that it was hardly worth while for southern slave owners to appeal to the Fugitive Slave Law. The northern state governments would not assist in sending a hunted fugitive back to lifelong captivity for no crime except that of being born a black slave.

256. PRESIDENT PIERCE AND CUBA (1852–1855)

So far the slavery question had had little effect on parties, except for the group of Free-soilers (§ 234), who cast only 300,000 votes in 1848. Still the two old parties were losing vitality. No serious issue existed between them: the Whigs no longer insisted on a United States bank, or national internal improvements, or a protective tariff; while inside each party there was a strong and fierce division on slavery.

In the political campaign of 1852 the Whigs nominated Winfield Scott of Virginia, a good soldier, but a weak candidate. The Democratic convention, after a fierce competition, nominated an inconspicuous man, Franklin Pierce of New Hampshire, who had been in Congress and had served creditably in the Mexican War. Pierce received 254 electoral votes to 42 for Scott, though the Whigs succeeded in polling nearly 1,400,000 popular votes against 1,600,000 for the Democratic ticket and 155,000 for the Free-soil Democrats, which was the name taken by the antislavery party.

President Pierce made William L. Marcy of New York Secretary of State, and Jefferson Davis of Mississippi Secretary of War. In his inaugural address he showed a strong leaning toward slavery by proposing to annex Cuba, a rich slaveholding island (§ 190). This was not a new idea. President Polk in vain offered Spain a hundred million dollars for the island in 1848, and from 1849 to 1851 several expeditions of "filibusters" — that is, of volunteer adventurers — were fitted out in New Orleans, to land men in Cuba. One of them, under Lopez, was captured by the Spaniards, and Lopez with about fifty of his followers was executed.

President Pierce appointed Pierre Soulé, of Louisiana, as minister to Spain. He was an ardent "fire eater," as extreme advocates of slavery were called, and he bent all his energies to acquire Cuba. The time for a war of conquest seemed to have arrived when the American steamer *Black Warrior* was seized in Havana for a technical violation of the customs regulations (March, 1854).

While this question was pending, Soulé and two other foreign ministers drew up the "Ostend Manifesto" (October, 1854), which was an open avowal that Cuba must be annexed in order to protect slavery. If Spain should refuse to sell Cuba for a fair price, the manifesto declared, "then by every law, human and divine, we shall be justified in wresting it from Spain if we possess the power [lest] we permit Cuba to be Africanized." Marcy's influence was against annexation, and the United States accepted a settlement of the *Black Warrior* difficulty (February, 1855). This proved to be a deathblow to the plan of annexation.

257. DOUGLAS AND THE NEBRASKA BILL (1854)

The main reason for holding back from Cuba was the trouble that Pierce's administration had with the Nebraska question. After 1820 the region west of the Missouri River remained without a territorial government, which was much needed when the overland travel to California began on a large scale in 1849 (§ 232). Senator Stephen A. Douglas of Illinois, chairman of the committee on territories, introduced a bill for the organization of Nebraska Territory (January 4, 1854). The Missouri Compromise prohibited slavery there, but Douglas asserted that that compromise had been set aside by the New Mexico and Utah bills in the Compromise of 1850 (§ 236), and he insisted on "popular sovereignty" or "squatter sover-

eignty"; that is, the right of the people of a territory to make
their own laws, like the people of the states. After various
twists and turns he was compelled to come into the open and
declare in the text of his bill that the antislavery clause of
the Missouri act "is hereby declared inoperative and void."
The point in dispute was whether the "principle" of the act
of 1850, which in terms applied only to the annexation of 1848,
could "supersede" the details of the act of 1820, which in
terms applied only to the Louisiana cession.

In this controversy
Douglas represented a
strong influence which
eastern men did not
understand. Born in
Vermont in 1813, he
early went to Illinois,
where he held various
state offices, including
that of judge of the
Supreme Court. In
1847 he was sent from
Illinois to the Senate,
and there represented
those crude but deter-
mined political forces
which had earlier made
Jackson President. He

STEPHEN A. DOUGLAS, ABOUT 1850.

came from a constituency which was accustomed to care for
itself, and which therefore thought it as reasonable that the
people of a territory should settle the question of slavery
as that they should settle the question of schools. Later
in his career he made the significant admission that he "did
not care whether slavery was voted down or voted up"; but
he was very ambitious, and there is no doubt that he was
looking forward and hoped to convince the southern Democrats

that he would be a safe and powerful candidate for the presidency in the next election. Still Douglas was one of the few statesmen interested in the future of the West. His theory of "squatter sovereignty" fitted in with the general principles of democracy.

Of all American public men, Douglas was the fiercest debater. Though a short man, he had a big voice which poured forth anything that came into his mind, especially a coarse and effective personal abuse of those who opposed him. He was quick and forcible, and never much concerned himself about accuracy or consistency. His main defect was that he could not understand the moral opposition to slavery.

258. TROUBLE IN KANSAS (1854–1856)

In the course of the discussion about the Nebraska bill, the measure was amended so as to divide the new territory into two territories, Kansas and Nebraska, showing a plain expectation that Kansas, which lay immediately west of Missouri, would become a slaveholding community to balance California. In spite of the bitterest opposition, ably led by Chase, Douglas got 37 votes for his bill in the Senate against 14, and then forced the bill through the House by a vote of 108 to 100. He had already arranged with President Pierce, who duly signed the bill (May 30, 1854). Perhaps Douglas began to see his error in allowing slavery to enter a free area when, on the test vote on the Kansas-Nebraska Bill in the House, half the northern Democrats refused to go with him; and still more when in the Congressional election in the fall of 1854 most of the half who supported him lost their seats.

The difficulty with Douglas's principle of "popular sovereignty" was that it put upon the first rush of settlers in a new territory the responsibility of deciding whether the future state should be free or slaveholding. Hundreds of Missourians saw this chance and at once crossed over into Kansas and entered up land for farms which most of them did not mean to occupy. On the antislavery side, several emigrant aid companies were founded in New England, and within about three years sent out six thousand free-state men, as permanent settlers, many of them armed with a new weapon of precision, the Sharps rifle. In the first Kansas election for members of the territorial legislature (March, 1855) 2905 legal voters were somehow credited with 6307 votes. Hundreds of armed Missourians came over into Kansas, and set up or drove away election officers at their will. Thus they elected a large majority of the legislature, which passed a code of laws to establish slavery.

To protect themselves against this minority rule, the antislavery people attempted to set up a free-state government. The rival settlers and neighbors came to civil war in the spring of 1856. About two hundred lives were sacrificed and the free-state town of Lawrence was sacked. Among the most reckless of the free-state people was a man named John Brown, who turned out whenever there was a fight; and in May, 1856, he directed his men to seize and kill some proslavery neighbors at Osawatomie. President Pierce took sides in favor of the bogus territorial legislature and broke up the free-state government at Topeka (July 4, 1856).

259. NEW REPUBLICAN PARTY (1854-1856)

Both the Whig party and the Democratic party were split by the Kansas-Nebraska Bill, and a great effort was made to form a new party. It first took the form of a short-lived American party, created on the principles of dislike of Catholics and distrust of foreigners. This organization was backed by a powerful secret society, the members of which always replied to any question about their society, "I know nothing about it," and they were commonly called "Know-nothings." They carried the state government of Massachusetts, and extended into the southern states, but they soon broke into factions over the slavery question. Horace Greeley said that you might as well try to form an "anti-potato-rot party" as an anti-foreign party.

The antislavery men could count on their 155,000 voters in the election of 1852 (§ 256), and were a lively element in a new and strong political combination with those "anti-Nebraska" Whigs and Democrats who opposed Douglas's squatter sovereignty. To this new party the name "Republican" was given, probably for the first time, at Jackson, Michigan (July, 1854). Their main principle was to put a stop to the extension of slavery. By all sorts of fusions and coalitions of Know-nothings, Republicans, Whigs, and Democrats, the anti-Nebraska people carried fifteen states in 1854, and elected eleven senators and a small majority of the House of Representatives.

In 1856 the Republicans, who were called by their opponents "Black Republicans," girded themselves up for the presidential election. Instead of nominating Seward, their ablest man, they put up John C. Frémont (§§ 227, 231) who was popularly supposed to have conquered California. To the grief of Stephen A. Douglas, the Democrats passed him over, precisely because he had roused such opposition by helping the South in his Kansas-Nebraska Bill; instead they nominated for the presidency James Buchanan of Pennsylvania.

In the election of 1856 Buchanan received 174 electoral votes to 114 for Frémont, and the Republicans failed to secure the House for 1857-1859. Yet Frémont had 1,300,000 votes against 1,800,000 for Buchanan; and carried every northern state except New Jersey, Pennsylvania, Indiana, and Illinois.

260. PRESIDENT BUCHANAN AND THE TERRITORIES

When James Buchanan was inaugurated as President in March, 1857, there was a temporary lull in the controversy between the sections. Upon the face of it, the quarrel was no more serious than the earlier struggles over the bank or the tariff or internal improvements. The northern and southern states had about the same kind of state governments, appealed to the same principles of the equal rights of all free men. The only pressing trouble was the condition of Kansas; and President Buchanan appointed Robert J. Walker of Mississippi as territorial governor, with a promise that the people might choose a convention to form a state constitution, which was then to be submitted to the voters in the territory.

One other territorial question proved troublesome to Buchanan: this was a serious disturbance in the territory of Utah. At that time, most of the overland traffic to California

MORMON CHURCH BUILDINGS, SALT LAKE CITY. (Tabernacle, built 1870; Temple, built 1893.)

went by wagon roads which passed near Great Salt Lake. That neighborhood was settled by the Mormons (§ 205), who, under their new prophet Brigham Young, came out to Salt Lake in 1847, laid out farms, began an irrigation system, and founded a city. Young publicly announced that he had received a direct revelation from the Almighty, by which polygamy was to be part of the Mormon religious system. The Mormons furnished a battalion of United States troops for the Mexican War, and made no objection to the cession of 1848, which brought them within the United States. When Utah Territory

was created in 1850 (§ 236), Brigham Young was made the
first governor.

The Mormons wanted to be let alone, and made trouble for
the federal officials. In 1857 Buchanan appointed a new territorial governor, and sent with him 1500 troops to support
his authority over the Mormons, who were reported to have
burned the court records, and to be in a state of rebellion.
Governor Brigham Young declared there was no rebellion or
disorder; he forbade the troops to enter the territory, and
called out the militia, which captured some of the government
supply trains and tried to starve out the federal troops. The
following year, however, the new governor was peacefully in-
stalled, Buchanan proclaimed amnesty for the Mormons, and
the troops entered the territory unmolested.

261. KANSAS AND THE DRED SCOTT DECISION (1857)

Before the plan for relieving what the antislavery people
called "Bleeding Kansas" could be carried out, the antislavery
spirit was much intensified by a decision of the Supreme Court
on the question of territorial slavery. Congress had failed to
settle that question by the Kansas-Nebraska Act, and the
settlers in Kansas had vainly tried to settle it by a little civil
war. Yet the Supreme Court attempted to put an end to the
controversy by a decision in the famous case of Dred Scott vs.
Sandford. The facts were that Dred Scott, the slave of a Dr.
Emerson, had been taken from Missouri, first to Illinois, which
was covered by the Northwest Ordinance (§ 115), and then to
what is now southern Minnesota, a region covered by the
Missouri Compromise (§ 185). Dred Scott without objection
then accompanied his master to Missouri, but some years later
he sued for his freedom on the ground that his master had
voluntarily taken him into regions where slavery was prohibited.

The case went through three trials in lower courts. In
March, 1857, six of the nine judges of the United States Supreme
Court united in the assertion that the Missouri Compromise

was no protection to Dred Scott, because that act had always been unconstitutional, inasmuch as Congress had no power to deal with slavery in the territories. So far the opinion agreed with Douglas's report on the Kansas-Nebraska Bill; but at least four of the judges turned down the Douglas doctrine of popular sovereignty (§ 257), by holding that neither Congress *nor a territorial legislature* could prohibit slavery in a territory. That is, the Court, so far as it could, supported slavery as a national institution, which was normal in every territory and could be ended only by a regular state government. Chief Justice Taney also laid down the principle that Dred Scott could not sue, because no negro could be a citizen of the United States, and added that at the time of the Revolution negroes "had no rights which the white man was bound to respect."

Curtis and McLean, two judges from northern states, denied all these conclusions and especially the unfounded statement that negroes had been shut out of the political community at the time of the Revolution (§ 112). The result was that Dred Scott remained a slave, but in fact he was immediately set free by his legal owner. The decision was so drastic that the antislavery men and the leaders of the Republican party declared that they would not be bound by it.

While the Republicans were in a state of rage and suspicion on account of the Dred Scott decision, a proslavery territorial convention met at Lecompton and drew up a constitution for the future state of Kansas (1857). Contrary to Buchanan's promise (§ 260), the convention did not submit their work to popular vote, but instead offered merely a choice of two clauses concerning slavery: the voters were to cast their ballots only for "Constitution with Slavery" or for "Constitution with no Slavery" but not against the Constitution; and whichever form might carry, the slaves then in the territory were to remain slaves. The "free-state" Kansans refused to cast any vote on what they considered to be a fraudulent constitution; so it easily carried "with Slavery." In the territorial election,

meanwhile, they had secured a majority of the territorial legislature, which ordered another election to vote on the Lecompton
constitution; and in that election the constitution was rejected
altogether by a very large vote. Nevertheless, Buchanan insisted that the Democratic majority of Congress should force
Kansas into the Union under the proslavery Lecompton constitution (1858). On a final test ordered by Congress, the
people of Kansas by a crushing vote refused to be made a
slave state against their will, and therefore they remained a
territory till 1861.

262. RISE OF ABRAHAM LINCOLN (1809-1858)

The effort to make Kansas a slave state was flatly against
Douglas's doctrine of popular sovereignty, and he refused to
support it. His term in the Senate was about to expire; and
in the campaign in Illinois a rival claimant appeared for the
seat, in the person of Abraham Lincoln of Springfield. At this
time, he was an obscure country lawyer who wrote up his
autobiography as follows:

"Born, February 12, 1809, in Hardin County, Kentucky;
"Education defective;
"Profession a lawyer;
"Have been a captain of volunteers in the Black Hawk War;
"Postmaster at a very small office;
"Four times a member of Illinois Legislature;
"And was a member of the lower house of Congress."

Lincoln rose steadily from the squalor of a poor white family,
living in Kentucky, then in Indiana, and later in Illinois. After
trying surveying and storekeeping, he practiced law, went to
the legislature, was an early Whig and became known throughout the state for his good stories, homely sayings, and honest
attention to the cases intrusted to him. In 1841 he visited the
South, and he called slavery "a thing which has, and con-
tinually exercises, the power of making me miserable." From
1847 to 1849 he sat in Congress (§ 230).

When the Kansas-Nebraska question arose, Lincoln came out firmly for the antislavery cause. When designated by the Illinois Republicans as their candidate for the senatorship against Douglas (1858), he accepted in a magnificent speech, of which the text was: "A house divided against itself cannot stand. I believe this government cannot endure permanently half slave and half free."

He next took the bold step of challenging Douglas to a

LINCOLN STUDYING LAW.

series of public joint debates. In this contest, Douglas accused Lincoln of seeking the social equality of the negro, to which Lincoln replied: "In the right to eat the bread without the leave of anybody else, which his own hand earns, he is my equal, and the equal of Judge Douglas, and the equal of every living man." Lincoln skillfully compelled Douglas to put forth what was called the "Freeport doctrine," to the effect that the people of a territory might actually prevent slavery by "unfriendly legislation." This was in accordance with "popular sover-

cignty," but was contrary to the Dred Scott decision (§ 261).
Partly because of his "Freeport doctrine," Douglas was reelected to the Senate; but when he went back to Washington he
found that the southern Democrats, who controlled the party
organization, refused to recognize him as an associate in the party.

263. JOHN BROWN'S RAID (1859)

The most striking event of the year 1859 was the attempt of
John Brown (§ 258) to cause a slave insurrection by establishing a camp for runaway negroes in the southern mountains.
He secured money and counsel from some New England friends,
recruited twenty-two men, and descended upon Harpers Ferry
(October 16). He seized the United States arsenal, sent out
parties to capture some of the white planters, and tried to
rouse the neighboring slaves, who were expected to carry
off a quantity of the government arms. The whole countryside was in an uproar; but the negroes did not rise, and the
engine house in which Brown had fortified himself was finally
taken by United States marines under Colonel Robert E.
Lee. Brown was wounded and captured, and ten of his men
were killed.

It is greatly to the credit of Virginia that Brown had a fair
and open trial. He was duly convicted of murder and treason
against Virginia, and was sentenced to be hanged. He somehow won the respect of his jailers and southern visitors; but
he never had the slightest feeling of remorse or guilt, and went
to his death without fear. In his last letter to his family he
solemnly said, "John Brown writes to his children to abhor,
with undying hatred also, that sum of all villanies, slavery."
Moderate northern people condemned Brown's methods, but
could not help admiring his heroic spirit. John Brown probably did more than any other man to convince the South that
slavery was no longer safe within the federal Union, so long as
abolitionists were willing to sacrifice their own lives to free
other people's slaves.

264. REVIEW

Congress was again driven into the slavery struggle by its power to legislate on slavery in the federal District, on the slave trade, on fugitive slaves, and on slavery in the territories. The aid given by the abolitionists to fugitive slaves, including violent rescues in several cases, aroused the slave owners.

Franklin Pierce, as President, set out to annex Cuba. This plan, which led to the Ostend Manifesto of 1854, was interrupted by a bill introduced by Douglas for a new territory. He proposed to allow slavery there on the ground that the Compromise of 1850 "superseded" the Missouri Compromise.

The Kansas-Nebraska Bill became law; but the antislavery men at once seized upon this new principle of "popular sovereignty," by colonizing Kansas.

After a brief attempt by the Know-nothings to found an anti-foreign party, the Republican party appeared. The various opponents of the Kansas-Nebraska act elected a majority in the House in 1854, but in the presidential election of 1856 the Democrats elected Buchanan as President.

The Supreme Court decided in the Dred Scott Case (1857) that neither Congress nor the people of a territory could prevent slavery in a territory. This aroused the Republicans, who also objected to the Lecompton Constitution, made by a pro-slavery convention and not submitted to a popular vote.

Abraham Lincoln of Illinois came forward in 1858 as an antislavery champion in a series of debates with Douglas. The next year the whole country was aroused by the attempt of John Brown to raise a slave insurrection in Virginia.

References Bearing on the Text and Topics

Geography and Maps. See maps, pp. 384, 403. — Chadwick, *Causes of the Civil War*, 80. — Dodd, *Expansion and Conflict*, 180, 237.

Secondary. Bassett, *U.S.*, 485–504. — Brown, *Lower South*, 50–82; *S. A. Douglas.* — Chadwick, *Causes of the Civil War*, chs. i, iii–vi; *U.S. and Spain*, I. chs. xii, iii. — Fish, *Am. Nationality*, 327–354. — Foster, *Century of Diplomacy*, 335–356. — Hart, *Foundations of Am.*

Foreign Policy, 108, 127; *S. P. Chase*, 130–177. — Johnson, *S. A. Douglas*, chs. x–xvii. — Linn, *Mormons*, 458–542. — Lothrop, *W. H. Seward*, chs. vi–x. — McMaster, *U.S.*, VIII. 45–68, 133–442. — Morse, *Abraham Lincoln*, I. 93–160. — Nicolay and Hay, *Abraham Lincoln*, I. chs. xviii–xxv, II. chs. i–xi. — Pendleton, *A. H. Stephens*, chs. vi–viii. — Rhodes, *U.S.*, I. 207–302, 384–506, II. 1–416. — Schouler, *U.S.*, V. 202–454. — Siebert, *Underground Railroad*. — Villard, *John Brown*.

Sources. *Am. Hist. Leaflets*, nos. 2, 17, 23. — Ames, *State Docs. on Fed. Rels.*, 272–310. — Harding, *Select Orations*, nos. 19–22. — Hart, *Contemporaries*, IV. §§ 29–48; *Patriots and Statesmen*, V. 130–250. — Hill, *Liberty Docs.*, ch. xxi. — Lincoln, *Works*, passim. — MacDonald, *Select Docs.*, nos. 85–92.

Illustrative. Brooks, *Boy Settlers* (Kan.). — Cable, *Strange True Stories of La.* — McLaws, *The Welding.* — Morgan, *The Issue.* — Orpen, *Jay-Hawkers* (Kan.). — Paterson, *For Freedom's Sake* (Kan.). — Sherlock, *Red Anvil* (fugitives). — Stedman, *How Old John Brown took Harper's Ferry.* — Stowe, *Dred; Uncle Tom's Cabin* (slavery). — Trowbridge, *Neighbor Jackwood* (fugitives). — Whittier, *Antislavery Poems*, 159–213; *Brown of Osawatomie.*

Pictures. Sparks, *Expansion.* — Wilson, *Am. People*, IV.

Topics Answerable from the References Above

(1) Personal Liberty Bills. [§ 253] — (2) Slave-trading ships after 1830. [§ 254] — (3) Public career of *one* of the following: John P. Hale; Sumner; Seward; Thurlow Weed. [§ 254] — (4) Details of *one* of the following fugitive slave cases: Shadrach; Gorsuch; Burns; Hamlet; Jerry; Crafts; Williamson. [§ 255] — (5) Public career of *one* of the following: Pierce; Marcy; Jefferson Davis; Douglas. [§ 256] — (6) Account of the New England Emigrant Aid Society. [§ 258] — (7) John Brown at Osawatomie. [§ 258] — (8) Early history of the Republican party. [§ 259] — (9) Mormon migration to Utah. [§ 260] — (10) Abraham Lincoln from 1849 to 1857. [§ 262] — (11) Lincoln-Douglas debate. [§ 262] — (12) John Brown's raid. [§ 263]

Topics for Further Search

(13) Influence of *Uncle Tom's Cabin*. [§ 252] — (14) Why was a territorial bill needed for Nebraska? [§ 257] — (15) Was the Missouri Compromise superseded by the Compromise of 1850? [§ 257] — (16) Objections to the Kansas-Nebraska Bill. [§ 258] — (17) The Know-nothing party. [§ 259] — (18) Contemporary criticisms of the Dred Scott decision. [§ 261] — (19) What was the " Freeport doctrine "? [§ 262]

CHAPTER XXIV

DIVISION BETWEEN NORTH AND SOUTH (1860–1861)

265. ELECTION OF 1860

A NEW contest for the presidency began as soon as Buchanan was elected in 1856; for the Republicans had great hopes of carrying all the northern states in 1860. The Dred Scott decision, the Lecompton controversy, and the Lincoln-Douglas debate all helped them in their policy as an antislavery party. They had a small majority in the House of Representatives from 1859 to 1861, but the Senate remained strongly Democratic. Jefferson Davis of Mississippi, leader of the extreme proslavery party, introduced a series of resolutions into the Senate (February, 1860), which after some debate were passed by 35 to 21 votes. They declared: (1) that Congress ought to interfere, if necessary, to protect slavery, thus going beyond the Dred Scott decision (§ 261); (2) that the northern states ought to stop public agitation by the abolitionists; (3) that the states were sovereign.

In effect, the resolutions gave notice that the election of a President who opposed those principles might be made an excuse for breaking up the Union; further, that unless these extreme views were accepted by the federal government, the slaveholding states would have a constitutional right to break up the Union. Hence the whole country watched the regular Democratic convention which met at Charleston, South Carolina in April. Douglas had a majority of the delegates, but the southerners insisted that he should accept a platform which was substantially the Davis resolutions. Douglas was willing to pledge himself to "abide by the decisions of the Supreme Court"; but he could not promise to support any plan for forcing slavery into an unwilling territory.

On that difference the convention split; the delegates of most of the southern states withdrew, and the convention adjourned. It reconvened at Baltimore in June, and, after another split, Douglas was there nominated, on the platform proposed by his

PROGRESSIVE DEMOCRACY PROSPECT OF A SMASH UP.

ELECTION CARTOON OF 1860.

friends at Charleston. The southern bolters met separately and nominated John C. Breckinridge, then Vice President of the United States.

Many of the old southern Whigs, and the northern Whigs who had not become Republicans, united in what they called the Constitutional Union party, and nominated John Bell of Tennessee, on the brief platform, "The Constitution of the country, the union of the States, and the enforcement of the laws."

The Republican convention met in Chicago (May 16), in an immense hall, with thousands of spectators. It was gen-

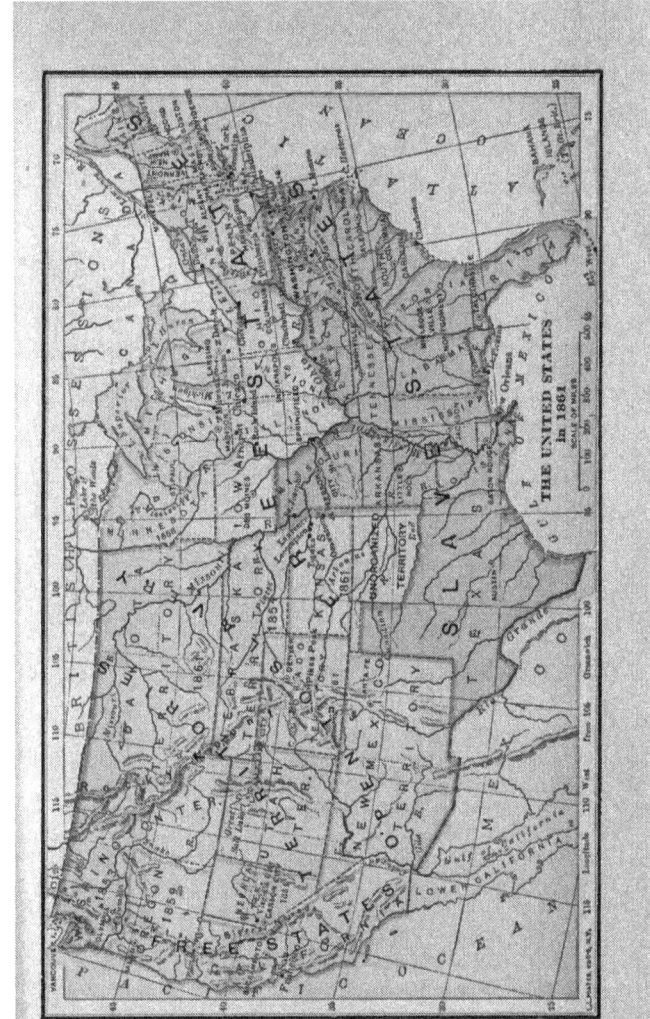

erally expected that Seward would be nominated, but he was thought too radical; what was wanted was a moderate western man who could carry the doubtful states of Pennsylvania, Ohio, Indiana, and Illinois. Abraham Lincoln was the most available among such men; and on the third ballot he was nominated.

The campaign was fierce and exciting. On election day (November 6), 180 Lincoln electors were chosen against 72 for Breckinridge, 39 for Bell, and 12 for Douglas. Lincoln had the necessary majority of all the electoral votes, though of the popular vote, he had only 1,900,000 against 1,400,000 for Douglas, 850,000 for Breckinridge, and 600,000 for Bell. Yet if his opponents had concentrated on any two, or any one, of the other candidates, the result of the election would have been the same; for the Republicans had a majority in every northern state except New Jersey, California, and Oregon.

266. Secession of Seven States (1860-1861)

During the campaign it was freely predicted that the election of Lincoln would lead to secession. To most northern men the threat seemed preposterous. Nevertheless, on the day after the national election, the South Carolina legislature took steps toward calling a secession convention, and within a few days the principal federal officers in South Carolina resigned their offices. Hardly a Union man could be found in the whole state; not one was elected to the convention.

During the next seven weeks South Carolina was in turmoil; federal buildings and supplies were seized, and companies of men were drilled. The excitement culminated when the secession convention at Charleston, by a unanimous vote (December 20, 1860), passed an ordinance declaring that South Carolina was no longer a part of the Union. A member of the convention said, "We have carried the body of this Union to its last resting place, and now we will drop the flag over its grave."

In this awful crisis the country hardly had a President.

Buchanan had long stood on the same political ground as the radical southerners, and he called in Jefferson Davis to advise

ABRAHAM LINCOLN IN 1860.

him. The President's message to Congress (December 3) was a helpless document; he laid all the trouble to "the incessant and violent agitation of the slavery question throughout the North for the last quarter of a century." As for secession, Seward neatly summed up the message as follows: "The President has conclusively proved two things: (1) that no state has a right to secede unless it wishes to; and (2) that it is the President's duty to enforce the laws unless somebody opposes him."

After secession, the South Carolina government immediately demanded the surrender of the forts within its borders; and while the question was pending, Major Anderson, in command of the scanty force in Charleston harbor, moved his troops (December 26) from the exposed Fort Moultrie into the strong, isolated Fort Sumter. Floyd, Secretary of War, insisted that he should give up Fort Sumter. Jeremiah Black, Secretary of State, and Edwin M. Stanton, who had just entered the Cabinet, declared that in that case they would resign. "You don't give me any time to say my prayers," said Buchanan; "I always say my prayers when required to act upon any great state affairs." In the end he yielded to his northern advisers, and Anderson was left in Fort Sumter.

It was understood from the first that other states would follow South Carolina, and between January 9 and February 1, six other state conventions, specially chosen for that purpose, voted secession ordinances. The six additional states were Mississippi, Florida, Alabama, Georgia, Louisiana, and Texas. In two of them, Alabama and Georgia, there was a strong opposition and a close vote. In all these states, before secession, most of the United States mints, posts, arsenals, forts, public buildings, and public property were seized. All that remained in federal hands were Fort Pickens, below Pensacola, Key West and the Dry Tortugas on detached islands, and Fort Sumter in the harbor of Charleston.

The next step was to combine the seceded states into a union.

In February, 1861, a convention of delegates from six states met at Montgomery, Alabama, drew up a "provisional constitution" for "The Confederate States of America," and elected Jefferson Davis of Mississippi President of the new Confederacy, and Alexander H. Stephens of Georgia Vice President. A Cabinet was duly appointed by President Davis. The convention reorganized as a provisional Congress and sat for a year. During that time a permanent constitution was framed.

267. SOUTHERN AND NORTHERN GRIEVANCES

The whole North was convulsed by the seven secessions, and asked what were the reasons for breaking the Union. The grievances of the South were expressed in addresses of conventions, in pamphlets, newspapers, public speeches, and statements by southern members of Congress from their seats; their charges against the North were numerous and angry. The most important grievances may be stated as follows:

(1) General hostility. That the North was bent on making money for itself, and was no longer interested in the general welfare of the Union. The charge was later made that the existing tariff discriminated against the South; but in 1860 the South made no such complaint; in fact all the South Carolina members of Congress had voted for that tariff.

(2) Breach of the Constitution. That the North misinterpreted the Constitution, and would not admit the doctrine of state rights and secession; that the Republicans meant to overturn the Dred Scott decision; and that, by the personal liberty laws, the northern states defied the Constitution.

(3) Antislavery. That the North hated slavery and allowed abolition meetings and newspapers and members of Congress to speak abusively of the slaveholders; and that the northern people approved of John Brown's insurrection.

(4) Territorial slavery. That the North would not admit any more slave states or allow the annexation of slaveholding

territory, and was trying to draw a "cordon of free states" around the South and thus slowly to strangle slavery.

(5) Election of Lincoln. That the choice of an antislavery President was an act of hostility to the South and would result in an attack on slavery in the states.

In this list the main and deciding grievance is briefly that the North disliked slavery, wanted to check it, and allowed people to discuss it. As Robert Toombs of Georgia put it, "What is wanted is that the North shall call slavery right." It is also true that the South was fast losing strength in Congress. By the admission of Minnesota in 1858, Oregon in 1859, and Kansas (34th state) in 1861, the number of free states was raised to 19, as against 15 slaveholding states.

A feeling of injury and wrath was also widespread in the North because of grievances expressed substantially as follows:

(1) Territory. That the southerners had for years been forcing the annexation of territory in order to strengthen slavery.

(2) Free speech. That the South had arrogantly attempted to put down free speech and a free press in the northern states, and even in Congress.

(3) Citizenship. That by the South Carolina negro seamen act of 1820 and other statutes against the movement of free negroes, the southern states violated rights of northern negro citizens which were guaranteed by the Constitution.

(4) Violence in Kansas. That the Kansas episode showed a determination to foist a slavery constitution by fraud and violence on the people of a practically free territory.

(5) Political control. That the slave power had ever since 1829 practically controlled the presidency, the Supreme Court, the Senate, and the House (except for two Congresses), and now wanted to leave the Union when other people began to come into control.

(6) Secession. That the South entertained doctrines of secession which were contrary to the Constitution and destructive to the Union.

268. BASIS OF SECESSION

Were there no Union men in the South? There were thousands. A few were permanent Union men, such as Sam Houston of Texas, and James L. Petigru of South Carolina, who marched out of St. Michael's Church, in Charleston, when prayers were first offered for the President of the Confederacy; but most of them, like Alexander H. Stephens, yielded when their states seceded. Stephens, born in 1812, educated in North Carolina, entered Congress as a Whig in 1843. Though little and boyish in appearance, he was soon recognized as one of the strongest men in Congress. When the crisis of 1861 came, Stephens headed the opposition to the secession of his state, Georgia. He urged that the southern people had not been entirely blameless, and that the only real ground for secession was the personal liberty laws, which would probably be withdrawn if a proper effort were made.

Nearly all southerners admitted that the majority in each state should decide whether there was sufficient reason for secession; but they upheld the principle that if there was sufficient reason, there was an undeniable right to withdraw from the Union; and they felt that such a secession ought not to be looked upon by the North as a breach of the Constitution or as a hostile act. The southern theory of secession can be traced back to the Virginia and Kentucky Resolutions (§ 152) and the nullification doctrine (§ 201). It was, in effect, that secession was not war, but a constitutional and practical way of getting rid of the controversy between the sections.

Even admitting that secession was right, many serious questions were left undecided:

(1) The constitutionality of secession was not self-evident, though it was accepted not only by southern public men, but by some in the North. Once admit that the states were sovereign and the Constitution only a compact, and any state

was undoubtedly entitled to leave the Union whenever it wished. But had the states ever been sovereign?

(2) The expediency of secession, even if it were constitutional, depended on what the secessionists wanted. Some preferred to go out of the Union, so as to put a pressure on the North to readmit them on such terms as they might dictate; but Davis and other leaders from the first intended to form a permanent southern government, and they confidently expected all the slave states to join them.

(3) Secession under any circumstances was really a solution of the problem only if it did not lead to war. Most southern leaders thought the North would not fight; others foresaw a long war, notwithstanding the arguments for the constitutional right of secession, but were sure that the South would be successful in the end.

(4) The most potent reason for the whole doctrine of secession was clearly that it offered a means of relieving slavery from the dangers that were growing up under the Union. When the Georgia convention declared for secession, Stephens announced that he would go with his state, and later made a famous speech in which he said of the Confederate constitution: "Its foundations are laid, its corner stone rests upon the great truth, that the negro is not equal to the white man; that slavery . . . is his natural and normal condition." This left unanswered the question whether slavery would be protected by a war between South and North.

269. Attempted Compromise (1860–1861)

As soon as the danger of secession was realized, four desperate attempts were made to stop it by framing a compromise, something like those which had averted trouble in 1820, 1833, and 1850 (§§ 185, 218, 236):

(1) Special committees of the House and Senate were appointed (December, 1860), to try to prepare bills or constitutional amendments that would hold the Union together.

In the Senate committee, the Republicans offered a proposition (which we now know was drafted by Abraham Lincoln) to the effect that neither the federal government nor the free-state governments should interfere with slavery in the states; but they added the very unwelcome clause that fugitive slaves should have a jury trial. Jefferson Davis, as the southern spokesman in the committee, demanded that the free states should be put under obligation to protect slave owners who might wish to carry slaves across free territory or to hold them there for short periods.

(2) The House committee submitted the "Corwin Amendment" against interference by Congress with slavery in the states, and both houses approved it but it never was ratified — it was too weak and too late. Plainly, neither side really desired compromise.

(3) As yet the secession movement had not spread to the five "border states" — Delaware, Maryland, Virginia, Kentucky, and Missouri — nor to the next tier of southern states — North Carolina, Tennessee, and Arkansas. Senator Crittenden of Kentucky brought forward a set of constitutional amendments intended to keep these doubtful states in the Union. The plan included a division of future territory between freedom and slavery; and against it Lincoln, as President-elect, used all his personal influence over the Republicans in Congress. He felt that any compromise which recognized, extended, and perpetuated territorial slavery was an admission that the Republican party had no reason for existence.

(4) A fourth attempt at compromise was a "Peace Congress," called by the border states at Washington in February, 1861. This body sat for a month and made a report, which was substantially the Crittenden compromise; but it could make no headway.

Neither side would give way in Congress or outside on the main issue, which was whether the federal government would thereafter throw its influence for or against slavery. The

Republicans would not agree to let slavery alone; and the South would not agree to accept any limitation of slavery by the federal government.

If the North would neither consent to secession nor make a compromise, what was left but to keep the seceding states in the Union by force? To this remedy there were many objections. Thousands of people in the North, especially some of the abolitionists, thought the country would be better off without the slaveholding states; the army and navy were small and scattered; and President Buchanan argued that there was no way of "coercing a state." Yet some action had to be taken, because the sites of the few southern forts still in possession of the United States had been formally ceded by the states to the Union, and to give them up would be an acknowledgment of the right of secession.

Fort Sumter, which lay in the sea channel of Charleston, became the storm center. When the merchant ship *Star of the West*, carrying the stars and stripes, appeared with provisions and reënforcements for the fort (January 9, 1861), she was fired upon by a South Carolina battery, and compelled to turn back. Major Anderson wisely referred the whole matter to the government in Washington; and the South waited for the new Lincoln administration to declare its position.

270. LINCOLN'S PURPOSES (1860–1861)

For three months after his election, Lincoln remained quietly at his home in Springfield, arranging his Cabinet, receiving delegations, listening to office seekers, and keeping his eye on Congress. He early selected Seward to be his Secretary of State, and gave Chase of Ohio and Cameron of Pennsylvania to understand that they could come into his Cabinet. He also sent word to General Scott (December 21, 1860), asking him to be prepared "to either hold or retake the forts, as the case may require, at and after the inauguration."

In February, 1861, Lincoln started eastward, and made a

series of speeches in which he foreshadowed his future policy. "On what rightful principle," said he, "may a state, being not more than one fiftieth part of the nation in soil and population, break up the nation?" March 4, 1861, Lincoln appeared at the Capitol, took the oath of office, and in his inaugural address sounded the keynote of his administration. "I hold that in contemplation of universal law and of the Constitution, the Union of these states is perpetual . . . and to the extent of my ability I shall take care . . . that the laws of the Union be faithfully executed in all the states. . . . Physically speaking, we cannot separate. We cannot remove our respective sections from each other, nor build an impassable wall between them."

Lincoln's first official act was to select his Cabinet, and he showed his political wisdom by choosing about equally among former Whigs and former Democrats. To

LINCOLN DELIVERING HIS INAUGURAL ADDRESS, 1861.

Chase of Ohio, the ablest of the political abolitionists, he assigned the treasury. Simon Cameron of Pennsylvania, rather against Lincoln's judgment, was made Secretary of War. Edward Bates of Missouri, Attorney-General, was a southern Republican; Gideon Welles of Connecticut, Secretary of the Navy, was a former New England Democrat. Caleb B. Smith of Indiana was Secretary of the Interior, and Montgomery Blair of Maryland was Postmaster-General.

271. CAPTURE OF FORT SUMTER (1861)

The question of Fort Sumter could not be long postponed, because commissioners of the Confederate government ap-

INTERIOR OF FORT SUMTER AFTER BOMBARDMENT, APRIL, 1861.

peared and demanded its surrender. The President, therefore, asked for written opinions from the members of his Cabinet, on provisioning Fort Sumter. Montgomery Blair was the only member of the Cabinet who advised using force. Seward unwisely assumed that he was to be the real head of the administration, and took it upon himself to say through third parties to the southern commissioners that he was sure that the fort would be given up. A few days later (April 1) Seward sent to the President a remarkable letter, in which he proposed to take charge of the government, and make war on Spain, France, and England, so as to bring back the seceders to defend the United States. Lincoln replied that the President must do whatever was done, and Seward at last accepted the fact that the President was his chieftain.

Lincoln was convinced that even if he gave up the forts, it could only postpone war; for the old questions of fugitive slaves, of boundaries, and of the territories would instantly come up again, and the new separate Confederacy was certain to demand more than was expected by the southern states before secession.

Batteries were by this time constructed around Charleston Harbor, commanding Fort Sumter. When Lincoln at last sent a notice that he purposed to forward a supply of provisions to Sumter, he threw on Jefferson Davis and the Confederate states the responsibility of firing the first gun. Even the extreme southerner Robert Toombs objected and said to Davis: "Mr. President, at this time it is suicide, murder, and will lose us every friend at the North. . . . It is unnecessary; it puts us in the wrong; it is fatal."

He was overruled, and instructions were given to General Beauregard, in command of the Charleston district, to reduce Fort Sumter. At 4 : 30 A.M. of April 12, 1861, the first shell was fired. With his sixty men and a few laborers, Anderson defended himself against forts manned by seven thousand men. After thirty hours of bombardment, Fort Sumter was knocked about his ears, while the relief expedition lay helpless outside the bar. Further resistance being useless, Anderson surrendered the fort, April 14, marching out with colors flying and drums beating, and saluting his flag with fifty guns.

272. MAKING READY FOR WAR

April 15, 1861, President Lincoln issued a proclamation calling on the state governors to send 75,000 state militia, and this action invited the border states to take sides with either South or North. Virginia at once seceded; Arkansas, Tennessee, and North Carolina followed. Not so the other border states, although their governors all refused to send militia. Thus the governor of Missouri replied, "The requisition is illegal, unconstitutional, and revolutionary in its object, inhuman and diabolical, and cannot be complied with." Delaware remained quiet. Maryland for a time seemed likely to secede; and the Sixth Massachusetts Regiment, while passing through the city of Baltimore (April 19), was attacked by a mob and several men were killed — the first blood of northern troops shed in the Civil War. In Kentucky, the legislature had already voted that "Kentucky should maintain a strict neutrality." Later there was a nominal secession legislature, but the regular government of the state remained loyal throughout the war. In Missouri a camp of secessionists was formed in St. Louis, but the Germans in the city remained loyal, were drilled and organized, and under Captain Lyon broke up the camp (May 10).

Who shall describe the excitement, wrath, and grief in the North while Fort Sumter was under bombardment? On Sunday, the day of surrender, hundreds of northern ministers called on their congregations to support the government. Next day the members of the militia companies hurried to their armories; the states opened their arsenals for arms and military supplies; banks offered millions of dollars in loans to the state governments; the legislatures appropriated unheard-of sums for military supplies; the women joined with the men in fitting out the soldier and bidding him Godspeed. As the need grew more urgent, the flower of American youth volunteered, and some colleges were almost broken up by loss of students. Even the President's old enemy, Stephen A. Douglas, came to him, and offered any service that he could give for the preservation of the Union.

The first full regiment to report was the Sixth Massachusetts, raised among the farmers and townspeople around Lexington and Concord, and its reception in New York is typical of the popular feeling all over the Union. "We saw the heads of armed men, the gleam of their weapons, the regimental colors, all moving on, pageant-like; but naught could we hear save that hoarse, heavy surge — one general acclaim, one wild shout of joy and hope, one endless cheer, rolling up and down, from side to side, above, below, to right, to left."

Meantime in the South there was a like enthusiasm — regiments in gray marched to the front amid the shouts and prayers of the people. Both sides were sure they were right. Which side would win?

273. REVIEW

In 1860 the Democratic party divided into two factions: one nominated Douglas and the other Breckinridge, an extreme proslavery man. The Republican convention nominated Abraham Lincoln. Part of the old Whigs formed a Constitutional Union party and nominated Bell. Lincoln was elected by carrying nearly all the northern states. A few weeks later, South Carolina passed an ordinance of secession and was followed by six other states. Buchanan was helpless, but under great pressure left the federal garrison in Fort Sumter, inside the harbor of Charleston. The seven seceded states formed "The Confederate States of America."

The two sections were thoroughly aroused, each accusing the other of attempting to use the federal government for its sectional advantage. The main grievance was that the election of Lincoln showed that the North intended to prevent any more slave territory or slave states. Many southern leaders were opposed to secession, but when their state conventions declared for withdrawing from the Union, nearly all of them "went with their states."

Several efforts were made in Congress to frame a constitutional amendment that would stop secession; but the two sides could not agree, and Lincoln opposed a compromise. When he became President he declared against secession and announced that he meant to execute the laws.

Some of his Cabinet were in favor of giving up Fort Sumter, but he finally decided to send supplies and men to hold it. The Confederate authorities therefore ordered an attack on Fort Sumter, which was taken after a few hours' bombardment. Amidst great excitement the President called for volunteers to protect the government, and four more southern states seceded. The four other border states remained in the Union, and later furnished men and aid for the war.

References Bearing on the Text and Topics

Geography and Maps. See maps, pp. 403. 436–437. — Chadwick, *Causes of the Civil War*, 132, 244. — Dodd, *Expansion and Conflict*, 264, 291. — *Epoch Maps*, nos. xii, xiii. — Fish, *Am. Nationality*, 356.

Secondary. Brown, *Lower South*, 83–152. — Chadwick, *Causes of the Civil War*, chs. vii–xix. — Curry, *Govt. of the Confed. States*, chs. i–iv, ix. — Dodd, *Expansion and Conflict*, 260–281; *Jefferson Davis*, chs. xi–xiv. — Fite, *Presidential Campaign of 1860*. — Hapgood, *Abraham Lincoln*, 151–208. — Hart, *S. P. Chase*, 178–211. — Johnson, *S. A. Douglas*, chs. xviii, xix. — Lee, *General Lee*, 52–98. — Lothrop, *W. H. Seward*, 203–262. — Morse, *Abraham Lincoln*, I. chs. vi–viii. — Nicolay, *Outbreak of the Rebellion*, 1–81. — Nicolay and Hay, *Abraham Lincoln*, II. chs. xii–xxix, III, IV. chs. i–xiii. — Paxson, *Civil War*, chs. ii, iii. — Phillips, *Robert Toombs*, chs. viii, ix. — Rhodes, *U.S.*, II. 416–502, III. 115–415. — Schouler, *U.S.*, V. 454–512, VI. 1–50. — Shaler, *Kentucky*, ch. xv. — Trent, *R. E. Lee*, 31–48.

Sources. *Am. Hist. Leaflets*, nos. 12, 18. — Ames, *State Docs. on Fed. Rels.*, 310–320. — Beard, *Readings*, §§ 143–148. — Caldwell, *Survey*, 108–117. — Century Co., *Battles and Leaders*, I. 7–98. — Hart, *Contemporaries*, IV. §§ 40–74, 76, 77, 96, 97; *Patriots and Statesmen*, V, 261–305. — Johnson, *Readings*, §§ 143–148. — Johnston, *Am. Orations*, III. 230–329, IV. 16–81. — Lincoln, *Works*, passim. — MacDonald, *Select Docs.*, nos. 93–96; *Select Statutes*, no. 1. — See New Engl. Hist. Teachers' Assoc., *Hist. Sources*, § 87; *Syllabus*, 353.

Illustrative. Barton, *Pine Knot* (Ky. and Tenn.). — Churchill, *The Crisis* (Lincoln). — Conway, *Pine and Palm.* — Fox, *Little Shepherd of Kingdom Come.* — Morris, *Aladdin O'Brien.* — Whittier, *Antislavery Poems.*

Pictures. Century Co., *Battles and Leaders*, I. — *Frank Leslie's Weekly.* — *Harper's Weekly.* — Wilson, *Am. People*, IV.

Topics Answerable from the References Above

(1) Public services of *one* of the following: Breckinridge; Bell; Floyd; Black; Stanton; Stephens. [§§ 265, 266] — (2) Republican convention of 1860. [§ 265] — (3) Incidents of the secession of *one* of the first seven seceding states. [§ 266] — (4) First Confederate Congress. [§ 266] — (5) Admission of *one* of the following states: Minnesota; Oregon; Kansas. [§ 267] — (6) Opinions of *one* of the following statesmen on compromise: Lincoln; Davis; Seward; Greeley. [§ 269] — (7) *Star of the West* incident. [§ 270] — (8) Public services of *one* of the following statesmen: Crittenden; Cameron; Bates; Welles; Smith; Blair. [§ 270] — (9) Capture of Fort Sumter. [§ 271] — (10) Account of the secession of *one* of the last four seceding states. [§ 272] — (11) War sentiment in the South in 1861. [§ 272] — (12) Secession sentiment in *one* of the four loyal border states. [§ 272]

Topics for Further Search

(13) Why did the Democratic convention split? [§ 265] — (14) Why did not President Buchanan stop secession? [§ 266] — (15) Northern arguments in favor of, or against, secession. [§ 267] — (16) Southern arguments in favor of secession. [§ 267] — (17) Union men in the South. [§ 268] — (18) Did Fort Sumter belong to the United States in April, 1861? [§ 271] — (19) Effect of the fall of Fort Sumter on northern sentiment. [§ 272]

CHAPTER XXV

NORTH AND SOUTH IN 1861

274. POPULATION OF THE TWO SECTIONS (1861)

THE result of the Civil War depended on the relative strength of the contestants, measured in men, resources, business organization, and moral force. In population, the North, which included the West and Northwest, far surpassed its rival.

A LOG HOUSE IN THE BACKWOODS.

In 1790 the North and the South had each 2,000,000 people; in 1830 the numbers were 7,000,000 and 6,000,000 respectively; but in 1860 the free states and territories counted 19,000,000, and the slaveholding states and territories 12,000,000. There were 3,500,000 foreign-born persons in the North, as against 300,000 in the seceding states; for immigrants disliked going into the South where there were few cities and few manufactures, and where manual labor was despised.

When the crisis came, four of the slaveholding states stayed with the nineteen free states; these were Maryland, Delaware, Kentucky, and Missouri, with a total population of 3,100,000.

Probably 500,000 of the inhabitants of these states adhered to the South; but West Virginia (not yet a state) and eastern Tennessee stood by the Union and nearly made good that loss. The total population of the region controlled by secession was therefore about 8,900,000 as against 22,100,000 for the area supporting the Union. Out of the 8,900,000, 3,500,000 were slaves and 140,000 free negroes, leaving a white population of about 5,300,000, of whom about 1,300,000 were white men between eighteen and sixty years old, presumably capable of military service. The twenty-three states that adhered to the Union contained about 5,500,000 men from eighteen to sixty years old, of whom about 500,000 were foreign-born.

275. FARMING AND DEMOCRACY

For the support of an army, the North had many advantages. Much more land was under cultivation than in the South; and farm machinery, fertilizers, and improved methods made farming more productive. Hence, as far west as southern Wisconsin, much of the country was as thickly settled and prosperous as the rural parts of New England. It was a period of rising prices — in part because of the influx of gold from California. If the condition of the wage earners at any time was not satisfactory in the East, it was possible for them to take up land in the West and make a living there. The Bureau of Agriculture, established at Washington in 1862, showed how much the government appreciated the farmer.

In the South, plantations of hundreds or thousands of acres were numerous, but the South did not raise all its own food, and was buying corn and other food products in large quantities from the Northwest. The staple crop was cotton, of which the South exported a value of $191,000,000 in 1860. Most of the profits of southern farming appear to have gone to the slaveholding planters.

The rise of city and factory populations in the eastern states developed a democracy very like that of the West. The manufacturers and heads of corporations, many of whom had risen from the ranks of labor, were now leaders in American industry. The South supposed that this was a timid class, which would never permit a war for fear of losing its profits, and that workmen and clerks were "mudsills," who could be trodden on, but would not and could not fight. Yet from such men came a great part of the victorious northern armies. In the West there was a genuine and wide-awake democracy, which knew no such

thing as family prestige and was not controlled by the commercial class.

In the South, slaves were almost the only form of great wealth, and the 300,000 slaveholding families were as much a governing class as in colonial times. Out of those families came also nearly all the doctors, lawyers, and ministers in the South. The most numerous type of the southern white was that of the "crackers," or "poor

A MOUNTAIN WHITE, SPINNING. (From a Kentucky photograph.)

whites," illiterate and unprogressive, but born fighting men. Most of them believed that the interest of slavery was their interest also, and therefore supported the planter at the polls and in the trenches. Nevertheless, the mountain whites along the west slope of the Appalachians had no slaves, hated the slaveholders, and constantly opposed them in the state governments.

276. STATE AND CITY GOVERNMENT

During the period from 1840 to 1860 the state constitutions, both North and South, grew more and more democratic.

People showed a striking change of feeling by the loss of confidence in the legislatures, which they tried to tie down by amendments to the state constitutions. Much new legislation was required to meet the new problems of business and social life. In the South the states legislated less for social welfare than in the North; partly from long habit, partly because there was no class of free mechanics to demand such legislation.

Party management grew more and more elaborate, especially in the populous North; and in a few states certain political managers, whom we should call bosses, got control — such men as Thurlow Weed of New York and Simon Cameron of Pennsylvania. Still the candidates for state offices were usually nominated in conventions where the result was not arranged beforehand, and there was plenty of discussion in state legislatures. In purity of politics the South was better off than any other part of the country, for the use of money at elections was there uncommon. The one question which could not be discussed there, and on which nobody was allowed to disagree with his neighbor, was slavery.

The census of 1860 showed 158 cities of 8000 or more people, which together contained about a sixth of the total population. Of these, 137 were in the states that adhered to the Union, and 21 within the later southern Confederacy. New Orleans, with a population of 168,000, lived largely on down-river trade from the Northwest; the largest southern city that was supported wholly by southern commerce was Charleston, with 41,000 people.

In the North, many of the old towns expanded into crude, irregular, and ugly cities, and nobody seemed to foresee how fast they would increase. The cities were poorly policed, and riots were frequent. Washington, the capital city, was an unpaved bog in time of rain, in which ran half-wild hogs. Most of the firemen were volunteers, who pumped with their little hand engines while the fire burned; but some of the large cities were using steam fire engines. In the large cities politics were

very unsavory; New York and San Francisco were notorious
for their corrupt and disorderly governments, and for fraud and
violence at elections.

Nevertheless, great public improvements were on foot.
Most of the large cities now had public water supplies: Phila-
delphia began a system of city waterworks in 1801, New York
built its Croton aqueduct in 1835–1842, and Boston turned on
Cochituate water in 1845. Parks were established. In 1857
New York laid out Central Park, the first great municipal pleas-

BROADWAY, NEW YORK, ABOUT 1850.

ure ground in the country. Horse cars began to be widely
used about 1845. In 1857 the city of New York organized the
first "metropolitan police" of uniformed and disciplined men.
The western cities were now growing fast: Cincinnati, St.
Louis, and Chicago were still rude and dirty, but had populations of 161,000, 161,000, and 109,000 respectively. Next to
them in importance were Louisville (68,000), Pittsburgh (49,000),
Detroit, Milwaukee, and Cleveland (each about 45,000).

277. PUBLIC AND PRIVATE EDUCATION

For public education, the cities developed a system of free graded schools, in which pupils of about the same age and experience could be gathered into one room; and (about 1850) they began to appoint trained superintendents to direct their schools. The country district schools were still taught by farmers' sons and daughters, who often had no other training than that of the district school itself. Still, even the remote prairie farmer had a schoolhouse near at hand to start his boys and girls in education. Some of the northern cities had public high schools, for boys and girls; in a few places there were separate girls' high schools (§ 207). "Female seminaries" and other large boarding schools for girls were numerous but not very effective.

The colleges were still small; none of them counted over 530 undergraduate students in 1860. College athletics made a beginning at this time, with the boat races between Harvard and Yale. The sport spread to other eastern colleges. The animal spirits of most students still found vent in all sorts of tricks and horseplay. True universities were now appearing: some of the older colleges added departments such as a theological school here, a law school there, a school of mines in another place; and the new western state universities from the beginning included schools for the training of doctors, lawyers, and scientific men. In 1862 Congress made a large gift of land to found an agricultural college in each state, and that gave a chance for a new kind of training. The University of Iowa took the bold step of admitting women to the various parts of the university (1856), an example later followed by all the western state universities.

Southern education was on a different footing. In 1860 about four times as many children were at school in the North as in the South; but the slaves and free negroes had no form of education, and the country poor whites had little or none.

In the towns the public schools had small funds and few trained teachers. Secondary schools were few: the most successful were military academies, the best known of which were the famous "Citadel" in Charleston and the Virginia Military Institute at Lexington, Virginia. Little colleges abounded in which the instruction was much like that of the larger colleges, and the University of Virginia was a strong institution.

Some of the well-to-do families sent their sons to southern state or denominational colleges, or abroad, or to northern colleges, and the ruling class was highly educated and intellectual.

278. LITERATURE AND THE CHURCHES

The year 1860 falls about in the middle of the golden age of American literature, in which flourished Whittier, the author

NATHANIEL HAWTHORNE.

of pathetic poems about slavery and suffering; Longfellow, the sunny-minded and graceful; Oliver Wendell Holmes, the wit of his time; and Ralph Waldo Emerson, whose *Essays*, full of deep thought put in masterful English, had been published almost twenty years earlier. Nathaniel Hawthorne, perhaps the greatest of all American writers, died in 1864.

The *North American Review* was the oldest review of literature and politics; *De Bow's Review* was an excellent southern periodical in questions of business, trade, and politics. Among magazines in a lighter vein were *Harper's Monthly*, started in 1850, and soon after made an illustrated magazine; and the *Atlantic Monthly*, founded in November, 1857, under the editorship of James Russell Lowell. Lowell was renowned as a poet, essayist, and critic; but he will always be best remembered for his *Biglow Papers*, the keenest of satires on slavery.

A new school of American historians was at the height of its activity in 1860; to George Bancroft and William H. Prescott were added John Lothrop Motley with his *Rise of the Dutch Republic* (1856). Francis Parkman, greatest of all American historians, about 1850 began his life work of describing "the romance of the woods"; that is, the relations of the Indians, the French, and the English in the New World.

EDGAR ALLAN POE IN 1849.

The fierce contest of the Civil War developed many political humorists. Among the more genial was Artemus Ward, who invented an ingenious misspelling which did not hide the humor of his thought. It was he who was willing "to send all his wife's male relatives to the war."

In this active intellectual life the South had at that time little part. Aside from some able political writers, it raised no body of defenders of slavery equal to opponents like Mrs. Stowe, Whittier, and Lowell; and no essayists, poets, satirists, or historians who affected northern public opinion. Edgar Allan Poe, born a southerner, was one of America's greatest writers; he died in 1849. William Gilmore Simms wrote novels in the style of Walter Scott on southern themes, but they were not much read outside of the South. There was no large southern school of writers who appealed to the whole people of the section.

With the passing of the years, the great national churches grew larger, stronger, and wealthier. The Catholic Church was steadily enlarged by the immigration of Irish and German Catholics. Though the Presbyterians, Baptists, and Methodists were split by the slavery question (§ 205) the factions flourished. The Congregational, Unitarian, Episcopalian, and Catholic churches were never formally divided by slavery. Theology was in general milder than in 1830, and there was less preaching on future punishment, and more on present duty. Benevolent organizations were now very active: Bible societies, tract societies, foreign missionary societies, education societies, helped to raise the moral standards of the people.

The South, more than the North, made its churches intellectual and social centers. It had many good church buildings, large congregations, and eloquent ministers, perhaps the most renowned of whom was Bishop William Meade of Virginia. In both city and country the negroes had separate churches, usually with a minister of their own race; and there is a tradition that one such church bought and owned its minister.

279. INDUSTRIES

People were learning what immense resources the country possessed in other products than those of the farm. Lumber was still very cheap, and a great business was developed in supplying the white pine of Michigan and Wisconsin to the treeless prairie states. Oil always floated on the surface of Oil Creek, a tributary of the Allegheny River, and in 1859 it was discovered that, by putting down drill holes along this creek, a porous rock containing this valuable substance could be tapped; and new methods of refining this petroleum turned the product into a fluid that gave a beautiful light.

Mining grew to be a great industry, and many states provided geological surveys of their territory so as to get at the minerals. Many discoveries of valuable minerals were made after 1850. Rich copper deposits were found south of Lake Superior, and more gold in California. In 1858 gold was found near Pikes Peak, and the city of Denver quickly sprang up. In 1859 silver was discovered in great abundance at Virginia City, Nevada; and in 1861, gold in Montana.

The South was equally rich in stores of timber, in coal, iron, oil, and the natural wealth of the soil; but the profits of industry went into buying slaves and raising cotton, and there was no labor adapted to manufacturing. Hence, in the whole seceding South the only coal mines worked on a large scale were those on the upper James in Virginia.

Like progress was made in commercial organization (§ 248). Corporations of every kind rapidly increased, though all were small as measured by the standards of to-day. In 1848 the first clearing house was organized in New York to simplify the banking business. Labor also began to organize into trades unions, which demanded a shorter day; in 1840 the United States made ten hours the legal day for its employees. Manufactures developed rapidly because of cheap fuel, brought down from the Pennsylvania mines to the Hudson and the Delaware, so that it could be distributed all along the seaboard, for use in factories and houses. In the West the bituminous coal furnished a great trade down the Ohio from Pittsburgh to Cincinnati, Louisville, St. Louis, and many other places. Soon after 1860 Lake Superior iron ore began to come down the Lakes; and before long places convenient to both coal and iron, especially Cleveland and Pittsburgh, became great iron-manufacturing centers.

In this development also the South had but a small share. The only very large iron works in the South was the Tredegar at Richmond; there was only one other large southern rail mill; and the southern water powers were not developed. Some cotton and woolen mills were built, and a large amount of southern capital was invested in banks, which gave credit to the small planter and the farmer. Of the imports from abroad one tenth came to the South in 1860, and nine tenths to the North.

280. Progress of Invention

The progress of invention in the previous thirty years has already been described (§ 244). This progress was increasingly rapid in the forties and fifties. The manufacture of cloth was changed, all the way from the farm to the wearer's back, by improvements in carding, spinning, weaving, and dyeing. In 1846 Elias Howe made his first practicable sewing machine, clumsy enough, but provided with a needle with the eye near the point, a device which has revolutionized sewing. In 1844 Goodyear discovered a means of "vulcanizing" rubber, so as to make it up into shoes, garments, and hard articles. These and like inventions came into use slowly.

HOWE'S FIRST SEWING MACHINE.

The French inventor Daguerre in 1839 announced a method of taking self-recorded sun pictures called daguerreotypes. They required an exposure of about twenty minutes, and the result was a single picture on a silvered plate. An American, Dr. Draper, at once discovered that the process could be applied to portraits; a few years later an Englishman named Archer found that a negative could be fixed on a glass plate, from which any number of prints could be made. Thus photography sprang into being.

The greatest new discovery in methods of communication

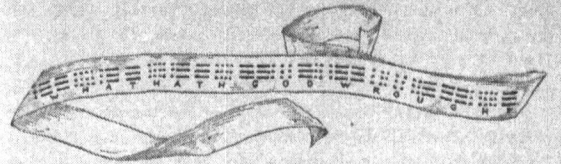

THE FIRST TELEGRAPHIC MESSAGE.

of intelligence was the electric telegraph, first discovered in 1835, and worked out and applied by Samuel F. B. Morse and Alfred Vail in 1844. It carried the news of the nomination of James K. Polk (§ 228) from Baltimore to Washington. Telegraph lines rapidly spread through the country, and in 1851 the first electric fire alarm telegraph was set up. Machinery began to be applied to many new purposes. The first steam fire engine was constructed about 1853. In 1847 Richard Hoe invented a rotary printing press, run at great speed and delivering a continuous stream of newspapers.

The South had little use for these inventions, for factories and workshops were few, and most manufactures were imported. Not a fortieth part of the southern cotton was manufactured in the South. Mowers and reapers were of no use

FIRST PORTRAIT MADE BY PHOTOGRAPHY.
Daguerreotype by Dr. Draper, 1839.)

where there was so little hay or grain. The only widely distributed labor-saving machine was the cotton gin (§ 125).

281. TRANSPORTATION

Railroads as yet profited little from the inventions of the period. Nearly all the American railroads were single-tracked as many are to-day; the trains were slow, the stations small and dirty, the locomotives weak. From New York to Chicago the fastest schedule time in 1860 was thirty-eight hours — about twice the time now required for the fastest trains. The cars were small and comfortless, but sleeping cars had been introduced for the long routes. Railroad accidents were frequent and destructive. Freight rates were so high that long distance traffic was small; and as there were several different gauges in use, it was hard to make through shipments.

The South fell behind the North in transportation; the railroads were lighter in construction, ran less regularly, and charged higher fares. The tributaries of the Mississippi were provided with light-draft steamers, but the South built very few vessels, and the seagoing coasters were mostly northern property.

The railroad and steamboat quickened the carrying of the mails; and several reforms were made in the postal service. Official adhesive stamps were introduced (1847); the postage was reduced to five cents (1845), and then to three cents (1851). Unfortunately neither the post office nor the railroad undertook the plain duty of carrying parcels. In 1839 a young man named Harnden conceived the idea of carrying packages back and forth between Boston and New York, and he thus began the express business in the United States. The Adams Express Company was formed in 1854. In the fifties Wells, Fargo, and Company organized an express system on the Pacific coast; and Butterfield and Company introduced a "pony express" for letters and valuables, which covered the nineteen hundred miles from St. Joseph on the Missouri to Sacramento in ten days.

282. REVIEW

At the outbreak of the Civil War, the population that adhered to the Union was about 22,000,000 and that which supported the Confederacy about 9,000,000. The North had a greater diversity of industry and trades. The northern workmen and business men turned out to be excellent soldiers. In the South the chief wealth came from the cultivation of cotton, and went to a small number of slaveholding families; but they, and also the so-called "poor whites," proved to be good fighters.

The North abounded in cities, some of which were badly governed, but they were supplied with uniformed police and with water, gas, and other conveniences. The South was largely a rural country. All the northern states had free public schools, including many high schools, and they provided for the education of girls. There were also numerous colleges. The South cultivated an intellectual life, but had fewer schools and colleges. Most of the literature of the period was written by northerners, especially Longfellow, Holmes, Emerson, and Lowell; but there were some southern writers, of whom Poe was the greatest.

In industry the North led, because most of the factories and mines were in northern states, the South not yet having developed its natural resources. Invention went on steadily in the North, but the South built few factories, and its staple crops could not be aided by farm machinery. Both sections built railroads; but the North showed the larger mileage. Most of the commercial and business organization of the country was centered in the North, except in the cotton cities of New Orleans, Savannah, and Charleston.

References Bearing on the Text and Topics

Geography and Maps. See maps, pp. 436-437. — Bogart, *Econ. Hist.*, 297, 349. — Chadwick, *Causes of the Civil War*, 8, 20, 160. — Coman, *Indust. Hist.*, 211, 281. — Dodd, *Expansion and Conflict*, 188, 190, 191, 193, 196, 197. — Fish, *Am. Nationality*, 266.

Secondary. Chadwick, *Causes of the Civil War*, ch. ii. — Coman,

Indust. Hist., 232–279. — Dodd, *Expansion*, chs. x, xi. — Hosmer, *Appeal to Arms*, ch. i. — McMaster, *U.S.*, VII. 99–134, VIII. 68–132. — Raymond, *Peter Cooper*, 52–95. — Rhodes, *U.S.*, III. 1–114. — Smith, *Parties and Slavery*, chs. v, xix, xx. — See also references to chs. xix, xxii.

Sources. Bogart and Thompson, *Readings*, 282–285, 291–293, 295–308, 404, 542–558. — James, *Readings*, §§ 74, 77, 83. — Olmsted, *Seaboard Slave States*. — Smedes, *Southern Planter*.

Illustrative. Baker, *The New Timothy*. — Beecher, *Norwood* (N.E.). — Cable, *Dr. Sevier* (New Orleans). — Cary, *Clover-nook* (Middle West). — Clemens, *Life on the Mississippi; Huckleberry Finn*. — E. Eggleston, *Mystery of Metropolisville* (Minn.). — G. C. Eggleston, *Irene of the Mountains*. — Gilmore, *Among the Pines*. — Howells, *A Boy's Town*. — Moore, *Rachel Stanwood* (South). — Morris, *Hist. Tales*, 225–269 (telegraph). — Page, *In Ole Virginia*. — Pryor, *Colonel's Story*. — Roberts, *Down the O-hi-o*. — Sargent, *Peculiar* (slavery, Mo.). — Smith, *Fortunes of Oliver Horn* (Md. and N.Y.). — White, *Blazed Trail; Riverman* (northern frontier). — See also references to ch. xix.

Pictures. *Leslie's Weekly*. — *Harper's Weekly*. — *Mentor*, serial no. 29.

Topics Answerable from the References Above

(1) Life in *one* northern city during the Civil War. [§ 276] — (2) Life in *one* southern city during the Civil War. [§ 276] — (3) Public high schools in New England, *or* in the West, in 1861. [§ 277] — (4) A day in a district school about 1861. [§ 277] — (5) Literary career of *one* of the following writers: Holmes; Emerson; Hawthorne; Motley; Parkman; Simms; Artemus Ward. [§ 278] — (6) Coal trade down the Ohio River. [§ 279] — (7) Career of *one* of the following inventors: McCormick; Elias Howe; Goodyear; Draper; Morse; Vail; Hoe. [§ 280] — (8) Railroad travel in the North, *or* in the South, about 1861. [§ 281] — (9) Steam travel on the Great Lakes, *or* on the Mississippi, about 1861. [§ 281] — (10) Beginnings of the express business. [§ 281]

Topics for Further Search

(11) Why did so few immigrants go into the South? [§ 274] — (12) Conditions of the mountain whites about 1861. [§ 275] — (13) Agricultural college land grants. [§ 277] — (14) Account of the character and influence of *one* of the leading newspapers, *or* weeklies, *or* monthly magazines, *or* reviews of the Civil War period. [§ 278] — (15) Influence on the community of *one* of the following clergymen: Beecher; Hughes; Finney; Meade; Storrs. [§ 278] — (16) Account of mining of copper, *or* gold, *or* silver, *or* coal, *or* iron ore. [§ 279]

CHAPTER XXVI

THE MILITARY SIDE OF THE CIVIL WAR (1861–1865)

283. WHAT KIND OF WAR WAS IT?

THE Civil War practically began April 12, 1861, when the Confederates fired on Fort Sumter. The official Confederate point of view was that the North was trying to conquer the South. The northern point of view was that the southerners were in rebellion against their lawful government and could not excuse themselves by any theory of "sovereign states," or a "Confederacy"; that the states were still in the Union, and hence every individual was liable to execution for treason, if he made armed resistance against the authority of the federal government.

In practice it was impossible to treat Confederates in uniform, acting under orders of their superiors, as anything but soldiers; if captured, they were prisoners of war. By a proclamation of April 19, 1861, for the blockade of the southern ports, President Lincoln virtually admitted that there was a government on the other side, carrying on civilized war.

What was the place of slavery in the contest? The national House of Representatives and the Senate separately voted (July 22, 25, 1861): "That this war is not waged upon our part in any spirit of oppression, or for any purpose of conquest or subjection, or purpose of overthrowing or interfering with the rights or established institutions of those States, but to defend and maintain the supremacy of the Constitution and to preserve the Union with all the dignity, equality, and rights of the

435

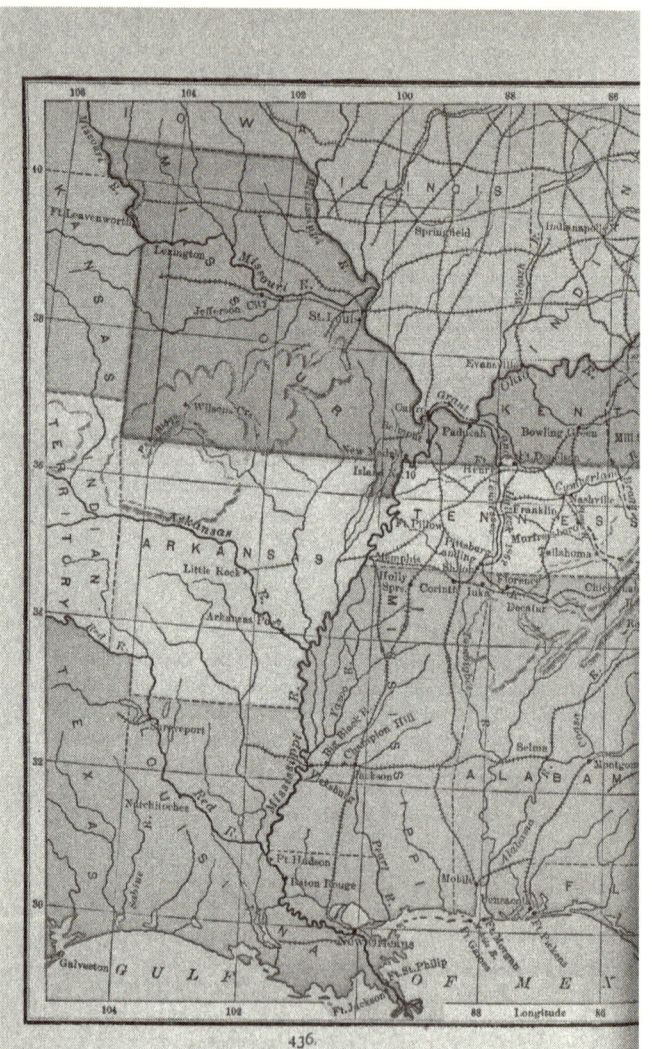

436.

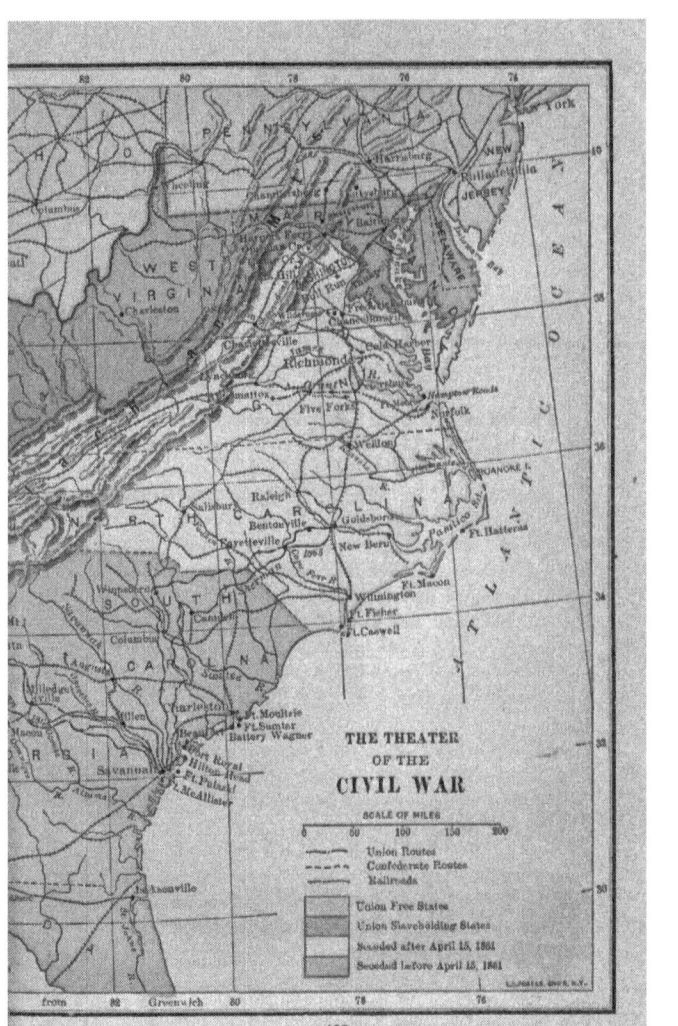

THE THEATER
OF THE
CIVIL WAR

SCALE OF MILES

0   50   100   150   200

Union Routes
Confederate Routes
Railroads

Union Free States
Union Slaveholding States
Seceded after April 15, 1861
Seceded before April 15, 1861

437

several States unimpaired." The war was called "the War between the States" by the South, and "the Rebellion" by the North. In fact, it was neither; it was a genuine Civil War carried on between two parts of the same nation, two sections of the same people.

284. The Field of War

The only way to break up the Confederacy and to bring the states back into the Union, was to invade the South, a region naturally very strong. Now an invading army is like a serpent which can strike only with its head, and as it moves forward leaves the length of its body exposed. Such an army must follow some kind of highway over which supplies and reënforcements may be sent up to the front; hence the rough and impassable Appalachian Mountains covered the middle of the Confederate lines and seemed a sure protection. Most of the fighting was in the extreme east and in the west. At the beginning of the war, the Confederate military frontier ran south of Fort Monroe on the James, then followed a little to the south of the Potomac River, and through the mountains of West Virginia and Kentucky; it ran to the two Confederate forts of Donelson and Henry, on the Cumberland and Tennessee rivers; it touched the Ohio at Paducah, crossed the Mississippi at Belmont, and then passed about midway through Missouri.

That strong line of defense was weakened by four routes into the interior of the Confederacy, and along them were fought most of the campaigns of the Civil War: (1) the lower Mississippi River, which was deep enough to admit ships from the sea; (2) the middle Mississippi, a great national waterway, abounding in steamers; (3) the line of railroad from Louisville to Nashville, and thence across the mountains to Chattanooga and Atlanta; (4) a strip of territory lying east of the mountains in Virginia, which was traversed by several railroads leading south from Washington.

285. THE TWO ARMIES

To fight its battles, the South had a population accustomed to outdoor life, to the use of firearms, and to the management of horses; and it had also commanders trained in the national military school of West Point and in the wars of the Union. Since the negroes did the hard work at home, nearly all the able-bodied white men could be enlisted. According to Colonel T. S. Livermore, the authority on this question, over 1,230,000 different men were enlisted in the Confederate army and they rendered 3,240,000 years of military service.

Though the North was not considered to be a military people, the first call for militia brought out 92,000 "citizen soldiers"; and during 1861, 660,000 men were enlisted for three years. At first volunteers continued to pour in, but in 1863 this impulse lost strength and a draft was ordered, which, however, produced only 36,000 men. In the course of the whole war about 2,500,000 adult men were in the military service of the Union, of whom about 400,000 reënlisted at least once. The total year's services were about 4,670,000, which made the actual fighting force one half greater than the Confederate force. To raise, organize, and supply such enormous forces required a great man as Secretary of War. In January, 1862, Lincoln practically removed Simon Cameron from that department, and appointed instead Edwin M. Stanton, chosen for his loyalty to the Union, his rugged honesty, and his great ability, although he had the worst of tempers and would occasionally defy the President.

286. THE TWO NAVIES

The regular navy was at first disorganized, because more than a third of the officers resigned to join the Confederacy, and all the navy yards in the southern states were seized by the Confederacy, with the vessels that happened to be in port. Of the Union navy, only seven steamers and five wooden cruisers

were available when the war began. The President's proclamation of a "blockade" (§ 283) was a notice to foreign ships
that squadrons would be placed outside all the southern ports,
to capture vessels going in or running out. Thus, began the
celebrated "anaconda policy" of pressing on the Confederacy
from all sides at once. To form the necessary blockading squadrons, merchant vessels, both sail and steam, were hastily bought
and equipped, naval volunteers were enrolled, and in a few
months squadrons were actually blockading the coast and
making frequent captures.

To evade the fleet, small and very swift steam "blockade
runners" were built abroad, to run from the near-by Bahama
and Bermuda islands to Confederate ports, carrying in military stores and miscellaneous cargoes, and carrying out cotton, compressed into small bulk. Many of these vessels were
captured, but their profits were so great that two successful
trips would pay for a vessel. As the war advanced, the blockade grew more and more effective; in all about 1500 captures
were made by the Union fleet, and the trade of the South with
the rest of the world was nearly throttled.

The Confederate authorities made every possible effort to
build a navy. They did construct several fleets for harbor defense, but their only seagoing ships were the "commerce de-
stroyers." The South at once began to issue commissions to
private ships to capture Union merchantmen, and also sent out
cruisers, or public armed ships. At first the United States tried
to make out that the crews of such vessels were pirates, and
several of these men were convicted and sentenced to death;
but President Davis threatened to execute an equal number of
Union soldiers held as prisoners, and the United States finally
decided to treat them as prisoners of war.

Several vessels were also fitted out as Confederate ships of
war in British ports; of these the principal one was the *Alabama*, which was built at Liverpool for the Confederacy. Although Minister Adams steadily protested, she slipped away to

sea (July, 1862), her crew and guns coming out to her on another ship. The *Alabama* and other Confederate ships, following the precedents of the Revolution and War of 1812 (§§ 93, 171), found a rich prey in the Union merchant ships, of which the total number captured was 260, valued at $20,000,000. Gradually the United States navy hunted out and blockaded, took, or sank all these vessels except the *Shenandoah*, which was still at work when the war ended. Claims were at once filed against Great Britain for these losses.

287. CAMPAIGNS OF 1861

As in previous wars, the military events were important, not for themselves, but because they decided the issue of the war — whether the northern or the southern way of thinking should prevail. And campaigns and battles are less important than the character and action of the leading soldiers. Nevertheless, it is necessary to know something about the main military events, because they prepared the way for acts of Congress and proclamations and the great social and economic changes brought about by the Civil War.

The first significant battle was fought at Bull Run. A few weeks after the fall of Fort Sumter, Washington was strongly fortified because it was in danger of surprise by a Confederate force under General Beauregard which was lying at Manassas Junction, only thirty miles away. The country loudly called for somebody to break up that army. Against the judgment of the military men, a force of 30,000 Union troops, under General McDowell, attacked the line at Bull Run (July 21, 1861), not knowing that Joseph E. Johnston was bringing more men from the Shenandoah valley, the first time in history that soldiers were carried into battle by railroad.

In the midst of the battle, a Confederate officer cried to his men, "There are Jackson and his Virginians standing like a stone wall!" and as "Stonewall" Jackson that general has gone down in history. Nevertheless the Confederate army was weakening when fresh troops arrived and broke the Union lines. Says an eyewitness, "For three miles hosts of Federal troops, all detached from their regiments, all mingled in one disorderly rout, were fleeing along the road."

The North profited by Bull Run more than the South, for it was forced to realize the task before it. President Lincoln held his courage, and within three days was making preparation for new campaigns in both East and West. General George B. McClellan was at once put in command of the army in front of Washington, and in November became

"STONEWALL" JACKSON, IN 1863.

commander of all the armies of the United States. He devoted himself to organizing an "Army of the Potomac." Day after day, week after week, the only news from that part of the front was the stereotyped telegram, "All quiet on the Potomac."

288. WESTERN CAMPAIGNS OF 1862

In the West, the two contestants lined up across central Kentucky and Missouri. Early in 1862, General Ulysses S. Grant, who had shown his ability in a little expedition down the Mississippi to Belmont, moved forward in conjunction with Flag Officer Foote. Together they accomplished the first great Union victory by capturing Forts Henry and Donelson, with 14,500 men (February, 1862). The Confederates thereupon abandoned Kentucky, and Nashville, the capital of Tennessee, fell to the Union forces without a blow. A provisional state government was set up for Tennessee, with Andrew Johnson as governor.

Farther west the Confederates retreated down the Mississippi to a strong position called Island No. 10, which, however, was captured in April. The Confederate army west of the Mississippi had just been broken up at the battle of Pea Ridge. The result of three months' campaigning was, therefore, the gain by the Federals of a strip of territory a hundred miles wide and more than five hundred miles long.

General Halleck was put in general command and sent Grant's army up the Tennessee River, and he ordered Buell to unite his forces with Grant's. Before Buell could get up, General Albert Sidney Johnston with 40,000 Confederates suddenly attacked Grant's army of 43,000 (April 6) at Shiloh, near Pittsburg Landing. The Union troops, surprised and as yet little experienced in fighting in line, were driven back almost to the river. General W. T. Sherman, one of the division commanders, fought gallantly. The Confederates were startled by the death of Johnston, killed on the field. Next morning Buell's army of 20,000 arrived to reënforce Grant, the tables were turned, and the Confederates were driven from the field.

Halleck, taking personal command, moved southward and captured Corinth, Mississippi (May 30), which commanded the railroads east from Memphis, and thus gave to the Union forces control of the Mississippi River as far south as the strongly fortified town of Vicksburg. The career of victory was interrupted by a Confederate invasion of Kentucky under General Bragg, who started for Louisville. The Union army under Buell met Bragg at Perryville (October 8) and after a hot fight the Confederates withdrew. General Rosecrans, then appointed to the Union command, attacked Bragg in the bloody battle of Stone River or Murfreesboro (December 31, 1862, January 2, 1863), and compelled him to retire.

289. NAVAL WARFARE OF 1862

Meanwhile, in the spring of 1862, Flag Officer David G. Farragut was sent out with a fleet to force an entrance into the lower Mississippi. Farragut was born in 1801, of Scotch descent, entered the navy when ten years old, and served as a midshipman in the War of 1812. Though he lived in Virginia, he stood by the old flag in the Civil War. After entering the mouth of the Mississippi, he signaled for close action, "conquer or be conquered." He boldly led his fleet up the river (April 24), which was defended by strong forts. A fire-ship came down against his flagship *Hartford,* but half the sailors kept up the fight, while the other half put out the fire.

JOHN ERICSSON. (Inventor of the *Monitor.*)

At the end of the fight a boom across the river was destroyed, the vessels were beyond the forts, and there was nothing to stop them. They shortly anchored in front of the city of New Orleans, and the forts soon surrendered. A large force of Union troops soon after took possession of New Orleans, under command of General B. F. Butler, who for a year ruled the city like a conquered province.

By March, 1862, the Army of the Potomac had grown to 185,000 men, eager to move "on to Richmond." After many delays, McClellan marched up the peninsula between the James and York rivers. The Confederates at Norfolk were rebuilding the former United States frigate *Merrimac* into a powerful ironclad called the *Virginia;* and to meet this danger the new iron ship *Monitor* was sent down from New York. This craft was the invention of John Ericsson, a little "cheese-box on a raft," with a revolving iron turret carrying two heavy guns, mounted on a deck almost flush with the water. She was built in one hundred days, and none too soon.

The *Merrimac* unexpectedly came out (March 8, 1862),

steamed slowly but steadily to the Union fleet in Hampton Roads, and destroyed the wooden sloop of war *Cumberland* and the frigate *Congress*. Next morning the *Merrimac* appeared again, but found, in front of the rest of her prey, the little *Monitor*, which had arrived during the night. For five hours the two ships pounded each other; neither could destroy her adversary, but the *Merrimac* finally retired. One of the greatest dangers of the whole war was safely passed, for not another vessel in the world could have coped with the Confederate ship. She never made another attack, and later was scuttled and burned by her own crew, to prevent her capture by Union forces.

290. CAMPAIGNS IN VIRGINIA IN 1862

When McClellan was at last ready to attack (April, 1862), to his deep disappointment the President detached McDowell with 40,000 troops to cover Washington. McClellan's army wasted about a month in the scientific siege of Yorktown, which was defended in part with "Quaker guns," made of painted logs of wood. By May 31, he reached a point only seven miles from Richmond. The official returns later showed that McClellan had about 115,000 present for duty against about 90,000 in the Confederate army, which was commanded by Joseph E. Johnston. McClellan was checked at the battle of Seven Pines or Fair Oaks, when Johnston was wounded, and next day Robert E. Lee took command of the Confederate army. Meanwhile Stonewall Jackson, in a brilliant campaign in the Shenandoah valley, threatened Washington and kept McDowell's corps from reaching McClellan. Jackson thereupon suddenly joined Lee; so that McClellan found himself attacked. Then followed the terrible "seven days' fighting," in which McClellan was forced to give way and retreat (June 26 to July 1) to the James River, ending at Malvern Hill.

In thirty-one days McClellan had lost over 21,000 men and the enemy about 27,000; but they had saved their capital and the Confederacy for the time. In the sting of defeat McClellan telegraphed to Secretary Stanton: "I have lost this battle because my force was too small. . . . If I save this army now, I tell you plainly that I owe no thanks to you or to any other persons in Washington. You have done your best to sacrifice this army." McClellan was a brave man and a natural leader, always heartily trusted and loyally obeyed by his subordinates, and he knew how to handle troops; but he was misled by his secret-service agents, who reported that the Confederate army was much larger than his own; he was never willing to attack unless he was sure that he would win; and he was exceedingly unjust to Stanton and Lincoln.

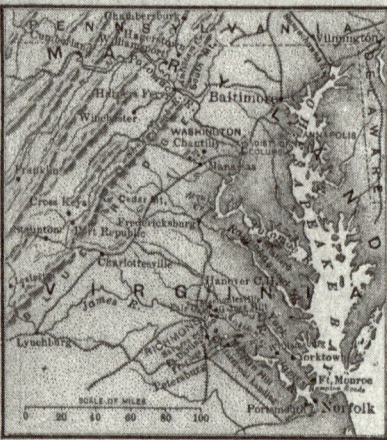

THE WAR IN VIRGINIA.

Lincoln (July 1862) called for 300,000 more men; and 420,000 soon responded. McClellan had lost the confidence of the administration, and General Halleck became the confidential adviser to the President. During the next six months, the Army of the Potomac fought three more unsuccessful battles with Lee's army:

(1) General Pope received command of most of the eastern army. He was little known to his subordinates, few of whom liked or trusted him. Pope was attacked by Stonewall Jack-

son's "foot cavalry" and fought three days near the old battlefield of Bull Run (August 28–30). He was so badly defeated
that the army was withdrawn to the neighborhood of Washington.

(2) Lee saw the first chance to carry the war into the North,
and crossed the Potomac. McClellan was again put in active
command and attacked Lee on the Antietam near Sharpsburg,
Maryland (September 17). This was the best opportunity
of the war for destroying Lee's army; but after a day of
terrible fighting, and another day's delay, Lee's army was .
allowed to withdraw across the Potomac unmolested.

(3) McClellan was soon removed, and General Burnside was
appointed to succeed him. Burnside marched to the Rappa-
hannock River, beyond which Lee with 80,000 men intrenched
himself. The Union army of 113,000 men attacked Lee's
intrenchments in front near Fredericksburg (December 13, 1862)
and was defeated in one of the bloodiest battles of the war,
with a heavy loss and without the slightest military advantage.

291. VICKSBURG AND GETTYSBURG (1863)

The year 1863 began with 918,000 men under arms on the
Union side and 466,000 on the southern. The campaign opened
in the West, where General Grant tried various schemes of
opening a communication through shallow bayous around
Vicksburg. Finally he marched seventy miles down the back
country on the west side of the river, crossed the Mississippi
south of Vicksburg, and then pushed northeast, defeated his
enemy right and left, and closed in on Vicksburg from the east.
Thus by boxing the compass south, east, north, and west, Grant
cut Vicksburg off from all help.

After vain attempts to take the place by assault, Grant
regularly invested the city and bombarded it. As the seven
weeks of siege progressed, the inhabitants came down to pea meal
mixed with cornmeal, of which they made a sort of bread. The
streets were full of débris, wounded men, and houseless people.

The inhabitants moved to caves in the bluffs, dug out bomb-proofs, and lived there day and night. July 4, 1863, Vicksburg surrendered unconditionally with 29,000 men, the largest number of prisoners taken by either side during the entire war. A week later a freight steamer from St. Louis arrived in New Orleans, and President Lincoln said, "The Father of Waters again goes unvexed to the sea."

The Army of the Potomac fought as bravely as the western armies, but with smaller success. General Joseph Hooker

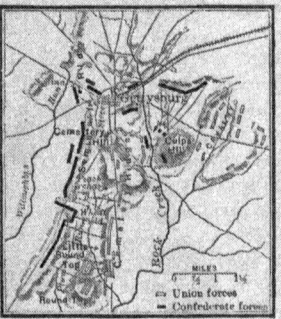

BATTLE OF GETTYSBURG.

was put in command (January 25) and assembled his army at Chancellorsville, where it was confronted by Lee's much smaller force and suddenly thrown back in confusion (May 2). Jackson was accidentally shot by his own men—a terrible blow to the South — but Hooker was badly beaten.

Lee now had his greatest opportunity during the whole war. He crossed the Potomac, and reached southeastern Pennsylvania. At this critical moment the command of the Union army was transferred from Hooker to General Meade. The two armies came together near Gettysburg and for three days (July 1-3) fought the greatest battle of the Civil War. The Union army took its stand on a crescent-shaped hill, ending with the strong position of Round Top.

At one o'clock on the third day, the Confederates opened fire against the ridge; at the end of two hours, a division of 15,000 men, under command of Pickett, burst into the open and came surging up the slope into the Union lines on Cemetery Ridge. This was the so-called "High Tide of the Confederacy," the most critical moment of the war. A few of the

assailants got over the breastworks; and could they have held
their ground, the Union army must have broken in disorder, and
Philadelphia, Baltimore, or Washington might have been the
prize of Lee's army. But the Union lines held steady, the
remnants of Pickett's division fell back, and Lee was defeated.

Of the 88,000 Union troops engaged, more than one man in
four went down, killed or wounded. The Confederate army
of 75,000 men lost 23,000, or almost a third of its number.
On the night of the next day Lee slowly retreated, and the
Union army let him cross the Potomac; it was the last chance
to invade the North in large force.

292. CHICKAMAUGA AND CHATTANOOGA (1863)

Two more terrible battles were fought in the West before the
year 1863 ended. To Rosecrans, with the Army of the Cumberland, was assigned the task of advancing to Chattanooga
while Burnside moved up from Kentucky to Knoxville, to give
support to the large population of Union men in East Tennessee.
Bragg attacked Rosecrans on the Chickamauga (September 19,
1863) with a heavy force. The next day the attack was renewed, and the Union line was broken, but the army of
Thomas stood its ground. Two days later the whole army
returned to Chattanooga.

No soldier on either side was more passionately admired than
General George H. Thomas. After graduation at West Point
in 1840, he served in the Mexican War. He was sent to Kentucky, beat Zollicoffer in 1861, and served as an excellent subordinate to Buell and Rosecrans. Thomas was a quiet, reserved
man, shy and proud; but he had a wonderful gift of inspiring
his men with confidence and devotion, and he was commonly
called "Pap Thomas" by his troops.

Thomas's great national reputation was gained at Chickamauga. General Garfield.said, "I shall never forget my amaze-
ment and admiration when I beheld that grand officer holding
his own with utter defeat on each side, and such wild disorder

in his rear." From that unflinching courage Thomas got the name which he carried the rest of his life, "the Rock of Chickamauga."

Rosecrans was now penned up in Chattanooga by the Confederates under Bragg, who occupied the neighboring heights of Missionary Ridge and Lookout Mountain. River communication by the Tennessee was closed by the enemy, and soon the

FIELD GUN GOING INTO ACTION. (From a war-time lithograph by Forbes.)

army was almost starving. Grant was now placed in command of the combined forces of Sherman and Thomas, who superseded Rosecrans, and at once began to extricate the army.

In three successive days (November 23–25) the Confederate army was driven out of its strong positions above Chattanooga. First, Thomas took the works at the foot of Missionary Ridge. Next day Sherman attacked the north end of Missionary Ridge, and took position on the enemy's flank; and in the dramatic "Battle above the Clouds," Hooker drove Bragg's troops off Lookout Mountain. On the third day Thomas's army attacked the Confederates at the foot of Missionary Ridge. Without orders the troops went on up the hill, and in an hour cleared that mountain of enemies. There is no more stirring incident in the annals of war than the lines of bluecoats, in sight of thousands of their fellows, dashing up the slope, capturing batteries, guns, and men, and raising the stars and stripes on the summit. Bragg retreated in great confusion.

293. GRANT'S CAMPAIGN OF 1864

For the eastern campaign of 1864, Lincoln selected Grant, who had made the most brilliant record in the West. He was made lieutenant-general with the authority of general in chief of all the armies in the country. Grant selected the Army of the Potomac, which remained under direct command of Meade, as his own fighting force; and he took the field (May 4) with 102,000 effective men against Lee's army of 61,000. The next day he was attacked by Lee in the wooded region of northern Virginia known as the Wilderness, and withdrew only after three days of blind, confused, and bloody fighting.

Up to this time the Army of the Potomac had always retreated after such a check; and as the army marched southward, the whole length of the column rang with cheers, for the men realized that they were to fight it through this time.

Grant now moved southward parallel with Lee's army, both sides intrenching every night. In seventeen days after beginning his campaign, he lost over 30,000 men. At Cold Harbor, fifteen miles from Richmond, he found the enemy strongly intrenched in what was really a great fort. He attacked (June 3) and within an hour had lost 7000. His purpose was to wear Lee out, and he could have afforded to give two men for one, to break up that opposing army then and there.

Once more Grant edged southward, and attempted to seize Petersburg, the key of eastern Virginia. A vain effort to entice him from his grip was made by the Confederate general Early, who, in a sudden dash northward, reached the edge of the city of Washington, which he could have taken, had he known how few its defenders were. He then raided and burned Chambersburg. After the failure of an attempt by a mine to break through the Confederate defenses of Petersburg at a spot thereafter called the Crater (July 30), the Union troops settled down to a slow siege of Petersburg which lasted nearly a year.

294. GENERAL GRANT AND GENERAL LEE

From this time the eyes of the whole North were on Grant. Ulysses S. Grant was a man of the plain people, a descendant

of an early colonist of Massachusetts, probably of Scotch ancestry. The son of a tanner, he was born in Ohio (April 27, 1822), was brought up first to farm work, then graduated in 1843 at West Point. Two years later he was sent to Taylor's army and distinguished himself in the Mexican campaign. He resigned from the army in 1854, and then tried various kinds of business in St.

ULYSSES S. GRANT.

Louis and Galena, Illinois, and fell into obscurity. When the war broke out, Grant returned to the army. From 1861 to 1863 his name was connected with most of the successful operations in the West, till Lincoln said of him: "I can't spare this man; he fights."

Grant was a very taciturn man, slow to express an opinion; he disliked writing, and sometimes got into trouble because he would not report. Yet he coined some apt phrases, as in his demand for the surrender of Fort Donelson: "No terms except an unconditional and immediate surrender can be ac-

cepted. I propose to move immediately upon your works";
and in 1864, "I propose to fight it out on this line if it takes all
summer."

Grant's greatest characteristic was his indomitable grit.
After the terrible discouragements of the campaign of 1864,
he wrote, "I want Sheridan put in command of all the troops
in the field [of the Shenandoah], with instructions to put himself south of the enemy and follow him to the death. Wherever
the enemy goes let our troops go also." This intense determination kept in action the forces that brought the war to an
end. Grant did not stake all on one battle; he was not daunted
or discouraged by defeat; he simply kept at it till his enemy
was vanquished.

Grant's most dangerous opponent was Robert E. Lee, who was
born in 1807, of an old and aristocratic Virginia family; he
graduated from West Point
(1829), and spent thirty-two
years in the regular army;
he distinguished himself in
the Mexican War.   Just
before the Civil War broke
out he wrote to a friend,
"If the Union is dissolved
and the government dis-
rupted, I shall return to
my native state and share
the miseries of my people,
and, save in defense, will
draw my sword on none."
A few days after the fall of
Fort Sumter he was offered
the command of the United

ROBERT E. LEE.

States army, and declined it.   He resigned, and, after Virginia
seceded, accepted a Confederate commission.

For a year Lee saw little active service; then he took command of the Confederate army in the East and for nearly three years was the unquestioned leader of that army. His brilliant division and corps commanders, Stonewall Jackson, Gordon, Longstreet, A. P. Hill, D. H. Hill, Ewell, Early, and J. E. B. Stuart, remained with him with few exceptions till the end of the struggle. The things that made Lee a great soldier were his skillful preparations, his watchfulness, and his ability to accomplish much with small resources. In this respect he greatly resembled Washington, with whom he has often been compared. He had great power over men, and his soldiers had perfect confidence in "Uncle Robert."

295. GEORGIA AND ALABAMA CAMPAIGNS (1864)

On the same day that Grant moved south in 1864, Sherman began an advance from Chattanooga to Atlanta, 135 miles through

SHERMAN MONUMENT, NEW YORK.

the mountains; his opponent was Joseph E. Johnston, till he was superseded in July by the more dashing Hood. During four months Sherman worked his way southward, skillfully flanking Johnston's smaller army from point to point. He was at last able to telegraph (September 3), "Atlanta is ours, and fairly won."

General Johnston was of Scotch descent, born in 1807; he was a classmate of Lee at West Point, and then served against the Indians and the Mexicans. In 1860 he was made quartermaster general of the United States army, but followed his state of Virginia when it seceded. He was one of the first generals appointed by the Confederacy, commanded in the Shenandoah valley, at Bull Run, in the Peninsular Campaign, and against Grant outside of Vicksburg. Johnston's most remarkable service was in 1864, when with about 70,000 men he tried to hold Sherman's army of 113,000. His policy was to avoid general engagements, but to wear the invaders out by a long campaign, and by attacking their ever lengthening line of communications.

The Union navy shared in the hard work of 1864, especially by Farragut's attack in August, on the powerful defenses of Mobile Bay. Farragut fastened himself to the rigging of his flagship, the *Hartford*. As his fleet went in, his monitor *Tecumseh* was torpedoed, and instantly sank, but the admiral signaled "Go ahead!" The Union vessels succeeded in passing the forts at the entrance of the bay. They then dashed at the big iron-clad ram *Tennessee*, firing their heavy guns, and they pounded her till she surrendered. The forts were taken, one after the other, so that the port of Mobile was closed to the blockade runners.

Farragut's determination never ceased throughout the war; he was one of the most careful commanders that ever lived; he made all his preparations beforehand, weighed the risks, and then nothing could stop him short of the sinking of his vessel; and his courage affected everybody in the fleet. So perfect were his discipline and his coolness, that in his great fights he always came out safe with a small loss of men.

Fort Fisher was taken by the navy and the army (January, 1865) and the port of Wilmington, North Carolina, was closed. Thereafter there was no large port open to the blockade runners except Charleston.

296. MARCHING THROUGH GEORGIA (1864)

Sherman's strong imagination suggested to him that the next step was to cut the Confederacy in two by marching eastward from Atlanta to Savannah through the heart of the country. He started in November with 62,000 men. There was no army in front of him and no militia that could oppose him. His troops lived on the country, and as Sherman passed through he left it devastated, so far as he could. The main army was followed by "Sherman's Bummers," several thousand stragglers who paid very little attention to the orders against looting private houses; and thousands of negro "contrabands" joined in the procession on foot or in wagons. The railroads were destroyed for miles; even the rails were heated and twisted up. Sherman reached and took Savannah (December 21), and Lincoln wrote to him, "The honor is all yours."

General William T. Sherman (born in 1820), as a man and a soldier, was a striking figure. He was a member of a distinguished family, and all his life long was acquainted with public affairs. Sherman graduated at West Point (1840), and was sent out to California in 1846. In 1855 he resigned, and when the war broke out, was superintendent of a military school in Louisiana. Sherman served at Bull Run, then in the West, and won his first renown at Shiloh. Then he commanded large forces in the Vicksburg and Chattanooga campaigns. In 1864, Sherman was put in command of most of the western armies, and acted in perfect accord and harmony with his chieftain, Grant. As a military man Sherman's chief characteristic was his skill in forecasting what the enemy was likely to do. He was a great strategist, and in his many fights and campaigns always tried to get a good position before he attacked. His men admired him and called him "Old Billy"; but he was too brusque and fiery for the warm personal love which they poured out on McClellan and Thomas.

297. VALLEY AND TENNESSEE CAMPAIGNS (1864)

Both east and west, subsidiary campaigns went on parallel with the marches and sieges of Grant and Sherman. General Philip H. Sheridan came to the front in 1864. Born in New York of Irish parents, he was a graduate of West Point, and

SHERMAN'S MARCH TO THE SEA. (From a drawing by Darley.)

457

served on the western frontier. He was put in command of a brigade, and soon after of a division in Buell's army (1862). He fought at Perryville, Stone River, Chickamauga, and Chattanooga, and in 1864 was made chief of the cavalry corps of the Army of the Potomac. Later he was sent into the valley of the Shenandoah, against Early, where he devastated the country so that it should no longer feed the Confederate army. The enemy drove Sheridan's army out of its camp at Cedar Creek (October 19) while General Sheridan was about twenty miles to the north. He hurried to the sound of the guns and found a number of demoralized men on the road, but a large part of the troops were still in line. As he galloped along the line he shouted, "We are all right. . . . Never mind, boys, we'll whip them yet, we'll whip them yet. We shall sleep in our quarters to-night." He pushed the enemy back, and actually reoccupied his old camp at Cedar Creek that night.

When Sherman started in his "march to the sea" (§ 296) Thomas was left in command of the forces strung all the way along from Nashville to Atlanta. Hood struck northward and intrenched himself south of Nashville, where Thomas made ready for a great battle. He would not move till his army was fully prepared. In vain did orders follow day after day from Grant, bidding him attack. When he at last was ready (December 15) he drove Hood from his lines, and the Confederate army was routed and dispersed in two days' fighting. This battle practically ended the war in the West, and vindicated Thomas's prudence and generalship.

From Savannah, Sherman marched northward to Columbia, and the town was burned as his forces entered it (February 17, 1865). Neither Sherman nor any other officer gave orders to burn it, but he was not made unhappy by the catastrophe. Charleston could no longer be defended and was occupied by other Union forces (February 18, 1865). The battle of Bentonville (March 19) was the last serious fight.

298. END OF THE WAR (1865)

The Army of the Potomac, during these brilliant movements, was losing thousands of men before Petersburg, but slowly wore down Lee, who could not replace his losses. He even proposed to President Davis to levy negro regiments; but the time was too short to carry out the plan. Lee forced a series of fights to cover his preparations for a retreat; he then aban-

SURRENDER OF LEE.

doned Petersburg and Richmond and struck westward along the Appomattox River. Next day, April 3, 1865, Richmond was occupied by the Union troops.

Grant followed close after Lee, and Sheridan closed in the net. A week after leaving his intrenchments, Lee was surrounded at Appomattox, and (April 9) he surrendered his command, which had now dwindled to 27,000 men. Lee's parting speech to his troops was simply, "Men, we have fought through the war together; I have done my best for you." A few days later, Johnston surrendered his army to Sherman, at Raleigh;

and the Civil War was practically at an end.   Two weeks later
Jefferson Davis was captured while trying to escape.

Many suggestions had been made during the war, looking
toward terms of peace.   Foreign governments tried in vain to
mediate.   In 1864 some overtures were made to President
Davis, who replied, "You may 'emancipate' every negro in
the Confederacy, but we will be
free, we will govern ourselves."
Just before the collapse Lincoln
met Vice President Stephens of
the Confederacy at Hampton
Roads; but Lincoln was firm
that the only conditions of
peace were for the South to return to the Union and for
slavery to cease; and on those
issues the conference failed.

After Richmond fell, Lincoln
took pains to notify General
Grant that he was not to make
any pledges for the future of
the South.   Nevertheless, Grant
released Lee's men, "not to
be disturbed by the United
States authority so long as they
observed their paroles and the laws in force where they reside."
He also won the respect and gratitude of the southern officers
and soldiers by allowing them to take their horses home for
their farm work.   Sherman, in receiving Johnston's surrender,
undertook to make pledges about the reorganization of the
states; but this action was disavowed by the government at
Washington.

MONUMENT TO GENERAL ROBERT
E. LEE, AT RICHMOND.

299. REVIEW

The Civil War began with the attack on Fort Sumter, April
12, 1861.   The far South was protected by the ranges of the

Appalachian Mountains, but there was much fighting east and west of the mountains, especially in Virginia, along the railroad line from Louisville to Atlanta, and along the Mississippi River.

About twice as many individuals enlisted in the North as in the South; but they served on the average a shorter time, so that the proportion of men in the field was usually about three Union men to two Confederates. The North retained most of the navy and two thirds of the regular military and naval officers, and blockaded the southern coast. The South fitted up a few ships in its own ports and others in England, and made many captures of American merchant ships.

The principal battles of the war were as follows:

1861. (1) Bull Run (July 21), Confederate victory.

1862. (2) Forts Henry and Donelson (Feb.), Union victory by Grant. (3) *Monitor-Merrimac* (March 8), Union victory. (4) Shiloh (April 6), drawn battle. (5) New Orleans (April 24), Union victory by Farragut. (6) Peninsular Campaign (May 31-July 1), Confederate victory, McClellan defeated by Johnston and Lee. (7) Second Bull Run (Aug. 28-30), Confederate victory, Pope defeated by Lee and Stonewall Jackson. (8) Antietam (Sept. 17), drawn battle, McClellan against Lee. (9) Perryville (Oct. 8), Union victory, Bragg defeated by Buell. (10) Fredericksburg (Dec. 13), Confederate victory, Burnside defeated by Lee. (11) Stone River (Dec. 31, Jan. 2), Union victory, Bragg defeated by Rosecrans.

1863. (12) Chancellorsville (May 2), Confederate victory, Hooker defeated by Lee. (13) Gettysburg (July 1-3), Union victory, Lee defeated by Meade. (14) Vicksburg (July 4), Union victory, surrender to Grant. (15) Chickamauga (Sept. 19), Confederate victory, Rosecrans defeated by Bragg. (16) Chattanooga (Nov. 23-25), Union victory, Bragg defeated by Grant.

1864. (17) Wilderness (May 5-7), Confederate victory, Grant defeated by Lee. (18) Mobile Bay (Aug. 5), Union victory, forts passed by Farragut. (19) Atlanta (Sept. 3), Union victory, captured by Sherman.   (20) Cedar Creek (Oct. 19), Union victory, Early defeated by Sheridan.   (21) Nashville (Dec. 15, 16), Union victory, Hood defeated by Thomas. (22) Savannah (Dec. 21), taken by Sherman.

1865.   (23) Appomattox (April 9), Union victory, Lee surrendered to Grant.

The outcome of the war depended in large degree upon the abilities of the commanders; but in the end it was won by wearing the South down to the point where it could no longer raise men and keep up the necessary supplies.

References Bearing on the Text and Topics

Geography and Maps. See maps, pp. 436–437, 446, 448. — Brigham, *Geogr. Influences*, ch. vii. — Century Co., *Battles and Leaders.* — Dodd, *Expansion and Conflict*, 313, 327. — Fish, *Am. Nationality*, 388. — Hosmer, *Appeal to Arms; Outcome of the Civil War.* — Semple, *Geogr. Conditions*, ch. xiv. — Shepherd, *Hist. Atlas*, 208. — Special war maps in Atlas of *Official Records of the Rebellion.* — See also maps in Dodge, Rhodes, Ropes and Livermore, Wood and Edmonds, cited below.

Secondary. Bassett, *U. S.*, 518–520, 526–571. — Dodge, *Bird's Eye View.* — Fiske, *Mississippi Valley in the Civil War.* — Hosmer, *Appeal to Arms*, chs. iii–xiii, xv–xix; *Outcome of the Civil War*, chs. ii, iii, v–vii, x–xii, xiv, xvii. — Hovey, *Stonewall Jackson.* — Lee, *General Lee*, 99–399, 420–424. — Maclay, *U.S. Navy*, II. 159–559. — Mahan, *Admiral Farragut*, chs. vii–x, xii. — Morse, *Lincoln*, I. 298–367, II. 31–94, 134–169, 276–285, 328–341. — Nicolay and Hay, *Abraham Lincoln*, IV–X passim. — Paxson, *Civil War*, 54–72, 91–102, 113–172, 208–213, 222–244. — Rhodes, *U.S.*, III–V passim. — Ropes and Livermore, *Civil War.* — Schouler, *U.S.*, VI passim. — Scribner, *Campaigns of the Civil War; Navy in the Civil War.* — Wilson, *General Grant*, 74–343. — Wood and Edmonds, *Am. Civil War.*

Sources. *Am. Annual Cyclop.*, 1861 to 1865. — Century Co., *Battles and Leaders.* — Eggleston, *Rebel's Recollections.* — Goss, *Recollections of a Private.* — Grant, *Personal Memoirs*, I. 229–584, II. — Hart, *Contemporaries*, IV. §§ 84–95, 103–123, 132–140; *Source Book*, §§ 116–125. — Hosmer, *Color Guard; Thinking Bayonet.* — Lincoln, *Works*, passim. — Longstreet, *Manassas to Appomattox.* — MacDonald, *Select Statutes*, nos. 1, 2, 5, 8, 26, 31, 40. — Wormeley, *Other Side of War.* — See New Engl. Hist. Teachers' Assoc., *Hist. Sources*, § 88; *Syllabus*, 354–356.

Illustrative. Benson, *Who Goes There?; Friend with the Countersign.* — Brady, *The Patriots* (Lee). — Cable, *The Cavalier.* — Eggleston, *Am. War Ballads,* I. 167–226, II. — Johnston, *Long Roll; Cease Firing.* — King, *Rock of Chickamauga.* — Matthews, *Poems of Am. Patriotism,* 127–277. — Moore, *Lyrics of Loyalty; Rebel Rhymes.* — Page, *Among the Camps; Two Little Confederates; Burial of the Guns.* — Trowbridge, *Drummer Boy.* — Webster, *Traitor and Loyalist* (blockade).

Pictures. Century Co., *Battles and Leaders.* — *Frank Leslie's Weekly.* — Forbes, *Artist's Story of the Great War.* — *Harper's Pictorial History of the Rebellion.* — Johnson, *Campfire and Battlefield.* — Miller, *Photog. Hist. of the Civil War.*

Topics Answerable from the References Above

(1) Noted ships of the Union navy. [§ 286] — (2) Life on blockade runners, *or* blockading ships. [§ 286] — (3) Adventures of *one* of the following Confederate cruisers: *Nashville; Florida; Alabama; Shenandoah.* [§ 286] — (4) Fight between the *Merrimac* and *Monitor.* [§ 289] — (5) Grant's Vicksburg campaign. [§ 291] — (6) Accounts of *one* of the following battles: Chancellorsville; Gettysburg; Chickamauga; Lookout Mountain; Chattanooga; The Wilderness; Cold Harbor; Petersburg; Mobile Bay; Fort Fisher; Savannah; Nashville. [§§ 291–297] — (7) Sherman's March to the Sea. [§ 296] — (8) Surrender of Lee at Appomattox. [§ 298]

Topics for Further Search

(9) Map of the military line dividing North and South at various dates during the Civil War. [§ 284] — (10) Incidents and results of *one* of the following battles: Balls Bluff; Bull Run; Belmont; Henry and Donelson; Island No. 10; Shiloh; Corinth; Perryville; Stone River; New Orleans; Seven Pines; Malvern Hill; Second Bull Run; Antietam; Fredericksburg. [§§ 287–290] — (11) Military services of *one* of the following commanders: U. S. Grant; Halleck; Buell; McDowell; A. S. Johnston; Sherman; Bragg; Rosecrans; Farragut; R. E. Lee; J. E. Johnston; Stonewall Jackson; Pope; Burnside. [§§ 288–290] — (12) Building the federal navy. [§ 289] — (13) Military services of *one* of the following generals: Thomas; Garfield; Hooker; Sheridan; Porter; Hancock; Franklin; Longstreet; A. P. Hill; D. H. Hill; Ewell; Early; Stuart; Hood. [§§ 292–294] — (14) Lincoln's conference at Hampton Roads. [§ 298]

CHAPTER XXVII

CIVIL SIDE OF THE WAR (1861–1865)

300. Union Government

During the long and fearful war, both sides kept up their governments, made every effort to influence foreign powers, raised money, and carried on their business and domestic life. The United States Congress and the other parts of the federal government sat regularly in Washington, which was uncomfortably near the scene of hostilities. Though the war was fought to vindicate the Constitution, the country was subjected to many arbitrary methods of government, some of them plainly unconstitutional:

(1) In the territory actually occupied by the army, including the city of Washington, martial law — that is, the will of the commander in chief — was declared; civilians could be arrested simply by the order of a military commander, were imprisoned without charge of crime or right of trial, and in some instances were tried by military courts.

(2) Under an order of the President (April 27, 1861) the writ of *habeas corpus* was suspended. Several thousand people first and last were arrested in a haphazard manner, often without knowing the charge against them; and they could get free only through the request of some man of influence.

(3) Provost marshals were appointed in the northern cities, hundreds of miles away from hostilities; and they arrested thousands of people under military law.

(4) In 1864 a military commission condemned to death Dr. Milligan of Indiana for taking part in a traitorous secret society.

(5) In the border states, and even in the North, military officers sometimes shut up churches, dissolved societies, or stopped the publication of newspapers. It is true that the papers abounded in war gossip, war news, and war stories, and the correspondents often revealed military secrets.

These measures, though reluctantly supported by President Lincoln, helped to swell the strong party which was opposed to the war. The "Peace Democrats" at the beginning favored letting the South secede. They accepted the name of "Copperhead," bestowed by their opponents, and wore as badges the heads cut out of copper cents; or butternuts cut in sections, because the butternut was the ordinary dye for the clothing worn by Confederate soldiers. They also formed dangerous secret societies, such as the Knights of the Golden Circle, with thousands of members in Ohio and Indiana.

One of the leaders of the Peace Democrats was Clement L. Vallandigham, member of Congress from Ohio, who boasted that he never voted a dollar or a man for the war. In May, 1863, he was convicted by a military court-martial and sentenced to imprisonment for a cutting speech against martial law; but Lincoln sent him across the lines into the Confederacy — a practical joke which to many people seemed bad policy.

An act of Congress for drawing recruits by lot from among the able-bodied men led to terrible "draft riots" in the city of New York (July, 1863). The opposition turned into a savage mob which hunted down and stoned to death many harmless negroes and white people, and burned colored orphan asylums. The next step was to attack buildings which represented any kind of government, especially police stations and armories. The police fought desperately, but were too few to resist such a rising. Federal troops were hastily summoned, and after three days of riot the mob was put down by musket and bayonet. About a thousand people lost their lives as victims of the mob, or by the shots of the defenders of order, and the money damage was many millions.

301. CONFEDERATE GOVERNMENT

The Confederate government moved from Montgomery to Richmond after Virginia seceded. The "permanent constitution," which went into effect February 18, 1862, was a revision of the old federal Constitution, with the significant change that the word "slave" was freely used. In practice, many parts of this constitution never went into effect; for instance, the Supreme Court was never formed. The President overshadowed the rest of the government, and state rights were often disregarded.

(Copyright, 1867, by Anderson.)

JEFFERSON DAVIS.

President Jefferson Davis, the head and type of the Confederacy, was born in Kentucky (1808) not far from the birthplace of Abraham Lincoln. He was educated at West Point and served seven years as lieutenant in the army. From 1845 to 1851 he was in Congress, and as a soldier in the Mexican War he served with distinction. From 1853 to 1857 he was Pierce's Secretary of War, and then as senator from Mississippi came forward as the leader of the ultra proslavery men in Congress. After the election of Lincoln, Davis used his place and influence, before resigning from the Senate of the United States, to bring about the breakup of the Union. During the war he was almost a civil dictator, acting through his influence on the Confederate Congress; his veto was overridden but once in four years.

In his speeches and public papers, Davis simply assumed as a matter of course, not subject to argument, that negroes were no part of the political community; he also tacitly assumed that the ruling class, of which he was a member, were entitled to govern their fellow white men. In both respects he satisfied the public sentiment of the South, which, on the whole, loyally supported him to the end. He was an example of the resolute, masterful, slaveholder statesman.

302. FOREIGN RELATIONS

The government of the United States continued to hold to the former treaties and diplomatic relations with foreign powers. Charles Francis Adams, son of President John Quincy Adams, was sent as minister to Great Britain, but on the day before he reached London, the British government issued (May 13, 1861) a proclamation of neutrality in the contest between "The United States of America, and certain states styling themselves the 'Confederate States of America.'" Other European governments took similar action. This was a formal and justified recognition that a belligerent power was in existence in the southern states, with a government that directed armies in the field, and with warships on the sea which were entitled to the same treatment in foreign ports as the public ships of the Union. Although President Lincoln's proclamation of blockade (§ 283) practically recognized this "belligerency," the North long cherished wrath against Great Britain for thus treating the Civil War as a war, instead of as a domestic rebellion.

To the Confederacy the action of Great Britain seemed far too weak; and in 1861 commissioners were sent to Europe to ask for full recognition as an independent nation. The commissioners, Mason and Slidell, while on their way through the West Indies in the British merchant steamer *Trent*, were forcibly taken off by Captain Wilkes in the United States ship of war *San Jacinto* (November 8). The country and Congress were

delighted at the capture; but Lincoln pointed out that the
search of neutral ships was just what drove the United States
to war in 1812 (§§ 163, 167). Lord Palmerston, the British
prime minister, prepared a dispatch which might have led to
immediate war; but Queen Victoria insisted that a more peaceful tone should be taken. On the other side, Lincoln and the
Cabinet saw that to stand out meant war with Great Britain
and the consequent success of the Confederacy; and they pru-
dently decided that it was doubtful whether Mason and Slidell
were rightfully taken; therefore the two men were finally given
up. These and other Confederate agents in Europe strove hard
but in vain to persuade foreign powers, especially Great Britain
and France, to recognize the independence of the South. Napoleon III, Emperor of the French, was favorable to the Confederacy, but dared not act alone.

By this time it became necessary to prove to foreign nations
that the North was making war on behalf of freedom, and not
simply for the sake of ruling the South. Napoleon III was
trying to conquer Mexico and had no liking for the North.
The English were hard hit because the blockade cut off the
raw material for their cotton manufactures, and thousands
of mill hands were thrown out of work. The ruling aristocracy of England made no secret of its hope that the South
would succeed. A brilliant young statesman, William E.
Gladstone, publicly said, "Jefferson Davis and other leaders
of the South have made an army; they are making, it
appears, a navy; and they have made, which is more important than either . . . a nation."

After the defeat of McClellan and Pope in 1862 (§ 290),
Lord Palmerston was on the point of offering a "mediation,"
which would have meant something very like recognition;
but there was a strong Union sentiment in England, especially
among the workmen in the cotton mills, who felt that the
rights of free labor were involved; and they were represented in Parliament by the orator John Bright, who was

a great friend of the United States government. The defeat of the ironclad *Merrimac*, the battle of Antietam, and still more the campaigns in the West during 1862 (§ 288), took away the pretexts for immediate recognition; and the success of the Union arms in 1863 and 1864 made it impossible without arousing the enmity of the United States of America.

303. FINANCES

It was as hard for both sides to raise the necessary means as to fight in the field. The federal Congress met in special session, July 4, 1861, to provide for the war. The "Morrill tariff" had already passed in March, after many southern members had withdrawn from Congress; it restored the general scale of rates of the tariff of 1846 (§ 229), but it added some high protective duties. At various times throughout the war the tariff was raised and raised again. Congress also began to lay new taxes of many kinds, such as the old-fashioned excise on liquor (§ 139); duties on incomes (bringing in $347,000,000 in all); duties on manufacturing; stamp duties in many ingenious forms; in fact, taxes on almost everything that could be reached. The proceeds of the taxes rose from $40,000,000 in 1860 to $490,000,000 in 1865; but they did not keep pace with the expenditures, which were $66,000,000 in 1860, and $1,290,000,000 in 1864. To meet the deficits, heavy loans were secured; and the government debt grew from $90,000,000 in 1861 to nearly $3,000,000,000 in 1866, bearing an interest of $133,000,000 a year.

Another great change was a complete revolution in currency and banking. In 1862 Congress authorized the issue of "legal tender notes"; that is, paper money which must be accepted if offered by debtors to creditors. These "greenbacks" gradually grew to over $450,000,000. Congress in 1863 chartered a system of national banks with a currency which was secured by government bonds. In order to increase the demand for the bonds through the new banks, Congress in 1864 laid a tax of ten per cent on the notes of the state banks, which drove those notes out of circulation, and caused many of the banks to accept national bank charters.

In all these financial measures the North had the great advantages of support by a rich community and of easy access to Europe, where military supplies were bought in large quantities. The southern Confederacy had no such reserves of wealth and was shut in by the blockade. The specie in the banks and in private hands was quickly spent. It was hard to raise large sums by taxation, and great quantities of paper money were issued by Confederate states and the Confederate government.

304. CONTRABANDS AND ABOLITION BY CONGRESS (1861-1862)

Early in the struggle it became evident that the purpose of the war could not be limited by the resolution of July, 1861 (§ 283). The Union could never be restored just as it was, because slavery could not be kept out of the contest. It was easy to take advantage of the weakness of a system under which the laborers could not be soldiers. Several different measures were directed against the slaveholders:

(1) Since a recognized measure of war against a slaveholding country is for the invading commander to declare the slaves of his enemy free, Congress (August, 1861) made partial use of this "war power" against slavery. It passed a confiscation act, providing that if slaves were used in promoting any insurrection, the owner should "forfeit his claim to such labor."

(2) As soon as the armies began to move, hundreds of negroes took matters into their own hands by running away and coming into the federal camps. General B. F. Butler, in command at Fort Monroe, found more than a thousand such refugees. When he was asked to surrender some fugitives to their masters, who came from within the Confederate lines to claim them, he replied, "I shall detain the negroes as contraband of war." The phrase struck the popular fancy, and from

that time to the end of the war "contraband" meant a southern slave, usually a refugee.

(3) Two Union generals tried to go further. General Frémont (August, 1861) and General Hunter (May, 1862) issued
proclamations freeing the slaves in their military districts, and
even beyond; but President Lincoln disavowed both the proc-

NEGROES FLEEING TO FORT MONROE. (From a magazine sketch of 1861.)

lamations, because slavery was too large a question to be settled by subordinates.

(4) The abolitionists and antislavery people were joined by
many thousands of people who had up to that time been apathetic, but who wanted to weaken the South by destroying the
value of slave labor; and the feeling was reflected in Congress,
which outran the President, and in 1862 passed three sweeping
emancipation acts: (a) The 3000 slaves in the District of Co-

lumbia were set free (April 16), and their masters were given a compensation of about $300 for each one. (b) In flat contradiction to the Dred Scott decision of 1857, Congress passed a statute (June 19) immediately abolishing slavery in every territory, without compensation. (c) The strong feeling of personal wrath against the leaders on the other side caused Congress to provide, in a second confiscation act (July 17), for the seizure of all the property of people convicted of treason, or who "engaged in armed rebellion," including such slaves of rebel owners as might in any manner come inside the Union lines. Lincoln signed the bill; and as fast as the Union lines extended, thousands of slaves flocked to their camps, and thus became free.

305. PRESIDENT LINCOLN

A few months' experience showed that the man for this crisis was Abraham Lincoln, the one indispensable figure in the Civil War. Two characteristics made him the greatest man of his time: his practical common sense went straight home to the essential point in everything that he was considering; and his quick sensitive heart knew by instinct the beliefs and hopes of his fellow countrymen. Toward the weak and needy, Lincoln had a tender feeling. He could not bear even to sign the death warrant of a deserter, for, he said, "I am trying to evade the butchering business." The same sympathy and sweetness of character were shown in a thousand ways to the people who beset the White House with their little personal errands — the poor woman whose only son was sick in the hospital, or the boy who wanted a commission, or the stranger who came in from mere curiosity.

Although Lincoln always distrusted his own military judgment, he learned to understand the conditions of war better than most of his commanders. His writings are full of quaint telegrams to his generals; for example: "Fight him, too, when opportunity offers. If he stays where he is, fret him and

fret him." To General Grant he once telegraphed: "I have
seen your dispatch expressing your unwillingness to break your
hold where you are. Neither am I willing. Hold on with a
bulldog grip, and chew and choke as much as possible." On
another side of his character, Lincoln was the shrewdest politician of his time; he was very keen in judging election returns;
he knew how to keep congressmen good-natured with offices.

During the first three years of the war, Lincoln was criticized by many members of his own party, who thought him
weak and indecisive because he held a temperate middle course,
avoiding extremes. Only by degrees did people begin to understand that this plain, homely man in the White House had a
spirit of surpassing wisdom, and an unselfish care for his
country's welfare. Patient in defeat, calm in victory, Abraham
Lincoln came to be recognized as a true father of his country.

306. Emancipation by Proclamation (1862–1864)

Throughout 1862 President Lincoln was brooding over the
question of his duty to his country, and his power as commander in chief to declare free all the slaves in the Confederacy.
Lincoln was born in a border slave state, understood the southern people, and was anxious not to take any step that would
drive Kentucky and Missouri out of the Union. Therefore he
sent to Congress a message (March, 1862) urging that the federal government coöperate with the states in setting the slaves
free, with a money payment to the masters.

Lincoln said of himself: "I am naturally antislavery. If
slavery is not wrong, nothing is wrong"; and at another time,
"You must not expect me to give up this government without
playing my last card." In August, 1862, Horace Greeley came
out in the *New York Tribune* with what he called the "Prayer
of Twenty Millions," violently abusing the President for his
"mistaken deference to rebel slavery." The President replied in a public letter, "My paramount object . . . is to save
the Union, it is not either to save or to destroy slavery."

Slowly Lincoln made up his mind that the best way to save the Union was to free the slaves. Calling his Cabinet together (September 22, 1862), he read them the draft of a preliminary Proclamation of Emancipation, which declared that "On the first day of January, in the year of our Lord one thousand eight hundred and sixty-three, all persons held as slaves within any State or designated part of a State, the people whereof shall then be in rebellion against the United States, shall be then, thenceforward, and forever free." As a military measure the proclamation had no immediate effect; it roused only defiance in the South and was at first coldly received in the North. In the elections of congressmen a few weeks later, the Republican party barely kept a majority in the House of Representatives.

Nevertheless, on January 1, 1863, the President issued his second and final proclamation, which applied to all the seceded states except Tennessee and those parts of Louisiana and Virginia which were then occupied by Union troops. Then Lincoln set himself to the task of persuading the border-state slaveholders to free their slaves and take a compensation. They might have had about a hundred million dollars in bonds, but they refused to admit that slavery was wrong, even by giving it up. In the border states thousands of slaves ran away. By act of Congress (in 1862) the troops were forbidden to return them; and in 1864 Congress repealed the Fugitive Slave Act. After that time the slave who stayed with his master in the border states did so only because he liked him.

307. Emancipation and Politics (1862–1864)

The good effects of the proclamation were at once seen abroad, where the friends of the Union in England in 1863 thwarted a last effort to have Great Britain and France "mediate" in the struggle (§ 302). When two ironclad ships of war, the "Laird rams," were ordered for the Confederacy in England, our minister, Adams, protested, and used the grim phrase, "It would be superfluous in me to point out to your

Lordship that this is war." The British government had already decided to hold the vessels, and they were never delivered to the Confederacy.

Three of the loyal border states, which were practically under military rule, settled the slavery question for themselves: (1) The new state of West Virginia in 1863 adopted an anti-slavery constitution. (2) A constitutional ordinance in Missouri provided for gradual emancipation (1863). (3) A new Maryland constitution abolished slavery outright (1864). Lincoln tried to help the process by finding some place in Central America where the former slaves could be colonized; but the experiment did not work.

Both the confiscation act of 1862 and the final Emancipation Proclamation authorized the enlistment of negro troops. The first full negro regiment in service was the First South Carolina Volunteers, commanded by Colonel T. W. Higginson, a New England abolitionist. In the summer of 1863 the government ordered a draft, and states began to fill up their quotas by recruiting negroes in the federal camps on the coast. One of these regiments, the Fifty-fourth Massachusetts, took part in a bloody assault on Battery Wagner near Charleston (July, 1863). Its colonel, Robert G. Shaw, was killed; and the enemy "buried him with his niggers." The 186,000 negro troops eventually received the pay and treatment of white troops.

The state elections of 1863 responded to the victories at Vicksburg and Gettysburg by giving good Republican majorities. Though Lincoln had the confidence of the people, in 1864 a clique of disaffected Republican politicians, including Secretary Chase, wanted to set him aside. Nevertheless the regular Republican convention was practically unanimous for Lincoln, on a platform that slavery must be destroyed. Andrew Johnson of Tennessee was put on the ticket as the candidate for Vice President, in order to strengthen it in the border states. The Democrats nominated for the presidency General George B. McClellan, as representative of the war Democrats and as a soldier candidate; but declared in their platform that there "had been four years of failure to restore the Union by the experiment of war."

The failure of Grant to break up Lee's army in June, 1864 (§ 293), had a damaging effect on the campaign, and Lincoln was deeply discouraged, for he miscalculated the people's affection for their President. To the eighteen free states in the Union in 1860 had been added Kansas (1861), West Virginia (1863), and Nevada, the 36th state (1864). Lincoln carried all the twenty-one except New Jersey; and also Maryland and Missouri out of the four border states in the Union. He secured 212 electoral votes to 21; and 2,200,000 popular votes against 1,800,000 for McClellan. The reëlection of Lincoln made it certain that the war would be fought to a finish, and enabled the government to find men to recruit Grant's army before Petersburg (§§ 293, 298).

308. How the North and the South Lived

Life was exciting in Civil War times. People opened the morning papers with dread, for after the battles there were long lists of killed and wounded, which carried woe to thousands of families. Then came a flood of wounded and sick pouring back from the front; thousands of them died in the hospitals, other thousands went maimed about the streets.

Northern people were always doing things for the soldiers. In almost every village and city there was a ladies' aid society, in which the women scraped lint for wounds, made bandages and comfortable clothing, haversacks, mittens, and articles for the sick, and collected provisions, clothing, and blankets for the soldiers. Two large charitable societies, the Sanitary Commission and the Christian Commission, took these supplies, moved them to the front, and distributed them to the needy.

People had to learn the use of several new kinds of money. After the banks suspended specie payments in December, 1861, a gold coin was a curiosity; and presently the silver

also went out of circulation. For months the only small change
was sticky postage stamps, till Congress provided the little
"shinplasters," or fractional currency. Early in 1862 appeared the crisp and beautiful new legal tender "greenbacks"
(§ 303), and as they came pouring out they began to fall in gold
value; and prices correspondingly rose to double, once almost to
triple, the old rates. Yet business was good in most parts of
the country, crops were large, manufactures increased, the
railroads were busy, and many business men were happy.

Behind the Confederate lines life was just as exciting as in
the North, though much less comfortable. Throughout the
South there was the same passionate support of the soldiers as
in the North, the same fervent prayer to the Almighty to bless
their cause. By severe conscription acts every able-bodied white
man between seventeen and fifty years was called into the army,
so that General Grant said, "They robbed the cradle and the
grave." The ne-
groes on the plan-
tations raised the
crops and took
care of the women
and children, and a
slave insurrection
would have dis-
solved the Confed-
erate army; but
the negroes never
rose.

CONFEDERATE MONEY.

The war brought
dire poverty on
the South. The blockade cut down the cotton export from
$191,000,000 in 1860 to $19,000,000 in 1862. Confederate
paper notes (§ 303) were never legal tender, but they were put
out by hundreds of millions, and toward the end of the war
their value fell to a cent on the dollar: cornmeal sold in Rich-

mond for $80 a bushel in paper; flour at $1000 a barrel; a
newspaper cost a dollar.

As the war progressed the South could no longer replace
its men who fell or were made prisoners; and therefore the
North refused to exchange, even though a hundred thousand
northern soldiers remained in southern prisons. The commissary of the Confederate army was ill managed; and there were
few supplies in the country. Libby Prison for officers in Richmond, and various prisons farther south, were all badly mis-
managed. The prison stockade at Andersonville was in the
hands of a small garrison, officered by men of the overseer type,
who were in constant fear lest the prisoners should break loose.
Hence, in a country abounding in timber and with plenty of
good water, the prisoners were confined in a treeless stockade
on a foul stream, and were fearfully overcrowded, with no materials to build proper houses. They had the same kind of food
that was provided for the jails and the negro quarters, and often
for the Confederate troops at the front — chiefly cornmeal,
sometimes ground cob and all.

309. BEGINNINGS OF RECONSTRUCTION (1861–1865)

The war soon showed the difficulty of assuming that the
seceding states were still in the Union. The forty mountain
counties of western Virginia settled the problem for themselves
by refusing to secede with Virginia. They held a convention,
formed a reorganized government of Virginia, and later framed
a constitution for the new state of West Virginia, and asked
to be admitted into the Union. As the Constitution provides
that no state shall be divided "without the consent of the
Legislatures of the states concerned," Congress accepted the
fiction that the legislature at Wheeling could give such a consent in the name of the whole state of Virginia; and in June,
1863, West Virginia became a separate state.

In 1861 to 1863, under the direct and earnest insistence of
President Lincoln, so-called state governments were formed in

Virginia, Arkansas, Louisiana, and Tennessee; governors were elected by a handful of voters, legislatures were chosen, senators and members of the House appeared in Washington, and several were actually admitted to Congress for a short period, though at the same time these states were represented in the Confederate Congress at Richmond. By a formal proclamation (December 8, 1863) Lincoln offered to all persons who had "participated in the existing rebellion," except the leaders, pardon and amnesty "with restoration of all rights and property except as to slaves"; and he promised to recognize new state governments in any of the seceded states, if formed by one tenth or more of the voters, provided they would take an oath of allegiance to the United States.

The success of the Union arms raised Lincoln in 1865 to the highest point in his whole life. He had the people behind him and could have struck out a policy for restoring the Union which Congress must have followed. He was himself a southern man by birth, understood the southern people, and in his great nature there was no room for enmity toward those who had fought bravely and were beaten. The difficult problem of reconstruction seemed ready for him to solve.

Terrible, therefore, was the blow that fell upon the whole country when, just four years from the surrender of Fort Sumter, the President was shot in a box at Ford's Theater, during a play, by the organizer and head of a band of conspirators. The next morning the President's life ebbed away, and he died (April 15, 1865) at the height of his service and power.

The whole country felt that Lincoln had died for his country as truly as if he had been in the front line at Gettysburg. The work that he did will live imperishably, for he rescued the Union and he destroyed slavery. The principles of his life he summed up a few days before his death: "With malice toward none; with charity for all; with firmness in the right, as God gives us to see the right, let us strive on to finish the work we are in; to bind up the nation's wounds; to care for him who shall have borne the battle, and for his widow, and his orphan — to do all which may achieve and cherish a just and lasting peace among ourselves, and with all nations."

310. COST OF THE CIVIL WAR

What was the cost of the Civil War? In men, 360,000 on the Union side were killed or died of disease, and about 258,000 on the Confederate side. In money, the United States paid out during the Civil War, for other purposes than its ordinary civil expenses, $3,660,000,000; the Confederacy probably spent $1,500,000,000 measured in gold. As for destruction of property, no free territory was invaded, except Indiana, Pennsylvania, and Ohio for a few days; and the destruction of northern merchant vessels amounted to only $20,000,000. The border states of the Union, as well as the seceding South, however, were invaded at many different points and devastated by marching armies, both Union and Confederate. Thousands of houses were burned, the business of cities was for months suspended, the cotton crop was nearly a dead loss. The South was commercially ruined, while the North, in spite of its immense expenses, had more men, more capital, and more money at the end of the war than at the beginning.

MEMORIAL OF THE CIVIL WAR AT NEWBURYPORT, MASS.

The South felt also that it had lost four million slaves whom it valued in 1860 at $2,000,000,000. The slaveholding

families did lose the opportunity of turning their human property into cash; but most of the negroes were still on the
ground and ready to work the land; and the community was
no poorer for the change.

Was this enormous expenditure of life, treasure, and national
forces worth while? Yes, for it did several vital things: (1) It
taught forever the lesson that there is no such thing as peace-
able secession, for we are now sure that any future attempt
at secession would at once lead to war. (2) It proved once for
all that slavery is an institution that weakens the economic
and social forces of a country; for example, the South was deprived of the use in the field of a third of its able-bodied men.
(3) It opened to four million negroes the opportunity to prove
what they could do for themselves if they had a fair chance.
(4) It proved the courage and self-sacrifice of the people of
the United States, both North and South — all the people,
not soldiers merely, but men, women, and children. (5) It put
an end to the project of dividing the strength and influence of
the United States between two federations. One Union, one
government, one nation, one country — that was the result.

The war was worth what it cost, because it led at last to a
recognition of the rights of all men, and to an understanding
that all alike are citizens of one great and enduring country.
It benefited the South as much as the North, by setting it free
from the cramping, wasteful, and undesirable system of slavery.

311. REVIEW

Both the Union and the Confederate governments during
the war went far beyond the ordinary law by authorizing the
arrest of civilians, imprisonment without trial, or trial by a
military commission. These methods seemed necessary against
secret societies in sympathy with the Confederacy. Draft
riots in New York were put down by military force. The
Confederate government used similar dictatorial methods.

Both the North and the South tried to influence European

HART'S NEW AMER. HIST. — 30

governments. Several difficulties arose with England, especially the British proclamation of neutrality, the *Trent* affair, and the disposition to recognize the Confederacy. Recognition was prevented largely by the attitude of the British workmen.

To support the war, heavy taxes were laid by Congress, paper money was issued, and a new system of national banks was chartered. The South borrowed what it could and issued great quantities of government paper notes.

Congress passed many acts relating to slaves and fugitives, including two confiscation acts and emancipation acts for the District of Columbia and the territories. Several Union generals tried to set slaves free; but President Lincoln took over that question and issued two proclamations of emancipation, and most of the loyal border states passed emancipation acts. Large numbers of negro troops were raised.

In both North and South, the war came close home to civilians through their interest in the soldiers and prisoners. Union governments were formed in several of the seceded states, and Lincoln was making plans for adjusting the problems arising from the war when he was assassinated. The war cost about 600,000 lives and \$5,000,000,000; but it restored the country.

References Bearing on the Text and Topics

Geography and Maps. Hosmer, *Appeal to Arms*, 204. — Shepherd, *Hist. Atlas*, 206. — See also references to ch. xxvi.

Secondary. Adams, *C. F. Adams*, chs. ix–xvii. — *Cambridge Mod. Hist.*, VII. chs. xviii, xix. — Coman, *Indust. Hist.*, 279–285. — Curry, *Govt. of the Confed. States*, chs. v–viii. — Dewey, *Finan. Hist.*, §§ 117–140. — Dodd, *Expansion and Conflict*, 281–293, 304, 305, 309–328; *Jefferson Davis*, chs. xv–xxi. — Fish, *Am. Dipl.*, 304–323. — Fite, *Social and Indust. Conditions.* — Hapgood, *Abraham Lincoln*, 201–419. — Hart, *S. P. Chase*, 211–318. — Hosmer, *Appeal to Arms*, chs. ii, xiv, xx; *Outcome of the Civil War*, chs. i, iv, viii, ix, xiii, xv, xvi. — McCall, *Thaddeus Stevens*, chs. viii–xiii. — Morse, *Lincoln*, I. 272–298, 368–387, II. 1–30, 95–133, 170–275, 286–327, 341–357. — Nicolay and Hay, *Abraham Lincoln*, IV–X passim. — Paxson, *Civil War*, 72–222 passim. — Rhodes, *U.S.*, III–V passim. — Schouler, *U.S.*, VI passim. — Schwab, *Confed. States.* — Wilson, *Am. People*, IV. 214–312 passim.

Sources. *Am. Annual Cyclopædia*, 1861–1865. — *Am. Hist. Leaflets*, nos. 18, 26. — Avary, *Va. Girl in the Civil War.* — Brooks, *Washington in Lincoln's Time.* — Carpenter, *Six Months at the White House.* — Chesnut, *Diary from Dixie.* — Hart, *Contemporaries*, IV. §§ 75–83, 96–101, 124–131; *Patriots and Statesmen*, V. 307–342; *Source Book*, §§ 118, 120, 124, 126. — Hill, *Liberty Docs.*, ch. xxii. — Johnson, *Readings*, §§ 153–169. — Johnston, *Am. Orations*, IV. 51–148. — Lincoln, *Works* passim.

Illustrative. Alcott, *Hospital Sketches.* — Browne, *Artemus Ward: His Book; Artemus Ward: His Travels.* — De Forest, *Miss Ravenel's Conversion.* — Dickinson, *What Answer?* (draft riots). — Harris, *On the Plantation.* — Harrison, *The Carlyles.* — Holmes, *In War Time.* — Howe, *Memory of Lincoln* (poems). — Lowell, *Biglow Papers* (2d. ser.); *Commemoration Ode.* — Trowbridge, *Cudjo's Cave.* — Thruston, *Called to the Field.* — Whittier, *Antislavery Poems*, 219–258.

Pictures. *Frank Leslie's Weekly.* — *Harper's Weekly.* — *Harper's Monthly.* — *Mentor*, serial no. 52. — Wilson, *Am. People*, IV.

Topics Answerable from the References Above

(1) Draft riots in New York. [§ 300] — (2) Incidents of the Confederate government at Richmond. [§ 301] — (3) Charles Francis Adams as minister to England. [§ 302] — (4) Capture of the *Trent*. [§ 302] — (5) First national banks. [§ 303] — (6) Confederate use of paper money. [§ 303] — (7) Butler, *or* Frémont, *or* Hunter, on freeing slaves. [§ 304] — (8) Abraham Lincoln: in the White House; *or* with McClellan; *or* in Cabinet meetings; *or* in his relations with Seward; *or* in his relations with Greeley. [§§ 305, 306] — (9) Emancipation Acts of *one* of the following states: West Virginia; Missouri; Maryland. [§ 307] — (10) Lincoln's colonization plan for the negroes. [§ 307] — (11) Election of 1864. [§ 307] — (12) Shinplaster fractional currency. [§ 308] — (13) High prices in the South. [§ 308] — (14) Assassination of President Lincoln. [§ 309]

Topics for Further Search

(15) Secret societies of southern sympathizers in the North. [§ 300] — (16) English workingmen as friends of the North. [§ 302] — (17) Why were the confiscation acts passed? [§ 304] — (18) Hospitals and care of the wounded; *or* Sanitary Commission; *or* Christian Commission. [§ 308] — (19) Conscription of soldiers in the South, *or* in the North. [§ 308] — (20) Was the South made poorer by emancipation? [§ 310]

CHAPTER XXVIII

RECONSTRUCTION OF THE UNION (1865-1876)

312. SOUTHERN WHITES

THE result of the war was to break down the army and navy of the South. The government of the Confederacy at once collapsed, and the secession state organizations were suppressed. How could the southern people and their governments be restored to their former share in the Union? This perplexing question included three issues: the status of the individual whites before the law, the future of the negroes, and the relations of the states to the Union.

The southern whites were nearly all connected with what the North commonly called the "Rebellion," and therefore the penalties for treason were hanging over them all. From that danger, the military men were practically freed by the terms of surrender of Lee's and Johnston's armies. When warrants were issued for Lee and others in order to try them for treason, General Grant would not permit the arrests.

Out of the many who had been civil officers of the Confederacy and the seceded states, the only man actually held for treason was Jefferson Davis. Lincoln would probably have stood firmly against any kind of punishment for the common people of the South, whether soldiers or civilians; but Congress had confiscated the property of some of the leaders (§ 304); and by the Fourteenth Amendment (adopted later) many of those who had taken a leading part, either civil or military, were excluded from office.

484

313. SOUTHERN NEGROES

At the end of the war, most of the slaves within the boundaries of the United States had been declared free by one or another of the following methods: (1) Congress prohibited slavery in the District of Columbia and the territories (§ 304). (2) The President emancipated the slaves in the eleven seceded states, except Tennessee and certain counties of Louisiana and Virginia (§ 306). (3) Maryland, West Virginia, and Missouri passed immediate or gradual emancipation acts for themselves (§ 307). (4) The loyal governments of Louisiana, Virginia, and Arkansas (§ 309) adopted constitutions that freed the slaves; and Tennessee in 1865 passed a special emancipation act. That left Delaware and Kentucky the only areas in which slavery was still legal in April, 1865.

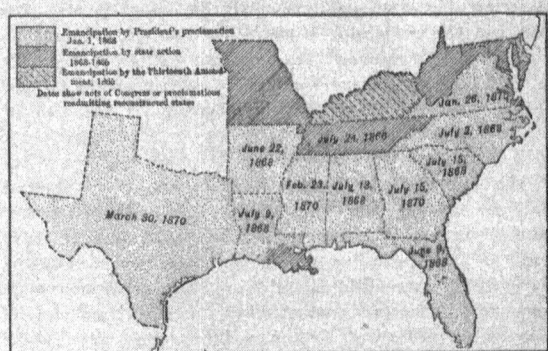

EMANCIPATION AND RECONSTRUCTION.

For the thousands of negroes who had left their old homes and flocked into the Union camps, Congress passed an act for a Freedmen's Bureau (March 3, 1865), which was intended, through military officers, to protect the negroes from injustice, to find work for them, to keep them from starving, and to start schools for their education. This bureau was taking a limited responsibility for individuals within the states, which the United States government had never before attempted.

To prevent any question that the former slaves were forever free, a Thirteenth Amendment to the Constitution was carried through both houses of Congress (January, 1865) by the personal influence of President Lincoln, who said in a public speech, "It winds the whole thing up." Three fourths of all the states, through their legislatures, ratified this amendment, which became a part of the Constitution, December 18, 1865. It provided that "Neither slavery nor involuntary servitude, except as a punishment for crime whereof the party shall have been duly convicted, shall exist within the United States, or any place subject to their jurisdiction." This amendment made freedom the only legal condition in all the United States. The slaves in Kentucky and Delaware were set free by it against the will of their masters. Thenceforth it was out of the power of any state to set slavery up again. Whatever else the war did, it put an end to legal slavery forever.

314. THEORIES OF STATE RECONSTRUCTION (1865–1866)

The question of the eleven states which had tried to withdraw from the Union was the most difficult of all. Did they at once come back into their former place? Would they still have "all the dignity, equality, and rights of the states unimpaired," as set forth by the resolution of 1861 (§ 283)? If so, their senators and representatives would help to settle their own future. The northern theory of the war from first to last was that the states always remained in the Union and could not get out of it; that secession simply had not occurred; that the whole trouble was made by certain individuals who traitorously resisted the United States, on the unfounded claim that their states so ordered. Yet, at the end of the war the individuals went practically unpunished; while the seceded states, as political communities, for years were not allowed to resume their previous relations to the Union. Even after furnishing eight of the twenty-seven ratifications needed to carry the Thirteenth Amendment (§ 313), they were held to be not really in the Union, not capable of sending members to Congress nor of taking part in an election for President.

Four main theories were put forth to explain this singular state of things and to provide a method of "reconstructing" the southern states: (1) The "presidential theory," held by Lincoln, was that the states were entitled to come back and send members to Congress, as soon as the President decided that they had repented. (2) The "state suicide theory," urged by Charles Sumner, was that by secession the states lost statehood and became territories. (3) The "conquered provinces theory," for which Thaddeus Stevens was responsible, was that Congress could deal with the South exactly as if it were a part of a conquered foreign country; it was even suggested that South Carolina be divided between Georgia and North Carolina and thus be obliterated from the map. (4) The "forfeited rights theory" was that the states still existed and were members of the Union, but through their traitorous acts, acting as a community, had made themselves subject to some punishment which would reach them *as states*.

The first theory to be applied was the presidential, which after Lincoln's death was carried on by Andrew Johnson, who succeeded to the presidency. Though a southern man, he was a mountain white and hated the planters. By an amnesty proclamation (May 29, 1865) Johnson undertook to shut out the old southern leaders, and to leave the poor whites to form new state governments. Accordingly, during the year 1865, while Congress was not in session, Johnson appointed civil governors for the southern states. These governors called constitutional conventions, which formed antislavery constitutions, and new elections were then held for members of Congress, and governors, and for legislatures which chose United States senators. In December,

1865, members-elect appeared from all the seceded states except Texas, and demanded seats in Congress.

315. RECONSTRUCTION BY CONGRESS (1866–1867)

Unfortunately for the South, some of the states passed statutes on "vagrancy" and "labor contracts" which made the negro field hands subject to masters for terms of many months. The North believed that if those states were left to themselves they would after a few years reënslave the negro; and that if their members were admitted to Congress, a large part of the work of the Civil War would be undone. Congress, therefore, took the question of reconstruction into its own hands by a joint resolution of both houses (March 2, 1866) to the effect that neither house would admit senators or representatives from a seceding state, until Congress as a whole should decide that the state was again to be represented.

President Johnson's plan of reconstruction was thus quite set aside. He was a coarse, blustering man, who did not know how to get on with other people, who had no powerful friends, and who was not trusted by the antislavery people. The Republican leaders were backed by a two-thirds majority in both branches of Congress, and openly broke with the President by passing over his veto a Civil Rights Act (April 9), which placed the negroes under the protection of the federal government.

In order to put it out of the power of a later Congress to give up the principles of the Civil Rights Act, the two houses in 1866 submitted the Fourteenth Amendment. The main principles of this amendment are four: (1) For the protection of the negro, all persons born or naturalized in the United States are declared to be citizens of the United States and also of the state in which they reside; and states are forbidden to "deprive any person of life, liberty, or property without due process of law," or to "abridge the privileges or immunities of citizens of the United States." Thus a great field of power

over persons was transferred from the states to Congress. (2)
In order to favor negro-suffrage, any states which cut off adult
male citizens from voting, were to lose part of their representation in Congress. (3) To punish the leaders in the Confederacy,
many of them were excluded from state or national office (§ 312).
(4) To set a stigma forever on secession, the Confederate and
state debts incurred "in aid of insurrection or rebellion against
the United States" were declared void.

In a formal Reconstruction Act (March 2, 1867) Congress
passed over the "state suicide theory," and accepted a compromise between the "conquered provinces" and "forfeited
rights" theories (§ 314), by providing that the seceded states
before they could come back into the Union must frame new
constitutions, must give the negro the suffrage, and must ratify
the Fourteenth Amendment and thereby consent to punish
their own leaders.

316. MOTIVES OF RECONSTRUCTION (1866–1869)

These were harsh terms, and it has often been charged
that their purpose was to crush the South and put the intelligent people there under control of the most ignorant part of
the population. Perhaps that was the motive of the man most
responsible for the measure, Thaddeus Stevens of Pennsylvania.
He was a lawyer who went into politics as a Whig, and declared
that he was hostile to slavery "in every form and place." When
the war broke out, Stevens was chairman of the Committee on
Ways and Means, and legislative leader of the House. When
people talked about the Constitution, he said in the House,
"I hold that none of the states now in rebellion are entitled
to the protection of the Constitution." Stevens was one of
the best debaters who ever sat in Congress, but he was absolutely one-sided in politics and thought everybody on the
other side a scoundrel. He was strongly in favor of emancipation, not so much to help the slaves as to hurt the slaveholders;
and he insisted on enlisting negroes in the army, for he said:

"The only place where they can find equality is in the grave. There all God's children are equal." He favored negro suffrage because it would "continue the Republican ascendancy."

Most northern people, though they felt that secession was a crime, were willing to let the states come back into the Union, and to allow the South to recover its prosperity, if they could be sure that the negroes would have a fair chance. This point of view was represented in the Supreme Court, which was much altered by President Lincoln's appointment of five new judges under the leadership of Chief Justice Chase, former Secretary of the Treasury. The Court made a series of decisions on the war and reconstruction (1866 to 1869), in which the right of the Union to make war on rebellious states was affirmed, and the right of Congress to reconstruct such states after the war was supported. In the famous Texas vs. White case (1869) the court dwelt on "an indestructible Union composed of indestructible States." As for individuals, Chief Justice Chase held that the usual penalties for treason were superseded by the Fourteenth Amendment, and Jefferson Davis was therefore set free after two years of imprisonment.

317. Process of Reconstruction (1867-1871)

While the southern states were reorganizing, they remained under the authority of military commanders, who vetoed laws, removed civil governors, dismissed legislatures, issued orders where the legislatures did not pass acts, made ordinances for the cities, and in general exercised many of the powers of despotism. Yet, with few exceptions, they were moderate and just rulers. Reconstruction under the acts of Congress was a slow process. Members of Congress from Tennessee were readmitted in 1867, from six more states in 1868, from Virginia, Mississippi, and Texas in 1870; Georgia, the last of the eleven seceding States, after being twice set back, was at last allowed to reënter the complete Union in 1871. Several of the border states, though not covered by the Reconstruction Act, went into the hands of Republican majorities, who disfranchised former Confederates. By ratifications of twenty northern states and ten southern states, the Fourteenth Amendment was declared (July 28, 1868) to be a part of the Constitution.

The Freedmen's Bureau was allowed to lapse in 1869; but, in order to put negro suffrage out of the control of the southern states, a Fifteenth Amendment was framed by Congress (1868). It forbade any state to withhold the suffrage on account of "race, color, or previous condition of servitude." It was duly ratified by the aid of reconstructed legislatures and became a part of the Constitution (March 30, 1870).

When the southern states were fully restored, the adult negro men had the suffrage. Every legislature had negro members, and some of them a negro majority. Most of these negroes were ignorant men who were controlled by two classes of whites, called "scalawags" (southern Republicans) and "carpetbaggers" (northern men who had gone to the South to get into politics). Taxes were increased, debts ran up, and the extravagance and corruption of some of the legislatures surpass belief. The state debt of Alabama swelled from $8,000,000 to $25,000,000 in six years; the South Carolina legislature spent $350,000 in one session for "supplies, sundries, and incidentals." These losses came on states already impoverished by four years of war — states in which almost the whole community, white and black, was poor and struggling.

318. QUARREL WITH PRESIDENT JOHNSON (1866-1868)

Several efforts were made to induce the Supreme Court to stop the course of the reconstruction acts passed by Congress, by a judicial decision, but the court refused to interfere. President Johnson therefore felt bound to carry out most of these laws. Meantime he was engaged in a violent quarrel with Congress and tried to arouse public sentiment by coarse and abusive speeches, especially during the political campaign of 1866, when he said, "We have seen hanging upon the verge of the

Government, as it were, a body called, or which assumes to be, the Congress of the United States."

He did himself more harm than good; for in 1866 a Republican and anti-Johnson two-thirds majority was again elected to both houses of Congress. Johnson kept up the fight by vetoing in all 21 bills, 15 of which were carried over his veto. He also tried to head the Democratic party — just at that time called Conservatives. The Republican House of Representatives went so far as to present articles of impeachment against President Johnson (1868), and the trial before the Senate lasted over two months. Discarding many trifling charges, the managers selected for a test vote the charge that Johnson had tried to remove Secretary Stanton, contrary to a Tenure of Office Act which had been passed over his veto. Thirty-five senators (all Republicans) voted for conviction; nineteen senators (twelve Democrats and seven Republicans) voted for acquittal. The impeachment failed, though a change of one vote would have made the necessary two-thirds vote. There is now no doubt that the dissenting Republican senators saved the country from the dangerous precedent of removing a President because he differed with and quarreled with Congress.

319. SEWARD'S FOREIGN POLICY (1861–1869)

During the Civil War, the United States found itself in several difficulties which were settled after peace came:

(1) Mexico. The first of these was caused by a French occupation of Mexico. Napoleon III, emperor of the French, took advantage of the embarrassment of the Union in 1861 to send an expedition to collect damages from Mexico, and extended it into a war of conquest. A French army set up what they called an Empire, with Maximilian, an Austrian archduke, as emperor (1864). This occupation of Mexico was very offensive to the United States; and Secretary Seward many times warned the French not to force a monarchical government on an American republic. At the end of the Civil War a large

force of Union troops was sent to Texas, as a hint to the undesirable invaders across the Mexican boundary. Seward's
firmness compelled the French to withdraw in 1867. Maximilian was taken prisoner by his subjects, and shot; and that
was the end of the Empire of Mexico.

(2) Central America and the West Indies. Another group
of foreign questions related to the Isthmus route to California
and to a naval station in the West Indies. Secretary Seward
made treaties with Honduras and Nicaragua, looking toward
a canal. Then he turned to the West Indies, and pressed upon
the Danish government a treaty of purchase for the little
islands of St. Thomas and St. John (1867); but the Senate declined to ratify the treaty, in which there was little public interest. Then he tried hard to annex Samaná Bay in the island
republic of Santo Domingo — but the Senate would not listen.

(3) Alaska. Another project of annexation was successful.
Russia, during the Civil War, had been extremely friendly;
and when it became known that Russia would like to dispose
of Russian America, Seward surprised the whole country by

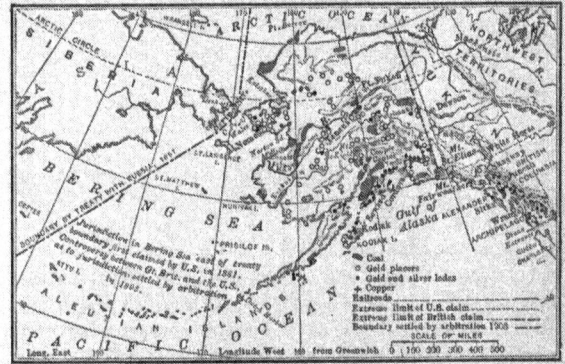

ALASKA.

arranging a treaty for the purchase of the whole region for $7,200,000; and it was ratified by the Senate (April 9, 1867). People knew very little about the region, which is now named Alaska; but it comprised half a million square miles of land, a valuable seal fishery, and a rich gold-mining region.

320. GRANT AND RECONSTRUCTION (1869-1873)

The presidential election of 1868 gave the approval of the majority of the actual voters to the Congressional plan of reconstruction. The Republicans nominated General Grant; the Democrats put up Horatio Seymour of New York. Two of the eight states just readmitted to the Union voted for Seymour, but Grant received 214 electoral votes to 80, and a popular majority of 300,000.

President Grant came into office in March, 1869, and had a stormy administration. He was absolutely honest and truthful and a sincerely patriotic man, but he had an unwavering belief in those whom he selected as friends. He wanted to give orders himself; and his friends made him believe that he was essential to the salvation of the country. Like General Jackson, Grant made a vigorous fight for the rights of the President; and he used his veto power forty-three times, principally against special pension and relief bills. Grant was the first President after John Quincy Adams who desired a nonpartisan civil service. He was opposed to the practice of removing the civil officers of the government, down to floor scrubbers, every time a new President came in; and he induced Congress in 1871 to pass a civil service reform act. He tried to carry it out in good faith, till Congress three years later cut off the appropriations and the scheme collapsed.

Throughout Grant's first administration (1869-1873) reconstruction was dragging along. The South was protesting against the carpetbag governments, and many northern Democrats proposed to wipe out the three amendments if they could come into control of the national government. Within five years after the last of the states was readmitted (§ 317), something very like a "second rebellion" arose; and the result was that three of the main principles of reconstruction ceased to work.

321. FAILURE OF RECONSTRUCTION (1869–1874)

The failure of reconstruction included the defeat of all three of the main objects of the whole system of severe laws, and also a serious limitation of negro suffrage in the lower South.

(1) The very moderate punishment of individuals under the Fourteenth Amendment (§ 315) ceased; for Congress used its power to pass an amnesty act (1872) by which all but about three hundred former Confederate leaders were restored to political rights. Many of those excepted were restored by special acts, but none ever reached Jefferson Davis or Robert E. Lee.

(2) The punishment of the states came to an end when they were admitted to their former full share in the Union.

(3) The special protection of the negro, supposed to be embedded in the Fourteenth Amendment, was much weakened by decisions of the Supreme Court, which ruled (1869) that the amendment was not "intended to bring within the power of Congress the entire domain of civil rights, heretofore belonging exclusively to the states." Congress then passed a Civil Rights Act (1875) to give the negroes the same privileges as white people in hotels, railroad cars, and so on; but it was some years later held unconstitutional by the Supreme Court.

(4) Negro suffrage was broken up in many states by violence, through the Ku-Klux Klan movement (begun in 1868). Young men, masked and disguised, rode about the country at night, threatening the negroes, and dragging out and whipping or even shooting their leaders. White men also, especially the "carpetbaggers," were terrorized and sometimes driven out. Congress in vain attempted to protect the negroes by the "Force Bills" of 1870 and 1871, under which the President had authority to send troops to protect the polling places in the South.

The Ku-Klux Klan gave the Republicans a new campaign
issue for the presidential election of 1872. The Democrats
combined with the Liberal Republicans (an anti-Grant organization) to nominate Horace Greeley, the old-time abolitionist
and hater of the Democratic party. Grant was easily reëlected

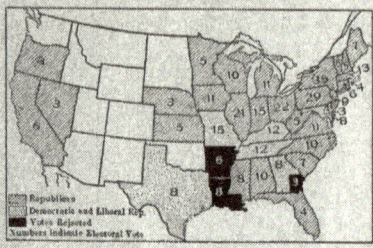

by the Republi-
cans by 286 elec-
toral votes to 63;
and he had a pop-
ular majority of
700,000.

In the South
the effort of the
Democrats to get
the state govern-
ments out of the
hands of the "car-

ELECTION OF 1872.

petbaggers" brought about several little civil wars, especially
in Louisiana, where for weeks two legislatures, each supporting a governor, sat in halls a few squares from each other.
The whole country was weary of the squabbles. In the so-
called "tidal wave" of congressional elections in 1874, a large
number of Democratic members were elected to the House
from the South. From that time nearly all the negroes in
the lower South were prevented by persuasion, or fraud, or
force, or by new state constitutions from influencing any southern election where their vote could affect the result; in the
former border states, and in Texas and Tennessee, they continued to vote till after 1890. The white voters, under their
war-time leaders, were again in the saddle.

322. PUBLIC FINANCE (1865–1875)

Besides the political reconstruction of individuals and states,
the finances of the federal government and of the northern and
southern states had to be reorganized.

Both South and North came out of the war with very heavy public debts. The Fourteenth Amendment disposed of the Confederate debts, and also of debts contracted by seceding states in aid of the war, by providing that they should never be paid (§ 315). The southern states, under the lead of the "carpetbag" legislatures, issued a new set of bonds for borrowed money; but some of the bonds were fraudulent, and several states, including Virginia, simply refused to pay this debt.

The northern state governments were more prudent and by 1885 they owed, taken together, only about $100,000,000. On the other hand the cities of the North were borrowing money right and left; and the result was that the total public debt — national, state, and local — constantly increased. Still the country was growing in prosperity and wealth and did not feel the burden of the interest payments.

The outstanding national debt in 1870 was $2,481,000,000 and the local debts were $270,000,000. The national government at once began to pay off its obligations. Till 1893 every year showed a surplus of receipts over expenses, available for that purpose. The lowest point reached was $839,000,000 net debt in 1893. "Internal revenue" on liquors and tobacco furnished about a third of the national income, customs duties about two thirds; and there was a little from the public lands.

A very serious question was that of the paper money. After Congress forced the state chartered banks to stop issuing notes the currency was made up of "greenbacks" (§ 303), national bank notes, and paper small change, for all of which the federal government took the responsibility. Greenbacks in 1865 were worth about seventy cents on the dollar, measured in gold; by 1871 they rose to ninety cents.

At first it was intended that the greenbacks should be paid off in hard money, but in 1866 there was a small commercial panic, and then came an outcry that the bondholders had paid greenbacks for their bonds, and ought to be repaid in the same paper money; that is, that the national debt should be paid with a different kind of debt. A political movement began, called the "Ohio Idea," or by its enemies the "Rag Baby," which startle l Congress into voting (February 4, 1868) that the greenbacks should not be reduced below $350,000,000. A year later, however, Congress voted that the bonds should be paid in " coin."

An effort was made to compel Congress to redeem the greenbacks by showing that there was no constitutional power to issue them. In 1870 the Supreme Court held, in the Legal Tender cases, by four judges to three, that the greenbacks were unconstitutional. In a few months two vacancies occurred in the Supreme Court; two new judges were appointed; and by a majority of five to four the court held greenbacks justified under the war power, thus reversing the previous decision. Thirteen years later, the court ruled that legal tenders could be issued at any time, without regard to the war power.

323. CURRENCY QUESTIONS (1869–1875)

Paper money was for ten years the most difficult question before Congress.

(1) What was meant by "coin" in the Act of 1869? At that time both gold and silver bullion could be presented at the United States mint, which would return the weight (less a small deduction for coinage) in gold or silver coin.

(2) In a long act on coinage (February 12, 1873) a brief clause was introduced — later dubbed the "Crime of 1873" — by which the coinage of the silver dollar was legally given up. At the time nobody objected, because no silver dollars were then in circulation. Gold coin was for five years the only coin struck by the mint which could be offered in large amounts as "legal tender" in payment of debt. Gold became by this act the legal standard of values, in which greenbacks were to be redeemed.

(3) Instead of calling in and paying off the greenbacks, vigorous efforts were made to add to the paper currency. A bill passed both houses of Congress (1874) for the issue of about fifty millions more of greenbacks; but President Grant vetoed

it because "inflation of the currency" by issue of more paper money was contrary to the policy of the government.

(4) Congress at last (1875) came to a decision to bring the greenbacks up to gold value, and passed an act for accumulating a specie reserve so as to be ready for resuming specie payments.

324. GRANT'S PEACE POLICY (1869-1877)

Several foreign questions of great importance went over to Grant's administration, and were settled under the influence of Hamilton Fish, Grant's able Secretary of State. Most important of these was the question of the *Alabama* Claims, which interfered with good relations with Great Britain during all the years from 1862 to 1872. These were claims against Great Britain for damages of several kinds, especially: (1) the recognition of the belligerency of the Confederacy (§ 302); (2) captures of American merchantmen by the *Alabama* and other cruisers built or fitted out in British ports (§ 286); (3) hospitality to Confederate war ships in British ports, and allowing them to coal and refit; (4) "indirect damages," for the supposed prolonging of the war through British sympathy.

Public feeling ran high and some bold spirits clamored for war. The heads of the British government gradually made up their minds to admit that a mistake had been made. Hence they agreed to the Treaty of Washington (May, 1871) in which Great Britain made a formal apology "for the escape, under whatever circumstances, of the *Alabama* and other vessels from British ports." A Commission of Arbitration to fix the amount of the damages met at Geneva (1872), examined the evidence, and adjudged the sum of $15,500,000 to be paid by Great Britain to the United States.

Another arbitration with Great Britain settled a long-pending controversy over the national ownership of the San Juan group of islands between Vancouver and the mainland; they were awarded to the United States. A dispute over the northern fisheries led to a third arbitration commission, which decided

GRANT'S TOMB, NEW YORK.

(1877) that for certain privileges desired by American fishermen on the coasts of Canada, for a period of ten years, the sum of $5,-500,000 should be paid by the United States.

One of the lessons of the Civil War was that the United States needed naval stations in the West Indies. Grant and Fish revived Seward's policy as to the negro republic of Santo Domingo, and a treaty of annexation was drawn up in 1869; but Senator Charles Sumner of Massachusetts (§ 254) used his personal influence to defeat it.

On other West Indian questions Grant was more moderate. In 1868 the native Cubans rebelled against the Spanish rule. On both sides it was a war of atrocities: the insurgents burned the sugar plantations; the Spaniards shot the insurgents like wild beasts. Our government remained neutral and tried to prevent filibusters (§ 256) from slipping over to aid the Cubans. In 1873 the filibustering steamer *Virginius* was captured by a Spanish cruiser and eight Americans were shot. There would have been war but that President Grant was determined to have peace, and the Spanish government made due amends.

325. REVIEW

Though the Civil War lasted only four years, it took eight years more to restore the Union. The main difficulties were:

(1) The southern whites. Should they be punished for their share in the war? (2) The negroes, who were set free as the result of the war. What would become of them? (3) The seceded states. Were they already in the Union or must they be brought back by a new process?

Congress refused to accept its former doctrine that the states had never been out of the Union, and eventually passed several acts under which those states had to allow the negroes to take part in public affairs. Those men who had been most active in the Confederacy were excluded from public office, but no one was tried for treason.

Congress sought to make the results of the war permanent by submitting three constitutional amendments: (1) the Thirteenth (1865), forever prohibiting slavery; (2) the Fourteenth (1868), intended to make the negroes citizens and to protect them in personal rights; (3) the Fifteenth (1870), protecting negro suffrage. Some of the southern states came under the influence of "carpetbaggers" and "scalawags" who could control the negro vote. When President Johnson set himself against Congress he was all but impeached by the Senate.

Secretary Seward initiated a policy of influence and expansion by causing the French to leave Mexico; by attempting annexations in the West Indies; and by securing Alaska (1867).

General Grant became President in 1869, and tried to reform the administration. Reconstruction broke down because the Supreme Court took the pith out of the Fourteenth Amendment by its decisions; and the organization known as the Ku-Klux Klan prevented the negroes from voting. Most of the southern states went over to the Democratic party.

The Confederate and southern state debts were shut out, but the Union carried a heavy public debt. The greenbacks were continued, and an effort was made to pay off the bonds in that currency. Silver ceased to be coined by an act of 1873. President Grant was successful in settling the claims against Great Britain, and pursued a policy of peace.

References Bearing on the Text and Topics

Geography and Maps. See maps, pp. 343, 485, 493, 533. — Bogart, *Econ. Hist.*, 389. — Dunning, *Reconstruction*, 4, 82, 114, 158.

Secondary. Adams, *C. F. Adams*, ch. xix. — Bancroft, *W. H. Seward*, II. 419–500. — Bassett, *U.S.*, 594–652, 660–664, 668–674, 782–784. — Brown, *Lower South*, 191–225. — Burton, *John Sherman*, chs. vii–xi. — Dewey, *Finan. Hist.*, §§ 142–158, 163–170. — Fish, *Am. Dipl.*, chs. xxiii–xxv; *Am. Nationality*, 407–431, 443–446. — Hart, *S. P. Chase*, chs. xiii–xvi. — Haworth, *Reconstruction and Union*, 7–71. — Linn, *Horace Greeley*, 214–259. — Lothrop, *W. H. Seward*, ch. xxi. — Paxson, *New Nation*, 27–66, 75–80. — Rhodes, *U.S.*, V. 516–626, VI, VII. 1–194. — Stanwood, *J. G. Blaine*, chs. v, vi; *Presidency*, I. chs. xxiii, xxiv.

Sources. *Am. Annual Cyclopædia*, 1865 to 1875. — Caldwell and Persinger, *Source Hist.*, 469–483. — Fleming, *Doc. Hist. of Reconstruction*. — Harding, *Select Orations*, nos. 29–32. — Hart, *Contemporaries*, IV. §§ 141–157, 173–176; *Source Book*, §§ 127–132, 134. — Hill, *Liberty Docs.*, ch. xxiii. — Johnson, *Readings*, §§ 168–192. — Johnston, *Am. Orations*, IV. 149–188. — MacDonald, *Select Statutes*, nos. 44–95, 99. — Smedes, *Southern Planter*, 231–341. — Welles, *Diary*, II, III.

Illustrative. Cable, *John March, Southerner*. — De Forest, *Honest John Vane* (Washington). — Glasgow, *Voice of the People*. — Hale, *Mrs. Merriam's Scholars*. — Locke, *Struggles of Petroleum V. Nasby*. — Lowell, *Biglow Papers* (2d. ser.). — Page, *Red Rock*. — Thanet; *Expiation*. — Tourgée, *Fool's Errand*; *Bricks without Straw*.

Pictures. Andrews, *Last Quarter Century*. — *Frank Leslie's Weekly*. — *Harper's Weekly*. — Wilson, *Am. People*, V.

Topics Answerable from References Above

(1) Robert E. Lee, *or* General Grant, *or* Jefferson Davis, in reconstruction. [§ 312] — (2) Debates on the Thirteenth, *or* Fourteenth, *or* Fifteenth Amendment. [§§ 313, 315, 317] — (3) Public career of Thaddeus Stevens. [§ 316] — (4) Process of reconstruction of any *one* of the eleven seceding states. [§ 317] — (5) Impeachment of Andrew Johnson. [§ 318] — (6) Incidents of the Ku-Klux Klan movement. [§ 321] — (7) Incidents of the Geneva arbitration. [§ 324] — (8) San Juan Islands. [§ 324] .

Topics for Further Search

(9) The Freedmen's Bureau. [§ 313] — (10) Why did Congress break with President Johnson? [§ 315] — (11) Why did the French leave Mexico? [§ 319] — (12) Why did Russia sell Alaska? [§ 319] — (13) Rival governments in Louisiana, *or* Arkansas. [§ 321] — (14) Greenback movement. [§ 322] — (15) Resumption of specie payments. [§ 323]

CHAPTER XXIX

SOCIAL AND ECONOMIC CHANGES (1865–1885)

326. NEW CONDITIONS

WHILE political reconstruction was going on and the government of the United States was slowly returning to the former condition of a Union including all the states, the business of the country was going through a series of changes which were almost as significant. The economic conditions of the two sections were very different. The North was prosperous during most of the war. The eastern states grew rapidly, and at the same time population pushed out to new frontiers; towns and cities sprang up from end to end of the country; railroads were extended; and new mines and factories were opened. It was this prosperity which made it possible for the nation to pay high taxes during the war and to carry the tremendous national debt.

So long as fighting continued, and for ten years afterward, the South was in a bad economic condition. The principal export, cotton, could not be sent to market except in small quantities. Most of the banks and large business houses were ruined. Stocks of goods were entirely exhausted. Long stretches of railroads were torn up by invading armies. The seaports were in decay as a result of the blockade. The South as a community was bankrupt at the end of the war.

Still, the natural resources of both North and South were enormous. The southern land was there and produced cotton which fortunately commanded an unusually high price. In the North, wheat, oats, corn, and all sorts of agricultural products abounded. Both sections were rich in coal and iron, and the western plateau region was beginning to produce silver and gold. Above all, millions of laborers were on hand to make available these gifts of nature. Fully 1,500,000 able-bodied men returned from the war, ready to take their places as farmers, workmen, professional men, and business managers. The North had money to lend, and part of its savings could be invested in the South. Europe was also ready to lend and to invest, on a great scale, the money that was so much needed for the development of the North and the restoration of the South. Such force and vigor required only a proper organization of business to make all parts of the country rich.

327. LABORERS AND IMMIGRANTS

Laborers were numerous. In the South the mountaineers kept up their farms in much the same shiftless fashion as before the war, barely supporting their families from year to year. The old class of substantial families tilling their own land remained in the border states, and in North Carolina, Tennessee, and Texas. The rough work of the towns and cities, together with much of the building of every kind, continued to be done by negroes. They also cut most of the timber, built the railroads, worked as section hands and farmers, and did the crude labor for the factories. In the fields, they furnished nearly all the hired labor, for the South was obliged to adopt something approaching a wage system. The negro hands were not very efficient, but still they were on the ground, knew the tasks, and raised probably two thirds or more of the annual crop of cotton.

Northern labor was on a far better footing. The farmer owning and working his own land was considered the normal, usual worker in the open country. Hired farm laborers were few, for there was such a demand for labor in mines and factories and on lines of transportation that any good man could find a job at attractive wages. Many of the farmers' sons found their way to the cities, where the most energetic and able became foremen, managers, owners of shops, stores, and factories, bankers, and proprietors of railroads and other corporations.

Northern labor and industry were greatly aided by foreign immigration, which was resumed on a large scale as soon as the Civil War ended. Irish and German immigration was heavy. English, Welsh, Scotch, Scandinavians, and Swiss also came in large numbers. Wars in central Europe between Prussia on one side and Denmark, Austria, and France in turn on the other (1864-1870) led most European nations to require that every able-bodied young man should have military training for at least a year or two. Hence when German and other immigrants went back to visit friends, if they had originally come away without having served the required term in the army, they were liable to arrest, even though naturalized citizens of the United States.

To get rid of this trouble, a set of treaties was negotiated (beginning in 1868) with the various German states, and with Belgium, Austria, Great Britain, and several small powers, by which if a native of those countries comes to the United States and stays five years, he loses his native citizenship, whether naturalized here or not; but if he goes back to his mother country and lives there two years, he may lose his American citizenship.

The welcome to immigrants extended across the Pacific. Chinese laborers drifted to California and Oregon, and thousands of them were employed in the construction of the Pacific railroads (§ 329). In 1868 the "Burlingame Treaty" specifically promised that our government would protect Chinese in this country in the enjoyment of the same rights as those enjoyed by citizens of other countries. Nobody then seemed to doubt that immigration of any kind added to the prosperity and happiness of the United States.

328. DEVELOPMENT OF THE FAR WEST (1861-1876)

The immigrants helped to develop the West, into which settlers were pouring by hundreds of thousands. Many were attracted by the Homestead Act, passed in 1862, under which any head of a family, native or foreign born, might take up 160 acres of government land, and at the end of five years' residence receive a title to it free of cost. Within ten years 28,000,000 acres of land were thus "homesteaded"; and 9,000,000 acres were given away under an act of 1873, granting "tree claims"

A WESTERN HOMESTEAD, ABOUT 1875.

to settlers who would plant and keep alive a certain number of trees.

Another cause for the rush to the West was the discovery of new mines — copper at Butte, Montana (1864), gold in the Black Hills of Dakota and Wyoming (1874), silver at Leadville, Colorado (1876). Between 1861 and 1876 it was found desirable to organize three new western states: Nevada (1864), Nebraska (1867), and Colorado (1876), raising the total number to thirty-eight. Congress also set up the territories of Dakota, Idaho, Arizona, Montana, and Wyoming.

Much of the western country was still unknown to white men when, in 1869, Major Powell, with a dare-devil boat expedition, went down the Colorado River, and revealed the wonders of its Grand Canyon. In 1870 an exploring party reached the upper Yellowstone valley, and made known the canyons, hot springs, and spouting geysers which are among the greatest of our natural wonders.

The Indian reservations established in the Northwest in Jackson's time (§ 240) were hard pressed by the wave of white settlement. President Grant set on foot a "peace policy" in 1869, by which he hoped to civilize the Indians. Many reservations were placed under agents nominated by religious societies. Nevertheless, Indian wars could not be stopped. The little Modoc tribe in the lava beds of northern California for many months (1872–1873) defied the whole United States government; and the Sioux of the upper Missouri country, under the leadership of Chief Sitting Bull, in 1876 totally

AN ARMY AMBULANCE ON THE WESTERN PLAINS.

destroyed a force of about two hundred troops with their commander, General Custer; but this was the last dangerous contest with the Indians in the Northwest.

329. RAILROADS

The rapid settlement of the West was made possible by the railroads. All the eastern roads had state charters, which could give no rights outside the state limits. Hence "parent companies" were formed to lease or operate local lines. Foremost were the Pennsylvania Company, which now holds at least thirty charters in twelve states, and the New York Central. Many short lines in the West were merged into great systems such as the Chicago and Northwestern, and the Chicago Burlington and Quincy. In this process there was plenty of "stock watering"; that is, issuing of shares to an amount greater than the cost of the property, and then trying to earn dividends on the whole capital.

Up to the Civil War most of the railroads were organized in

lengths of a few hundred miles at most. Cornelius Vanderbilt, a steamboat king, bought an interest in several railroads
branching out from New York, and in 1869 made a union
between the Hudson River Railroad and the New York Central, which gave an all-rail line, under one management, from
the wharves of New York to the wharves of Buffalo. The
Pennsylvania Railroad, till then running from Philadelphia to
Pittsburgh, absorbed the Fort Wayne route to Chicago (1869),
and the Pan Handle route to Cincinnati and St. Louis; and in

A TRANSATLANTIC STEAMER IN 1875. (Steamship *Wyoming* of the
Guion Line.)

1875 changed its eastern terminus to New York. It also
founded an "American Line" of steamers (1873) sailing from
Philadelphia to Liverpool.

The delay and expense of ferry transfers across broad rivers
led to the building of great railroad and highway bridges. The
first bridge across the middle Mississippi was built at Rock
Island, Illinois, in 1856. Between 1865 and 1880 that river was
bridged at a dozen other places, and in 1874 the Eads steel
arch railway bridge was constructed at St. Louis. In 1867 a
wagon suspension bridge was built across the Ohio from Cin-

cinnati to Covington; and the river was bridged for a railroad at Parkersburg in 1871. The greatest work of this kind was the suspension bridge from New York to Brooklyn, 1595 feet span, and 135 feet above the water level, begun in 1870, and opened for travel in 1883.

During the Civil War it became plain that a railroad across the continent to California was necessary if California was to be held in the Union. For this purpose (beginning in 1862) Congress chartered the Union Pacific, Northern Pacific, Atlantic and Pacific, and Texas and Pacific companies; Congress also granted lands and privileges to these roads and to the Central Pacific, Kansas Pacific, Southern Pacific, and the short Western Pacific and Sioux City and Pacific roads.

Construction was pushed rapidly on the most direct of the trunk lines, that from Omaha via Great Salt Lake to California; and in 1869 the last spike was driven at Ogden, Utah, and a through rail connection was thus established, 1917 miles long, from Omaha to San Francisco. State-chartered roads filled the gap from Chicago to Omaha.

By 1885 the companies mentioned above had built four lines to the Pacific coast: the Northern Pacific from Lake Superior to Puget Sound; the Union Pacific and Central Pacific from Omaha and Kansas City to San Francisco; the Southern Pacific from New Orleans to San Francisco via El Paso; and the Atchison Topeka and Santa Fe from Kansas City to San Diego.

These roads were not like the former state-chartered roads. They all had a connection with the federal government: (1) The long through lines were chartered by Congress, which prevented the states from interfering with their through business. (2) Most of them had land grants — half the government land lying in a strip twenty miles wide, in some instances forty miles wide, along their whole length, amounting in all to 117,000,000 acres. (3) The government lent large sums to the Union, Central, Kansas, Western, and Sioux City and Pacific roads to an amount finally of $64,000,000.

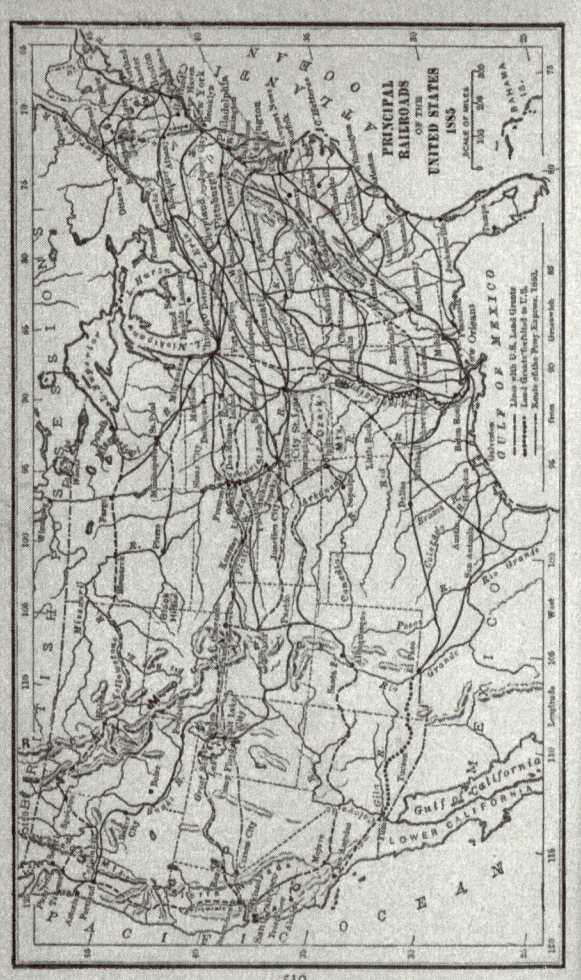

PRINCIPAL
RAILROADS
OF THE
UNITED STATES
1885

Scale of Miles

Lines with U.S. Land Grants
Land Grants forfeited to U.S.
Route of the Pony Express, 1860.

330. COMMERCIAL QUESTIONS (1865-1885)

Business increased by leaps and bounds throughout the Union, and a new commercial system grew up to meet the needs of the time.

(1) Banking was much changed. About half the banking capital was owned by national banks, chartered by a general act of Congress; they deposited government bonds in Washington and received national bank notes which were as acceptable as greenbacks, and therefore were at par in gold after 1879 (§ 335). Some state chartered banks kept on without issuing any notes (§ 303), and private banking houses acted as finance agents. The Drexel firm in Philadelphia, the Morgan firm of New York, and the Lee-Higginson firm in Boston are examples. A new kind of banks called "trust companies" began to operate in the great money centers. They did a regular banking business and also aided in the transactions of large corporations.

(2) The savings of the country were invested in all kinds of ways. Great numbers of people bought farms or town houses; other people put their savings into mortgages. The savings banks became very important; their total deposits were $1,095,000,000 in 1885. Life insurance was also developed as a means of saving and of providing for families. From 1865 to 1886 the policy holders and the amounts invested increased nearly ten times over. The insurance companies and savings banks made a business of lending money on good real estate security, and that helped the building of towns and cities.

(3) Corporations now became the usual form of great enterprises of every sort, and many private firms found it convenient to change into stock companies, which could bring together the capital of many persons and hold them free from unlimited liability for the corporation's debts. Manufacturers, miners, and owners of steamship companies and many other industries chose this form of investment.

(4) A new type of corporation was the great monopoly controlling some large line of business. In 1870 was chartered in Ohio a corporation called the Standard Oil Company, directed principally by John D. Rockefeller, for the purpose of manufacturing illuminating oil out of petroleum (§ 279). In a few years it became one of the largest and most profitable companies in the country. It consolidated with other companies; it had special contracts with the railroads, and was soon able to force most of its rivals out of business; and its property, which in 1870 was about $1,000,000, rose in 1885 to an amount estimated at $150,000,000.

Just after the Civil War came a period of fierce speculation: 24,000 miles of new railroad were built in four years; great losses came in the Chicago fire (1871) and in the Boston fire (1872), and a commercial crisis in 1873 caused failures to the amount of about $225,000,000. Several instances of fraud seemed to show a lax morality in business and in the public service. It was found (1872) that the Credit Mobilier, a corporation formed to build the Union Pacific Railroad, had offered bribes in the form of its stock to members of Congress. A Whisky Ring was unearthed (1875), which was defrauding the government by false accounts. Secretary Belknap, of the War Department, was detected in selling the privilege to trade at army posts; an attempt was made to impeach him, but he resigned, and the impeachment broke down for lack of a two-thirds vote (1876).

331. Mechanical Improvements

The foundation of business prosperity was the ability of the nation to produce every year more than was needed to carry it through the year, for the surplus could be put into new enterprises. One of the ways of increasing the profits was to use machinery in place of hand labor, and the Americans of the time were notably ingenious in labor-saving devices. Cheap machinery required cheap iron; and the blast furnaces for

making pig iron were enlarged and provided with more powerful machinery for blowing in air. Another great improvement
was caused by the introduction of the
Bessemer process for making steel direct
from pig iron (1864).

Bessemer steel furnished cheap and
substantial railroad rails; the stronger
wheel base made it possible to run
heavier cars, carrying loads still heavier,
and thus transportation was cheapened.
After 1880 the track gauges of almost all
the railroads were made uniform, so that
through freight and passenger cars could
be more widely used. Pullman and other
sleeping, dining, and parlor cars came
into use. Passenger rates on through
routes were reduced, mileage tickets were
introduced, and better stations erected.

A SHOE-SEWING
MACHINE.

New methods of sending intelligence came into use. The
Western Union Telegraph Company absorbed a number of
small companies, and
spread a net of wires
and offices over the
Union; and in 1866
the first permanently
successful Atlantic ca-
ble was laid. The mail
system also underwent
three improvements:
delivery of mails by
carriers (1863), postal
money orders (1864),

STEEL MANUFACTURE.

and mail cars in which clerks sort the mail while *en route* (1864).

Hundreds of new inventions and improvements in old ones
were made for the betterment of home life and business. Among

them were systems of heating buildings by hot air, steam, and hot water; artificial ice; barbed wire fencing and wire nails; house drainage; building paper; elevators for storing and loading grain; passenger elevators in high buildings; asphalt and wooden-block pavement; plate glass windows of large dimensions; improved firearms, especially the automatic machine guns of Hiram Maxim and others; new explosives, especially dynamite; sulky plows and other farm machinery; compressed

air drills for mining; steel safes and bank vaults; chemical dyestuffs; and new metals and alloys. The present form of bicycle was evolved from earlier patterns in 1884. The typewriter, first put on the market in 1874, furnished a new employment for thousands of men and women. Typesetting and typecasting machines, perfected after 1890, have

AN EARLY FORM OF TYPEWRITER.

quickened and cheapened the process of making books and newspapers.

The greatest inventive leap was in the use of electricity, especially in four forms: (1) electric lights — first the arc, then the incandescent — pushed into use by Charles F. Brush and Thomas A. Edison, who took out at Washington more than one thousand patents for various inventions; (2) the telephone, first exhibited by Professor Alexander Graham Bell in 1876; (3) electric trolley cars taking power from a wire, made practicable about 1884; (4) electric motors for fixed machinery and for wheeled vehicles.

Many new safety appliances were adopted in the steam railroad service, especially the air brake, introduced by George

Westinghouse (1868), the automatic coupler, the continuous car platform and vestibule, telegraphic train dispatching, and automatic switches and signals.

The system of "assembling" machines out of parts, each of which is made by the thousand in standard dimensions, wonderfully cheapened many lines of manufacturing; it was applied all the way from watch-making to locomotive building. It led, however, to subdivision and specialization of labor, and tended to diminish the all-round training of mechanics.

332. LABOR AND STRIKES (1865–1885)

The rolling up of capital in big units was paralleled by a combination of labor. The labor organizations began to seek various improvements of their condition which might be gained by action of the state legislatures. They urged

LINOTYPE MACHINE. (Casts a line of type in one piece, from matrices "set" by use of a keyboard and afterwards "distributed" automatically.)

laws making ten hours the normal day's work. They secured from Congress in 1885 a bill preventing the immigration of "contract laborers"; that is, of men and women who came over under an agreement to work for a certain sum from an employer here. They began to demand inspection of factories, and relief from the bad conditions to which women and children were subjected.

Trades unions were active long before the Civil War, and in 1869 the order of Knights of Labor was founded, as a general society open to workmen of all trades; but its power was little felt before 1883. Contests between employers and organizations of workmen in particular trades, led to a series of terrible strikes, the worst of which was the railroad strike of 1877 at Pittsburgh and other places. The railroads were paralyzed, trains and stations were set on fire, and millions of dollars' worth of property destroyed. The state authorities could not stop this

A COAL MINER'S MODEL DWELLING.

disorder, and United States troops were eventually called in, and put it down.

The greatest triumph of labor was the stopping of Chinese immigration (§ 327). The census of 1880 showed 105,000 Chinese in the United States, chiefly on the Pacific coast. There a prejudice arose against them, especially among white laborers. An agitator named Dennis Kearney, "the Sand Lots Orator," headed a movement expressed in the last words of his every speech, "The Chinese must go!" In 1879 Congress passed a bill to restrict the coming of the Chinese. Notwithstanding vetoes by President Hayes and President Arthur the immigration of Chinese laborers was "suspended" for ten years, — a principle to which the Chinese consented by treaty. Similar bills were passed from time to time to make the exclusion practically permanent. The action of Congress prevented the coming of hundreds of thousands of men who would have brought about a race difficulty like the negro question in the South.

333. REVIEW

At the end of the Civil War, the South was practically ruined, while the North was prosperous and rich. The negroes were employed on a new wage system, which took time to develop. The North offered many opportunities for laborers and drew a heavy immigration from abroad, including Chinese on the Pacific coast. The West was built up partly by the ease of acquiring land under the Homestead Act, and partly by the attraction of rich mines. As the frontier pressed upon the Indians, fierce wars broke out with several tribes.

Many railroad lines were consolidated into systems, especially the great through lines from the seaboard to Chicago. The great rivers were bridged and, with the aid of the government, several railroads were constructed to the Pacific coast.

As the country grew richer, banks increased and trust companies and savings banks were founded. Stock companies multiplied, and great corporations controlling whole branches of industry began to appear. Speculation brought on corruption in government and heavy losses in business.

The main causes for prosperity were the inventive genius of the Americans, the introduction of the Bessemer steel process, better systems of mail and telegraphy, and all kinds of inventions for the home and the office, particularly electrical devices. The skilled laborers banded together in organizations, at first in a single trade, then under the Knights of Labor, into a national union. An era of serious strikes came on, beginning with the railroads; and the labor men on the Pacific coast made a determined and successful effort to stop the immigration of Chinese.

References Bearing on the Text and Topics

Geography and Maps. Bogart, *Econ. Hist.*, 357, 490. — Dunning, *Reconstruction*, 142, 224. — Paxson, *New Nation*, 23, 146, 147. — Shepherd, *Hist. Atlas*, 210. — Sparks, *Nat. Development*, 20, 266. — U. S. Tenth Census, *Atlas*.

Secondary. Bassett, *U.S.*, 664–667, 676–691. — Beard, *Contemp. Am. Hist.*, ch. ii. — Bogart, *Econ. Hist.*, chs. xxii, xxiv, xxvii, xxx. — Buck, *Granger Movement.* — Coolidge, *Chinese Immigration.* — Dunning, *Reconstruction*, ch. ix. — Forsyth, *Story of the Soldier*, chs. vi–xvi. —

Haney, *Congressional Hist. of Railroads*, II. chs. vi–xii. — Hebard, *Pathbreakers*, chs. vii–ix. — Hough, *Story of the Cowboy*. — McLaughlin, *My Friend, the Indian*. — O'Neill, *Labor Movement*, ch. v. — Parrish, *Great Plains*, 173–382. — Paxson, *Last Am. Frontier*, chs. ix–xxii; *New Nation*, 20–27, 67–74, 92–97, 119–124, 142–151. — Shinn, *Story of the Mine*. — Warman, *Story of the Railroad*. — Wilson, *Am. People*, V. 115–141, 164–169. — Wright, *Indust. Evolution*, 159–309.

Sources. Bogart and Thompson, *Readings*, 601, 739, 749, 752, 779–781, 811, 815, 842. — Hart, *Contemporaries*, IV. §§ 162, 163; *Source Book*, § 138. — James, *Readings*, §§ 96, 97. — MacDonald, *Select Statutes*, nos. 106, 107, 110. — See also contemporary magazines and newspapers.

Illustrative. Adams, *Log of a Cowboy*. — Anderson, *Heart of the Ancient Firs* (Wash.). — Bindloss, *Cattle-Baron's Daughter*. — Birge, *Awakening of the Desert*. — Brooks, *The Reservation* (Minn.). — Carr, *The Iron Way*. — Churchill, *Coniston*. — Clemens, *Roughing It*. — Garland, *Moccasin Ranch; The Little Norsk* (northwest farming). — Grey, *Riders of the Purple Sage* (Mormons). — Overton, *Heritage of Unrest* (Indians). — White, *The Westerners*. — Wister, *The Virginian*.

Pictures. Bogart, *Econ. Hist.* — *Century*. — Dunbar, *History of Travel in Am.* — *Harper's Weekly*. — *Mentor*, serial nos. 85, 87. — *Scribner's*.

Topics Answerable from the References Above

(1) Admission of Colorado. [§ 328] — (2) Account of *one* of the following territories: Idaho; Montana; Wyoming; Dakota; Arizona. [§ 328] — (3) Powell's voyage down the Colorado River. [§ 328] — (4) Modoc War. [§ 328] — (5) Custer massacre. [§ 328] — (6) On a Pacific railroad crossing the plains; *or* frontier towns. [§ 329] — (7) Chicago fire. [§ 330] — (8) Bessemer steel process. [§ 331] — (9) Development of *one* of the following inventions: sleeping cars; telegraph; firearms; locks and safes; typewriter; typesetting machines; electric lights; telephones; electric trolley cars; train equipments; railroad signals. [§ 331] — (10) Railroad strikes. [§ 332]

Topics for Further Search

(11) Life of a former slaveholder's family after the War. [§ 327] — (12) Use of the Homestead Act. [§ 328] — (13) Industrial career of Cornelius Vanderbilt. [§ 329] — (14) Land grants to Pacific railroads. [§ 329] — (15) Early savings banks; *or* early life insurance. [§ 330] — (16) Early history of the Standard Oil Company. [§ 330] — (17) The Knights of Labor. [§ 332] — (18) Prohibition of Chinese immigration. [§ 332]

CHAPTER XXX

POLITICS AND ADMINISTRATION (1876-1896)

334. ELECTION OF 1876

AN opportunity to measure the great social and commercial advance came in 1876, when the Americans commemorated the hundredth anniversary of the nation by a Centennial Exposition held at Philadelphia. Machines and products of every kind were shown; millions of people had their first opportunity to see spinning, weaving, printing, paper manufacture, and like processes, actually performed before their eyes. Schools and colleges showed their methods and results. Foreign exhibitors brought over their wares, and the whole land was stirred by new ideas.

SAMUEL J. TILDEN, ABOUT 1876.

When the time came to nominate a President in 1876, the Republican convention passed over the most prominent candidate, James G. Blaine, recently Speaker of the House, who was strongly opposed by the friends of President Grant. They finally settled on a compromise candidate, General Rutherford B. Hayes, governor of Ohio. The Democrats nominated Samuel J. Tilden, recent governor of New York, an honest and

519.

conservative man, the ablest in the party. An organization
of the western farmers, under the name of Patrons of Husbandry
— oftener called "Grangers" — which was formed in 1867,
now made itself felt. A third party candidate was nominated
by the "Greenback party," which stood for the views of the
Grangers in favor of more paper money. The thing most
discussed in the
campaign was the
alleged disloyalty
of the South and
its friends after
the war was over.

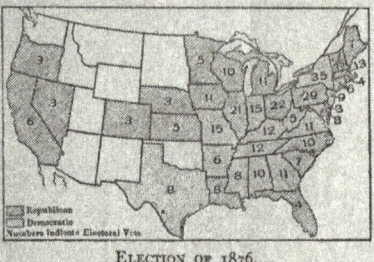

ELECTION OF 1876.

On the morning
after election day
Tilden was cred-
ited with a plural-
ity of 250,000,
and appeared to
have 203 electoral votes to Hayes's 166. The Republicans, who
had a majority in the Senate, at once claimed that the legal
votes in South Carolina, Florida, Louisiana, and Oregon were
for their candidate, and that the Senate was to supervise the
count and decide the contest; the Democratic House insisted
that the two houses must unite in counting the vote. The
question was complicated, because in the three disputed
southern states many Democratic ballots were thrown out by
Republican "returning boards." On the other hand, the Republicans were sure that if the negro voters in the South had
been freely allowed to vote, they would have cast sufficient
votes to carry those states for Hayes.

335. ADMINISTRATION OF PRESIDENT HAYES (1877-1881)

As the inauguration day approached without a settlement
of the dispute, public excitement ran high. After fierce discussion, an act of Congress was passed (January 29, 1877) for

a special Electoral Commission of fifteen members, five each to be chosen by the House, the Senate, and the Supreme Court. It was understood that the choice should fall to seven Republicans, seven Democrats, and one Independent; but instead of the Independent a Republican was chosen. In the deliberations of the commission, every one of the disputed questions was decided for the Republican contention by a majority of eight to seven. The result was that on March 2, Hayes was declared elected by 185 electoral votes to 184.

Before the commission finished its work, Hayes intimated that he did not mean to keep federal troops in the South any longer; and in a few weeks the soldiers were removed and never were sent again. The Democrats continued to hold a majority in the House from 1875 to 1881, and controlled the Senate from 1879 to 1881. They tried to force the Republican President's hand by adding to the army appropriation act a "rider"—that is, a clause not necessary for the purpose of the act—against the use of federal election supervisors, such as was authorized by the anti-Ku-Klux act of 1871 (§ 321). The President won by vetoing seven such bills in succession. Eventually the rules of the House were so changed as to restrict the practice of attaching riders. In 1879, however, an act was passed formally forbidding the use of federal troops at the polls.

From 1878 to 1882 was in general a period of prosperity. The high war tariff stood after most of the other taxes were reduced; and the United States had a surplus nearly every year, and was buying gold to get ready for the resumption of specie payments, which came about almost without incident, January 1, 1879. John Sherman, Secretary of the Treasury, had accumulated $140,000,000 in gold to redeem any greenbacks that might be presented. When the people knew that they could get a hundred cents in gold value for every dollar, they preferred the greenbacks. Inasmuch as the paper notes that were redeemed were reissued in payment of government expenses, the amount of greenbacks issued by the Treasury stood fast at $346,000,000, and still stands at that figure to-day.

336. SILVER COINAGE (1877–1885)

Just as the country was coming back to a specie basis, the question arose, what was specie? Silver sold in London for sixty pence an ounce in gold in 1872, and for only fifty-three pence in 1878; and the silver mine owners of the far West felt sure that the act of 1873 demonetizing silver (§ 323) was causing the fall in the price of their product. The Greenback party (§ 334) cast 1,000,000 votes in the state and congressional elections of 1878; and one of their main demands was that the United States again coin silver dollars. Meanwhile Mr. Bland, a Missouri congressman, introduced a bill which passed over Hayes's veto (February, 1878), providing that the United States should buy and coin "not less than two million dollars' worth [of silver bullion] per month nor more than four million dollars' worth" into silver dollars at the old ratio of 16 to 1. During the next twelve years the mint struck 370 million of these "cart wheel dollars"—called in jest "the dollar of our daddies."

The act, however, did not restore the old right which had existed from 1792 to 1873, of "free coinage" of silver; that is, of exchanging silver bullion at the treasury for its weight in silver dollars (§ 140). Free coinage of gold was continued, and in effect, therefore, gold remained the single standard of money. The silver dollars circulated freely at their face value because everybody thought that somehow the government would make every "dollar" that it issued good at the best value; and in the end their confidence was justified.

337. GARFIELD AND ARTHUR (1881–1885)

In the election of 1880 the Democrats, who had never ceased to call Hayes "the fraud President," hoped to be successful beyond all dispute. They found a soldier candidate in General Winfield S. Hancock, one of the bravest and soundest soldiers of the war. In the Republican convention the leading candidates were Grant and Blaine, but again as in 1876 (§ 334) a compromise candidate was nominated, General James A. Garfield of Ohio, a good soldier and the Republican leader in the House. General Hancock seemed likely to be elected, till he wrote a letter in which he said that the tariff was "a local issue." He carried every southern state — the first instance of the so-called "solid South" — and New Jersey, Nevada, and California. Though about even with Garfield in the popular vote, he received only 155 electoral votes to 214.

President Garfield soon found himself in a quarrel within his own party over the offices; before he was fairly settled in his administration, he was shot by a half-crazed aspirant for office and died some weeks later (September 19, 1881). He was succeeded by the Vice President, Chester A. Arthur of New York.

The difficulties and death of Garfield centered public attention on the system of political removals introduced in Jackson's time (§ 216), by which the subordinate places were distributed by favor, usually as a reward for political service. Men were constantly being removed to make room for new appointees; and it was a regular custom to demand from the government employees a certain proportion of their salaries, for the national party campaign funds. To meet these abuses, Congress passed the Pendleton Civil Service Act (January 16, 1883), under which (1) appointments to certain clerkships and other subordinate places in the government, commonly called "the classified service," were to be made only on competitive examinations; (2) removals for refusal to contribute to a party fund were forbidden; (3) political assessments by a government official or in a government building were prohibited. Arthur began to carry out the act in a small way and it is still the law of the land.

After 1879 money again piled up in the treasury and there was a popular demand, in which Garfield shared during his lifetime, for a reduction of the tariff. The discussion came to a head in 1882 and Congress authorized a commission to report on the tariff — the first case of the kind in our history. They presented a bill which was discussed, revised, and essentially altered by Congress so that the final outcome, the tariff of 1883, reduced duties on some kinds of goods but raised the average rate of duty from about 43 per cent to about 45 per cent. It left unsettled the main issue of whether the Republican party would make high protection a political issue.

338. PUBLIC INTEREST IN LATIN AMERICA (1875–1885)

After the settlement of the *Alabama* claims (§ 324) several serious questions of foreign policy arose in Latin America. President Grant threatened in 1875 to call on the great European powers to unite with us in intervention in Cuba; and under this pressure Spain made peace with the Cubans in 1878. The colonial government was continued, but negro slavery was abolished in Cuba; but as a participant in the rebellion afterward said, "We went to work to save money for another revolution."

The old question of an isthmian canal (§ 233) arose in a new form when in 1878 the government of Colombia granted a "concession" to a French company to construct a canal across the Isthmus of Panama. The leading spirit was Ferdinand de Lesseps, an engineer who had recently constructed the Suez Canal, and who had the confidence of French investors. He designed a tide-level canal through a divide about 300 feet high; and the company at once began to raise money. Vainly did President Hayes try to arouse the people of the United States to a sense of danger at the prospect of a canal to be controlled by Europeans. In a message to Congress (1880) he said that such a canal would be a great ocean thoroughfare between our Atlantic and our Pacific shores, and "virtually a part of the coast line of the United States." Neither Congress nor the people at large took alarm; they were willing to wait and see what the French could accomplish.

From March to December, 1881, James G. Blaine was Secretary of State under Presidents Garfield and Arthur. In those few months he attempted to found an American policy which should bring about three desirable things: leadership among the American states, trade reciprocity with those states, and an isthmian canal under the control of the United States.

(1) Blaine was struck by the losses and confusion caused by the wars among the Latin American powers. War broke out between Peru and Chile in 1879. After an exhausting struggle, when the Peruvians were at the mercy of Chile, Blaine instructed our ministers to Peru and Chile (1881) to use their influence to soften the demands of the conquerors. The ministers went beyond their instructions, and threatened Chile, which paid no heed to their suggestions. The other Latin American states were much disturbed at what they thought a spirit of meddling with their concerns.

(2) Blaine believed that it was for the interest both of the United States and of the countries south of us to build up mutual trade by special "reciprocity treaties," reducing the tariff duties on both sides; but he could not persuade Congress to heed his policy of pushing trade with Latin America.

(3) Blaine was very anxious to make it clear that the Panama Canal was the special concern of the United States; and he tried to get rid of the troublesome Clayton-Bulwer treaty (§ 233). Great Britain simply stood by the treaty and he made no progress. A private company was formed in New York (1884) to build a rival canal by the Nicaragua route, and made some preliminary surveys. The French Panama Canal Company was at work from 1881 to 1889; but after spending $100,000,000 on the canal and $160,000,000 more on salaries, commissions, interest, and nobody knew what else, the company failed (December, 1888) and the work was suspended.

339. CHANGE OF POLITICAL ISSUES (1881–1885)

Hayes's withdrawal of the troops in the South (§ 335) was an admission that the era of force was over. The presidential election of 1884 marks the time when the two national parties

at last gave up the outworn issues of the Civil War and reconstruction, and began to divide on the pressing questions of
revenue, expenditure, currency, trusts, and especially the
protective tariff. The Republican candidate was at last
James G. Blaine (§§ 337, 338), an able man who had many
enemies in his own party. The Democrats put up Grover
Cleveland, who had come to the front by triumphantly carrying
New York in a campaign for the governorship.

The campaign abounded in fierce personalities. Blaine's
enemies secured and published certain "Mulligan Letters,"
which, they considered, showed that he had used his office of
Speaker for the private advantage of himself and his friends.
Cleveland was supported not only by his own party, but also by
the "Mugwumps," or independent Republicans, who expected
him to stand for purer politics.

Without the vote of New York, Cleveland could not be elected,
but in that state he had a plurality of 1149, in a total vote of
1,167,000. This with Indiana, New Jersey, Connecticut, and the
"solid South" gave 219 electoral votes against 182 for Blaine.

As Cleveland was the first Democratic President since Buchanan, his election seemed to his opponents a revolution, and
it was freely predicted that he would pay off the Confederate
debt or even reduce the negroes again to slavery. He was a
resolute President who vetoed 301 bills, and followed Grant in
defeating many private bills; but the Republicans held a
majority in the Senate, and the President could do little to
secure legislation to carry out the purposes of his party.

340. Cleveland's First Administration (1885–1889)

As President, Cleveland showed a rugged will and a strong
sense of public duty. Great pressure was put on him to remove
the Republicans who held public office. He poured out his
wrath upon those who were guilty of "offensive partisanship" —
that is, who used their offices in behalf of their party — and he
removed many of them; but he stood by Arthur's "classified

list" (§ 337) and added many others to this category of public officers, who under the Pendleton Law were appointed on competitive examination.

Cleveland was much concerned by the extravagance of Congress, which voted large sums for public buildings, river and harbor improvements, and pension bills. This last outgo was partly in consequence of promises made to the soldiers during the Civil War — that they

GROVER CLEVELAND, ABOUT 1890.

and their families should not suffer want because of their service. Pensions were liberally voted to the widows and minor children of soldiers killed, and to the living veterans suffering from permanent wounds or disability contracted in the service, if they needed help. In addition Congress passed hundreds of bills, some of them over the President's veto, granting pensions to men and women who were not entitled to them under the general law; in 1889 the pensioners numbered 490,000 and drew $89,000,000 a year. A Dependent Pension Bill passed both houses (January 31, 1887), granting a pension to every survivor of those who had served in the war, if not able to support himself by physical labor. Cleveland vetoed it on the ground that there was no public need for pensioning men who had means or could be supported by their children.

The lavishness of Congress was caused partly by the surplus of revenue over current expenses. Of course there was an immense unpaid debt, to which the surplus might go, but it was not easy to call in bonds before they were due. A further reason for the surplus was the heavy proceeds of the high tariff of 1883 (§ 337). If the tariff were reduced, the surplus would disappear. President Cleveland set the political issue for the campaign of 1888 in his annual message of 1887, in which he discussed only the tariff: "It is a condition which confronts us — not a theory," said he. The "condition" was the annual surplus which, in 1887, reached $56,000,000.

341. HARRISON AND THE TARIFF (1888–1890)

The Republicans accepted this challenge and for the presidential election of 1888 nominated Benjamin Harrison, who had been senator from Indiana. For the first time the Republicans in their platform declared that high protection was a party principle. The Democratic convention unanimously renominated Cleveland. By a plurality of 13,002 votes in New York, Harrison carried that state, and thus secured 233 electoral votes to 168, and was elected; though the Cleveland men cast about 100,000 more popular votes than the supporters of Harrison, in the whole country.

The first Congress under Harrison had a Republican majority in both houses, and began in 1890 to vote money still more freely than before for public buildings in small cities, for money subsidies in aid of American ships, and for dependent pensions. The outgo for pensions jumped up to an average of $140,000,000 a year. A new navy was already begun, and in 1893 the country possessed a "white squadron" of steel armed cruisers.

In accordance with the Republican platform of 1888, a new tariff was drawn up by the Committee of Ways and Means, of which William McKinley was chairman; and the bill took its name from him. The Republicans argued the necessity of protecting American manufacturers and laborers from foreign competition, and of reserving "the home market" for American producers; the Democrats contended that the tariff kept up the prices to the consumer of protected products, was class legislation, and brought in an unnecessary and dangerous surplus. The tariff of 1883 on dutiable goods averaged about 45 per cent; the McKinley tariff (October 1, 1890) raised it to about 49 per cent; but the non-dutiable "free list" was larger in the McKinley bill than in the previous tariff.

342. BLAINE'S FOREIGN POLICY (1889-1892)

Harrison was not a leader. The strong man in his administration was James G. Blaine (§ 339), who again became Secretary of State. Blaine was born in Pennsylvania in 1830, settled in Maine, went to Congress in 1863, was Speaker from 1869 to 1875, and then senator from Maine. He was always a strong partisan, believed in his own side, and hated and attacked his political opponents. He was an effective debater, but made many enemies by saying bitter things — as when he called Senator Conkling of New York "a turkey cock." Blaine has often been compared with Henry Clay, whom he much resembled in his strong assertion of the rights of America, his power of making personal friends, and his long and unsuccessful ambition to be President; but he was too quick and aggressive to be a good diplomat. Blaine resigned in 1892, and died not long after, a disappointed man.

In 1890 he took the lead in a Pan-American Congress at Washington, which recommended a Pan-American bank, a Pan-American railroad, and commercial reciprocity treaties. Blaine agreed with our Latin American neighbors, but the Senate would not back him. The difficulty of keeping on good terms with these neighbors was shown by a dispute with Chile in 1891. Some of the men of the United States ship *Baltimore* were attacked on the streets of Valparaiso and one was killed. As a suitable apology was not made, President Harrison sent a message to Congress suggesting war; but on the same day the long-delayed apology came, and hostilities were avoided.

Blaine was involved in another dispute which required several years to settle. The United States had for some years claimed the right to seize Canadian vessels which took seals in the open

sea near Alaska. Blaine insisted that the Bering Sea belonged
to the United States as a part of the Alaska purchase (§ 319).
In 1893 the controversy was settled by a board of arbitration
in Paris, which decided against the United States.

343. FREE SILVER AND THE TARIFF (1890–1894)

Frequent debates on the trusts, railroads, and banks and on the
tariff brought out the fact that the South and West felt — with

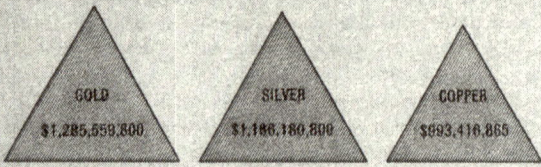

COMPARATIVE VALUE OF THE GOLD, SILVER, AND COPPER MINED IN THE
UNITED STATES FROM 1870 TO 1900.

some reason — that they received less than their share of the results of the nation's prosperity. Hence the formation (1887) of a
political Farmers' Alliance, which carried the stanch Republican
states of Kansas and Nebraska; and a National People's party
was soon formed (May, 1891). The silver-producing states —
Colorado, Montana, Wyoming, Idaho, and Nevada — joined
the movement, because the price of their product went down
from 89 cents in gold, for the weight of a standard silver dollar
in 1878, to 73 cents in 1889, and 67 cents in 1892.

The combination showed its strength in 1890 by introducing
a bill for the free coinage of silver at the ratio of 16 to 1; this
would have enabled owners of silver bullion to turn it into legal
tender silver dollars. To head off this bill, Congress passed
the Sherman Silver Act (July 14, 1890), which provided that the
Secretary of the Treasury should buy 4,500,000 ounces of silver
bullion each month at the market price, paying for it in a new
kind of paper notes. Thus a market was given to the silver
producers, and the currency was increased to satisfy the West
and South.

Under the Mc-
Kinley tariff the
prices of silk,
woolen, and cot-
ton goods of every
kind suddenly
rose, and thus
brought its effect
home to thou-
sands of buyers.
Hence the Demo-
crats went hope-

ELECTION OF 1892.

fully into the campaign of 1892, on the tariff issue, and again
nominated Cleveland, who won a sweeping victory. He had
277 electoral votes to 145 for Harrison and 22 for a People's
party candidate; his popular plurality was 380,000 and his
party elected a majority in both the House and the Senate
which would sit in 1893-1895. This was the first Congress
since 1859 that was Democratic in both houses.

When Cleveland was a second time inaugurated (March 4,
1893) a severe commercial crisis was impending. A general
crash was prevented only by the banks standing by one another.
As always happens in hard times, the tariff revenues fell off;
the expenses of the government increased, and the gold in the
treasury ran down till it looked as if the holders of greenbacks
would make a run on the treasury by demanding redemption
in gold. Congress reluctantly listened to President Cleveland,
and (November 1, 1893) stopped the silver purchases under the
Sherman Act. It took several years to return to prosperity.

The Democrats kept their campaign promise of making a new
tariff, which was framed in 1894 by William L. Wilson, chairman of the Ways and Means Committee. The Senate added
so many protective duties that the President would not sign the
bill, but let it become an act without his signature. The act
included an income tax which of course bore hardest on the

wealthy eastern and middle states. On a test case, the Supreme Court decided (May, 1895) that the tax as levied was
unconstitutional because it was a direct tax not distributed in
proportion to the population of the states (see Constitution,
Article I, Section 2, Clause 3). A revenue of about $40,000,000
a year was thus cut off. The customs dropped so that there
was a deficit amounting to $70,000,000, and for several years
similar deficits followed. The public debt slowly increased,
and the government was for a time in financial straits.

344. END OF CLEVELAND'S ADMINISTRATION (1895-1897)

The Democratic party was badly split by the controversy over
free silver (§ 343), and when President Cleveland insisted on
stopping the silver purchases, a considerable part of the western
and southern Democrats accused him of being a "gold bug."
Some of the Democrats, especially in Pennsylvania and a few
states of the South, were in favor of protection. During the
last two years of his administration, therefore, Cleveland was
no longer recognized as the great Democratic leader.

He showed his characteristic toughness of fiber by taking up
a long-standing boundary controversy between Venezuela and
the British colony of Guiana. His Secretary of State, Richard
Olney, served notice upon Great Britain that the refusal of
that country to arbitrate on this question was an attempt to
control part of an American state, and hence contrary to the
Monroe Doctrine. "To-day the United States," said Olney,
"is practically sovereign on this continent, and its fiat is law
upon the subjects to which it confines its interposition." The
President made this correspondence public in an unexpected
message (December, 1895) and threatened war if Great Britain
did not yield. The British government was taken aback by
this sudden interest in a dispute which seemed far removed from
any danger to the United States; but on reflection it yielded and
accepted arbitration. The arbitrators decided (1899) that
Great Britain was entitled to most of the territory in dispute.

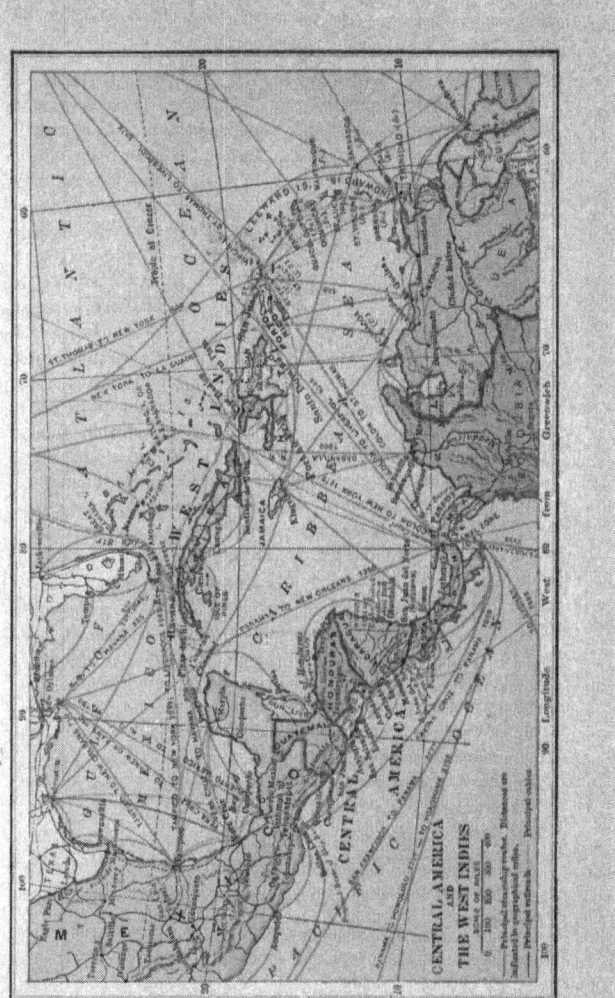

CENTRAL AMERICA
AND
THE WEST INDIES

533

Meantime the election of 1896 drew near. The Democrats were sharply divided on the silver question. Their regular

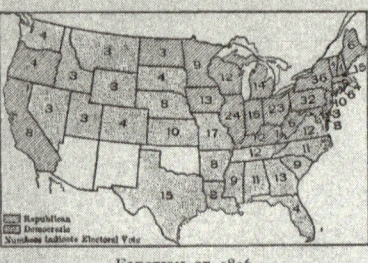

ELECTION OF 1896.

convention (July, 1896) declared for the free coinage of silver at the ratio of 16 to 1 (§ 336), and nominated William J. Bryan of Nebraska, who came suddenly to the front in the convention as a remarkable speaker and leader. The People's party (§ 343), which included many former Republicans, also supported Bryan for President on a separate ticket. A fraction of the Democratic party organized as "Sound Money Democrats" and made an opposing nomination. In the Republican nominating convention, William McKinley of Ohio was the logical candidate because of his attractive personality and his service as a champion of protection. The platform declared against the free coinage of silver unless the principal nations of the world would agree to it.

In the campaign of 1896 the principal issue was free coinage, for the low prices of silver, wheat, and cotton had kept the West and South poor. But wheat suddenly rose in price and some of the western farming states went over to McKinley, together with four southern states. He was elected by a plurality vote of 600,000 and 271 electoral votes to 176. So far as could be judged from this election, a considerable majority of the voters wished high protection and were against free coinage of silver.

345. REVIEW

The Republicans nearly lost their hold on the national government in the election of 1876. Disputed returns were settled

by a special electoral commission and the Republican candidate
was declared elected by 185 electoral votes to 184. Hayes
had a long fight with Congress over conditions in the South.
In 1878 the mine owners and other "friends of silver" forced
Congress to resume the coinage of silver, though gold remained
the standard.

General Garfield was elected President over Hancock in 1880
but was assassinated in 1881. Under his successor, Arthur,
Congress passed an act for improving the Civil Service, and the
tariff of 1882 was passed.

Secretary Blaine tried to make the United States the leader
among the Latin American powers and to secure control of the
Isthmian Canal.

In 1884, Grover Cleveland was elected President, the first
Democrat since 1861. He stood by the reform of the Civil
Service, and opposed enlarging the expenditures for pensions
and other drafts on the treasury. He made an issue of the tariff,
and on that issue was narrowly defeated in the election of 1888
by Harrison. The Republicans then passed the more highly
protective McKinley tariff of 1890. Blaine again became Secretary of State and, without much effect, urged friendship and
an understanding with the Latin American states. The steady
fall of silver caused a continuation of the silver agitation; and
by the Sherman Act of 1890 Congress ordered the buying of
more silver for coinage by the government.

Cleveland was reëlected President in 1892, and the commercial
panic of 1893 compelled the stopping of the silver purchases.
In 1894 a moderately protective tariff was passed by the Democrats. In his second term, Cleveland quarreled with Great
Britain over a question of Venezuelan boundary. William J
Bryan, a free silverite, was the Democratic candidate in 1896,
and was defeated by William McKinley of Ohio.

References Bearing on the Text and Topics

Geography and Maps. See maps, pp. 520, 531, 534, 566. Bogart,
Econ. Hist., 395. — Coman, *Indust. Hist.*, 338. — Dewey, *Nat. Prob-*

lems. — Dunning, *Reconstruction*, 310. — Paxson, *New Nation*, 76, 77, 186, 227.

Secondary. Bassett, *U.S.*, 652–817 passim. — Beard, *Contemp. Am. Hist.*, chs. iv–vii. — Burton, *John Sherman*, chs. xii–xvi. — Carpenter, *America in Hawaii*, chs. xi–xv. — Dewey, *Finan. Hist.*, §§ 159–161, 171–196; *Nat. Problems*, chs. ii, iv, v, vii–xi, xiii–xvii. — Dunning, *Reconstruction*, chs. xix–xxi. — Fish, *Am. Diplomacy*, chs. xxvi–xxviii. — Hart, *Monroe Doctrine*, 169–206. — Haworth, *Disputed Election; Reconstruction and Union*, 72–174. — Johnson, *Panama Canal*, chs. vi, vii. — McCall, *T. B. Reed*, chs. vi–xix. — Paxson, *New Nation*, 80–256 passim. — Rhodes, *U.S.*, VII. 194–291. — Sparks, *Nat. Development*, chs. vi–xix. — Stanwood, *Am. Tariff Controversies*, II. 192–304; *J. G. Blaine*, chs. vii–xii; *Presidency*, I. chs. xxv–xxxi. — Taussig, *Tariff Hist.*, 230–409. — Williams, *R. B. Hayes*, I. chs. xxiv–xxvi, II. chs. xxvii–xxxviii. — Wilson, *Am. People*, V. 104–204. — Woodburn, *Polit. Parties*, chs. viii, xviii, xix.

Sources. *Am. Hist. Leaflets*, nos. 6, 34. — *Appletons' Annual Cyclopædia*, 1876 to 1897. — Beard, *Readings*, §§ 42–44, 83–87. — Bogart and Thompson, *Readings*, 711–763. — Hart, *Contemporaries*, IV. §§ 158–173; *Source Book*, §§ 133–140. — MacDonald, *Select Statutes*, nos. 96–98, 100–105, 108, 109, 111–113, 121–123, 125, 126.

Illustrative. Anon., *Democracy*. — Atherton, *Senator North*. — Burnett, *Through One Administration*. — Ford, *Honorable Peter Stirling*.

Topics Answerable from the References Above

(1) Public services of *one* of the following: Blaine; Hayes; Tilden; Arthur; Cleveland; Harrison; Sherman. [§ 334] — (2) Election of 1876 [§ 334], *or* of 1880 [§ 337], *or* of 1884. [§ 339] — (3) Debates on the Pendleton Civil Service Act of 1883, *or* the tariff of 1883 [§ 337], *or* the Tariff of 1890. [§ 341] — (4) First Cuban War. [§ 338] — (5) Vetoes by President Cleveland. [§ 340] — (6) Pan-American Congress of 1890. [§ 342] — (7) National People's party. [§ 343] — (8) Debates on the Sherman Silver Act, *or* the tariff of 1894. [§ 343] — (9) Public services of *one* of the following statesmen: Olney; Bryan; McKinley. [§ 344]

Topics for Further Search

(10) Effects of the Centennial Exposition. [§ 334] — (11) Patrons of Husbandry. [§ 334] — (12) Electoral commission of 1877. [§ 335] — (13) What was meant by free coinage? [§ 336] — (14) System of military pensions. [§ 340] — (15) Claim to part of Bering Sea. [§ 342] — (16) Controversy over Venezuela. [§ 344]

CHAPTER XXXI

REGULATION OF BUSINESS (1885–1895)

346. POPULATION IN 1890

By the year 1885, the economic effects of the Civil War had almost disappeared. The South (as will be shown in a later chapter) was more prosperous than ever before, and an immense new area had been opened up beyond the Mississippi. The population of the country, as shown by the census of 1890, had increased in a hundred years from 3,900,000 to 62,600,000, which showed that the population had almost precisely doubled in every period of twenty-five years. Both the older and the newer parts of the country shared in this remarkable growth. New England and the middle states had 17,500,000 people, the South had 22,300,000, and the great block of states from Ohio to Kansas had 19,600,000. Of the total about 7,000,000 were negroes, mostly living in the southern states; and 10,000,000 were immigrants, most of whom were in the northern states. More than one fourth of all the people, especially in the northern states, lived in cities and towns.

This rapid growth of population could hardly be paralleled in the history of the world. It was possible for two reasons. The first was the natural increase of families in regions where there was so much wild land and so much demand for labor. The other was the foreign immigration, which sprang up again on a large scale before the Civil War was fairly over. From 1861 to 1870, 2,300,000 immigrants arrived; from 1871 to 1880, 2,800,000; from 1881 to 1890, 5,200,000. (See page 362.) They helped to make up the rapid growth of the whole population.

As in the earlier period of immigration, the newcomers helped to build up the cities. The Irish and Germans and their descendants formed a large fraction of the populations of the coast cities of Boston, New York, Philadelphia, and Baltimore; and were almost as numerous in proportion in the interior cities that were now growing up, such as the five Lake cities of Buffalo, Cleveland, Detroit, Milwaukee, and Chicago, and the seven large northern river cities, St. Paul and Minneapolis, St. Louis, Cincinnati, Louisville, Kansas City, and Pittsburgh. The one large southern city was New Orleans. On the Pacific coast, San Francisco was still the only considerable city, but the beginnings of great ports appeared at various points along the Pacific coast; and Salt Lake City and Denver grew up in the interior.

347. AMERICAN CITIES (1865-1895)

Throughout the Union, villages were expanding into towns; towns into cities; small cities into great cities. The building

"THE POINT," PITTSBURGH.

and the government of these new centers of population were outside the previous experience of Americans born in this country, and the greater part of the immigrants had been tillers of the soil in their own country, and could contribute little to the problems of city government, while they added very much to the difficulties of taking care of the population.

All the cities were perplexed by the presence of masses of people who were not born within their limits, nor even within the state in which the city was situated. A constant stream poured from the farming districts into the cities, furnishing thousands of capable citizens, but it took them a long time to learn how to care for the welfare of their communities.

Few of the cities foresaw their own growth, and nearly all were badly planned. The example of Philadelphia in laying out the streets in a gridiron of squares with few or no diagonal thoroughfares was followed in most of the new places, such as Buffalo, Chicago, and St. Louis. Even in San Francisco, with its hilly site, the streets were laid out on the same inconvenient plan. The railroads were allowed to enter the cities on the same grade as the streets, and in many cases ran right through the middle of the thoroughfares; as their business grew, they greatly interfered with the city traffic.

The stone pavements were ragged and uneven, and many of the western cities laid down pavements of wooden blocks, which rapidly wore out. Most of the cities were dirty and slovenly, and no city till about 1890 was regularly and systematically cleaned. Few were provided with sufficient sewers and an abundant water supply. In the rich city of Philadelphia, many houses still turned their waste into

A DOUBLE-DECK HORSE CAR, ABOUT 1875.

the city by surface drainage. Horse cars had long been running in many cities and the lines were extended to carry people into the suburbs. The growth of the cities led to rapid changes in the centers of business, so that old wholesale streets were abandoned, and old residential quarters were invaded by business buildings. Most cities were proud of fine residence streets such as Euclid Avenue in Cleveland and Michigan Avenue in Chicago, with their handsome houses and broad and beautiful grounds; but the coal smoke brought dirt and grime even in the best quarters.

The city governments never caught up with their immense tasks. From 1868 to 1871 a terrible object lesson was given to the whole country as to what might happen in the richest cities whenever a set of thieves managed to get hold of the machinery of the city government. A gang arose in New York known as the "Tweed Ring," headed by "Boss Tweed," a bad character who began life as a fighting fireman and managed to worm himself into the government of the county and city of New York. They systematically plundered that great city out of about $100,000,000. These official criminals controlled and falsified the count of the votes,

WAITING FOR THE STORM TO BLOW OVER. (Cartoon by Thomas Nast. The largest vulture represents Boss Tweed.)

so that it seemed impossible to turn them out of office. Two of the newspapers of the time fought the bandits, notwithstanding big offers if they would hold their peace. George Jones, proprietor of the *New York Times*, belabored them in his paper, and Thomas Nast, one of the first cartoonists in the country, from week to week pictured the thieves in *Harper's Weekly*. Samuel J. Tilden, a democratic leader in the city and state (later candidate for President, § 334), took the field against them, organized a political movement, and by a desperate effort the property owners and voters in New York recovered control of their own city. The ring was broken up, the conspirators scattered, and Tweed was sent to prison.

Other cities, especially Philadelphia, suffered from similar organized plundering. The trouble was that the city governments were not efficient for their purpose. The mayors were, by this time, nearly all elected by popular vote and there were regular police departments, fire departments, and school departments; but there were too many officials over whom the mayor had no control, the city councils were badly organized, most of them in two parts which quarreled with each other. There was not a single city in the land that had a city government strong and wise enough to take charge of the activities that were rapidly increasing. They allowed mean slums to grow up. They fell behind on their schools. They all ran into debt.

348. CORPORATIONS AND TRUSTS

The defects in city government, and also the defects in state, county, and village government, were the more amazing because American business men showed such remarkable skill in organizing great business concerns. They found no danger in putting the control of great private enterprises into the hands of men who showed the greatest ability and skill. Yet in their governments they made little effort to reap the benefits of doing things on a big scale by strong men. The most striking feature of this time was the growth of corporations and the development of the very large and powerful corporations which came to be called trusts.

This system of corporations, which grew steadily from the time of the first United States Bank (§ 141), proved to be well suited for the conditions of the immense business which was developing in the United States. With the exception of national banks, corporations which carried on business in the District of Columbia, and some of the Pacific railroads, Congress chartered none of these companies. As early as 1820 some of the states provided a system of general laws, under which those who wished to form a company could do so without going to the legislature for a special charter.

Business corporations of all kinds enjoyed several valuable privileges: (1) They had the right to hold property and use it for their purposes, like individuals and firms. This included the important right to carry on business in other states than that in which they were chartered. (2) They could sue and be sued just as if they were persons. (3) The stockholders were not liable for the debts of the corporation, except to the amount of their own holdings in the corporation, and in some states, a fixed proportion beyond that. (4) Corporations could be stockholders and managers in other corporations, and that made it easy to roll up great businesses and large capital. (5) Under an early decision of the United States Supreme Court, the charter of a company was considered a "contract," which could not be repealed or otherwise impaired by the state which had granted it (Constitution, Article 1, Section 10, Clause 1). To meet that difficulty many of the states passed laws providing that charters thereafter granted should contain a clause making them subject to repeal. In addition any charters could be taken away by the courts, if it could be shown that they were misused by the companies that held them; but that was a difficult and expensive process. The great advantages of corporations have been discussed elsewhere (§§ 141, 248, 330). They enabled the small investor to place his money under guidance of able business men; they could do business freely all over the Union; they relieved the stockholder from the risk of losing his all.

Till after the Civil War, the state and national governments paid little attention to the corporations, except the railroads. These companies were very powerful in some communities.

As an example, humorists used to call New Jersey "the State
of Camden and Amboy," referring to a railroad that crossed
the state. In the sixties, the states began to set up railroad
commissions — executive bodies which made rules for the
operation of the roads, and in some cases fixed the rates; and
about that time the country woke up to the fact that some other
corporations were becoming so powerful that they threatened
to override the rest of the community. (1) A corporation might
be so rich and powerful that it simply ignored the laws intended
to regulate it. (2) The corporation, though acting within
the law, might acquire a monopoly of some line of business,
and thus extinguish competition. (3) One corporation might
own another corporation, and mix up the accounts of the concerns, often to the disadvantage of the small owners of stocks,
as in the case of certain steamship companies. (4) To float
new enterprises, great bankers and capitalists sometimes formed
"syndicates" with secret and complicated interests and obligations. (5) Occasionally several corporations, instead of combining, made an agreement that the stock of all the corporations
should be held and voted "in trust" by a body of trustees.
Only in the last case should the term "trust," strictly speaking, be applied; but the name was loosely used for any
large corporation or combination of corporations which tried
to control a large line of business. A very common form of
"trust" was a company or group of companies which controlled some public service, such as water, gas, or traction.
Such a group of men might hold a city or state at its mercy.

349. PUBLIC CONTROL OF RAILROADS

The great corporations most in the public eye down to 1885
were still the railroad companies. Railway kings like William
H. Vanderbilt of the New York Central, Jay Gould of the Erie,
Edgar Thomson of the Pennsylvania, and C. P. Huntington
of the Southern Pacific, performed a public service by consoli-
dating small roads into systems thousands of miles in extent,

especially eight or nine "trunk lines" from Chicago to New
York, and the Southern Pacific transcontinental routes. The
only public control regulating the railroads was that of the
state governments, which passed acts on the speed of trains,
frequency of stops, and other working details, and also tried
to reduce rates for passengers and freight. The states, however, had no legal control over traffic passing from one state to
another, for "interstate commerce" was, by the text of the Constitution, subject only to the control of the federal government.

By ancient principles of the common law of England, which
were applied in most states, a "common carrier" is obliged
to accept on equal terms any passengers and freight that offer.
This is only fair, inasmuch as the railroads have many valuable
privileges, such as the right to condemn and purchase private
property necessary for their roadbed. Nevertheless, the railroads, especially the big ones, looked upon their service as a
private business which they could control as they liked. Hence
they fell into the habit of making discriminations between shippers: (1) They gave special — often secret — rates to large
shippers and favored friends. (2) They charged higher freights
for a shorter distance — say from Chicago to Pittsburgh —
than for a longer distance on the same route — say from Chicago to New York. (3) They formed "pools" or agreements

JETTIES AT THE MOUTH OF THE MISSISSIPPI RIVER.

by which all the freight offered was arbitrarily divided among competing roads.

One reason why the federal government for many years let the railroads alone was that it was putting its energy and money on waterways. Every year or two after 1870 a river and harbor bill passed Congress, containing appropriations for sea and lake harbors and for improving rivers, many of which were of small account. Congress spent large sums on the Mississippi River and Great Lakes. In 1879 Captain Eads built a system of jetties at the mouth of the Mississippi, which made New Orleans a deep-sea harbor. For the enormous Lake trade in iron ore, coal, grain, and lumber, the government built

LOCKS OF THE "SOO" (SAULT STE. MARIE) CANAL, COMPLETED IN 1896.

ship canals between Lake Superior and Lake Huron, around the falls of Sault Ste. Marie, and through St. Clair Lake and the Detroit River.

350. REGULATION OF RAILROADS BY CONGRESS (1887–1890)

Eventually public sentiment, headed by Senator Cullom of Illinois, forced Congress to pass the "Interstate Commerce Act" (February 4, 1887) regulating commerce between the

states, on the following principles: (1) Railroads operating in
more than one state were forbidden to make a higher charge to
one customer than to another for the same service. (2) They
were forbidden to form "pools." (3) All freight rates were
to be publicly posted and could be neither raised nor lowered
without notice. (4) Unreasonable rates could be reviewed by
the commission. (5) By the "short haul clause," no railroad
could charge more for carrying freight a shorter distance than
it charged for carrying freight over the same line to a greater
distance. (6) The roads were obliged to make sworn reports
of their business to the government.

How should these new and drastic regulations be carried out?
Other acts of Congress, such as the land laws, were put into
action by officials whose duties and powers were clearly set
forth by statute. The ordinary criminal laws were made
effective by suits brought before the courts. Here was a new
problem, for it was absolutely necessary to provide a body of
men expert in railroad affairs, to decide what was, and what was
not, reasonable in railroad business. At the same time it was
necessary to create something like a court, which could hear
complaints and make decisions, such as the regular courts had
been making.

Congress solved this new problem by creating a new kind of
agency for the federal government, following the example of
some of the state railroad commissions. It created the Interstate Commerce Commission of five members. This powerful
body, which was to control the railroads for the government,
was not attached to any of the great departments such as that
of Justice, or of the Interior. It was responsible only to Congress. On the other hand, though the commissioners could
hold court and examine witnesses and make legal decisions,
they were subject to appeals to the regular United States
courts on many points.

Hence the Interstate Commerce Commission was obliged
to go slowly and ask Congress for amendments to the Inter-

state Commerce Law from time to time. Congress gradually increased the powers of the commission, limited the right of appeal to the ordinary courts, and passed several additional statutes on railroad business. For instance, by the so-called "Original Package Law" (1890) Congress made it possible to prevent the carrying of liquor into states which prohibited the sale of it. By the statute of 1893, the railroads were compelled to adopt and use a uniform car coupler, so as to eliminate the numerous accidents from the old method. The very important act of 1895 forbade the carrying of mail or express matter by the United States Post Office or by express companies if intended for lotteries or gift concerns. Congress also (1899) made a settlement with those Pacific roads (§ 329) which had received money aid from the government. In 1899 they owed $64,000,000 on original bonds and $72,000,000 of interest paid by the United States. Rather reluctantly, the roads finally repaid nearly the whole of this great sum to the government.

351. REGULATION OF TRUSTS BY CONGRESS (1890)

The success of the Interstate Commerce Act led Congress to try its hand at regulating large corporations, for up to this time the only way of dealing with corporations was by state laws. Many such laws proved successful for business carried on wholly within the limits of one state. Public commissions were set up to regulate gas, electric light, and water companies and to control street car companies and other so-called "public utilities" which were serving great numbers of persons. Commissions or commissioners were also appointed to regulate insurance, banking, and other sorts of private business. In many cases, the price for lights and for carrying passengers by city transit systems was fixed by law. Even railroad passenger fares were established in many states at so many cents a mile.

Popular feeling was such that Congress, by the so-called "Sherman Antitrust Law" (July 2, 1890) extended some of the principles of the Interstate Commerce Act to all corporations which carried on a business from state to state or from the United States to a foreign country. The act provided that any attempt by such corporations to "monopolize" any line of business should be punishable by both criminal and civil suits. This applied to manufacturing and trading companies and also to railroads; and the law made no distinction between cases where such combinations "in restraint of trade" were hurtful to the public, and those cases where the merger of business concerns and the joint action of corporations were an advantage to the community. "Good corporations" and "bad corporations" were both forbidden to combine so as to secure a monopoly.

One method of bringing corporations to book was to compel them by law to keep their accounts on a uniform system. Another way was by taxes, which required them to pay for their privileges and also to reveal the amount and profit of their business. In New York, as in other states also, many of the traction companies received from the cities without payment, the immensely valuable privilege of using the streets, and then issued bonds on the money value of that privilege. The state government in 1899, under Governor Roosevelt, taxed the traction companies on the capitalized value of this privilege which they had received from the public. Some cities even attempted to take over the traction lines and make them a public service. Municipal subways built by the cities of Boston (beginning in 1898) and New York (beginning in 1904) were owned by the cities, but were leased to private companies to operate.

These measures checked and guarded some of the corporations which had become dangerously powerful, but had no effect upon that part of the business of corporations which passed from one state to another. Business men, firms, and small corporations were being driven out of business. In some cases, prices were cut down in a particular state or city till the small competitors were killed out and then the big corporation had a monopoly.

352. REGULATION OF LABOR (1880–1895)

The laborers, especially those employed in manufacturing and transportation, felt the pressure of these great organizations and did their best to meet it by powerful organizations of their own. For many years they had been managing large unions made up of all the men that would join out of a particular trade. Most of them paid sick benefits and burial expenses, but their main purpose was to improve the conditions of work hours and wages. The most successful of these unions was the Brotherhood of Locomotive Engineers, which readily secured favorable conditions of work and pay, with very few strikes. The idea of one general controlling union was still alive. The Knights of Labor (§ 332) could not hold their ground in that direction, but in 1886 the American Federation of Labor was formed to unite so far as possible the special trades unions into a national body, which should have authority to order men in one trade to strike in order to help strikers in another trade. The Federation through strikes pressed the issue whether employers would "recognize the union" — that is, would make agreements with their employees only through officers of the union — and would establish the "closed shop" — that is, would employ only union hands.

From this time the labor unions became an important factor in business. They accumulated funds for strike benefits and other purposes, by laying high initiation fees and dues on members. They issued "union cards" to members in good standing, without which, in some trades, no one could get a job. They made every effort to raise the wages of laborers employed by the various governments so as to create a high standard of earnings for private employment. They avoided politics, for they saw that they were not numerous enough to make a successful national party of their own and therefore remained divided between the main parties.

The laws had long since ceased to hold strikes to be a breach of the peace. Nobody was liable to be punished for refusing to do the work which he had agreed to do, except soldiers and sailors; and if two men, or any larger number of men, united in a strike — that is, in refusing to work — they were not committing any offense. If, however, such men attempted to compel others to strike by threats or violence, they could be dealt with by the law, and some courts even punished men and women for "picketing"; that is, for standing near the entrance of factories trying to persuade the hands to give up their jobs.

Another labor method was the "boycott," which was an agreement not to buy goods from the concerns against which there was a strike. In some street car strikes, people were beaten or killed because they patronized the cars which were run by non-union employees. The courts at that time almost always held that the boycott was not legal, although they did not deal so severely with the "black list," which was an agreement between employers not to give work to individuals who they thought were having a bad influence on their hands.

The labor men were successful in putting several kinds of work on the footing of state regulated industries. Examination boards were created for such trades as plumbing, running stationary engines, and barbering, and nobody could obtain work who was not certified by those examiners. The states also began to legislate for the welfare of laborers by reducing the legal hours of labor and passing acts to compel employers to make dangerous machinery safe.

In some trades the result was a kind of war between the employers and the employed, each striving to build up a powerful organization, with plenty of reserve money to use to support strikes or lockouts. Some manufacturers joined in a sort of union to protect themselves. The factory of the president of that union was put on the "unfair list" by the American Federation of Labor. The natural tendency of the unions was to raise wages and to compel the payment of wages in cash instead of in "store pay"; that is, goods from stocks carried for that purpose by the companies.

353. ERA OF STRIKES

A test of the power of the new labor unions was a series of great strikes. The first came in 1886 on the Gould system of

POST OFFICE, CHICAGO.

railroads leading southwest from St. Louis. In 1892, in a fearful strike at the Homestead Iron Works near Pittsburgh, a body of private guards, furnished by a detective agency and sworn in as constables, were fired upon by the strikers, several of them were killed, and wounded men were put to death by infuriated men and women. There were many strikes during 1893 and 1894, of which the worst began in a strike at the Pullman Car Works near Chicago. The American Railway Union, through their president, Eugene V. Debs, took up the dispute, and demanded that the company settle it with them, as representing organized labor. When the company refused, Debs called out the railroad men on a "sympathetic strike." On one road after another they refused to handle, first Pullman cars, then the cars of the "tied-up roads," till the whole railway business of Chicago, and indeed of the whole great country west of Chicago, was in confusion. Nonunion men (called "scabs" by the strikers) who were employed by the railroads were beaten, and some of them killed. The unions disclaimed responsibility for these acts of violence.

All these great strikes at last broke down. As the government of Illinois did not keep order, President Cleveland made use of the only organized force adequate for such cases by calling out United States troops to prevent the obstruction of United States mails and of interstate commerce (July 8, 1894). This broke the strike, and the Pullman Company then came to an understanding with its employees. A federal court served an injunction on Debs, forbidding him to interfere with interstate commerce. As he ignored this injunction, Debs was imprisoned for contempt of court, and the Supreme Court of the United States held the sentence good.

354. REGULATION OF IMMIGRATION

A large part of the wage earners by this time were immigrants or their children, for the number of immigrants was greatly increasing (§ 346). In the single year 1882 it ran up to nearly 800,000. (See page 362.) When times were hard, as after the commercial panic of 1873 and the financial crisis of 1893, immigration dropped off; but as business increased, the numbers were enlarged.

Down to about 1885 nearly all the immigrants came from Scandinavian countries, Germany, Great Britain, and Canada, but from that time on these elements all diminished in number and their place was taken by a large immigration from Italy,

THE LANDING OF IMMIGRANTS.

Austria-Hungary (mostly Slavic peoples), and Russia. Under the operation of the Chinese exclusion laws (§ 332), the importation of Chinese was cut off; but about 1894 began a Japanese immigration which increased till it was 30,000 a year.

Among the immigrants were many French Canadians, who found ready employment in the textile mills of New England. For a time they saved their money and went back to Canada, but before 1890 they began to settle as permanent residents of our country. They furnished the first considerable movement of people of the Latin races into the United States. Alongside of it went an increasing immigration of Italians, who soon became the most dependable source of rough labor by large gangs, work which previously had been done by men of the English stock, the Irish, and the Germans. The Italians also furnished many skilled laborers in artistic industries, such as the molding of plaster.

The carrying of immigrants was a part of commerce between foreign nations and the United States, which was under the exclusive control of the federal government. National regulation began (1848) with laws for the proper accommodation and treatment of immigrants while on board ship. Then in 1884 Congress created an immigration commissioner. The first law for limiting immigration was an act prohibiting the entrance of persons convicted of crimes in their own country "other than political" (1875). "Coolie" (Chinese) laborers were also excluded. Down to 1882 nobody else was shut out, but in that year Congress forbade the coming in of "any lunatic, idiot, or any person unable to take care of himself or herself." In 1885, under the influence of the labor unions, Congress prohibited the bringing in of "contract laborers" (§ 332). In 1891 the list was extended to include insane persons, paupers, persons ill of contagious diseases, and polygamists. In 1903, after the assassination of McKinley, anarchists were added. Congress also laid a head tax beginning at 50 cents but raised to $4 per head (1907).

Though several thousand people were sent back every year because they were found to be included in this list, the number of immigrants continued to grow till, in 1907, it reached the high-water mark of 1,285,349 in a single year. (See page 362.) As the immigrants saved money, many of them went back to visit their old homes, but nearly all returned to the United States. The Italians and some other races showed a desire to return home and live there, so that in a single year over 300,000 people have sometimes gone back. They sent or took with them their savings, but of course they left behind the buildings and roads and bridges that they had built and the manufactured goods which they had helped to produce.

355. POLITICAL REFORMS (1885–1895)

While thus endeavoring to control powerful corporations and to pay attention to the rising demands of the laborers, the national and state governments also took in hand some of the defects of their own system. The most striking instance of political reform was the progress in improving the civil service of the United States. President Cleveland did not disturb the " classified " service as he found it (§ 340), but outside of that limited number he allowed thousands of removals to make room for party friends. Under Cleveland's successor, President Harrison, Theodore Roosevelt became chairman of the National Civil Service Commission and made it the business of the commission to follow up instances of violation of the rules. It was he who gave the name of " merit system " to the method of admitting to the public service those who had passed among the highest in a competitive examination. By the time Cleveland came in again in 1893, 44,000 offices had been placed in the classified service, and he made further additions to the classified list.

Several other defects in the workings of the federal government were corrected in this period. A Presidential Succession Act (1886) provided that in case of the death or disability of the President and Vice President, the Secretary of State (if constitutionally eligible to the office) should fill the vacancy, and if he were disabled, some other member of the Cabinet, in a specified succession. The danger felt in 1877 in the count of electoral votes for President was removed by an act (1887) for accepting the certificate of state authorities as final in determining the electors chosen by each state. The Tenure of Office Act of 1867, which led to the impeachment of President Johnson (§ 318), was completely repealed (1887). The House of Representatives often found its business blocked by " filibustering " motions and by amendments which were intended only to kill time; and under the leadership of the Speaker, Thomas B. Reed, one of the ablest men of his time, adopted in 1890 a new code of rules giving the Speaker more power to prevent such practices.

The states felt the reforming spirit, and two of them — New

York (1883) and Massachusetts (1884) — passed statutes for the merit system; and it was later introduced into Chicago (1895) and other cities. The cities tried to improve their governments by securing new charters from the legislatures. New York and Brooklyn and several smaller places united in 1897 in the city of "Greater New York," which at once became second in population and wealth only to London. Nevertheless the state and city governments were still clashing, principally because the governors and mayors were not allowed to be business managers like the heads of great corporations, but had to work with other officials whom they had not appointed and could not control. Hence it was hard to secure efficiency.

356. REVIEW

Side by side with the political questions after 1884, went a great change of public sentiment with regard to the relations of government to business. Population showed nearly 63,000,000 in 1890, including several million immigrants, distributed all over the Union. The cities did not take sufficient pains to provide for their future population, and suffered from many scandals, especially in New York, which was looted in the seventies by the "Tweed Ring."

The system of corporations was greatly extended. Companies were formed for all kinds of business and enjoyed great privileges of trade, granted by the states. About 1865 the states began to regulate railroads, and then other corporations. Some were so great and powerful as to defy public control, and the name of "trust" was applied to them, and loosely to all large corporations.

The railroads could be regulated by the states on "intrastate" business but not on "interstate" business. Some of them granted special rates and facilities to particular places or corporations. Congress made attempts to develop water transportation so as to compete with the railroads. Then it passed the so-called "Sherman Act" (1890), which provided for punishment of attempts to "monopolize" any line of interstate business.

The laborers, on their side, were founding powerful unions in many great lines of trade; and the American Federation of Labor became a central authority. They urged the states and Congress to improve the conditions of labor, and made use of strikes and boycotts. Antagonisms grew up between the trades unions and the employers, leading to violent strikes, in which many strikebreakers were killed. President Cleveland and the Supreme Court used the authority of the federal government to stop this violence.

Conditions of immigration changed: fewer people came from English-speaking countries, and more from French Canada and eastern and southern Europe. Beginning in 1875, Congress passed a series of laws shutting out various classes of undesirables from immigration.

Several defects in the national government were corrected during this time. President Cleveland and his successors followed out the civil service reforms of President Arthur; and definite acts were passed regulating the presidential succession, count of the electoral vote, and tenure of office. Some improvements were also made in state and city governments.

References Bearing on the Text and Topics

Geography and Maps. See maps, pp. 362, 510. — Bogart, *Econ. Hist.*, 378, 433, 482, 490, 529. — Fish, *Am. Nationality*, 438. — Semple, *Geogr. Conditions*, chs. xv-xvii.

Secondary. Bassett, *U.S.*, 731-744, 774-777. — Beard, *Contemp. Am. Hist.*, ch. iii. — Bogart, *Econ. Hist.*, chs. xxiii, xxv, xxviii, xxix, xxxi. — Coman, *Indust. Hist.*, 347-374. — Dewey, *Nat. Problems*, chs. i, iii, vi, xii, xviii. — Hall, *Immigration*. — Latané, *Am. as a World Power*, ch. xvii. — Munro, *Govt. of Am. Cities*, 15-27. — Paxson, *New Nation*, 135, 157-168, 172, 177-187, 244-251. — Wilson, *Am. People*, V. 184-187, 264-269. — Woodburn, *Polit. Parties*, chs. xvi, xvii. — Wright, *Indust. Evolution*, ch. xxvi.

Sources. Antin, *Promised Land* (immigration). — Beard, *Readings*, §§ 52, 53, 143-148. — Bogart and Thompson, *Readings*, 608-622,

768-776, 781-790, 817, 840. — Hart, *Contemporaries*, IV. §§ 165, 197, 200-202. — MacDonald, *Select Statutes*, nos. 114, 120, 124, 127.

Illustrative. Churchill, *Mr. Crewe's Career.* — Harris, *The Bomb.* — Hay, *The Breadwinners.* — Luther, *The Henchman.* — Merwin and Webster, *Calumet "K"; Short-Line War.* — Norris, *The Octopus; The Pit.* — Payne, *Money Captain; Mr. Salt.* — Riis, *How the Other Half Lives.* — Smith, *Tom Grogan.* — Thanet, *Heart of Toil.* — Webster, *Banker and the Bear.* — White, *A Certain Rich Man.*

Pictures. Bogart, *Econ. Hist.* — Coman, *Indust. Hist.* — *Harper's Weekly.* — *McClure's.* — *Scientific American.*

Topics Answerable from the References Above

(1) Immigrants in some particular city. [§ 346] — (2) Incidents of the "Tweed Ring." [§ 347] — (3) Service of *one* of the following railroad magnates: William H. Vanderbilt; Jay Gould; Edgar Thomson; C. P. Huntington; James J. Hill. [§ 349] — (4) Account of the Eads jetty system. [§ 349] — (5) Ship canals in the Great Lakes region. [§ 349] — (6) American Federation of Labor. [§ 352] — (7) *One* of the following strikes: Railroad of 1886; Homestead of 1892; Pullman of 1894. [§ 353] — (8). Roosevelt's public service previous to 1901. [§ 355] — (9) Reed as czar of the House. [§ 355]

Topics for Further Search

(10) Debates on the Interstate Commerce Act, *or* the Original Package Law, *or* the Sherman Antitrust Law. [§§ 350, 351] — (11) Notable boycotts by union labor. [§ 353] — (12) Laws limiting immigration. [§ 354] — (13) Refusal of admission to immigrants. [§ 354] — (14) Creation of Greater New York. [§ 355]

CHAPTER XXXII

THE SPANISH WAR AND ITS RESULTS (1895–1903)

357. TROUBLES IN CUBA (1895–1898)

A NEW era of national history began when our territory was extended by war with Spain in 1898. After the end of the Cuban insurrection in 1878 (§ 338) Cuba quickly recovered prosperity, till the island had an export trade of $100,000,000 a year, most of it to the United States. Yet many of the native-born Cubans were discontented, for in government and society they were considered inferiors by the "peninsulars," or native Spaniards; taxes were high; and the trade of the island was, so far as possible, kept in the hands of Spanish merchants.

An insurrection broke out in Cuba in 1895, aided by a "Junta" — a council of wealthy Cubans in the United States — who within three years sent from the United States several filibustering expeditions, with arms and men for the insurgents. The war was savage on both sides; the sugar plantations were devastated, and neither party could beat the other. The Spaniards held the western end of the island, and ordered the people outside the towns to come within the Spanish lines into *reconcentrado* camps, where many of them miserably perished. Property was destroyed, often that of American citizens; and some American residents and newspaper correspondents were arrested on suspicion that they were helping the insurgents.

A natural sympathy with a people struggling for independence led a Senate committee to investigate conditions in Cuba (1896). Part of the American press stirred up the trouble as much as possible and helped to drive from his post the Spanish minister De Lome, who was supposed to have spoken slightingly of the President and the government in a private letter.

Demonstrations against the Americans in Havana led our government to send the battleship *Maine* on a friendly visit to that city. The *Maine* was blown up by an explosion (February 15, 1898) which killed 260 of the men; and an American naval board of inquiry later reported that the ship was destroyed by a mine. It was thought that Spaniards were responsible, though our consul-general at Havana, Fitzhugh Lee, said : "I do not think it was put there by the Spanish government. I think probably it was an act of four or five subordinate officers."

War was so likely that Congress placed at the disposal of the President $50,000,000 for national defense (March 9). President McKinley and Thomas B. Reed, Speaker of the House, were both anxious to prevent war; but there was a strong public feeling that Spain could not keep order in Cuba, could not subdue the insurgents, and could not protect American property or even the shipping in Cuban harbors. The time seemed to have come to end the Spanish government in the western world. Senator Proctor of Vermont added to the flame by a speech (March 17, 1898) describing the horrors he had seen in Cuba.

358. OUTBREAK OF WAR (1898)

After some months of negotiation, in which promises of reform in Cuba were proposed by Spain, President McKinley sent a message to Congress (April 11, 1898) in which he described the loss of property and life, and said : "In the name of humanity, in the name of civilization, in behalf of endangered · American interests, which give us the right and the duty to speak and act, the war in Cuba must stop." Accordingly a joint resolution was passed (April 19) directing the President to use the military and naval forces of the United States to compel Spain to leave Cuba. To this measure was added the Teller Resolution against conquest, in the words:

"That the United States hereby disclaims any disposition
or intention to exercise sovereignty, jurisdiction, or control
over said island except for the pacification thereof, and asserts
its determination, when that is accomplished, to leave the government and control of the island to its people."

On the outbreak of war, Commodore George Dewey, in command of the American vessels in the Pacific, was ordered to find
and fight the Spanish fleet that
was stationed in the Philippine
Islands. He had a small fleet of
six modern steel vessels with
which to confront the weak
Spanish fleet; and he attacked
under the guns of the Spanish
forts of Cavite, in Manila Bay
(May 1, 1898). After four hours'
spirited fight he set the Spanish
fleet on fire, and sent home a
brief dispatch to the effect that
he had destroyed eleven vessels
and the fort, with trifling loss to
his fleet.

THE PHILIPPINES.

Dewey anchored off the city of
Manila, which for some time
remained in the hands of the
Spaniards. He shortly brought to the island, Aguinaldo, a
Philippine native of influence, who had been engaged in an
insurrection against the Spanish power, and who now renewed
the insurrection and raised a Philippine army. Manila was
attacked by sea and land, and eventually taken (August 13,
1898) by a fleet under Dewey, and an American army under
General Merritt. Aguinaldo expected that he would have the
opportunity to found a Philippine state, though no such promise
was ever made to him; and his troops remained in the trenches
before Manila, confronting the Americans.

359. Campaigns in Cuba and Porto Rico (1898)

Cuba was very soon blockaded by a fleet under the command of Admiral Sampson, but the Spaniards could be forced to leave the island only by an army. As the United States then had only about 26,000 regular troops, Congress authorized an

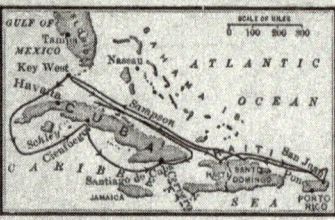

ROUTES OF FLEETS TO SANTIAGO DE CUBA.

increase to 63,000, besides the volunteers called for by the President. In a few weeks about 200,000 men were enlisted in the volunteers, consisting in part of state militia commands. The navy was well organized; but the new army was not trained for campaigning, and the War Department was not prepared to handle, clothe, or feed so many men. Secretary of War Alger said, "It is doubtful if any nation rated as a first-class power ever entered upon a war of offense in a condition of less military preparation." Meanwhile a second small Spanish fleet left Spain for Cuba. Admiral Schley with a flying squadron was sent out to look for the Spaniards, and with some difficulty ascertained that they had slipped into the harbor of Santiago de Cuba. Admiral Sampson then took command and blockaded the port.

A small force of 17,000 men was brought together in Tampa Bay under General Shafter, and with great confusion and difficulty landed on the south coast of Cuba. It then marched up to capture Santiago from the Spaniards. The army had no proper transportation or medical supplies, and the food was poor and sometimes scanty. No army of Cuban patriots could be found. The principal fight was at San Juan Hill (July 1, 1898) in which good service was done by the "Rough Riders," part of Colonel Roosevelt's dismounted cavalry regiment.

The Spanish fleet under Admiral Cervera at last made a dash out of Santiago (July 3, 1898). Admiral Sampson's flagship, the *New York*, was out of range to the eastward, and Admiral Schley was next in command. In execution of Sampson's standing orders the American ships dashed at the enemy, and in a running fight forced ashore and destroyed all four of the cruisers and two torpedo boats, with little damage to any of the American ships. The credit for this victory is due to the vim and dash of all the officers and men engaged, and also to the foresight of Admiral Sampson, who made preparations to receive just such an attack. The troops now pushed nearer to Santiago, and that city with its garrison

A ROUGH RIDER, 1898.

surrendered (July 17, 1898). The island of Porto Rico was taken by 17,000 men under command of General Miles, who landed (July 25) on the southwest coast, moved eastward and took the city of Ponce, and then crossed the island to San Juan. There was little resistance, and the people welcomed the invaders.

360. END OF THE WAR (1898)

The Spaniards still had a force of about 50,000 men at Havana, and the little American army at Santiago was already seized with fever. It was not properly supplied with hospital tents and medicines, and ten of the general officers united in a so-called "round robin" addressed to General Shafter, to say, "This army must be moved at once or it will perish." Accordingly it was transported from Cuba to Long Island (August 7). Spain was in no condition for further fighting, and (August 12) a "protocol," or agreement, was signed, under which Spain was to

evacuate Cuba and to cede Porto Rico to the United States; the
future of the Philippines was to be settled by a later treaty of peace.
The protocol came too late to stop hostilities at Manila, for the
city surrendered (§ 358) before the news of peace arrived.

For the definite treaty of peace, President McKinley appointed
a special commission which met the Spanish representatives
in Paris. The negotiators found a troublesome question in the
Philippines, which were very distant from the United States,
and had a mixed population ranging from head-hunting savages to highly civilized Spanish-speaking gentlemen. Should
the United States return the islands to Spain? or turn them
over to Aguinaldo's government? or annex them outright?

The arguments for annexation were: (1) The islands were a
rich and fertile region, which the United States would be glad
to possess. (2) The war with Spain had destroyed the government of the Philippines and made it the duty of the United
States to give the people a just and orderly government.
(3) The Philippines were so near the coast of Asia that the possession of them would give the United States great influence
with China and eastern Asia.

For some time the President hesitated. Annexation of distant islands seemed a departure from all the previous policy
of the government; but both McKinley and his new Secretary of State, John Hay, agreed that it was the course most
likely to bring peace to the islands, and to give the United
States a position in the Pacific. The treaty of peace, signed
at Paris, December 10, 1898, provided that "Spain relinquishes
all claim of sovereignty over and title to Cuba," and ceded
outright Porto Rico, Guam in the Ladrones, and the Philippine
Islands. The United States was to pay $20,000,000 to Spain.

For some time it was doubtful whether the Senate would
ratify the treaty. Bryan, as a Democratic leader, came to
Washington and used his influence with Democratic senators
in favor of the treaty. It was ratified by the Senate (February
6, 1899) and was proclaimed by the President, April 14, 1899.

361. WILLIAM McKINLEY, PRESIDENT (1897-1901)

During and after the war, President McKinley came more and more to the front as a man of power. He was born in Niles, Ohio, in 1843, served with gallantry in the Civil War, and rose from a private to a major. In 1877 he was sent to Congress, where he grew in reputation, and in 1889 was made chairman of the Ways and Means Committee; that is, leader of his party on the floor of the House. To him was committed the task of drafting the new tariff in 1890 (§ 341). By a "gerrymander" he lost his seat in Congress, but in 1891 he was elected governor of Ohio, and he was the logical candidate of his party for

WILLIAM McKINLEY.

the presidency in 1896. His intimate friend, Marcus A. Hanna, came into the Senate from Ohio, and was the President's right-hand man. McKinley was one of the most gracious and genial men who ever sat in the White House.

He cannot be held responsible for the war with Spain, which he felt was demanded by public opinion; but he made the decision for taking the Philippines. He also urged upon Congress a new tariff and settlement of the currency question.

Immediately after his inauguration (1897) McKinley called a special session of Congress, in which the Republicans controlled both houses. Dingley of Maine, chairman of the Committee of Ways and Means, engineered the making of a new tariff (July 24, 1897), the third one passed since 1889. The scale of duties of the McKinley Tariff of 1890 was restored and somewhat increased. The cry was raised that certain manufacturers who wanted their products protected had

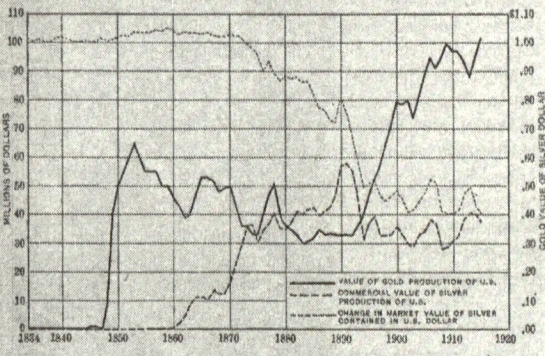

VALUE OF THE GOLD AND SILVER MINED IN THE UNITED STATES, AND THE CHANGE IN THE MARKET PRICE OF SILVER.

been allowed to write paragraphs of the measure, because they had made large contributions to the party campaign fund.

The silver controversy was much affected by a great increase in the output of gold, so that all over the world there was gold enough to serve as a standard for the world's business, and Congress finally passed an act definitely establishing the single gold standard (March 14, 1900). Under it all outstanding paper money was redeemable in gold coin.

McKinley was reëlected in 1900 over Bryan, again the Democratic candidate (§ 344), by an electoral vote of 292 to 155, and began his second term with a prestige and influence which no President had enjoyed for many years. He urged a liberal tariff policy which would aid trade in our manufactured goods abroad, but before Congress met he was shot (September 6, 1901) by an obscure fanatic. He died lamented by all his countrymen, and was succeeded by Vice President Roosevelt.

362. NEW DEPENDENCIES (1899–1902)

After the capture of Manila, Aguinaldo still hoped for independence, and kept up his forces outside the city of Manila (§ 358). He and his officers grew discontented, and their soldiers brought on a fight (February 4, 1899). For two years Aguinaldo kept together an organized force, until he was made a prisoner; and the insurrection continued until 1902.

The treaty of 1899 declared that "the civil rights and political status of the native inhabitants of the territories hereby ceded to the United States shall be determined by the Congress." Accordingly a modified form of territorial government was created for Porto Rico (April, 1900), in which the members of the upper house of the legislature were appointed by the President; but the act did not make the island part of the United States. In 1917 Porto Rico received a larger degree of self-government and Porto Ricans were made citizens of the United States. For the temporary government of the Philippines

HUSKING COCONUTS IN PORTO RICO.

the President, on his own responsibility, appointed two successive commissions of civilians, and Congress later authorized him
to establish a government at his discretion (March 2, 1901).
He continued the former commission under Judge Taft of Ohio;
and that commission organized a government for the islands
and set up local governments wherever it was safe.

Trouble at once arose over the question whether the United
States tariff applied to these new dependencies. The question,

VILLAGE IN THE PHILIPPINE ISLANDS.

so far as it concerned Porto Rico, was settled by an act of
Congress (April 12, 1900), providing a special tariff for that
island, but allowing it speedily to come into the regular tariff
system of the United States; that is, to be free from all duties
on trade with the states. In 1901 the Supreme Court supported
this legislation by decisions in the "Insular Cases." The majority of the court (5 to 4) agreed: (1) that Congress had the
right to make a separate tariff for the dependencies; (2) that
Porto Rico and the Philippines were not foreign countries;
(3) that they were also not complete parts of the United States,
unless Congress should choose to incorporate them.

Acting on those principles, Congress made a special tariff of import duties into the Philippines (March 8, 1902), and fixed the duties on imports from the Philippines into the United States at three fourths the rates on similar imports from other countries. By another act (July 1, 1902) a bill of rights was adopted which contained substantially the guarantees of personal liberty set forth in the federal Constitution (§ 137), except the clauses for jury trials and for keeping and bearing arms. A permanent form of government was created by Congress — substantially the same as that framed by the commission. Judge Taft was appointed civil governor, and provision was made for an Assembly of elected representatives.

363. RELATIONS WITH CUBA (1898–1903)

As Cuba was completely disorganized by the war, United States troops were left in the island. General Leonard Wood was appointed military governor, and within a few months the island was restored to order; roads and telegraphs were built, hundreds of schools were opened, and prosperity slowly returned. What were to be the future relations of the United States to Cuba? Annexation was out of the question, in view of the Teller Resolution of 1898 (§ 358). The President and Cabinet drew up a set of regulations for Cuba which were passed by Congress under the name of the "Platt Amendment" (March 2, 1901). It contained as bases for the future government of Cuba the following principles: (1) Cuba must make no foreign agreements contrary to the interests of the United States. (2) Cuba must not incur a debt that she could not pay. (3) Sites were to be ceded on the Cuban coast for United States naval stations. (4) Cuban ports must not be allowed to be breeding places of disease. (5) The United States was to have the right to occupy Cuba, if necessary to keep order.

A Cuban constitutional convention agreed to these conditions (June 12), and formed a republic of which General Palma was elected first president. The control of the island was formally given up to the new government (May 20, 1902), and the United States troops were withdrawn.

Next came the question of the commercial relations of the two countries. The Cubans had lost their former market in Spain, and expected that the United States would make a reduction on the regular tariff duties on imports from Cuba. As the House paid no attention to urgent messages from both President McKinley and his successor, President Roosevelt, a treaty was negotiated (1903) for a 20 per cent reduction on regular import duties, and was ratified by the Senate with a proviso that it be subject to the approval of the House of Representatives, a very unusual method of securing a treaty.

364. THE UNITED STATES IN THE PACIFIC (1897–1913)

The United States reached far beyond the boundaries of the Pacific coast states. To the northward lay Alaska, annexed from Russia in 1867 and provided with a government in 1884 as "a civil and judicial district." It was an immense region, extending from the North Pacific to the Arctic Ocean and westward to Bering Sea, together with the Aleutian Islands which reach almost to the coast of Asia. For many years the only source of wealth in Alaska was the fur seals, caught on and near the Pribilof Islands in Bering Sea. Then in 1897 gold was discovered on the headwaters of the Yukon River, mostly in Canadian territory. The result was a stampede of prospectors and gold diggers. Gold was also found on the sea beaches at Nome, almost on the Arctic Circle. The population of Alaska increased slowly, and in 1912 Congress at last created a regular territorial government for it.

The interest of the United States in the Pacific led to several annexations of island territory. The Hawaiian Islands had for many years enjoyed a favorable commercial treaty with us; and in 1893, with the aid of marines landed from a United States ship, a party which included most of the people of American descent in the islands, revolted from the native monarchy and set up a republic. President Cleveland would not agree to annexation; but during the Spanish War a joint resolution of Congress (July 7, 1898) brought the Hawaiian Islands into the United States, and they were organized as a territory (1900). This important group in the mid-Pacific is especially valuable as a naval station.

The United States, Great Britain, and Germany all had interests in the Samoan Islands; hence a tripartite treaty had been agreed on (June 14, 1889), by which the three powers administered the islands together. The natives tried to fight out their own quarrels, and this led to such confusion that in 1899 the three powers made a division treaty, by which the United States took the island of Tutuila and five other small islands, with the harbor of Pago Pago, one of the best in the Pacific. Various small islands, Baker, Midway, Wake, Howland, and others, which lay in the mid-Pacific and had never been claimed by any other power, were annexed by the United States, to be used as landing or telegraph stations.

365. THE UNITED STATES IN ASIA

The results of the war of 1898 gave the United States a new place in the world's councils. In a conference held at the Hague, in Holland, to discuss means of preventing war (1899), the influence of the United States was high among the twenty-seven nations represented, and helped to bring about a general treaty providing courts of arbitration.

That influence was also strong in China, where France, Great Britain, Germany, Japan, and Russia were all trying to take and keep Chinese territory. The interest of the United States in China was heightened by the great opportunity for commerce with that populous nation, which offered a market for American flour, piece goods, machinery, railway material, and other exports. For the growing commerce with Japan and China, the main ports were Seattle, Tacoma, Portland. and San Fran-

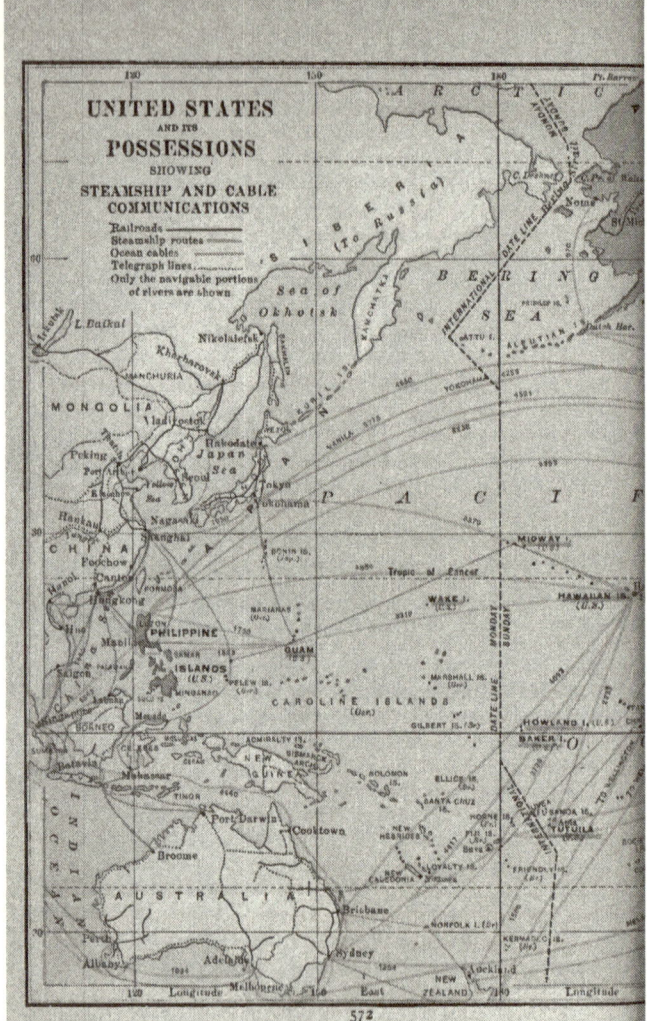

UNITED STATES
AND ITS
POSSESSIONS
SHOWING
STEAMSHIP AND CABLE
COMMUNICATIONS

Railroads
Steamship routes
Ocean cables
Telegraph lines
Only the navigable portions
of rivers are shown

572

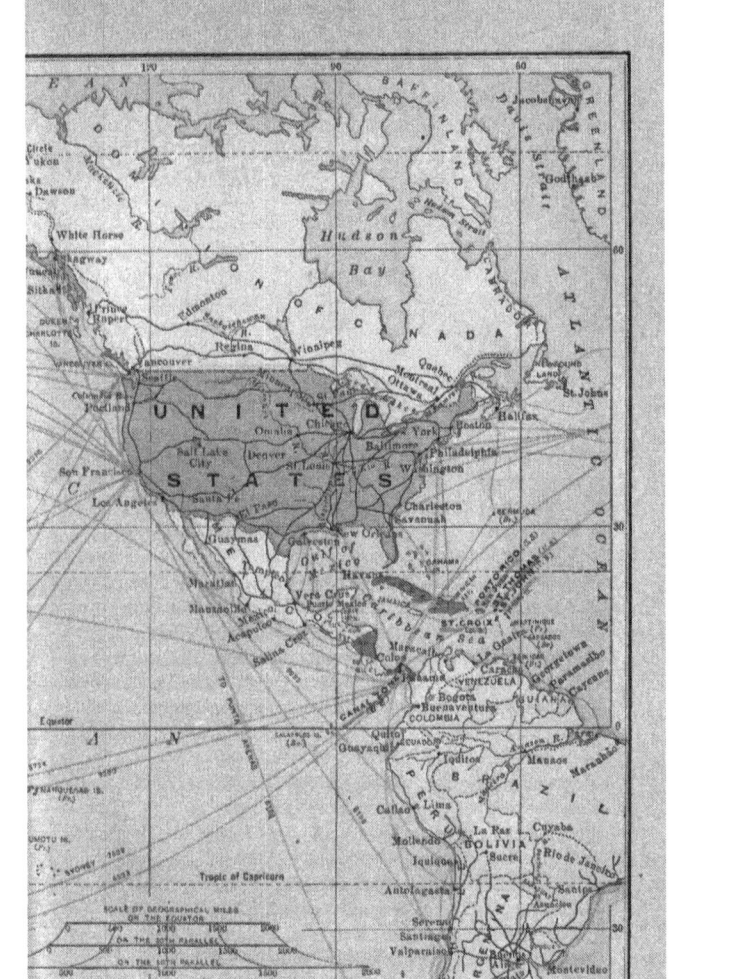

cisco. American, Japanese, and British steamer lines ran from these ports and also from Vancouver in British Columbia,

carrying out timber, flour, cotton cloth, and various manufactures, and bringing back tea, silk, and other Oriental products.

The ownership of the Philippines caused the United States to feel some responsibility for happenings

A PHILIPPINE BOAT WITH OUT-RIGGERS.

in eastern Asia. Therefore, a small body of American troops in 1900 joined similar detachments of British, French, Russian, Italian, and Japanese troops in a march from the coast to Peking; there they defeated the Chinese Boxers and rescued the diplomats who had for weeks been besieged in the city. Secretary Hay proposed the policy of "the open door," by which he meant the right of all foreign nations to trade on equal terms in all parts of China, and the European powers accepted this principle. Secretary Hay also did his best to hold back the European powers from greedy demands for a large money indemnity from the Chinese, after the Boxer Rebellion.

366. REVIEW

Unsatisfactory government of Cuba by Spain led to an insurrection there in 1895. American property and citizens suffered, and the battleship *Maine* was blown up (February, 1898) in the harbor of Havana. To end the oppression of the Cubans, Congress authorized intervention (April, 1898), at the same time promising not to annex Cuba.

The significant military events of the war which followed were: (1) Admiral Dewey's defeat of the Spanish fleet in Manila

Bay (May 1); (2) later capture of Manila; (3) blockade of Cuba; (4) attack on Santiago by Shafter's army (San Juan Hill); (5) destruction of the Spanish fleet as it tried to escape; (6) capture of Santiago (July); (7) capture of Porto Rico.

The Spaniards did not care to prolong the fighting and signed a preliminary treaty (August 12). Negotiations at Paris resulted in a treaty of peace (December 10) by which Spain ceded Porto Rico, the Philippine Islands, and the island of Guam, and "relinquished sovereignty" over Cuba.

For this treaty, President McKinley was responsible, and he became one of the most popular men in the country. Not long before the war the Dingley tariff of 1897 was passed. Congress established the gold standard for our paper money (1900). McKinley was reëlected President, but was assassinated.

Aguinaldo, a Filipino leader, headed a fight for the independence of the Philippine Islands (1899). Meanwhile Porto Rico was organized; and the Hawaiian Islands, which had been annexed in 1898, were also organized. In the "Insular Cases" the Supreme Court held that annexations made by conquest were not complete parts of the United States, till "incorporated" by Congress.

An American army was left in Cuba, and it pacified and reorganized the island. In 1902, Cuba set up an independent government under an agreement called the "Platt Amendment." The United States annexed several small islands in the Pacific and part of the Samoan group. The Pacific possessions led to a new interest in eastern Asia; and in 1900 the United States joined a military expedition into China and demanded the "open door" for Chinese trade.

References Bearing on the Text and Topics

Geography and Maps. See maps, pp. 493, 561, 562, 572–573. — Chadwick, *U. S. and Spain*, II, III. —Latané, *Am. as a World Power*, 4, 46, 102, 132. — Paxson, *New Nation*, 77, 259. — Semple, *Geogr. Conditions*, 397–435.

Secondary. Bassett, *U.S.*, 784–813, 822–824. — Beard, *Contemp.*

Am. Hist., ch. viii. — Brooks, *War with Spain.* — Carpenter, *Am. Advance*, 288–331. — Chadwick, *U. S. and Spain*, I. chs. xx–xxix, II, III. — Coolidge, *U. S. as a World Power*, chs. vi–viii, xvii–xix. — Fish, *Am. Dipl.*, chs. xxix, xxxii. — Griffis, *Am. in the East.* — Hart, *Obvious Orient*, chs. xxiv–xxvi. — Haworth, *Reconstruction and Union*, chs. vii, viii. — Latané, *Am. as a World Power*, chs. i–x. — McCall, *T. B. Reed*, ch. xx. — Maclay, *U. S. Navy*, III. 39–440. — Olcott, *Wm. McKinley*, I. chs. xvi–xxiii, II. — Thayer, *John Hay*, II. chs. xxiii–xxvii, — Titherington, *Span.-Am. War.*

Sources. *Appletons' Annual Cyclopædia*, 1898 to 1902. — Beard, *Readings*, §§ 154–158. — Caldwell, *Terr. Development*, 213–255. — Hart, *Contemporaries*, IV. §§ 180–196; *Source Book*, §§ 141–145. — Hill, *Liberty Docs.*, ch. xxiv. — *International Year Book*, 1898 to 1902.

Illustrative. Crane, *Wounds in the Rain.* — Dean, *Promotion* (Philippines). — Dunne, *Mr. Dooley in Peace and in War; Mr. Dooley in the Hearts of His Countrymen.* — Hyatt, *Little Brown Brother.* — Lewis, *Gunner aboard the Yankee.* — Wood, *Spirit of the Service.*

Pictures. *Century. — Collier's Weekly. — Harper's Pictorial Hist. of the War with Spain. — Leslie's Official Hist. of the Span.-Am. War. — McClure's. — Mentor*, serial no. 89. — *Scribner's Magazine.* — Worcester, *The Philippines.*

Topics Answerable from the References Above

(1) Battle of Manila Bay [§ 358], *or* of Santiago. [§ 359] — (2) Public career of *one* of the following: Proctor; John Hay; Hanna; Dingley. [§§ 357, 360, 361] — (3) Military service of *one*: Dewey; Miles; Wood; Roosevelt. [§§ 358, 359] — (4) Debates on the tariff of 1897. [§ 361] — (5) Election of 1900. [§ 361] — (6) Philippine War. [§ 362] — (7) Military occupation of Cuba. [§ 363] — (8) Alaska from 1867 to 1897. [§ 364] — (9) Discovery of gold in Alaska. [§ 364] — (10) Attempt to annex Hawaii, 1893, *or* annexation of Hawaii, 1898. [§ 364] — (11) Annexation of small Pacific islands, 1899. [§ 364]

Topics for Further Search

(12) Could the war with Spain have been prevented? [§ 358] — (13) Public career of Aguinaldo. [§ 358] — (14) Why was the United States unprepared for the Spanish War? [§ 359] — (15) Why did the United States annex the Philippines? [§ 360] — (16) Why was the Platt Amendment adopted? [§ 363] — (17) First Peace Congress at the Hague. [§ 365] — (18) Americans in the Boxer Rebellion. [§ 365]

CHAPTER XXXIII

NEW SOUTH AND FAR WEST (1885-1916)

367. THE SECTIONS AFTER 1885

THE history of the United States for nearly a hundred years after the Revolution abounded in rivalries between the different sections. New England quarreled with the middle states and the South. New England and the middle states felt jealous of the rising West. Then New England and the middle states and the West of that time united into the North and fought the Civil War against the South. It took a long time to free the land from the rivalry between North and South; but by 1885 those two sections had come to understand that they were both parts of the same Union, and that they had similar aims and interests, and could go hand in hand. When the country continued prosperous and peaceful under Grover Cleveland, a Democratic President who was supported by the solid South, the feelings of hatred and suspicion died out on both sides.

One reason for the more cordial feeling was that northern and southern people traveled more widely. Florida became a winter pleasure resort and drew northern visitors who stopped over in the southern states along their route. Some northerners settled on southern plantations or took places as teachers, college professors, business and professional men in the southern cities. On the other side, well-to-do southerners spent their summers in the North, and southern students entered northern colleges, both eastern and western. Some of the ablest business men in the South settled in northern cities.

In 1885, the West was stretching far beyond the Missouri River. A belt of new communities appeared in and beyond the Rocky Mountains, which came to be called the far West. Both North and South helped to build up this far West. Southerners found their way to all the northwestern, southwestern, and Pacific states; and the native stock from New England, the middle states, and the middle West furnished a large element of the population, which was further swelled by hundreds of thousands of foreigners.

By this time, five or six railroads had been completed to the Pacific coast, and eastern money poured in to open the mines, cut the forests, and develop the cities. In 1885 a large part of the far West was still in the hands of Indian tribes; and the last of the great herds of buffaloes had just disappeared. The newcomers found the same kind of opportunities for hard work and wealth in Montana and Utah and California that their fathers had found earlier in Michigan and Missouri. The far West was for a time the frontier of the United States, but a frontier abounding in railroads and growing towns.

The far West felt little sense of rivalry with the East. It had its own ports on the Pacific, its own industries, such as cattle raising, mining, and fruit and grain growing. The same kind of men and women lived there as in the older states; but there was a livelier spirit of freedom and adventure, especially in California, which made the far West different from the older parts of the Union.

368. ADMISSION OF NEW STATES (1889-1912)

In 1888 there were no organized states west of the Rockies except California, Oregon, Nevada, and part of Colorado. In 1912, twenty-four years later, the whole continental area was blocked out in communities which took their places as sisters of the older states. This process of western state making began in 1889, when Congress provided for the admission of North Dakota, South Dakota, Montana, and Washington. The two Dakotas, having duly adopted state constitutions, were formally admitted November 2. They were created out of the Territory of Dakota, including a vast prairie region and also the mining district of the Black Hills. These two states very much resembled their older neighbors, Nebraska and Minnesota.

A few days later, the two states of Montana (November 8) and Washington (November 11) came into the Union. Montana is one of the largest of all the states, stretching for 500 miles from the Rocky Mountains eastward, including most of the valleys of the upper Missouri and Yellowstone rivers.

ALTMAN, COLORADO, A WESTERN MINING TOWN.

Washington is the northwestern part of that broad Oregon country which was assured to the United States in 1846 (§ 229). It includes two very different regions, separated from each other by the Cascade Range. The eastern part is the middle valley of the Columbia, with large areas of volcanic desert, and also the splendid wheat-growing area of the Palouse, often called "The Inland Empire." The western part extends from the Columbia River around the superb Puget Sound to the British boundary. It contains some of the finest harbors on the Pacific Ocean, which furnish a point of departure for the Oriental trade.

These four states at the time of admission had together only about 1,000,000 inhabitants, but rapidly increased and are destined to be populous members of the Union.

Two more states were added in 1890, Idaho and Wyoming. Idaho is a mountain state, lying mostly on the slope from the Rocky Mountains westward to the Snake River, with enormous water powers, valuable mines, and much good agricultural land in the valleys. Wyoming, the 44th state, is the only state in the Union except Colorado that boasts exactly rectangular boundaries. The chief industry of this region is stock raising and mining, including valuable coal mines.

WHEAT FIELD IN THE PALOUSE COUNTRY, WASHINGTON. (A combined harvester and thresher.)

Utah territory was for a time more populous than any of these six neighbors, but was held back from statehood by a long controversy with the federal government about polygamy. Plural marriages, as the system was called in Utah, were practiced in the territory in spite of special acts of Congress prohibiting them. In 1896 Utah was admitted as a state, with a pledge in the state constitution that polygamy should never be allowed.

In 1907 the two territories of Indian Territory and Oklahoma were united into the state of Oklahoma. This is the only one

of the new admissions which can be counted as distinctly southern; for in climate, productions, and people, it much resembles
the states immediately to the eastward. Few states in the
Union are so rich in natural resources as Oklahoma. It has some
timber and abounds in coal, oil, and natural gas. The western
end of the state runs up into a mountain range; the central and
eastern parts teem with corn, wheat, fruit, and cotton. It is
a garden spot.

The only two territories left in the main part of the United
States were New Mexico and Arizona. Congress wanted to
be rid of the whole question of organized territories, and both
were admitted as states in 1912. Their population was rather
small and included many Mexican immigrants. Their admission
completed the process of state making, which began in 1776
when New Hampshire framed the first state constitution (§ 100).

369. MATERIAL PROSPERITY OF THE SOUTH

During this whole period, from 1885 onward, the South was
steadily gaining in population and wealth. In 1890 there were
22,700,000 people in the southern states, including Missouri
and Oklahoma. In 1910 there were 32,700,000. The most
valuable southern product was corn, most of which was con-
sumed on the spot as food for man and beast. Cotton always
attracted more attention, because it was the staple export crop
that brought in cash. By 1881 the crop reached 6,580,000
bales — an amount larger than at any time previous to the Civil
War. The area of cotton land was broadened by the use of
fertilizers, which brought into use large tracts in the hill country
and also made more available some of the lands of the " Black
Belt," which stretches across Alabama and Mississippi. The
crop rose to 8,650,000 bales in 1900 and 16,700,000 bales in 1914.

The South also took advantage of its magnificent uncut timber, much of it yellow pine, which found a ready market. The
rich coal deposits of Tennessee, Alabama, and some other states
were at last developed, and also the iron ore beds, so that great

centers for blast furnaces and rolling mills arose at Chattanooga,
Birmingham, Greensboro, and elsewhere. The manufacturers
boasted that they could make pig iron cheaper than anybody
else in the world. In 1901 immense deposits of oil were discovered in Texas, and afterwards in Oklahoma, furnishing a
cheap fuel for locomotives and useful for many purposes. The
tobacco of Kentucky and other states, the rice of Louisiana,

ROUNDING UP CATTLE ON A TEXAS RANCH.

Texas, and Arkansas, and the "truck farming" of the Atlantic
coast and eastern Texas, all added to the wealth of the South.
Immense quantities of early vegetables were shipped to the northern cities, and orange raising became a regular industry of Florida.

The South at last became a manufacturing region. Besides
the iron works, there were some great machine-making industries, such as the Richmond Locomotive Works. The greatest
industrial gain for the South was the building up of a great
manufacture of cotton cloth. The attempt to use negro labor

in cotton mills failed wherever it was tried, but the "poor whites" were drawn from their little farms into mill towns, many of which were built on the splendid water powers of the Carolinas, Georgia, and Alabama. Mill towns quickly arose, such as Columbia (South Carolina), Columbus (Georgia), and Tallassee (Alabama). These towns furnished a market for the products of the farmers who had stayed on their land, and the whole region was prosperous.

To provide money for such great enterprises, northern and European capital flowed in. Banks sprang up all over the South, and the planters and manufacturers soon found that their savings furnished a vast capital belonging to the South which could be used to develop the region. This prosperity reacted on the cities. Such places as Norfolk, Savannah, Atlanta, Montgomery, Mobile, and Memphis grew populous and rich. New Orleans, as the largest southern port and as the center of a network of railroads, profited by these improvements. Beyond the Mississippi appeared such prosperous cities as Oklahoma City, Houston, Dallas, Fort Worth, and San Antonio.

370. LABOR IN THE SOUTH

All this growth of the new South would have been impossible but for a new labor system. The South drew very few immigrants from foreign countries; skilled laborers did not seem to like their social conditions; and except a few thousand Italians, foreigners could not be induced to work on the plantations. For the crude, rough labor of the country both in the shop and in the field the main reliance was upon the negroes. Though the cotton-mill hands were all white, great numbers of negroes were employed on the railroads, and in the iron works, tobacco factories, cotton gins, oil mills, etc.; and they did most of the heavy work in the cities of the lower South.

As for farming, fully half the crops of the South were raised by farmers, most of them whites, who worked their own land or took up farms as renters. The other half was produced by negroes working on the plantations, raising corn, cotton, tobacco, rice, garden truck, and fruit. Stock raising was never a large industry in the South. The negro's greatest success had always been as a farmer, but it proved very hard to adapt his labor to the needs of the large plantations, which by this time were run mostly for owners who did not live on the place. On many

BALING COTTON IN A COTTON GIN.

such plantations the laborers were hired by the year and were commonly paid by a share of the crop. Cotton must be planted eight or ten months before the crop can be picked and sold, and so the laborers had to be taken care of till the crop was made. This obliged the employers to "make advances" for provisions and supplies, for which they were usually obliged to borrow money from banks, and thus they practically mortgaged their growing crop for these loans. This system came

down from the time before the Civil War and was expensive
for the owner. Moreover, if a negro broke his contract in the
middle of the season and threw up his job, it might be impossible to find another to take his place.

Some unscrupulous employers found means to compel negro
hands, and sometimes white men, to work for them against
their will. This was called "peonage" and had to be broken
up by prosecutions of the worst offenders. The jails and state
prisons held large numbers of negro convicts who were often
treated much like the former slaves. Even in communities
which were otherwise highly civilized, the custom of "lynching"
was practiced; that is, persons accused of crime, usually negroes
but often white men, were seized by mobs, and were barbarously
killed, frequently by burning at the stake.

371. Intellectual Growth of the South

One of the evidences of advance in the South was a great
improvement in education. In reconstruction times every
southern state provided a common school system both for the
towns and for the open country. Some states were never willing to spend enough money for good schools. Others, like
Louisiana, built up a first-class system. The main difficulty
was in the back country, where the children were few and the
schools were often very poor. Another trouble was that the
school days in the year for the country schools were often only
about two thirds as many as in the northern states.

For higher education new endowed universities appeared,
such as Tulane University in New Orleans and Rice Institute
in Houston. The state universities were brought up to a much
higher standard, especially in Virginia, North Carolina, and
Texas. Agricultural and mechanical colleges were built in
every state, and they educated young men for science and
engineering. Normal schools for men and women prepared
the teachers of the lower schools. Southern educators took a
high place in the national associations. Several excellent

southern writers made a national reputation, especially Joel
Chandler Harris and Thomas Nelson Page, who wrote on
southern subjects. Societies like the Confederate Veterans and
the Daughters of the Confederacy kept warm the memories
of the Civil War. Southern statesmen in Congress and in the
Cabinet took places alongside the eastern and western men.

In this intellectual growth the negroes had a slender share.
Few of them could expect higher education. The negro schools
did not carry children
so far as the white
schools did. Excel-
lent high schools for
white boys and girls
were opened all over
the South, but many
towns and cities pro-
vided no public higher
instruction for ne-
groes. For their
needs, however, spe-
cial normal schools
were established and

VIEW ON THE CAMPUS AT TUSKEGEE.

some technical schools were provided by the states. Twenty-
five or thirty negro institutions existed, called colleges, mostly
supported by gifts from the North: the most successful were
Atlanta University, Hampton Institute in Virginia, and Tuskegee in Alabama, at the head of which was Booker T. Washington, for a long time the most eminent member of his race.
Some two hundred private and endowed schools were founded
for negroes. The negroes shared in the general prosperity.
Negro business men and bankers appeared. A few negroes
gathered together large estates of plantation land which they
rented; and there were always a few trained leaders who edited
newspapers, headed negro institutions, and aroused a sense of
the possibilities for their race.

OKLAHOMA CITY ON THE DAY THE LAND WAS OPENED TO SETTLEMENT,
APRIL 22, 1889.

372. GROWTH OF THE FAR WEST

The South in this period was made up mostly of old settled
communities. The far West was planted on new land, some
of which had to be won from the Indians. In 1886 the Apaches,
the scourges of the Southwest, who had been the most ferocious
of the Indian enemies of the United States, were at last subdued. The next year, Congress passed the "Severalty Act"
which offered free farms to Indians who would leave their tribes
and become citizens. In 1889, when a great area of good farm
land was opened for settlement in a part of Indian Territory
(later set off as the territory of Oklahoma), the applicants
for lands were so much more numerous than the opportunities,
that there was a frantic rush from the border line to the interior, where the farms and town lots could be taken up.

One of the great industries of the Southwest and part of the
Northwest was cattle raising, which required not only grass but
convenient water. Hence ranchmen who had possession of the
river fronts could prevent anybody from taking up public land
which lay behind them, and used that method to keep large
areas of government land under their control. In some cases,

OKLAHOMA CITY FOUR WEEKS LATER.

they had the effrontery to fence in government land and prevent others from making use of the common advantage.

Another source of trouble was the system of irrigating lands. The first comers often took up river fronts and then dug irrigating canals to carry the water to the back lands. Later comers would take water farther up the river and thus reduce the flow so that the earlier farmers lost their supply of water. This gave rise to endless difficulties and lawsuits.

In 1902 the government stepped in to develop the opportunities for storing water on the public lands, so as to provide for irrigation. To protect government timber and keep the streams from drying up, the government in 1891 began to set off various forest reserves and national parks.

Except the two Dakotas, which were a part of the middle West, and Oklahoma, which was southern, all the new states admitted after 1889 belonged to the far western group. They occupied the broad and confused mountain mass of the Rocky Mountains, the so-called Great Basin, the valleys of the Colorado and Columbia, and the Pacific slope. This region included many broad and fertile valleys, but no grassy, extended plains like the prairies of the middle West. Fully three fourths of this area was barren mountain or desert. Most of the coast strip received plenty of rain, but through eastern Washington and Oregon, Nevada, southern California, and the states farther east, lay immense areas of desolate, rainless land. Some of

the principal railroads, such as the line from Salt Lake City to Los Angeles, passed for hundreds of miles through rocky or sandy wildernesses. The Colorado River had worn its way thousands of feet down below the level of a sterile plateau.

A GOLD DREDGER.

Nevertheless there were many beautiful and rich spaces, such as the so-called "parks" of the Rocky Mountains, the Willamette valley in Oregon, and the great interior valleys of California, in which grain, vegetables, and fruit came to perfection. The state governments all made it a point to foster the industries of the state, whether fisheries, grain growing, fruit growing, mining, or lumbering.

373. TRAVEL AND SCENERY IN THE FAR WEST

The first necessity of the scattered settlements was railroads, and the local traffic was cared for by the through lines from the Pacific coast eastward. Besides the various land grant roads which reached the Pacific — the Northern Pacific, Union Pacific, Southern Pacific, and Atchison Topeka and Santa Fe — several through lines were built by private capital, particularly the Denver and Rio Grande and the Western Pacific; the Great Northern — the work of James J. Hill — and the Milwaukee St. Paul and Pacific routes from Lake Superior and Lake Michigan to Puget Sound; and the Oregon Short Line from the neighborhood of Salt Lake City to Portland. Several different railroads combined to make a continuous line of rail from the British boundary, near Vancouver, south to San Diego. The Chicago and North Western and the Chicago Burlington and Quincy railroads built from Chicago westward to the Rocky Mountains.

One of the great assets of the far West is its magnificent natural scenery, which has for many years drawn visitors from all over the world. The Grand Canyon of the Arkansas and the canyon of the Feather River offer magnificent views from the car window. The whole Pacific coast abounds in picturesque cliffs and bays and islands and harbors. Among the superb areas reserved by the United States government for perpetual pleasure grounds, are the Yellowstone National Park in and near northwestern Wyoming, the Glacier Park on the Canadian border, and Rocky Mountain Park near Denver.

JAMES J. HILL.

The Columbia River is one of the most magnificent navigable streams in the world. From Mt. Shuksan in Washington to Mt. Shasta in northern California, there is a procession of the most magnificent glacier-covered volcanic peaks such as Mt. Rainier, otherwise called Mt. Tacoma, Mt. Adams, Mt. St. Helens, and Mt. Hood. The lofty Sierra Nevada does not rise in startling peaks, but it contains unrivaled valleys, especially the Yosemite, which is not to be matched in the whole world

for the height and beauty of its waterfalls, the grandeur of its
cliffs, and the contrast between the granite mountains and the
green wooded floor of the valley. In the neighborhood are
several groves of the marvelous Big Trees, which rise as high as
four hundred and sixty feet. Farther east lies the Grand Canyon
of the Colorado, which offers the most superb natural scenery on
earth. Instead of standing at the foot of a mountain and looking up five thousand feet, the observer stands on the brink of
an abyss and looks down five thousand feet to the boiling river.

374. THE PEOPLE OF THE FAR WEST IN 1910

In no large area of the country was the population so mixed
as in the far West. According to the census of 1910, 1,400,000
persons, out of the western population of 6,800,000, were born
outside the United States; 1,700,000 were children of foreigners;
2,100,000 were born in the United States of native white stock
but outside of the states in which they then resided. Only
1,600,000 were born in the states in which they lived. Some
cities, like Portland and Los Angeles, were made up chiefly of
people who immigrated from the eastern states. Others abounded
in foreign immigrants. For instance, in 1890 Denver contained
forty-seven per cent foreign born or children of foreigners, and
San Francisco contained sixty-eight per cent — more than two
thirds. Whatever their origin, the people had a strong sense
of pride in, and devotion to, their own states as well as a love for
their section. They were great travelers, freely moving about
in their own neighborhood, which might be a thousand miles wide.
They traveled across the continent to "The States," as they
called any place east of Denver. In the mountains, where the
chief industry was mining, large numbers of foreign workingmen were found. The far West was the only part of the
country in which there was any considerable Asiatic population.
46,000 of the 72,000 Chinese, and 58,000 of the 72,000 Japanese
in the United States in 1910, were living in the three states of
Washington, Oregon, and California. Hence those states were

the centers of the protest against admitting immigrants from any Asiatic country.

The far West was very proud of its schools and universities. In every state there was a complete system of schools, so that even in the most remote mountain regions, children might have the opportunity of an education. Public high schools were of a high grade, and every state had a public university, which was aided by the government. The University of California

STADIUM OF THE TACOMA HIGH SCHOOL, TACOMA, WASHINGTON.

was the oldest in the far West. In Washington there were practically two universities, one in the eastern section and one in the western. The agricultural, mining, and academic universities of Colorado were situated in three towns a few miles apart.

375. THE SOUTH AND THE WEST IN POLITICS

Both the South and the far West had interests which affected their point of view on political questions. After reconstruction the South was determined that the negroes should have no deciding part in elections. They were frightened away from the polls in some states by the Ku-Klux Klan (§ 321); later in some states, as South Carolina, perplexing laws were passed for the purpose of making it difficult for the negro to vote.

Beginning in 1890 a new system was devised by which the suffrage of the negroes was much diminished: New constitutions or amendments were adopted in the seven states of North Carolina, South Carolina, Alabama, Mississippi, Louisiana, Virginia, and Oklahoma by which no one could vote who could not prove that he possessed rather difficult qualifications. He must show a receipted tax bill; or prove to the satisfaction of an election board that he could understand clauses of the state constitution, or that he was descended from a person who was a voter before the Civil War. This last provision, the so-called "Grandfather clause," led to lawsuits in which the Supreme Court of the United States held that such clauses were unconstitutional. These provisions were nominally the same for negro and white voters, but were intended to be so applied as to shut out the colored voters and leave all or nearly all the white men free to vote.

Notwithstanding these precautions, the fear that the negroes might dominate in politics kept the "solid South" (§ 337) together. Negroes were still allowed freely to vote in Tennessee, Florida, Texas, and Missouri, and there were some Republican white voters in all the southern states. Still, not a single southern state chose Republican electors in 1892. Only Kentucky, Maryland, and West Virginia were Republican in 1896, and in 1912 and 1916 every southern state again was Democratic. In Kentucky and Tennessee a Republican governor was occasionally elected, but in most cases no one in the South could expect to be chosen to a high state or city office except Democrats. Inasmuch as the South could be depended upon to vote for any Democratic candidate in national elections it was not thought necessary to put southern candidates on the Democratic ticket either for President or for Vice President, except that in 1904 a West Virginia man was nominated with Bryan. In some parts of the South there was a strong feeling in favor of the tariff, especially among the cotton and iron manufacturers and the sugar growers of Louisiana, but it was hard to give this interest expression without throwing over the Democratic ticket.,

The far West was the home of experiments in popular government. The direct primary, initiative, referendum, and recall of officials, discussed in a following chapter, either began in the far West or were enthusiastically taken up there. From 1878 to 1900 the silver-producing states of the far West were strong advocates of free silver, and the Pacific coast was the seat of the movement against the immigration of Asiatics.

376. REVIEW

The sections in the Union after 1885 were: New England, the middle states, the South, the middle West, and the far West, all of them on terms of intimate friendship and kinship. From 1889 to 1896, seven new states were admitted into the Union: the two Dakotas, Montana, Washington, Idaho, Wyoming, and Utah. Oklahoma was added in 1907 and New Mexico and Arizona in 1912, thus making a total of forty-eight states.

The South began to flourish again after 1885; it included about a third of the inhabitants of the United States and was raising immense crops of cotton and developing its resources of timber, oil, and farming products. Manufactures were developed, capital was brought in, and cities grew prosperous.

The negroes, though not employed in textile and similar manufactures, did much of the rough labor and raised about half the crops. The South suffered from a vicious system of money advances to cotton growers and to laborers. Some attempts were made to secure forced labor from negroes and others by peonage. Lynchings often interfered with the course of justice. The southern states built up a good system of grade

schools, high schools, and universities, of which few were
open to the negroes.

In the far West, the Indians ceased to be troublesome.
The question of water rights gave concern to both the stock
holders and the farmers on irrigated land. Excellent railroads
were built from east to west across the Rocky Mountains,
and along the Pacific coast. These brought travelers into touch
with the magnificent scenery of the mountains and the coast.
Population in the far West was still sparse and included great
numbers of foreigners. The people, however, set up an excellent system of public education.

In some of the southern states, laws or constitutions, including the "Grandfather clause," were made so as to shut out a
great part of the negro vote. Most of the southern states,
united as the "solid South," usually cast their votes for Democratic governors, senators, and presidential electors. In the
West many new political methods were tried out, and there
was great agitation in politics.

References Bearing on the Text and Topics

Geography and Maps. See map, p. 578. — Brigham, *Geogr. Influences*, chs. viii–x. — Paxson, *New Nation*, 53. — Shepherd, *Hist. Atlas*,
203.

Secondary. Beard, *Contemp. Am. Hist.*, ch. i. — Brown, *Lower
South*, 247–271. — Cable, *Negro Question.* — Coman, *Indust. Hist.*,
307–312. — Eastman, *Indian To-day.* — Hart, *Southern South.* —
Haworth, *America in Ferment*, ch. v. — Kephart, *Southern Highlanders.*
— Leupp, *Indian and his Problem.* — Markham, *California*, chs. xiii–xix. —
Murphy, *Present South.* — Paine, *Greater America.* — Paxson, *New
Nation*, 151–157, 192–207. — Ralph, *Dixie; Great West.* — Smythe,
Conquest of Arid America. — Wilson, *Am. People*, V. 136–140, 199–204,
210–214.

Sources. Bogart and Thompson, *Readings*, 605, 622–629, 640–
643, 750. — DuBois, *Souls of Black Folk.* — Grady, *New South.* —
Harding, *Select Orations*, nos. 33, 34. — Herbert, *Why the Solid South?*
— King, *Mountaineering in the Sierra Nevada.* — MacDonald, *Select
Statutes*, nos. 115, 116, 118, 119. — Muir, *Mountains of California.*
— Van Dyke, *The Desert.* — Washington, *Up from Slavery.*

Illustrative. Atherton, *Ancestors*. — Craddock, *Prophet of the Great Smoky Mountains*. — Chesnutt, *Marrow of Tradition* (negroes). — Dunbar, *Folks from Dixie* (negroes); *Lyrics*. — Foote, *Chosen Valley* (irrigation). — Moore, *Bishop of Cottontown*. — Page, *The Southerner*. — Rayner, *Handicapped among the Free*. — Sanborn, *A Truthful Woman in Southern California*. — Smith, *Colonel Carter*. — Stewart, *Letters of a Woman Homesteader*. — Wister, *Lady Baltimore*. — Wright, *Winning of Barbara Worth*.

Pictures. *Century*. — *Collier's Weekly*. — Dunbar, *Hist. of Travel in Am*. — *Harper's Weekly*. — *Independent*. — *Literary Digest*. — McKinley, *Illus. Topics for Am. Hist*. — *Mentor*, serial nos. 60, 72, 83, 92, 116. — *National Geographic Magazine*. — *National Parks Portfolio*. — *Outlook*. — *Review of Reviews*. — *Survey*. — *World's Work*.

Topics Answerable from the References Above

(1) Admission of *one* of the following states: North Dakota; South Dakota; Montana; Washington; Utah; Oklahoma. [§ 368] — (2) Cultivation of corn, *or* cotton, *or* wheat. [§ 369] — (3) Discoveries of oil in the Southwest. [§ 369] — (4) Plantation laborers: negro *or* white. [§ 370] — (5) Southern farmers: white *or* negro. [§ 370] — (6) Education in the South: common schools; *or* normal schools; *or* colleges; *or* state universities. [§ 371] — (7) Literary career of: Joel Chandler Harris; *or* Thomas Nelson Page; *or* Hopkinson Smith. [§ 371] — (8) Negro education in the South: common schools *or* colleges. [§ 371] — (9) Educational career of Booker T. Washington. [§ 371] — (10) Account of *one*: national parks; national monuments; national forests. [§ 372] — (11) A railroad trip from the Atlantic to the Pacific about 1900. [§ 373] — (12) Grand Canyon of the Colorado. [§ 373] — (13) Description of: western mining town; *or* western fruit ranch; *or* western summer resort. [§ 374]

Topics for Further Search

(14) Early northern visitors to the South. [§ 367] — (15) Southern students in northern colleges. [§ 367] — (16) Southern cotton mill towns. [§ 369] — (17) Why are there few foreign immigrants in the South? [§ 370] — (18) Description of peonage. [§ 370] — (19) Tribal Indians in Indian Territory. [§ 372] — (20) Cattle raising in the Southwest. [§ 372]

CHAPTER XXXIV

BROADENING OF THE GOVERNMENT (1901–1912)

377. PRESIDENT ROOSEVELT

A NEW note was struck in public affairs when Theodore Roosevelt became President. No man for many years had come

THEODORE ROOSEVELT.

to that place so free from obligations to party leaders, so little hampered by the political traditions of Congress and the White House. Theodore Roosevelt was born in New York in 1858, of Dutch, German, Irish, and English descent. He graduated from Harvard College in 1880, and in 1883 was a member of the New York legislature, where he distinguished himself as a fighter for cheaper fares on the New York elevated roads. Then he carried on a cattle ranch in North Dakota and wrote several books on open-air life and American history.

From 1889 to 1895 he was the leading spirit of the National Civil Service Commission (§ 355). For two years he was a Police Commissioner in the city of New York. In 1897–1898 he was Assistant Secretary of the Navy, but resigned to enter the army, and was one of the few men who, in the Spanish War, attracted popular attention by military services on land. The reputation thus gained practically made him governor of New York (1899); he was very outspoken and active in that office; and the New York political leaders thought it wise to shelve him by making him Vice President (1901). Roosevelt's distinguishing qualities in his various offices were the courage to hold and express an opinion for himself, quick resolution, firmness of decision, public criticism of opponents, and a fixed policy of openness and publicity in all that he did, that left no opportunity for private understandings and deals.

378. INTERNAL AFFAIRS (1901–1904)

For a time, President Roosevelt continued in office the Cabinet left by McKinley. John Hay remained Secretary of State till his death in 1905, when Elihu Root of New York succeeded him. Gradually a new set of heads of departments came in; and a new Cabinet position was created by the organization of the Department of Commerce and Labor (1903). Besides the members of the Cabinet, the President consulted with a group of young men who held government positions; they were often called the "Tennis Cabinet." In fact the President consulted with everybody: with senators and representatives, with party leaders, with thousands of visitors to the White House. Having filled up his mind with information from all sources he then made his decisions so swiftly and energetically that many people thought him impulsive.

As a former chairman of the Civil Service Commission, Roosevelt was especially interested in improving the national public service. He found 84,000 government employees in the "classified service," entrance to which was to be had only through competitive examination. By 1904, this number was raised to 143,000, which was about half of all the civil employees of the government. Outside of this list, 7000 officials held their places on "presidential appointments," which required confirmation by the Senate; and 85,000 were country postmasters and mail clerks, who were not considered subject to the reformed system.

Roosevelt was much interested in the diplomatic and consular service. He made it a point to follow the unusual method of transferring good foreign ministers to higher diplomatic posts. He also began an improvement in the consular service, by keeping experienced men in their places, and in 1906 directed that all the higher posts in the consular service should be filled by promotions from lower places.

President Roosevelt was specially confronted by a question which had been difficult for forty years — that of nominating colored men for office. Such appointments were frequent in the northern states; but though there were several hundred thousand negro voters in the South, notwithstanding the effect of the new suffrage laws (§ 375), only a few responsible and well-paid offices were held by them in that section. Roosevelt continued the practice of nominating a few such men and declared in a public letter that he would not "shut the door of opportunity" on the members of the negro race.

The President proceeded on the Jacksonian theory (§ 215) that he represented the people at large, and in 1902 came forward as a mediator in a great coal strike. The anthracite miners in eastern Pennsylvania struck for higher wages, and the eastern states were left without the necessary supply of fuel at the beginning of the winter. The state government was unable to deal with the matter, and there was then no national machinery for that purpose. John Mitchell, a labor leader, worked for a settlement, and President Roosevelt, by consent of both sides, appointed an informal commission which settled the strike by arranging for an increase of wages. The price of coal rose in proportion.

The great question of trusts and monopolies was still in confusion. A few ineffective prosecutions had been brought by McKinley's administration under the Sherman Antitrust Act of 1890 (§ 351). Roosevelt directed that other corporations

be prosecuted, and especially pushed a suit to prevent the "merger" — that is, the consolidation — of the Great Northern, the Northern Pacific, and the Chicago Burlington and Quincy railroads which tended to make a monopoly of the railroad business in the North-

TYPES OF AMERICAN LOCOMOTIVES IN 1876, 1903, AND 1914.

west. The Supreme Court (1904) held that the Sherman Act applied to monopolies of railroads as well as to other corporations, and quashed the merger. This decision seemed likely to put a stop to the consolidations of railroads.

Meanwhile a more stringent antitrust act was passed in 1903, under which the United States government required corporations which were doing any interstate business to allow the inspection of their accounts. It was believed that many of the evils of trusts and combinations would disappear if the trusts could be compelled to tell the public what they were doing. The new Department of Commerce and Labor established a Bureau of Corporations whose business it was to gather information, investigate abuses, and apply the laws.

379. The Isthmian Canal (1898–1904)

These changes and reforms were obscured in the public mind by exciting events which brought about the building of an Isthmian Canal, under the ownership and control of the United States. The voyage of the battleship *Oregon* in 1898, when it was compelled to steam 15,000 miles from San Francisco to join the fleet in the West Indies, called attention to the need of a shorter route from ocean to ocean. The French Panama Canal Company, after its breakdown in 1889 (§ 338), was reorganized and made a second attempt to complete the canal and thus to save the capital that had gone into it, but again suspended operations in 1899. Nevertheless it held the land on the canal route and the concession to build the canal, and it owned the Panama Railroad.

A rising sentiment in the United States demanded that the only way to build a canal or to make a canal worth while to the world, was for the United States to undertake the task. The American Nicaragua Company (§ 338) had done little work on the more northern route, and asked Congress to take their work and concessions off their hands. In order to act intelligently Congress authorized a special commission of experts, and the President appointed five of the ablest engineers in the land. They made the first trustworthy surveys of the isthmus routes and reported (1900) that the United States ought to build on the Nicaragua route, because the French Panama Company would not come to any reasonable terms for the purchase of their property and rights. Between the lines it was clear that the commission thought the Panama route the more desirable one.

A serious obstacle in the way of any American route was the Clayton-Bulwer treaty (§ 233) under which the British govern-

ment had an equal interest with the United States in any canal
that might be built. The British in 1882 had taken possession
of Egypt and become controlling owners of the Suez Canal;
and it did not seem fair that they should also control a half
interest in an American canal. Inasmuch as during the Spanish War the British government and people showed warm
sympathy with the United States, and plainly desired to remove any jealousies between the two English-speaking countries, the United States proposed that the Clayton-Bulwer
treaty be given up. By the Hay-Pauncefote treaty (November
18, 1901), Great Britain agreed to make no claims to take part
in the construction or control of the canal; in return, it was
agreed that the tolls charged should be equal for all nations.
So far as foreign nations were concerned, the United States was
then free to handle the matter for itself. Public sentiment
demanded an American canal built with the funds of the
United States government.

The French company offered to sell out for $40,000,000 cash.
The only obstacle to the wishes of the United States was that
the Panama route ran through the territory of Colombia. A
strong movement in the United States favored settling the
matter by taking the Nicaragua route, where the local government was eager to have a canal. Congress, therefore,
passed an act (June 28, 1902) authorizing the President to
accept the French company's offer, provided Colombia would
cede the control of the necessary land strip "within a reasonable time and upon reasonable terms." Otherwise he
was directed to begin construction of the canal on the Nicaragua
route.

This pressure caused the government of Colombia to draw
up and offer a treaty, by which the United States, for a stipu-
lated payment, was to acquire the desired control over the line
of the canal. The Colombian Congress, however, refused ratification of this treaty, either because it wanted more money,
or because it expected the French grant to lapse so that the

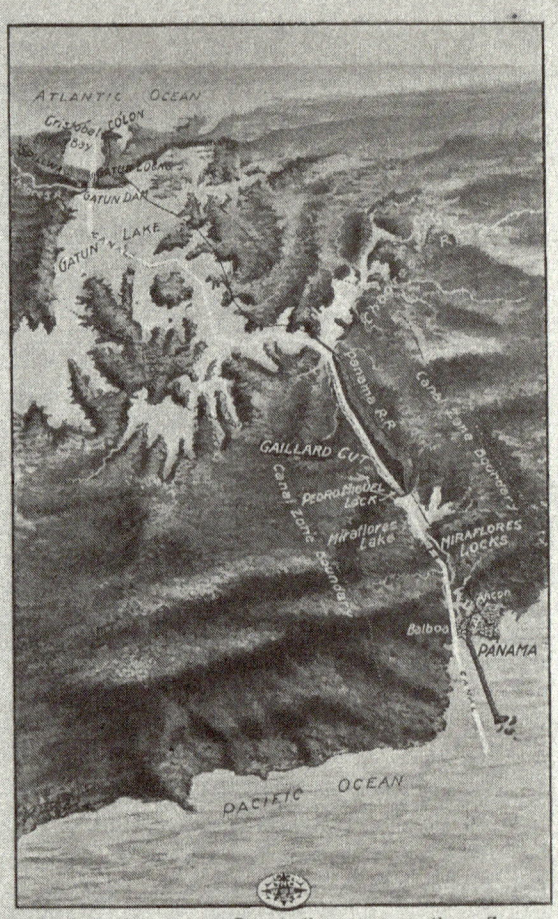

BIRD'S-EYE VIEW OF THE PANAMA CANAL AND THE CANAL ZONE.

604

$40,000,000 would go to Colombia. About six weeks later an insurrection broke out in Panama, which was then a state of the United States of Colombia. The insurrection would have probably failed but for the presence of United States marines, who headed off the Colombian troops. A republic of Panama was set up (November 3, 1903). Within three days, the republic was recognized by the United States, and later by European nations. The new government of Panama hastened to negotiate a treaty on the same lines as that with Colombia (February, 1904). It ceded a "Canal Zone" ten miles wide in which the United States was to have sovereign control. The United States paid $10,000,000 down and agreed to pay $250,000 a year to Panama. Having thus prepared the way, the President appointed civilian engineers, put them in charge, and urged them to "make the dirt fly."

380. INTERNAL AFFAIRS (1904–1908)

When the Panama question was thus settled to the mind of the government, the two main political parties prepared for the presidential election of 1904. Roosevelt was renominated by the Republicans without opposition. The Democratic party was divided between the Free Silverites headed by Bryan, and those who were ready to accept the gold standard as permanent. The latter were able to control the nominating convention and to nominate Judge Alton B. Parker of New York, who stood distinctly on the gold basis.

The currency question being thus out of the way, the main issues of the campaign were "Imperialism" (which meant the question of the Philippines), the tariff, and the relation of the two great parties to the trusts. In the election, Judge Parker carried the "solid South" except Missouri and one elector in Maryland. Roosevelt carried all the other states in the Union, and had 336 electoral votes to 140, and a popular plurality of about 2,500,000 votes. The Socialist candidate, Eugene V. Debs, received 400,000 votes; the People's party candidate, Thomas E. Watson, had 120,000 votes; and the Prohibition candidate, Silas Swallow, had 260,000 votes.

The population was growing and the country was very prosperous. Even the loss of $400,000,000 worth of property in a great fire at San Francisco following an earthquake (April 18, 1906) did not check the general growth of business. In spite of the laws regulating railroads (§ 350) it was found hard to secure convictions of railroads or their officials for the giving of special rates, or rebates from the regular rates, to favored shippers. The President, therefore, urged upon Congress an act which was finally passed (June 29, 1906) as the "Hepburn Act," bestowing larger powers on the Interstate Commerce Commission, increasing the number of commissioners to seven, fixing new penalties for the offense of allowing special rates to anybody, and abolishing free passes — all applying of course only to interstate or foreign traffic.

One of the most important lines of business in the country was the preparation of food products on a large scale, including enormous quantities of tinned meats, fruits, and vegetables. Some states passed laws for inspecting meats, and a popular novelist roused the whole country by describing in lurid fashion the dirt and carelessness in certain packing houses where dressed meats were put up. The result of this popular interest was an act of Congress (June 30, 1906), which was based on the right of Congress "to regulate commerce with foreign nations, and among the several states." By this statute all manufacturers of meat products must have their products inspected and marked by federal officials, in case they were intended for shipment outside the state. Akin to this act was the Pure Food Act of the same date, which forbade the carrying of food products, drugs, liquors, etc. from one state to another unless they bore labels showing their real nature and the proportion of alcohol or narcotics. Many states passed similar pure food laws for intrastate business. These acts showed that both national and state governments were infused with a new idea of what ought to be done for the health and safety of the people. They showed also that Congress, through its power over interstate commerce, could bring about a fairly uniform system in such matters as pure food products.

381. WORLD POLITICS (1905–1909)

Ever since the Spanish War the people of the United States felt that they had a place as a great power, which ought to share in settling the world questions of the time. An evidence of the respect felt for this country by foreign nations was the agreement of Russia and Japan, after a year's warfare in Korea and Manchuria, to accept President Roosevelt's suggestion that they attempt to make peace on American soil. The result was the Treaty of Portsmouth (September, 1905), which ended the war.

In 1906 the United States sent a diplomatic representative to the conference of Algeciras (Spain), which was held to decide whether France and England were willing that Germany should secure a foothold in Morocco. The weight of American influence was thrown toward a peaceful settlement, and a convention was negotiated in which, however, the German hopes were not realized. That failure to gain what the Germans felt to be a national ambition was one of the causes of the Great War of 1914.

Nearer home, the United States took a more direct and important part in several international affairs. Trouble arose in 1902 over the relations between Venezuela on one side and Germany, Great Britain, and Italy on the other. Subjects of these three powers had claims against the Venezuelan government for destruction of property, or personal injuries. Since they could get no satisfaction in any other way, the three governments gave notice that they would send fleets to collect the bill. This was very unwelcome to the United States, and President Roosevelt insisted that Germany give a pledge not to land on Venezuelan soil. The fleets, therefore, did nothing but blockade

harbors and capture a few coasters. Venezuela gave way so
far as to consent to arbitrate the claims before the Hague
Court which had been set up by the peace conference of 1899
(§ 365).

The Cuban government established in 1902 (§ 363) continued
after the departure of the American troops, till in 1906 a revolution broke out. The regular government under President Palma
could not protect itself, and the only way to keep order was
for the United States, acting under the Platt Amendment,
to take control of the country for a time. A provisional governor, Magoon, was appointed from Washington, and acted till
it was announced that an orderly government was again in
force, whereupon the United States troops for the second time
withdrew (1909).

The naval power of the United States was made prominent by
a voyage of sixteen battleships and some smaller vessels around
the world (1907–1909) — the first voyage of the kind ever
made by so powerful a fleet. On the other hand the delegates
of the United States to the second Hague Conference (1907)
took a strong position for peace and aided in framing and ap-
proving several conventions which it was hoped would prevent
wars from breaking out and would take away much of their
horror if they did occur. In this meeting, as in that of 1899,
the American representatives secured a statement that nothing in the conventions should be taken to affect the "traditional
policy of the United States"; and that phrase was understood
to mean the Monroe Doctrine (§ 193).

382. APPLYING THE MONROE DOCTRINE (1902–1913)

The Venezuelan difficulty is closely connected with the objections of the United States to foreign influence in America, to
which the name Monroe Doctrine is usually applied. The
affair brought out that it was very inconvenient and undesirable
for foreign fleets to use force in American waters. On the
other hand, what was to be done when some weak American

powers failed to protect foreigners resident in their borders
and declined to pay damages if they were ill treated? Was there
any effective remedy except to occupy their territory?

When in 1906 there was another of the many political up-
heavals in the republic of Santo Domingo, the administration
at Washington was sure that some European power was about
to interfere in behalf of its citizens. President Roosevelt made
up his mind that the only way to prevent trouble was for the
United States to step in, restore order, and guarantee the payment of just debts. He therefore landed a force, made a treaty
with the men who happened to be in control of the little republic, and put an American official into the customhouse to
collect the money and take out enough to pay the interest on
the debt of Santo Domingo and eventually to pay the principal.
After a long delay the Senate of the United States ratified the
treaty and thus gave its approval to this method of dealing
with Latin American states. Since Panama and Cuba were
practically no longer sovereign, but protectorates of the
United States, the United States then had three dependencies
besides Porto Rico and the Philippine Islands. President
Roosevelt stated this new form of the Monroe Doctrine in
several messages and speeches. He virtually promised Europe
that the United States would undertake to set to rights any
American power against which there were just grievances.
Such a course would make it unnecessary for European powers
to intervene. This is the policy of "the international police-
man" or "the big stick." The same policy was followed out
in the next administration by President Taft, who negotiated a
treaty with Nicaragua similar to that with Santo Domingo.

The Panama Canal had a close connection with the Monroe
Doctrine, since it would be a new bond of communication and
influence with the Central American and South American
states. For some time the construction lagged, because the
American engineers had to contend with the dreadful unhealth-
fulness of the isthmus. Fortunately, skilled American medical

men in Cuba had discovered that yellow fever is carried by a
mosquito, and it was already known that malaria is carried
by another mosquito. Acting on this knowledge, Colonel
Gorgas was put in charge of the sanitary conditions of the
working force. On his recommendation, all the underbrush
was cut along the line of the canal, for about half a mile back
on each side, and a pure water supply was introduced. The
result was that the engineers and laborers on the canal were as
free from disease as anybody else in the world. In 1907 Major
George W. Goethals of the United States army was made chief
engineer of the canal; and under the management of army
officers the work was carried on rapidly. The original plan of
a sea level canal from ocean to ocean was changed to a lock
canal, with a great central lake.

383. CONSERVATION (1909–1913)

For many years it had been the policy of the United States
government to get rid of the public lands as fast as possible.
The old Preëmption Act of 1841 (§ 239) was repealed, but under
the Homestead Act of 1862, great quantities of land went directly
into the hands of farmers. The land grants to the railroads
and to the states, besides tracts supposed to be unfit for farming, passed into the hands of capitalists. By 1901 there was
very little government land left that was available for farming, though Uncle Sam still owned hundreds of thousands of
square miles of desert and mountain and forested areas. Much
of this land was valuable for its timber, its coal and other minerals, its oil and its water powers, which became useful through
the invention of systems for transmitting electric power to long
distances.

The idea naturally sprang up that these advantages ought
not to be allowed to pass into the hands of speculators or even
investors; that they were immense bounties of nature which
somehow ought to be saved for the public benefit. The system of saving them came to be called " conservation."

(1) Forests. To preserve the forests, the government adopted
the method of "forest reserves" (beginning in 1891). Large
areas which either bore trees or were probably capable of
bearing trees, were taken out of the land available for settlement and kept as permanent public tracts. A system of for-
estry was developed which kept down fires, prevented the cutting of timber without leave from the government, and began
to reforest areas that needed it. A main argument for these
reserves was that the forests held heavy rains and thus pro-

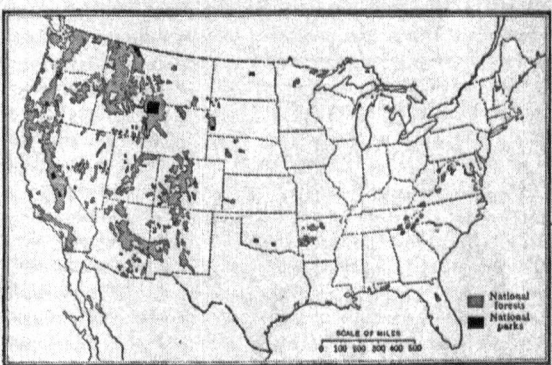

NATIONAL FORESTS AND PARKS.

tected the sources of navigable rivers and prevented floods. This
argument was applied to the Appalachian mountain ranges
in 1911, when Congress appropriated $6,000,000 to buy for-
est lands in that region; by 1915, 1,285,000 acres were thus
acquired, principally in the White Mountains and southern
mountains.

(2) Minerals. The government had a system of selling ledges
containing valuable ore to those who could mine them, usually
in very small tracts. If land was sold as farm land, timber
land, or for any other purpose, and coal or any other minerals

were subsequently discovered, those riches belonged to the owner of the soil. Sharp speculators would locate many blocks of land through employees or dummies, and thus hold large tracts for the sake of the minerals they contained. In 1910, Congress passed an act by which farm lands could be sold, reserving as government property the coal and other minerals beneath the surface. Great pains were taken to prevent the coal deposits in Alaska from falling into the hands of private owners.

(3) Water powers. It had been the practice all over the Union for the man who could buy or homestead a waterfront,

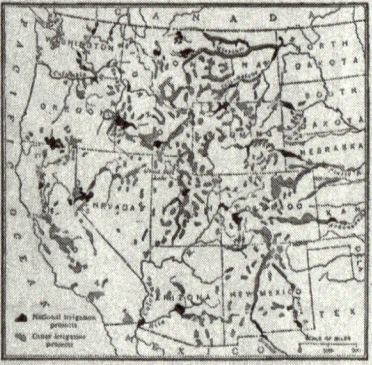

to take possession of the water powers that might exist there. In 1910 the government took the precaution to reserve a large number of water powers on the public domain until some general law should be passed, by which they could be kept as government property, and could be

WESTERN IRRIGATION PROJECTS.

leased to those who were best able to develop them.

(4) Irrigation. In parts of the West and far West, some lands could be made rich and productive by bringing irrigation water to them. Many such privileges were taken up by individuals or land companies. By the Newlands Act (1902), Congress adopted the policy of spending whatever money was received for public lands in certain states, for the building of irrigation works. The land served by these new systems was

to be sold in small tracts, at prices which were intended to pay for the works. This policy required the government to hold the stretches of the mountain streams necessary for filling the reservoirs, and to use the water power drained from these dams.

384. PRESIDENT TAFT (1909–1913)

Few of the questions agitated during the two terms of President Roosevelt (1901–1909) divided Congress on party lines. Public sentiment called for such measures as the Pure Food Act and acts for regulating railroads and other corporations, and the only question was how far-reaching they should be. The President looked upon himself as the representative of the people at large (§ 378) and he had the habit of writing messages to Congress and expressing his mind in conversations, upon what he considered to be the duty of Congress. In numerous instances he thus compelled Congress to follow his lead. Many people believed that Roosevelt could have been reëlected in 1908, but he made no effort to secure a third term, and threw his influence in favor of William H. Taft, then Secretary of War.

In the campaign (1908) there were no very distinct party issues. The currency issue had faded out. As for the tariff, both of the great parties favored a revision of the Dingley tariff of 1897 (§ 361), against which there was rising opposition in the West. William J. Bryan was for the third time the Democratic candidate, and carried the "solid South" and four western states, with a total of 162 electoral votes. Taft received 321 electoral votes and a plurality of 1,270,000 popular votes. The Socialist vote rose to 420,000 and the Prohibition vote was 250,000.

William H. Taft was a man of wide and varied experience. He served the public, first as judge of a United States court in Ohio; then as Governor General of the Philippines, where he had a large part in framing the successful insular government

(§ 362); then as Secretary of War, where he was still in charge of the Philippine administration. As President he carried out

WILLIAM H. TAFT.

many of the policies of previous Presidents, particularly the regulation of corporations and transportation and the reform of the federal service.

President Taft at once after his inauguration summoned Congress to meet in special session for the purpose of revising the tariff. The members of his party disagreed as to whether the promise to revise meant to "revise downward." Eventually a measure called the Payne-Aldrich tariff was passed (1909); it reduced some duties and somewhat increased others, especially on cotton goods. President Taft signed the measure and afterwards presented it as "the best tariff bill that has been passed." To make up for any possible loss of revenue, Congress added to the bill a tax of one per cent on the net earnings of corporations having a net income above $5000 a year. This tightened the hold of the administration on corporations, because they were obliged to make statements of their transactions to serve as the basis for the tax.

385. PROGRESSIVE REPUBLICAN MOVEMENT (1910–1912)

Though the Republican party seemed firmly seated in the national government, serious differences of opinion arose in

several states and made their appearance in Congress. Some
of the Republicans were greatly disappointed by the Payne-
Aldrich tariff. Others were angered by what they thought to
be high-handed methods of Joseph G. Cannon, who since 1903
had been Speaker of the House of Representatives. They accused him of refusing to grant committee appointments and
other favors to Republican members who did not agree with
him. Another group of dissatisfied Republicans was headed
by Robert LaFollette of Wisconsin, who had defied and finally
beaten the old-time heads of the party in his state; after being
governor he was elected to the United States Senate (1910),
and there he defied the traditions of that august body.

The members of Congress who joined in this movement, which
grew to be a revolt, were called by their enemies "insurgents,"
but they called themselves "Progressives" or "Progressive
Republicans." The regular Republicans, who had control of
the national committee and of most of the state committees
of the party, were called "Standpatters." In March, 1910,
about forty insurgents joined with the Democrats in voting to
take away some of the most important powers of the Speaker.
Other Standpatters lost their seats in Congress or declined to
stand for reëlection.

In 1911, a struggle arose over an act of Congress offering favorable trade to Canada. President Taft favored it and pushed
it through Congress, but the Canadians refused to accept it.
A special Tariff Commission was appointed, to find out if
possible the difference of cost in making goods in the United
States, as against that of other countries. It reported in favor
of the lowering of certain wool duties; but the President vetoed
the bills on that subject passed by Congress.

Taft urged the strengthening of the Interstate Commerce
Commission; and, following his lead, Congress gave the commission larger powers and placed the Pullman car service and
the private express companies under its authority to investigate and alter rates (June 18, 1910). The President also set on

foot prosecutions of some of the largest corporations, on the charge that they were not observing the Sherman Antitrust Act. This resulted in a decision of the Supreme Court (1912) against the Standard Oil Company and American Tobacco Company. Both were held to be guilty of "restraint of trade and monopolization," by their practical control of two great lines of business. They were ordered to break up the holding companies into which they were divided, after which they might continue their regular business under their former charters. The decision included the "rule of reason"; that is, the Court said that it was not reasonable to suppose that the Sherman Act of 1890 applied to corporations which did not set up a monopoly dangerous to the public interests.

The administration of President Taft thus followed in the same line as that of President Roosevelt, in pressing steadily for stronger acts of Congress against fraud and monopoly in business; in inviting Congress to enlarge the powers of the courts and the Interstate Commerce Commission, so as to regulate business and especially corporations; and in urging suits before the Supreme Court intended to compel corporations to live up to the laws as understood by the federal government.

386. REVIEW

When Theodore Roosevelt became President of the United States in 1901, the country was ready for novelties in government, foreign policy, and economic organization. The President placed many more federal employees in the classified service. He urged Congress to improve the consular service, and mediated a coal strike in Pennsylvania. He successfully pushed a suit against railroad consolidation, and began to investigate corporations.

On the Isthmian Canal an official commission reported (1900) that the United States ought to control such a canal. Great Britain gave up the Clayton-Bulwer Treaty of 1850 and the United States was left free to act. A treaty was negotiated with Colombia for a canal through Panama; but the Colombian Congress refused to ratify. A Republic of Panama, set up by revolution, agreed to a canal treaty.

In 1904, Roosevelt was reëlected, over Judge Parker of New York, the Democratic candidate. Congress passed several new acts enabling the Interstate Commerce Commission to deal more effectively with the railroads, and providing for sanitary meat packing and pure food and drugs.

In 1902, President Roosevelt objected to foreign powers taking any territory of Venezuela. The United States acted as a kind of mediator between Japan and Russia in 1905. The conditions in Cuba led to an occupation of that republic (1906-1909). The United States was active in the Second Hague Conference of 1907, and advanced the Monroe Doctrine to new applications. Panama and Santo Domingo practically became dependencies.

Under a new policy of conservation, the government set up forest reserves, held back part of the minerals under the surface of farming lands, held up water powers, and provided for irrigation on a large scale.

William H. Taft was urged as Roosevelt's successor, and he was elected in 1908 by the Republicans, over W. J. Bryan, the Democratic candidate. He continued the policy of regulation of transportation and corporations. He approved of the Payne-Aldrich tariff of 1909. "Progressive Republicans" arose who opposed the "Standpatters." The powers of the Interstate Commerce Commission were still further advanced.

References Bearing on the Text and Topics

Geography and Maps. See maps, pp. 611, 612. — Bogart, *Econ. Hist.*, 371, 490, 511. — Coman, *Indust. Hist.*, 350, 384, 388, 394, 404. — Hart, *Am. Ideals*, 46, 240, 264. — Latané, *Am. as a World Power*, 200, 210, 274. — Paxson, *New Nation*, 77, 120, 153.

Secondary. Bassett, *U.S.*, 817–822, 825–843, 849–852. — Beard, *Contemp. Am. Hist.*, chs. ix–xii. — Bogart, *Econ. Hist.*, chs. xxxii, xxxiii. — Coolidge, *U. S. as a World Power*, chs. x–xvi. — Coman,

Indust. Hist., ch. xi. — De Witt, *Progressive Movement*, pts. i, ii. — Duncan-Clark, *Progressive Movement.* — Edwards, *Panama*, chs. xxix–xxxiv. — Fish, *Am. Dipl.*, 429–453; *Am. Nationality*, 496–514, 517–531. — Hart, *Monroe Doctrine*, 214–242. — Haworth, *Reconstruction and Union*, ch. ix. — Johnson, *Panama Canal*, chs. viii–xviii. — Latané, *Am. as a World Power*, chs. xi–xvi, xviii. — Laughlin, *Indust. America.* — Paxson, *New Nation*, 283–335. — Thayer, *John Hay*, II, chs. xxviii–xxxi. — Van Hise, *Conservation.* — Washburn, *Roosevelt*, chs. ii, iii, v.

Sources. *Am. Year Book*, 1910 to 1912. — Beard, *Readings*, §§ 105, 149–153. — Bogart and Thompson, *Readings*, 598–853 passim. — Foraker, *Notes of a Busy Life*, II, chs. xxxv–xlviii. — *International Year Book*, 1907 to 1912. — James, *Readings*, §§ 101, 102, 104. — Orth, *Readings.* — Roosevelt, *Autobiography*, chs. x–xv.

Illustrative. Dillon, *The Leader.* — Gale, *Friendship Village* (Middle West). — Grant, *Chippendales.* — Hurt, *Scarlet Shadow* (labor).

Pictures. *Mentor*, serial no. 15. — See also references to ch. xxxiii.

Topics Answerable from the References Above

(1) Theodore Roosevelt as a boy and young man. [§ 377] — (2) Public services of *one* of the following public men: Roosevelt; Root [§ 378]; Parker; Debs [§ 380]; Cannon; LaFollette. [§ 385] — (3) Formation of the republic of Panama. [§ 379] — (4) The Canal Zone. [§ 379] — (5) Election of 1904 [§ 380], *or*, of 1908. [§ 384] — (6) San Francisco fire. [§ 380] — (7) Occupation of Santo Domingo, 1906. [§ 382] — (8) Construction of the Panama Canal. [§ 382] — (9) Forest reserves in the East. [§ 383] — (10) Debates on the Payne-Aldrich tariff. [§ 384]

Topics for Further Search

(11) What is the "classified service"? [§ 378] — (12) Anthracite strike and settlement. [§ 378] — (13) French Panama Canal Company. [§ 379] — (14) What is the need of pure food laws? [§ 380] — (15) Blockade of the Venezuelan ports. [§ 381] — (16) Second Hague Peace Conference. [§ 381] — (17) Effects of the Newlands Act. [§ 383] — (18) Proposed reciprocity with Canada. [§ 385]

CHAPTER XXXV

THE UNITED STATES AS A WORLD POWER (1912–1917)

387. POLITICAL METHODS

BEHIND the controversies in Congress, the White House, and
the Supreme Court, behind the Progressive movement, was
a feeling of unrest which showed itself all over the country.
The great political parties were managed by small groups of
men, some of them holding state or national office, others without
any official connection with the government. In some states,
notably New York and Pennsylvania, single "bosses" practically
nominated the candidates, dictated the platforms, and made the
appointments to office. In others, railroads and public service
corporations were in alliance with bosses and saw to it that nobody was nominated to any important office who was unfavorable to them. The principal difficulties of the political system
were the following:

(1) *Nomination of candidates by local and state conventions,*
sometimes under the absolute control of a single man. This
led to the so-called "direct primary," beginning in Wisconsin
in 1903. By this system the members of each party vote at
special elections conducted by the state authorities, for the person whom they desire to see nominated for a particular office.
The man who receives the most votes on his party ticket is
then entered on the ballot as the only candidate of his party
at the regular election. This reform applies especially to state
and local officers, but in some states the members of each
party can vote on the selection of candidates for President.

(2) *Lack of responsibility of members of the legislature.* In
some states, bosses or corporations could control a majority

of the state legislature, and could thus secure acts against which there was strong popular sentiment. A system of "referendum"—that is, appeal to the popular vote—had been familiar for many years in votes on state constitutions, on the issuing of liquor licenses, and other matters. In several states it was now applied to any legislative acts, on petition of a certain number of votes. To meet the case of a legislature which will not pass measures that it is supposed the electorate wants, the "initiative" was contrived, by which a certain number of voters can place on the ballot the text of a statute which they desire and have that voted upon without referring it to the legislature at all.

(3) *Weak city governments.* Many of the city governments were clumsy and weak. Hence a movement to simplify and strengthen them began at Galveston, Texas, in 1901. Under this "commission" plan, the whole government of a city is placed in the hands of a board of commissioners, usually five, who act both as a city council to make ordinances and as an executive board to carry them out. This puts all the affairs of the city in the control of a few persons, who presumably are known to the electors.

(4) *Campaign expenses.* Though the expense of printing ballots and holding elections was borne by the states, large sums were raised and spent by candidates and party committees. Most of the money went for public meetings, bands, speakers, and "getting out the vote." Some was used for bribing voters. To meet this evil, laws were passed by most states and by Congress limiting the amounts that might be spent and compelling managers to file statements of their accounts.

(5) *Irresponsibility of officers.* Sometimes mayors, members of commissions, governors, or other officers performed acts which their constituents did not wish. Therefore, several states, beginning with California, now allow a certain number of voters to place upon the ballot the question whether a particular official shall be "recalled"—that is, deprived of his

office — so that some one may be elected who does represent
the majority. In a few states, judges can be recalled.

None of the new methods of government have worked perfectly. The direct primary brings forward many small men as
candidates, and public men miss the advantage of personal
acquaintance through conventions. The initiative and referendum lead to putting so many different propositions on the
ballot that it is hard to secure the voters' attention. Commission government proved so popular that by 1916 there were
about 400 cities and villages in which it was established; and a
still more concentrated plan of "city manager" was devised,
by which the greater part of the government of a city may be
placed in the hands of a single man, selected for his skill in city
government. Publicity of campaign expenses has been avoided
in many cases by tricks and evasion. The recall works irregu-
larly and there is some danger that judges may be recalled
simply because they make decisions according to their con-
victions. Long experience has shown that no political method
will do much good, unless the voters take an interest in their
own public affairs.

388. PRESIDENTIAL ELECTION OF 1912

In general, the Progressive Republicans in Congress and in
the states supported these new ideas in government and also
more stringent regulation of railroads and other corporations
(§ 378). They brought their views to a test in the Republican national convention of June, 1912, where President Taft
had the support of most of the Standpat party leaders for
renomination, and Theodore Roosevelt was the candidate of
the Progressive Republicans.

Many rival sets of Taft delegates and Roosevelt delegates
appeared, claiming to be the properly elected representatives
of the same districts. Most of these contests were settled in
favor of the Taft men, who proved to have a majority in the
convention and renominated their candidate. The supporters of

Roosevelt insisted that their man had been deprived of votes that justly belonged to him, and called another convention, which adopted the name of Progressive party, nominated Roosevelt, and drew up a platform calling for social and political reforms.

The Democratic convention had before it as candidates Champ Clark of Missouri, Speaker of the House of Representatives, and Woodrow Wilson, then governor of New Jersey. After seven days and forty-six ballots, the deadlock between these candidates was broken by the choice of Woodrow Wilson, chiefly through the influence of William J. Bryan, who had great power in the convention.

The resulting election was the most exciting for many years. Taft received about 3,500,000 popular votes, and 8 electoral votes; Roosevelt received 4,120,000 popular votes and 88 electoral votes; Wilson received 6,300,000 popular votes, and 435 electoral votes, and was elected. Both branches of the Congress which would sit from 1913 to 1915 showed Democratic majorities.

389. President Woodrow Wilson (1913–1917)

President Wilson, in his speeches during the campaign, set forth ideas of government which were very close to those of the Progressive party. He scored the bosses, protested against the usual methods of state legislation, and declared that the trusts "are so great that it is almost an open question whether the government of the United States can dominate them or not." In selecting his Cabinet, he made Bryan Secretary of State as being, next to the President, the most distinguished member of the party.

Woodrow Wilson was born at Staunton, Virginia, in 1856, the son of a southern family. He was educated at Princeton and at Johns Hopkins University, practiced law a short time, and became a professor of history at several colleges. He was one of the first writers to point out the weakness of the committee system in Congress. In 1902 he became president of Princeton University and a recognized leader in education.

In 1910 he was elected as a Democratic governor of New Jersey, where he secured bills for direct primaries, a state commission on corporations, and other measures of a progressive kind. His success in this office led to his nomination for President.

Wilson had a remarkable gift of vigorous speaking and writing, was a good campaigner, and his messages and state papers were always to the point. In addition to the members of his Cabinet — now ten in number by the separation of the Department of Commerce and Labor into two departments (1913) — President Wilson had a few confidential advisers, something like Roosevelt's "Tennis Cabinet" (§ 378). With these exceptions, he sought advice from few people; and he made his own decisions. He carried on the methods of his predecessors in forcing the attention of Congress to measures which he thought necessary, and went a little further by going in person to the halls of Congress and making addresses there — thus reviving the practice of Presidents Washington and Adams — instead of sending in written messages. He was very successful in bringing his party friends in both houses to see the force of his ideas.

WOODROW WILSON.

390. BANKS, TARIFF, AND CORPORATIONS (1913–1917)

The two old questions of the protective tariff and national banks, which had been discussed for nearly a hundred years, came straight to the front again in Wilson's administration.

(1) At once he called Congress in special session, to pass a new tariff, which was introduced by Oscar W. Underwood of Alabama, as Chairman of the Committee on Ways and Means. This tariff was intended first of all to produce revenue, then to discourage monopolies. The main manufactures which were not monopolistic received moderate protection, but the time seemed to have come for a large export trade in manufactured goods, so that less protection was needed. Most of the Republicans opposed the bill and it was very difficult to get the Democrats to act together; but this Underwood tariff became law October 3, 1913.

(2) Alongside the tariff discussion went a long debate on the reorganization of the national banks, which took the form of an immense central bank directed by a Federal Reserve Board, and subdivided into twelve regional Reserve Banks. The bill was signed December 23, 1913, and was called the Owen-Glass Federal Reserve bill, from the two Congressmen who steered it through the Senate and the House.

The President also urged new and stricter legislation against the trusts, and with some difficulty induced Congress to pass an act (September 26, 1914) for a Federal Trade Commission. The main purpose was to prevent "unfair methods of competition in commerce." A few weeks later (October 15) was passed the Clayton Antitrust Act, "to supplement existing laws against unlawful restraints and monopolies." Among other things it forbade any one to sell goods on condition that the purchaser should not buy anything of other firms in the same line; and prohibited "holding companies" so far as they tended to make a monopoly.

These statutes were the high-water mark of an agitation that had been going on ever since the first Interstate Commerce Act of 1887 (§ 350). They went about as far as laws could usefully go in curbing transportation companies, banks, and other great corporations. The states also set up public utility commissions, or corporation commissions, to deal with concerns that were doing a business within the limits of one state and therefore did not come under the regulating acts of Congress. This left in many cases what Roosevelt called "the twilight zone," in which neither the Union nor the state had sufficient power. Still the country began to feel that enough laws had been passed on that subject, and that the great corporations, and especially the railroads, were so tied up that it was hard for them to render good service.

391. CONSTITUTIONAL AMENDMENTS (1909-1913)

An objection to lowering the tariff was that the government needed the revenue. To meet this point, in 1894 the Wilson tariff act contained a clause for taxing incomes, but this clause was held void by the Supreme Court (§ 343). The long discussion of banks and corporations again called attention to the immense amount of interest-bearing securities held in the eastern states. Hence it became possible to secure a two-thirds majority in both Houses of Congress in 1909, for a Sixteenth Amendment to the Constitution authorizing Congress to lay an income tax. It was accepted by the necessary three fourths of the states by February, 1913. The Underwood tariff contained a clause taxing all incomes above $3000 a year (or $4000 for married couples), with higher rates for incomes above $20,000.

A Seventeenth Amendment was added in May, 1913, which transferred the election of United States senators from the legislatures to the voters of each state, acting directly.

Congress was also strongly urged to adopt an amendment granting suffrage throughout the Union to women, but the proposition was voted down in both houses. The first territory or state to grant equal suffrage to women was Wyoming in 1869;

and by 1917 constitutional provisions gave them the vote in eleven states, and they also received it by act of the legislature in Alaska Territory and (for most offices) in Illinois, Indiana, and North Dakota. Besides these states, about twenty others gave some sort of limited suffrage to women.

Pressure was applied to Congress for a national amendment prohibiting the sale of alcoholic liquors. In August, 1917, the liquor traffic was stringently regulated by Congress, as a war measure. Down to 1917 there were twenty-three states in which this traffic was prohibited, besides many others in which cities, counties, or separate municipalities might refuse to grant a license if the majority of the voters so desired.

392. RELATIONS WITH MEXICO (1913–1917)

When President Wilson came into office, he found a war going on in Mexico. General Porfirio Diaz, who had for about thirty years been the dictator of that country, was forced out of office by a revolution headed by Madero (1911). Two years later President Madero was deposed and imprisoned by General Huerta; and then, while in the custody of Huerta's officials, was murdered (February, 1913). Civil war was renewed. Thousands of Americans and hundreds of millions of American property in Mexico sorely needed protection by somebody.

President Wilson refused to recognize Huerta, on the ground that there was no evidence that the Mexicans wanted him for their president. Carranza and Villa raised a force of friends of the former Madero government, and after several defeats Huerta withdrew (July, 1914).

Not only Americans but many other foreigners were caught in Mexico, and some of them were murdered by Villa or by other insurgents or bandits. The United States was unwilling that any other power should enter Mexico, and used its influence for the protection of all non-Mexicans who were in that country. In April, 1914, Wilson thought it necessary to send a military expedition to Vera Cruz. The troops remained several months

and then withdrew without accomplishing anything in particular. Meanwhile Villa made war on Carranza, but was defeated. After much negotiation with the representatives of the
A. B. C. powers (Argentina, Brazil, and Chile), Carranza was
recognized in 1915 as head of the republic of Mexico, although
parts of the country were still held by bandits.

In 1916, an attack on the American town of Columbus, by
Villa, caused the government to send a force of about 15,000
men under General Pershing into Mexico to hunt for the
bandit. When Carranza protested, 150,000 militia were called
out and stationed on the border, but a few months later both
forces were withdrawn without reaching Villa.

393. POLICY OF DEPENDENCIES

With other Latin-American countries, closer relations were .
established. In 1906, a Pan-American Congress was held in
Rio de Janeiro and another in 1910 in Buenos Aires; and suggestions were made that the time had come for a " Pan-American
union" between the United States and the twenty neighboring
republics.

This policy of union was much disturbed by the attitude of
the United States toward some of the small and weak near-by
powers. After the withdrawal of American troops in 1902,
Cuba remained practically a dependency of the United States,
subject to the Platt Amendment (§ 363). Santo Domingo (the
Dominican Republic) remained practically under the direction
of the United States after the customhouse was taken over in
Roosevelt's administration (§ 382). Haiti was disturbed in
much the same way, and in 1915 a treaty was negotiated by
which the finances and the police of that negro republic were
placed under American control. With Nicaragua, President
Taft proposed a treaty very similar to the arrangement with
Cuba but including a payment of $3,000,000 to the little neigh-
bor. After much discussion the Haitian treaty was ratified
in 1916 and a new one with Nicaragua the same year. Inas-

much as the Republic of Panama was from its beginning subject
to the will of the United States government, five of the twenty
republican neighbors were practically not independent countries.

394. THE GREAT WAR IN EUROPE (1914–1916)

The most difficult problems of Wilson's administration were
caused by the terrific war which broke out in Europe August 1,
1914. Though none of the various reasons for the war directly
affected the United States, this country was at once caught in

UNITED STATES BATTLESHIPS.

the circle of hostile operations. The allied powers — Russia,
Great Britain, France, later Japan and Italy, with Belgium,
Serbia, Montenegro, and Portugal — showed such a superiority
at sea, that all the German and Austrian merchant ships
were driven from the seas and some of them took refuge in
our ports. In the protection of these ships, and in all other
details, our government fulfilled the duties of strict neutrality.

The chief difficulty arose from our trade across the ocean.
The United States claimed for its citizens the right to trade
with any of the powers that were at war, just as in times of
peace, except so far as American ships might be carrying con-

traband of war or might break an established blockade (§ 146). Great Britain made new rules of contraband, including copper, rubber, iron ore, cotton, and all kinds of oils; and scores of American vessels were seized for carrying these goods. In 1915 she declared what amounted to an interdict on all commerce to Germany. The Germans sank some of our ships for carrying contraband, and sent out a swarm of submarines with orders to sink British merchant ships on sight. On May 7, 1915, such a craft sank the British merchant steamer *Lusitania*, and about 1200 people were drowned, including 114 Americans. By international law these Americans had the right to take passage on a British merchant ship; and in case the ship was sunk, were entitled, like all the passengers and crew, to sufficient time and opportunity to save their lives.

In the United States a newspaper warfare raged almost as violently as that of bullets and shells in Europe. The friends of Germany defended the *Lusitania* sinking, as well as all other German deeds, and urged that it was a breach of neutrality for Americans to ship any munitions of war, inasmuch as none could reach German ports. The friends of Great Britain, as well as neutral Americans, denied this and pointed to the fact that Germany had not hesitated in time of war to send munitions to Spain, the Balkan powers, and other nations.

The President and Secretary Bryan framed and sent a succession of notes of protest, especially on the *Lusitania* matter; but they got little satisfaction from either belligerent. Mr. Bryan thought the administration too firm in its insistence on American rights, and resigned (June, 1915). Robert Lansing of New York then became Secretary of State.

All kinds of foodstuffs brought a very high price, and there was a great market for clothing, copper, steel, machinery, and munitions of war. The exports of the United States jumped up from $2,365,000,000 in 1913–1914 to $2,769,000,000 in 1914–1915, and $4,333,000,000 in 1915–1916.

395. Review

For several years the energy of a large part of the country went into the discussion of political methods. Many legislatures set up a new system of "direct primaries" for nomination of state officers. The system of "initiative" and "referendum" was devised, to enable the people to pass laws over the heads of the legislature. Hundreds of cities adopted "commission governments." Laws were passed regulating campaign expenses. In a few states the "recall" of public officials by a majority vote of the electors was made legal. None of these reforms worked as completely as had been hoped.

In 1912, Taft was renominated by the Republicans; the followers of Roosevelt organized a separate Progressive party. Woodrow Wilson was put up by the Democrats and was elected. As President, Wilson followed the lead of his predecessors in putting great pressure on Congress to pass legislation. He had a large influence in the Underwood tariff which became law; in a new Federal Reserve Bank system (1913); in the creation of a Federal Trade Commission (1914); and in an enlarged antitrust act (1914).

By the Sixteenth Amendment (1913), it became possible to lay an income tax; by the Seventeenth Amendment (1913), the election of senators was to be determined by popular vote.

An insurrection broke out in Mexico in 1910 which kept that country in anarchy. A United States military expedition was sent to Vera Cruz in 1914; and another into northern Mexico in pursuit of Mexican bandits (1916).

Several Pan-American conferences were held between 1901 and 1915 which looked toward some sort of understanding with the United States. Cuba, Santo Domingo, Haiti, Panama, and Nicaragua practically became dependencies. A fearful war broke out in Europe in 1914 and brought upon the United States many controversies and differences affecting its neutral trade and security.

References Bearing on the Text and Topics

Geography and Maps. See map, p. 533. — Fish, *Am. Dipl.*, 445. — Hart, *Monroe Doct.*, front. — Paxson, *New Nation*, 77, 340.

Secondary. Beard, *Contemp. Am. Hist.*, ch. xiii. — Chamberlin, *Philippine Problem.* — De Witt, *Progressive Movement*, pts. iii, iv. — Duncan-Clark, *Progressive Movement*, chs. iv-vi, xvi. — Fish, *Am. Dipl.*, chs. xxxiv, xxxv. — Ford, *Woodrow Wilson.* — Hart, *Monroe Doct.*, chs. xv-xxiv. — Hecker, *Women's Rights.* — Hepburn, *Currency*, chs. xxii-xxv. — Koren, *Alcohol and Society.* — McLaughlin and Hart, *Cyclopædia of Am. Gov.* — Reed, *Insurgent Mexico.* — Stanwood, *Presidency*, II. ch. iv. — Woodburn, *Polit. Parties*, chs. xxi, xxii.

Sources. *Am. Year Book*, 1912 to 1916. — Beard, *Readings*, §§ 45, 54, 93, 94. — Beard and Shultz, *Docs. on the Initiative.* — Bogart and Thompson, *Readings*, 709, 765. — *International Year Book*, 1912 to 1916. — Roosevelt, *New Nationalism; Progressive Principles.* — Wilson, *New Freedom.*

Pictures. See references to ch. xxxiii.

Topics Answerable from the References Above

(1) Presidential election of 1912. [§ 388] — (2) Account of *one* of the conventions of 1912: Republican; Progressive; Democratic. [§ 388] — (3) Public services of *one* of the following statesmen: Champ Clark; Bryan; Wilson; Underwood. [§§ 388-390] — (4) Debates on *one* of the following bills: Underwood tariff; Federal Reserve Act; Federal Trade Commission; Clayton Antitrust Act; Child Labor Act. [§ 390] — (5) The Sixteenth Amendment; *or* the Seventeenth Amendment. [§ 391] — (6) Expedition to Vera Cruz; *or* Pershing's expedition. [§ 392] — (7) Occupation of Haiti. [§ 393]

Topics for Further Search

(8) Arguments for and against *one* of the following: Referendum; Initiative; Commission Government; Campaign Expense Laws; Recall; City Manager. [§ 387] — (9) Woman suffrage in the U. S.: beginnings; *or* extension; *or* arguments for and against. [§ 391] — (10) Prohibition legislation: beginnings; *or* extension; *or* arguments for and against. [§ 391] — (11) Why was there a revolution in Mexico against Diaz? [§ 392] — (12) The A. B. C. powers. [§ 392] — (13) Pan-American congresses since 1890. [§ 393] — (14) What are the duties of a neutral power in time of war? [§ 394]

CHAPTER XXXVI

WHAT AMERICA HAS DONE FOR THE WORLD

396. The American Race

THE history of our beloved country can be understood only by thinking of it as the story of the effort to make great principles and ideals prevail. We may now sum up for ourselves what the United States of America has accomplished that is worth handing on to the next generation.

First of all, the United States has taught the world how to make a great modern nation out of a variety of races and peoples.

According to the federal census of 1910, in the total population of 92,000,000 people in the main part of the United States, about 14,000,000 were born in other countries, and 19,000,000 were children of foreigners. Probably 25,000,000 more were descended from non-English races and 10,000,000 were negroes, leaving about 24,000,000 who were descended solely from the English stock that was in the country before the Revolution.

Though we have as many race elements as any other country in the world, we have succeeded in holding to a common set of political traditions and methods.

From the earliest times, the people of the United States have been grouped in communities, first called colonies and later states. There were thirteen of these at the end of the Revolution and there are now forty-eight, besides the District of Columbia; the Canal Zone; the four outlying territories and dependencies of Alaska, the Hawaiian Islands, the Philippine

Islands, and Porto Rico; some small islands; and five protectorates. The forty-eight states are grouped as follows:

(1) New England, 66,000 square miles and 6,600,000 people, inhabited in about equal numbers by people of the old New England stock, immigrants now living, and the descendants of the earlier immigrants.

(2) The four middle states, with 105,000 square miles and 19,500,000 population, have more wealth than any other part of the Union because of their immense manufactures and their great cities.

(3) The South, with 969,000 square miles and sixteen states, had a population in 1910 of 32,500,000. Of these states West Virginia, Missouri, and Oklahoma are almost as much western as southern.

TYLER DAVIDSON FOUNTAIN, CINCINNATI.

(4) The middle West, with seven states extending west and northwest from Ohio to Minnesota, includes 389,000 square miles and a population in 1910 of 22,600,000. This region is now about as rich and as closely settled as the eastern · states.

(5) The far West, made up of twelve states, from the Missouri River west to the ridge of the Sierra Nevada, contains 1,173,000 square miles and 6,700,000 population. This region includes much mountain and desert, and is still underpopulated.

(6) The three Pacific coast states of Washington, Oregon, and California, contain 324,000 square miles and 4,200,000 population. They abound in natural resources and form the gateway to the Pacific and Asia.

397. TERRITORIAL EXPANSION

The people of the United States live on an area which increased from about 369,000 square miles in 1776 to about 3,744,000 square miles by the following additions of territory (maps, pages viii, 572–573):

(1) The Northwest Territory of 275,000 square miles, in part conquered by George Rogers Clark in 1778 (§ 104), in part ceded in 1782 (§ 108); and the area south of the Ohio River with 205,000 square miles, which was in part previously occupied by frontiersmen (§ 102), but was chiefly gained by the clever diplomacy of our envoys in 1782 (§ 108).

(2) The Louisiana Purchase, 885,000 square miles, secured from France in 1803 (§ 159).

(3) The Oregon country, 285,000 square miles, discovered in 1792, explored in 1805, occupied by a trading post in 1811 (§ 160), occupied by settlers after 1831, and confirmed by the treaty of 1846 (§ 229).

(4) West Florida, 600 square miles, claimed from 1803 (§ 159) but added by military conquest from 1810 to 1813.

(5) East Florida, 59,000 square miles, purchased by the treaty of 1819 with Spain (§ 190).

(6) Texas, previously an independent state, annexed in 1845, with 389,000 square miles (§ 228).

(7) New Mexico and California, 529,000 square miles, conquered in 1846, and ceded by Mexico in 1848 (§ 231).

(8) Gadsden purchase of 30,000 square miles, bought from Mexico in 1853 (§ 231).

(9) Alaska, bought in 1867 from Russia (§ 319), with 591,000 square miles.

(10) The Hawaiian Islands, 6500 square miles, previously an independent country, annexed by Congress in 1898 (§ 364).

(11) Porto Rico, Guam, and the Philippines, 119,000 square miles, conquered from Spain in 1898 (§ 360).

(12) Part of the Samoan Islands, 77 square miles, claimed

after 1878, and confirmed by treaty with Germany and Great Britain in 1899 (§ 364).

(13) Several small Pacific islands, especially Wake, Baker, Howland, and Midway, earlier discovered but formally recognized as part of the United States in 1898 (§ 364).

(14) Panama Canal Zone, 474 square miles, annexed by purchase from Panama in 1903 (§ 379).

(15) Three of the Virgin Islands (St. Thomas, St. John, St. Croix), 138 square miles, bought from Denmark in 1917.

CITY AND HARBOR OF CHARLOTTE AMALIE, ST. THOMAS.

In addition the United States between 1906 and 1916 obtained a protectorate over the neighboring Latin American states of Cuba, Haiti, Panama, Santo Domingo, and Nicaragua (§ 393). Altogether, those five states included 157,000 square miles and 6,600,000 people.

398. DEVELOPMENT OF THE FRONTIER

With the exception of the island possessions, nearly all the annexations since 1776 have been in an unsettled territory which had to be developed by new settlers. In 1800 Indiana and Mississippi were the frontier communities. In 1821 Mis-

souri was admitted as the first state west of that river except
Louisiana. In 1850 there was still little population beyond the
Missouri River and the frontiers of Arkansas and Texas. Then
the settled area began to work backward from the Pacific coast,
till in 1890 a continuous block of states extended across the
continent from east to west.

The Indian tribes, once the sole owners of all this magnificent country, were pushed aside by the onset of settlers. In
the conflict of 1811, the northwestern Indians were practically
dispossessed from Indiana (§ 167). The wars under Jackson
and others cleared lower Georgia and Alabama, and the Indians
of northern Georgia were moved west soon after 1830 (§ 240).
The northwestern and southwestern tribes continued a series
of bloody wars in the far West till about 1885, when their
power was destroyed forever.

As the wheat fields and cornfields advanced, the forests fell,
swamps were drained, roads created, streams bridged, houses
built, schoolhouses provided. Never before had mankind
seen such a speedy and complete conquest of a wilderness.
America has taught the world how to push into a new country,
take up the land, build cabins, found towns, establish schools,
and change the wilderness into a great civilized land.

399. SOCIAL DEVELOPMENT

The immense growth of the United States in the agricultural
regions has been equaled by the rise of great cities. In 1916
there were more than sixty cities, each having a population
of more than 100,000. The great wealth of those places is
shown by miles of lofty flats and business structures, and the
palatial homes of rich people, by docks and wharves and
enormous railroad terminals, by costly public buildings and
great factories.

Much of the wealth of the country is concentrated in the
great cities because they offer attractive homes to the rich,
and because they are seaports, or full of factories and business

houses. The eager spirit of the United States finds its opportunity in these vast cities. The total property value of the city of New York is over 8000 millions, which is more than that for the whole of New England.

These cities are "melting pots" in truth. In some of them more than half the residents were born outside the United States. In large cities with a varied population such as Chicago and San Francisco, nearly all the languages of Europe and some of Asia are spoken. Upon the city governments is placed the great responsibility of educating the children of the immigrants and of preparing them for citizenship.

400. PERSONAL FREEDOM

The westward movement gave a fine opportunity to carry into effect the great principle that the people of a country are the proper governors of that country. By long experience, the United States has learned how to make popular government a reality and it has put in practice the following, among many principles of free government:

(1) The foundation of all democratic government is the right of personal freedom; that is, the right of every normal man and woman to be free from the personal control of any other human being. This means that there shall be no slavery such as was practiced in all the English colonies (§ 75). During and just after the Revolution, about half the new states rid themselves of this curse (§ 112). Then, as new states were brought in during the period from 1800 to 1850, they were admitted to the Union in pairs, one free and one slave, to balance each other (§§ 183, 235). As a result of the Civil War, slavery was prohibited by the Thirteenth Amendment in every part of the United States and every place under its jurisdiction (§ 313). This ended the long struggle to keep up a system which in its nature was opposed to American principles.

(2) To this freedom from bondage is added freedom from arbitrary arrest and imprisonment, from unfair trials and

cruel punishments. With these go the broad right to everybody to move about within the United States, to pass from place to place, to engage in any trade or profession for which one is qualified, to find opportunities for whatever ability one may have. In the United States, children are not obliged to follow the calling of their fathers. No one is subject to the will of the landowner or the magistrate. No one can be imprisoned for debt. Nobody has any privileges of rank, title, or nobility.

(3) The United States has gone further than any other large country in acknowledging that women are a part of the make-up of the nation and are entitled to a share in the public national life. Public schools for girls appeared soon after the Revolution, and later high schools and colleges. In addition, many private secondary schools and universities have been established for women. Having these equal educational opportunities, women can enter many employments which were formerly reserved almost entirely for men; they can serve as clerks, bookkeepers, stenographers, librarians, teachers in schools and colleges, workers in factories, stores, and various outdoor pursuits, and as physicians and lawyers. Many women are trustees or officers of public charitable institutions, and a few are state or city officials and members of legislatures. In most states, laws have been changed so as to give to women the right to hold property and to carry on business without the control of their husbands. In a majority of the states of the Union, women have suffrage in school or municipal affairs or both, and in about one quarter of the states of the Union they can vote and hold office on equal terms with men (§ 391). Beyond these legal privileges and rights, women in the United States have a share in public discussions and an influence in public affairs unknown in any other large country in the world.

401. FREEDOM OF THE MIND

Freedom of the body and the right to vote would be of little value without an opportunity to form and express one's own opinion and to discuss matters with one's neighbors. In this respect, the United States has taught a lesson to the world.

(1) Any person here may express his mind on any public question, provided he does not tell malicious untruths about his neighbors or public men. He may call his neighbors together in a public meeting to discuss, protest, and petition, and he may print his views in a newspaper.

(2) This invaluable freedom extends to religious belief, teaching, and utterance. This is the first great country in the world in which men and women have been allowed freely to preach and practice any form of religion which does not interfere with the morals or the welfare of the community.

(3) Americans also have had the freest opportunity of education. The community has provided public schools where all children who so desire may be educated at the expense of the state. Thus every child has a chance to make the most of himself; while the state on its side has the advantage of a population in which people know something, can express their ideas, and can act upon reason. No other country in the world has encouraged so many boys and girls to make use of public schools, colleges, universities, and professional schools.

(4) The people of the United States enjoy a freedom hardly known on the continent of Europe, to form societies for any legal purpose. Thousands are members of college fraternities and similar societies; millions of members belong to the secret fraternities. The churches, besides their religious purposes, form social organizations for common benefits. Workingmen, business men, and scientific and professional men are grouped in national societies. Such organizations, which extend from state to state, tend to make the people realize that they belong to one country and have one purpose.

Besides all these societies, some of which number their membership by hundreds of thousands, there is one organization within the United States to which everybody belongs, which is supreme over every other society, corporation, or union, and which comes first, must be loved most, and obeyed first. That society is our country itself, the United States of America; the "American Commonwealth," as organized in its various forms of local and city governments, state governments, and the national government.

402. FREEDOM OF LABOR

No government can be carried on, no country can be kept alive, without the hard and systematic labor of millions of men and women. It may take the form of a wage system, such as prevailed in England during the eighteenth century, where each workman made his own bargain, and a hard bargain it was. It may be organized upon the idea that workmen are free to make individual contracts or, if they prefer, may unite in trades unions for what is called "collective bargaining."

On this freedom of labor are many limitations. The states and the national government have a right to fix the number of hours that make a day's labor. Eight hours is the legal day in government employment and on government work. Ten hours

A MONUMENT TO LABOR. (Designed by Tilden, San Francisco.)

is the legal amount in many states, and there is a great effort to reduce it to eight hours. In some states there are special laws as to the hours and conditions of the labor of women. Again, in many states, children cannot lawfully be employed under a fixed age, and not then except for a limited number of hours. Employers of labor are required both by national and by state laws to look out for the safety of their workmen and to compensate them if injured by accidents while at work.

Trades unions, which are powerful in many parts of Europe, have been developed to a high degree in the United States. The labor unions are usually eager to enroll all those skilled in their trade. Hence they feel that the man who will not join the union is acting against them. The laws everywhere recognize the right to "strike" — that is, to stop working by a common agreement; and the trades-unionist feels that a non-union man who keeps on at work, or who takes the place of the union man who strikes, is stealing his job and taking the bread out of his mouth. Several states and also the United States have set up boards of conciliation or arbitration, which are intended to bring the strikers and their employers into accord. The laws of many states also provide that nobody shall engage in certain sorts of work, such as that of barbers, stationary engineers, and plumbers, without a certificate issued by the state on examination, and that is of course a protection to those trades. Certain kinds of business, such as the sale of liquors and dangerous drugs, are restricted or prohibited outright.

With these exceptions and with the practical exception of the power of the labor unions to control trades in which they are very strong, a man or woman who wishes to make a living with the labor of hands or brain, may go anywhere throughout the land and engage in any kind of work for which he is fitted. This freedom of work, combined with high wages, has drawn millions of immigrants from other countries.

403. FREEDOM OF BUSINESS

The same right of free choice extends to the business man. He may go to any part of the country and engage in any kind of lawful business. He may form firms, partnerships, and corporations.

This ability of any man to try the thing he thinks he can do best has caused amazing wealth and prosperity for the United States. For instance, the railroad business has been revolutionized by American cheap steel and American railroad management. The average trainload of freight, moved by one engineer, one fireman, one conductor, and a small train crew, was in 1916 two or three times as large in America as in Europe.

American corporations and trusts, with all their dangers, have shown a great capacity to organize business on a large

TRANSFERRING AN AEROPLANE TO A TRAIN.

scale. They succeed because in many lines of business they bring about a saving in the cost of manufacture and in the expenses of management and of selling goods. On the other hand, no country has shown more success in curbing great combinations of capital.

Among modern nations, none is so quick as the United States to use labor-saving machinery and devices for factory, office, farm, and home. Americans have taught the world how to save human labor by the use of farm machinery, including such marvels as the thirty-horse harvester which goes through a field of standing wheat, and leaves behind it bags of grain ready for shipment. The same expertness in machinery extends to the factories. The willingness of American workmen to invent tools and adapt themselves to new machinery is one of the reasons for the prosperity of this country. The telegraph, electric traction, electric light, and the telephone are all American inventions. No other nation approaches the Americans in the use of the telephone and of electric light. The use of motor cars on a great scale at low prices began in the United States. The first practicable flying machine was American.

In transportation, the United States has learned much from the rest of the world, and has taught much. The first steam locomotives were English, but the first practical steamboat was American (§ 178). From end to end of the United States, there were in 1916, one post office system including a parcel post, two telegraph companies, one system of currency, one general method of transportation of through freight and through passengers. Free trade existed throughout the Union and no state could hinder it.

404. POPULAR GOVERNMENT

Perhaps the largest contribution that America has made to the world is the proof, for the first time in history, that popular government is possible for a nation of great extent, with a large population. This success is in part due to some of the following peculiarities of our American form of government:

(1) The breadth of the suffrage, which is based upon the idea that if a man has a vote he will think about public affairs.

(2) Equal representation of districts of equal population — a plain, comprehensible method, which keeps people satisfied.

(3) Organized parties and party politics, which help to keep government moving, so long as they are not looked upon as the real government themselves.

(4) Frequent elections, making it possible to bring public opinion to bear in a quick and effective way.

In practice, popular government has had to contend with many difficulties. People change their residences so often that they do not come to know each other well. Political organization and action is complicated and can often be managed by a few men. Popular government has sometimes been almost destroyed, as by the Tweed Ring in the city of New York (§ 347).

Nevertheless popular government has so far found means to keep possession of its rightful authority by the following methods: (a) safeguarding the ballot by voting devices such as the Australian Ballot and by limiting the amount that may be spent by candidates for office and their friends; (b) giving the people a greater share in the government by direct vote on constitutional amendments and on legislative acts (§ 387); (c) guarding more carefully the nomination machinery, by supervising the conventions or by primary elections (§ 387); (d) giving greater power to a few officials, such as the mayors of cities, the President, and the heads of city commission governments, and then encouraging men of high character and reputation to stand for those offices.

405. SUCCESS OF FEDERAL GOVERNMENT

Perhaps the most striking lesson which the United States has taught the rest of the world is the success of the federal system, which has been drawn upon as a model by the German, Swiss, Canadian, Australian, and South African confederations. This result seems due chiefly to the following:

(1) The national government is well organized in a well-balanced Congress, a strong President with the most efficient civil service in the country, and Federal Courts of weight and dignity. Under the Constitution this government has shown that it possesses powers enough for national purposes, such as foreign commerce and war, federal taxes, banking, currency, and internal commerce and regulation of citizenship.

(2) The states have shown by an experience of more than

a hundred years that they can exercise very large authority over business confined to the boundaries of one state, over labor, education, public improvements, and the "police power"; that is, the relations of men with each other and with the government. Differences between the state and national governments about their fields of authority are finally settled by the Supreme Court of the United States.

(3) The local governments — towns, boroughs, villages, and cities — are all created by the states. This is the weakest part of American government and has little to teach the rest of the world, because many of the cities are badly governed, and are unfavorably affected by state and national politics.

(4) A new type of government has sprung up since 1898 in the dependencies — which are really colonies of the United States, with the important exception that hardly any settlers go out from the continental United States to live in them. Such colonies are honestly and carefully governed, but it is difficult to make them fit into the principle of "local self-government" which prevails in the United States, or into the idea of government by the "consent of the governed" which inspired the men of the Revolution.

406. SUMMARY — MEANING OF AMERICAN HISTORY

Of what advantage to the pupil has been this study of American history? Is it simply a tale that is told, which stores the mind with some knowledge of the men and events of our history? Or has it left impressions that will make American citizens helpful in carrying on the nation in the next generation? As we follow the story, all the way from the days of our exploring, sea-fighting, and colonizing forbears, the three things most important to remember and apply are the principles which the French have tried to express in their national motto — "Liberty, Equality, Fraternity."

Liberty means in the United States, not the freedom to do whatever one likes, but — with due respect to the rights of others — to take part in life as one judges best, to act for oneself. That is what has made the great inventors, educators, and statesmen; they have worked out their own problems.

Equality in the United States means an equal privilege before the law for every man, woman, and child. It is the just boast of our country that all people who have their own way to make, enjoy a better chance here than anywhere else in the world.

Fraternity means combination; and in the whole history of America, perhaps the most wonderful thing is the spirit of orderly union. The Pilgrims on the *Mayflower* agreed to act together and to obey the majority; the patriots of the Revolution created state and national governments; the Federal Convention enlarged and strengthened the Union; the spirit of union saved the government from destruction by the Civil War, and has brought the two sections together again.

Liberty, equality, and fraternity are all parts of one great idea — the happiness and safety of the individual under the protection of law and order. Americans do not look upon "The State" as something different from themselves. The state exists only in order to make individuals as free and happy as possible. The state, by its methods of discovering and applying the popular will, makes it possible for the nation to grow and to bring about necessary changes and reforms by an appeal to the fairness and moral sense of the people.

As Lincoln said in his first inaugural: "Why should there not be a patient confidence in the ultimate justice of the people? Is there any better or equal hope in the world?" Ours be Lowell's pledge of patriotism: —

> "O Beautiful! my Country! . . .
> What were our lives without thee?
> What all our lives to save thee?
> We reck not what we gave thee;
> We will not dare to doubt thee,
> But ask whatever else, and we will dare!"

CHAPTER XXXVII

THE UNITED STATES IN THE GREAT WAR

407. PRESIDENTIAL ELECTION OF 1916

DURING the year 1916 relations with Europe grew steadily more serious. When several Americans were killed by a German submarine while crossing the English Channel in the British ship *Sussex*, the German government apologized, and finally agreed not to destroy merchant ships without warning; that is, without giving passengers and crew a chance to escape in lifeboats. Notwithstanding many attacks, both in the press and in Congress, President Wilson earnestly sought to preserve peace.

No other serious candidate appeared for the Democratic nomination but President Wilson. In the Republican party several states put forward their favorite sons: Root in New York, Burton in Ohio, Fairbanks in Indiana, Sherman in Illinois, and others. The Progressives appointed delegates to meet in Chicago on June 7, the same day as the Republican convention. They hoped that the Republicans would nominate Roosevelt. When the conventions met, the Republicans refused to accept Roosevelt, and nominated Charles E. Hughes, Justice of the Supreme Court. The Progressive convention named Roosevelt for President, but he declined the nomination, and supported Hughes in the campaign. The Democratic convention at St. Louis a few days later renominated Wilson and supported his policy in Mexico and in protecting the citizens of the United States in the European war. Hughes made long campaign trips through the country, but the campaign was rather quiet. Wilson's position as to war and peace satisfied the majority of the voters, and he was reelected by a very close electoral vote, 276, to 255 for Hughes. The total popular vote showed about 600,000 plurality for Wilson. The vote was very close in some states; out of nearly

PRESIDENT WILSON ADDRESSING CONGRESS.

1,000,000 votes in California Wilson's plurality was 3773, and Hughes's plurality in Minnesota was 392. The election was won by a combination of the solid South with New Hampshire, Ohio, and most of the far western states.

The reëlection of Wilson meant that every honorable effort would be made to keep out of the European war, and in January, 1917, President Wilson in a public address to both houses of Congress demanded in behalf of the neutral nations "A peace

without victory." By this he meant a peace in which none of
the European powers was to be crushed or deprived of the power
of governing itself. His ideas seemed to promise relief from
the terrible burden of war; when the German government
announced that beginning with February it would capture any
vessels that ventured to approach the coasts of the Allies in
Europe, no matter what their flag, whence they came, whither
they were bound, or what their cargo. All such vessels, cargoes,
and the persons on board were to be sunk without warning and
without mercy by German submarines.

408. BEGINNING OF THE WAR WITH GERMANY

This raised anew the question of the rights and duties of the
United States. The action of Germany was virtually a declaration of war, and the only way to avoid active hostilities
was for the United States to give up commerce with Europe,
so long as it pleased Germany to ignore our rights. The success
of Germany would mean, therefore, the setting up of a great
world power which would hold the seas in control; a power
which looked upon the United States as an enemy because it
furnished food and munitions to the Allies.

In this great crisis President Wilson made an address to
Congress in which he announced that the United States could
not accept such dictation and that the time had come to declare war. In spite of the opposition of the "pacifists," Congress on April 6 passed a declaration of war against Germany.
From that moment the two countries were public enemies.

Almost the first hostile step was to seize the German merchantmen, then lying in the American ports, many of which had been
deliberately damaged by their crews. A naval force was shortly
sent to Europe to join in hunting out the submarines. Merchant
ships were armed, so that they might protect themselves if
possible.

A bill was at once introduced for raising a great national army.
An act of 1916 already had provided for an increase in the regular

army to about 250,000 and of the state militia to about 400,000. The new bill, passed in May, created a new national army to be called in successive waves of about 500,000 each, and to be chosen by draft out of the able-bodied men between 21 and 31 years of age. This was followed up by a tremendous tax bill which more than doubled the annual amount paid by the people of the United States. A loan bill, also, provided for borrowing still larger sums. For all kinds of war preparations, Congress provided for spending about twenty billion dollars.

A registration of the men between 21 and 31 showed nearly

A MILITARY AËROPLANE.

10,000,000 men, out of which, after proper exemptions were made, the national army could be drafted. Within a few weeks commissions came over from England, France, Italy, Belgium, and Russia and created great enthusiasm wherever they went. The War Department established camps for the training of officers and men in various parts of the country, the navy was enlarged, and arrangements were made to build a fleet of merchant ships and a vast number of aëroplanes. The country was aroused by the mighty preparations to a sense of the great task in hand.

APPENDIX A

BRIEF LIST OF DESK BOOKS

(These books, obtainable at moderate cost, are well adapted for constant use on the teacher's desk. At least one work out of each of the five groups should be available for pupils' use.)

I. Methods and Materials. American Historical Association, Committee of Seven, *The Study of History in Schools.* (N. Y., Macmillan, 1899.)

Bourne, H. E., *The Teaching of History and Civics in the Elementary and Secondary School.* (N. Y., Longmans, 1902.)

Channing, E., Hart, A. B., and Turner, F. J., *Guide to the Study and Reading of American History.* (Bost., Ginn, 1912.)

History Teachers' Magazine (monthly). (Phila., McKinley, 1909.)

New England History Teachers' Association, *A History Syllabus for Secondary Schools.* (Bost., Heath, 1904. Part IV, on American History, sold separately.)

New England History Teachers' Association, *Historical Sources in Schools.* (N.Y., Macmillan, 1902.)

II. Collections of Sources. Ames, H. V., ed., *State Documents on Federal Relations.* (N. Y., Longmans, 1906.)

Caldwell, H. W., ed., *Survey of American History.* (Chic., Ainsworth, 1900.)

Caldwell, H. W., and Persinger, C. E., eds., *Source History of the United States.* (Chic., Ainsworth, 1909.)

Hart, A. B., ed., *American History told by Contemporaries.* (4 vols., N. Y., Macmillan, 1897-1901.)

Hart, A. B., ed., *American Patriots and Statesmen.* (5 vols., N. Y., Collier's, 1916.)

Hart, A. B., ed., *Source Book of American History.* (N. Y., Macmillan, 1900.)

Hart, A. B., and Channing, Edward, eds., *American History Leaflets.* (36 nos., N. Y., Simmons, 1892-1910.)

Hill, Mabel, ed., *Liberty Documents, with Contemporary Exposition and Critical Comments.* (N. Y., Longmans, 1901.)

MacDonald, Wm., ed., *Documentary Source Book of American History.* (N. Y., Macmillan, 1908.)

III. Brief Histories. Bassett, J. S., *Short History of the United States.* (N. Y., Macmillan, 1913.)

Sparks, E. E., *The United States of America.* (2 vols., N. Y., Putnams, 1904.)

ix

IV. Short Series of Histories. *Epochs of American History.* (3 vols., N. Y., Longmans. Rev. eds., about 1914.)
   1. Thwaites, R. G., *The Colonies.*
   2. Hart, A. B., *Formation of the Union.*
   3. Wilson, Woodrow. *Division and Reunion.*
Home University Library of Modern Knowledge. (5 vols., N. Y., Holt, 1911–14.)
   1. Andrews, C. M., *The Colonial Period.*
   2. Smith, T. C., *The Wars between England and America.*
   3. MacDonald, Wm., *From Jefferson to Lincoln.*
   4. Paxson, F. L., *The American Civil War.*
   5. Haworth, P. L., *Reconstruction and Union.*
The Riverside History of the United States. (4 vols., Bost., Houghton Mifflin, 1915.)
   1. Becker, C. L., *Beginnings of the American People.*
   2. Johnson, A., *Union and Democracy.*
   3. Dodd, W. E., *Expansion and Conflict.*
   4. Paxson, F. L., *The New Nation.*
A Short History of the American People. (2 vols., N. Y., Am. Book Co.)
   1. Greene, E. B., *The Foundations of American Nationality.* (In preparation.)
   2. Fish, C. R., *The Development of American Nationality.* (1913.)

V. Biographical Series. *American Crisis Biographies.* (15 vols., Phila., Jacobs, 1907–14.)
American Statesmen. (31 vols. and additional vols., Bost., Houghton Mifflin, 1907–14.)
Beacon Biographies. (31 vols., Bost., Small, Maynard, 1899–1901.)
Riverside Biographical Series. (14 vols., Bost., Houghton, 1900–02.)

APPENDIX B

GENERAL BIBLIOGRAPHY

(Containing exact titles of the most important books to which reference is made in the chapter bibliographies.)

Adams, Henry, *History of the United States, 1801–1817.* (9 vols., N. Y., 1889–91.) — *John Randolph.* (Amer. Statesmen, Bost., 1900.)
Addams, Jane, *Twenty Years at Hull-House.* (N. Y., 1910.)
Allen, G. W., *Our Naval War with France.* (Bost., 1909.) — *Our Navy and the Barbary Corsairs.* (Bost., 1905.)
American Annual Cyclopædia, 1861–1874. (N. Y., 1862–75.) Continued as *Appletons' Annual Cyclopædia,* 1875–1902. (N. Y., 1876–1903.)
American Review of Reviews. Monthly Mag. (N. Y., 1890–.)
American Year Book, 1910–. (Annual, N. Y., 1911–.)
Ames, H. V., ed., *State Documents on Federal Relations.* (N. Y., 1906.)

Andrews, C. M., *Colonial Self-Government.* (Amer. Nation, N.Y., 1904.) — *Colonial Period.* (Home Univ. Lib., N.Y., 1912.)

Avery, E. M., *History of the United States and Its People.* (7 vols., Cleveland, 1904-10.)

Babcock, K. C., *Rise of American Nationality.* (Amer. Nation, N.Y., 1906.)

Bassett, J. S., *Federalist System.* (Amer. Nation, N.Y., 1906.) — *Life of Andrew Jackson.* (2 vols., N.Y., 1911.) — *Short History of the United States.* (N.Y., 1913.)

Battles and Leaders of the Civil War. (4 vols., N.Y., 1888.)

Beard, C. A., *Contemporary American History, 1877-1913.* (N.Y., 1914.) — *Readings in American Government and Politics.* (Rev. ed., N.Y., 1913.)

Becker, C. L., *Beginnings of the American People.* (Riverside, Bost., 1915.)

Bogart, E. L., *Economic History of the United States.* (N.Y., 1907.)

Bogart, E. L., and Thompson, C. M., eds., *Readings in the Economic History of the United States.* (N.Y., 1916.)

Bourne, E. G., ed., *Narratives of the Career of Hernando de Soto.* (Trail Makers, 2 vols., N.Y., 1904.) — *Spain in America.* (Amer. Nation, N.Y., 1904.)

Brigham, A. P., *Geographic Influences in American History.* (Bost., 1903.)

Brooks, E. S., *Story of Our War with Spain.* (Bost., 1899.)

Brown, W. G., *Andrew Jackson.* (Riverside Biogr., Bost., 1900.) — *The Lower South in American History.* (N.Y., 1902.)

Bruce, P. A., *Social Life of Virginia in the 17th Century.* (Richmond, 1907.)

Caldwell, H. W., ed., *American Territorial Development.* (Chic., 1900.) — *Survey of American History.* (Chic., 1900.)

Caldwell, H. W., and Persinger, C. E., eds., *Source History of the United States.* (Chic., 1909.)

Carlton, F. T., *History and Problems of Organized Labor.* (Bost., 1911.)

Chadwick, F. E., *Causes of the Civil War.* (Amer. Nation, N.Y., 1906.) — *Relations of the United States and Spain.* (3 vols., N.Y., 1909-11.)

Channing, Edward, *History of the United States.* (4 vols., N.Y., 1905-.) — *Jeffersonian System.* (Amer. Nation, N.Y., 1906.)

Chittenden, H. M., *American Fur Trade in the Far West.* (3 vols., N.Y., 1902.)

Collier & Son, P. F., Pub., *Story of the Great War.* (5 vols., N.Y., 1916-.)

Coman, Katharine, *Economic Beginnings of the Far West.* (2 vols., N.Y., 1912.) — *Industrial History of the United States.* (Rev. ed., N.Y., 1910.)

Curry, J. L. M., *Civil History of the Government of the Confederate States.* (Richmond, 1901.)

Dana, R. H., *Two Years before the Mast.* (N.Y., 1840, and later editions.)

Dewey, D. R., *Financial History of the United States.* (Amer. Citizen Ser., 5th ed., N.Y., 1915.) — *National Problems, 1885-1897.* (Amer. Nation, N.Y., 1907.)

De Witt, B. P., *Progressive Movement.* (Citizen's Library, N.Y., 1915.)

Dodd, W. E., *Expansion and Conflict.* (Riverside Hist., Bost., 1915.) — *Jefferson Davis.* (Amer. Crisis Biogr., Phila., 1907.)

Du Bois, W. E. B., *Souls of Black Folk.* (Chic., 1903.)

Dunbar, P. L., *Folks from Dixie.* (N. Y., 1898.) — *Lyrics of Lowly Life.* (N. Y., 1896.)

Dunne, F. P., *Mr. Dooley in Peace and in War.* (Bost., 1898.) — *Mr. Dooley in the Hearts of His Countrymen.* (Bost., 1899.)

Dunning, W. A., *Reconstruction.* (Amer. Nation, N. Y., 1907.)

Earle, A. M., *Child Life in Colonial Days.* (N. Y., 1899.) — *Colonial Dames and Goodwives.* (Bost., 1895.) — *Curious Punishments of Bygone Days.* (N. Y., 1896.) — *Home Life in Colonial Days.* (N. Y., 1898.) — *Sabbath in Puritan New England.* (N. Y., 1891.) — *Stage-Coach and Tavern Days.* (N. Y., 1900.) — *Two Centuries of Costume in America.* (2 vols., N. Y., 1903.)

Eastman, C. A., *Indian Boyhood.* (N. Y., 1902.) — *Indian To-day.* (N. Y., 1915.)

Eggleston, G. C., ed., *American War Ballads and Lyrics.* (2 vols., N. Y., 1889.) — *A Rebel's Recollections.* (N. Y., 1905.) — *Irene of the Mountains.* (Bost., 1909.)

Fish, C. R., *American Diplomacy.* (Amer. Hist. Ser., N. Y., 1915.) — *Development of American Nationality.* (N. Y., 1913.)

Fiske, John, *American Revolution.* (2 vols., Bost., 1891.) — *Beginnings of New England.* (Bost., 1889.) — *Critical Period of American History.* (Bost., 1888.) — *Discovery of America.* (2 vols., Bost., 1892.) — *Dutch and Quaker Colonies.* (2 vols., Bost., 1899.) — *Mississippi Valley in the Civil War.* (Bost., 1900.) — *New France and New England.* (Bost., 1902.) — *Old Virginia and Her Neighbors.* (2 vols., Bost., 1897.)

Ford, H. J., *Woodrow Wilson.* (N. Y., 1916.)

Ford, P. L., *Honorable Peter Stirling.* (N. Y., 1894.) — *Janice Meredith.* (N. Y., 1899.) — *The Many-sided Franklin.* (N. Y., 1899.) — *The True George Washington.* (Phila., 1902.)

Foster, J. W., *Century of American Diplomacy.* (Bost., 1900.)

Franklin, Benjamin, *Autobiography.* (Many editions.)

Garrison, G. P., *Texas.* (Amer. Commonwealths, Bost., 1903.) — *Westward Extension.* (Amer. Nation, N. Y., 1906.)

Grant, U. S., *Personal Memoirs.* (2 vols., N. Y., 1885–86.)

Greene, E. B., *Provincial America.* (Amer. Nation, N. Y., 1905.) — *Provincial Governor in English Colonies of North America.* (N. Y., 1898.)

Griffis, W. E, *America in the East.* (N. Y., 1899.) — *Sir William Johnson and the Six Nations.* (Makers of Amer., N. Y., 1891.)

Hapgood, Hutchins, *Paul Jones.* (Riverside Biogr., Bost., 1901.)

Hapgood, Norman, *Abraham Lincoln.* (N. Y., 1899.) — *Daniel Webster.* (Beacon Biogr., Bost., 1899.)

Harding, S. B., and Clapp, J. M., eds., *Select Orations Illustrating American Political History.* (N. Y., 1909.)

Harris, J. C., *On the Plantation.* (N. Y., 1892.) — *Uncle Remus, His Songs and His Sayings.* (N. Y., 1880.)

Hart, A. B., *Actual Government.* (Amer. Citizen Ser., 3d ed., N. Y., 1908.) — *American Nation, a History; from Original Sources by Associated Scholars.* (ed., 28 vols., N. Y., 1904–17.) — *American History Told by*

Contemporaries. (4 vols., 1897–1901). — *American Patriots and Statesmen.* (Collier Classics, ed., 5 vols., N. Y., 1916.) — *Epoch Maps Illustrating American History.* (4th ed., N. Y., 1910.) — *Formation of the Union.*
(Epochs of Amer. Hist., rev. ed., N. Y., 1915.) — *Foundations of American Foreign Policy.* (N. Y., 1901.) — *Monroe Doctrine : an Interpreta-
tion.* (Bost., 1916.) — *National Ideals Historically Traced.* (Amer.
Nation, N. Y., 1907.) — *Obvious Orient.* (N. Y., 1911.) — *Salmon Port-
land Chase.* (Amer. Statesmen, Bost., 1900.) — *Slavery and Abolition.*
(Amer. Nation, N. Y., 1906.) — *Source Book of American History.* (ed.,
N. Y., 1900.) — *Source Readers in American History.* (ed., 4 vols.,
N. Y., 1902–03.) — *Southern South.* (N. Y., 1910.) — *War in Europe.*
(N. Y., 1914.)
Haworth, P. L., *America in Ferment.* (Indianapolis, 1915.) — *Hayes-Tilden
Disputed Presidential Election of 1876.* (Cleveland, 1906.) — *Recon-
struction and Union.* (Home Univ. Lib., N. Y., 1912.)
Hawthorne, Nathaniel, *Blithedale Romance.* (Bost., 1852.) — *Grandfather's
Chair.* (Bost., 1840.) — *Old News* in *Snow Image and Other Twice-
Told Tales.* (Bost., 1852.) — *Septimius Felton.* (Bost., 1872.) — *Twice-
Told Tales.* (2 vols., Bost., 1851; also later eds.)
Hill, Mabel, ed., *Liberty Documents.* (N. Y., 1901.)
Hinsdale, B. A., *Old Northwest.* (2 vols., N. Y., 1888.)
Holmes, O. W., *Poetical Works.* (In many editions.)
Howells, W. D., *Boy's Town.* (N. Y., 1890.)
Hunt, Gaillard, *John C. Calhoun.* (Amer. Crisis Biogr., Phila., 1908.) —
James Madison. (N. Y., 1902.)
International Year Book. 1898–1902, 1907–. (Annual, N. Y., 1899–1903,
1908–.)
James, J. A., ed., *Readings in American History.* (N. Y., 1914.)
Johnson, Allen, ed., *Readings in American Constitutional History, 1776–1876.*
(Bost., 1912.) — *Stephen A. Douglas.* (N. Y., 1908.) — *Union and De-
mocracy.* (Riverside Hist., Bost., 1915.)
Johnston, Alexander, and Woodburn, J. A., eds., *American Orations : Studies
in American Political History.* (4 vols., 1896–97.)
King, Grace, *Jean Baptiste Le Moyne, Sieur de Bienville.* (Makers of Amer.,
N. Y., 1892.)
Latané, J. H., *America as a World Power, 1897–1907.* (Amer. Nation, N. Y.,
1907.)
Leland, C. G., *Algonquin Legends of New England.* (Bost., 1884.)
Lodge, H. C., *Alexander Hamilton.* (Amer. Statesmen, Bost., 1900.) —
Daniel Webster. (Amer. Statesmen, Bost., 1900.) — *George Washing-
ton.* (Amer. Statesmen, 2 vols., Bost., 1900.) — *Story of the Revolution.*
(2 vols., N. Y., 1898; also in 1 vol., 1903.)
Longfellow, H. W., *Poetical Works.* (1893, and many editions.)
Lummis, C. F., *Some Strange Corners of Our Country.* (N. Y., 1892.) —
Spanish Pioneers. (Chic., 1893.)
McCall, S. W., *Life of Thomas Brackett Reed.* (Bost., 1914.) — *Thaddeus
Stevens.* (Amer. Statesmen, Bost., 1900.)

MacDonald, William, *From Jefferson to Lincoln.* (Home Univ. Lib., N. Y., 1913.) — *Jacksonian Democracy.* (Amer. Nation, N. Y., 1906.) — *Select Charters and Other Documents Illustrative of American History, 1606–1775.* (ed., N. Y., 1899.) — *Select Documents of United States History, 1776–1861.* (ed., N. Y., 1898.) — *Select Statutes and Other Documents Illustrative of the History of the United States, 1861–1898.* (ed., N. Y., 1903.)

McKinley, A. E., *Illustrated Topics for American History.* (Phila., 1912.)

McLaughlin, A. C., *Confederation and Constitution.* (Amer. Nation, N. Y., 1905.) — *Lewis Cass.* (Amer. Statesmen, Bost., 1900.)

Maclay, E. S., *History of the United States Navy.* (3 vols., N. Y., 1901–02.)

McMaster, J. B., *History of the People of the United States.* (8 vols., N. Y., 1883–1913.)

Merwin, H. C., *Aaron Burr.* (Beacon Biogr., Bost., 1899.) — *Thomas Jefferson.* (Riverside Biogr., Bost., 1901.)

Morse, J. T., *Abraham Lincoln.* — *Benjamin Franklin.* — *John Adams.* — *John Quincy Adams.* — *Thomas Jefferson.* (Amer. Statesmen, Bost., 1900.)

Munro, W. B., *Government of American Cities.* (N. Y., 1912.) — *Selections from the Federalist.* (ed., Cambridge, Mass., 1914.)

Nicolay, J. G., and Hay, John, *Abraham Lincoln: A History.* (10 vols., N. Y., 1890.)

Olcott, C. S., *Life of William McKinley.* (2 vols., Bost., 1916.)

Parkman, Francis, *Conspiracy of Pontiac.* (Rev. ed., 2 vols., Bost., 1870.) — *Count Frontenac and New France under Louis XIV.* (Bost., 1877.) — *Half-Century of Conflict.* (2 vols., Bost., 1892.) — *Jesuits in North America.* (Bost., 1867.) — *La Salle and the Discovery of the Great West.* (Rev. ed., Bost., 1887.) — *Old Régime in Canada.* (Rev. ed., Bost., 1895.) — *Pioneers of France in the New World.* (Bost., 1887.)

Paxson, F. L., *American Civil War.* (Home Univ. Lib., N. Y., 1911.) — *Last American Frontier.* (N. Y., 1910.) — *The New Nation.* (Riverside Hist., Bost., 1915.)

Phillips, P. C., *West in the Diplomacy of the Revolution.* (Urbana, Ill., 1914.)

Ralph, Julian, *Dixie; or Southern Scenes and Sketches.* (N. Y., 1896.) — *Our Great West.* (N. Y., 1893.)

Rhodes, J. F., *History of the United States.* (7 vols., N. Y., 1893–1906.)

Roosevelt, Theodore, *Autobiography.* (N. Y., 1913.) — *Gouverneur Morris.* (Amer. Statesmen, Bost., 1900.) — *Naval War of 1812.* (3d ed., N. Y., 1883.) — *New Nationalism.* (N. Y., 1910.) — *Progressive Principles.* (N. Y., 1913.) — *Strenuous Life.* (N. Y., 1901.) — *Thomas H. Benton.* (Amer. Statesmen, Bost., 1900.) — *Winning of the West.* (4 vols. N. Y., 1889–96.)

Schouler, James, *Americans of 1776.* (N. Y., 1906.) — *History of the United States.* (Rev. ed., 7 vols., N. Y., 1894–1913.) — *Thomas Jefferson.* (Makers of Amer., N. Y., 1893.)

Schurz, Carl, *Henry Clay.* (Amer. Statesmen, 2 vols., Bost., 1900.)

Seawell, M. E., *Decatur and Somers.* (N. Y., 1894.) — *Little Jarvis.* (N. Y., 1890.) — *Midshipman Paulding.* (N. Y., 1891.)

Semple, E. C., *American History and Geographic Conditions.* (Bost., 1903.)

Shepherd, W. R., *Historical Atlas.* (Amer. Hist. Ser., N. Y., 1911.)

Simms, W. G., *Border Beagles.* (Phila., 1840.) — *Cassique of Kiawah.* (N. Y., 1860.) — *Eutaw.* (N. Y., 1856.) — *The Forayers.* (N. Y., 1855.) — *Katherine Walton.* (Phila., 1851.) — *Mellichampe.* (N. Y., 1836.) — *The Partisan.* (N. Y., 1835.) — *Richard Hurdis.* (Phila., 1838.) — *Vasconselos.* (N. Y., 1856.)

Sloane, W. M., *French War and the Revolution, 1756–1783.* (Amer. Hist. Ser., N. Y., 1893.)

Sparks, E. E., *Expansion of the American People.* (Chic., 1900.) — *National Development, 1877–1885.* (Amer. Nation, N. Y., 1907.)

Stockton, F. R., *Buccaneers and Pirates of Our Coasts.* (N. Y., 1898.) — *Kate Bonnet.* (N. Y., 1902.)

Taussig, F. W., *Tariff History of the United States.* (6th ed., N. Y., 1914.)

Thayer, J. B., *John Marshall.* (Riverside Biogr., Bost., 1901.)

Thayer, W. R., *Life and Letters of John Hay.* (2 vols., Bost., 1915.)

Thwaites, R. G., *The Colonies, 1492–1750.* (Epochs of Amer. Hist., rev. ed., N. Y., 1910.) — *Daniel Boone.* (N. Y., 1902.) — *Father Marquette.* (N. Y., 1902.) — *France in America.* (Amer. Nation, N. Y., 1905.)

Titherington, R. H., *Spanish-American War of 1898.* (N. Y., 1900.)

Trowbridge, John, *Samuel Finley Breese Morse.* (Beacon Biogr., Bost., 1901.)

Tyler, L. G., *England in America.* (Amer. Nation, N. Y., 1904.)

Tyler, M. C., *American Literature during the Colonial Time.* (2 vols., N. Y., 1897.) — *Literary History of the American Revolution.* (2 vols., N. Y., 1897.) — *Patrick Henry.* (Amer. Statesmen, Bost., 1900.)

Van Tyne, C. H., *American Revolution.* (Amer. Nation, N. Y., 1905.) — *Loyalists in the American Revolution.* (N. Y., 1902.)

Villard, O. G., *John Brown.* (Bost., 1910.)

Von Holst, Hermann, *John C. Calhoun.* (Amer. Statesmen, rev. ed., Bost., 1909.)

Washington, B. T., *Up from Slavery.* (N. Y., 1901.)

Weeden, W. B., *Early Rhode Island.* (N. Y., 1910.) — *Economic and Social History of New England.* (2 vols., Bost., 1891.)

Wendell, Barrett, *Cotton Mather.* (Makers of Amer., N. Y., 1891.) — *Literary History of America.* (Library of Lit. Hist., N. Y., 1900.)

Whittier, J. G., *Complete Poetical Works.* (Cambridge ed., Bost., 1894.)

Wilson, Woodrow, *Division and Reunion.* (Epochs of Amer. Hist., rev. ed., N. Y., 1910.) — *History of the American People.* (5 vols., N. Y., 1902.) — *New Freedom.* (N. Y., 1913.)

Winsor, Justin, *Cartier to Frontenac.* (Bost., 1894.) — *Christopher Columbus.* (Bost., 1891.) — *Memorial History of Boston.* (4 vols., Bost., 1880–81.) — *Mississippi Basin.* (Bost., 1895.) — *Narrative and Critical History of America.* (8 vols., Bost., 1886–89.) — *Westward Movement.* (Bost., 1897.)

Woodburn, J. A., *American Politics.* (Rev. ed., N. Y., 1914.)

APPENDIX C
STATES OF THE UNION

		ADMISSION			POPULATION			NUMBER OF REPRESENTATIVES, 1913
		ENABLING ACT	ADMISSION	PREVIOUS STATUS	CENSUS FOLLOWING ADMISSION	CENSUS OF 1910	LARGEST CITY 1910	
22	Alabama	March 2, 1819	Dec. 14, 1819	Territory	127,901	2,138,093	Birmingham	10
48	Arizona	June 20, 1910	Feb. 14, 1912	Territory	—	204,354	Tucson	1
25	Arkansas		June 15, 1836	Territory	97,574	1,574,449	Little Rock	7
31	California		Sept. 9, 1850	Unorganized territory	92,597	2,377,549	San Francisco	11
38	Colorado	March 3, 1875	Aug. 1, 1876	Territory	194,327	799,024	Denver	4
5	Connecticut			Original state	237,946	1,114,756	New Haven	5
1	Delaware			Original state	59,096	202,322	Wilmington	1
27	Florida		March 3, 1845	Territory	87,445	752,619	Jacksonville	4
4	Georgia			Original state	82,548	2,609,121	Atlanta	12
43	Idaho		July 3, 1890	Territory	84,385	325,594	Boise	2
21	Illinois	April 18, 1818	Dec. 3, 1818	Territory	55,211	5,638,591	Chicago	27
19	Indiana	April 19, 1816	Dec. 11, 1816	Indiana Territory and part of Michigan Territory	147,178	2,700,876	Indianapolis	13
29	Iowa		Dec. 28, 1846	Part of Iowa Territory	192,214	2,224,771	Des Moines	11
34	Kansas		Jan. 29, 1861	Part of Kansas Territory	364,399	1,690,949	Kansas City	8
15	Kentucky		June 1, 1792	Part of Virginia	220,955	2,289,905	Louisville	11
18	Louisiana	Feb. 20, 1811	April 30, 1812	Territory of Orleans	153,407	1,656,388	New Orleans	8
23	Maine		March 15, 1820	Part of Massachusetts	298,335	742,371	Portland	4
7	Maryland			Original state	319,728	1,295,346	Baltimore	6
6	Massachusetts			Original state	475,327	3,366,416	Boston	16
26	Michigan		June 26, 1837	Part of Michigan Territory	212,267	2,810,173	Detroit	13

	State						City	
32	Minnesota	Feb. 20, 1857	May 11, 1858	Part of Minnesota Territory	172,023	2,075,708	Minneapolis	10
20	Mississippi	March 1, 1817	Dec. 10, 1817	Territory	75,448	1,797,114	Meridian	8
24	Missouri	March 6, 1820	Aug. 10, 1821	Part of Missouri Territory	66,557	3,293,335	St. Louis	16
41	Montana	Feb. 22, 1889	Nov. 8, 1889	Territory	132,159	376,053	Butte	2
37	Nebraska	April 19, 1864	March 1, 1867	Territory	122,993	1,192,214	Omaha	6
36	Nevada	March 21, 1864	Oct. 31, 1864	Territory	42,491	81,875	Reno	1
9	New Hampshire	—	—	Original state	141,885	430,572	Manchester	2
3	New Jersey	—	—	Original state	184,139	2,537,167	Newark	12
47	New Mexico	June 20, 1910	Jan. 6, 1912	Territory	—	327,301	Albuquerque	1
11	New York	—	—	Original state	340,120	9,113,614	New York	43
12	North Carolina	—	—	Original state	393,751	2,206,287	Charlotte	3
39	North Dakota	Feb. 22, 1889	Nov. 2, 1889	Part of Dakota Territory	184,719	577,056	Fargo	3
17	Ohio	April 30, 1802	Feb. 19, 1803	Part of Northwest Territory	230,760	4,767,121	Cleveland	22
46	Oklahoma	June 16, 1906	Nov. 16, 1907	Indian Territory and Oklahoma Territory	790,391	1,657,155	Oklahoma City	8
33	Oregon	—	Feb. 14, 1859	Part of Oregon Territory	52,465	672,765	Portland	3
2	Pennsylvania	—	—	Original state	434,373	7,665,111	Philadelphia	36
13	Rhode Island	—	—	Original state	68,825	542,610	Providence	3
8	South Carolina	—	—	Original state	249,073	1,515,400	Charleston	7
40	South Dakota	Feb. 22, 1889	Nov. 2, 1889	Part of Dakota Territory	328,808	583,888	Sioux Falls	3
16	Tennessee	—	June 1, 1796	Territory South of the Ohio	105,602	2,184,789	Memphis	10
28	Texas	—	Dec. 29, 1845	Independent state	212,592	3,896,542	San Antonio	18
45	Utah	July 16, 1894	Jan. 4, 1896	Territory	270,749	373,351	Salt Lake City	2
14	Vermont	—	March 4, 1791	Semi-independent state	154,465	355,956	Burlington	2
10	Virginia	—	—	Original state	747,610	2,061,612	Richmond	10
42	Washington	Feb. 22, 1889	Nov. 11, 1889	Territory	349,390	1,141,990	Seattle	5
35	West Virginia	—	June 19, 1863	Part of Virginia	442,014	1,221,119	Wheeling	6
30	Wisconsin	Aug. 6, 1846	May 29, 1848	Part of Wisconsin Territory	305,391	2,333,860	Milwaukee	11
44	Wyoming	—	July 10, 1890	Territory	60,705	145,965	Cheyenne	1

APPENDIX D

DECLARATION OF INDEPENDENCE

(AGREED TO, JULY 4, 1776)

[From a facsimile of the original parchment]

IN CONGRESS, JULY 4, 1776

THE UNANIMOUS DECLARATION OF THE THIRTEEN UNITED STATES OF AMERICA

When in the Course of human events, it becomes necessary for one people to dissolve the political bands which have connected them with another, and to assume among the powers of the earth, the separate and equal station to which the Laws of Nature and of Nature's God entitle them, a decent respect to the opinions of mankind requires that they should declare the causes which impel them to the separation. We hold these truths to be self-evident, that all men are created equal, that they are endowed by their Creator with certain unalienable Rights, that among these are Life, Liberty and the pursuit of Happiness. — That to secure these rights, Governments are instituted among Men, deriving their just powers from the consent of the governed. — That whenever any Form of Government becomes destructive of these ends, it is the Right of the People to alter or to abolish it, and to institute new Government, laying its foundation on such principles and organizing its powers in such form, as to them shall seem most likely to effect their Safety and Happiness. Prudence, indeed, will dictate that Governments long established should not be changed for light and transient causes; and accordingly all experience hath shewn, that mankind are more disposed to suffer, while evils are sufferable, than to right themselves by abolishing the forms to which they are accustomed. But when a long train of abuses and usurpations, pursuing invariably the same Object evinces a design to reduce them under absolute Despotism, it is their right, it is their duty, to throw off such Government, and to provide new Guards for their future security. — Such has been the patient sufferance of these Colonies; and such is now the necessity which constrains them to alter their former Systems of Government. The history of the present King of Great Britain is a history of repeated injuries and usurpations, all having in direct object the establishment of an absolute Tyranny over these States. To prove this, let Facts be submitted to a candid world. — He has refused his

xviii

Assent to Laws, the most wholesome and necessary for the public good. — He has forbidden his Governors to pass Laws of immediate and pressing importance, unless suspended in their operation till his Assent should be obtained; and when so suspended, he has utterly neglected to attend to them. — He has refused to pass other Laws for the accommodation of large districts of people, unless those people would relinquish the right of Representation in the Legislature, a right inestimable to them and formidable to tyrants only. — He has called together legislative bodies at places unusual, uncomfortable, and distant from the depository of their public Records, for the sole purpose of fatiguing them into compliance with his measures. — He has dissolved Representative Houses repeatedly, for opposing with manly firmness his invasions on the rights of the people. — He has refused for a long time, after such dissolutions, to cause others to be elected; whereby the Legislative powers, incapable of Annihilation, have returned to the People at large for their exercise; the State remaining in the mean time exposed to all the dangers of invasion from without, and convulsions within. — He has endeavoured to prevent the population of these States; for that purpose obstructing the Laws for Naturalization of Foreigners; refusing to pass others to encourage their migrations hither, and raising the conditions of new Appropriations of Lands. — He has obstructed the Administration of Justice, by refusing his Assent to Laws for establishing Judiciary powers. — He has made Judges dependent on his Will alone, for the tenure of their offices, and the amount and payment of their salaries. — He has erected a multitude of New Offices, and sent hither swarms of Officers to harrass our people, and eat out their substance. — He has kept among us, in times of peace, Standing Armies without the Consent of our legislatures. — He has affected to render the Military independent of and superior to the Civil power. — He has combined with others to subject us to a jurisdiction foreign to our constitution, and unacknowledged by our laws; giving his Assent to their Acts of pretended Legislation: — For quartering large bodies of armed troops among us: — For protecting them, by a mock Trial, from punishment for any Murders which they should commit on the Inhabitants of these States: — For cutting off our Trade with all parts of the world: — For imposing Taxes on us without our Consent: — For depriving us in many cases, of the benefits of Trial by Jury: — For transporting us beyond Seas to be tried for pretended offences: — For abolishing the free System of English Laws in a neighbouring Province, establishing therein an Arbitrary government, and enlarging its Boundaries, so as to render it at once an example and fit instrument for introducing the same absolute rule into these Colonies: — For taking away our Charters, abolishing our most valuable Laws, and altering fundamentally the Forms of our Governments: — For suspending our own Legislatures, and declaring themselves invested with power to legislate for us in all cases whatsoever. — He has abdicated Government here, by declaring us out of his Protection and waging War against us. — He has plundered our seas, ravaged our Coasts, burnt our towns, and destroyed the Lives of our people. — He is at this time transporting large Armies of foreign Mercenaries to compleat the works of death, desolation and tyranny, already begun with circumstances of Cruelty & perfidy scarcely paralleled in the most barbarous ages, and totally unworthy the Head of a civilized nation. — He has constrained our fellow Citizens taken Captive on the high Seas to bear Arms against their Country, to become the executioners of their friends and Brethren, or to fall themselves by their Hands. — He has excited domestic insurrections amongst us, and has endeavoured to bring on the inhabitants of our frontiers, the merciless Indian Savages, whose known rule of warfare, is an undistinguished destruction of all ages, sexes and conditions. In every stage of these Oppressions We have Petitioned for Redress in the most humble terms: Our repeated Petitions have been answered only by repeated injury. A Prince, whose character is thus marked by every act which may define a Tyrant, is unfit to be the ruler of a free people. Nor have We been wanting in attentions to our Brittish brethren. We have warned them from time to time of attempts by their legislature to extend an unwarrantable jurisdiction over us. We have reminded them of the circumstances of our emigration and settlement here. We have appealed to their native justice and magnaninity, and we have conjured them by the ties of our common kindred to disavow these usurpations, which, would inevitably interrupt our connections and correspondence. They too have been deaf to the voice of justice and of consanguinity. We must, therefore, acquiesce in the necessity, which denounces our Separation, and hold them, as we hold the rest of mankind, Enemies in War, in Peace Friends. —

We, therefore, the Representatives of the united States of America, in General Congress, Assembled, appealing to the Supreme Judge of the world for the rectitude of our intentions, do, in the Name, and by Authority of the good People of these Colonies, solemnly publish and declare, That these United Colonies are, and of Right ought to be, Free and Independent States; that they are Absolved from all Allegiance to the British Crown, and that all political connection between them and the State of Great Britain, is and ought to be totally dissolved; and that as Free and Independent States, they have full Power to levy War, conclude Peace, contract Alliances, establish Commerce, and to do all other Acts and Things which Independent States may of right do. — And for the support of this Declaration, with a firm reliance on the protection of divine Providence, we mutually pledge to each other our Lives, our Fortunes and our sacred Honor.

JOHN HANCOCK.

[Signatures of representatives of the thirteen States, affixed under date of August 2, 1776.]

APPENDIX E

CONSTITUTION OF THE UNITED STATES OF AMERICA (1787)[1]

(SUBMITTED SEPT. 17, 1787 ; IN FORCE APRIL 30, 1789)

[The following text of the Federal Constitution, including the Amendments thereto, is reprinted with the accompanying notes from *American History Leaflets*, No. 8, for which the original parchment rolls were compared.]

WE THE PEOPLE of the United States, in Order to form a more perfect Union, establish Justice, insure domestic Tranquility, provide for the common defence, promote the general Welfare, and secure the Blessings of Liberty to ourselves and our Posterity, do ordain and establish this CONSTITUTION for the United States of America.

ARTICLE. I.

SECTION. 1. All legislative Powers herein granted shall be vested in a Congress of the United States, which shall consist of a Senate and House of Representatives.

SECTION. 2. [§ 1.] The House of Representatives shall be composed of Members chosen every second Year by the People of the several States, and the Electors in each State shall have the Qualifications requisite for Electors of the most numerous Branch of the State Legislature.

[§ 2.] No Person shall be a Representative who shall not have attained to the Age of twenty five Years, and been seven Years a Citizen of the United States, and who shall not, when elected, be an Inhabitant of that State in which he shall be chosen.

[§ 3.] Representatives and direct Taxes shall be apportioned among the several States which may be included within this Union, according to their respective Numbers, [which shall be determined by adding to the whole Number of free Persons,][2] including those bound to Service for a Term of Years, and excluding Indians not taxed, [three fifths of all other Persons].[3] The actual Enumeration shall be made within three Years after the first Meeting of the Congress of the United States, and within every subsequent

---

[1] There is no title in the original manuscript.
[2] Modified by Fourteenth Amendment.
[3] Superseded by Fourteenth Amendment.

Term of ten Years, in such Manner as they shall by Law direct. The Number of Representatives shall not exceed one for every thirty Thousand, but each State shall have at Least one Representative; [and until such enumeration shall be made, the State of New Hampshire shall be entitled to chuse three, Massachusetts eight, Rhode-Island and Providence Plantations one, Connecticut five, New-York six, New Jersey four, Pennsylvania eight, Delaware one, Maryland six, Virginia ten, North Carolina five, South Carolina five, and Georgia three.][1]

[§ 4.] When vacancies happen in the Representation from any State, the Executive Authority thereof shall issue Writs of Election to fill such Vacancies.

[§ 5.] The House of Representatives shall chuse their Speaker and other Officers; and shall have the sole Power of Impeachment.

SECTION. 3. [§ 1.] The Senate of the United States shall be composed of two Senators from each State, chosen by the Legislature thereof,[2] for six Years; and each Senator shall have one Vote.

[§ 2.] Immediately after they shall be assembled in Consequence of the first Election, they shall be divided as equally as may be into three Classes. The Seats of the Senators of the first Class shall be vacated at the Expiration of the second Year, of the second Class at the Expiration of the fourth Year, and of the third Class at the Expiration of the sixth Year, so that one third may be chosen every second Year; and if Vacancies happen by Resignation, or otherwise, during the Recess of the Legislature of any State, [the Executive thereof may make temporary Appointments until the next Meeting of the Legislature, which shall then fill such Vacancies.][2]

[§ 3.] No Person shall be a Senator who shall not have attained to the Age of thirty Years, and been nine Years a Citizen of the United States, and who shall not, when elected, be an Inhabitant of that State for which he shall be chosen.

[§ 4.] The Vice President of the United States shall be President of the Senate, but shall have no Vote, unless they be equally divided.

[§ 5.] The Senate shall chuse their other Officers, and also a President pro . tempore, in the Absence of the Vice President, or when he shall exercise the Office of President of the United States.

[§ 6.] The Senate shall have the sole Power to try all Impeachments. When sitting for that Purpose, they shall be on Oath or Affirmation. When the President of the United States is tried, the Chief Justice shall preside: And no Person shall be convicted without the Concurrence of two thirds of the Members present.

[§ 7.] Judgment in Cases of Impeachment shall not extend further than to removal from Office, and disqualification to hold and enjoy any Office of honor, Trust or Profit under the United States: but the Party convicted shall nevertheless be liable and subject to Indictment, Trial, Judgment and Punishment, according to Law.

SECTION. 4. [§ 1.] The Times, Places and Manner of holding Elections for

---

[1] Temporary clause.   [2] Superseded by Seventeenth Amendment.

Senators and Representatives, shall be prescribed in each State by the Legislature thereof; but the Congress may at any time by Law make or alter such Regulations, except as to the Places of chusing Senators.

[§ 2.] The Congress shall assemble at least once in every Year, and such Meeting shall be on the first Monday in December, unless they shall by Law appoint a different Day.

SECTION. 5. [§ 1.] Each House shall be the Judge of the Elections, Returns and Qualifications of its own Members, and a Majority of each shall constitute a Quorum to do Business; but a smaller Number may adjourn from day to day, and may be authorized to compel the attendance of absent Members, in such Manner, and under such Penalties as each House may provide.

[§ 2.] Each House may determine the Rules of its Proceedings, punish its Members for Disorderly Behaviour, and, with the Concurrence of two thirds, expel a Member.

[§ 3.] Each House shall keep a Journal of its Proceedings, and from time to time publish the same, excepting such Parts as may in their Judgment require Secrecy; and the Yeas and Nays of the Members of either House on any question shall, at the Desire of one fifth of those Present, be entered on the Journal.

[§ 4.] Neither House, during the Session of Congress, shall, without the consent of the other, adjourn for more than three days, nor to any other Place than that in which the two Houses shall be sitting.

SECTION. 6. [§ 1.] The Senators and Representatives shall receive a Compensation for their Services, to be ascertained by Law, and paid out of the Treasury of the United States. They shall in all Cases, except Treason, Felony and Breach of the Peace, be privileged from Arrest during their Attendance at the Session of their respective Houses, and in going to and returning from the same; and for any Speech or Debate in either House, they shall not be questioned in any other Place.

[§ 2.] No Senator or Representative shall, during the Time for which he was elected, be appointed to any civil Office under the Authority of the United States, which shall have been created, or the Emoluments whereof shall have been encreased during such time; and no Person holding any Office under the United States, shall be a Member of either House during his Continuance in Office.

SECTION. 7. [§ 1.] All Bills for raising Revenue shall originate in the House of Representatives ; but the Senate may propose or concur with Amendments as on other Bills.

[§ 2.] Every Bill which shall have passed the House of Representatives and the Senate, shall, before it become a Law, be presented to the President of the United States; If he approve he shall sign it, but if not he shall return it, with his Objections to that House in which it shall have originated, who shall enter the Objections at large on their Journal, and proceed to reconsider it. If after such Reconsideration two thirds of that House shall agree to pass the Bill, it shall be sent, together with the Objections, to the other House, by which it shall likewise be reconsidered, and if approved by two thirds of that House, it shall become a Law. But in all such Cases the Votes of both Houses shall be determined by yeas and Nays, and the Names of the Persons voting for and against the Bill shall be entered on the Journal of each House respectively. If any Bill shall not be returned by the President within ten Days (Sundays excepted) after it shall have been presented to him, the same shall be a Law, in like Manner as if he had signed it, unless the Congress by their Adjournment prevent its Return, in which Case it shall not be a Law.

[§ 3.] Every Order, Resolution, or Vote to which the Concurrence of the Senate and House of Representatives may be necessary (except on a question of Adjournment) shall be presented to the President of the United States; and before the same shall take Effect, shall be approved by him, or being disapproved by him, shall be repassed by two thirds of the Senate and House of Representatives, according to the Rules and Limitations prescribed in the Case of a bill.

SECTION. 8. The Congress shall have Power [§ 1.] To lay and collect Taxes, Duties, Imposts and Excises, to pay the Debts and provide for the common Defence and general Welfare of the United States; but all Duties, Imposts and Excises shall be uniform throughout the United States;[1]

[§ 2.] To borrow Money on the credit of the United States;

[§ 3.] To regulate Commerce with foreign Nations, and among the several States, and with the Indian tribes;

[§ 4.] To establish an uniform Rule of Naturalization, and uniform Laws on the subject of Bankruptcies throughout the United States;

[§ 5.] To coin Money, regulate the Value thereof, and of foreign Coin, and fix the Standard of Weights and Measures;

[§ 6.] To provide for the Punishment of counterfeiting the Securities and current Coin of the United States;

[§ 7.] To establish Post Offices and post Roads;

[§ 8.] To promote the Progress of Science and useful Arts, by securing for limited Times to Authors and Inventors the exclusive Right to their respective Writings and Discoveries;

[§ 9.] To constitute Tribunals inferior to the supreme Court;

[§ 10.] To define and punish Piracies and Felonies committed on the high Seas, and Offences against the Law of Nations;

[§ 11.] To declare War, grant Letters of Marque and Reprisal, and make Rules concerning Captures on Land and Water;

[§ 12.] To raise and support Armies, but no Appropriation of Money to that Use shall be for a longer Term than two Years;

[§ 13.] To provide and maintain a Navy;

[§ 14.] To make Rules for the Government and Regulation of the land and naval Forces;

[§ 15.] To provide for calling forth the Militia to execute the Laws of the Union, suppress Insurrections and repel Invasions;

[§ 16.] To provide for organizing, arming, and disciplining, the Militia, and for governing such Part of them as may be employed in the Service of the United States, reserving to the States respectively the Appointment of the

[1] Extended by Sixteenth Amendment.

Officers, and the Authority of training the Militia according to the discipline prescribed by Congress;

[§ 17.] To exercise exclusive Legislation in all Cases whatsoever, over such District (not exceeding ten Miles square) as may, by Cession of particular States, and the Acceptance of Congress, become the Seat of the Government of the United States, and to exercise like Authority over all Places purchased by the Consent of the Legislature of the State in which the same shall be, for the Erection of Forts, Magazines, Arsenals, dock-Yards, and other needful Buildings; — And

[§ 18.] To make all Laws which shall be necessary and proper for carrying into Execution the foregoing Powers, and all other Powers vested by this Constitution in the Government of the United States, or in any Department or Officer thereof.

SECTION. 9. [§ 1.] [The Migration or Importation of such Persons as any of the States now existing shall think proper to admit, shall not be prohibited by the Congress prior to the Year one thousand eight hundred and eight, but a Tax or duty may be imposed on such Importation, not exceeding ten dollars for each Person.][1]

[§ 2.] The Privilege of the Writ of Habeas Corpus shall not be suspended, unless when in Cases of Rebellion or Invasion the public Safety may require it.

[§ 3.] No Bill of Attainder or ex post facto Law shall be passed.[2]

[§ 4.] No Capitation, or other direct, Tax shall be laid, unless in Proportion to the Census or Enumeration herein before directed to be taken.

[§ 5.] No Tax or Duty shall be laid on Articles exported from any State.

[§ 6.] No Preference shall be given by any Regulation of Commerce or Revenue to the Ports of one State over those of another: nor shall Vessels bound to, or from, one State be obliged to enter, clear, or pay Duties in another.

[§ 7.] No Money shall be drawn from the Treasury, but in Consequence of Appropriations made by Law; and a regular Statement and Account of the Receipts and Expenditures of all public Money shall be published from time to time.

[§ 8.] No Title of Nobility shall be granted by the United States: And no Person holding any Office of Profit or Trust under them, shall, without the Consent of the Congress, accept of any present, Emolument, Office, or Title, of any kind whatever, from any King, Prince, or foreign State.[3]

SECTION. 10. [§ 1.] No State shall enter into any Treaty, Alliance, or Confederation; grant Letters of Marque and Reprisal; coin Money; emit Bills of Credit; make any Thing but gold and silver Coin a Tender in Payment of Debts ; pass any Bill of Attainder, ex post facto Law, or Law impairing the Obligation of Contracts, or grant any Title of Nobility.

[§ 2.] No State shall, without the Consent of the Congress, lay any Imposts or Duties on Imports or Exports, except what may be absolutely necessary for executing its inspection Laws: and the net Produce of all Duties and

[1] Temporary provision.
[2] Extended by the first eight Amendments.
[3] Extended by Ninth and Tenth Amendments.

Imposts, laid by any State on Imports or Exports, shall be for the Use of the Treasury of the United States; and all such Laws shall be subject to the Revision and Controul of the Congress.

[§ 3.] No State shall, without the Consent of Congress, lay any Duty of Tonnage, keep Troops, or Ships of War in time of Peace, enter into any Agreement or Compact with another State, or with a foreign Power, or engage in War, unless actually invaded, or in such imminent Danger as will not admit of delay.[1]

ARTICLE. II.

Section. I. [§ I.] The executive Power shall be vested in a President of the United States of America. He shall hold his Office during the Term of four Years, and, together with the Vice President, chosen for the same Term, be elected, as follows

[§ 2.] Each State shall appoint, in such Manner as the Legislature thereof may direct, a Number of Electors, equal to the whole Number of Senators and Representatives to which the State may be entitled in the Congress: but no Senator or Representative, or Person holding an Office of Trust or Profit under the United States, shall be appointed an Elector.

[The Electors shall meet in their respective States, and vote by Ballot for two Persons, of whom one at least shall not be an Inhabitant of the same State with themselves. And they shall make a List of all the Persons voted for, and of the Number of Votes for each ; which List they shall sign and certify, and transmit sealed to the Seat of the Government of the United States, directed to the President of the Senate. The President of the Senate shall, in the Presence of the Senate and House of Representatives, open all the Certificates, and the Votes shall then be counted. The Person having the greatest Number of Votes shall be the President, if such Number be a Majority of the whole Number of Electors appointed; and if there be more than one who have such Majority, and have an equal Number of Votes, then the House of Representatives shall immediately chuse by Ballot one of them for President ; and if no Person have a Majority, then from the five highest on the List the said House shall in like Manner chuse the President. But in chusing the President, the Votes shall be taken by States, the Representation from each State having one Vote ; A quorum for this Purpose shall consist of a Member or Members from two thirds of the States, and a Majority of all the States shall be necessary to a Choice. In every Case, after the Choice of the President, the Person having the greatest Number of Votes of the Electors shall be the Vice President. But if there should remain two or more who have equal Votes, the Senate shall chuse from them by Ballot the Vice President.][2]

[§ 3.] The Congress may determine the Time of chusing the Electors, and the Day on which they shall give their Votes ; which Day shall be the same throughout the United States.

---

[1] Extended by Thirteenth, Fourteenth, and Fifteenth Amendments.
[2] Superseded by Twelfth Amendment.

[§ 4.] No Person except a natural born Citizen, or a Citizen of the United States, at the time of the Adoption of this Constitution, shall be eligible to the Office of President; neither shall any Person be eligible to that Office who shall not have attained to the Age of thirty-five Years, and been fourteen Years a Resident within the United States.

[§ 5.] In Case of the Removal of the President from Office, or of his Death, Resignation, or Inability to discharge the Powers and Duties of the said Office, the Same shall devolve on the Vice President, and the Congress may by Law provide for the Case of Removal, Death, Resignation, or Inability, both of the President and Vice President, declaring what Officer shall then act as President, and such Officer shall act accordingly, until the Disability be removed, or a President shall be elected.

[§ 6.] The President shall, at stated Times, receive for his Services, a Compensation, which shall neither be encreased nor diminished during the Period for which he shall have been elected, and he shall not receive within that Period any other Emolument from the United States, or any of them.

[§ 7.] Before he enter on the Execution of his Office, he shall take the following Oath or Affirmation : —

" I do solemnly swear (or affirm) that I will faithfully execute the Office of " President of the United States, and will to the best of my Ability, preserve, " protect and defend the Constitution of the United States."

SECTION. 2. [§ 1.] The President shall be Commander in Chief of the Army and Navy of the United States, and of the Militia of the several States, when called into the actual Service of the United States; he may require the Opinion, in writing, of the principal Officer in each of the executive Departments, upon any Subject relating to the Duties of their respective Offices, and he shall have Power to grant Reprieves and Pardons for Offences against the United States, except in Cases of Impeachment.

[§ 2.] He shall have Power, by and with the Advice and Consent of the Senate, to make Treaties, provided two thirds of the Senators present concur; and he shall nominate, and by and with the Advice and Consent of the Senate, shall appoint Ambassadors, other public Ministers and Consuls, Judges of the supreme Court, and all other Officers of the United States, whose Appointments are not herein otherwise provided for, and which shall be established by Law : but the Congress may by Law vest the Appointment of such inferior Officers, as they think proper, in the President alone, in the Courts of Law, or in the Heads of Departments.

[§ 3.] The President shall have Power to fill up all Vacancies that may happen during the Recess of the Senate, by granting Commissions which shall expire at the End of their next Session.

SECTION. 3. He shall from time to time give to the Congress Information of the State of the Union, and recommend to their Consideration such Measures as he shall judge necessary and expedient; he may, on extraordinary Occasions, convene both Houses, or either of them, and in Case of Disagreement between them, with Respect to the Time of Adjournment, he may adjourn them to such Time as he shall think proper; he shall receive Ambassadors and other public Ministers; he shall take Care that the Laws be faithfully executed, and shall Commission all the Officers of the United States.

SECTION. 4. The President, Vice President, and all civil Officers of the United States, shall be removed from Office on Impeachment for, and Conviction of, Treason, Bribery, or other high Crimes and Misdemeanors.

ARTICLE. III.

SECTION. 1. The judicial Power of the United States, shall be vested in one supreme Court, and in such inferior Courts as the Congress may from time to time ordain and establish. The Judges, both of the supreme and inferior Courts, shall hold their Offices during good Behaviour, and shall, at stated Times, receive for their Services, a Compensation, which shall not be diminished during their Continuance in Office.

SECTION. 2. [§ 1.] The judicial Power shall extend to all Cases, in Law and Equity, arising under this Constitution, the Laws of the United States, and Treaties made, or which shall be made, under their Authority; — to all Cases affecting Ambassadors, other public Ministers and Consuls; — to all Cases of admiralty and maritime Jurisdiction; — to Controversies to which the United States shall be a Party; — to Controversies between two or more States; — between a State and Citizens of another State; [1] — between Citizens of different States, — between Citizens of the same State claiming Lands under Grants of different States, and between a State, or the Citizens thereof, and foreign States, Citizens or Subjects.

[§ 2.] In all Cases affecting Ambassadors, other public Ministers and Consuls, and those in which a State shall be Party, the supreme Court shall have original Jurisdiction. In all the other Cases before mentioned, the supreme Court shall have appellate Jurisdiction, both as to Law and Fact, with such Exceptions, and under such Regulations as the Congress shall make.

[§ 3.] The Trial of all Crimes, except in Cases of Impeachment, shall be by Jury; and such Trial shall be held in the State where the said Crimes shall have been committed; but when not committed within any State, the Trial shall be at such Place or Places as the Congress may by Law have directed.

SECTION. 3. [§ 1.] Treason against the United States, shall consist only in levying War against them, or in adhering to their Enemies, giving them Aid and Comfort. No Person shall be convicted of Treason unless on the Testimony of two Witnesses to the same overt Act, or on Confession in open Court.

[§ 2.] The Congress shall have Power to declare the Punishment of Treason, but no Attainder of Treason shall work Corruption of Blood, or Forfeiture except during the Life of the Person attainted.

ARTICLE. IV.

SECTION. 1. Full Faith and Credit shall be given in each State to the public Acts, Records, and judicial Proceedings of every other State. And the Congress may by general Laws prescribe the Manner in which such Acts, Records and Proceedings shall be proved, and the Effect thereof.

[1] Limited by Eleventh Amendment.

SECTION. 2. [§ 1.] The Citizens of each State shall be entitled to all Privileges and Immunities of Citizens in the several States.[1]

[§ 2.] A Person charged in any State with Treason, Felony, or other Crime, who shall flee from Justice, and be found in another State, shall on Demand of the executive Authority of the State from which he fled, be delivered up, to be removed to the State having Jurisdiction of the Crime.

[§ 3.] [No Person held to Service or Labour in one State, under the Laws thereof, escaping into another, shall, in Consequence of any Law or Regulation therein, be discharged from such Service or Labour, but shall be delivered up on Claim of the Party to whom such Service or Labour may be due.][2]

SECTION. 3. [§ 1.] New States may be admitted by the Congress into this Union; but no new State shall be formed or erected within the Jurisdiction of any other State; nor any State be formed by the Junction of two or more States, or Parts of States, without the Consent of the Legislatures of the States concerned as well as of the Congress.

[§ 2.] The Congress shall have Power to dispose of and make all needful Rules and Regulations respecting the Territory or other Property belonging to the United States; and nothing in this Constitution shall be so construed as to Prejudice any Claims of the United States, or of any particular State.

SECTION. 4. The United States shall guarantee to every State in this Union a Republican Form of Government, and shall protect each of them against Invasion; and on Application of the Legislature, or of the Executive (when the Legislature cannot be convened) against domestic Violence.

ARTICLE. V.

The Congress, whenever two thirds of both Houses shall deem it necessary, shall propose Amendments to this Constitution, or, on the Application of the Legislatures of two thirds of the several States, shall call a Convention for proposing Amendments, which, in either Case, shall be valid to all Intents and Purposes, as Part of this Constitution, when ratified by the Legislatures of three fourths of the several States, or by Conventions in three fourths thereof, as the one or the other Mode of Ratification may be proposed by the Congress; Provided [that no Amendment which may be made prior to the Year One thousand eight hundred and eight shall in any Manner affect the first and fourth Clauses in the Ninth Section of the first Article; and][3] that no State, without its Consent, shall be deprived of its equal Suffrage in the Senate.

ARTICLE. VI.

[§ 1.] All Debts contracted and Engagements entered into, before the Adoption of this Constitution, shall be as valid against the United States under this Constitution, as under the Confederation.[4]

[1] Extended by Fourteenth Amendment.
[2] Superseded by Thirteenth Amendment so far as it relates to slaves.
[3] Temporary provision.
[4] Extended by Fourteenth Amendment, Section 4.

[§ 2.] This Constitution, and the Laws of the United States which shall be made in Pursuance thereof; and all Treaties made, or which shall be made, under the Authority of the United States, shall be the supreme Law of the Land; and the Judges in every State shall be bound thereby, any Thing in the Constitution or Laws of any State to the Contrary notwithstanding.

[§ 3.] The Senators and Representatives before mentioned, and the Members of the several State Legislatures, and all executive and judicial Officers, both of the United States and of the several States, shall be bound by Oath or Affirmation, to support this Constitution; but no religious Test shall ever be required as a Qualification to any Office or public Trust under the United States.

ARTICLE VII.

The Ratification of the Conventions of nine States, shall be sufficient for the Establishment of this Constitution between the States so ratifying the Same.

[Note of the draughtsman as to interlineations in the text of the manuscript.]
Attest
    WILLIAM JACKSON,
    Secretary.

DONE in Convention by the Unanimous Consent of the States present the Seventeenth Day of September in the Year of our Lord one thousand seven hundred and Eighty seven and of the Independence of the United States of America the Twelfth **In Witness** whereof We have hereunto subscribed our names.
    Go WASHINGTON —
    Presidt and deputy from Virginia.

[Signatures of members of the Convention.][1]

[AMENDMENTS.]

ARTICLES in addition to and Amendment of the Constitution of the United States of America, proposed by Congress, and ratified by the Legislatures of the several States, pursuant to the fifth Article of the original Constitution.[2]

[ARTICLE I.][3]

Congress shall make no law respecting an establishment of religion, or prohibiting the free exercise thereof; or abridging the freedom of speech, or of the press; or the right of the people peaceably to assemble, and to petition the Government for a redress of grievances.

[ARTICLE II.]

A well regulated Militia, being necessary to the security of a free State, the right of the people to keep and bear Arms, shall not be infringed.

[1] These signatures have no other legal force than that of attestation.
[2] This heading appears only in the joint resolution submitting the first ten amendments.
[3] In the original manuscripts the first twelve amendments have no numbers.

[ARTICLE III.]

No Soldier shall, in time of peace be quartered in any house, without the consent of the Owner, nor in time of war, but in a manner to be prescribed by law.

[ARTICLE IV.]

The right of the people to be secure in their persons, houses, papers, and effects, against unreasonable searches and seizures, shall not be violated, and no Warrants shall issue, but upon probable cause, supported by Oath or affirmation, and particularly describing the place to be searched, and the persons or things to be seized.

[ARTICLE V.]

No person shall be held to answer for a capital, or otherwise infamous crime, unless on a presentment or indictment of a Grand Jury, except in cases arising in the land or naval forces, or in the Militia, when in actual service in time of War or public danger; nor shall any person be subject for the same offence to be twice put in jeopardy of life or limb; nor shall be compelled in any criminal case to be a witness against himself, nor be deprived of life, liberty, or property, without due process of law; nor shall private property be taken for public use, without just compensation.

[ARTICLE VI.]

In all criminal prosecutions the accused shall enjoy the right to a speedy and public trial, by an impartial jury of the State and district wherein the crime shall have been committed, which district shall have been previously ascertained by law, and to be informed of the nature and cause of the accusation; to be confronted with the witnesses against him; to have compulsory process for obtaining witnesses in his favor, and to have the Assistance of Counsel for his defence.

[ARTICLE VII.]

In suits at common law, where the value in controversy shall exceed twenty dollars, the right of trial by jury shall be preserved, and no fact tried by a jury shall be otherwise re-examined in any Court of the United States, than according to the rules of the common law.

[ARTICLE VIII.]

Excessive bail shall not be required, nor excessive fines imposed, nor cruel and unusual punishments inflicted.

[ARTICLE IX.]

The enumeration in the Constitution, of certain rights, shall not be construed to deny or disparage others retained by the people.

[ARTICLE X.]

The powers not delegated to the United States by the Constitution, nor prohibited by it to the States, are reserved to the States respectively or to the people.[1]

[ARTICLE XI.][2]

The Judicial power of the United States shall not be construed to extend to any suit in law or equity, commenced or prosecuted against one of the United States by Citizens of another State, or by Citizens or Subjects of any Foreign State.

[ARTICLE XII.][3]

The Electors shall meet in their respective states, and vote by ballot for President and Vice-President, one of whom, at least, shall not be an inhabitant of the same state with themselves; they shall name in their ballots the person voted for as President, and in distinct ballots the person voted for as Vice-President, and they shall make distinct lists of all persons voted for as President, and of all persons voted for as Vice-President, and of the number of votes for each, which lists they shall sign and certify, and transmit sealed to the seat of the government of the United States, directed to the President of the Senate; — The President of the Senate shall, in the presence of the Senate and House of Representatives, open all the certificates and the votes shall then be counted; — The person having the greatest number of votes for President, shall be the President, if such number be a majority of the whole number of Electors appointed; and if no person have such majority, then from the persons having the highest numbers not exceeding three on the list of those voted for as President, the House of Representatives shall choose immediately, by ballot, the President. But in choosing the President, the votes shall be taken by states, the representation from each state having one vote; a quorum for this purpose shall consist of a member or members from two-thirds of the states, and a majority of all the states shall be necessary to a choice. And if the House of Representatives shall not choose a President whenever the right of choice shall devolve upon them, before the fourth day of March next following, then the Vice-President shall act as President, as in the case of the death or other constitutional disability of the President. — The person having the greatest number of votes as Vice-President, shall be the Vice-President, if such number be a majority of the whole number of Electors appointed, and if no person have a majority, then from the two highest numbers on the list, the Senate shall choose the Vice-President; a quorum for the purpose shall consist of two-thirds of the whole number of Senators, and a majority of the whole number shall be necessary to a choice. But no person

[1] Amendments First to Tenth appear to have been in force from Nov. 3, 1791.
[2] Proclaimed to be in force Jan. 8, 1798.
[3] Proclaimed to be in force Sept. 25, 1804.

constitutionally ineligible to the office of President shall be eligible to that of Vice-President of the United States.

ARTICLE XIII.[1]

SECTION 1. Neither slavery nor involuntary servitude, except as a punishment for crime whereof the party shall have been duly convicted, shall exist within the United States, or any place subject to their jurisdiction. SECTION 2. Congress shall have power to enforce this article by appropriate legislation.

ARTICLE XIV.[2]

SECTION 1. All persons born or naturalized in the United States, and subject to the jurisdiction thereof, are citizens of the United States and of the State wherein they reside. No State shall make or enforce any law which shall abridge the privileges or immunities of citizens of the United States; nor shall any State deprive any person of life, liberty, or property, without due process of law; nor deny to any person within its jurisdiction the equal protection of the laws.

SECTION 2. Representatives shall be apportioned among the several States according to their respective numbers, counting the whole number of persons in each State, excluding Indians not taxed. But when the right to vote at any election for the choice of electors for President and Vice President of the United States, Representatives in Congress, the Executive and Judicial officers of a State, or the members of the Legislature thereof, is denied to any of the male inhabitants of such State, being twenty-one years of age, and citizens of the United States, or in any way abridged, except for participation in rebellion, or other crime, the basis of representation therein shall be reduced in the proportion which the number of such male citizens shall bear to the whole number of male citizens twenty-one years of age in such State.

SECTION 3. No person shall be a Senator or Representative in Congress, or elector of President and Vice President, or hold any office, civil or military, under the United States, or under any State, who, having previously taken an oath, as a member of Congress, or as an officer of the United States, or as a member of any State legislature, or as an executive or judicial officer of any State, to support the Constitution of the United States, shall have engaged in insurrection or rebellion against the same, or given aid or comfort to the enemies thereof. But Congress may by a vote of two-thirds of each House, remove such disability.

SECTION 4. The validity of the public debt of the United States, authorized by law, including debts incurred for payment of pensions and bounties for services in suppressing insurrection or rebellion, shall not be questioned. But neither the United States nor any State shall assume or pay any debt or obligation incurred in aid of insurrection or rebellion against the United

[1] Proclaimed to be in force Dec. 18, 1865. Bears the unnecessary approval of the President.
[2] Proclaimed to be in force July 28, 1868.

States, or any claim for the loss or emancipation of any slave; but all such debts, obligations and claims shall be held illegal and void.

SECTION 5. The Congress shall have power to enforce, by appropriate legislation, the provisions of this article.

ARTICLE XV.[1]

SECTION 1. The right of citizens of the United States to vote shall not be denied or abridged by the United States or by any State on account of race, color, or previous condition of servitude.

SECTION 2. The Congress shall have power to enforce this article by appropriate legislation.

ARTICLE XVI.[2]

The Congress shall have power to lay and collect taxes on incomes, from whatever source derived, without apportionment among the several States, and without regard to any census or enumeration.

ARTICLE XVII.[3]

The Senate of the United States shall be composed of two Senators from each State, elected by the people thereof, for six years; and each Senator shall have one vote. The electors in each State shall have the qualifications requisite for electors of the most numerous branch of the State legislatures.

When vacancies happen in the representation of any State in the Senate, the executive authority of such State shall issue writs of election to fill such vacancies: *Provided*, That the legislature of any State shall empower the executive thereof to make temporary appointments until the people fill the vacancies by election as the legislature may direct.

This amendment shall not be so construed as to affect the election or term of any Senator chosen before it becomes valid as part of the Constitution.

[1] Proclaimed to be in force Mar. 30, 1870.
[2] Proclaimed to be in force Feb. 25, 1913.
[3] Proclaimed to be in force May 31, 1913.

INDEX

Diacritic marks: ă as in *late*; ā as in *fat*; ä as in *far*; â as in *care*; À as in *last*; ạ as in *full*; o, eh as in *cask*, *charm*; ç as in *ice*; ö as in *me*; ĕ as in *met*, *berry*; ḡ as in *veil*; ĕ as in *term*; g as in *gem*; g̱ as in *go*; ī as in *tin*; ĭ as in *police*; N, the French nasal; ó as in *note*; ŏ as in *not*; ô as in *son*; ä as in *for*; ọ as in *do*; ạ as in *news*; th as in *the*; û as in *tune*; ŭ as in *nut*; ạ as in *rude* (= ọ); ụ as in *full*; ü = French u; ẏ as in *my*. Single Italic letters are silent.

www.ingramcontent.com/pod-product-compliance
Lightning Source LLC
Chambersburg PA
CBHW020242010726
47475CB00001B/13